CRITICALLY THINKING ABOUT MEDICAL ETHICS

CRITICALLY THINKING ABOUT MEDICAL ETHICS

ROBERT F. CARD
State University of New York, Oswego

Upper Saddle River, New Jersey 07458

Library of Congress Cataloging-in-Publication Data
Card, Robert F.
Critically thinking about medical ethics / Robert F. Card.
p. cm.
ISBN 0-13-182484-8 (alk. paper)
1. Medical ethics. 2. Critical thinking. I. Title.

R724.C346 2004
174.2—dc21 2003054836

Senior Acquisitions Editor: Ross Miller
Editorial Director: Charlyce Jones-Owen
Assistant Editor: Wendy Yurash
Editorial Assistant: Carla Worner
Senior Marketing Manager: Chris Ruel
Marketing Assistant: Kimberly Daum
Managing Editor (Production): Joanne Riker
Production Liaison: Joanne Hakim
Manufacturing Buyer: Christina Helder
Cover Art Director: Jayne Conte
Cover Design: Bruce Kenselaar
Cover Illustration/Photo: Diana Ong/SuperStock
Cover Image Specialist: Karen Sanatar
Composition/Full-Service Project Management: Fran Daniele/Preparé Inc.
Printer/Binder: R.R. Donnelly & Sons

Credits and acknowledgments borrowed from other sources and reproduced, with permission, in this textbook appear on appropriate page within text.

Pearson Education LTD., London
Pearson Education Singapore, Pte. Ltd
Pearson Education, Canada, Ltd
Pearson Education–Japan
Pearson Education Australia PTY, Limited
Pearson Education North Asia Ltd
Pearson Educación de Mexico, S.A. de C.V.
Pearson Education Malaysia, Pte. Ltd
Pearson Education, Upper Saddle River, New Jersey

10 9 8 7 6 5 4

ISBN 0-13-182484-8

CONTENTS

PREFACE

The inspiration for this book stems from my dissatisfaction with other currently available texts. An acceptable textbook must reflect the breadth and depth of the debate it addresses, but should also prepare students to *engage* this debate. To do this requires providing resources to help students develop critical thinking skills. My fundamental belief is that students in a medical ethics/bioethics course should learn not only *content* regarding different thinkers' positions on the issues but also a philosophical or logical *method* that can be used to think more clearly about the ethical challenges posed by medicine. This book aims to make elements of this philosophical method explicit as it introduces students to the dialogue concerning central issues in medical ethics.

The dialogue in medical ethics is shaped in part by various ethical viewpoints. While thinkers accept different views, it is worth noting that bioethicists never defend their position by appealing to, say, Ethical Subjectivism. Philosophers understand why this is the case, and this is so natural that it probably goes unnoticed. Yet students deserve to know that this is not merely an accident. In order to explain and philosophically justify why thinkers in medical ethics explicitly rely on a relatively small number of ethical outlooks when presenting their views, this book includes a comprehensive introduction to ethical perspectives (Chapter 1).

Also, philosophical thinkers in medical ethics presume more than a passing familiarity with arguments when presenting their case. This book includes a separate introductory chapter (Chapter 2) on critical thinking, which will help students become more careful critics and make them more reflective about their own thinking. Chapter 1 contains *Critical Thinking Interludes*, which present and discuss case studies that are then related to important facets of the ethical perspectives just explained. The purpose of these Critical Thinking Interludes is to naturally awaken students' dormant analytical powers before a more formal introduction to critical thinking occurs in Chapter 2. The explanation and discussion of the case study are completely self-contained. These Critical Thinking Interludes serve as "helping hands" that model for students the type of questions relevant to a philosophical examination of an issue.

The critical thinking theme is not simply forgotten once the introductory chapters are completed. The sections containing the readings are divided into four units, and each unit consists of two chapters that are unified by a common "Critical Thinking Tool" that is explained and applied to several readings from that unit. These "Critical Thinking Tools" relate to the background critical thinking material explained in Chapter 2, yet are also independent since their explanation and application is contained within the Unit Introductions. For example, Unit II contains readings on the topics of surrogacy and abortion. This Unit Introduction contains a detailed explanation of analogies that then highlights and analyzes several examples of analogies from the readings in that Unit.

In addition, Unit Introductions contain an overview of the readings in that Unit, with particular emphasis on how the thinkers on each topic are responding to one another in a common dialogue. Serious effort has been expended to ensure that a balanced selection of readings representing different viewpoints are included. Further, the text contains enough readings on each topic to allow a philosophically respectable discussion of the issues.

This text contains more resources than can likely be used in a one semester medical ethics or bioethics course. I believe that is a favorable aspect of the text, since it allows flexibility in course design. In my experience, the selections contained in this text can be easily tailored to meet the needs of students of varying aptitudes and backgrounds.

The overarching goal of this text is to construct a cohesive philosophy textbook in medical ethics that offers the best in classic and contemporary readings (with a number of readings not contained in other texts). The critical thinking elements introduced and applied in the text are freestanding, and instructors who do not wish to incorporate critical thinking pedagogy in their courses are encouraged to use the text as well.

This collection offers an ample number of readings on each topic to allow for an informed discussion of the relevant issues that incorporates different viewpoints. The intention is to offer students structure to assist them in developing the skills necessary for engaging in philosophical thinking while allowing instructors the freedom to teach their courses as they see fit.

I would greatly appreciate comments and suggestions from those who use the book to learn how it might be improved. Communications may be directed to me either via email at rcard@oswego.edu or by postal mail at Department of Philosophy; State University of New York, Oswego; Oswego, NY 13126.

I would like to acknowledge those authors who have allowed me to reproduce their work in this textbook. Additionally, sincere thanks to the reviewers of this text: John J. Paris, S. J. Boston College, Anthony Preus, Binghamton University, and Louis I. Katzner, Bowling Green State University.

I believe there is reason to be proud of the sophisticated dialogue that has developed in medical ethics. It is my hope that the thinkers included in this text feel that their contributions have been accorded proper merit both in the presentation of their selections as well as in the discussion of their views. Both Ross Miller, Prentice-Hall's Acquisitions Editor for philosophy, and Carla Worner, Editorial Assistant at Prentice-Hall, have provided just the right amount of support to foster this project. Finally, I thank my wife, Peggy, and our daughter, Noelle, for the special encouragement that only a loving family can provide.

FEATURES OF THE BOOK

(1) This book does not assume that students have any background in philosophy or in medicine: it is completely *self-contained*. It provides a thorough introduction to the ethical theories that philosophical thinkers in medical ethics employ as a backdrop in their discussions. In addition, it offers a basic introduction to logical arguments and critical thinking. This reader satisfies all the requirements for a medical ethics course; there is no need for supplementary texts.

(2) The readings have been selected to create a true *dialogue* among the writers and the various positions and arguments on the relevant issues in medical ethics. A concise overview of the key arguments and their relations to one other is provided in an introduction to each chapter.

(3) There is a *sufficient number of readings* for each topic. Currently, popular readers in medical ethics provide only a small number of selections for each subject, and hence do not allow the depth of treatment that is necessary for a philosophically respectable examination of the ethical issues in medical practice. This text remedies this problem by offering a mixture of classic and contemporary readings, including readings not contained in other medical ethics textbooks.

(4) Each unit consists of two chapters, and a *critical thinking tool* that appears prominently in the readings in each unit is applied in the chapter introductions. This feature builds on the foundation established in Chapter 2 on logical reasoning, and establishes a link between critical thinking and the ethical issues discussed in each chapter. Sufficient background on a relevant critical thinking tool is provided, and these tools encourage critical analysis of the readings contained in each unit. This also establishes a pedagogical theme within each unit.

(5) This reader allows *sufficient flexibility* in course design. The readings may be used to teach a general elective course that uses (for example) the introductory Chapters 1 and 2, as well as the chapters on surrogacy, abortion, and euthanasia. It may also be used to teach an upper-level course in biomedical ethics by using (for instance) the introductory Chapters 1 and 2, and the chapters on genetics, HIV/AIDS, medical professionalism, and experimentation on human subjects. This text is also well suited for a course on contemporary moral issues focused on life and death issues.

(6) While the readings in each unit are conceptually related to one another, this text allows *ample freedom* when choosing the order in which readings will be discussed. The readings from one unit also connect naturally to readings from other units. For example, readings in Chapter 4 (abortion) can be naturally related to readings in Chapter 6 (reproductive risk and prenatal diagnosis). Readings in Chapter 5 (end of life issues) connect naturally to readings in Chapter 8 (medical professionalism; informed consent and competence) and Chapter 10 (allocation of medical resources). Readings in Chapter 7 (HIV/AIDS) relate closely to readings in Chapter 9 (biomedical research; clinical research in the third world).

ORGANIZATION OF THE BOOK

Chapter 1

This chapter provides a solid introduction to various moral perspectives. It explains and analyzes various ethical theories to assist students in understanding why certain perspectives have become dominant in writings on morality and ethics. It explains and critically analyzes ethical relativism, divine command ethics and natural law theory, psychological egoism, and ethical egoism. This is used to set the stage for a philosophical discussion of the perspectives of utilitarianism, Kantian and rights-based ethics, virtue/aretaic ethics, and the Rawlsian theory of justice. This chapter also contains a novel feature called critical thinking interludes. In these interludes, a case study is briefly presented, followed by a critical thinking question that relates the case study to the ethical perspective under discussion. A brief, critical discussion of the question follows. The purpose of these interludes is to spur the development of critical thinking skills in a natural way, before the main logical concepts are introduced in Chapter 2.

Chapter 2

This chapter provides essential background on critical thinking. Descriptive statements are distinguished from normative statements, since this distinction is central to understanding the nature of ethical claims. The fundamentals of arguments, as well as a discussion of the difference between facts, opinions, and ideas, is included. The chapter also details types of logical arguments, the concepts of validity and soundness, and presents and explains selected logical fallacies. Numerous illustrations are offered to help students become accustomed to the logical method employed in the readings.

Chapter 3

Surrogacy contracts and discussion of other reproductive technologies are the focus of this chapter. This chapter can be used to provide students with an excellent introduction to the type of issues present in medical ethics. Concerns about women's autonomy, the introduction of a profit motive into reproduction, the societal consequences of access to reproductive technologies, and the acceptability of paternalism are expressed and examined in the readings contained in this unit. Since most students do not initially express a strong commitment to one position on surrogacy arrangements, this topic helps students to begin to appreciate the role that ethical argument can play in forming one's view on a moral issue.

Chapter 4

Abortion remains one of the most divisive moral issues in the United States. Yet this divisiveness is reason to make a serious effort to understand the rationale of different perspectives on this controversy. Legal background is provided, as well as readings that express different reasoned views (conservative, liberal, and moderate views) on the moral status of the fetus and women's rights and responsibilities regarding the fetus.

Chapter 5

Euthanasia and physician-assisted suicide remains one of the most pervasive moral issues affecting the medical profession. This chapter provides crucial legal background on euthanasia, discusses the moral distinction between "passive" and "active" euthanasia, and examines the viability of a social policy allowing voluntary active euthanasia. Unlike most texts, it contains a reading on the practice of euthanasia in the Netherlands, which aids in discussion of claims about the long-term effects of social policies allowing euthanasia. Also, unlike other readers, the chapter also discusses differences between physician-assisted suicide and euthanasia.

Chapter 6

The implications of the Human Genome Project for our lives are potentially revolutionary. The moral issues associated with prenatal diagnosis and reproduction in conditions of genetic risk are explored in the readings, as are the moral questions surrounding genetic engineering and cloning. Special features not included in other medical ethics readers include discussions of whether insurance companies can justifiably use genetic testing to determine eligibility or rates for insurance coverage, as well as selections that present conflicting opinions on whether or not genes for human diseases should be patented.

Chapter 7

This chapter discusses whether medical professionals have a duty to treat HIV-positive patients, questions surrounding professionals' duty to disclose information about patients, and ethical questions surrounding the limits of confidentiality and the right to know. The chapter closes with readings that examine the ethical quandaries stemming from drug treatment of pregnant HIV-positive women.

Chapter 8

The health care provider/patient relationship itself generates a number of important ethical questions worthy of consideration. Questions broached in earlier chapters—such as whether medical professionals may honor patients' requests for euthanasia or whether they have a moral duty to treat HIV-positive patients—rely on a conception of the provider/patient relationship. The chapter opens with a discussion of whether forcible medical treatment is ever justified if it is refused based on religious reasons. Issues concerning informed consent, determinations of competence, and telling patients the truth are examined from different perspectives.

Chapter 9

This chapter concerns the ethical issues involved with medical research performed on human subjects. The chapter opens with several important statements of research ethics, including *The Nuremberg Code*. A selection on the Tuskegee syphilis study makes clear the human cost incurred as a result of morally irresponsible research. The chapter contains selections that examine the central moral issues surrounding the usage of randomized clinical trials and determinations of when (and whether) the benefits to subjects participating in a study are sufficiently great to justify conducting and continuing the research.

Chapter 10

Issues of justice are prevalent within medical ethics. This chapter focuses on the moral issues surrounding the just allocation of scarce resources, such as organs for transplant, as well as more general questions surrounding the justice of cost containment programs and initiatives that limit the employment of expensive medical treatment. The last part of the chapter broaches the issue of medical errors, a topic not covered by other current medical ethics anthologies. The remainder of the readings concerns the question of how to address the fallout from medical mistakes in a just manner.

Robert F. Card
State University of New York, Oswego

UNIT ONE

INTRODUCTION TO ETHICS AND CRITICAL THINKING

CHAPTER 1

INTRODUCTION TO ETHICAL THEORY

CHAPTER GOALS:

- To provide an introduction to philosophical ethics, medical ethics, and ethical theories
- To illustrate the relative advantages and disadvantages of different ethical perspectives in order to explain why some theories are currently dominant within the field of philosophy
- To apply these ethical perspectives to case studies in order to naturally spur the development of critical thinking skills

OVERVIEW: TYPES OF QUESTIONS IN THE ETHICAL LANDSCAPE

This chapter serves as a concise introduction to moral philosophy. Before we can begin to explore what it means to take a philosophical approach to morality, we should ask: "What is philosophy?" In general, the term "philosophy" can suggest two main things. First, philosophy is a method of inquiry. When we ask the question "What is philosophy?" we are in effect doing philosophy because we are engaging in conceptual analysis to discover what we think this notion *means.* Asking questions is the focus in philosophy, but this does not mean that philosophers think there are no acceptable answers to these questions. One central part of philosophy is setting general standards for what constitutes a reasonably good answer to a philosophical question. Philosophers emphasize the point that you must ask the right questions to get the right answers. The activity of *philosophy as a method* requires that *you* get involved by weighing all of the relevant factors to arrive at a defensible position consistent with your beliefs.

Philosophy also refers to a *field of study* or a *subject matter* in which various positions and views are defended regarding questions of fundamental importance.

Areas of philosophy include *metaphysics*, which explores questions such as, "What exists in the universe—physical substances, minds, spirit?," "Does the soul exist?," and "Are we free to act as we wish?" Other areas of philosophy are *political philosophy*, which asks, "What is a just society?" and "When is a government legitimate?" and *philosophy of religion*, which examines such questions as, "Does God exist?" and "Is there an afterlife?" Our focus will be on *ethics*, which examines questions such as, "What is right or wrong?," "What makes a person or action good or bad?," and "What is the basis for such judgments?" There exists an area of philosophical inquiry for almost any field of study. This philosophical area consists of asking and addressing those questions at the foundation of the discipline. Ethics is simply one area within the larger discipline of philosophy itself. Exploring the ethical questions raised by medicine will also require thinking about other types of philosophical questions, such as those from the areas of metaphysics, political philosophy, and philosophy of religion. In this way, different areas of philosophy are interconnected.

Within the study of ethics there are several general types of inquiry that are relevant.

I. Empirical Questions

These questions concern factual matters; for example, the question, "How many students are in this semester's class?" is an empirical question. Factual questions bear on moral judgments, but they are fundamentally different from ethical questions. Ethical questions involve a normative element; this refers to what *should* be done (not necessarily to what is or was in fact done). An example of an ethical question is, "Was it morally right for the United States to use nuclear weapons against Japan in 1945?" To address this question would require weighing a number of factors, and having the answer to certain factual questions would be valuable. For instance, we might want to know the answer to factual questions such as, "Did this help to end World War II?," and "How many lives did this action save overall?" This example suggests that it is sometimes very difficult to get the type of factual information that bears on moral questions.

II. Conceptual Questions

To be able to think clearly about moral questions, we must gain a proper understanding of the concepts involved in these questions. For instance, if a central moral tenet is that all persons are granted equal moral rights, we must know what is meant by "person" and how we are to understand the notion of a "right." Only then could we evaluate this piece of moral advice and use a moral rights theory in a particular case.

III. Particular Moral Issues

Particular moral issues are practical examples of ethical controversies, such as the issues of abortion and capital punishment. Providing a thorough examination of the central points in practical moral controversies involves answering Type I and Type II questions, as well as applying general moral rules and principles to the case at hand. Particular moral issues are the focus in applied ethics, and will be our central concern.

IV. General Moral Principles

The focus at this level is on the characteristics that make an action or policy morally right/wrong or good/bad in general. Different philosophers have different ideas on what factors need to be emphasized from the moral point of view.

One element of morality concerns what is good in itself. This is often summed up in the philosophical question, "What is the Good?" To ask this question is to ask what is of *intrinsic value*, or valuable in itself, and therefore fundamentally makes other things possess value. For example, suppose you value eating an ice cream cone on a hot, sunny day. Why is this experience valuable? You might say that you value the ice cream cone because it makes you feel cooler when it is hot outside. Why is feeling cooler valuable? You may say that this is a good thing because when you feel cooler you enjoy your outdoor activities more. Why is it valuable to get more enjoyment from your activities? This is valuable, you may think, because getting more enjoyment makes you happy or provides you with pleasure. At this point, some philosophers would point out that the chain of explanation ends. Some even say that to ask the next question ("Why is getting pleasure a good thing?") is nonsense, because it literally makes no sense to ask why or whether pleasure is good since it is of its very nature a good thing. These philosophers may even argue that if you think carefully, you will notice that inherent in every valuable activity is the element of pleasure, and this is the characteristic that makes such actions good. For this reason, such thinkers believe that pleasure is an acceptable answer to the question of what makes something good in itself. This theory is known as *philosophical hedonism*. On one moral perspective that incorporates philosophical hedonism, we ought to strive to produce in our actions as much pleasure as possible for all persons affected by our actions. This serves as an example of a general moral principle that is meant to guide our actions. The other main question at Level IV concerns the principles, rules, or character traits that contribute to right actions or to proper conduct. We will examine theories that attempt to address this question later in this chapter.

V. Questions About Moral Skepticism versus Moral Cognitivism

Moral skepticism is the view that no moral knowledge is possible. To be a skeptic is really just to be agnostic, to believe that there may be a true answer to whether or not an action is morally right or wrong, but to think that we cannot know what the truth about that fact is. Cognitivism is the opposing view that holds that we possess or could possess moral knowledge. Notice that these Level V questions are of a different type than the previous questions, since they are questions *about* the nature of morality generally. These are often referred to as *metaethical* questions, to distinguish them as one level "higher" than normative questions such as those at Level IV or Level III. This means that regardless of what general moral principle (Level IV) or particular ethical controversy (Level III) concerns you, the position of either moral skepticism or moral cognitivism will apply to all of the issues under examination, since these are more general questions about the nature of moral knowledge.

VI. Questions About Relativism versus Objectivism

Relativism is the position that there is no fact of the matter regarding morality. That is, there is no one or best answer about whether an action or policy is morally right or wrong, but instead, that answer is relative to an individual thinker or culture. If moral relativism is true, there is no such thing as facts in the realm of morality. In opposition to this view is the position known as objectivism, which states that there is a fact of the matter regarding the moral status of an act, policy, or principle. The answers to moral questions are not simply a matter of one's personal beliefs, since on objectivism a person could in fact be mistaken concerning their view on a moral question.

Level VI questions, like Level V questions, are metaethical questions. In Level V, the question is whether we can or cannot know moral subject matter. In Level VI, the question is whether there is or is not an objective moral subject matter at all. Notice that these two types of questions are logically distinct: it could be that there exists some objective moral subject matter but it may be very hard for us to know something about it. Even if one were skeptical about our ability to gain moral knowledge, one could still believe that objective answers to moral questions exist (but are unfortunately out of our human grasp). We will now turn to discuss ethics, and the area of medical ethics, in particular.

THE FIELD OF MEDICAL ETHICS

The field of medical ethics is one area of ethical inquiry that focuses on a set of particular ethical controversies (Level III questions). *Medical ethics* aims to offer a logical analysis of ethical issues in an effort to clarify the relevant concerns and suggest appropriate policies. Standard issues discussed in medical ethics include the morality of ending a patient's life at his or her request, the ethical status of genetic modifications to humans, and the moral issues involved in human experimentation. This field is sometimes referred to as *bioethics*, yet since this text is concerned more with issues in medical practice than issues in biomedical research and biotechnology, I shall use the term "medical ethics" to describe the field of study within which the writers in this anthology are engaged. It is also worth noting that the issues discussed in this text are faced not only by physicians, but by all medical staff including nurses and allied health personnel. The dialogue constructed by the readings in this text aims to include many voices, and takes as essential the experience and practical input from professionals in the field. The time at which medical ethics became a distinct area of study within the field of ethics is typically marked by the creation of the Hastings Center, an organization for research in medical ethics, in 1969. Since this time, a sea change has occurred within medicine, with movement from a paradigm in which patients were expected to simply follow doctors' advice without question to a new model in which patients are granted significant latitude in determining the course of their treatment. *Patient autonomy*, the freedom for individuals to guide the course of their lives according to their preferences and deepest values, has become a central focus in medicine and in discussions of medical ethics.

Medical ethics is a truly interdisciplinary field of study, because it involves addressing questions of all types from within philosophy, including metaphysical, social, religious, and ethical queries. Medical ethics is at the intersection of morality, law, social/political philosophy, and public policy. It is also interdisciplinary in that it depends on input from fields outside philosophy such as medicine, medical research, and biotechnology. The selections in this textbook reflect the interdisciplinary nature of this dialogue by including writing not only by academic philosophers, but also from physicians, judges, attorneys, hospital ethics committees, and others. This field has become a central area of study at the advent of the twenty-first century; hardly a day goes by in which a news story reporting a development in medical treatment or medical research is not discussed in the media. With the huge advances made in the development of medical technology, and given the institutional pressures caused by an aging population in the United States as well as heightened concerns about legal liability, medical ethics has assumed an increased importance within the field of philosophy.

ETHICAL PERSPECTIVE #1: ETHICAL RELATIVISM

The remainder of this chapter discusses philosophical approaches to ethics. The first theory we shall discuss regarding what makes an action morally right or wrong in general is called ethical relativism. This theory claims that a person's "say-so" or approval is what makes an action morally right: this is referred to as a belief in *conventionalism* about morality, and this belief is at the heart of ethical relativism. Ethical relativism comes in two forms: individual ethical relativism, often called *ethical subjectivism*, and *cultural ethical relativism.*

Ethical subjectivism works from the basic belief that morality is not grounded in reasoning, and therefore states that a person's *feelings* or *beliefs* are the only possible means for morally justifying an action. So, if I enjoy lying to people to steal money from them, according to ethical subjectivism it is morally acceptable for me to lie and steal. Of course, if you do not approve of this behavior, then given your moral standards you should not follow my example. Proponents of this view find it appealing since it reflects the truth that there is no decisive way to settle moral disputes. Ethical subjectivists believe that this truth points to the only plausible view of morality, a view that holds that a person's feelings and beliefs make an action right for that person.

Even if we accept the idea that there is no decisive way to settle moral disputes, this does not imply that ethical subjectivism is true. This foundational point suggests only that individuals must ask themselves what values they most cherish and they should then try to arrive at a solution to a moral problem that they can live with; it does not suggest that there are no means whereby we can judge a moral belief to be better or worse. Yet the ethical subjectivist believes precisely this, since it is the case that as long as one feels that an action is acceptable, it is morally permissible. The idea that some ethical standards exist that are "external" to the individual also suggests that deeper problems affect this view. These problems include the following:

On Ethical Subjectivism, One's Actions Cannot Be Morally Criticized

Since ethical subjectivism is based on how a person feels about an action, if a person believes that the action is morally acceptable, it is morally acceptable. So, if convicted serial killer Ted Bundy thought that abducting and murdering young women was the right thing to do, it is not possible to criticize this decision. On this view, one could acceptably harm others and not need to offer a justification for these actions. The only possible way that a person's actions are judged as wrong on ethical subjectivism is if he acted in a way inconsistent with his own beliefs. But even then, he must have approved of his own actions in some way, at least at the time the action was performed, and therefore, the action is a correct action on this view. This view's hands-off approach is quite extreme since we judge the actions of murderers and other criminals to be morally wrong. If their actions are judged to be morally acceptable, this poses a problem with the imposition of punishment for such crimes. It is clearly reasonable to consider murderers to be deserving of punishment such as prison time for their crimes.

On Ethical Subjectivism, There Is No Reason to Be Tolerant of Other Persons' Beliefs or Actions

Adopting a general attitude of tolerance regarding others' behavior is crucial for living together in society. Since this view emphasizes the personal aspect of morality, it may seem that it would encourage each of us to be tolerant of the moral beliefs and decisions of others. However, this view is quite puzzling in that if it were to do so, it would be advocating a belief that is "external" to the personal decisions of moral agents. To put the point another way, on ethical subjectivism, one needs to be tolerant of others only if one feels this is a good thing. This is paradoxical since ethical subjectivism places such a high premium on an individual's personal beliefs that it makes them the basis of morality, yet this theory cannot necessarily encourage individuals to respect or tolerate the moral beliefs of other persons.

Ethical Subjectivism Does Not Properly Explain the Moral Status of Actions

According to ethical subjectivism, an action is right simply based on an individual person's feelings or beliefs, yet this explanation is not plausible. For one thing, an action could be morally right, such as keeping a promise, and this is not the case simply because of one's feelings toward the matter. Even if a person feels that keeping the promise is good, there are wider explanations available for why doing so is a moral requirement. For instance, keeping promises is part of maintaining trust in society, which is a good thing. It is part of being a virtuous person. On the other hand, an action could be wrong, despite the fact that a person has feelings that support the performance of the action. For instance, if a depraved rapist believes that his actions are acceptable and has strong positive feelings about his behavior, this may serve as a further indictment of his decisions, not as a justification of his harmful actions. While our feelings about the morality of performing an action possess some importance, the implications of considering them as the basis of morality are deeply problematic and hence ethical subjectivism is an unacceptable moral perspective.

The other form ethical relativism may take is cultural ethical relativism. This view is similar to ethical subjectivism in that it is *conventionalist* and therefore holds that morality is made by humans and not discovered. Yet it is different in that the basis of morality is founded in the norms of a culture or a society, not in the personal feelings and beliefs of an individual. This view holds that an action is morally right if it accords with the norms of that person's culture, and morally wrong if it does not. According to cultural ethical relativism, we cannot morally criticize the actions of persons in other cultures who act on the basis of their society's norms—we can only morally assess actions within our own culture by appealing to our society's norms.

Cultural ethical relativism does possess advantages over ethical subjectivism, since on this view, it is the case that a person's actions or behavior is not necessarily morally right by definition. According to cultural ethical relativism, a person's actions are wrong if they are not in conformity with the norms of their culture. So, if I engage in polygamy (marriage to more than one person at a time) and my culture does not approve of this practice, then my action is judged to be morally wrong on this view. Proponents of cultural ethical relativism find this view appealing since it builds from the idea that different societies have different cultural norms, and hence, different moral codes. This idea is often defended by referring to striking examples of different cultural practices. For instance, sociologists discuss Eskimo peoples who engaged in practices that resulted in the death of aged members of their group when these members were no longer productive. To the cultural relativist, this belief serves as proof of their theory about the nature of morality since in the United States we do not engage in the killing of our elderly parents. This is meant to suggest that there is quite a difference in the cultural beliefs of these two societies. The cultural relativist takes this as evidence of the claim that the norms in each society serve as the basis for morality in each culture: engaging in the killing of one's elderly parents in Eskimo culture is morally acceptable, while doing this in United States culture is morally unacceptable. According to the cultural relativist, their view is the only ethical perspective that can account for the diversity of cultural practices and moral codes.

While cultural ethical relativism initially looks more promising than ethical subjectivism, it possesses significant problems. First, its central belief, that different societies have different cultural norms and hence different moral codes, is not obviously true. This can be illustrated by looking at the example concerning the Eskimo peoples more closely. One writer[1] discusses the Kabloona, a culture in the Canadian Arctic that had a cultural practice in which an elderly member of the group would ask members of their family for help to ready for an expedition, say, to go seal hunting. The members of the family would agree, even though they were aware that the elderly member was not in any condition for hunting. In one reported case, a blind, elderly man made such a request, and after being properly outfitted, the man was led to the seal hunting grounds where he walked through a hole in the ice and disappeared. It is important to understand that the Kabloona were a nomadic people who survived by living off of the seal population. Each member of the group needed to be capable of doing his or her part in the activities to sustain the group. Insisting that an elderly member remain part of the group could endanger the safety and survival of the whole family. It is also important to notice that the family members did not initiate the actions that resulted in the elder's death; these were decided on by the elder himself. Thus, accepting the elder's decision was a form of respect, and allowed the rest of the family to retain loyalty to the elder while also allowing the elder to die with dignity while out on a seal hunt.

By looking more closely at this example, it is not so clear that the Kabloona possess a moral compass all that different from people in our culture. In this country, we show respect for our elders by ensuring their well-being in ways that were not available to a nomadic people such as the Kabloona (caring for them in our own homes or placing them in health care facilities). We share the principle of respect for elders, but given our environment and circumstances, we apply those principles differently. This underscores the point that significant *moral* differences may not exist between peoples as seemingly different as the Kabloona and Americans. To put the point in another way, while significant factual differences may exist between the Kabloona and Americans with regard to their parents, the cultural relativist seems to overlook the point that both peoples appear to subscribe to a similar moral principle. Relying on such examples seems curious when one takes a closer look: while the cultural relativist wishes to use such examples as illustrations of moral difference, this only works if one examines the cultural practice from a surface level. Looking for the reasons and moral principles behind the practices of such cultures significantly weakens the support that the cultural relativist's position receives from citing such examples.

Cultural ethical relativism also has a number of serious internal problems. These objections are generated by simply getting clear about the implications of adopting this ethical view. These difficulties include the following:

On Cultural Ethical Relativism, It Is Not Possible to Criticize Other Cultures

If we were to engage in criticism of another culture's practices, this would mean that we are making precisely the type of cross-cultural judgment barred by cultural relativists. However, we believe that the practices of many cultures are in fact morally unacceptable, and are willing to make a moral judgment that, for example, ethnic cleansing or torture of political prisoners is morally unacceptable. Accepting cultural ethical relativism implies that we must remain silent regarding such practices. The only form of criticism possible consists of pointing out that members of a culture are not adhering to their own norms. According to this theory, as long as the members of a society are acting in a manner consistent with their own culture's beliefs, their behavior is beyond reproach.

On Cultural Ethical Relativism, We Cannot Criticize Our Own Cultural Standards

According to this view, our culture's norms are morally correct since they serve as the basis for morally right action. How exactly should we identify what counts as a cultural standard within a particular society? This itself is a difficulty for cultural ethical relativism, but we could simplify the view by maintaining that if the majority of people in a culture support a practice, then that practice is the norm. However, even making this simplifying assumption, most of us think that our society could improve and is not completely right in all of its practices and policies. For instance, in the United States, it is still the case that racist practices exist in some areas and that women are paid significantly less for doing the same work as men. Even if we assume that the simple majority of persons in our culture support these practices, this still does not put these practices beyond moral questioning. However, by accepting cultural ethical relativism, one is unable to criticize such societal norms and practices.

On Cultural Ethical Relativism, There Is No Standard by Which We Can Judge Moral Changes in Society as Better or Worse

Suppose someone pointed out that the moral practices of the United States have improved (though they are not perfect) and cites as evidence for this claim that slavery and the subjection of women are now considered to be morally wrong. One may take this as evidence that the United States has progressed morally. However, if questioning racism and sexism is viewed as an improvement over earlier periods in our society's history, then we cannot adopt cultural ethical relativism. According to this view, there is no criticism of past societies, even of the past incarnations of our own society, and hence no comparison is possible. All a cultural relativist can say is that U.S. society is now different than it used to be, and that this is no better or worse than it was before. If our culture found slavery to be morally acceptable once again, that would simply mean that the culture has changed, not that it has gotten worse. If this belief became a norm, slavery would become morally acceptable in our society.

On Cultural Ethical Relativism, Moral Reformers Are Always Morally Wrong

Many consider Abraham Lincoln to be a hero since he helped to abolish slavery or Martin Luther King a visionary since he imagined how our country might look if it did away with the evils of institutionalized racism. However, according to cultural ethical relativism, moral reformers such as Lincoln and King are always morally wrong in their actions because moral reformers criticize and attempt to change the dominant practices of their society. Are Lincoln and King considered to be wrong in retrospect on cultural ethical relativism, even now, when slavery and racism are considered to be morally evil? The relativist, looking backward, is still committed to the wrongness of their actions: how can the relativist say that the norms supporting slavery and racism were wrong, if all that determines their rightness is acceptance by that culture? If the cultural relativist would say that those beliefs were wrong at that time, then this would suggest that some other standard was operating, some standard existing independently of mere cultural acceptance. To make this admission would undermine the cultural relativist's own position.

Cultural Ethical Relativism Recommends Inconsistent Courses of Action

In this discussion of cultural ethical relativism, the term "culture" has been used as an unanalyzed notion. How are the boundaries of culture determined? The boundaries are far from sharp, and this raises questions regarding how many cultures of which we are each members. Regardless of the definition of "culture" we settle on, we are each members of many different cultures. If these cultures have conflicting standards and norms, then cultural relativism recommends inconsistent moral judgments and courses of action. For instance, a person could be a member of Amnesty International, a group that supports social justice and holds that the death penalty as applied in the United States is unjust. This person could also be a member of the broader U.S. culture; according to recent surveys, the simple majority of Americans (approximately 60%) support capital punishment. Hence, according to cultural relativism (given the simplification concerning majority preference), this is a cultural norm. According to cultural ethical relativism, what is one to think regarding the death penalty, if one has cultural memberships that both recommend and oppose the death penalty? The cultural relativist does not possess any resources to address this dilemma, since this theory does not allow appeals to standards wider than cultural practices themselves. If we consider ethics to be a practical endeavor, then we need an acceptable moral perspective to provide guidance for us regarding the most important decisions about how to live our lives. Cultural ethical relativism lacks the resources for dealing with conflicting practices within a culture stemming from multiple cultural memberships.

Cultural ethical relativism reinforces the idea that context is important when thinking about what is morally acceptable. This critical discussion should not be understood as rejecting the importance of culture in shaping one's moral beliefs. The main point has been that cultural ethical relativism bases all of morality on cultural practices, yet it lacks support for its main premise and has unacceptable consequences. For these reasons, the vast majority of philosophical thinkers have abandoned cultural ethical relativism.

Critical Thinking Interlude: The Case of the "Guinea Pigs"

It was recently revealed that the Kennedy Krieger Institute conducted a study in the mid-1990s in which researchers enticed landlords to recruit 108 families with healthy children to live in houses with varying degrees of lead paint contamination. The purpose of the study was to measure the effectiveness of projects in poor areas to remove lead contamination from older buildings. It was thought that this study could benefit other families who may have children at risk for lead paint contamination. The families were not told that the houses contained lead paint, and even as children got sick, researchers did not tell parents what the potential cause of the illness was. As one mother said, "I feel betrayed ... my children were used as guinea pigs."

Critical Thinking Question: How would an ethical relativist who supported cultural ethical relativism assess the researchers' behavior in this case? On cultural ethical relativism, are the researchers' actions morally right or wrong? What reasons support the conclusions you reach?

Discussion: We have learned that on cultural ethical relativism, an act is morally right only if it accords with the norms of that person's culture. One may be tempted to respond in the following manner: "Clearly, in the United States, we do not accept such behavior as ethical, and therefore, it is not morally right." To use this response as a cultural ethical relativist's analysis of this case study, several points must be clarified. First, this reasoning applies only if the Kennedy Krieger Institute is located in the United States. If it is located in another country, its actions should be assessed based on different cultural norms. As it turns out, the Kennedy Krieger Institute is affiliated with Johns Hopkins University in Baltimore, Maryland, and therefore is located within the United States. Even so, for the actions to be assessed as morally right or wrong, we may have to look to the norms of the Kennedy Krieger Institute itself, since the institute may constitute its own culture. (As already discussed, the definition of "culture" is quite fluid.) If this is the case, then appealing to U.S. norms in general to judge the researchers' behavior would be mistaken from the perspective of cultural ethical relativism, since this would be to judge their behavior on the basis of norms external to their culture. Similarly, to judge the researchers' actions based on the assessments of the families who were exposed to the lead paint would also be misguided from the perspective of cultural ethical relativism. Again, assessments based on the cultural norms of such families (if they constituted their own culture) would be irrelevant in judgments of the researchers' actions from this ethical perspective. The researchers' actions would be morally right if the institute adopted the norm that it was acceptable to perform experiments on persons without securing their informed consent. Their actions would be morally wrong if the institute did not consider it morally acceptable to risk others' health without receiving their permission.

ETHICAL PERSPECTIVE #2: DIVINE COMMAND THEORY

Addressing the question of whether religion serves as the basis for morality is the central issue in this section. Our discussion will stem from a dialogue named *Euthyphro* in which the ancient Greek philosopher Socrates investigates this question. In this discussion, we will try to see the general points about the relationship between religion and morality to which Socrates' questioning may lead us. These general points will be illustrated by using Christianity as an example of the religion in question, although the conclusion reached is perfectly general so it applies to other religions as well.

The ethical perspective we will consider is the *Divine Command Theory*, a theory about the nature of moral rightness and wrongness. On this theory, "morally right" means, by definition, "commanded by God," and "morally wrong" means, by definition, "forbidden by God." In essence, this view states that God's will or approval determines what is morally right and morally wrong. Of course, if one was an atheist, one would reject such a view, since this person does not believe that God exists in the first place. If one rejects the Divine Command Theory on the basis of a belief in atheism alone, then the debate shifts to a dispute about whether or not God exists. To avoid changing the subject, we will avoid a philosophical discussion of arguments for and against God's existence, and instead look for deeper, internal reasons for determining whether this theory is true or false.

As he examines the relationship between religion and morality, Socrates' discussion suggests the following crucial question: are actions right/good because God commands them, or does God command right/good actions because they are right/good? It is central that we recognize the different meanings and implications of the two parts of this question, which is often referred to as the *Euthyphro question*. It may help to restate the question in two distinct portions:

(1) Are actions right/good *because God commands them,*

or

(2) Does God command right/good actions *because they are right/good?*

Let's now draw out the difference between the two parts of this question. Part (1) suggests that God *makes* acts morally right by commanding them or approving of them. Part (2) implies that whether an act is right relies on a standard existing *independently of* God's will. To bring these two different points into focus, imagine that God possessed a divine stamper that is used to determine the moral status of actions. According to part (1) of the question, it is simply God's approval of an action that makes it morally right—if God stamps the action "morally right" with the divine stamper, this is literally what makes the action morally right. According to part (2), however, this implies that things are morally right *prior to* God commanding them or not. It is not the act of using the divine stamper that determines the action to be right or wrong. Instead, on this understanding, since God is good, all-knowing, and wise, God perfectly recognizes the rightness of acts and places the divine stamp of approval only on those actions that possess the inherent property of moral rightness and goodness.

Socrates possessed great skill in using questioning to uncover interesting and sometimes unusual implications of proposals. If we examine each part of the *Euthyphro question* carefully, we can see that each of these options presents a serious problem for the Divine Command Theory's interpretation of the view that morality is based on religion. Let's begin with part (1) of the question, the portion that corresponds to the Divine Command Theory. If we take the (1) view, then understanding the nature of rightness in this way makes God's commands perfectly *arbitrary*. On this conception, any action is just as likely to be right as it is wrong; all actions are morally neutral and their moral status completely depends on God's command. On this conception, independently of God's approval of something, it is not right or wrong. It is true by definition that God's approval of X automatically makes X right, no matter what it is that God loves, evil or good. This makes the will of God arbitrary, since according to this view, God can make any action—even terrible actions such as murder, theft, or torture—right or good by willing those actions.

To focus the problem, we can ask whether God approves of what He approves of (a) because of certain qualities in those actions, or (b) because of nothing in particular. If we accept (1) as the definition of moral rightness, then we must also accept (b)—God's judgments are based on "raw" approval, meaning that God has no reasons for commanding what He commands apart from the fact that He commands it! If this is the case, then moral rightness is nothing in particular—it simply depends on the whims or moods of the divine authority. This conception is not acceptable even from the religious perspective, since it has impious results. If we are to have a *reasoned* account of morality, then the proper account of the relationship between religion and morality must connect moral rightness instead to (a)—that rightness depends on certain qualities of actions or persons (for example, whether the act causes others pain or whether the person is intentionally mean to others). If God is to have good reasons for choosing what is right or good, then God's decisions must relate to something inherent in the actions. With matters like morality and justice, we want to know *why* things are right or good, and to do this, we must look to reasons grounded in the nature of the thing itself. Because view (1) does not allow a reasoned account of morality and makes God's commands arbitrary, this understanding of the relationship between religion and morality is not acceptable even from a theological point of view.

On the view built from part (2) of the question, God commands right conduct because it is right. This conception avoids the problems with the first option. On this view, God's commands are not arbitrary: God commands acts because they possess certain good qualities that God recognizes. Since on this view rightness depends on inherent qualities of actions, it is not the case that any action can be made morally acceptable simply because it is commanded. For instance, if the act of murder is inherently evil, then, as an all-knowing and perfectly good being, God would disapprove of this action and would not command it.

The conclusion that Socrates reaches in his examination of the relationship between religion and morality is that the second option is left standing: it may be correct, and does not possess the problems with the first option. This may seem to be a rather modest conclusion, but it is still valuable. First, to know what is false is important, and by questioning and clarifying, we have arrived at a powerful indictment of the option stemming from part (1) of the *Euthyphro* question. Second, this conclusion points us in the right direction and provides a valuable insight: we can pursue the examination of rightness or value ourselves, *since divine commands only indicate or reflect what is morally right or wrong, they do not determine it.* Even assuming that God's commands are perfectly correct, as we must if we accept the conception of God as all-knowing and all-powerful, we should still look to the moral principles that explain the basis of the rightness and wrongness of actions. It is precisely these principles that explain in general what is morally right and morally wrong.

If what is morally right is not determined by God's commands, then how can we as humans figure out how to guide our lives? The answer to this question is that we must use *reason* to determine for ourselves what are the most acceptable moral rules and principles. As fallible human beings, we have no direct pipeline to the truth, but by thinking for ourselves and using reasoning to examine arguments concerning moral principles and issues, we can gather the best evidence for what is morally right and wrong.

It is possible to imagine several important objections to the argument based on Socrates' reasoning. First, we have seen that option (1) is not acceptable since it would imply that God could make any action (including murder and torture) morally acceptable if such actions were to be willed. One could object to this argument by emphatically stating, "God would never will such things, because God is good!" Since this is the case, one could claim that the argument is not relevant since the circumstance on which it is based will never in fact occur. On the Christian conception of God as a perfect, all-knowing being, of course God would never actually recommend and command terrible actions. However, this remark misses the point of the argument stated above. The question raised by Socrates' reasoning is how to account for the wrongness of such actions since by definition, on view (1) such actions would be considered automatically right in virtue of being commanded. The central point is that we have located an implication of view (1), and since this implication is troubling, we need to see what resources the view possesses to address this problem. To object on the basis that God is good and therefore would not command actions such as murder or theft, one would have to be operating with a different notion of goodness than the one inherent in the Divine Command Theory. According to the definition of rightness and goodness on view (1), what counts as right or good is simply left open and strictly depends on what God wills. To state that God is inherently good and therefore could not will "bad" actions such as murder or rape is to adopt an independent conception of goodness that undercuts the Divine Command Theory itself.

Another important objection one may raise is that if option (2) is adopted, as Socrates' argument suggests, then this makes moral standards "higher than" God and therefore is unacceptable. One may think this since if God's commands do not determine what is morally right or wrong, but instead involve certain inherent properties of actions and moral principles, then it may seem that morality is somehow "greater" than God and hence out of God's reach. It is possible to offer a reply to this objection that shows that on the Christian conception of God, there is no such problem. If our conception of divinity is that of a perfect being (as it was not for the ancient Greeks), then by adopting Socrates' reasoning, we can view God as willing perfectly in accord with moral principles of rightness or goodness, because perfection is of God's essence. The argument discussed in this section does not in any way "subordinate" God to moral standards: if perfection is of God's essence, then God wills perfectly in accord with the correct moral principles. This is not a limitation placed on God, since a thing's essence is not a constraint on it, but is simply part of its nature. If God did not possess this essence, then God would simply be a different thing from the perfect being we have been discussing.

The root worry here is that rejecting the Divine Command Theory somehow makes religion unimportant, but that does not logically follow if we accept Socrates' reasoning and adopt option (2) as a viable understanding of morality. Even if we accept option (2), as we should even from the theological perspective, religion can serve as a source of moral guidance in that it provides good advice on how to live an upright life. It is consistent (in principle) with the rejection of the Divine Command Theory that every word of the Bible is true, and in general we should encourage everyone to seek out all sources of good moral guidance. All we are committed to thinking if we reject the Divine Command Theory is that the foundational explanation of rightness and wrongness does not reside in God's commands, but lies in, for example, moral principles and the inherent moral qualities of action themselves.

Closely related to the Divine Command Theory is Natural Law Theory, which holds that everything in nature has a purpose, and that purpose is determined by God. We have just finished discussing Socrates' argument for the conclusion that morality cannot be determined on the basis of God's commands. Many Christian thinkers accept the conclusion of this argument and therefore reject the Divine Command Theory. (This includes the great Christian theologian Saint Thomas Aquinas.) However, the Natural Law Theory serves an important role in the Christian conception of the relationship between religion and morality, and hence it is worthy of a brief examination. This conception depends on a *teleological* view of science and nature, one that posits built-in ends for all things, including humans. This view makes a normative claim by stating that things are as they ought to be when they are serving their natural purposes. The essential claim is that humans should favor activities that are natural, and shun those that are "unnatural" or run counter to their God-given purpose. On this view, human reason is thought to be able to divine these natural purposes, and therefore, to discern the actions that are required by the Natural Law Theory.

The central tenets of this view possess significant problems. First, the teleological conception of Natural Law Theory is based on outmoded scientific beliefs. The view that everything has a purpose is dubious as reflected in the basis of modern science founded on the work of Galileo, Newton, and Darwin. Natural phenomena such as thunderstorms are not best thought of as divine waterings of planet earth, but are instead explainable by appeal to the workings of physical laws. On this widely accepted conception, there are no inherent values in nature. A defender of Natural Law Theory may claim that things are as they ought to be since the natural state of affairs is that in which *homo sapiens* is the only human species to roam the earth. However, to make such a claim is to appeal to a science that has been discredited; natural selection does not work according to some grand plan, but instead, through random mutations. It works "blindly" without a specific purpose in mind. Anyone who accepts these widely held scientific beliefs will reject the Natural Law Theory.

In addition, privileging the notion of a "natural" activity is itself problematic. On this view, any form of sexual activity that is not procreative, such as masturbation, oral sex, and homosexual sex, would be morally wrong since it is not in keeping with the "natural" purposes of sexual activity. To analyze this notion further, ask yourself the following question: "What is meant by the term 'natural?' " When I look at my cereal box in the morning, it states on the front, "All Natural." When I look through the list of ingredients, I find a whole list of chemicals that I cannot even pronounce. It would seem that on this conception of "natural," anything that comes from the Earth is natural, even if it has been processed or modified by techniques engineered by humans. On this conception, however, then everything counts as natural; there is nothing on the Earth that could be "unnatural." As such, this conception does not mark off such "natural" products or activities as morally special.

Alternatively, to be "natural" may mean to be untouched by human intervention. If this is the case, it is difficult to see why "natural" things are to be held in such high esteem. Over the course of the twentieth century, the average life expectancy at birth of humans in the United States increased by over twenty-five years. This has been accomplished largely because of advances in medical treatments and pharmaceuticals. If it is the case that humans are now living an "unnaturally" long life span, then what is so bad about things that are "unnatural?" In thinking about it, medicine itself is fundamentally "unnatural" at some level, since it attempts to intervene in the natural course of an illness. While disease itself may viewed as upsetting the natural state of the body, it is still the case that sickness itself is to be expected as a "natural" part of life. The following dilemma arises: It is difficult to specify a notion of the "natural" that does not either prevent us from esteeming products or activities that we reasonably find to be valuable, or does not allow us to avoid a notion that becomes so generic that it fails to ground the normative superiority of products or activities that the Natural Law Theory wishes to endorse. In addition, as we have discussed, Natural Law Theory relies on dubious assumptions about the existence of purposes in the universe. For these reasons, this conception has fallen out of favor as a serious philosophical theory.

Critical Thinking Interlude: The Case of "Jodie" and "Mary"

In 2000, two conjoined twins given the fictitious names of "Jodie" and "Mary" were born. The childrens' parents were from the island of Gozo, part of Malta, and the parents traveled to England to have the twins to ensure good medical care. Jodie and Mary were joined at their lower abdomens, but were capable of lying flat on their back. Their spines were fused yet their legs were independently formed and criss-crossed one another. Upon medical examination, it was discovered that Mary's brain and body were less developed than Jodie's. Mary exhibited very little activity, and experts reported that her brain was "extremely primitive" and found that she had no realistic chance at living on her own. However, the medical team caring for the twins also determined that it was highly probable that if left unseparated, both twins would die within six months, due to the strain put on Jodie's heart. It was also believed that Jodie would have a good quality of life and a substantial possibility of a normal life expectancy if she were separated from Mary. The children's parents did not wish for the surgery to be performed; as Roman Catholics, they decided that they could not kill one daughter to allow the other one to live. As they put it, "Now that things have gone very badly wrong and we find ourselves in this very difficult situation ... [W]e believe that [if] it's God's will that both our children should not survive then so be it."

Critical Thinking Question: The parents in this case are opposed to the surgery to separate the twins since they believe this would in effect be intentionally "killing" Mary, and this violates the religious prohibition on murder. However, given the alternatives faced, what can be said in favor of the decision to perform the surgery? Could it be the case that a "killing" occurs no matter whether the surgery is performed or not? Discuss.

Discussion: The central moral issue in this case is whether or not the surgery can be morally justified, all things considered. The parents' remarks could be interpreted as consistent with some form of the Divine Command Theory on which God's commands determine the right decision, or may stem from a Natural Law component of a form of religious ethics on which we should not interfere with the "natural" course of events.

What are the relevant alternatives? We might vote in favor of *no surgery*, which could be described as a case in which Jodie is killed (?) and Mary continues to live for a longer time (until both then die in approximately six months). Or, we may support *performing the surgery*, in which case we might say that Mary is killed (?) and Jodie lives (given the best medical evidence).

These descriptions of the options demand further discussion and clarification. The parents in this case believe that their view implies that it is better not to attempt the separation, since this would involve "killing" Mary. On this view, if we perform the surgery and know that on the best medical evidence, Mary's death will be hastened, we are "killing" Mary. But notice that on the same score, if we do not perform the surgery and know that on the best medical evidence, Jodie's death will be hastened, then this can be construed as "killing" Jodie. (This is the case if at some point not using a medical intervention to save a life becomes a "killing," just as using a medical intervention that hastens the end of a life is a "killing.") If both options may properly be said to involve killing, it is unclear which option a religious ethic would favor.

At this juncture, one would likely introduce the distinction between killing and allowing to die, and argue that Jodie is merely being allowed to die, since nothing is done to kill her (but merely withholding the surgery). By the same token, however, it could be said that Mary is allowed to die as well: this is clearest if we consider Jodie to be a form of human "life-support" for Mary and the medical procedure that enacts the separation is simply a complex form of withdrawing Mary from life-support. (On such a view, withdrawing from life-support is a paradigm case of letting one die.) So, in tracking out this line of argument, either both options represent killings and both are morally wrong, or both simply consist in letting one die, and can be morally acceptable.

This way of setting up the problem moves a bit too quickly, and there are many more things that would need to be explored to reach a stable and defensible description of the alternatives. There are also additional questions one needs to raise. For example, is it the case that Mary, even though she is innocent, could be said to *kill* Jodie? If so, the surgery could be justified on grounds of self-defense, and Jodie's parents may be morally obliged as third party guardians to exercise this right on Jodie's behalf. This discussion suggests that even from the perspective of religious ethics, it is not obvious that God's will is only expressed by the "no surgery" option. (Perhaps from this perspective, God approves of the use of medical technology to expand the length and quality of life, and that is why such technology has developed as a product of human reason.) The lack of certainty created by critically reflecting on questions such as those above suggest that much deeper thought is needed before a reasoned opinion can be reached concerning this case. The issues in this case are not able to be resolved simply by subsuming them under a rule such as "Thou shalt not kill."

PSYCHOLOGICAL EGOISM AND ETHICAL PERSPECTIVE #3: ETHICAL EGOISM

A common view about human nature that bears on a full discussion of ethics states that humans always put themselves first. This view, referred to by philosophers as Psychological Egoism, holds that people do always (and cannot but) promote or maximize their self-interest. The suggestion is that given the way that humans are constituted, they have no choice but to give first priority to satisfying their own interests. Let's begin by clarifying some central points about this view.

First, psychological egoism is a *descriptive* theory: it attempts to offer a "deep" psychological fact about human motivation. It is not a *normative* theory that offers a justification for how we *ought* to act. Sometimes, psychological egoism is presented as an empirical claim that is used to support the view that we ought to be concerned exclusively about our own interests. This latter view is generally referred to as *ethical egoism*, which states that an act is morally right only if it maximizes the self-interest of the individual. If it is the case that humans are not psychologically capable of putting others' interests first, then an acceptable moral theory must reflect this fact by not requiring them to do so. It is in this way that some defenders of ethical egoism attempt to use psychological egoism as support for their theory, since they believe that ethical egoism is the only realistic theory given the nature of humans.

Second, psychological egoism is a theory about humans' ultimate or fundamental motivations. It is consistent with this theory that humans have *instrumental* desires for all sorts of things—to listen to music, go for a walk, or climb a mountain—but at bottom all of these things are desired simply because one seeks to satisfy one's self-interest. What this suggests is that if psychological egoism is true, human beings can desire that their friends be happy, and can help them to have a pleasant life, but the psychological egoist only does this because she sees this as in her self-interest. If helping her friends did not contribute to her own happiness in a particular instance, or if she did not believe that her friends would eventually "pay her back" for her help, she would not be motivated to help her friends. It is important to see that when thinking about the truth or falsity of psychological egoism, appearances can be deceiving: one may think from the outside that persons are acting in an altruistic way, but that may not necessarily be true. Persons may be helping their friends simply because they believe that this is in their own best interest, and if they are motivated in this way, this is completely consistent with psychological egoism. To say that on psychological egoism, all persons are selfish, is not to refer to the common usage of "selfish," which means being "stingy." Instead, selfishness means being motivated *egoistically*; according to this view, persons cannot ever be motivated *altruistically*, that is, by an ultimate desire to promote another person's interests.

Third, psychological egoism intends to be a doctrine about our true motivations, not simply about what we would like to believe about our deepest motivations. We may engage in rationalization all the time, so that we think we are good at heart, when at bottom we really are out for ourselves. Finally, the focus in the discussion of psychological egoism is on *intentional* or *voluntary* acts. These are acts about which it makes sense to talk of a person's motivations. A knee-jerk reaction is not an intentional action—it is not an action for which we formed an intention on the basis of a desire that we have. The class of actions we are discussing when considering the truth of psychological egoism is limited to intentional acts.

While psychological egoism is an empirical theory about human motivations, proponents of this view do not present empirical surveys or studies to support it. Instead, they employ various arguments to establish their theory. For this reason, philosophical analysis can be an enlightening method for examining psychological egoism.

One argument offered in support of this view begins with the claim that persons always do what they most want to do. This statement is meant to imply that persons always act on their strongest desire, and this statement is assumed to be true. From this, proponents of this argument think it follows that persons always act in their own self-interest, and therefore, that psychological egoism is true. The idea that is intended to link the two statements is that if persons always act on their strongest desire, then they simply must be doing what they want most to do, and this is the same as what they view as in their self-interest. This argument merits some critical commentary. First, the statement that persons always do what they most want to do may be false: we may not always act on our strongest desire. Each time a student comes to class on a beautiful, sunny day, this may not be what he or she most wants to do. In response, one could point out that while the student may not most strongly desire coming to class on those days, if she did not truly value completing her education, then she simply would not come to class. The point is that in a larger sense, she is doing what she most wants to do by coming to class since she values getting an education, completing her college work, or having the type of career afforded by a university degree. So, it may still be true that we always do what we most want in light of our long-term goals.

However, even though this part of the argument is not obviously false, it is still far from clear that the argument is successful. Even if one always does what he most wants to do, this may not be the action that is in fact in his own best interest. This would be true only if persons desire what is best for them in the long-run, yet this is false. Most defenders of psychological egoism do not wish to make their theory of self-interest completely subjective by assuming that whatever a person desires is in fact best for him. That is, most proponents of this view assume that persons can be wrong about what is in their best interest. For this reason, it does not follow from the fact that one always acts on his strongest desire that this will be the action that is in his self-interest. The conclusion of the argument does not follow from the premise.

Another argument proposed in support of psychological egoism maintains that all "unselfish" actions are accompanied by the pleasure of feeling good about oneself. Since this is the case, one simply does such acts for the resulting pleasure, and psychological egoism is true. This interpretation of the argument assumes a simple hedonistic view of self-interest that is defined in terms of pleasure. Notice that this argument assumes that if doing an action that helps another results in the person who performs the action feeling good, then this must be the purpose of the action. In general, this assumption is false, since our actions have many unintended *results*, and each of these results is not necessarily the *purpose* of the action. One result of giving money to the Salvation Army person who rings the bell outside the department store during the holidays is that my wallet is somewhat lighter. However, even though that is a result, we cannot necessarily assume that I give the money to reduce the bulk of my wallet. Similarly, a predictable result of giving money to charity may be that I get a good feeling about myself. Even though this is a result, we cannot necessarily assume (as the psychological egoist does) that this is the purpose of my action of donating to charity.

The main argument offered in support of this psychological theory is the *strategy of reinterpreting motives.* This strategy maintains that any action whose motivation appears to contradict psychological egoism can be redescribed to fit the theory. Can you think of any action whose description does not fit the theory? One possible example of an unselfish act might be that of a firefighter who rushes into a burning building to save a child. A defender of psychological egoism may claim that the firefighter's motivation is to show his strength and perhaps be featured in the newspaper as a hero. If we think about it, almost any action that appears "unselfish" from the outside likely gives the person who performs the action a good feeling, and hence, provides some pleasure that may be seen as being in his or her self-interest. From a critical perspective, all this point demonstrates is that it is *possible* to reinterpret any action in egoistic terms, not that these egoistic explanations are any better or more accurate than competing non-egoistic explanations.

There is a deeper problem with this argument, as suggested by one recent philosopher.[2] If I make the claim that Shaquille O'Neal cannot stand up straight in my basement, then there must be a way to prove or disprove this. I could invite Shaq over to my house and see if he can do so without putting his head through the first floor. (Or, more simply, I could find out his height from an NBA website and measure the basement from floor to ceiling.) This example underscores the point that empirical claims must be testable. Now, consider a different example. Imagine that an expert on swans has proclaimed that after a lifelong research project, his studies have revealed with certainty that all swans are white. When confronted with evidence that black swans are found in Australia, this researcher says, "Those swans do not count; they are not white." What becomes clear is that this researcher, based on this theory, has simply built "whiteness" into the definition of "swan." To him, nothing non-white can be properly classified as a swan, even if the relevant bird shares similar biological and genetic features, can successfully mate with the white birds, and so on. The researcher's claim, at least initially, seemed to be an empirical claim, yet on examination it has become true by definition that all swans are white. No proposed counterexample could ever be successful, given this theory's conception of "swanhood," since the claim is no longer *testable in principle*.

An analogous point applies to psychological egoism. Recall that this theory purports to make an empirical claim concerning the nature of humans. However, if it is the case that any and all proposed counterexamples could be redescribed to fit the theory, this theory loses its interest as an empirical claim and instead becomes a kind of conceptual definition. The requirement that empirical claims must be testable is sometimes referred to as the requirement of *falsifiability in principle*. Of course, if a theory is in fact true, it will never be falsified, but the theory must remain falsifiable *in principle*; for psychological egoism, it must at least be possible to realistically specify the conditions in which a person fails to act egoistically. The psychological egoist's approach to viewing evidence of altruistic behavior, however, is to reinterpret all possible cases of altruism in a way that make them consistent with their view. This theory no longer qualifies as an empirical hypothesis, and if it becomes true by definition that all human actions are essentially motivated by self-interest, then this view loses its interest as a theory about human nature that has potential impact on our conception of morality. We have critically examined only the main arguments typically offered in support of psychological egoism. This discussion suggests, at the very least, that these standard arguments do not offer good reasons to subscribe to psychological egoism.

Ethical Egoism is a normative theory that states, in its most generic formulation, that an act is morally right only if it maximizes an individual's self-interest. The common formulation of the view suggests that everyone ought to do those acts that will best serve his or her self-interest. So, one is obligated on this moral theory to do what is in one's best interest no matter what, even if this harms other persons or many other people.

To begin our evaluation of the viability of ethical egoism, it is worth noting that some arguments for this theory appeal to the truth of psychological egoism for support. The claim is that psychological egoism as an empirical hypothesis supports the moral perspective of ethical egoism. As we saw earlier in this section, however, psychological egoism is subject to a number of difficulties that call its truth into question. One could object by stating that the arguments offered against psychological egoism are not conclusive. It is worth asking, then, that if psychological egoism were true, would this imply that ethical egoism is true?

First, psychological egoism could be true and ethical egoism could be false. If psychological egoism were true, this would rule out all ethical theories that posited altruistic duties for individuals, since human beings would simply not be capable of performing such duties. Many philosophers accept the idea that "ought" implies "can." If humans are morally required to perform an action, it must be possible in the relevant sense for them to do so, otherwise we cannot require this action. It is simply unfair to require humans to perform impossible actions. Even though this is the case, the fact that we *do* behave in a certain way does not imply that we *ought to* act in that way. For example, many persons have acted in disrespectful ways toward other drivers when on the road, yet it does not follow from this that this is morally acceptable behavior. In addition, psychological egoism could be true, and the proper account of morality could be (for example) nihilism, the view that there are no morally right or wrong actions at all, because there are no moral standards. This suggests that while the truth of psychological egoism implies the falsity of all non-egoistic moral perspectives, it does not necessarily follow that ethical egoism is true.

Also, psychological egoism can be false and ethical egoism can be true. For instance, it could be the case that humans can perform purely altruistic acts, so that psychological egoism is false, yet all such non-egoistic actions are morally wrong. In other words, ethical egoism could be true, in that you would be doing wrong by not promoting your best interests at all times, even though at times persons simply do not follow its dictates. The upshot of these remarks is that the truth or falsity of psychological egoism cannot be used to establish anything necessarily regarding the truth of ethical egoism.

While some persons find ethical egoism to be an ethical perspective that possesses natural appeal, the discussion of the relationship between psychological egoism and ethical egoism leaves us with no good reason to believe that ethical egoism is true. One alternative supporting reason could be that ethical egoism conforms to our commonsense ethical thinking: it is not uncommon to hear a "me first" attitude expressed in ethical discussions in the public media. While this is the case, one must realize that according to ethical egoism, any action could be considered morally acceptable if it serves that person's best interests. So, if an individual takes pleasure in torturing animals or in defrauding senior citizens, these actions could be morally permissible on this view, which is very different from what commonsense morality holds. Persons who wish to defend this implication would stress the fact that ethical egoism is sometimes offered as a revisionary ethical view: it seeks to change our common beliefs about the root of morality. With this defense, however, defenders of ethical egoism can no longer appeal to the conformity of their theory with commonsense ethical thinking. One way to defend ethical egoism without losing this reason for supporting the view is to instead argue that in the long-run, actions such as torturing animals are not truly in a person's best interest. These actions will eventually get one in trouble with the law and make one a bad person; perhaps it is in one's own best interest to treat others kindly in most cases and to generally obey society's rules and regulations.

Even given this reply, defenders of ethical egoism still have difficulty offering a clear justification for the main point underlying ethical egoism, that each individual's ethical obligations stop with himself or herself. Why believe that I am so different from everyone else and therefore have no moral obligations toward others? One recent thinker points out that ethical egoism amounts to a form of unacceptable ethical discrimination against others.[3] First, a moral perspective that uniformly assigns greater weight to the interests of one group over another seems to be unacceptably arbitrary, unless there is some reason that justifies the different treatment of the members of the two groups. This discussion of ethical egoism makes clear that this view requires that individuals assign greater weight to their own interests than to the interests of others. However, the defender of ethical egoism offers no general, morally relevant difference that justifies persons in putting their interests above those of other persons in all cases. For this reason, ethical egoism is unacceptable since its basis relies on an arbitrary and unfounded assignment of superiority to the interests of oneself over the interests of others.

How could one attempt to defend this distinction? The ethical egoist seems to suggest on the one hand that we are all very similar in that each of us should focus on maximizing our own self-interest. On the other hand, perhaps we are quite different in that each of us is the "owner" of our personal interests. Given that these are our interests, I might argue that putting my own interests above others' interests at all times is justified precisely because I can better promote my interests since they are *mine*.

I simply know myself better and will do a superior job in looking after myself. While it is true that I may know myself better than I know others' interests, this does not imply that there are not lots of situations in which I can easily discern what others need and what it would take to satisfy those needs. In many instances, I can further a child's interests or assist a person who is more unfortunate than I am, knowing that in most cases I am performing an action that truly helps this other person. With a little effort I can realize that others' needs are in many cases very similar to my own, and especially in cases where others' needs are more pressing than mine, I should act to promote these other persons' interests. This insight that all humans have very similar basic needs, even though the means to satisfying these needs may take various forms, suggests that ethical egoism is not a promising moral perspective. This critical treatment of ethical egoism does not reach a solely negative result, since it suggests that a promising moral view should weight the interests of others on a par with our own since human beings possess similar needs. We will discuss theories that embody this idea later in this chapter.

Critical Thinking Interlude: The Case of the Kansas City Pharmacist

Recently, a pharmacist in Kansas City, Missouri, was accused of diluting chemotherapy drugs dispensed to cancer patients. Authorities became suspicious when they realized that the pharmacy had not ordered the needed amount of raw materials to concoct the volume of chemotherapy drugs dispensed by the pharmacy. It is suspected that the cancer treatments consisted mostly of saltwater. According to a news reports, court filings say the pharmacist admitted to diluting the chemotherapy drugs out of greed. A federal magistrate suggested the pharmacist may have been motivated by a $600,000 tax bill. The pharmacist's wealth was estimated by prosecutors to be approximately $10 million. The case is still pending in court, but the pharmacist has recently pleaded innocent to a 20-count indictment charging that he misbranded and adulterated the drugs.

Critical Thinking Question: According to ethical egoism, assuming that the pharmacist did in fact intentionally dilute the drugs, would his actions be morally right or morally wrong? Present the reasons that could be offered in support of both conclusions. Then, explain which conclusion you believe the ethical egoist would reach concerning the pharmacist's actions.

Discussion: An ethical egoist may argue that the pharmacist's actions are acceptable from the perspective of ethical egoism, since clearly the pharmacist has been very successful, having amassed a fortune of approximately $10 million. Also, the chances of this being found out are probably relatively low, especially if the record-keeping system in the pharmacy could be reworked to avoid alerting authorities.

Alternatively, an ethical egoist may argue that the pharmacist's actions are not acceptable. Several reasons could be offered to support this conclusion. First, the fact that the pharmacist's action of watering down the drugs has been discovered may cause his customers to doubt whether he is giving them the correct pharmaceutical dosage, even if they are not cancer patients. This may lead them to fill their prescriptions at other pharmacies, and therefore may hurt his business. Second, if the pharmacist is in fact convicted on the charge, then he will likely lose his fortune and spend a considerable amount of time in prison. This will obviously have a negative effect on his self-interest. Overall, given the drastic consequences of being found out, even granting the low probability of this occurring, an ethical egoist would likely argue that from his or her perspective it is not best overall for the pharmacist to dilute the drugs. Since it is likely that the pharmacist could make a good living without having to take this risk, it would be best overall not to dilute the drugs.

ETHICAL PERSPECTIVE #4: UTILITARIANISM AND CONSEQUENTIALISM

Consequentialism is a moral perspective that holds that only the consequences or results of one's actions matter intrinsically. Utilitarianism is the most popular form of consequentialism. Utilitarianism states that an action is right only if it produces overall results at least as good as any available action for everyone involved.

On utilitarianism, the best consequences are interpreted in terms of *happiness*, and happiness is understood in terms of maximizing pleasure and minimizing pain. (As discussed earlier, this view of value is called *philosophical hedonism*.) According to this perspective, we are to aim at promoting the happiness of all persons affected by the action, not just ourselves. Utilitarianism looks toward producing the best *overall* consequences in the long-run. We are to try to figure out as best we can what will happen as a result of our actions, weigh the alternatives, and perform the best possible action from those alternatives. Finally, utilitarianism is a revisionary perspective that does not determine the morality of actions on the basis of divine commands or inflexible rules. What is right can vary depending on what will produce the most happiness in general. This perspective constantly challenges us to rethink our traditional beliefs and does not simply subscribe to current social practices and norms.

This theory, while intuitively appealing to a number of philosophers, has been the subject of a number of objections. In what follows we will consider only the most serious of these criticisms. The first objection maintains that utilitarianism cannot accommodate "backward-looking" reasons.[4] For example, defenders of this objection would argue that utilitarianism would approve of breaking a promise to meet your friend in front of the movie theater for a trivial reason (for instance, simply because you felt like staying home and watching TV). What reason is there for thinking this? Critics maintain that because utilitarianism is a "forward-looking" theory, in that only the future results of an action matter, promises would not be considered important on utilitarianism. When one performs an action on the basis of a promise, this refers to a "backward-looking" reason, since this action stems from a reason based on a past event that (it is claimed) has no inherent significance on utilitarianism.

In response, utilitarians argue that this criticism is weak. They admit that if you have a very significant reason to break the appointment (suppose you must rush a friend to the hospital), that would very likely be acceptable according to utilitarianism. However, many people would agree that in such an emergency it is morally right to break the promise to save a life. But to claim that this view would approve of breaking promises for trivial reasons is a serious misunderstanding. First, even if you must cancel the appointment due to an unforeseen event, you should still notify the person if you can. For instance, you could contact the person before she leaves to meet you, or reach her on her cellular telephone. The utilitarian would stress that better alternatives exist than simply allowing the friend to wait outside the theater alone. Further, utilitarians would stress that there is nothing special about "backward-looking" reasons which makes it the case that they are incompatible with their theory. The fact that you made a promise to your friend *does* in itself affect future events. To cancel the appointment for a trivial reason would have bad effects on your friendship, and this is very important in utilitarian terms. For these reasons, utilitarians appear to be able to offer a powerful response to this first objection.

The second objection states that utilitarians cannot accommodate justice or moral rights. A current controversy could be used to illustrate this possible objection. In the wake of the September 11 terrorist attacks on the United States, law professor Alan Dershowitz discussed on the television show "60 Minutes" the possibility that the U.S. government may use torture on prisoners to obtain information about terrorist networks. Dershowitz was not necessarily endorsing this idea, but his claim is that since it was likely that this would be done, we should establish standards within the legal system to determine the (rare) cases in which this is a justified action. Dershowitz used a "ticking bomb" case to make his point vivid: in this scenario, either one person could be caused great pain in order to force this person to tell when and where the terrorist act will occur, or a great number of innocent persons (say, 10,000) will die if the bomb detonates. Dershowitz discussed the idea of "torture warrants," which would allow very painful procedures to be administered to persons to prevent a great loss of human lives. For instance, sterilized needles could be put under prisoners' fingernails, which would cause them great pain but no permanent physical harm or disfigurement. From a moral perspective, one might point out that utilitarianism cannot accommodate moral rights or justice since it could approve of using torture on prisoners in certain cases. Since this is unjust and violates fundamental human rights, one could argue that this constitutes a major objection to utilitarianism.

Utilitarians have developed a number of replies to this objection. One line of response takes a radical strategy and argues that some acts that violate rights may in fact be morally right according to utilitarianism. As it turns out, in extreme cases such as this we see clearly the utilitarian foundation of moral rights. According to this response, we need to revise our moral feelings in such instances: we should realize that this situation is a moral dilemma in which either many innocent persons will suffer, or one innocent person will suffer. Regardless of what we do, someone who is innocent will be harmed. We have a strong psychological aversion to using torture, which is a good thing since it prevents this from being used in all but the most desperate cases. Yet, in some cases we need to overcome this psychological aversion. The utilitarian asks that we imagine vividly those other persons who will be hurt due to no fault of their own. Since we can at least minimize the amount of harm that occurs, though we cannot completely prevent it, the utilitarian responds by arguing that it is not so implausible to say that in such extreme cases we may need to violate some persons' rights in order to minimize the number of rights' violations that will occur.

Further, utilitarians will stress that in general, moral rights can be overridden. When living in society, in some cases rights must be curtailed for the greater good. For instance, American citizens have a constitutional right to freedom of speech. However, if it is reasonable to think that what you say will incite listeners to riot, then your right to free speech can be limited and you can be legally required to stop speaking. Citizens have a right to freedom of movement and freedom of association. Yet, in times of crisis, a curfew can be enacted and enforced by the National Guard, even though this serves to curtail fundamental rights. The overarching point is that there are already widely accepted limitations on the exercise of moral rights. The utilitarian invites you to look more closely at the reasons that lie behind these limitations, and argues that these limits exist because it is believed that they will improve the overall level of well-being in society. So, it is generally acceptable to exercise one's right to free speech, but this is not the case if doing so endangers the safety of others or leads to terrible results. This response emphasizes that the critic of utilitarianism is simply misled in thinking that moral rights are the fundamental ethical notion. Even though rights are often viewed as if they are a primary moral concept, that is simply because in most cases, allowing the free exercise of rights has the best overall results.

The alternative line of response offered by utilitarians is less radical. On this response, no actions that violate rights are in fact ever right according to utilitarianism. This response emphasizes that while it is always possible that the overall results could be best achieved by using torture, in the real world this never really is the case. First, if we use torture, we would get a lot of misinformation, since persons subjected to such treatment will say anything under these conditions to make the torture stop. This misinformation will not only hinder law enforcement, but also may allow real criminals to continue to harm others. Second, and perhaps more importantly, we will then live in a country that itself uses the "terrorist" tactics we reject. This may have negative effects on citizens' respect for their government, and this decision in itself may lead to further human rights abuses in our own land.

The final objection to utilitarianism we shall discuss maintains that utilitarianism is too demanding. This objection can be interpreted in several ways. One aspect of this worry may be that utilitarianism will dictate every aspect of our lives to ensure that we always perform the action that has the best overall results. For instance, one could argue that in a utilitarian society, perhaps all children should be tested to determine their abilities and then assigned to careers that are best suited to their capacities. That way, each individual would make the largest possible contribution to society by best using his or her natural talents and abilities. While we feel that choice of career is a personal matter that each of us should be free to make, the objector points out that the utilitarian may find it is best to modify this social practice. This sort of policy suggests that utilitarianism is an unduly controlling moral theory.

The utilitarian can offer the following response to this worry. He or she would likely argue that there are good utilitarian reasons to not dictate every aspect of our lives. If we assign persons to careers based on a battery of tests, even though they may not be interested in pursuing those careers, it is quite likely that many persons will be miserable. If persons are miserable in their jobs, they are not happy in general and will take no interest in doing good work. This will have terrible effects. Of course, if the utilitarian calculation were perfect, it would take all of this into account—and this is precisely the point, that perhaps leaving people alone for the most part in such personal decisions actually leads to the best results! On the basis of this argument, it is not true that utilitarianism is overly demanding in the sense that it would approve of such oppressive practices, and hence this objection fails.

One could argue that utilitarianism is too demanding since it would never allow us to rest; instead, we should always be acting to help others. For instance, when I am sleeping, I could instead be helping to feed the poor, which would have very good results. If I look individually at each instant of my life, it may be true that when I am sleeping, I could be doing something more productive with my time. This is sometimes referred to as the "no rest" version of the objection that utilitarianism is too demanding.

Utilitarians have a ready reply to this second version of the objection as well. On utilitarianism, should we rest? The answer to this question is, "Yes!" How much? The answer is "the optimal amount." People who never take time to rest get burned out and over the course of their lives do not accomplish as much as they could have overall at a more moderate pace. Utilitarianism does not advocate that we look at each of our individual actions blindly, that is, without thinking how they would affect one's life in the long-run. Since a person who has not slept in two weeks is good for nothing, the utilitarian can easily argue that a policy of "no rest" has terrible results and therefore is not recommended. Utilitarianism proves itself to be a resourceful and resilient philosophical theory, and for this reason it has become one of several currently dominant ethical perspectives.

ETHICAL PERSPECTIVE #5: DEONTOLOGY: KANTIAN AND RIGHTS-BASED ETHICS

Deontological theories are those ethical theories that do not base the morality of actions on consequences, but instead, on respect for persons. The German philosopher Immanuel Kant (1724–1804) was a primary defender of this ethical perspective. This ethical theory contrasts sharply with consequentialist views. For instance, for deontologists such as Kant, morality has to do with following rules and acting from good intentions. Utilitarians, on the other hand, would feel free to question rules and will allow exceptions to rules when this produces the best results. Since deontologists do not base the morality of actions on their consequences, they are not fundamentally concerned about producing the best results in each action they perform. Further, utilitarians are not concerned directly with persons' intentions, but only with the outcome of the action. On utilitarianism, if a person performs an action that has horrible effects, even though the person had good intentions and did not wish to harm anyone, the action still remains a bad action (though the person's character may not be bad by virtue of performing this action). Similarly, if a person's action produces good results even though she had bad intentions, this action would still remain a good action according to utilitarianism. Deontologists do not agree with these assessments, since for them, what matters is that a person does the action because they believe it is the right thing to do, not because they believe that it will produce good effects or make persons happy. If the emphasis on deontology is not on producing happiness, then what is its focus?

Kant's main principle is called the *Categorical Imperative*. An "imperative" is a command. Kant's idea is that as imperfectly rational creatures, we need some sort of a command containing an "ought" to signify that we have overcome sensuous inclination to perform an action for the sake of moral duty. The term "categorical" can have several meanings, which include (1) "does not depend on a person's desires or inclinations" and (2) "that moral rules are exceptionless." I will return to discuss these different meanings below. By contrast, a *hypothetical imperative* is an imperative that guides conduct only if you want some further goal. For this reason, the force of a hypothetical imperative depends on a person possessing a desire for the goal in question. For Kant, morality consists only of categorical imperatives, since he does not wish his system of ethics to depend on whether or not a person has the desire necessary for doing the right thing. Kant believes that this alternative basis for ethics is, quite simply, too flimsy. In the case of an ethical command, persons are not motivated by the fact that they wish to satisfy some further desire, but they perform the action since they think that it is important in itself to do one's duty.

Kant offers several formulations of his main principle, the categorical imperative. He makes it clear that all of these formulations are simply intended to be different ways of expressing the same foundational idea, though this point is a matter of dispute among philosophers. In what follows I shall discuss only the two most popular versions of the categorical imperative. The first is often referred to as the formula of universalization. This formulation states the following: "Act only according to that *maxim* whereby you can at the same time will that it should become a universal law." A maxim is a rule or subjective principle of action. In other words, it is a description of the agent's action from the point of view of the agent. This maxim is the rule that the person has in mind when he or she is acting. The main idea here is that you are to ask yourself whether your maxim or rule could become a general policy governing all others in similar circumstances. To determine whether or not the rule could be universalized, ask yourself, "What if everyone in similar circumstances followed this rule?"

Kant provides an example to illustrate how this system of ethical reasoning is to work. In this example, a person needs money and has no other means to get it besides borrowing it and making a false promise to pay it back. In this example of the lying promise, then, the person makes the promise knowing that they will not be able to keep it. For Kant, we must always know the maxim on which the person is acting, which in this case is the following: (A) "When I believe myself to be in need of money, I will borrow money and promise to pay it back, although I know I can never do so." Can this maxim be universalized? If it is not possible that all others in similar circumstances do the same without some form of contradiction arising, then the action is not morally acceptable. If the action passes the test of universalization, then the action is permissible to perform.

In his discussion of the lying promise example, Kant argues that maxim (A) is not universalizable and hence that making the lying promise is not permissible. Kant first asks you to think about what would result if everyone in a similar circumstance adopted this as a rule of action: what would happen? It seems clear that no one will believe promises made by others if everyone acts as if they can make a lying promise whenever needed. As Kant puts it, everyone who attempts to borrow money on the basis of a promise would simply be laughed at. Quite simply, this would destroy the trust on which the acceptance of promises depends. If this is the case, then the maxim in essence defeats itself, and rules that defeat themselves illustrate that their associated actions are *irrational*. In this case, the rule defeats itself because the person attempts to enter into the promise to receive the money, yet by subjecting this rule to the test of morality, it becomes clear that this rule does not allow him to receive the money. In Kant's eyes, to will this rule is self-contradictory since to act on the basis of such a rule frustrates the central purpose one has for acting on the basis of this rule. The test of the categorical imperative shows that it is irrational to will such a thing, and since the maxim fails, the action is impermissible.

It is worth noting that Kant is not saying that the action is wrong simply because of the bad consequences that result if no one believes promises. If this were true, his argument would be a consequentialist argument, not a deontological one. The reason the action is wrong is that by virtue of willing this maxim, the person is in effect willing (1) a world in which he wishes promises to be taken seriously and (2) a world in which promises will not be taken seriously. This is what Kant calls a practical contradiction in the will, which suggests that the action will not pass the categorical imperative and is irrational. Since a person cannot embrace such a contradiction rationally, the associated action is morally unacceptable. As Kant himself says with regard to such cases of actions that fail the categorical imperative:

> If we attend to ourselves in any transgression of a duty, we find that we actually do not will that our maxim should become a universal law .... We only take the liberty of making an exception to the law for ourselves (or just for this one time) .... (Kant, *Groundwork*, 424)[5]

Simply put, what Kant realizes is that when the maxim of our actions fails, we "want it both ways"—we wish the maxim to be a universal law (so that it will be a valid rule and will be believed, so we get our money) yet we want to opt out of adhering to that rule in order to satisfy our own needs. In doing so, we are trying to "make an exception of ourselves," since we want all others to adhere to morality while allowing ourselves to ignore it.

In his writings on ethics, Kant draws a distinction between mere things and persons: things have conditioned value, while persons have unconditional value. Kant believes that something in the universe must have an unconditioned value: if all value were conditioned then there would be no basic intrinsic moral value. If nothing possesses fundamental moral value, then the chain of explanation would never end, but would simply move from one value to the value underlying that value, to the value underlying that value, and so on. For Kant, the source of value is found in persons by virtue of their rationality. Rational beings are persons—they have purposes of their own, and are not to be used for others' purposes. In this way, persons are unlike mere things such as an automobile. If you own a car, you may use it for whatever you wish, since it has no purposes of its own. This contrast between things and persons sets the stage for the second formulation of Kant's categorical imperative, which is as follows: Never treat a person *merely* as a means, but also always as an end. This is often referred as the *formula of respect for persons.* The main idea behind this principle is that since persons possess inherent purposes, they cannot be used by others without first securing their consent or approval.

Note the word "merely" in this principle. While it is perhaps inevitable that we will use other persons as a means to our ends in one way or another as members of society, we are never to use others *merely* as a means. For instance, since I lack the relevant skills, I may have to use a plumber as a means to unclog the kitchen drain in my home. On Kant's view, there is nothing morally questionable about this decision. However, if I invited the plumber into my home to remove the blockage from my drain and then refused to pay for this service, I would be using the plumber *merely* as a means to fixing my pipes and this would be morally unacceptable. By inviting the plumber into my home to do the work, I am agreeing to pay him for services rendered.

By failing to do this, I am not acknowledging that this person is a rational agent who possesses interests and purposes of his own. To use another person merely as a means is to only consider the ways in which he or she can benefit you without thinking about the manner in which he or she deserves to be treated as a rational being. On the Kantian view of morality, you can never use another person merely as a means to your personal ends or to promote the greater good.

There have been a number of important objections raised against Kant's moral theory. We will discuss two objections that are most potentially damaging. The first objection claims that Kant's view never allows exceptions to moral rules generated by the categorical imperative, and as such, it is too rigid to be realistically used in everyday life. It is simply implausible to defend an absolutist theory that states that moral rules have no exceptions. In addition, there may be conflicts between rules that require that we violate one of them, which means that we must create exceptions to rules, yet Kant's deontological theory may not allow this.

This first objection is all the more damaging in that Kant himself appears to adopt such an absolutist view in one of his writings. In this writing, he discusses a case in which an innocent person comes to our door and asks to hide in our house to escape from those who intend to harm him (imagine that these persons are criminals or gangsters). You believe his story and, since you sympathize with his plight, let him into your home. Then, one of the gangsters knocks on your door and, after providing a detailed description of the person you have just let in, asks whether the person is inside your home. To many people, it would seem that I would be morally justified in lying to the gangster to protect the fugitive. However, if Kant truly believes that moral rules are absolute, then we have a moral duty not to lie that allows for no exceptions. Another way to look at this case is to view it as involving a conflict of duties. In letting the person into our home, we seem to have made an implicit promise to not give him up to those from whom he is hiding. In addition, we have a duty to not lie. So, in this case we have a duty to keep our promise and a duty to tell the truth, yet these duties conflict. If we tell the truth we break our promise, and if we keep our promise we fail in our duty to tell the truth. If we possess both of these duties and these duties are absolute, Kant's theory simply lacks the resources to address a fundamental problem and this is a serious objection to it.

As a preface to offering a response to this objection, let's clarify the options available to the homeowner at the door. The possible options are as follows: he may (1) tell the gangster the truth about the location of the fugitive, (2) he may lie about this, or (3) he may keep quiet when asked. For purposes of simplicity, I am going to assume (as Kant does in his discussion) that the homeowner must answer the question. (One could add that perhaps remaining silent would cause the gangsters to barge past him and search the house for the fugitive.) By eliminating option (3) in this discussion, this removes the possibility of the homeowner "opting out" of this moral dilemma.

While critics believe that Kantian moralists must support rules such as "never lie," this is simply not true. Even though some think that Kant himself suggests this in one of his writings, this is not a position that a defender of this ethical perspective must accept. First, let's remind ourselves of what Kant concluded in his discussion of the lying promise example. In that example, Kant showed us that given a particular maxim, one is not morally permitted to make lying promises. He did not establish that one should never lie under any circumstances in his discussion of the lying promise case. To examine what is morally permissible in the fugitive case, we must have the maxim on which the person is acting. This has not been provided, nor is it provided in Kant's own discussion of this case. A reasonable maxim is as follows: "When I can save an innocent person's life by lying, I will do so." We are now to ask: "What if everyone in similar circumstances acted on the basis of this rule?" We must think through the likely chain of events and determine whether universalizing this maxim results in self-contradiction.

One may argue that the gangster case is analogous to the lying promise case—telling the lie would undermine the trust needed for utterances to be believed by others. Following this line of reasoning, you are trying to will (1) a world in which your statements would be believed yet are in effect willing (2) a world in which your statements are not believed. Hence, this results in a contradiction in the will, since subjecting this rule to the test of morality undermines your own purposes. While this is the case, the line of argument from the lying promise case does not seem to apply to the gangster example. This becomes clear if we ask: In how many cases are persons faced with this as their purpose? Cases in which a lie is necessary to save an innocent person's life are rare, to say the least. Is this case relevantly similar to the lying promise case? It seems not, since it would not lead to a general disbelief in a person's statements if people only lied in precisely these rare cases. What this means is that the gangster at the door would not have any reason to disbelieve you even if your maxim was followed by everyone in similar circumstances. Even if the gangster realized that good individuals will not give up innocent victims to criminals, the gangster at the door simply does not know if you are a good individual who has chosen to protect an innocent person or if the person simply is not inside your home. This feature of the case distinguishes it from the example of the lying promise in which no one would believe other persons' promises if the relevant maxim were universalized. In fact, it is difficult to find anything like the Kantian contradiction if one attempts to universalize this maxim in the gangster case.[6]

A second important objection is that Kant's different formulations of the categorical imperative are not in fact interchangeable, as Kant himself claims. If this is true, then this is damaging for Kant since the different versions of his main principle may come into conflict because they have different implications. This objection, if successful, would establish that Kant's moral theory does not arrive at a consistent set of answers to moral issues, and this calls its credibility into question. At the most general level, this objection calls the conceptual unity of Kant's ethical theory into question.

It would be a significant task to attempt to address this objection in its various forms. For the purposes of this discussion, however, I can offer a more limited reply. I have only discussed two formulations of Kant's categorical imperative, and in an attempt to blunt the force of this criticism, I will offer a brief sketch of how these two formulations can be seen to be two different ways to say something similar. In the first formulation, the Formula of Universalization, one is to ask the question, "What if everyone in similar circumstances acted on the basis of that rule?" Suppose your rule was the following: "Whenever I want to, I will not pay my taxes so that I can spend the money on luxuries for myself." What would happen if this maxim were universalized? It seems obvious that this would have very bad effects—almost no one would pay their taxes, and our basic public services would collapse. This would have awful results, but of course that is not what makes it wrong for Kant. What makes it wrong is that it is self-contradictory once it is universalized. I am considering adopting this rule as a way to secure luxuries for myself, yet if I have no public roads to travel on, no street lights, no fire and police service, and so on, I will not be able to direct the money I save toward buying luxuries. Instead, I will spend this money (and probably more) in an attempt to acquire the services that the state once provided. In this case, you are attempting to "make an exception of yourself"—you can only get away with such an action if most other persons hold up their end of the deal by paying their taxes. Only in such a situation would your strategy work. As soon as most others follow suit and adopt this maxim as well, the rule undermines itself.

Notice that this description of the reasoning in this case ties closely to the second formulation, the Formula of Respect for Persons. In this case, you are in essence using these other persons merely for your own purposes of acquiring luxury items and are not taking into account that they have their own ends and would probably like to avoid paying taxes as well. This suggests that the second formulation brings out an idea latent in the first formulation of the categorical imperative. When you subject the maxim of your actions to the test of universalization, you are making sure that you are not attempting to make an exception of yourself in your decisions. By making sure that you are not trying to make an exception of yourself in your actions, you ensure that you are not using others merely as a means to your own purposes. This insight illustrates that there is a central theoretical unity between the Formula of Universalization and the Formula of Respect for Persons, and therefore suggests that these two versions of Kant's central principle are not as disconnected as defenders of this objection believe.

Kant's theory supports the notion of moral rights, and this is illustrated by his distinction between perfect and imperfect duties. For Kant, an imperfect duty is a duty that admits there are exceptions in the interest of inclinations. In essence, it is a duty over which a person possesses a certain amount of latitude in meeting his or her moral obligations. For instance, Kant believes that we have an imperfect duty to develop our talents and abilities. This suggests that persons need not develop all of their abilities, since this could be impossible. For example, it may be the case that a particular person could be either a great writer or a great jazz saxophonist, but the time commitments required for intensively writing each day and for practicing the instrument may not allow the person to cultivate both sets of skills. In such a case, for Kant it would be up to the person to decide which career to pursue. By contrast, a perfect duty is a duty that holds regardless of one's inclinations. It is important to stress that this does not imply that all such perfect duties are absolute; as discussed above, we must refer to the maxim in question. For instance, Kant believes that we have a perfect duty to others not to make lying promises. Since in this case we have a *duty* to be truthful, others have a *right* to our truthfulness with regard to lying promises. For Kant, then, perfect duties generate *correlative obligations*: for every such duty there is a corresponding right on the part of others.

Kant is one philosopher among many who believe that individual persons are valuable, and as such, people should act in ways that respect that value by granting them moral rights that are justified on a non-consequentialist basis. Another philosopher who supports moral rights theory is John Locke (1632–1704). Modern-day followers of Locke argue that all persons (not simply adult, white males) possess rights, and generally ground moral rights in reason itself (and do not argue that such rights are God-given). In the main, Locke supported rights to life, liberty, and property. For Locke, a right is a protection against others interfering with one of our vital interests. One acts ethically if one acknowledges others' rights and unethically if one violates the rights of other persons. This conception is often referred to as a "negative rights" view, since this perspective stresses the fact that to have a right is for others to not interfere with your actions. For example, a right to life for Locke is understood as a duty on all others to not kill you. A right to property protects one's control over their property and forbids the interference by others with the benefits stemming from possessing that property.

A broader conception of moral rights views rights not only as protections but also grants the existence of "positive" rights or entitlements. For instance, the United Nation's Universal Declaration of Human Rights (1948) considers a basic education to be a right of all human beings. On this conception, the possession of this right implies that others bear duties of positive assistance. In other words, the state does not satisfy its moral obligations simply by failing to prevent individuals from receiving a basic education, but must provide some programs (such as a tuition-free education plan) or other means to ensure that citizens can in fact receive a basic education if they so choose. If one possesses a "positive" right to life, then this suggests not only that others have a duty not to kill this person, but also that others are obligated in some ways to provide assistance to this person in sustaining his or her life. Moral rights theories serve as a direct counterpoint to utilitarian theories, since they maintain that moral consideration in the form of moral rights is not fundamentally rooted in consequentialist notions of producing the best overall results.

Critical Thinking Interlude: The Nash Case

Lisa and Jack Nash were both carriers of a recessive gene for Fanconi anemia and therefore had a twenty-five percent chance of producing a baby with the disease. Fanconi anemia prevents the afflicted person from producing his or her own bone marrow. This disease will significantly shorten the affected person's life; half of those with Fanconi anemia experience bone-marrow failure by age 7. Their first child, Molly, did receive the gene for Fanconi, and at age six was already experiencing serious health problems. The best treatment for Fanconi is a transfer of stem cells derived from a sibling.

The Nashes chose to have another child using reproductive technology. They created embryos by *in vitro* fertilization, where ova are fertilized in the laboratory. The embryos were subject to a unique series of tests. First, they were screened to ensure that the embryos that would be implanted in the mother's womb did not have the genetic disease. Second, those embryos that passed this first test were screened also for traits that allowed a match for helping Molly Nash—the new sibling could help her by providing cells to help Molly produce her own bone marrow. (This is better than a transplant of bone marrow, which is painful and involves a chance of rejection.) From this process, Adam Nash was created and born. Molly was given radiation treatment to kill her diseased bone narrow. Stem cells—which are cells that can become any cells in the body—were taken from blood in the umbilical cord after Adam's birth and were programmed to replace the decimated bone marrow. Then the stem cells in the blood were infused into Molly. The procedure was a success—shortly after the transfusion, Molly began to make her own bone marrow cells.

Critical Thinking Question: How would a Utilitarian assess the Nashes' decision to have another child? How would a Kantian assess the Nashes' decision to have another child? (Suppose the Kantian specifically referred to the second formulation of the Categorical Imperative.)

Discussion: We have learned that a Utilitarian assesses an action based on whether it produces the best overall results for everyone involved. What possible good and bad effects, both short-term and long-term, flow from the Nashes' decision to have a second child using reproductive technology in this way? Some straightforward good results are, first, the fact that the resulting child, Adam, is born free of this serious genetic disease. Second, Molly is helped by the procedure performed after Adam's birth in which she received the stem cells isolated from the umbilical cord blood. Third, the parents were successful in having an additional child who was free of the disease. Finally, one might point to wider societal benefits: this procedure prevents disease so that the Nashes' child never requires medical treatment for Fanconi anemia. One could argue that this is a social benefit in that it allows medical resources to be redirected to other diseases that are not preventable at this time.

By contrast, one could argue that allowing such procedures to be used at parents' discretion allows for the creation of "designer babies," and this represents an illegitimate tampering with nature. Also, if such pre-implantation genetic diagnosis becomes standard practice, then persons that possess a serious disease that is undetected by a screening process before they are born may be subject to discrimination and mistreatment. Third, the embryos that did not pass the screening process were not gestated and were frozen. Depending on one's view of when moral status and moral rights are ascribed to early human life, this may be morally equivalent to murder. There are many more possible positive and negative effects resulting from the Nashes' decision, but these are among the most central.

What would a utilitarian say in making a judgment about the Nashes' decision? The utilitarian would likely emphasize the fact that the good results have a high degree of certainty attached to them, while the possible negative effects are long-term and are less certain to occur. Of course, long-term results do matter from the utilitarian perspective, yet the utilitarian would also "discount" them given the fact that each of these effects is somewhat speculative. In addition, a trend of discrimination against persons with certain diseases would not be a sole result of the Nashes' decision itself, yet it is true that their decision could contribute in some way to supporting such a trend. Overall, the results are quite positive for Molly Nash, who has the most serious interests at stake since her life is in danger, and the results are favorable for Adam, Lisa, and Jack Nash as well. Since the long-term results are quite speculative, and the immediate results are quite favorable, it is very likely that from the utilitarian perspective the Nashes' decision is morally acceptable.

To the surprise of the Nashes, however, they were subject to a lot of public criticism for their decision to use reproductive technology in this way. While many consider it ethical to screen embryos for genetic diseases, since this is best for the child, in this case the screening occurred to select for traits that would benefit another person besides Adam Nash. One could make the objection that this use of reproductive technology in some way represents a misuse or violation of Adam Nash. This connects with Kant's second formulation of the Categorical Imperative, which states that we ought never treat a person merely as a means, but also always as an end. How does this principle apply to the case, and what does this case suggest about the principle itself?

One approach for spelling out the notion of what it is to use Adam Nash merely as a means is in terms of the parties' *motivations*: The parents' motivations in this case must be consistent with respecting the child's humanity in itself, to desire the child in some unqualified sense. However, some pressing questions exist concerning this interpretation. If we hold these parents to such a standard, we should also presumably apply this idea to all parents. Yet do persons typically approach reproduction and parenting in this way, where the child is desired in some completely unqualified sense? Or can other desires figure into the decision to reproduce, consistent with the decision being a morally defensible one?

It seems that potential parents aim to satisfy desires other than those referring to the desire for the child itself when making reproductive decisions and this does not necessarily make it the case that the parents are doing something morally wrong. For example, the parents' motivations may be complex; they may just want the child itself, or they may want to have a child so that their first child has someone to grow up with or play with, or they want to have a child because all of their friends are having children at this stage in their lives, or they may want to appease their parents' desire for a grandchild. In addition, if we did use such a standard—where the parents had to desire the child in some completely unqualified sense—and we used this to set public policies to determine which parents could have access to reproductive technologies, how could we know when this condition was satisfied? The parents could simply "mouth the words" and report these motivations, even if this report was not true.

Further, is it really the case that Adam Nash is used merely as a means to the end of helping Molly Nash, on this interpretation? Interestingly enough, the Nashes' motivations appear to be complex as well. They wanted additional children, but were afraid to conceive since they may have another child with the disease. Lisa Nash adds that "We wanted a healthy child ... [a]nd it doesn't hurt him (Adam) to save her (Molly's) life." Their motivation is not accurately described by saying that they had a child simply to use cells from him to save their other child's life. To use embryo screening to prevent *Adam* from getting the genetic disease certainly does not use him merely as a means. Given that the parents wanted to have a child in the first place, and then used embryo selection to achieve a "dual purpose" that also helped their other child, perhaps it is more accurate to say that Adam is a means for helping Molly Nash. But then this decision does not violate Kant's principle, since the principle disallows treating others *merely* as a means.

Considering this case and its relation to the Kantian ethical principle raises other interesting interpretative questions. One may argue that while Adam Nash is not used merely as a means, perhaps the embryos that are tested and not gestated are used merely as a means. What are we to think about this? This sheds light on the issue of what it means on Kantianism to "use" another person. If we test an embryo, it fails the test, and is then frozen, was it "used?" This question may be complicated by the question of whether the embryo is considered a person from a Kantian perspective. Even putting that question to the side, and granting for the sake of argument that it is a person, it is still not clear what constitutes "usage" of another person. Suppose (to modify Kant's famous example) that I am heading out for a long night of making lying promises to others, and to save time, I devise a test that I use first to determine whether my prey is sufficiently gullible to be ensnared by my tactic. If I administer this test and the person is not sufficiently gullible, I do not even attempt the lying promise, but simply move on to someone else. It is not clear that I have "used," in the relevant sense for Kant, those who fail the test and hence are not subject to my lying promise. Even granting that if someone were used in this way that person would be treated as a mere means, since it is unclear that "usage" occurs in the first place, it is not clear how to construct a case for the moral wrongness of this activity on this basis.

Further, how do we determine exactly *who* is being used merely as a means (assuming that we grant that use would constitute use merely as a means)? A Kantian theorist may maintain that *Adam Nash* is used merely as a means, yet we must be clear about the facts of the case to determine whether or not this is true. The umbilical cord blood is all that is used in this procedure; are the cells that are found in the cord blood (which would otherwise be simply destroyed) part of Adam Nash, or part of his mother, or both? At the very least, it is ambiguous whether *Adam* is the one being used in this case (if usage occurs at all). It would seem to be a different case if a family were to conceive a child that is free of disease, then after raising the child demand a transplant, say, of one of his kidneys, since these are a match for an ailing sibling. That would be using the child in an unacceptable way without regard to the possible harm to the child.

The question of harm to Adam Nash also seems to be important, and this suggests another way to interpret the categorical imperative that in some way involves the *effect* that one's acts have on the person who is putatively used merely as a means. This interpretation may be unacceptable to some followers of Kant since it seems too "utilitarian," but it does raise an interesting issue. In the typical examples of lying promises, another person is used merely as a means and it is the case that the person used is clearly harmed. What if a person is used merely as a means, but in cases such as Adam Nash's, no harm results directly from this since using the cord blood has no negative effects on him at all? Even if we could get clear on the fact that it is he who is used (and used merely as a means), if there is no harm, does the Kantian principle still intuitively ground the moral wrongness of such actions? If not, perhaps the Kantian stricture against using persons as a mere means reduces to the harm of being used in this way. This line of questioning sheds critical light on whether Kant's principle is a *foundational* moral principle. This critical exercise is enlightening concerning both the Nash case as well as concerning the second formulation of Kant's Categorical Imperative itself.

ETHICAL PERSPECTIVE #6: VIRTUE OR ARETAIC ETHICS

In its purest form, the ethical perspective known as virtue ethics is represented by Aristotle's master work *Nicomachean Ethics*. In a central passage, Aristotle (1113a30) says that, "[T]he excellent person judges each sort of thing correctly ... the excellent person is far superior because he sees what is true in each case, being a sort of standard and measure of what is fine and pleasant."[7] This passage suggests the main idea behind virtue ethics, that the morality of actions is defined in terms of what a person with an ideally virtuous disposition would do in that situation. Some philosophers make distinctions between the notion of character and virtue, and then offer arguments bearing on theories grounded on one or the other.[8] However, this section will refer to the dominant understanding of a virtue- or character-based perspective as a *pure aretaic ethic*. (The word for virtue in ancient Greek is *arete.*) An aretaic ethic treats virtues as traits of character and holds that valuable traits of character are those that are necessary to live a good life in the fullest sense. Aretaic perspectives make the distinctive claim that notions of character traits or virtue are primary; to understand whether an action is morally acceptable or not essentially requires discovering whether an ideally virtuous agent would perform that action in those circumstances.

The following is a workable list of the general features of a pure aretaic perspective. First, a reference to traits possesses primary importance in explanations and moral justifications of acts. A mere appeal to features of a situation is not sufficient to properly explain one's behavior. While some external conditions matter for the possession of a virtuous trait, it is the trait itself that is of primary importance. The virtuous agent does not rely on moral principles to determine what is morally acceptable. Instead, "robust" and long-lasting traits and habits of perception and feeling assist agents in determining the salient features in any circumstance, so that they "see" what is the right thing to do. Aristotle discusses this in his "doctrine of the mean," which is offered as a piece of practical advice for how to determine the virtuous action. Simply put, the virtuous action is one that avoids excess and deficiency. Bravery, Aristotle says, is a mean between foolhardiness (excess) and cowardice (deficiency). The agent's particular sensitivity will help him or her determine the appropriate behavior that represents the golden mean. Contemporary defenders of aretaic ethics emphasize this component of a virtue ethic, since they believe that Kantian and utilitarian theories place too much emphasis on using principles to "calculate" the correct course of action. Recent aretaic ethicists believe that it is impossible in principle to codify all of the factors that may matter in making a correct moral decision, and therefore are skeptical about putting so much emphasis on moral principles.

Second, simply performing the right outward action is not sufficient to support the claim that one is an upright moral agent. In addition, one must also be the right sort of person, and have the right motivations and feelings. On some versions of this perspective, possessing the proper traits will "silence" all competing considerations that may pull one toward performing the wrong action. These traits screen out the "noise" in the situation, so that even if all features of the situation would push an agent in one direction, and that direction is wrong, the properly attuned agent is capable of doing the right thing in that situation. Finally, these habits of perception, feeling, and action are inculcated by a process of character education. Young persons are provided training by a role model that will lead to the development of stable and virtuous dispositions. On this conception, the power to be a good or bad person is up to us, and we become good or bad persons by engaging in activities that aim to inculcate a certain type of character. This list of general features of a pure aretaic view, while only a thumbnail sketch, will be helpful in our discussion of this perspective.

There are several influential objections to this ethical perspective. First, if on Aristotle's conception (as suggested in the passage quoted above), the virtuous person is a sort of standard of what is best, then does this view represent a form of ethical relativism? To put the point in another way, since aretaic ethicists explicitly do not subscribe to a moral principle (or set of moral principles) to determine how one should behave in a certain situation, but instead base this on the virtuous individual's disposition, does this mean that what it is correct to do in a situation varies for each individual? Aristotle's doctrine of the mean seems to especially lend itself to this interpretation. If this is the case, then many of the troublesome implications discussed in the section on ethical relativism also apply to aretaic ethics, and this damages the credibility of this view. The defender of a view in the spirit of an aretaic ethic can offer the following reply to this objection. The response does not abandon the idea that the virtuous person perceives or "sees" what features in the situation lead to the correct course of action in that circumstance. However, the virtue ethicist can emphasize that these features exist independently of the perceiver, so that there is a proper course of action in each circumstance. As Aristotle (1106b30-35) says in connection with the doctrine of the mean and virtuous perception, "[T]here are many ways to be in error, since badness is proper to what is unlimited ... but there is only one way to be correct. That is why error is easy and correctness hard, since it is easy to miss the target and hard to hit it. And so for this reason also excess and deficiency are proper to vice, the mean to virtue."

This passage suggests that Aristotle does not advocate a form of ethical relativism. To clarify how this response works, consider the following analogy.[9] Philosophers since John Locke have pointed out that the experience of color is perceiver-dependent: blue does not exist objectively in the world, but instead, there are certain physical features of the world that cause suitably attuned perceivers to experience the color blue. If this perceiver-dependent view is not correct, then it is very difficult to explain how a blue object may appear (say) yellow to all suitably attuned perceivers when viewed under colored lights. Does the object suddenly change its physical properties? In addition, if we attempt to eliminate the perceiver from the relationship, does that mean that an object in a darkened room (which causes no experience of color in suitably attuned perceivers) loses its physical properties that give rise to color experience when the lights go out? While color is perceiver-dependent, no one denies that there is a correct answer as to whether an object is in fact blue or not. Similarly, an aretaic ethicist could maintain that there are objective features of situations that correspond to the proper course of action in that situation. However, this requires a suitably attuned perceiver to interpret these features. By analogy with the example concerning color experience, there may be a correct answer concerning the morality of an action. This line of response allows for the importance of a virtuous perceiver, yet avoids the objectionable relativity inherent in ethical relativism.

A second objection claims that defenders of virtue ethics are faced with a dilemma.[10] This dilemma is suggested by asking the following question: "On virtue ethics, how do we learn what to do?" As we discussed earlier, there is a process of education and training by which an individual is to learn how to be virtuous through practice. So, one answer to this question refers to the virtuous person who is providing the training—we should simply ask this person to tell us what would be the appropriate behavior in this instance. However, if virtue is a matter of "perception," of entering a situation and using personal judgment instead of utility calculations or deontological rules, then how is the virtuous person going to *tell* us what we are to do (and how we are to learn what we are to do)? He could simply share his "perception" of the matter with us, and tell us what to do. But then in every case with even the slightest difference we must again seek this person out. This is not only impractical, but it suggests that this theory is not helpful in guiding action for those of us that are *imperfectly virtuous*, which of course describes most of us! So, if the answer to how we are to determine the proper course of action relies solely on the perception of the virtuous person, then virtue ethics has a problem with action-guidingness.

If this is not the proper interpretation, perhaps instead the virtuous person will provide his student with the "pattern" or criteria that constitutes the "thread" that makes an action a virtuous one. Perhaps there are some general features that tend to make an action virtuous. If this is the case, it would undermine virtue ethics itself, since one can then do the right action without in fact being virtuous. If the virtuous person can reduce what virtuous action is to a number of rules or other guidelines, then the whole spirit of virtue ethics is defeated—the virtuous person, according to philosophers such as Aristotle, does not subsume each case under a rule or principle!

The defender of virtue ethics can offer a response to this objection as well by pointing out that this dilemma is generated by making assumptions that the virtue ethicist rejects. In essence, the criticism highlights the point that the virtue ethicist does not generate algorithmic moral principles that can help one to know what to do if one is not yet virtuous. However, it is precisely the possibility of such universally applicable moral principles that is questioned by aretaic thinkers. Virtue ethics focuses on providing moral guidance in a different way—not on the basis of principles, but by building certain habits and character traits. If we look realistically at the practical helpfulness of the "algorithms" provided by utilitarians and Kantians, virtue ethicists claim that we should not be impressed. Certainly, says the virtue ethicist, we should not view a lack of principle formulation as a reason to reject virtue ethics. Defenders of this view would claim that the modest account of action-guidingness afforded by virtue ethics is the more realistic one. It is the case on all ethical perspectives that determining what is morally acceptable is a difficult matter.

Critical Thinking Interlude: The Death Bed Promise Case

A middle-aged man is diagnosed by his family physician with a case of pneumonia and is given a course of antibiotics. The man's condition does not improve and he is admitted to a local hospital. After a full workup, including blood tests and chest X-rays, it is discovered that this man has a rare form of pneumonia, called pneumocystis carinii, which is associated with immunodeficiency and in particular with HIV infection.[11] The man's medical history does not reveal any risk factors for HIV infection. The medical team approaches the man to ask him further questions about his medical history, and in this discussion, the man reveals with some discomfort that he has had several homosexual experiences in his past. Blood tests reveal that the man is HIV-positive. The man is adamant that his wife and four children not find out that this is the likely cause of his illness. This man, whose condition is now life-threatening, secures a "death bed promise" from his attending physician to ensure that his family will not find out these elements of his past.

Critical Thinking Question: How would a virtue ethicist evaluate this "death bed promise?" Would a virtue ethicist think that the physician should not tell the patient's family? Offer reasons to support the conclusion you believe the virtue ethicist would reach.

Discussion: From the perspective of virtue ethics, the central thing to determine is how a virtuous person would view this scenario. Not (yet) being a virtuous person myself, I am reluctant to offer too many suggestions, but a few things seem to stand out. One question to consider is whether a virtuous person would ask someone else to withhold medical information on his behalf. We need not assume that this patient is for some reason ashamed of this homosexual experiences, but simply is concerned about how his family will react to this knowledge. It seems clear that this man's HIV-positive status, at the very least, has put his wife in danger of becoming seropositive. This fact seems especially salient, and should figure prominently in the virtuous patient's assessment of what should be done in this case. Similarly, this fact should play a central role in the virtuous physician's determination of what should be done. While this case is worthy of much more discussion, it is likely that a virtue ethicist would endorse telling the patient's family of his HIV-positive status. This would constitute a breach of a promise. However, since virtue ethicists do not put primary weight on rules or principles, it is unclear how much weight this point would receive from a virtue ethicist in support of maintaining confidentiality in this case. (Additionally, as discussed earlier, even deontologists can allow exceptions to moral rules such as those that concern keeping one's promises.)

ETHICAL PERSPECTIVE #7: RAWLS' THEORY OF JUSTICE

In his work *A Theory of Justice*, John Rawls develops a vision of a just society as one that is governed by principles that persons choose from an impartial standpoint. Rawls sees himself as developing an alternative to the dominant utilitarian theory of distributive justice by elaborating a social/political theory that applies principles of justice to institutions. A fundamental insight of Rawls' theory is that principles of justice are to be considered just if the procedures used and conditions of the agreement are fair. For the principles to be acceptable, they must be principles that free and rational individuals would pick in circumstances characterized by equality.

To make this vivid Rawls asks you to imagine a group of individuals meeting to discuss the organization of society behind what he calls a "veil of ignorance." These individuals are prevented from knowing a number of specific facts about their place in our world, including such things as social position, natural abilities, intelligence, strength, or special psychological propensities.[12] The idea is that during this hypothetical meeting, which occurs in what Rawls calls the Original Position, these individuals will enter into a social contract in which they select the principles that are to govern the "basic structure of society," the main political, social, and economic institutions in a culture. The assumptions present in the Original Position are intended to ensure impartiality and fairness—if one does not know one's own position in society, one will be disinclined to vote for a policy that disfavors one class of individuals, since one may be a member of that disfavored class in the resulting society. We are to assume that agents in the Original Position wish to get the most goods they can for themselves, and that they are rational in that they can pick the best means to the ends they choose. In such a situation of uncertainty, Rawls argues that the rational strategy is to adopt what thinkers in the economic discipline of game theory refer to as the *maximin principle*. Maximin directs us in situations of uncertainty to pick the alternative whose worst possible outcome is better than the worst possible outcome of the available alternatives.

Since the individuals in the Original Position know so little about themselves, it is unclear how they could evaluate an alternative as better or worse. To avoid this potential problem, Rawls introduces the notion of "primary goods," those goods that every rational person is presumed to want whatever else he or she wants. To decide which conception of justice is most to their advantage, the representatives in the Original Position assume that they prefer more rather than less primary goods, since these are useful in advancing everyone's life plans, whatever those turn out to be. Primary goods fall into two basic types: social primary goods and natural primary goods. Examples of social primary goods include basic rights and liberties, powers and opportunities, and income and wealth. Also included here are the social bases of self-respect. Other primary goods such as health, vigor, intelligence, and imagination are considered to be natural primary goods. The main difference between the two types of primary goods is that social primary goods are distributed by the basic structure of society, while the possession of natural primary goods, by contrast, is influenced by the basic structure of society, but is not directly under its control.

Rawls' claim is that the conditions for agreement present in the Original Position are fair, and in this situation the parties would agree on the following principles of justice:

> (1) Each person is to have an equal right to the most extensive total (fully adequate) system of *equal basic liberties* compatible with a similar system of liberties for all, and (2) social and economic inequalities are to be arranged so that they are both: (a) to the greatest benefit of the *least advantaged*, and (b) are attached to offices and positions open to all under conditions of *fair equality of opportunity*. Principle (1) is given priority over (2), and part (b) of the second principle is prior to part (a), which is called the *Difference Principle.*[13]

In the first principle, the concept of "liberty" refers to various political liberties, such as the right to vote or freedom of thought and religion. Since this principle is given priority over the second principle, Rawls' theory ensures an equal system of basic liberties and forbids trade-offs of liberty for social or economic benefits. In the second principle, part (b) ensures that all persons will have adequate opportunities to improve their social position. Fair equality of opportunity means that your chances of occupying various positions should have nothing to do with your position in society. A child in a just society should have the same probability of becoming a president of a corporation or a laborer no matter how wealthy his or her parents are. Of course, this will never be literally true, given the differential advantages that are transmitted in the family, and Rawls realizes this.

Part (a) of the second principle requires that distributions of the goods in the basic structure of society must be subject to the condition that they improve the position of those who occupy the worst social position. The social implications of this proposal are fairly radical. It is important to see that the goods to be redistributed are primary goods, and Rawls is not saying that we should maximize the position of the least well-off person. The Difference Principle applies to social groups; we want to increase the expectations and life prospects of this group as a whole as much as possible. In addition, note that the members of this group may not be the same in all instances—since there may be a variety of possible distributions, depending on which distribution we select, the members of the least advantaged group will likely change. Those who are least advantaged simply have the smallest index of primary goods of any members in society in relative terms, yet in absolute terms, they may have a decent quality of life overall. This last point makes clear that Rawls' system does allow for some inequalities to exist between members of society, as long as those inequalities can be justified because they stem from, for example, hard work by those who are more clever or resourceful. Such inequalities will serve to increase the amount of total resources in society as a whole, which will indirectly benefit the least advantaged class given the commitment to the Difference Principle.

Rawls' theory has been the subject of intensive philosophical discussion since his book published in 1971, and in later work, Rawls has further developed this theory in response to input by critics. There have been many different specific objections raised, but none of these objections are presently seen in the philosophical community as constituting a refutation of the theory itself. In general, there are two main types of objections. One set of objections concerns Rawls' methodology in this theory. Philosopher Michael Walzer objects to Rawls by pointing out that the Original Position is too "idealized." Walzer says that it is quite plausible that behind the veil of ignorance, with those conditions in place, we could come to a unanimous agreement on principles of justice. But once we stepped out from behind the veil, we would not ratify our hypothetical choice made in the Original Position. Walzer thinks this is not because we would then know our position in society and self-interest would take precedence. Instead, this would happen because we are "situated" individuals, with a distinctive culture and history and values, and these things matter when considering what principles of justice are right for us in our society. All of this is ignored in the Original Position—there is no reference to shared understandings of what is valued in our culture, yet Walzer believes that these should play a significant role in determining the distribution of goods in a society.

In response, in his later work Rawls develops his theory to be more responsive to differences between cultures. However, it is important to Rawls to maintain the power of his theory to revise a society's practices if these are fundamentally unfair. One could point out that on Walzer's view, if the oppression of women was part of the shared understandings of that culture, then these practices may be insulated from criticism, yet this is a problematic result. The upshot is that Rawls would wish to avoid this relativistic implication, and would plausibly argue that since we accept the conditions imposed in the Original Position as embodying our intuitions about fairness, we should also accept the principles generated by this fair procedure, even if later we may find that these lead us to revise some aspects of our societal practices.

The other main set of objections concerns the results of implementing Rawls' theory. Philosopher Robert Nozick[14] famously objects to Rawls' theory by pointing out that it is too restrictive. He proposes an example in which athlete Wilt Chamberlain receives a small fee paid by spectators as part of their admission charge to see him play in basketball games. In the course of a season, Chamberlain earns $250,000 dollars from this fee. Nozick points out that while it seems that Chamberlain is entitled to these earnings, since each fan has freely and knowingly paid the fee to him to see him exercise his talents, Rawls would say that Chamberlain is not entitled to this money. As we discussed earlier, Rawls does allow for an unequal distribution of earnings within society, yet giving the entire $250,000 to Chamberlain would seemingly violate the Difference Principle since this may not put the least advantaged group in the best possible position, relative to other possible distributions. Nozick argues that implementing Rawls' theory would be incredibly invasive, since it would demand constant redistributions of money, and is absurd since it bars "capitalism among consenting adults."

Rawls can offer an effective reply to this objection as well. It is true that Rawls questions conceptions of political equality on which persons may reap the full benefits of their natural abilities without any questions of fairness arising. He criticizes conceptions on which "... the strength of men's claims is directly influenced by the distribution of natural abilities, and therefore by contingencies that are arbitrary from the moral point of view," and says that the special advantages a person receives from the exercise of special talents are to be governed by the Difference Principle.[15] The idea here is that since the possession of such talents are "arbitrary from the moral point of view," it is not fair that the individual receives the full benefits that result from the exercise of these capacities. Saying this, however, is not the same as saying that Rawls is committed to taking the entire sum of money away from Chamberlain in Nozick's example. Rawls does wish to allow for incentives to exist in society, since the talents of persons such as Chamberlain or Bill Gates enrich society as a whole. He may be willing to redistribute a portion of these earnings, but any state with a system of taxation does essentially the same thing for the same reasons. (Nozick himself would question even this system of taxation.) More specifically, justice as fairness does not require constant interventions in the economic dealings of individuals, since Rawls' theory only concerns the basic structure of society. Once the principles of justice are agreed on and institutions are created in accord with these principles, Rawls simply allows these institutions to develop within society. As long as the "pattern" of institutions in society is in accord with the principles of justice as fairness, on Rawls' view, justice has been achieved.

Critical Thinking Interlude: Health Insurance in the United States

Presently in the United States, anywhere from 44 to 70 million citizens are not covered by health insurance, if the figures include those persons that go at least part of a year without health coverage, and 8.7 million persons buy health insurance through individually underwritten policies.[16] The Health Insurance Portability and Accountability Act (HIPAA) of 1996 prohibits discrimination against individual members of a *group* health insurance plan (such as those offered by employers) on the basis of current health status or some future disposition to a particular disease based on genetic testing. However, this law does not address the use of genetic information in the *individual* underwriting process. Therefore persons who must pay for their own health insurance are subject to increased premiums and even denial of coverage based on information gathered from genetic testing. Genetic information is presently being used for a variety of purposes; a September 2000 study by the Shriver Center in Massachusetts revealed 582 cases of persons who were turned down for employment or health insurance based on genetic factors. This number may seem small, until one realizes that victims of such discrimination are usually reluctant to come forward, fearing greater stigmatization, and companies who practice such policies are careful not to reveal them. The increasing knowledge of the relationship between genetic factors and disease afforded by the Human Genome Project will, it seems, lead to a greater number of persons who will become uninsured if genetic factors are used to determine eligibility and premiums for health insurance.

Critical Thinking Question: How would a supporter of a Rawlsian theory of justice assess the current situation with respect to health insurance in the United States? Offer reasons in support of your analysis.

Discussion: First, let's assume that we can apply Rawls' principles of justice to the present situation in the United States. Of course, the policy in the United States was not constructed on the basis of Rawls' principles of justice, yet suppose we use these principles to critically analyze the current situation. (The question of applying Rawls' theory is discussed more fully in "Genetic Information, Health Insurance, and Rawlsian Justice," contained in Chapter 6.) The principle that seems most relevant would be the Difference Principle, since this governs the distribution of social goods, and as discussed above, health is considered by Rawls to be a natural primary good. Health is a primary good since it is necessary for being able to pursue whatever else one values in life. It is a natural (as opposed to a social) primary good since institutions are not able to directly distribute good health itself. Rawls' Difference Principle states that we must select the distribution of goods, of all possible available distributions, which will put the least advantaged class in the best possible relative position.

Given this application, it seems clear that Rawls' principles could be used to criticize a system in which as many as approximately one-quarter of Americans at some point in a calendar year are without health insurance. Since health plays an important role in conceiving and implementing one's life plans, some form of health insurance has become a reasonable and necessary means for safeguarding one's most important aspirations and hopes. Due to the economic and psychological instability that is caused by uncertainty about meeting present or future health needs and the corresponding effect on one's life plans, justice as fairness would criticize a policy that did not provide a system that at least meets one's basic health needs, those necessary for being able to live one's life in a minimally flourishing manner. Hence, justice as fairness would provide a powerful indictment not only of the present health insurance system in the United States but could also be used to morally criticize the usage of genetic factors that may deprive more Americans of health insurance and fundamental health care.

CONCLUDING NOTE ON ETHICS

This chapter has offered an overview of the main philosophical ethical perspectives, as well as a logical analysis that details the advantages and disadvantages of each. This explains why certain ethical perspectives are viewed as more promising by contemporary philosophers and therefore have assumed a primary place in discussions of medical ethics. It is worth emphasizing that ethical perspectives are not pieces of "machinery" whose purpose is to simply crank out answers to moral questions. Each perspective emphasizes one aspect of the moral domain and develops a theory of moral thinking centered on that aspect. Critical thinking skills are necessary to use these ethical perspectives in practice; one must have practice in questioning, discerning the relevant features of a situation, generating alternatives, and reflectively arriving at a decision based on the best reasons in light of one's own values and preferences. This underscores the general idea that ethics itself is a process of thinking, not simply a set of established answers that need only be passively accepted.

The overarching view that underlies the examination conducted in this chapter is that ethics consists in the construction of a critically reflective morality. Ethics is *critical* since it leaves itself open to examining and reexamining reasons from all sources and disciplines. Ethics is *reflective* in that a conscientious moral agent is constantly trying to achieve a delicate balance that takes into account the effect of these reasons on his or her deepest values. By contrast, a morality, or set of mores, is a set of rules, norms, or understandings that may be followed even by a non-reflective person. So, while ethics is a form of morality, a morality is not necessarily ethical. To consider ethics as a critically reflective morality highlights the fact that ethics is a method of discovery and not strictly a body of knowledge. Ethics does not consist of knowing the answers but instead of knowing how to inquire; in particular, of knowing what counts as a possible answer, what questions are appropriate and constructive ones to ask, and what tendencies in one's own thinking need to be kept in check. Given this substantive conception of ethics as a critically reflective morality aimed at identifying, examining, and addressing practical problems, to become (better) ethical thinkers requires the development of critical thinking skills.

In its reasoned treatment of the different ethical perspectives as well as in its discussion of the critical thinking interludes, this chapter serves as an illustration of critical ethical thinking from a philosophical perspective. The next chapter grounds the discussion in this chapter by explaining some main concepts of informal logic. These critical thinking tools will help you gain more precision and depth in your reflections about both the issues in medical ethics discussed in this text as well as the various other intellectual challenges you face every day as a thinker.

Notes

1. de Poncins, G. *Kabloona* (New York: Reynal & Hitchcock, 1941). This example is mentioned in Brannigan and Boss, *Healthcare Ethics in a Diverse Society* (Mountain View: Mayfield Publishing, 2001), p. 13.
2. This point is made by Feinberg, Joel, "Psychological Egoism," which appears in Feinberg (ed.) *Reason and Responsibility,* Ninth Edition (Belmont: Wadsworth Publishing, 1996), pp. 497–507.
3. Rachels, James, *The Elements of Moral Philosophy*, Third Edition (New York: McGraw-Hill Publishing, 1999), Chapter 6.
4. This objection was made by Elizabeth Anderson in her book *Value in Ethics and Economics* (Cambridge, MA: Harvard University Press, 1993), Chapter 2.
5. Kant, I. *Grounding for the Metaphysics of Morals,* translated by James Ellington. (Indianapolis: Hackett Publishing, 1993).
6. This line of argument focused on identifying and applying the maxim to the actions is derived from Marcus G. Singer, *Generalization in Ethics* (New York: Alfred A. Knopf, 1961), Chapter IX.
7. Aristotle, *Nicomachean Ethics*, translated by Terence Irwin. (Indianapolis: Hackett Publishing, 1985).
8. For instance, see Sherman, N. *The Fabric of Character* (New York: Oxford University Press, 1989), and Kupperman, J. *Character* (New York: Oxford University Press, 1991).
9. McDowell, J. 1979. "Virtue and Reason." *The Monist* 62:331–350.
10. This point is made in Louden, R. *Morality and Moral Theory* (New York: Oxford University Press, 1983).
11. For a discussion of this condition, see Powell, J. *AIDS and HIV-Related Diseases: An Educational Guide for Professionals and the Public* (New York: Plenum Press, 1996), pp. 44–46.
12. Rawls, J. *A Theory of Justice* (Cambridge, UK: Belknap, 1971), p. 12; Rawls, J. *Political Liberalism* (New York: Columbia University Press, 1996), p. 79.
13. Regarding this passage, see Rawls 1996, pp. 331–334, Rawls 1971, pp. 284–293, and Rawls 1971, p. 302.
14. Nozick, R. *Anarchy, State, and Utopia* (New York: Basic Books, 1974), pp. 160–164.
15. On this, see Rawls 1971, pp. 510–511, 506–507.
16. Banja, J. D. 2000. "The Improbable Future of Employment-Based Insurance," *Hastings Center Report* (May/June), p. 17.

CHAPTER 2

CRITICAL THINKING TOOLS

CHAPTER GOALS:

- Introduce central critical thinking concepts to formalize the activity of logical reasoning
- Provide language to identify and describe types and components of arguments
- Present and analyze numerous arguments to begin development of the perceptual abilities necessary for identifying and describing the components of logical arguments
- Present and explain logical fallacies as a means to suggest acceptable evaluative standards for logical reasoning

OVERVIEW OF CRITICAL THINKING

This chapter provides a concise discussion of tools that will help you become a (more) critical thinker. You have already done this in thinking through the case studies discussed in the Critical Thinking Interludes interspersed throughout Chapter 1. I imagine that you may have found this activity a bit unusual at first, but after some effort discovered the tempo and rhythm of this process of inquiry. After "taking the plunge," you may have even found the discussion of the case studies to be quite natural, having anticipated some of the points even before they were discussed. Richard Paul and Linda Elder, leading experts in critical thinking, point out that for most people, thinking is a subconscious activity, one that is never put into words.[1] Paul and Elder distinguish between first-order and second-order thinking. First-order thinking is spontaneous and unreflective, and is the type of thinking that most persons use exclusively. Second-order thinking involves analyzing and reconstructing our thinking. The aim of this chapter is to describe, explain, and begin to inculcate this higher-order thinking.

Critical thinking itself involves learning how to monitor your own thought process. More particularly, it involves learning the standards for evaluating your own thinking and then attempting to internalize certain tools to improve your thinking by constantly engaging in reflection and self-assessment. It is important to note that thinking well is hard work! We face many barriers to clear thinking. We may have unreflectively accepted cultural or social norms or attitudes. Perhaps we have adopted from our family prejudiced attitudes toward certain groups of persons or biases concerning certain issues. We may have internalized obedient attitudes and therefore find it difficult to question what is said by authority figures, thinking that we cannot really make a difference by offering our thoughtful input. We may have limited access to the information relevant to our concerns, assuming that we have been able to discern what those concerns are. Or, more likely, all of these challenges may affect us to some degree. Each of us has picked up bad habits of thinking that are difficult to identify, examine, and (hopefully) change. Ask yourself the following questions: How often do I examine my own thinking? What, if anything, have I learned about my own thinking? What is the best way to assess my own thinking? If you are like most persons, you probably do not have clear answers to these questions.

The challenges to clear thinking, combined with lack of attention to this matter, are what most likely explain the difficulty of addressing these questions. The importance of addressing these questions underscores the relevance of this chapter. It is not enough, however, to learn that you may have acquired some bad habits of thought. You also need to learn what good habits should take their place. The critical thinking concepts explained in this chapter will help you to learn the structures inherent in good thinking, so that you will acquire a sense of better and worse ways to think. Critical thinking skills not only are relevant to ethics or to a philosophy class, but also are applicable to everything you do in your life.

DESCRIPTION, INFERENCE, AND NORMATIVE STATEMENTS

Critical thinking focuses on building the skills necessary to identify patterns of reasoning, as well as on providing the tools necessary for assessing the strengths and weaknesses of arguments. The basic purpose of this chapter is to provide students with constructive methods for attempting to understand and evaluate others' perspectives, for identifying what is being said and what is being used to support what is being said, and for picking out the background assumptions that are implicit in others' reasoning.

To begin, we should note the distinction between *description* and *inference*. When we describe something, we provide an objective statement of a set of facts. In other words, a description consists of relating an empirically verifiable state of affairs. An inference, by contrast, is a conclusion that we draw on the basis of observation or evidence. These two activities are close cousins, yet they are distinct. For example, suppose you drive home to visit your parents. You pull up in their driveway and see that the garage door is open and both cars are parked in the garage. The gate to the backyard is ajar, and the windows in the house are open. Up to this point, we have simply provided a description of the scene at your parents' house. What do you infer from this description? First, you may infer on the basis of your observations that your parents are home at this time. After all, the garage is open, the cars are parked in the garage, and the windows are unlocked and open. Further, you may infer that the family dog is inside the house with your parents, since the gate to the backyard is ajar. Or you may infer that the dog has escaped again, knowing that the dog is not allowed in the house. And so on. Each of these is an inference that is justified to a greater or lesser extent based on the evidence drawn from your observations. While inferences follow from observations, they are not the same thing. Sometimes, we observe things about which we draw no inferences at all, such as when we view a July 4th fireworks show. Descriptions are based on facts while inferences consist of taking an extra step based on those facts.

Descriptive statements are also different from *normative statements*. Descriptive statements focus on what *is* the case. This is the type of exploration an anthropologist or a physicist engages in. They conduct research by going on site to digs or by conducting experiments, and these are meant to describe, respectively, the forms of organization of past cultures or the physical constitution of the universe. Through anthropological research we know that certain cultures (such as ancient Greece) had slaves perform much of the work in the society. An anthropologist would offer a likely description of this culture's practices and support this claim with evidence. The anthropologist would not make a value judgment about this Greek practice a central part of her professional mission. Normative statements focus not on what *is* the case, but on what *ought to be* the case. Normative claims are the focus of moral philosophers. A moral philosopher would be centrally concerned with examining the reasons for and against making a value judgment such as, "The Greeks should not have had slaves, since this practice is morally wrong."

THE FUNDAMENTALS OF ARGUMENTS

Arguments consist of two or more statements or propositions, one, the conclusion, which is supported by the other(s), the premise(s). A *proposition* is a statement that expresses a complete thought and possesses a truth value; that is, it can be either true or false. The *premises* are the propositions that are intended to do the supporting work. They provide the evidence, the reasons to believe the conclusion. The *conclusion* is the claim intended to be supported by the premises. The premises provide the foundation for the argument, and premises can take the form of either descriptive statements or normative statements (in moral arguments).

Certain words serve as clues for picking out the premises and the conclusion when reading a text. The following list is not intended to be exhaustive, but words such as *because, since, for, for the reason that*, and *given that* serve as premise-indicators. Words such as *therefore, consequently, hence, subsequently, thus*, and *accordingly* serve as conclusion-indicators. Organizing an argument into its components has the virtue of making clear not only the structure of the argument, but also the possible sources of disagreement concerning the argument that may exist. Consider the following argument:

Argument 1.

(1) The medical profession is under an obligation to provide all services desired and requested by patients.

(2) Some terminally ill patients will request assisted suicide.

(3) Therefore, the medical profession is under an obligation to assist in the suicide of patients who request this.

In this argument, statements (1) and (2) are the premises, and (3) is the intended conclusion. Persons inside and outside of the medical profession often have heated disagreements about whether patients should have a request for assisted suicide honored. Looking at this as one possible argument in support of assisted suicide allows us to touch on some of the relevant issues necessary for reaching a reasoned conclusion on this controversy. In addition, being clear about the structure of the argument itself (premises-conclusion) allows a more disciplined discussion of the issues.

Suppose that we were critically analyzing this argument as part of a medical ethics class. A good place to start would be to think carefully about premise (1). Are there any questions or general difficulties with premise (1) that come to mind? For one thing, it is not clear that premise (1) is true in general. It is not clear that the medical profession is under an obligation to provide all services desired and requested by patients. What if a patient requested surgery that could be potentially disfiguring, or drug therapy that was highly addictive and not necessary for the medical treatment undergone? What if a person requested the removal of her appendix because she "felt" something may go wrong with it during her overseas vacation next summer, even though there is no medical basis for thinking this? Medical professionals have a responsibility to administer the medical care that is in the patient's best interest, and in at least some cases, the patient may not be fully informed about what is in his or her best interest. In some cases, a physician can refuse a patient's request for a particular service or procedure, since she believes that this is incompatible with her professional responsibility. On this basis, one could question the truth of premise (1). If premise (1) is found to be unsustainable, one may reject Argument 1 by claiming that one of its premises is false. This is one possible way to criticize Argument 1 from a logical point of view.

Assumptions, Facts, Opinions, and Ideas

We will discuss several specific ways to critically assess arguments later in this chapter. However, to critically analyze arguments it will be helpful to be familiar with several other concepts that are associated with arguments. First, there are *assumptions*, which function like hypotheses and not like the facts that are part of descriptive statements. Consider the following argument:

Argument 2.

(1) The use of "recreational" drugs may be potentially harmful to some persons.

(2) Therefore, "recreational" drug use should be made illegal.

Consider the structure of this argument and how proposition (1) relates to statement (2). Notice that for the premise (1) to "connect" properly to the conclusion (2), we would have to add at least one additional step to fill out the logic in the argument. What would be required is something like the following:

Argument 3.

(1) The use of "recreational" drugs may be potentially harmful to some persons.
[(1.5) Anything that is potentially harmful to some persons should be made illegal.]
(2) Therefore, "recreational" drug use should be made illegal.

In this case, statement (1.5) serves as an *unstated assumption* in Argument 2, and this is brought out explicitly in Argument 3. Once this unstated assumption is made clear, however, this could affect our critical assessment of the argument. At first glance, Argument 2 may seem to be a compelling argument. However, think carefully about the unstated assumption needed to "bridge the gap" between statements (1) and (2). Can you think of any questions or possible difficulties with the unstated assumption, statement (1.5)? We may be able to think of many things that are potentially harmful to persons, such as automobiles, bathtubs, and tall buildings, yet not think the fact that they pose a potential harm constitutes a sufficient reason to make them illegal. A defender of this argument would need to make clear exactly why the nature of the potential harm associated with "recreational" drugs is different from the potential harm associated with these other things. Until this is done, the argument as stated appears to be weak.

To critically assess arguments, you should be able to distinguish between facts, opinions, and ideas. *Facts* are propositions that are true. These can generally be proven by means of empirical testing. An example would be that water freezes at 32 degrees Fahrenheit. There may be certain mathematical or scientific axioms or theorems, such as Einstein's famous equation $E = mc^2$, for which an ordinary person may not be able to demonstrate the proof. Even though this is the case, such propositions may still operate as facts. As discussed earlier, facts differ from inferences; if I know that water freezes at 32 degrees Fahrenheit and I know that the temperature has been below 32 degrees Fahrenheit for the past week, I may infer that the pool of water behind my home is frozen. It seems reasonable to say that once I verify the truth of this proposition by walking outside and observing the pool, it is then a fact that the pool of water is frozen. Of course, this proposition may not be true, and hence it may not be a fact, if (for example) the pool is so large that it has not frozen.

Opinions are statements of belief that vary between people. One may believe that the water is too gross to swim in, while another person may think the water is just fine for swimming. Opinions can differ from inferences in that inferences are always based on facts, while one can hold an opinion that is not based on facts ("I dislike green beans."). However, opinions on substantive or intellectual matters, such as beliefs about assisted suicide or human cloning, should be informed by relevant facts. It is common to hear clichés such as, "That is just your opinion" or "I have a right to my opinion." However, to say this is not to relegate everything concerning such intellectual debates to being simply a matter of opinion. Instead, if we note that opinions about issues in fields such as medical ethics need to be based on reasons and facts, when confronted with an opinion with which we disagree, we should ask, "What reasons do you have in support of that opinion?" The picture looks like this:

Facts + Reasons → OPINION

We can then examine the facts and reasons in support of the opinion to see, first, if those facts are accurate, and second, to see if these serve as relevant reasons in support of that opinion. When one says, "I have a right to my opinion," in one sense this is true. No one wishes to be bullied into thinking one thing or another. Even if we do not have all of the answers to a critic's questions, we have the right to say that we would like to give our viewpoint more thought before engaging in further dialogue. Yet, to exercise a "right to one's opinion," if that is used to avoid explaining the facts and reasons in support of one's opinion, does not provide anyone else with good reason to take your opinion seriously.

Ideas differ from both facts and opinions. Ideas are mental constructions created on the basis of observations or facts. An example can help us see how these "mental leaps" differ from facts and opinions. One might become aware of certain facts concerning the chemical properties of asbestos, an insulating material that used to be put into homes and other buildings. One may form the opinion based on these facts that breathing the dust created by this insulating material is harmful to humans since it damages lung tissue and is linked to cancer. One might then have the idea of marketing a process whereby the insulating material is surrounded by a plastic lining, or covered over with sprayable protective paint. This process would not allow the dust to be breathed in by humans once the treatment was completed. This idea is distinct both from the facts and the opinion that led to its development. In general, an idea could be a solution to a problem, an improvement in a current product or process, or a plan of action.

Deductive Arguments: Validity and Soundness

The first major type of logical arguments are deductive arguments. A *deductive* argument is one in which the premises are intended to be sufficient for the drawing of the conclusion. There are two central concepts regarding deductive arguments. The first is the concept of validity. A valid argument is an argument such that **if** the premises are true, the conclusion is guaranteed to be true. Validity is a "structural" notion; to test for validity, look for the proper relationship to exist between the premises and the conclusion.

The other concept is that of *soundness*. A sound argument is one in which both (A) all the premises are true and (B) the truth of the conclusion is guaranteed by the truth of the premises. The concept of "truth" in this definition is best understood in simple terms, that the propositions fit the relevant facts or are sufficiently supported by relevant reasons. This definition implies that an argument is unsound if **either** (C) it includes at least one false premise or (D) the conclusion "does not follow" from the premises. To say that the conclusion "does not follow" from the premises is shorthand for stating that the truth of the conclusion is not guaranteed by the truth of the premises. Sound arguments deal with both the logical structure of the argument and the truth of the premises. Notice, then, that the concept of soundness encompasses the concept of validity; for an argument to be sound, it must also be valid, although a valid argument need not be sound.

These two concepts underscore the idea that arguments themselves as a whole are not properly described as "true" or "false." Individual propositions are properly described as true or false; deductive arguments are instead discussed in terms of validity and soundness. Let's discuss some examples concerning the notions of validity and soundness:

Argument 4.

(1) All humans will die.

(2) Wayne Newton is a human.

(3) Wayne Newton will die.

Is this argument valid? Ask yourself, "If the premises were true, would the conclusion be guaranteed to be true?" The answer to this question is "Yes." The conclusion logically follows from the premises. Is this argument sound? We already know that the argument is valid, so therefore, condition (B) of the soundness definition is satisfied. Is condition (A) of the soundness definition satisfied? This is the case only if the premises are true, and in this case, it is reasonable to hold that they are in fact true. The best evidence suggests that all humans will die, at least in the sense that their bodies will cease to engage in biological functioning and thereby show no signs of life. In addition, famous Las Vegas performer Wayne Newton is in fact a human. Argument 4 is both valid and sound.

Argument 5.

(1) All philosophers are unkempt in appearance.

(2) Robert Card is a philosopher.

(3) Robert Card is unkempt in appearance.

Is this argument valid? Recall that for an argument to be valid, it must be the case that *if* the premises are true, then the conclusion is guaranteed to be true. Notice that in this argument, premise (1) is (almost certainly) false: we could find at least one philosopher who is well dressed and properly coifed. However, this point is irrelevant to whether Argument 5 is valid, since it *is* the case that *if* the premises were true, the conclusion is guaranteed to be true. In other words, to ask "if" the premises are true is to say: "*Supposing* or *assuming* the premises to be true, would the truth of the conclusion be guaranteed?" Regarding Argument 5, the answer to this question is "Yes." However, since premise (1) is false, the argument is unsound. Argument 5 is valid yet unsound.

Argument 6.

(1) All pigs are dogs.

(2) All dogs are humans.

(3) All pigs are humans

Is this argument valid? Yes, it is. This argument is valid since it is the case that *if* (assuming) the premises are true, the conclusion is guaranteed to be true. The conclusion, as we say, logically "follows" from the premises. Is the argument sound? It satisfies condition (B) of the definition of soundness, since it is a valid argument. However, both of the premises are false. For this reason, it fails condition (A) of the soundness definition, and therefore is unsound. Argument 6 is valid yet unsound.

Argument 7.

(1) A triangle has three sides.
(2) Pigs have four legs.
(3) Humans are mortal.

Is this (rather strange) argument valid? It is not valid, since the conclusion does not "follow" from the premises. The premises are in no way related to the conclusion, and thereby, do not provide any support for the conclusion. For this reason, the truth of the conclusion is not guaranteed by the truth of the premises. Is it unsound? Yes. Since this argument is invalid, we know automatically that it is unsound since it fails condition (B) of the definition of soundness.

Argument 8.

(1) *Some* humans teach philosophy.
(2) Robert Card is a human.
(3) Robert Card teaches philosophy.

Is this argument valid? Answering this question requires careful thought. *If* (assuming) the premises are true, is the truth of the conclusion guaranteed to be true? In this case, one may point out that it is reasonable to think that premises (1) and (2) are true. And it is the case that the conclusion is related to the premises and is provided a degree of support by the premises. Yet, it is not the case that the truth of the conclusion is guaranteed by the truth of the premises. Even if *some* humans teach philosophy and Robert Card is a human, it need not necessarily be the case that Robert Card is one of the humans that in fact teaches philosophy. In assessing validity, we are concerned with the logical relation of the premises to the conclusion. Even if premises (1) and (2) were assumed to be true, the conclusion is not guaranteed to be true. Therefore, this argument is not valid. Since it thereby fails condition (B) of the definition of soundness, Argument 8 is unsound as well.

Major Kinds of Deductive Arguments

In this section, we will briefly discuss four major kinds of deductive arguments.

1. Categorical Syllogisms A syllogism is a three line argument consisting of two premises and a conclusion. The propositions are expressed in the form of categorical statements such as "All A's are B's," "Some A's are B's," or "No A's are B's."

Argument 9a.

(1) All men are humans.
(2) All humans are mortals.
(3) Therefore, all men are mortals.

Looked at more closely, we see the form expressed in this example:

Argument 9b.

A B
(1) All [men] are [humans.]

B C
(2) All [humans] are [mortals.]

A C
(3) Therefore, all [men] are [mortals.]

This form is an example of categorical syllogism, and as such is a valid deductive argument.

2. Modus ponens These are arguments of the form, "If A then B. A. Therefore, B."

Argument 10a.

(1) If the doctor cannot make it to the hospital, Michael's surgery will be postponed until tomorrow.
(2) The doctor cannot make it to the hospital.
(3) Michael's surgery will be postponed until tomorrow.

The form known as *modus ponens* is represented in this argument. We can see this explicitly by identifying and labeling each part of the argument as such:

Argument 10b.

A then B
(1) If [the doctor cannot make it to the hospital], [Michael's surgery will be postponed until tomorrow.]

A
(2) [The doctor cannot make it to the hospital.]

B
(3) Therefore, [Michael's surgery will be postponed until tomorrow.]

Since this is an example of *modus ponens*, this is a valid deductive argument.

3. Modus Tollens This third type of deductive argument takes the following form: "If A then B. Not B. Therefore, not A." *If A then B* is known as a *conditional* statement. A is called the *antecedent* of the conditional statement, and B is called the *consequent* of the conditional statement. The conditional statement maintains that if something happens (A) then something else (B) will occur. If B does not occur, we can infer that A has not occurred. To say "Not B" can be expressed as "−(B)," which is to put the negation sign (−) outside the parentheses in which B is contained. Negation signs in logic work in a way similar to the way they function in mathematics: −7 is 7 less than 0, while −(−7) would in fact be equal to 7 (7 greater than 0). Keeping this in mind, in the following expression, −(Mark did come home), we would be saying that Mark did not come home. Similarly, if we expressed the following, −(My neighbor was not home), we would be saying that it was *not* the case that (my neighbor was not home), meaning that this was the case—my neighbor was in fact home. Here is an example:

Argument 11a.

(1) If Ryan finishes the trim on the house today, then the entire outside of the house will be freshly painted.

(2) It is not the case that the entire outside of the house is freshly painted.

(3) Therefore, Ryan did not finish the trim on the house today.

The argument looks like the following after labeling its parts:

Argument 11b.

A **then** **B**
(1) If [Ryan finishes the trim on the house today], [the entire outside of the house will be freshly painted.]

Not **B**
(2) It is not the case that [The entire outside of the house is freshly painted.]

Not **A**
(3) Therefore, it is not the case that [Ryan finished the trim on the house today.]

As an instantiation of modus tollens, this is a valid argument. Such an argument is said to be "truth-preserving," since if its premises are true, the conclusion is in fact guaranteed to be true.

4. Disjunctive Syllogisms The final type of deductive argument we will discuss are disjunctive syllogisms. These are arguments of the following form: "Either A or B. Not A. Therefore B." Or, "Either A or B. Not B. Therefore A."

Argument 12a.

(1) Either they have built a bonfire in the backyard or the house is on fire.

(2) They have not built a bonfire in the backyard.

(3) Therefore, the house is on fire.

After labeling its components, it appears as such:

Argument 12b.

A **B**
(1) Either [they have built a bonfire in the backyard] or [the house is on fire.]

Not **A**
(2) It is not the case that [they have built a bonfire in the backyard.]

B
(3) Therefore, [the house is on fire.]

This section is a brief overview of major types of deductive arguments. At the very least, learning these basic logical forms will help you to be more aware of how to identify (and ultimately assess) the structure of the arguments you will encounter in the readings contained in this text.

Inductive Arguments

The other major type of logical arguments are *inductive* arguments. In an inductive argument, the truth of the premises makes the conclusion very likely to be true. In contrast to deductive arguments, with inductive arguments the truth of the premises does *not* guarantee the truth of the conclusion; there is always some degree of doubt with respect to the truth of the conclusion in an inductive argument. The truth of the conclusion in an inductive argument can be said to follow only with a certain likelihood or probability. Consider the following example. A restaurant owner recognizes that an average of fifty customers have come to eat dinner at the restaurant every Sunday night for the past six months. On this basis, she orders enough food to prepare fifty meals on Sunday evening. The argument for ordering this amount of food is inductive since it generalizes from past experience and it supports the conclusion that ordering this amount of food is reasonable. The argument can be represented as the following:

Argument 13.

(1) An average of fifty customers have come to eat dinner at the restaurant every Sunday night for the past six months.

(2) Therefore, order enough food to serve fifty customers for dinner this Sunday evening.

Notice that the premise in this argument could be true and the conclusion could be false. Even if the restaurant owner has properly computed the average number of dinner customers on past Sundays, this Sunday could be unrepresentative. Perhaps this Sunday is Super Bowl Sunday, when more persons will be at home in front of their televisions and will not go out for dinner. Or perhaps a special event in town will bring many more customers into the restaurant. Even though these contingencies are certainly possible, they do not constitute an objection to this argument since an inductive argument never purports to establish its conclusion with certainty.

Inductive arguments can take three main forms. They can be predictions, such as the argument just discussed, or can be based more generally on statistical reasoning.

Argument 14.

(1) Eighty percent of students live on campus.

(2) Daniel is a student.

(3) Daniel lives on campus.

In this argument, the first premise only covers 80% of the students, so there is the possibility that Daniel is one of the 20% of students who do not live on campus. The conclusion, while given some degree of support, clearly does not follow with certainty. Statistical arguments with a 10 to 15% range of uncertainty can be considered to offer strong statistical support for their conclusion.

Inductive arguments can also take the form of analogies. An analogical argument rests on a comparison between two things.

Argument 15.

(1) When I see John, he looks just like his brother Mark when he was young.

(2) When Mark was young, he liked to break dishes for fun.

(3) Therefore, I bet John likes to break dishes for fun.

To assess an argument by analogy, we must critically examine the similarities and differences that exist between the things being compared. In this case, the main similarity between John and Mark is their physical resemblance and the fact that they come from the same family. While there is a striking physical resemblance, it is likely that there are many differences between the two brothers. The fact that they look alike does not provide a compelling reason to believe that they will behave in the same way at the same age. While we would have to know more about John to conduct a careful study, it is likely that we could find sufficient differences that outweigh the relatively unimportant similarity concerning their physical appearance. If this is the case, then this analogy does not provide sufficient support for its conclusion.

Finally, inductive arguments can take the form of cause and effect arguments.

Argument 16.

(1) Drinking too much caffeine will cause persons to act in strange ways.

(2) Ed drank nine cups of black coffee this morning.

(3) Therefore, Ed's heavy caffeine consumption explains why he babbled incoherently during the meeting.

This argument posits a connection between heavy caffeine consumption and unusual behavior. This may provide some support for the conclusion, but it is worth noting that there may be other causes that are equally (if not more) important in explaining Ed's behavior. Perhaps Ed has newborn twins, and he drank nine cups of coffee this morning since he was up all night taking care of his children. If so, the cause of his incoherent behavior during the meeting is not his caffeine consumption, but his lack of sleep.

It is worth noting a few points in closing that relate to inductive arguments. First, the concepts of validity and soundness do not apply to inductive arguments—they are only relevant to deductive arguments. Since inductive arguments do not even attempt to establish a relation of certainty between the truth of the premise(s) and the truth of the conclusion, these concepts are simply irrelevant to inductive arguments. Second, it is possible for an argument to involve statistics, for instance, and not be an inductive argument. Consider the following variation on an argument discussed earlier:

Argument 17.

(1) One hundred percent of students live on campus.

(2) Daniel is a student.

(3) Daniel lives on campus.

There is no element of uncertainty in this argument; claims about all (or nothing) are universal claims and, therefore, this argument in fact takes the form of a deductive argument. The same would be true if the argument were modified as follows:

Argument 18.

(1) Zero percent of students live on campus.
(2) Daniel is a student.
(3) Daniel does not live on campus.

In an inductive argument, the conclusion never follows with certainty. In this case, however, the conclusion does purport to follow with certainty, and this argument is therefore a deductive argument.

This section provides a brief introduction to inductive arguments. We will return to discuss analogies and statistical arguments in more detail in the introductions to Units II and V, respectively. We will discuss material related to cause and effect arguments in the next section on logical fallacies.

Selected Informal Logical Fallacies

In this section, we will illustrate some common—and tempting—mistakes in reasoning. The overall point of doing so is to help you begin to develop a critical capacity to question and assess patterns of reasoning. Highlighting typical mistakes in reasoning will help you to put into words the suspicions you may already have concerning questionable arguments made in the public media. In addition, this will further bring into focus what constitutes acceptable evaluative standards for logical reasoning.

A fallacy is a fundamental flaw in one's pattern of reasoning that invalidates that reasoning. It is important to notice that a logical fallacy is a perfectly general kind of mistake. If one's reasoning is fallacious, then any reasoning that fits that pattern is logically invalidated, even if these other arguments are focused on a different subject matter. Identifying fallacies, then, focuses once again on the structural aspects of one's reasoning. *Formal fallacies* occur when the pattern of reasoning in a deductive argument is faulty. An argument that may be psychologically or emotionally appealing yet contains a logical error is referred to as an *informal fallacy.* We will focus on fifteen common informal fallacies that are most relevant to the issues raised in medical ethics. (More in-depth discussions related to these fallacies occur later in the book in the introductions to Units II, III, IV, and V.)

1. Ad Hominem The *ad hominem* fallacy occurs when one engages in a personal attack on the speaker instead of dealing directly with the person's argument for his or her claim. The attack is an attempt to discredit the person on the basis of some personal characteristic such as race, gender, age, or class, even though this characteristic is irrelevant to a reasoned assessment of this person's claim.

Sandra: I think that laws placing restrictions on a woman's right to choose to have an abortion are wrong.

Marcus: You only think that because you are a woman! Your opinion does not count.

This is a fallacy since the merits and demerits of the person's position are not carefully examined, but instead, the view under consideration is rejected by criticizing its source. "Ad hominem" is Latin for "to the man," which suggests that it is the person and not the person's position that is being directly criticized. It is the case that at times we may become skeptical regarding the credibility of a source. In that instance, we should not accept that person's claim, but should conduct a more detailed examination of the reasons offered for their position. To reject a person's viewpoint based simply on the fact that he or she possesses an irrelevant characteristic is a logical mistake.

2. Ad Populum This fallacy occurs when a position is defended simply because it is in accord with popular belief. This fallacy is sometimes referred to as "appeal to the masses."

Bernie: Most college students would agree that English literature courses involve too much reading. Hence, English professors should reduce the number of required books in literature courses.

While Bernie may have made a correct statement concerning the beliefs of college students, this appeal does not necessarily provide good reason to reduce the reading in English courses. This approach attempts to pressure a person to conform to what most others think. It is likely that literature professors have good reasons for requiring a substantial amount of reading material in English classes as a way to ensure that the objectives of the course are met. To support the claim in favor of reducing the reading load, there would have to be good reasons to support this common belief, such as a study that showed that an equal (or greater) amount of learning could occur with less reading. Not all appeals to popular belief necessarily involve fallacies. For instance, suppose you are visiting Europe and wish to know if wearing a bikini while visiting a cathedral is considered offensive. If you find that most Europeans do find this inappropriate, then this provides you with good reasons to modify your attire when visiting cathedrals. In general, it can make sense to rely on popular beliefs concerning such benign things as etiquette. The point inherent in the discussion of the *ad populum* fallacy is that common belief does not necessarily determine truth.

3. False Appeal to Authority This fallacy occurs when a famous person or authority is cited concerning a field other than their area of expertise.

Rollie: My pastor told me that gene therapy was dangerous and was a bad idea. Therefore, we should stop research into gene therapy this minute!

Certainly, one may look to a religious figure to discuss moral issues and their relation to one's faith, but in this case, a religious figure may not be in a position to know all of the facts concerning the possible harms and benefits stemming from genetic research. Since this is the case, basing our opinion on the testimony of such an "expert" would be a mistake. We should be sure to gather input from authorities in the discipline relevant to our interest, and should critically analyze the evidence presented by such experts. The fact that an expert in an area says something is the case does not make it so; instead, we should look to the evidence and reasons offered in support of the claim. In cases of controversial issues such as gene therapy, it may be best to look at the input from a number of researchers and thinkers in the field.

4. Ad Ignorantiam This fallacy occurs when it is argued that something is the case (either true or false) simply because it cannot be proved whether or not it is true or false.

Joanna: My medical ethics professor is a kleptomaniac—you cannot prove that I am wrong, so obviously I am right!

In this fallacy, the person bases his or her argument simply on the lack of proof to the contrary. This, however, provides no good reason to support the claim, since a failure to disprove something does not constitute positive proof of the opposite claim. The proper conclusion to draw from the fact of ignorance about whether or not something is the case is, quite simply, that you do not know what is true about that matter.

5. Tu Quoque This fallacy is also sometimes referred to as the fallacy of hypocrisy or "practice what you preach."

Doctor Marshall: You should really try to stop smoking, Paul. I believe your smoking habit is significantly hurting your health.

Paul: Give me a break, Doctor Marshall! I saw you in the parking lot behind the medical building smoking a cigarette when I walked in today.

This fallacious pattern of reasoning is premised on the claim that since the person does not follow their own advice, then their advice should be rejected. This is often a very tempting rhetorical maneuver. However, it is not an acceptable logical tactic, since the fact that a person does not follow his own guidance does not mean that the advice itself is not good advice. An adulterer may detail the harms involved in adultery, and even though he or she has not followed this guidance at least at some point in their lives, their advice could be quite valuable. The person's own behavior with respect to their advice and the quality of the advice itself are separable. While an individual's own behavior may serve as a reasonable basis for assessing the person, it is a logical error to reject their statement on this basis.

6. Hasty Generalization This fallacy involves an inference or principle drawn on the basis of a sample that is too small. In some cases, the logical mistake lies in drawing an inference on the basis of unusual cases.

Jon: Some people say that eating red meat is bad for your health. What a crock! My grandpa ate steak and potatoes for dinner every night since he was a young man. He is now 87 years old and is fit as a fiddle!

Defending a conclusion on such a basis is logically mistaken, since it generalizes from one case. Jon's grandpa may be unrepresentative in some important way; for example, he may have been a manual laborer who physically exerted himself on a daily basis. We may find that most men who followed a similar diet were prone to heart disease or colon cancer, yet Jon's grandpa's degree of physical fitness may explain his good health. Perhaps there are genetic factors that happen to protect Jon's grandpa from health problems related to his diet. The fact that we can point to one case in which eating substantial amounts of red meat has not resulted in disease provides no good reason to believe that eating steak for dinner every night poses no health risks.

7. Biased Statistics This fallacy involves the mistake of drawing an inference on the basis of a sample that is not diverse enough. A study attempts to draw a conclusion based on a "sample population," and this sample population is to support claims about the larger "target population." In this fallacy, there is "mismatch" between the sample populations and target populations that invalidates the proposed inference.

Stacy: A recent survey of doctors revealed that 70% of physicians do not believe that medical costs are too high. Therefore, 70% of Americans must not think that medical costs are too high.

The shift from a sample population of physicians, who are the only ones polled in this study, to the target population of all Americans represents the crucial mistake in the fallacy of biased statistics. To infer such a conclusion about all Americans' views on health care costs from such a sample lacks diversity in many ways, including age and socioeconomic class. This sample is not diverse enough to support the proposed generalization. The only acceptable manner in which to support this generalization so as to avoid this "mismatch" would be to look at a more representative sample of Americans. This fallacy differs from that of hasty generalization, since the sample size in the survey of physicians could have been sufficiently large to support claims regarding *doctors'* views on health care costs. The fallacy of hasty generalization stems from this mistake, while biased statistics stems from misusing even the results of a sufficiently large sample by misapplying these to a particular target population.

8. Bifurcation The fallacy of bifurcation is sometimes called "false dilemma" or "false either-or choice." This mistake in logic occurs when only a subset of choices is presented, yet there are truly other options that exist.

Doctor Noel: Your terminally ill brother has only two choices to address his disease. He can either opt for the best and most aggressive treatment until the very end of his life, or he can be a wimp, give up, and refuse all medical care. I would recommend that he opt for the best medical treatment.

This piece of reasoning is aimed at convincing a sibling to agree to the most aggressive medical care possible for one's brother, since the other option represents weakness. The mistake is that there are other options that go unmentioned. Perhaps the ill man could try some of the aggressive care, and if he does not respond after a certain time, he could simply ask to be put into hospice care and made comfortable. Intentionally withholding some available options to make a certain conclusion seem more appealing is manipulative. Of course, we do not often know or consider every possible option when making a decision. The fallacy of bifurcation consists in artificially limiting the number of options to two in an attempt to influence another person's thinking. If it is the case that there are truly only two reasonable alternatives, then framing the discussion in this way does not necessarily involve a logical error.

9. Begging the Question The fallacy of begging the question is often one of the most difficult fallacies to detect. This fallacy consists of the speaker assuming precisely what he or she needs to prove. Since this is circular reasoning, this pattern of reasoning is illegitimate.

Janna: Abortion is always morally acceptable since women have the right to decide whether or not they will carry a pregnancy to term.

This reasoning does not offer any argument in support of the notion that women possess an unlimited right to decide whether or not they will carry a pregnancy to term.

Instead, it merely asserts this. Of course, if this were true, then abortion would always be acceptable if a woman chose it, yet this point is precisely the central point that is in contention. In some cases, a debate can get rather technical, and we must be careful that we are not simply restating our premises. The conclusion must come out of the premises; simply restating the conclusion we wish to establish in different words in our premises does nothing to logically ground the conclusion.

A further example may help to illustrate the subtlety of this logical error:

Jack: Voluntary active euthanasia should not be legal because if there was nothing wrong with it, it would already be legal in the United States. However, it is not legal, which proves my point.

The "argument" presented by Jack needs some disentangling to discover its error. Jack's claim is that voluntary active euthanasia should not be legal. What reasons are presented to support this conclusion? Essentially, Jack supports this claim by pointing to the fact that voluntary active euthanasia is currently not legal. Precisely what is in question in this debate is whether the law should be changed to grant terminally ill persons more control over the dying process. Pointing to its current illegality to support the claim that voluntary active euthanasia should not be legal assumes precisely what is necessary to establish the relevant conclusion: that the law ruling out voluntary active euthanasia is justified and is not in need of change. In Jack's statement, no substantive reasons are offered to support his claim.

10. Post Hoc Ergo Propter Hoc This fallacy, when translated from the Latin, means "after this, therefore, because of this." The mistake in the *post hoc* fallacy is to presume a false causal relationship between two things: that just because one thing chronologically precedes something else, that thing is the cause of the later thing.

Doctor Jones: I ate a cheesesteak with onions before coming to work yesterday, and three of my patients passed away during my rounds. I will never eat a cheesesteak with onions before work again!

This fallacy occurs when no evidence is presented to support the causal link between the two things. The sequence of the events could be coincidental, and there is no reason in such cases to believe that a true causal connection exists. This fallacy is related to the next fallacy.

11. False Cause This fallacy also concerns a possible causal relationship between two things, yet it differs from the *post hoc* fallacy. As philosopher Wanda Teays[2] points out, in false cause, it may be the case that there is a causal relationship between the things being examined, but the argument rests on a mistaken assumption that they stand in a *direct* causal relationship. This fallacy, says Teays, may take two forms: that of confusing cause and effect, and that of separating out one causal factor and calling it the sole cause.

Mattie: Gloria ate a piece of strawberry pie. Later that night, she got a rash and vomited. Obviously, the rash caused her to vomit.

Ralph: Frank exercises two hours a day in the gym, runs three miles each morning, eats right, and gets eight hours of sleep each night. He has an excellent physique. That just shows you, if you want an excellent physique, get eight hours of sleep every night!

The first example illustrates confusing cause and effect: it is more likely to think that the strawberry pie was in fact the cause of the vomiting rather than the rash. In the second example, this mistakenly separates out one causal factor as the explanation for Frank's excellent physique. Hence, this line of reasoning illustrates the other version of the fallacy of false cause.

12. Red Herring In the fallacy of red herring, a speaker uses irrelevant information to avoid addressing the true point.

Patient: Dr. Fina, I do not think this treatment is working. I do not feel any better and my blood levels are worse than they were before the treatment began more than a month ago.

Dr. Fina: Well, while those things may be true, I can feel that your spirit is stronger than it was before. That counts for quite a lot, you know, to have a strong spirit!

In this scenario, Dr. Fina commits the fallacy of red herring by intentionally changing the subject with the intent to divert attention away from the patient's (pointed) remarks about his medical condition. Whenever this is done with the intention to deceive or redirect one's attention to another point that is unrelated to the speaker's concerns, this fallacy is present. The important point is to recognize that the subject has been changed with the intent to derail a discussion based on the relevant concerns.

13. Slippery Slope This fallacy occurs when a person presumes that one decision, which may in itself seem trivial, will set off a chain of events that issue in devastating results.

Professor Froid: If I allow students to make up examinations they missed when hospitalized, then I will have to allow them to make up work when seriously ill. Eventually, I will have to allow makeups when they are simply too tired to get out of bed to come to class. That's it, no makeups!

None of us can predict with perfect accuracy the long-term results of our actions. However, while this is the case, the fact that one cannot disprove that the proposed sequence of events will occur provides no good reason to think that they will. (This remark suggests that the slippery slope is related to the fallacy of *ad ignorantiam.*) The distinguishing characteristic of the slippery slope is that there is no specific evidence presented to document how the first step will lead to the devastating chain of events predicted by the speaker. If one (incorrectly) assumes the connections and does not offer any supporting proof, then the fallacy of slippery slope has occurred. If one offers proof for the connections between Event A, Event B, on to Event Z, but this evidence is uncertain, the fallacy of slippery slope has not occurred and normal standards of evaluating evidence apply to assess the worth of the speaker's claim. (This fallacy will be discussed in greater depth in the introduction to Unit III.)

14. Equivocation Some terms have several meanings, and as long as the context signals the appropriate meaning of the term and the meaning is used consistently, there is no logical problem. The fallacy of equivocation occurs when the different meanings of a single word or phrase are confused and different senses of the word or phrase are used in the same context.

Linda: All human research subjects have a right to be treated as well as possible in the course of a scientific study.

Bart: There is no law in the United States that specifically requires this; hence, research subjects have no such rights.

There are many different meanings for the term "right" that need to be clarified and used consistently to allow a reasoned discussion to occur. In Linda's remark, she is assuming a notion of rights that applies to persons simply by virtue of being human, whether these rights are part of enacted laws or not. Bart's remark seems to assume that humans have no rights except for those privileges enumerated in positive law. Since these are different meanings, there is no necessary conflict between Linda and Bart, yet there would have to be consistency in the use of the term "right" before an acceptable argument could be constructed.

15. Naturalistic Fallacy One commits the naturalistic fallacy when one assumes that because something is the case, then it ought to be that way. Related is the fallacy of *ad populum*, since in this fallacy it is assumed that simply because people currently believe something is the case, then things should be in accordance with that belief.

Brian: Men have a strong desire to procreate and are naturally more aggressive than women. Therefore, it is natural for a man to engage in sexual intercourse with a woman even if she does not wish to participate.

If we took this line of reasoning seriously, it may provide some justification (or even an excuse) for rape.[3] However, even granting the physiological facts cited concerning men, there is no compelling reason to support the notion that men ought to be allowed to behave in ways that violate womens' rights. In other words, even assuming the facts about men as stated, we can still morally criticize (and legally sanction) acts of rape. Moving directly from such descriptive claims to normative claims concerning morality is an instance of the naturalistic fallacy, and is a logical error. (Ideas associated with this fallacy will be further examined in the introduction to Unit IV.)

Notes

1. Paul, R., and Elder, L. *Critical Thinking: Tools for Taking Charge of Your Learning and Your Life* (Upper Saddle River, NJ: Prentice Hall, 2001), p. xii.
2. Teays, W. *Second Thoughts* (Mountain View, CA: Mayfield Publishing), p. 210.
3. For a critical analysis of this line of reasoning, see Barbara Ehrenreich, "How Natural Is Rape?" *Time*, January 31, 2000, p. 88.

UNIT TWO

REPRODUCTIVE ISSUES

CHAPTER 3: SURROGACY CONTRACTS AND CHAPTER 4: ABORTION

This unit looks at the moral issues surrounding reproduction. Chapter 3 concerns the morality of commercial surrogacy contracts, which are arrangements in which a woman agrees to have a child for another party in exchange for money. Chapter 4 concerns the ethical status of abortion.

There are two methods of conception commonly used in surrogacy arrangements. First, there is *artificial insemination*. In this method, sperm is placed in a syringe attached to a narrow tube or catheter. This catheter is inserted into the cervical canal, and semen is injected into the uterus. The woman remains in a prone position with her hips raised for approximately twenty minutes to maximize the chances of fertilization. With this method, fertilization occurs within the surrogate's body, and hence, she is the biological mother of the child. The other method is *in vitro fertilization*. In this method, ova are fertilized in a laboratory and then left to undergo cell division. Usually at the eight-cell stage, the fertilized egg is transferred to the uterus through the cervix by means of a hollow plastic tube. If all goes well, the egg will continue to divide, will attach itself to the wall of the uterus, and pregnancy will proceed normally until the child is born. When using this method, fertilization occurs outside of the human body, and the contract mother is not the biological mother of the child. In fact, when using *in vitro fertilization*, the child could have as many as five parents: if donor sperm and/or ova are used, the donors would be biological parents of the child. The person or persons who raise the child would be the adoptive parents. The contract mother, who in this case serves as the *gestational mother*, could also be considered a parent of the child.

The readings in the unit begin with a New Jersey Supreme Court Majority Opinion written by Judge Robert Wilentz regarding the case of Baby M. In this case, Mary Beth Whitehead became pregnant via artificial insemination, and agreed to relinquish the child at birth in exchange for a fee of $10,000. The Court ruled that the surrogacy contract between Mrs. Whitehead and William Stern was not legally enforceable. While the Supreme Court of New Jersey saw no legal problem with surrogacy contracts if there was no monetary fee involved, the Baby M arrangement violated New Jersey law. In its opinion, the Court raises a number of concerns about commercial surrogacy arrangements, including the possibility of coercion and exploitation of contract mothers.

There has not been to date a judgment handed down by the United States Supreme Court regarding the legality of surrogacy contracts. Hence, there is a patchwork quilt of laws across the United States concerning the status and enforceability of surrogacy contracts. It seems that there are three main options to consider concerning surrogacy contracts: (1) to outlaw them, meaning that even entering into such a contract is illegal; (2) to consider them legally unenforceable, meaning that no legal remedies are available to those who file lawsuits relating to surrogacy contracts, even though entering into the contracts is not itself illegal; and (3) to consider such contracts to be legally enforceable, but to regulate them.

Katha Pollitt argues in support of option (2) in her papers, "The Strange Case of Baby M" and "When Is a Mother Not a Mother?". Pollitt's presentation is packed with interesting analogies and numerous arguments. Pollitt's main point is that there are many contracts that the law either prevents individuals from making, or that the law refuses to enforce. For instance, the law does not allow individuals to "donate" a kidney in exchange for money. What this suggests is that even if all parties to the contract agree, there are conditions that must be satisfied for a contract to be morally binding. Pollitt seems to draw implicitly on such conditions in her argument that from a moral perspective, surrogacy contracts should not be considered enforceable. The conditions that must be satisfied for a contract to be morally binding are, roughly, as follows:

1. signing the contract must be *voluntary*
2. parties to the contract must be *well-informed*
3. the parties to the contract must be *competent*
4. the contract must not require anyone to do something that is *immoral*

Condition (1) suggests that if the person is coerced or forced into signing the contract, it is null and void. Condition (2) implies that there must be no fraud when representing the terms of the agreement. Condition (3) suggests that the persons entering the agreement must be of legal age and must possess the requisite mental capacity to carry out the terms of the contract. Condition (4) is difficult to state precisely (and without circularity), but the idea is clear enough. A contract to murder someone, even if it meets the other three conditions, cannot be binding and cannot be enforced because it requires one to do something that is immoral. The central question confronted in Chapter 3, then, is this: Are surrogacy contracts as binding as other acceptable contracts? The most powerful argument in favor of enforcing surrogacy contracts is what we could call *The Liberty Argument*: persons have the freedom to enter into any contracts they wish, subject to conditions (1)–(4). If these conditions are met, the contract is enforceable. Pollitt argues in her discussion, however, that surrogacy contracts do not meet the conditions for morally binding contracts.

Laws making surrogacy contracts illegal or non-enforceable raise the question of *paternalistic* restrictions on liberty. A paternalistic law is one whose rationale is centered on the fact that it will prevent persons from harming themselves. Pollitt herself alludes to paternalistic laws, citing seat-belt laws and laws that prevent persons from selling bodily organs. Laws that make surrogacy contracts unenforceable or illegal are often justified on paternalistic grounds, since they prevent women from entering into binding arrangements that they may come to regret. In "Paternalism," Gerald Dworkin offers a careful general discussion of whether and why paternalism may be justifiable. Dworkin's discussion offers several important distinctions concerning types of paternalism, and at the end of his article he offers a number of factors that must be considered in deciding whether paternalism is justified in a particular instance. While Dworkin does not specifically address the question of whether anti-surrogacy laws are justifiable or not, applying Dworkin's factors to the case of surrogacy suggests that laws against surrogacy may be justifiable on paternalistic grounds.

Some argue against the enforceability of surrogacy contracts by pointing out that adults need to meet no requirements to become parents by entering into a surrogacy contracts: they must only have enough money to pay the relevant costs. This is in stark contrast with the procedures necessary to adopt a child in the U.S. To ensure that those who will raise the child born out of a surrogacy agreement will be good parents, some maintain that there should be a screening process prior to allowing the arrangements to proceed. One could argue in response to this point that we do not screen persons who reproduce "naturally" before they become parents, so it is unfair to require this for those who become parents via surrogacy arrangements. (This point is especially forceful if the persons who use surrogacy do so because one of the partners is infertile, since the fact that they cannot reproduce "naturally" is beyond their control.) If we support screening for the potential (adoptive) parents in surrogacy arrangements, then perhaps we *should* screen all potential parents, whether they reproduce "naturally" or by way of reproductive technology. One way to implement this idea would be to require potential parents to acquire parenting licenses. While this idea may seem radical, in his thought-provoking selection "Licensing Parents," Hugh LaFollette argues that there are no convincing objections to this licensing proposal. This would suggest that screening procedures are justified for persons who become parents via surrogacy arrangements.

In her selection, Bonnie Steinbock argues that we ought to model surrogacy arrangements on adoption arrangements. Steinbock's position, then, is that surrogacy contracts should not be outlawed, but they should be enforceable and regulated in a way similar to adoption. (Option (3) outlined above.) Steinbock also discusses the question of whether surrogacy contracts constitute a form of exploitation, and she concludes that surrogacy contracts are not necessarily exploitative. Finally, in "The Case Against Surrogate Parenting," Herbert Krimmel addresses the ethics of surrogacy contracts. His main argument is that since it is morally wrong to separate the decision to create a child from the decision to rear a child, surrogacy arrangements should be considered morally wrong. This argument directly links to Steinbock's treatment, since Krimmel believes that surrogacy and adoption are fundamentally different. Adoption is acceptable, while surrogacy is not, since adoption does *not* involve separating the decision to create a child from the decision to rear a child. This is the case since the woman giving up the child does not conceive the child with the intention of allowing another to rear it, and the adoptive parents themselves are not involved in the decision to create the child. The morality of surrogacy contracts raises issues such as the relationship between legal reasoning and moral reasoning, paternalistic justifications for restrictions on liberty, and issues of exploitation. The selections in this unit represent a diverse sampling of positions as well as provide a unifying dialogue on this moral controversy.

Chapter 4 contains readings that construct a dialogue about abortion. The first two readings, selections from the United States Supreme Court decisions in *Roe* v. *Wade* (1973) and *Planned Parenthood of Southeastern Pennsylvania* v. *Casey, Governor of Pennsylvania* (1992), provide the social and legal backdrop necessary for discussing the debate regarding the morality of abortion in the United States. *Roe* v. *Wade* legalized abortion in the first two trimesters of pregnancy, and allowed abortion in the third trimester only if continued pregnancy constituted a significant threat to the woman's health or life. The *Casey* decision is the most recent legal challenge to *Roe* v. *Wade*. In this decision, the Court reaffirmed the substance of *Roe*, yet they directly ascribed legal importance to fetal viability, the point at which a fetus can (at least in principle) survive outside of the womb with available medical technology. The *Casey* decision also affirms the point that certain legal restrictions are compatible with the existence of abortion rights.

The selections then turn from the legal status to the moral status of abortion. There are three central positions in the abortion debate:

(1) **The Conservative View.** This position maintains that a fetus is a person from the moment of conception. Since moral rights or moral status are ascribed to human life at conception, defenders of this position hold that abortion is morally wrong in most cases, with the possible exception of cases in which the mother's life is endangered by continuing the pregnancy.

(2) **The Liberal View.** This position holds that the fetus does not have any significant moral status or moral rights throughout pregnancy; it only achieves this status after birth. Therefore, abortion is never wrong because it violates the moral rights of the fetus, and hence is morally permissible in most cases.[1]

(3) **The Moderate View.** This set of views is neither conservative nor liberal. On this view, the general questions regarding when abortion is permissible are, (1) Up to what point of fetal development is abortion morally acceptable? and (2) What reasons are acceptable for justifying an abortion?

Don Marquis is the most influential recent defender of the conservative view on abortion. In "Why Abortion is Immoral," Marquis offers the following general philosophical explanation for why it is morally wrong to kill a human being: killing is morally wrong because it deprives an individual of a future of value. Marquis then applies this general explanation of the moral wrongness of killing to the abortion debate by arguing that this theory explains the moral wrongness of taking fetal life with equal plausibility. Marquis' argument also serves as an implicit criticism of arguments in the abortion debate that center around the concept of personhood—what is important is that the fetus will be deprived of a future of value regardless of whether or not it is a person. In "On the Moral and Legal Status of Abortion," Mary Anne Warren defends the liberal view on abortion and contributes to the dialogue by arguing that defining the moral community is the central issue in the abortion debate. In her view, defining this membership is in essence to determine the conditions for personhood. After offering five criteria for personhood, Warren argues that fetuses do not fit these criteria, and hence, are not persons. According to her, abortion is morally permissible in most cases. In a postscript to her original article, Warren addresses the question of whether infanticide is morally permissible on her view. She argues that while infants are not persons, it is still not morally permissible to kill them. In his selection, Robert Card looks carefully at how Warren's original argument fits with the reasoning offered in the postscript, and argues that Warren must either accept that infanticide is morally permissible or must abandon her liberal view on abortion. The defense of the liberal view is rounded out by Susan Sherwin, who argues from a feminist perspective that since the fetus is not a separate individual, it lacks moral status and abortion is morally acceptable throughout pregnancy.

Judith Thomson enters the dialogue by explicitly defending a moderate view on abortion. Thomson acknowledges the importance of women's rights to control their own bodies, yet does not categorically approve of abortion throughout pregnancy. Thomson, then, is not a liberal. In addition, Thomson moderates the conservative view, and therefore does not think that abortion is morally wrong in most cases. By employing a number of thought-provoking arguments, Thomson argues that abortion is morally permissible in cases of rape and in cases of contraceptive failure. In her selection, Jane English offers a moderate view which she also defends by employing a number of interesting analogies. English denies the overwhelming importance placed on personhood in the abortion issue, since she thinks that we can only identify features of persons which are more or less *typical*—we cannot successfully construct a list of definitive conditions for personhood. Further, English argues that even if we assume that the fetus is a person from the moment of conception, it does not follow that abortion is morally wrong, since women possess a right to self-defense even when pregnant. If we suppose that the fetus is not a person, it does not follow that abortion is morally acceptable in all cases, argues English. This is the case since we cannot do whatever we wish to non-persons, since fetuses as well as non-human animals may still possess some degree of moral status. English extends the moderate view even further than Thomson by arguing that abortion is morally permissible even in cases in which it is necessary for a woman to protect herself from drastic injury to her career prospects.

Finally, L.W. Sumner moderates the conservative and liberal views on abortion, yet in a manner very different from Thomson's approach. Sumner argues that neither the liberal nor conservative view take account of the common sense factors that matter in determining the moral status of abortion. Neither the liberal nor the conservative view (strictly interpreted) ascribes importance to the gestational age of the fetus or the reason offered for the abortion in determining the morality of an abortion decision. Sumner offers a clearly articulated moderate view on which the fetus acquires moral interests when it becomes sentient, that is, is able to experience pleasant and unpleasant sensations. This view allows abortions early in pregnancy but is more restrictive late in pregnancy. Sumner's selection, then, serves as a "blueprint" of sorts for constructing a moderate view, and provides the moral justification for supporting the moderate view defended from a legal perspective in *Roe* v. *Wade*. The chapter closes with an article examining both sides of the question "Should abortions late in pregnancy be banned?"

CRITICAL THINKING TOOL: ANALOGIES

In this unit on surrogacy contracts and abortion, it will be helpful to be familiar with the workings of analogies. This critical thinking tool appears prominently in the writings contained in these two chapters. Analogies can be powerful argumentative tools, yet this is only the case if they are understood and used properly. Basically, arguments based on analogies are founded on a comparison between two things. An argument based on an analogy is successful to the extent that the similarities between the things being compared outweigh the differences.

An analogical argument is a form of inductive argument. As discussed in Chapter 2, an inductive argument is one in which the truth of premises makes the conclusion likely to be true only with a certain probability. An inductive argument by its very nature does not aim at establishing the truth of the conclusion with certainty. This means that all analogical arguments, as examples of inductive arguments, will provide at best incomplete support for their intended conclusion. The form of an analogy is as follows:

Case C = the case we create; that to which we compare the object of interest

Case C* = the case we are interested in

Form

1. In Case C, *a* is *F*.
2. In Case C*, *b* is like *a* in all respects relevant to *F*-ness.

---

3. Therefore, in Case C*, *b* is *F*.

Let's discuss some examples to clarify the form that analogies take. While this presentation may be somewhat oversimplified, sketching some examples will be useful for illustrating the workings of this critical thinking tool. In a memorable analogy, Mary Anne Warren compares an abortion to cutting one's hair. When confronted with an analogy, the first question you should ask yourself is, "What point is this person trying to make with this comparison?" In this case, Warren, as a supporter of the liberal view on abortion, wishes to suggest that abortion is a morally neutral act—that is the principle behind the comparison. So, we have the following:

Case C = case of cutting one's hair

Case C* = case of an abortion

1. In the case of cutting one's hair, the act is morally neutral.
2. In the case of abortion, abortion is similar to the act of cutting one's hair in the relevant respects.

---

3. Therefore, in the case of abortion, the act is morally neutral.

To analyze an analogy, we need to complete the following four steps:

1. **Clarify the comparison.** In this analogy, a comparison is drawn between getting a haircut and having an abortion.
2. **Clarify the principle behind the comparison.** In this analogy, the principle inherent in the comparison is that both haircuts and abortions are morally unproblematic actions, since morality simply does not apply to these decisions.
3. **List the similarities and differences between the things being compared.** In this analogy, some of the relevant similarities and differences are the following:

SIMILARITIES	DIFFERENCES
1. both hair and fetuses grow	1. fetuses are living organisms, hair is not living
2. both hair and fetuses are part of the human body	2. hair does not have the potential to grow into a human person
3. both are decisions that concern one's preferences or values	3. fetuses grow inside the human body
4. both generally require another person to help perform the action	

4. **Weigh the relevant similarities and differences and arrive at a conclusion.** The list of similarities and differences is not complete, but it provides a good place to start. If the relevant similarities outweigh the differences, then the analogy is successful. If the differences outweigh the similarities, then the analogy is not successful. In weighing the similarities and differences, it is important to note that this does not simply consist of counting up the number of each. If that were the case, in the comparison above, the similarities would outweigh the differences. Instead, to properly conduct the weighting, we must decide which of the similarities and differences are most important.

For instance, from the list above, the first and second differences stand out as very important. In performing the weighting necessary to reach a conclusion, this requires arriving at a *reasoned conclusion* regarding the relative merits of the similarities versus the differences. A reasonable weighting might be that similarities 1 and 2 are fairly substantial (and similarities 3 and 4 are less substantial), and differences number 1 and 2 are significant. Therefore, one might claim that the differences outweigh the similarities, and the analogy is unsuccessful, meaning that it does not give us sufficient reason to believe that an abortion is a morally unproblematic act on a par with getting a haircut. When critically examining an analogy, it is important to remember that analogies are not rigid pieces of machinery that necessarily lead to one answer; you must do your own thinking to arrive at a conclusion.

Let's discuss one more example of analogical reasoning; this time, let's use an example from the readings on surrogacy contracts. In "The Strange Case of Baby M," Katha Pollitt calls surrogacy contracts a form of "reproductive prostitution." What point is Pollitt trying to make with this comparison? Let's apply the four steps necessary to analyze this analogy:

1. **Clarify the comparison.** In this analogy, the comparison being drawn is that between surrogacy and prostitution.
2. **Clarify the principle behind the comparison.** In this analogy, the principle inherent in the comparison is that prostitution is immoral, and therefore, surrogacy is immoral.
3. **List the similarities and differences between the things being compared.** In this analogy, some of the relevant similarities and differences are the following:

SIMILARITIES	DIFFERENCES
1. both involve the use of one's body	1. length of time commitment for action
2. both are done in exchange for money	2. level of danger to the woman involved
3. both involve a private or intimate matter	3. range of options open to the women who participate
4. both involve "turning off one's feelings" in some important way	

4. **Weigh the relevant similarities and differences and arrive at a conclusion.** Our task is to attempt to determine which of the similarities and differences is most important. What do *you* think? Similarities 1, 3, and 4 and differences 2 and 3 seem to be important. Perhaps one reasonable conclusion is that the similarities outweigh the differences, since difference 2 is not as significant as one might first think. While prostitutes face dangers ranging from sexually transmitted diseases to physical abuse, contract mothers may also face significant health risks arising from pregnancy. The health consequences suffered by surrogate mothers may also be long-term in nature. Similarly, difference 3 may not be as important as it first seems, if it is the case that a disproportionate number of women who become contract mothers are from lower socioeconomic classes and have few employment opportunities. Yet, the relevant similarities do seem to apply. This provides some reason, though certainly not a conclusive reason, to think that surrogacy, like prostitution, is immoral.

One last point to mention about this analogy is that if the similarities outweigh the differences, then this provides some reason to consider surrogacy arrangements and prostitution in the same light. However, notice that this may not necessarily serve as an argument against surrogacy contracts. If the analogy does hold, one simply needs to treat the two activities in the same way: if one does not believe that prostitution is immoral, then one could embrace the analogy, treat the activities equally, and argue that surrogacy is not immoral as well. This particular analogy may involve a comparison with an activity that is just as controversial as the activity it hopes to teach us about.

Notes

1. It is worth pointing out that liberals may consider abortion to be wrong in some cases, for example, if performed on the basis of sex selection. However, the wrongness of the abortion is not explained in terms of a violation of the moral status of the fetus. In this case, abortion could be considered unacceptable because it is a sexist practice and sexism is morally wrong.

SURROGACY CONTRACTS

OPINION IN THE MATTER OF BABY M

Judge Robert N. Wilentz

In this matter the Court is asked to determine the validity of a contract that purports to provide a new way of bringing children into a family. For a fee of $10,000, a woman agrees to be artificially inseminated with the semen of another woman's husband; she is to conceive a child, carry it to term, and after its birth surrender it to the natural father and his wife. The intent of the contract is that the child's natural mother will thereafter be forever separated from her child. The wife is to adopt the child, and she and the natural father are to be regarded as its parents for all purposes. The contract providing for this is called a "surrogacy contract," the natural mother inappropriately called the "surrogate mother."

We invalidate the surrogacy contract because it conflicts with the law and public policy of this State. While we recognize the depth of the yearning of infertile couples to have their own children, we find the payment of money to a "surrogate" mother illegal, perhaps criminal, and potentially degrading to women. Although in this case we grant custody to the natural father, the evidence having clearly proved such custody to be in the best interests of the infant, we void both the termination of the surrogate mother's parental rights and the adoption of the child by the wife/stepparent. We thus restore the "surrogate" as the mother of the child. We remand the issue of the natural mother's visitation rights to the trial court, since that issue was not reached below and the record before us is not sufficient to permit us to decide it *de novo*.

We find no offense to our present laws where a woman voluntarily and without payment agrees to act as a "surrogate" mother, provided that she is not subject to a binding agreement to surrender her child. Moreover, our holding today does not preclude the Legislature from altering the current statutory scheme, within constitutional limits, so as to permit surrogacy contracts. Under current law, however, the surrogacy agreement before us is illegal and invalid.

New Jersey Supreme Court (1988). Reprinted with permission from 109 N.J. 396. Noted Omitted.

FACTS

In February 1985, William Stern and Mary Beth Whitehead entered into a surrogacy contract. It recited that Stern's wife, Elizabeth, was infertile, that they wanted a child, and that Mrs. Whitehead was willing to provide that child as the mother with Mr. Stern as the father.

The contract provided that through artificial insemination using Mr. Stern's sperm, Mrs. Whitehead would become pregnant, carry the child to term, bear it, deliver it to the Sterns, and thereafter do whatever was necessary to terminate her maternal rights so that Mrs. Stern could thereafter adopt the child. Mrs. Whitehead's husband, Richard, was also a party to the contract; Mrs. Stern was not. Mr. Whitehead promised to do all acts necessary to rebut the presumption of paternity under the Parentage Act. Although Mrs. Stern was not a party to the surrogacy agreement, the contract gave her sole custody of the child in the event of Mr. Stern's death. Mrs. Stern's status as a nonparty to the surrogate parenting agreement presumably was to avoid the application of the baby-selling statute to this arrangement.

Mr. Stern, on his part, agreed to attempt the artificial insemination and to pay Mrs. Whitehead $10,000 after the child's birth, on its delivery to him. In a separate contract, Mr. Stern agreed to pay $7,500 to the Infertility Center of New York ("ICNY"). The Center's advertising campaigns solicit surrogate mothers and encourage infertile couples to consider surrogacy. ICNY arranged for the surrogacy contract by bringing the parties together, explaining the process to them, furnishing the contractual form, and providing legal counsel.

The history of the parties' involvement in this arrangement suggests their good faith. William and Elizabeth Stern were married in July 1974, having met at the University of Michigan, where both were Ph.D. candidates. Due to financial considerations and Mrs. Stern's pursuit of a medical degree and residency, they decided to defer starting a family until 1981. Before then, however, Mrs. Stern learned that she might have multiple sclerosis and that the disease in some cases renders pregnancy a serious health risk. Her anxiety appears to have exceeded the actual risk, which current medical authorities assess as minimal. Nonetheless that anxiety was evidently quite real, Mrs. Stern fearing that pregnancy might precipitate blindness, paraplegia, or other forms of debilitation. Based on the perceived risk, the Sterns decided to forgo having their own children. The decision had special significance for Mr. Stern. Most of his family had been destroyed in the Holocaust. As the family's only survivor, he very much wanted to continue his bloodline.

Initially the Sterns considered adoption, but were discouraged by the substantial delay apparently involved and by the potential problem they saw arising from their age and their differing religious backgrounds. They were most eager for some other means to start a family.

The paths of Mrs. Whitehead and the Sterns to surrogacy were similar. Both responded to advertising by ICNY. The Sterns' response, following their inquiries into adoption, was the result of their long-standing decision to have a child. Mrs. Whitehead's response apparently resulted from her sympathy with family members and others who could have no children (she stated that she wanted to give another couple the "gift of life"); she also wanted the $10,000 to help her family...

... The two couples met to discuss the surrogacy arrangement and decided to go forward. On February 6, 1985, Mr. Stern and Mr. and Mrs. Whitehead executed the surrogate parenting agreement. After several artificial inseminations over a period of months, Mrs. Whitehead became pregnant. The pregnancy was uneventful and on March 27, 1986, Baby M was born.

Not wishing anyone at the hospital to be aware of the surrogacy arrangement, Mr. and Mrs. Whitehead appeared to all as the proud parents of a healthy female child. Her birth certificate indicated her name to be Sara Elizabeth Whitehead and her father to be Richard Whitehead. In accordance with Mrs. Whitehead's request, the Sterns visited the hospital unobtrusively to see the newborn child.

Mrs. Whitehead realized, almost from the moment of birth, that she could not part with this child. She had felt a bond with it even during pregnancy. Some indication of the attachment was conveyed to the Sterns at the hospital when they told Mrs. Whitehead what they were going to name the baby. She apparently broke into tears and indicated that she did not know if she could give up the child. She talked about how the baby looked like her other daughter, and made it clear that she was experiencing great difficulty with the decision.

Nonetheless, Mrs. Whitehead was, for the moment, true to her word. Despite powerful inclinations to the contrary, she turned her child over to the Sterns on March 30 at the Whiteheads' home.

The Sterns were thrilled with their new child. They had planned extensively for its arrival, far beyond the practical furnishing of a room for her. It was a time of joyful celebration—not just for them but for their friends as well. The Sterns looked forward to raising their daughter, whom they named Melissa. While aware by then that Mrs. Whitehead was undergoing an emotional crisis, they were as yet not cognizant of the depth of that crisis and its implications for their newly enlarged family.

Later in the evening of March 30, Mrs. Whitehead became deeply disturbed, disconsolate, stricken with unbearable sadness. She had to have her child. She could not eat, sleep, or concentrate on anything other than her need for her baby. The next day she went to the Sterns' home and told them how much she was suffering.

The depth of Mrs. Whitehead's despair surprised and frightened the Sterns. She told them that she could not live without her baby, that she must have her, even if only for one week, that thereafter she would surrender her child. The Sterns, concerned that Mrs. Whitehead might indeed commit suicide, not wanting under any circumstances to risk that, and in any event believing that Mrs. Whitehead would keep her word, turned the child over to her. It was not until four months later, after a series of attempts to regain possession of the child, that Melissa was returned to the Sterns, having been forcibly removed from the home where she was then living with Mr. and Mrs. Whitehead, the home in Florida owned by Mary Beth Whitehead's parents.

The struggle over Baby M began when it became apparent that Mrs. Whitehead could not return the child to Mr. Stern. Due to Mrs. Whitehead's refusal to relinquish the baby, Mr. Stern filed a complaint seeking enforcement of the surrogacy contract. He alleged, accurately, that Mrs. Whitehead had not only refused to comply with the surrogacy contract but had threatened to flee from New Jersey with the child in order to avoid even the possibility of his obtaining custody. The court papers asserted that if Mrs. Whitehead were to be given notice of the application for an order requiring her to relinquish custody, she would, prior to the hearing, leave the state with the baby. And that is precisely what she did. After the order was entered, *ex parte*, the process server, aided by the police, in the presence of the Sterns, entered Mrs. Whitehead's home to execute the order. Mr. Whitehead fled with the child, who had been handed to him through a window while those who came to enforce the order were thrown off balance by a dispute over the child's current name.

The Whiteheads immediately fled to Florida with Baby M. They stayed initially with Mrs. Whitehead's parents, where one of Mrs. Whitehead's children had been living. For the next three months, the Whiteheads and Melissa lived at roughly twenty different hotels, motels, and homes in order to avoid apprehension. From time to time Mrs. Whitehead would call Mr. Stern to discuss the matter; the conversations, recorded by Mr. Stern on advice of counsel, show an escalating dispute about rights, morality, and power, accompanied by threats of Mrs. Whitehead to kill herself, to kill the child, and falsely to accuse Mr. Stern of sexually molesting Mrs. Whitehead's other daughter.

Eventually the Sterns discovered where the Whiteheads were staying, commenced supplementary proceedings in Florida, and obtained an order requiring the Whiteheads to turn over the child. Police in Florida enforced the order, forcibly removing the child from her grandparents' home. She was soon thereafter brought to New Jersey and turned over to the Sterns. The prior order of the court, issued *ex parte*, awarding custody of the child to the Sterns *pendente lite*, was reaffirmed by the trial court after consideration of the certified representations of the parties (both represented by counsel) concerning the unusual sequence of events that had unfolded. Pending final judgment, Mrs. Whitehead was awarded limited visitation with Baby M.

The Sterns' complaint, in addition to seeking possession and ultimately custody of the child, sought enforcement of the surrogacy contract. Pursuant to the contract, it asked that the child be permanently placed in their custody, that Mrs. Whitehead's parental rights be terminated, and that Mrs. Stern be allowed to adopt the child, *i.e.*, that, for all purposes, Melissa become the Sterns' child.

The trial took thirty-two days over a period of more than two months. ... Soon after the conclusion of the trial, the trial court announced its opinion from the bench. It held that the surrogacy contract was valid; ordered that Mrs. Whitehead's parental rights be terminated and that sole custody of the child be granted to Mr. Stern; and, after hearing brief testimony from Mrs. Stern, immediately entered an order allowing the adoption of Melissa by Mrs. Stern, all in accordance with the surrogacy contract. Pending the outcome of the appeal, we granted a continuation of visitation to Mrs. Whitehead, although slightly more limited than the visitation allowed during the trial.

Although clearly expressing its view that the surrogacy contract was valid, the trial court devoted the major portion of its opinion to the question of the baby's best interests. ...

On the question of best interests—and we agree, but for different reasons, that custody was the critical issue—the court's analysis of the testimony was perceptive, demonstrating both its understanding of the case and its considerable experience in these matters. We agree substantially with both its analysis and conclusions on the matter of custody.

The court's review and analysis of the surrogacy contract, however, is not at all in accord with ours. ...

INVALIDITY AND UNENFORCEABILITY OF SURROGACY CONTRACT

We have concluded that this surrogacy contract is invalid. Our conclusion has two bases: direct conflict with existing statutes and conflict with the public policies of this State, as expressed in its statutory and decisional law.

One of the surrogacy contract's basic purposes, to achieve the adoption of a child through private placement, though permitted in New Jersey "is very much disfavored." Its use of money for this purpose—and we have no doubt whatsoever that the money is being paid to obtain an adoption and not, as the Sterns argue, for the personal services of Mary Beth Whitehead—is illegal and perhaps criminal. In addition to the inducement of money, there is the coercion of contract: the natural mother's irrevocable agreement, prior to birth, even prior to conception, to surrender the child to the adoptive couple. Such an agreement is totally unenforceable in private placement adoption. Even where the adoption is through an approved agency, the formal agreement to surrender occurs only after birth, and then, by regulation, only *after* the birth mother has been offered counseling. Integral to these invalid provisions of the surrogacy contract is the related agreement, equally invalid, on the part of the natural mother to cooperate with, and not to contest, proceedings to terminate her parental rights, as well as her contractual concession, in aid of the adoption, that the child's best interests would be served by awarding custody to the natural father and his wife—all of this before she has even conceived, and, in some cases, before she has the slightest idea of what the natural father and adoptive mother are like.

The foregoing provisions not only directly conflict with New Jersey statutes, but also offend long-established State policies. These critical terms, which are at the heart of the contract, are invalid and unenforceable; the conclusion therefore follows, without more, that the entire contract is unenforceable.

A. Conflict with Statutory Provisions

The surrogacy contract conflicts with: (1) laws prohibiting the use of money in connection with adoptions; (2) laws requiring proof of parental unfitness or abandonment before termination of parental rights is ordered or an adoption is granted; and (3) laws that make surrender of custody and consent to adoption revocable in private placement adoptions. ...

B. Public Policy Considerations

The surrogacy contract's invalidity, resulting from its direct conflict with the above statutory provisions, is further underlined when its goals and means are measured against New Jersey's public policy. The contract's basic premise, that the natural parents can decide in advance of birth which one is to have custody of the child, bears no relationship to the settled law that the child's best interests shall determine. ... The surrogacy contract guarantees permanent separation of the child from one of its natural parents. Our policy, however, has long been that to the extent possible, children should remain with and be brought up by both of their natural parents. ...

The surrogacy contract violates the policy of this State that the rights of natural parents are equal concerning their child, the father's right no greater than the mother's. ... The whole purpose and effect of the surrogacy contract was to give the father the exclusive right to the child by destroying the rights of the mother.

The policies expressed in our comprehensive laws governing consent to the surrender of a child stand in stark contrast to the surrogacy contract and what it implies. ...

Under the contract, the natural mother is irrevocably committed before she knows the strength of her bond with her child. She never makes a totally voluntary, informed decision, for quite clearly any decision prior to the baby's birth is, in the most important sense, uninformed, and any decision after that, compelled by a pre-existing contractual commitment, the threat of a lawsuit, and the inducement of a $10,000 payment, is less than totally voluntary. Her interests are of little concern to those who controlled this transaction. ...

Worst of all, however, is the contract's total disregard of the best interests of the child. There is not the slightest suggestion that any inquiry will be made at any time to determine the fitness of the Sterns as custodial parents, of Mrs. Stern as an adoptive parent, their superiority to Mrs. Whitehead, or the effect on the child of not living with her natural mother.

This is the sale of a child, or, at the very least, the sale of a mother's right to her child, the only mitigating factor being that one of the purchasers is the father. Almost every evil that prompted the prohibition on the payment of money in connection with adoptions exists here. ...

The main difference [between an adoption and a surrogacy contract], that the unwanted pregnancy is unintended while the situation of the surrogate mother is voluntary and intended, is really not significant. Initially, it produces stronger reactions of sympathy for the mother whose pregnancy was unwanted than for the surrogate mother, who "went into this with her eyes wide open." On reflection, however, it appears that the essential evil is the same, taking advantage of a woman's circumstances (the unwanted pregnancy or the need for money) in order to take away her child, the difference being one of degree. ...

In the scheme contemplated by the surrogacy contract in this case, a middleman, propelled by profit, promotes the sale. Whatever idealism may have motivated any of the participants, the profit motive predominates, permeates, and ultimately governs the transaction. The demand for children is great and the supply small. The availability of contraception, abortion, and the greater willingness of single mothers to bring up their children has led to a shortage of babies offered for adoption. The situation is ripe for the entry of the middleman who will bring some equilibrium into the market by increasing the supply through the use of money.

Intimated, but disputed, is the assertion that surrogacy will be used for the benefit of the rich at the expense of the poor. In response it is noted that the Sterns are not rich and the Whiteheads not poor. Nevertheless, it is clear to us that it is unlikely that surrogate mothers will be as proportionately numerous among those women in the top twenty percent income bracket as among those in the bottom twenty percent. Put differently, we doubt that infertile couples in the low-income bracket will find upper income surrogates.

In any event, even in this case one should not pretend that disparate wealth does not play a part simply because the contrast is not the dramatic "rich versus poor." At the time of trial, the Whiteheads' net assets were probably negative—Mrs. Whitehead's own sister was foreclosing on a second mortgage. Their income derived from Mr. Whitehead's labors. Mrs. Whitehead is a homemaker, having previously held part-time jobs. The Sterns are both professionals, she a medical doctor, he a biochemist. Their combined income when both were working was about $89,500 a year and their assets sufficient to pay for the surrogacy contract arrangements.

The point is made that Mrs. Whitehead *agreed* to the surrogacy arrangement, supposedly fully understanding the consequences. Putting aside the issue of how compelling her need for money may have been, and how significant her understanding of the consequences, we suggest that her consent is irrelevant. There are, in a civilized society, some things that money cannot buy. In America, we decided long ago that merely because conduct purchased by money was "voluntary" did not mean that it was good or beyond regulation and prohibition. Employers can no longer buy labor at the lowest price they can bargain for, even though that labor is "voluntary," or buy women's labor for less money than paid to men for the same job, or purchase the agreement of children to perform oppressive labor, or purchase the agreement of workers to subject themselves to unsafe or unhealthful working conditions. There are, in short, values that society deems more important than granting to wealth whatever it can buy, be it labor, love, or life. Whether this principle recommends prohibition of surrogacy, which presumably sometimes results in great satisfaction to all of the parties, is not for us to say. We note here only that, under existing law, the fact that Mrs. Whitehead "agreed" to the arrangement is not dispositive.

The long-term effects of surrogacy contracts are not known, but feared—the impact on the child who learns her life was bought, that she is the offspring of someone who gave birth to her only to obtain money; the impact on the natural mother as the full weight of her isolation is felt along with the full reality of the sale of her body and her child; the impact on the natural father and adoptive mother once they realize the consequences of their conduct. Literature in related areas suggests these are substantial considerations, although, given the newness of surrogacy, there is little information.

The surrogacy contract is based on principles that are directly contrary to the objectives of our laws. It guarantees the separation of a child from its mother; it looks to adoption regardless of suitability; it totally ignores the child; it takes the child from the mother regardless of her wishes and her maternal fitness; and it does all of this, it accomplishes all of its goals, through the use of money.

Beyond that is the potential degradation of some women that may result from this arrangement. In many cases, of course, surrogacy may bring satisfaction, not only to the infertile couple, but to the surrogate mother herself. The fact, however, that many women may not perceive surrogacy negatively but rather see it as an opportunity does not diminish its potential for devastation to other women.

In sum, the harmful consequences of this surrogacy arrangement appear to us all too palpable. In New Jersey the surrogate mother's agreement to sell her child is void. Its irrevocability infects the entire contract, as does the money that purports to buy it.

TERMINATION

We have already noted that under our laws termination of parental rights cannot be based on contract, but may be granted only on proof of the statutory requirements. That conclusion was one of the bases for invalidating the surrogacy contract. Although excluding the contract as a basis for parental termination, we did not explicitly deal with the question of whether the statutory bases for termination existed. We do so here.

As noted before, if termination of Mrs. Whitehead's parental rights is justified, Mrs. Whitehead will have no further claim either to custody or to visitation, and adoption by Mrs. Stern may proceed pursuant to the private placement adoption statute. If termination is not justified, Mrs. Whitehead remains the legal mother, and even if not entitled to custody, she would ordinarily be expected to have some rights of visitation. …

Nothing in this record justifies a finding that would allow a court to terminate Mary Beth Whitehead's parental rights under the statutory standard. It is not simply that obviously there was no "intentional abandonment or very substantial neglect of parental duties without a reasonable expectation of reversal of that conduct in the future," quite the contrary, but furthermore that the trial court never found Mrs. Whitehead an unfit mother and indeed affirmatively stated that Mary Beth Whitehead had been a good mother to her other children. …

CUSTODY

Having decided that the surrogacy contract is illegal and unenforceable, we now must decide the custody question without regard to the provisions of the surrogacy contract that would give Mr. Stern sole and permanent custody. …

… [T]he question of custody in this case, as in practically all cases, assumes the fitness of both parents, and no serious contention is made in this case that either is unfit. The issue here is which life would be *better* for Baby M, one with primary custody in the Whiteheads or one with primary custody in the Sterns.

The circumstances of this custody dispute are unusual and they have provoked some unusual contentions. The Whiteheads claim that even if the child's best interests would be served by our awarding custody to the Sterns, we should not do so, since that will encourage surrogacy contracts—contracts claimed by the Whiteheads, and we agree, to be violative of important legislatively stated public policies. Their position is that in order that surrogacy contracts be deterred, custody should remain in the surrogate mother unless she is unfit, regardless of the best interests of the child. We disagree. Our declaration that this surrogacy contract is unenforceable and illegal is sufficient to deter similar agreements. We need not sacrifice the child's interests in order to make that point sharper. …

Our custody conclusion is based on strongly persuasive testimony contrasting both the family life of the Whiteheads and the Sterns and the personalities and characters of the individuals. The stability of the Whitehead family life was doubtful at the time of trial. Their finances were in serious trouble (foreclosure by Mrs. Whitehead's sister on a second mortgage was in process). Mr. Whitehead's employment, though relatively steady, was always at risk because of his alcoholism, a condition that he seems not to have been able to confront effectively. Mrs. Whitehead had not worked for quite some time, her last two employments having been part-time. One of the Whiteheads' positive attributes was their ability to bring up two children, and apparently well, even in so vulnerable a household. Yet substantial question was raised even about that aspect of their home life. The expert testimony contained criticism of Mrs. Whitehead's handling of her son's educational difficulties. Certain of the experts noted that Mrs. Whitehead perceived herself as omnipotent and omniscient concerning her children. She knew what they were thinking, what they wanted, and she spoke for them. As to Melissa, Mrs. Whitehead expressed the view that she alone knew what that child's cries and sounds meant. Her inconsistent stories about various things engendered grave doubts about her ability to explain honestly and sensitively to Baby M—and at the right time—the nature of her origin. Although faith in professional counseling is not a *sine qua non* of parenting, several experts believed that Mrs. Whitehead's contempt for professional help, especially professional psychological help, coincided with her feelings of omnipotence in a way that could be devastating to a child who most likely will need such help. In short, while love and affection there would be, Baby M's life with the Whiteheads promised to be too closely controlled by Mrs. Whitehead. The prospects for wholesome, independent psychological growth and development would be at serious risk.

The Sterns have no other children, but all indications are that their household and their personalities promise a much more likely foundation for Melissa to grow and thrive. There *is* a track record of sorts—during the one-and-a-half-years of custody Baby M has done very well, and the relationship between both Mr. and Mrs. Stern and the baby has become very strong. The household is stable, and likely to remain so. Their finances are more than adequate, their circle of friends supportive, and their marriage happy. Most important, they are loving, giving, nurturing, and open-minded people. They have demonstrated the wish and ability to nurture and protect Melissa, yet at the same time to encourage her independence. Their lack of experience is more than made up for by a willingness to learn and to listen, a willingness that is enhanced by their professional training, especially Mrs. Stern's experience as a pediatrician. They are honest; they can recognize error, deal with it, and learn from it. They will try to determine rationally the best way to cope with problems in their relationship with Melissa. When the time comes to tell her about her origins, they will probably have found a means of doing so that accords with the best interests of Baby M. All in all, Melissa's future appears solid, happy, and promising with them.

Based on all of this we have concluded, independent of the trial court's identical conclusion, that Melissa's best interests call for custody in the Sterns. ...

VISITATION

The trial court's decision to terminate Mrs. Whitehead's parental rights precluded it from making any determination on visitation. Our reversal of the trial court's order, however, requires delineation of Mrs. Whitehead's rights to visitation. It is apparent to us that this factually sensitive issue, which was never addressed below, should not be determined *de novo* by this Court. We therefore remand the visitation issue to the trial court for an abbreviated hearing and determination. ...

The fact that the trial court did not address visitation is only one reason for remand. The ultimate question is whether, despite the absence of the trial court's guidance, the record before us is sufficient to allow an appellate court to make this essentially factual determination. We can think of no issue that is more dependent on a trial court's factual findings and evaluation than visitation.

We have decided that Mrs. Whitehead is entitled to visitation at some point, and that question is not open to the trial court on this remand. The trial court will determine what kind of visitation shall be granted to her, with or without conditions, and when and under what circumstances it should commence. ...

CONCLUSION

... We have found that our present laws do not permit the surrogacy contract used in this case. Nowhere, however, do we find any legal prohibition against surrogacy when the surrogate mother volunteers, without any payment, to act as a surrogate and is given the right to change her mind and to assert her parental rights. Moreover, the Legislature remains free to deal with this most sensitive issue as it sees fit, subject only to constitutional constraints. ...

THE STRANGE CASE OF BABY M

Katha Pollitt

I think I understand Judge Harvey Sorkow's ruling in the Baby M case. It seems that a woman can rent her womb in the state of New Jersey, although not her vagina, and get a check upon turning over the product to its father. This transaction is not baby selling (a crime), because a man has a "drive to procreate" that deserves the utmost respect and, in any case, the child is genetically half his. The woman he pays for help in fulfilling that drive, however, is only "performing a service" and thus has no comparable right to a child genetically half hers. Therefore, despite the law's requirements in what the layperson might think are similar cases (women who change their minds about giving up a child for adoption, for example), a judge may terminate a repentant mother-for-money's parental rights forever without finding that she abused or neglected her child—especially if he finds her "manipulative, exploitive and deceitful." In other words, so-called surrogacy agreements are so unprecedented that the resulting human arrangements bear no resemblance to adoption, illegitimacy, custody after divorce, or any other relationship involving parents and children, yet, at the same time, bear an uncanny resemblance to the all-sales-final style of a used-car lot.

The State Supreme Court will hear Mary Beth Whitehead's appeal in September and has meanwhile granted her two hours of visiting time a week—a small sign, perhaps, that in jettisoning the entire corpus of family law, Judge Sorkow may have gone a bit too far. (*The New York Times* had trouble finding a single legal scholar who supported the judge's reasoning in full.) Maybe not, though. Despite the qualms of pundits, the outrage of many feminists and the condemnation of many religious leaders, every poll to date has shown overwhelming approval of Judge Sorkow's ruling. Twenty-seven states are considering bills that would legalize

Reprinted with permission of Katha Pollitt, from *The Nation*, May 23, 1987.

and regulate bucks-for-baby deals. What on earth is going on here?

Some of this support surely comes from the bad impression Mrs. Whitehead made every time she opened her mouth—most damningly, in her tape-recorded threat to kill Baby M and herself. And some comes from the ineptitude of her lawyer. (Where was the National Organization for Women? Where was the American Civil Liberties Union?) The Sterns said they would drag the Whiteheads through the mud, and they did. We learned as much about the Whiteheads' marital troubles, financial woes and quarrelsome relatives as if they were characters on *All My Children*. Distinguished experts testified that Mrs. Whitehead, who has raised two healthy, normal kids, is a bad mother and emotionally unbalanced: she was "overenmeshed" with her kids, disputed the judgment of school officials, gave Baby M teddy bears to play with instead of pots and pans (*pots and pans*?) and said "hooray" instead of "pattycake" when the tot clapped her hands. I know that, along with two-thirds of the adult female population of the United States, I will never feel quite the same about dyeing my hair now that Dr. Marshall Schechter, professor of child psychiatry at the University of Pennsylvania, has cited this little beauty secret as proof of Mrs. Whitehead's "narcissism" and "mixed personality disorder." Will I find myself in custody court someday, faced with the damning evidence of Exhibit A: a half-empty bottle of Clairol's Nice 'N' Easy?

Inexplicably, Mrs. Whitehead's lawyer never challenged the Sterns's self-representation as a stable, sane, loving pair, united in their devotion to Baby M. And neither did the media. Thus, we never found out why Dr. Elizabeth Stern claimed to be infertile on her application to the Infertility Center of New York when, in fact, she had diagnosed herself as having multiple sclerosis, which she feared pregnancy would aggravate; or why she didn't confirm that diagnosis until shortly before the case went to trial, much less consult a specialist in the management of M.S. pregnancies. Could it be that Elizabeth Stern did not share her husband's zeal for procreation? We'll never know, any more than we'll know why a disease serious enough to bar pregnancy was not also serious enough to consider as a possible bar to active mothering a few years down the road. If the Sterns's superior income could count as a factor in determining "the best interests of the child," why couldn't Mary Beth Whitehead's superior health?

The trial was so riddled with psychobabble, class prejudice and sheer callousness that one would have expected public opinion to rally round Mrs. Whitehead. Imagine openly arguing that a child should go to the richer parent! (Mr. Whitehead drives a garbage truck; Dr. Stern is a professor of pediatrics, and Mr. Stern is a biochemist.) And castigating a mother faced with the loss of her baby as hyperemotional because she wept! But Mrs. Whitehead (who, it must be said, did not help her case by perjuring herself repeatedly) made a fatal mistake: she fell afoul of the double standard of sexual morality. Thus, in the popular mind, Mrs. Whitehead was "an adult" who "knew what she was doing," while Mr. Stern, presumably, was not an adult and did not know what he was doing. Mrs. Whitehead was mercenary for agreeing to sell, but not Mr. Stern for proposing to buy. That victim-as-seducer mentality hasn't got such a workout since a neighborhood matron decided to stop for a drink at Big Dan's bar in New Bedford, Massachusetts.

The personalities of the Whiteheads and the Sterns, so crucial during the custody phase of the trial, will soon fade from public memory. The extraordinary welter of half-truths, bad analogies, logical muddles and glib catch phrases that have been mustered in defense of their bargain are apparently here to stay. If we are really about to embark on an era of reproductive Reaganomics—and most Americans seem to be saying, Why not?—we at least ought to clear away some of the more blatantly foolish things being said in support of it. For example:

Mary Beth Whitehead is a surrogate mother. "Mother" describes the relationship of a woman to a child, not to the father of that child and his wife. Everything a woman does to produce her own child Mary Beth Whitehead did, including giving it half the genetic inheritance regarded by the judge as so decisive an argument on behalf of William Stern. If anyone was a surrogate mother, it was Elizabeth Stern, for she was the one who substituted, or wished to substitute, for the child's actual mother.*

What's in a name? Plenty. By invariably referring to Mrs. Whitehead as a surrogate, the media, the courts and, unwittingly, Mrs. Whitehead herself tacitly validated the point of view of the Sterns, who naturally wanted to render Mrs. Whitehead's role in producing Baby M as notional as possible, the trivial physical means by which their desire—which is what really mattered—was fulfilled. And if Mrs. Whitehead was the substitute, then Dr. Stern must be the real thing.

Oddly enough, Mr. Stern, whose paternity consisted of ejaculating into a jar, was always referred to as the father or natural father or, rarely, biological father of Baby M, except by Mrs. Whitehead, who called him "the sperm donor." Although that is a far more accurate term for him than "surrogate mother" is for her (let alone "surrogate uterus," which is how the distinguished child psychologist Lee Salk referred to her), her use of it was widely taken as yet another proof of her irrational and cruel nature. Why was this harpy persecuting this nice man?

Surrogacy is a startling new technological development. This claim is a favorite of columnists and other instant experts, who, having solemnly warned that reproductive science is outstripping society's ability to deal with it, helplessly throw up their hands because—what can you do?—progress marches on. But a maternity contract is not a scientific development; it is a piece of paper. Physically, as Mary Beth Whitehead pointed out, it involves merely artificial insemination, a centuries-old technique which requires a device no more complicated than a turkey baster. And artificial insemination itself is a social contrivance, the purpose of which is to avert not infertility but infidelity.

What is new about contract motherhood lies in the realm of law and social custom. It is a means by which women sign away rights that, until the twentieth century, they rarely had: the right to legal custody of their children, and the right not to be bought, sold, lent, rented or given away. Throughout most of Western history and in many countries even today, there has been no need for such contracts because the father already owned the child, even if the child was illegitimate (unless the child's mother was married, in which case her husband owned the child). If a father chose to exercise his right to custody, the mother had no legal standing. In most societies, furthermore, a man in William Stern's position could have legally or semilegally acquired another female whose child, as per above, would be legally his: a second (or third or tenth) wife, a concubine, a slave, a kept woman. This is the happy state of affairs to which the maternity contract seeks to return its signers.

Those who comb history, literature and the Bible for reassuring precedents ignore the social context of oppression in which those odd little tales unfold. Yes, Sarah suggested that Abraham impregnate Hagar in order "that I may obtain children by her," but Hagar was a slave. What's modern about the story is that once pregnant, Hagar, like Mary Beth Whitehead, seemed to think that her child was hers no matter what anyone said. The outcome of that ancient domestic experiment was, in any case, disastrous, especially for Baby Ishmael. So perhaps the Bible was trying to tell us something about what happens when people treat people like things.

* In this article I will use the terms "contract mother," "maternity contract" and their variants, except where I am indirectly quoting others.

Surrogacy is the answer to female infertility. It has widely and properly been noted that only the well-to-do can afford to contract for a baby. (The Sterns, with a combined income of more than $90,000, paid $25,000 all told for Baby M, with $10,000 going to Mrs. Whitehead.) Less often has it been remarked that contract maternity is not a way for infertile women to get children, although the mothers often speak as though it were. It is a way for men to get children. Elizabeth Stern's name does not even appear on the contract. Had Mr. Stern filed for divorce before Baby M was born, had he died or become non compos, Dr. Stern would have been out of luck. Even after she became Baby M's primary caretaker, until the adoption went through, she had no more claim on the child than a baby sitter. Rather than empower infertile women through an act of sisterly generosity, maternity contracts make one woman a baby machine and the other irrelevant.

And there is no reason to assume that contracts will be limited to men married to infertile women—indeed, the Sterns have already broken that barrier—or even to men married at all. I can hear the precedent-setting argument already: Why, your honor, should a man's drive to procreate, his constitutional right to the joys of paternity, be dependent on the permission of a woman? No doubt, this further innovation will be presented as a gesture of female altruism too ("I just wanted to give him the One Thing a man can't give himself"). But take away the mothers' delusion that they are making babies for other women, and what you have left is what, in cold, hard fact, we already have: the limited-use purchase of women's bodies by men—reproductive prostitution.

So what? A woman has the right to control her body. The issue in contract motherhood is not whether a woman can bear a child for whatever reason she likes, but whether she can legally promise to sell that child—a whole other person, not an aspect of her body—to its father. Judge Sorkow is surely the only person on earth who thinks William Stern paid Mary Beth Whitehead $10,000 merely to conceive and carry a baby and not also to transfer that baby to him.

Actually, maternity contracts have the potential to do great harm to the cause of women's physical autonomy. Right now a man cannot legally control the conduct of a woman pregnant by him. He cannot force her to have an abortion or not have one, to manage her pregnancy and delivery as he thinks best, or to submit to fetal surgery or a Caesarean. Nor can he sue her if, through what he considers to be negligence, she miscarries or produces a defective baby. A maternity contract could give a man all those powers, except, possibly, the power to compel abortion, the only clause in the Stern-Whitehead contract that Judge Sorkow found invalid. Mr. Stern, for instance, seemed to think he had the right to tell Mrs. Whitehead's doctors what drugs to give her during labor. We've already had the spectacle of policemen forcibly removing 5-month-old Baby M from the arms of Mrs. Whitehead, the only mother she knew (so much for the best interests of the child!). What's next? State troopers guarding contract mothers to make sure they drink their milk?

Even if no money changed hands, the right-to-control-your-body argument would be unpersuasive. After all, the law already limits your right to do what you please with your body: you can't throw it off the Brooklyn Bridge, or feed it Laetrile, or even drive it around without a seat belt in some places. But money does change hands, and everybody, male and female, needs to be protected by law from the power of money to coerce or entice people to do things that seriously compromise their basic and most intimate rights, such as the right to health or life. You can sell your blood, but you can't sell your kidney. In fact, you can't even donate your kidney except under the most limited circumstances, no matter how fiercely you believe that this is the way you were meant to serve your fellow man and no matter how healthy you are. The risk of coercion is simply too great, and your kidney just too irreplaceable.

Supporters of contract motherhood talk about having a baby for pay as if it were like selling blood, or sperm, or breast milk. It is much more like selling a vital organ. Unlike a man, who produces billions of sperm and can theoretically father thousands of children at zero physical risk to himself, a woman can bear only a small number of children, and the physical cost to her can be as high as death. She cannot know in advance what a given pregnancy will mean for her health or for her ability to bear more children. (Interestingly, both the Sterns, who delayed parenthood until they found pregnancy too risky, and the Whiteheads, who foreclosed having more children with Mr. Whitehead's vasectomy, show just how unpredictable extrapolations from one's reproductive present are as guides to the future.) How can it be acceptable to pay a woman to risk her life, health and fertility so that a man can have his own biological child yet morally heinous to pay healthy people to sacrifice "extra" organs to achieve the incomparably greater aim of saving a life? We're scandalized when we read of Asian sterilization campaigns in which men are paid to be vasectomized—and not just because of the abuses to which those campaigns are notoriously subject but because they seem, by their very nature, to take advantage of people's shortsightedness in order to deprive them forever of something precious. Why is hiring women to have babies and give them away any better?

The question of payment is crucial because although contract mothers prefer to tell the television cameras about their longing to help humanity, studies have shown that almost nine out of ten wouldn't help humanity for free. (Well, it's a job. Would you do your job for free?) But women to whom $10,000 is a significant amount of money are the ones who live closest to the economic edge and have the fewest alternative ways of boosting their income in a crisis. Right now contract motherhood is still considered a rather *outré* thing to do, and women often have to talk their families into it. But if it becomes a socially acceptable way for a wife to help out the family budget, how can the law protect women from being coerced into contracts by their husbands? Or their relatives? Or their creditors? It can't. In fact, it can't even insure uncoerced consent when no money changes hands. *The New York Times* has already discovered a case in which a family matriarch successfully pressured one relative to produce a child for another.

If contract motherhood takes hold, a woman's "right to control her body" by selling her pregnancies will become the modern equivalent of "she's sitting on a fortune." Her husband's debts, her children's unfixed teeth, the kitchen drawer full of unpaid bills, will all be her fault, the outcome of her selfish refusal to sell what nature gave her.

A deal's a deal. This is what it's really all about, isn't it? To hear the chorus of hosannas currently being raised to this sacred tenet of market economics, you'd think the entire structure of law and morality would collapse about our ears if one high-school-dropout housewife in New Jersey was allowed to keep her baby. "One expects a prostitute to fulfill a contract," intoned Lawrence Stone, the celebrated Princeton University historian, in *The New York Times*. (Should the poor girl fail to show up at her regular time, the campus police are presumably to tie her up and deliver her into one's bed.) Some women argue that to allow Mrs. Whitehead to back out of her pledge would be to stigmatize all women as irrational and incapable of adulthood under the law. You'd think she had signed a contract to trade sow bellies at $5 and then gave premenstrual syndrome as her reason for canceling.

But is a deal a deal? Not always. Not, for instance, when it involves something illegal: prostitution (sorry, Professor Stone), gambling debts, slavery, polygyny, sweatshop labor, division of stolen goods and, oh yes, baby selling. Nor does it matter how voluntary such a contract is. So if your ambition in life is to be an indentured servant or a co-wife, you will have to fulfill this desire in a country where what Michael Kinsley calls "the moral logic of capitalism" has advanced so far that the untrained eye might mistake it for the sort of patriarchal semifeudalism practiced in small towns in Iran.

Well, you say, suppose we decided that contract motherhood wasn't prostitution or baby selling but some other, not flatly illegal, transaction: sale of parental rights to the father or some such. Then a deal would be a deal, right? Wrong. As anyone who has ever shopped for a co-op apartment in New York City knows, in the world of commerce, legal agreements are abrogated, modified, renegotiated and bought out all the time. What happens when contracts aren't fulfilled is what most of contract law is about.

Consider the comparatively civilized world of publishing. A writer signs up with one publisher, gets a better offer from another, pays back his advance—maybe—and moves on. Or a writer signs up to produce a novel but finds she'd rather die than see it printed, although her editor thinks it's a sure-fire best seller. Does the publisher forcibly take possession of the manuscript and print 100,000 copies because it's his property and a deal's a deal? No. The writer gives back the advance or submits another idea or persuades her editor she's such a genius she ought to be given even more money to write a really good book. And, somehow, Western civilization continues.

The closer we get to the murky realm of human intimacy the more reluctant we are to enforce contracts in anything like their potential severity. Marriage, after all, is a contract. Yet we permit divorce. Child-support agreements are contracts. Yet a woman cannot bar the father of her children from leaving investment banking for the less lucrative profession of subway musician. Engagement is, if not usually a formal contract, a public pledge of great seriousness. Yet the bride or groom abandoned at the altar has not been able to file a breach of promise suit for almost a hundred years. What have we learned since desperate spouses lit out for the territory and jilted maidens jammed the courts? That in areas of profound human feeling, you cannot promise because you cannot know, and pretending otherwise would result in far more misery than allowing people to cut their losses.

When Mary Beth Whitehead signed her contract, she was promising something it is not in anyone's power to promise: not to fall in love with her baby. To say, as some do, that she "should have known" because she'd had two children already is like saying a man should have known how he'd feel about his third wife because he'd already been married twice before. Why should mothers be held to a higher standard of self-knowledge than spouses? Or, more to the point, than fathers? In a recent California case a man who provided a woman friend with sperm, no strings attached, changed his mind when the child was born and sued for visitation rights. He won. Curiously, no one suggested that the decision stigmatized all his sex as hyperemotional dirty-dealers.

Fatherhood and motherhood are identical. It is at this point that one begins to feel people have resigned their common sense entirely. True, a man and a woman contribute equally to the genetic makeup of a baby. But twenty-three pairs of chromosomes do not a baby make. In the usual course of events the woman is then pregnant for nine months and goes through childbirth, a detail overlooked by those who compare maternity contracts to sperm donation. The proper parallel to sperm donation is egg donation.

Feminists who argue that respecting Mrs. Whitehead's maternal feelings will make women prisoners of the "biology is destiny" arguments should think again. The Baby M decision did not disclaim the power of biology at all; it exalted male biology at the expense of female. Judge Sorkow paid tribute to Mr. Stern's drive to procreate; it was only Mrs. Whitehead's longing to nurture that he scorned. That Baby M had Mr. Stern's genes was judged a fact of supreme importance—more important than Mrs. Whitehead's genes, pregnancy and childbirth put together. We might as well be back in the days when a woman was seen merely as a kind of human potting soil for a man's seed.

Speaking as a pregnant person, I find the view of maternity inherent in maternity contracts profoundly demeaning. Pregnancy and delivery are not "services" performed for the baby's father. The unborn child is not riding about inside a woman like a passenger in a car. A pregnant woman is not, as one contract mother put it, "a human incubator;" she is engaged in a constructive task, in taxing physical work. Some of this work is automatic, and no less deserving of respect for that, but much of it is not—an increasing amount, it would appear, to judge by doctors' ever-lengthening list of dos and don'ts.

Now, why do I follow my doctor's advice: swill milk, take vitamins, eschew alcohol, cigarettes, caffeine, dental X-rays and even the innocent aspirin? And why, if I had to, would I do a lot more to help my baby be born healthy, including things that are uncomfortable and wearisome (like staying in bed for months, as a friend of mine had to) or even detrimental to my own body (like fetal surgery)? It's not because I want to turn out a top-of-the-line product, or feel a sense of duty to the baby's dad, or have invested the baby with all the rights and privileges of an American citizen whose address just happens to be toy uterus. I do it because I love the baby. Even before it's born. I'm already forming a relationship with it. You can call that biology or social conditioning or a purely emotional fantasy. Perhaps, like romantic love, it is all three at once. But it's part of what pregnancy is—just ask the millions of pregnant women who feel this way, often to their own astonishment, sometimes under much less auspicious circumstances than Mrs. Whitehead's. It makes my blood boil when it is suggested that if contract mothers delivered under anesthesia and never saw their babies they wouldn't get a chance to "bond" and would feel no loss. I suppose the doctor could just tell them that they gave birth to a watermelon.

And so we arrive at the central emotional paradox of the Baby M case. We accept a notion that a man can have intense fatherly emotion for a child he's never seen, whose mother he's never slept with, let alone rubbed her back, or put his hand on her belly to feel the baby kick, or even taken her to the hospital. But a woman who violates her promise and loves the child she's had inside her for nine months, risked her health for, given birth to ... She must be some kind of nut.

Women need more options, not fewer. To suggest that female poverty can be ameliorated by poor mothers selling their children to wealthy fathers is a rather Swiftian concept. But why stop at contract motherhood when there's still a flourishing market for adoptive babies? Let enterprising poor women take up childbearing as a cottage industry and conceive expressly for the purpose of selling the baby to the highest bidder. And since the law permits parents to give up older children for adoption, why shouldn't they be allowed to sell them as well? Ever on the reproductive forefront, New Jersey recently gave the world the sensational case of a father who tried to sell his 4-year-old daughter to her dead mother's relatives for $100,000. Why he was arrested for doing what Mary Beth Whitehead was forced to do is anybody's guess.

Even leaving aside the fact that maternity contracts involve the sale of a human being, do women need another incredibly low-paying (around $1.50 an hour) service job that could damage their health and possibly even kill them, that opens up the most private areas of life to interference by a pair of total strangers, that they cannot get unless they first sign an ironclad contract forgoing a panoply of elementary human rights? By that logic, working in a sweatshop is an option, too—which is exactly what sweatshop employers have always maintained.

But people are going to do it anyway. Shouldn't they be protected? There are some practices (drinking, abortion, infidelity) so entrenched in mass behavior and regarded as acceptable by so many that to make them illegal would be both undemocratic and futile. Contract motherhood is not one of them. In ten years only about 500 women have signed up. So the argument that we should legitimize it because it's just human nature in its infinite variety is not valid—yet.

Now, it's probably true that some women will bear children for money no matter what the law says. In the privacy of domestic life all sorts of strange arrangements are made. But why should the state enforce such bargains? Feminists who think regulation would protect the mother miss the whole point of the maternity contract, which is precisely to deprive her of protections she would have if she had signed nothing. If the contracts were unenforceable, the risk would be where it belongs, on the biological father and his wife, whose disappointment if the mother reneges, though real, can hardly be compared with a mother's unwilling loss of her just-born child. The real loser, of course, would be the baby-broker. (Noel Keane, the lawyer who arranged for Baby M, made about $300,000 last year in fees for such services.) And that would be a very good thing.

But most surrogates have been pleased with their experience. Perhaps the Baby M trial is just a hard case making a bad law. It's possible to be horrified by what happened to Mary Beth Whitehead and still think that contract motherhood can be a positive thing if carefully regulated. If there had been better screening at the clinic, if the contract had included a grace period, if actual infertility had been required of Elizabeth Stern, we would never have heard of Baby M. If, if, if.

Regulation might make contract motherhood less haphazard, but there is no way it can be made anything other than what it is: an inherently unequal relationship involving the sale of a woman's body and a child. The baby-broker's client is the father; his need is the one being satisfied; he pays the broker's fee. No matter how it is regulated, the business will have to reflect that priority. That's why the bill being considered in New York State specifically denies the mother a chance to change her mind, although the stringency of the Stern-Whitehead contract in this regard was the one thing pundits assured the public would not happen again. Better screening procedures would simply mean more accurately weeding out the trouble-makers and selecting for docility, naïveté, low self-esteem and lack of money for legal fees. Free psychological counseling for the mothers, touted by some brokers as evidence of their care and concern, would merely be manipulation by another name. True therapy seeks to increase a person's sense of self, not reconcile one to being treated as an instrument.

Even if the business could be managed so that all the adults involved were invariably pleased with the outcome, it would still be wrong, because they are not the only people involved. There are, for instance, the mother's other children. Prospective contract mothers, Mrs. Whitehead included, do not seem to consider for two seconds the message they are sending to their kids. But how can it not damage a child to watch Mom cheerfully produce and sell its half-sibling while Dad stands idly by? I'd love to be a fly on the wall as a mother reassures her kids that of course she loves them no matter what they do; it's just their baby sister who had a price tag.

And, of course, there is the contract baby. To be sure, there are worse ways of coming into the world, but not many, and none that are elaborately prearranged by sane people. Much is made of the so-called trauma of adoption, but adoption is a piece of cake compared with contracting. Adoptive parents can tell their child, Your mother loved you so much she gave you up, even though it made her sad, because that was best for you. What can the father and adoptive mother of a contract baby say? Your mother needed $10,000? Your mother wanted to do something nice for us, so she made you? The Sterns can't even say that. They'll have to make do with something like, Your mother loved you so much she wanted to keep you, but we took you anyway, because a deal's a deal, and anyway, she was a terrible person. Great.

Oh, lighten up. Surrogacy fills a need. There's a shortage of babies for adoption, and people have the right to a child. What is the need that contract motherhood fills? It is not the need for a child, exactly. That need is met by adoption—although not very well, it's true, especially if parents have their hearts set on a "perfect baby," a healthy white newborn. The so-called baby shortage is really a shortage of those infants. (Shortage from the would-be adoptive parents' point of view; from the point of view of the birth mothers or Planned Parenthood, there's still a baby surplus.) What William Stern wanted, however, was not just a perfect baby; the Sterns did not, in fact, seriously investigate adoption. He wanted a perfect baby with his genes and a medically vetted mother who would get out of his life forever immediately after giving birth. That's a tall order, and one no other class of father—natural, step-, adoptive—even claims to be entitled to. Why should the law bend itself into a pretzel to gratify it?

The Vatican's recent document condemning all forms of conception but marital intercourse was marked by the church's usual political arrogance and cheeseparing approach to sexual intimacy, but it was right about one thing. You don't have a right to a child, any more than you have a right to a spouse. You only have the right to try to have one. Goods can be distributed according to ability to pay or need. People can't.

It's really that simple.

WHEN IS A MOTHER NOT A MOTHER?

Katha Pollitt

To the small and curious class of English words that have double and contradictory meanings—"moot," for example, and "cleave"—the word "mother" can now be added. Within the space of a single dazzling week this fall, this hoary old noun was redefined so thoroughly, in such mutually exclusive ways, that what it means now depends on which edition of the newspaper you read.

On October 23 in Orange County, California, Superior Court Judge Richard Parslow decided that the rightful mother of Baby Boy Johnson was not Anna Johnson, the black "gestational surrogate" who, for $10,000, carried him and birthed him, but Crispina Calvert, the wombless Asian-born woman who provided the egg from which, after in vitro fertilization with her (white) husband's sperm and implantation in Ms. Johnson, the baby grew. Declining, he said, to play Solomon and put the baby in the "crazy-making" position of having "two mothers"—or to follow California law, which defines the mother as the woman who gives birth to the child—Judge Parslow ruled that genes make the mom, as they do the dad. Anna Johnson was merely a kind of foster mother, a "home," an "environment."

One wonders what Judge Parslow would make of a headline two days later. "Menopause Is Found No Bar to Pregnancy" announced *The New York Times*, reporting that doctors had succeeded in making six prematurely menopausal women pregnant by implanting them with donated eggs fertilized in vitro with their husbands' sperm. By Judge Parslow's reasoning, of course, those women are merely foster mothers, homes and environments, but so far no one has

Reprinted with permission from Katha Pollitt from *The Nation*, December 31, 1990.

suggested this, much less called for a reevaluation of Johnson's claim in the light of new information about the value women place on pregnancy and childbirth and the persistent (if apparently erroneous) belief that the resultant babies belong to them.

To their credit, commentators have not regarded these developments with unalloyed rapture. Perhaps they learned something from the Baby M fracas (see Pollitt, "The Strange Case of Baby M," May 23, 1987). In that dispute, you will remember, many intelligent people persuaded themselves that the baby's rightful mother was a woman who had *no* biological connection to it, and that its real mother, Mary Beth Whitehead, was a grasping madwoman because she did not think she was, as child psychologist Lee Salk put it, a "surrogate uterus." The New Jersey Supreme Court disagreed and, lo and behold, none of the confidently predicted dire consequences ensued. Women are not regarded as too emotional to make binding contracts, as some feminists feared, nor has motherhood been more deeply consigned to the realm of instinct and mystification. The child, now a toddler, has not been destroyed or corrupted by contact with her mother. Mary Beth Whitehead, the supposed Medea of the Meadowlands, turns out to be such a good mom, in fact, that *New York Times* columnist Anna Quindlen, who observed one of the child's visits, felt moved to recant her earlier anti-Whitehead position. Indeed, the only consequences have been positive: The child knows both her parents; paid Baby M–style surrogacy has been outlawed in two states, the contracts declared unenforceable in three; Noel Keane, the infamous baby broker who boasted that he had made $300,000 in fees the year of the Baby M contract, has found another métier.

As our Eastern European friends are now reminding us, however, markets must be served. The New Jersey Supreme Court put a damper on Baby M–style contract motherhood—now commonly referred to as "traditional surrogacy," as though it came over with the Pilgrims—but it seems to have spurred science and commerce on to more ingenious devices. And so we have Baby Boy Johnson. Thanks to Baby M, we are a little sheepish, a little wiser. Ellen Goodman has called for the banning of gestational surrogacy for pay; like millions of other middle-aging moms, she wonders if being able to bear a child in one's 50s is really an unmitigated blessing. But we have not yet, as a society, begun fo face the underlying ideas about class, race, children and, above all, women that the new maternities rely on.

Take class. By upholding the Johnson-Calvert contract, Judge Parslow opens the door to the sale of poor women's bodies to well-off couples. It is disingenuous to claim, as does Polly Craig of the Los Angeles Center for Surrogate Parenting, that $10,000 is not enough money to motivate a woman to sell her womb, and that gestational surrogates simply enjoy being pregnant, want to help others, or wish to atone for a past abortion. Why offer payment at all, if it serves no function? And why, if gestational surrogacy is such an occasion for pleasure, altruism and moral purification, don't prosperous women line up for it? The Calverts—she a nurse, he an insurance broker—presumably possess a wide female acquaintanceship in their own income bracket, none of whom felt friendship required of them that they turn over their bodies to the Calvertian zygote. Instead the couple approached Johnson, a sometime welfare recipient, single mother and low-paid worker at Crispina Calvert's hospital.

No, money is the motivator here. Ten thousand dollars may not seem like a lot to Craig and her clients, but it's a poor person's idea of major cash—as much as 25 percent of American women earn in a whole year of full-time employment. It's quite enough to becloud good judgment. "You wave $10,000 in front of someone's face," said Anna Johnson, "and they are going to jump for it." By "someone," Johnson meant women like herself, shuttling between welfare and dead-end jobs, single, already supporting a child, with a drawerful of bills and not much hope for the future.

In a particularly nasty wrinkle, gestational surrogacy invites the singling out of black women for exploitation. It's not just that blacks are disproportionately poor and desperate, more likely to be single mothers and more likely to lack the resources to sue. It's that their visible lack of genetic connection with the baby will argue powerfully against them in court. (Indeed, about the Baby Boy Johnson case hovers the suggestion that the Calverts chose Johnson for precisely this reason.) Judge Parslow's comparison of Johnson to a foster mother is interesting in view of the fact that foster mothers who grow attached to their charges and try to keep them are regarded with much popular sympathy and sometimes even succeed. But it is safe to say that few American judges are going to take seriously the claims of a black woman to a nonblack child. Black women have, after all, always raised white children without acquiring any rights to them. Now they can breed them, too.

There are those who worry about the social implications of gestational surrogacy but who still think Judge Parslow made the right choice of homes for Baby Boy Johnson. Be that as it may, Anna Johnson wasn't suing for custody but for visitation. She wanted to be a small part of the child's life, for him to know her and for her to know him. Why would that be so terrible? As Dr. Michelle Harrison, who testified for Johnson, wrote in *The Wall Street Journal*, Judge Parslow wasn't being asked to divide the child between three parents; the Calverts had in fact so divided him when they chose to produce a baby with Johnson's help. Recent court decisions (not to mention social customs like open adoption, blended families and gay and lesbian co-parenting) have tended to respect a widening circle of adult relationships with children. Every state, for instance, gives grandparents access to grandchildren in the case of a divorce, regardless of the wishes of the custodial parent. Stepparents and lesbian co-parents are demanding their day in court. In 1986 California state courts upheld the right of a sperm donor to sue for parental rights when the artificial insemination did not involve a doctor (the old turkey baster method). Why isn't *that* prospect too "crazy-making" for California? Or, for that matter, mandatory joint custody, an innovation that California pioneered? Given the increasing number of children living outside the classic nuclear-family arrangement, and the equanimity with which the courts divide them up between competing adults, it seems rather late in the day to get all stuffy about Anna Johnson.

The most important and distressing aspect of Judge Parslow's decision, however, is that it defines, or redefines, maternity in a way that is thoroughly degrading to women. By equating motherhood with fatherhood—that is, defining it solely as the contribution of genetic material—he has downgraded the mother's other contributions (carrying the fetus to term and giving birth) to services rather than integral components of parenthood. Under this legal definition, a normally pregnant woman is now baby-sitting for a fetus that happens to be her own. "In a debate over nature vs. nurture, the winner is nature," read the *New York Times* pull-quote. But why define "nature" as DNA rather than as the physiological events of pregnancy and birth? There's nothing "natural" about egg donation, which involves the hormonal priming of an infertile woman, the extraction of an egg by delicate technology, fertilization in a dish with masturbated sperm and implantation of the zygote in another. And to call pregnancy and childbirth "nurture" seems a feeble way to describe the sharing of the body and the risking of health, well-being and even life itself that is required to bring another life into existence. Like "parenting," another fashionable buzzword, "nurture" is a bland social-sciency word that belittles a profound relationship and masks the role of women in gender-neutral language.

The picture of pregnancy as biological baby-sitting has many sources. It's as old as Aeschylus, who had Athena acquit Orestes of matricide in *The Eumenides* on the ground that mothers are merely "nurses" of men's seed, and as new as those ubiquitous photos of fetuses seeming to float in empty space. But its major proponents today are the antiabortionists. In order to maximize the claims of the fetus to personhood, they must obscure the unique status of the pregnant woman: She is not making a person, because the fertilized egg already *is* a person; she's only caring for it, or housing it, or even (as one imaginative federal judge recently wrote), holding it captive. Ironically, the movement that claims to celebrate motherhood is led by its own logic to devalue the physical, emotional and social experience of pregnancy. If unwanted pregnancy is just an "inconvenience," how serious an occasion can a *wanted* pregnancy be? If mass adoption is the answer to 1.6 million annual abortions, how strong can the ties be between mother and newborn? When ethicists fret that professional women may resort to gestational surrogacy to avoid "putting their careers on hold," they betray more than antiquated views about the capacities of pregnant women to get out of bed in the morning. They reveal their own assumption that pregnancy is a trivial, empty experience with nothing positive about it except the end product, the genetically connected baby. They then compound the insult by attributing this view to a demonized fantasy of working women—cold, materialistic, selfish, corrupted by "male values"—that is, those held by the ethicists themselves. Is there any evidence that working women—even MBAs, even lawyers—see pregnancy this way? Who do the pundits think are mobbing infertility clinics and signing on for donated eggs? A couple needs two incomes just to pay the doctors.

Why is the primacy of genetics so attractive? At the moment, genetic determinism is having one of its periods of scientific fashion, fueling the fear that an adopted baby will never "really" be yours. At the same time, hardening class distinctions make the poor, who provide most adoptive babies, seem scary and doomed: What if junior took after his birth parents? It's not an accident that sperm donors and now egg donors are largely recruited among middle-class professionals—they're not just white, they're successful and smart—and that the commercial aspects of the transaction ($50 for sperm, $1,500 for an egg) are disguised by calling it a "donation." You can buy a womb because wombs don't really matter, but if the all-important DNA must come from a third party, it should come as a gift between equals.

The main reason for our love affair with genes, though, is that men have them. We can't get all the way back to Aeschylus, with man as seed sower and woman as flowerpot (although we acknowledge it in our language, when we call women "fertile" or "infertile," like farmland). Women, we now know, have seeds too. But we can discount the aspects of procreation that women, and only women, perform. As the sociologist Barbara Katz Rothman has noted, Judge Parslow's decision follows the general pattern of our society, in which women's experience are recognized to the extent that they are identical with men's, and devalued or ignored to the extent that they are different. Thus, Mary Beth Whitehead won back her parental rights because the New Jersey Supreme Court acknowledged her *genetic* contribution: Baby M was half hers. And the postmenopausally pregnant, egg-donated women achieve parental rights by being married to the babies' fathers, not through their own contributions.

Of the two practices—actually a single practice with two social constructions—gestational surrogacy is clearly the more repellent, but to see its real meaning it must be looked at with egg donation as its flip side. Taken together they bring pregnancy into line with other domestic tasks traditionally performed by women—housework, child care, sex. Performed within marriage, for no pay, these activities are slathered with sentimentality and declared beyond price, the cornestone of female self-worth, family happiness and civilization itself. That is the world inhabited by prosperous married women now able to undergo pregnancy thanks to egg donation. That the egg is not their own is a detail; what counts is that they are able to have a profound and transforming life experience, to bond prenatally with their baby and to reproduce the genes of their husband. But look what happens when the checkbook and the marriage certificate are in the other hand: Now the egg is the central concern, pregnancy and childbirth merely a chore, prenatal bonding a myth. Like all domestic labor performed for pay—house-cleaning, baby-sitting, prostitution—childbearing in the marketplace becomes disreputable work performed by suspect, marginal people. The priceless task turns out to have a price after all: about $1.50 an hour.

What should happen now? Some suggest that new methods of parenthood require a new legal principle: pre-conception intent. Instead of socio-bio-ethical headaches—Who is the mother? Who is the father? What's best for the child? What's best for society?—we could have a simple rule of thumb: Let the seller beware. But at what cost to economic fairness, to principles of bodily integrity, to the nonmarketplace values that shape intimate life? Why not let the *buyer* beware? We cannot settle thorny questions by simply refusing to ask them.

A doctrine of pre-conception intent could, moreover, turn ordinary family law into fruit salad. Most pregnancies in the United States, after all, are not intended by either partner. They occur for dozens of reasons: birth-control failure, passion, ignorance, mixed messages, fear. The law wisely overlooks these sorry facts. Instead, it says Here is a child, here are the parents, next case. Do we really want to threaten a philosophy aimed, however clumsily, at protecting children from pauperism and abandonment? If pre-conception intent caught on with the general public, no single mother would be able to win child support; no single father could win parental rights. A woman's right to abortion could be conditioned on her pre-conception intent as evidenced, for example, by her use or neglect of birth control. In fact, in several states, laws have already been proposed that would restrict abortion to women who could prove contraceptive failure (a near impossibility, if you think about it, which is probably the point).

Perhaps the biggest problem with pre-conception intent, however, is that it ignores almost everything about the actual experience of becoming a parent of either sex. Planning to have a baby is not the same as being pregnant and giving birth, any more than putting on sexy underwear is like making love. The long months of pregnancy and the intense struggle of childbirth are part of forming a relationship with the child-to-be, part of the social and emotional task of parenthood. Not the only part, or even a necessary part—I am not suggesting that adoptive parents do not "really" become mothers and fathers. But is there a woman who feels exactly the same about the baby in the ninth month, or during delivery or immediately after, as she did when she threw away her diaphragm? When friends and relatives assure ambivalent parents-to-be not to worry, they'll feel differently about the baby when they feel it kick, or go through Lamaze together, or first hold their newborn in their arms, are they only talking through their hats? Whether or not there is a purely biological maternal instinct, more mothers, and more fathers, fall in love with their babies than ever thought they would. Indeed, if they did not, most babies would die of neglect in their cribs. How can we respect this emotional and psychological process—indeed, rely on it—and at the same time forbid it to the Mary Beth Whiteheads and the Anna Johnsons? I don't think we can.

Pre-conception intent would wreak havoc on everyone—men, women and children—and for what? To give couples like the Calverts a risk-free shot at a genetically connected baby. It makes more sense to assimilate surrogacy to already existing values and legal principles. In my view, doing so would make payment illegal and pre-birth contracts unenforceable. We don't let people sell their organs or work at slave wages; we don't hold new mothers to pre-delivery adoption arrangements; we don't permit the sale of children; we don't enforce contracts that violate human dignity and human rights. We respect the role of emotion and change and second thoughts in private life: We let people jilt their fiancées, and we let them divorce their spouses. True, we uphold prenuptial agreements (a mistake, in my opinion), but they're about property. If someone signed a premarital contract never to see his children again in the case of divorce, what judge would uphold it? Those children weren't even conceived when that contract was signed, the judge would point out—and furthermore they have rights that cannot be waived by others, such as the right to contact with both parents after divorce. The children of surrogates—even nongenetic surrogates like Anna Johnson—have the right to know the woman through whose body and through whose efforts they came into the world. We don't need any more disposable relationships in the world of children. They have quite enough of those already.

In order to benefit a very small number of people—prosperous womb-infertile couples who shun adoption—paid surrogacy does a great deal of harm to the rest of us. It degrades women by devaluing pregnancy and childbirth; it degrades children by commercializing their creation; it degrades the poor by offering them a devil's bargain at bargain prices. It creates a whole new class of emotionally injured children rarely mentioned in the debate: the ones the surrogate has already given birth to, who see their mother give away a newborn, or fight not to.

It is hard for Americans to see why they shouldn't have what they want if they can pay for it. We would much rather talk about individual freedoms and property rights, rational self-interest and the supposed sanctity of contracts, than about the common good or human dignity, or the depths below which no person should be allowed to sink. But even we have to call it quits somewhere. As we decided 130 years ago, the buying and selling of people is a very good place to draw the line.

PATERNALISM

Gerald Dworkin

> *Neither one person, nor any number of persons, is warranted in saying to another human creature of ripe years, that he shall not do with his life for his own benefit what he chooses to do with it.*
>
> Mill
>
> *I do not want to go along with a volunteer basis. I think a fellow should be compelled to become better and not let him use his discretion whether he wants to get smarter, more healthy or more honest.*
>
> General Hershey

I take as my starting point the "one very simple principle" proclaimed by Mill in *On Liberty* ... "That principle is, that the sole end for which mankind are warranted, individually or collectively, in interfering with the liberty of action of any of their number, is self-protection. That the only purpose for which power can be rightfully exercised over any member of a civilized community, against his will, is to prevent harm to others. He cannot rightfully be compelled to do or forbear because it will be better for him to do so, because it will make him happier, because, in the opinion of others, to do so would be wise, or even right."

This principle is neither "one" nor "very simple." It is at least two principles; one asserting that self-protection or the prevention of harm to others is sometimes a sufficient warrant and the other claiming that the individual's own good is *never* a sufficient warrant for the exercise of compulsion either by the society as a whole or by its individual members. I assume that no one with the possible exception of extreme pacifists or anarchists questions the correctness of the first half of the principle. This essay is an examination of the negative claim embodied in Mill's principle—the objection to paternalistic interferences with a man's liberty.

I

By paternalism I shall understand roughly the interference with a person's liberty of action justified by reasons referring exclusively to the welfare, good, happiness, needs, interests or values of the person being coerced. One is always well-advised to illustrate one's definitions by examples but it is not easy to find "pure" examples of paternalistic interferences. For almost any piece of legislation is justified by several different kinds of reasons and even if historically a piece of legislation can be shown to have been introduced for purely paternalistic motives, it may be that advocates of the legislation with an anti-paternalistic outlook can find sufficient reasons justifying the legislation without appealing to the reasons which were originally adduced to support it. Thus, for example, it may be that the original legislation requiring motorcyclists to wear safety helmets was introduced for purely paternalistic reasons. But the Rhode Island Supreme Court recently upheld such legislation on the grounds that it was "not persuaded that the legislature is powerless to prohibit individuals from pursuing a course of conduct which could conceivably result in their becoming public charges," thus clearly introducing reasons of a quite different kind. Now I regard this decision as being based on reasoning of a very dubious nature but it illustrates the kind of problem one has in finding examples. The following is a list of the kinds of interferences I have in mind as being paternalistic.

II

1. Laws requiring motorcyclists to wear safety helmets when operating their machines.
2. Laws forbidding persons from swimming at a public beach when lifeguards are not on duty.
3. Laws making suicide a criminal offense.
4. Laws making it illegal for women and children to work at certain types of jobs.
5. Laws regulating certain kinds of sexual conduct, e.g. homosexuality among consenting adults in private.
6. Laws regulating the use of certain drugs which may have harmful consequences to the user but do not lead to anti-social conduct.
7. Laws requiring a license to engage in certain professions with those not receiving a license subject to fine or jail sentence if they do engage in the practice.
8. Laws compelling people to spend a specified fraction of their income on the purchase of retirement annuities. (Social Security)
9. Laws forbidding various forms of gambling (often justified on the grounds that the poor are more likely to throw away their money on such activities than the rich who can afford to).
10. Laws regulating the maximum rates of interest for loans.
11. Laws against duelling.

In addition to laws which attach criminal or civil penalties to certain kinds of action there are laws, rules, regulations, decrees, which make it either difficult or impossible for people to carry out their plans and which are also justified on paternalistic grounds. Examples of this are:

1. Laws regulating the types of contracts which will be upheld as valid by the courts, e.g. (an example of Mill's to which I shall return) no man may make a valid contract for perpetual involuntary servitude.
2. Not allowing as a defense to a charge of murder or assault the consent of the victim.
3. Requiring members of certain religious sects to have compulsory blood transfusions. This is made possible by not allowing the patient to have recourse to civil suits for assault and battery and by means of injunctions.
4. Civil commitment procedures when these are specifically justified on the basis of preventing the person being committed from harming himself. (The D.C. Hospitalization of the Mentally Ill Act provides for involuntary hospitalization of a person who "is mentally ill, and because of that illness, is likely to injure *himself* or others if allowed to remain at liberty." The term injure in this context applies to unintentional as well as intentional injuries.)
5. Putting fluorides in the community water supply.

All of my examples are of existing restrictions on the liberty of individuals. Obviously one can think of interferences which have not yet been imposed. Thus one might ban the sale of cigarettes, or require that people wear safety-belts in automobiles (as opposed to merely having them installed) enforcing this by not allowing motorists to sue for injuries even when caused by other drivers if the motorist was not wearing a seat-belt at the time of the accident.

I shall not be concerned with activities which though defended on paternalistic grounds are not interferences with the liberty of persons, e.g. the giving of subsidies in kind rather than in cash on the grounds that the recipients would not spend the money on the goods which they really need, or not including a $1000 deductible provision in a basic protection automobile insurance plan on the ground that the people who would elect it could least afford it. Nor shall I be concerned with measures such as "truth-in-advertising" acts and the Pure Food and Drug legislation which are often attacked as paternalistic but which should not be considered so. In these cases all that is provided—it is true by the use of compulsion—is information which it is presumed that rational persons are interested in having in order to make wise decisions. There is no interference with the liberty of the consumer unless one wants to stretch a point beyond good sense and say that his liberty to apply for a loan without knowing the true rate of interest is diminished. It is true that sometimes there is sentiment for going further than providing information, for example when laws against usurious interest are passed preventing those who might wish to contract loans at high rates of interest from doing so, and these measures may correctly be considered paternalistic.

III

Bearing these examples in mind let me return to a characterization of paternalism. I said earlier that I meant by the term, roughly, interference with a person's liberty for his own good. But as some of the examples show the class of persons whose good is involved is not always identical with the class of persons whose freedom is restricted. Thus in the case of professional licensing it is the practitioner who is directly interfered with and it is the would-be patient whose interests are presumably being served. Not allowing the consent of the victim to be a defense to certain types of crime primarily affects the would-be aggressor but it is the interests of the willing victim that we are trying to protect. Sometimes a person may fall into both classes as would be the case if we banned the manufacture and sale of cigarettes and a given manufacturer happened to be a smoker as well.

Thus we may first divide paternalistic interferences into "pure" and "impure" cases. In "pure" paternalism the class of persons whose freedom is restricted is identical with the class of persons whose benefit is intended to be promoted by such restrictions. Examples: the making of suicide a crime, requiring passengers in automobiles to wear seat-belts, requiring a Christian Scientist to receive a blood transfusion. In the case of "impure" paternalism in trying to protect the welfare of a class of persons we find that the only way to do so will involve restricting the freedom of other persons besides those who are benefitted. Now it might be thought that there are no cases of "impure" paternalism since any such case could always be justified on non-paternalistic grounds, i.e. in terms of preventing harms to others. Thus we might ban cigarette manufacturers from continuing to manufacture their product on the grounds that we are preventing them from causing illness to others in the same way that we prevent other manufacturers from releasing pollutants into the atmosphere, thereby causing danger to the members of the community. The difference is, however, that in the former but not the latter case the harm is of such a nature that it could be avoided by those individuals affected if they so chose. The incurring of the harm requires, so to speak, the active cooperation of the victim. It would be mistaken theoretically and hypocritical in practice to assert that our interference in such cases is just like our interference in standard cases of protecting others from harm. At the very least someone interfered with in this way can reply that no one is complaining about his activities. It may be that impure paternalism requires arguments or reasons of a stronger kind in order to be justified since there are persons who are losing a portion of their liberty and they do not even have the solace of having it be done "in their own interest." Of course in some sense, if paternalistic justifications are ever correct then we are protecting others, we are preventing some from injuring others, but it is important to see the differences between this and the standard case.

Paternalism then will always involve limitations on the liberty of some individuals in their own interest but it may also extend to interferences with the liberty of parties whose interests are not in question.

IV

Finally, by way of some more preliminary analysis, I want to distinguish paternalistic interferences with liberty from a related type with which it is often confused. Consider, for example, legislation which forbids employees to work more than, say, 40 hours per week. It is sometimes argued that such legislation is paternalistic for if employees desired such a restriction on their hours of work they could agree among themselves to impose it voluntarily. But because they do not the society imposes its own conception of their best interests upon them by the use of coercion. Hence this is paternalism.

Now it may be that some legislation of this nature is, in fact, paternalistically motivated. I am not denying that. All I want to point out is that there is another possible way of justifying such measures which is not paternalistic in nature. It is not paternalistic because as Mill puts it in a similar context such measures are "required not to overrule the judgment of individuals respecting their own interest, but to give effect to that judgment: they being unable to give effect to it except by concert, which concert again cannot be effectual unless it receives validity and sanction from the law."

The line of reasoning here is a familiar one first found in Hobbes and developed with great sophistication by contemporary economists in the last decade or so. There are restrictions which are in the interests of a class of persons taken collectively but are such that the immediate interest of each individual is furthered by his violating the rule when others adhere to it. In such cases the individuals involved may need the use of compulsion to give effect to their collective judgment of their own interest by guaranteeing each individual compliance by the others. In these cases compulsion is not used to achieve some benefit which is not recognized to be a benefit by those concerned, but rather because it is the only feasible means of achieving some benefit which is recognized as such by all concerned. This way of viewing matters provides us with another characterization of paternalism in general. Paternalism might be thought of as the use of coercion to achieve a good which is not recognized as such by those persons for whom the good is intended. Again while this formulation captures the heart of the matter—it is surely what Mill is objecting to in *On Liberty*—the matter is not always quite like that. For example when we force motorcyclists to wear helmets we are trying to promote a good—the protection of the person from injury—which is surely recognized by most of the individuals concerned. It is not that a cyclist doesn't value his bodily integrity; rather, as a supporter of such legislation would put it, he either places, perhaps irrationally, another value or good (freedom from wearing a helmet) above that of physical well-being or, perhaps, while recognizing the danger in the abstract, he either does not fully appreciate it or he underestimates the likelihood of its occurring. But now we are approaching the question of possible justifications of paternalistic measures and the rest of this essay will be devoted to that question.

V

I shall begin for dialectical purposes by discussing Mill's objections to paternalism and then go on to discuss more positive proposals.

An initial feature that strikes one is the absolute nature of Mill's prohibitions against paternalism.

The structure of Mill's argument is as follows:

1. Since restraint is an evil the burden of proof is on those who propose such restraint.
2. Since the conduct which is being considered is purely self-regarding, the normal appeal to the protection of the interests of others is not available.
3. Therefore we have to consider whether reasons involving reference to the individual's own good, happiness, welfare, or interests are sufficient to overcome the burden of justification.
4. We either cannot advance the interests of the individual by compulsion, or the attempt to do so involves evil which outweighs the good done.
5. Hence the promotion of the individual's own interests does not provide a sufficient warrant for the use of compulsion.

Clearly the operative premise here is 4 and it is bolstered by claims about the status of the individual as judge and appraiser of his welfare, interests, needs, etc.

> With respect to his own feelings and circumstances, the most ordinary man or woman has means of knowledge immeasurably surpassing those that can be possessed by any one else.
>
> He is the man most interested in his own well-being: the interest which any other person, except in cases of strong personal attachment, can have in it, is trifling, compared to that which he himself has.

These claims are used to support the following generalizations concerning the utility of compulsion for paternalistic purposes.

> The interferences of society to overrule his judgment and purposes in what only regards himself must be grounded on general presumptions; which may be altogether wrong, and even if right, are as likely as not to be misapplied to individual cases.
>
> But the strongest of all the arguments against the interference of the public with purely personal conduct is that when it does interfere, the odds are that it interferes wrongly and in the wrong place.
>
> All errors which the individual is likely to commit against advice and warning are far outweighed by the evil of allowing others to constrain him to what they deem his good.

Performing the utilitarian calculation by balancing the advantages and disadvantages we find that:

> Mankind are greater gainers by suffering each other to live as seems good to themselves, than by compelling each other to live as seems good to the rest.

From which follows the operative premise 4.

This is clearly the main channel of Mill's thought and it is one which has been subjected to vigorous attack from the moment it appeared—most often by fellow Utilitarians. The link that they have usually seized on is, as Fitzjames Stephen put it, the absence of proof that the "mass of adults are so well acquainted with their own interests and so much disposed to pursue them that no compulsion or restraint put upon them by any others for the purpose of promoting their interest can really promote them."

Now it is interesting to note that Mill himself was aware of some of the limitations on the doctrine that the individual is the best judge of his own interests. In his discussion of government intervention in general (even where the intervention does not interfere with liberty but provides alternative institutions to those of the market) after making claims which are parallel to those just discussed, e.g.

> People understand their own business and their own interests better, and care for them more, than the government does, or can be expected to do.

He goes on to an intelligent discussion of the "very large and conspicuous exceptions" to the maxim that:

> Most persons take a juster and more intelligent view of their own interest, and of the means of promoting it than can either be prescribed to them by a general enactment of the legislature, or pointed out in the particular case by a public functionary.

Thus there are things

> ... of which the utility does not consist in ministering to inclinations, nor in serving the daily uses of life, and the want of which is least felt where the need is greatest. This is peculiarly true of those things which are chiefly useful as tending to raise the character of human beings. The uncultivated cannot be competent judges of cultivation. Those who most need to be made wiser and better, usually desire it least, and, if they desired it, would be incapable of finding the way to it by their own lights.

> ... A second exception to the doctrine that individuals are the best judges of their own interest, is when an individual attempts to decide irrevocably now what will be best for his interest at some future and distant time. The presumption in favor of individual judgment is only legitimate, where the judgment is grounded on actual, and especially on present, personal experience; not where it is formed antecedently to experience, and not suffered to be reversed even after experience has condemned it.

The upshot of these exceptions is that Mill does not declare that there should never be government interference with the economy but rather that

> ... in every instance, the burden of making out a strong case should be thrown not on those who resist but on those who recommend government interference. Letting alone, in short, should be the general practice: every departure from it, unless required by some great good, is a certain evil.

In short, we get a presumption not an absolute prohibition. The question is why doesn't the argument against paternalism go the same way?

I suggest that the answer lies in seeing that in addition to a purely utilitarian argument Mill uses another as well.

A consistent Utilitarian can only argue against paternalism on the grounds that it (as a matter of fact) does not maximize the good. It is always a contingent question that may be refuted by the evidence. But there is also a non-contingent argument which runs through *On Liberty*. When Mill states that "there is a part of the life of every person who has come to years of discretion, within which the individuality of that person ought to reign uncontrolled either by any other person or by the public collectively" he is saying something about what it means to be a person, an autonomous agent. It is because coercing a person for his own good denies this status as an independent entity that Mill objects to it so strongly and in such absolute terms. To be able to choose is a good that is independent of the wisdom of what is chosen. A man's "mode of laying out his existence is the best, not because it is the best in itself, but because it is his own mode."

> It is the privilege and proper condition of a human being, arrived at the maturity of his faculties, to use and interpret experience in his own way.

As further evidence of this line of reasoning in Mill consider the one exception to his prohibition against paternalism.

> In this and most civilised countries, for example, an engagement by which a person should sell himself, or allow himself to be sold, as a slave, would be null and void; neither enforced by law nor by opinion. The ground for thus limiting his power of voluntarily disposing of his own lot in life, is apparent, and is very clearly seen in this extreme case. The reason for not interfering, unless for the sake of others, with a person's voluntary acts, is consideration for his liberty. His voluntary choice is evidence that what he so chooses is desirable, or at least endurable, to him, and his good is on the whole best provided for by allowing him to take his own means of pursuing it. But by selling himself for a slave, he abdicates his liberty; he forgoes any future use of it beyond that single act.
>
> He therefore defeats, in his own case, the very purpose which is the justification of allowing him to dispose of himself. He is no longer free; but is thenceforth in a position which has no longer the presumption in its favour, that would be afforded by his voluntarily remaining in it. The principle of freedom cannot require that he should be free not to be free. It is not freedom to be allowed to alienate his freedom.

Now leaving aside the fudging on the meaning of freedom in the last line it is clear that part of this argument is incorrect. While it is true that *future* choices of the slave are not reasons for thinking that what he chooses then is desirable for him, what is at issue is limiting his immediate choice; and since this choice is made freely, the individual may be correct in thinking that his interests are best provided for by entering such a contract. But the main consideration for not allowing such a contract is the need to preserve the liberty of the person to make future choices. This gives us a principle—a very narrow one—by which to justify some paternalistic interferences. Paternalism is justified only to preserve a wider range of freedom for the individual in question. How far this principle could be extended, whether it can justify all the cases in which we are inclined upon reflection to think paternalistic measures justified remains to be discussed. What I have tried to show so far is that there are two strains of argument in Mill—one a straightforward Utilitarian mode of reasoning and one which relies not on the goods which free choice leads to but on the absolute value of the choice itself. The first cannot establish any absolute prohibition but at most a presumption and indeed a fairly weak one given some fairly plausible assumptions about human psychology; the second while a stronger line of argument seems to me to allow on its own grounds a wider range of paternalism than might be suspected. I turn now to a consideration of these matters.

VI

We might begin looking for principles governing the acceptable use of paternalistic power in cases where it is generally agreed that it is legitimate. Even Mill intends his principles to be applicable only to mature individuals, not those in what he calls "non-age." What is it that justifies us in interfering with children? The fact that they lack some of the emotional and cognitive capacities required in order to make fully rational decisions. It is an empirical question to just what extent children have an adequate conception of their own present and future interests but there is not much doubt that there are many deficiencies. For example it is very difficult for a child to defer gratification for any considerable period of time. Given these deficiencies and given the very real and permanent dangers that may befall the child it becomes not only permissible but even a duty of the parent to restrict the child's freedom in various ways. There is however an important moral limitation on the exercise of such parental power which is provided by the notion of the child eventually coming to see the correctness of his parent's interventions. Parental paternalism may be thought of as a wager by the parent on the child's subsequent recognition of the wisdom of the restrictions. There is an emphasis on what could be called future-oriented consent—on what the child will come to welcome, rather than on what he does welcome.

The essence of this idea has been incorporated by idealist philosophers into various types of "real-will" theory as applied to fully adult persons. Extensions of paternalism are argued for by claiming that in various respects, chronologically mature individuals share the same deficiencies in knowledge, capacity to think rationally, and the ability to carry out decisions that children possess. Hence in interfering with such people we are in effect doing what they would do if they were fully rational. Hence we are not really opposing their will, hence we are not really interfering with their freedom. The dangers of this move have been sufficiently exposed by Berlin in his Two Concepts of Liberty. I see no gain in theoretical clarity nor in practical advantage in trying to pass over the real nature of the interferences with liberty that we impose on others. Still the basic notion of consent is important and seems to me the only acceptable way of trying to delimit an area of justified paternalism.

Let me start by considering a case where the consent is not hypothetical in nature. Under certain conditions it is rational for an individual to agree that others should force him to act in ways in which, at the time of action, the individual may not see as desirable. If, for example, a man knows that he is subject to breaking his resolve when temptation is present, he may ask a friend to refuse to entertain his requests at some later stage.

A classical example is given in the Odyssey when Odysseus commands his men to tie him to the mast and refuse all future orders to be set free, because he knows the power of the Sirens to enchant men with their songs. Here we are on relatively sound ground in later refusing Odysseus' request to be set free. He may even claim to have changed his mind but since it is just such changes that he wished to guard against we are entitled to ignore them.

A process analogous to this may take place on a social rather than individual basis. An electorate may mandate its representatives to pass legislation which when it comes time to "pay the price" may be unpalatable. I may believe that a tax increase is necessary to halt inflation though I may resent the lower pay check each month. However in both this case and that of Odysseus the measure to be enforced is specifically requested by the party involved and at some point in time there is genuine consent and agreement on the part of those persons whose liberty is infringed. Such is not the case for the paternalistic measures we have been speaking about. What must be involved here is not consent to specific measures but rather consent to a system of government, run by elected representatives, with an understanding that they may act to safeguard our interests in certain limited ways.

I suggest that since we are all aware of our irrational propensities, deficiencies in cognitive and emotional capacities and avoidable and unavoidable ignorance it is rational and prudent for us to in effect take out "social insurance policies." We may argue for and against proposed paternalistic measures in terms of what fully rational individuals would accept as forms of protection. Now, clearly since the initial agreement is not about specific measures we are dealing with a more-or-less blank check and therefore there have to be carefully defined limits. What I am looking for are certain kinds of conditions which make it plausible to suppose that rational men could reach agreement to limit their liberty even when other men's interests are not affected.

Of course as in any kind of agreement schema there are great difficulties in deciding what rational individuals would or would not accept. Particularly in sensitive areas of personal liberty, there is always a danger of the dispute over agreement and rationality being a disguised version of evaluative and normative disagreement.

Let me suggest types of situations in which it seems plausible to suppose that fully rational individuals would agree to having paternalistic restrictions imposed upon them. It is reasonable to suppose that there are "goods" such as health which any person would want to have in order to pursue his own good—no matter how that good is conceived. This is an argument that is used in connection with compulsory education for children but it seems to me that it can be extended to other goods which have this character. Then one could agree that the attainment of such goods should be promoted even when not recognized to be such, at the moment, by the individuals concerned.

An immediate difficulty that arises stems from the fact that men are always faced with competing goods and that there may be reasons why even a value such as health—or indeed life—may be overridden by competing values. Thus the problem with the Christian Scientist and blood transfusions. It may be more important for him to reject "impure substances" than to go on living. The difficult problem that must be faced is whether one can give sense to the notion of a person irrationally attaching weights to competing values.

Consider a person who knows the statistical data on the probability of being injured when not wearing seat belts in an automobile and knows the types and gravity of the various injuries. He also insists that the inconvenience attached to fastening the belt every time he gets in and out of the car outweighs for him the possible risks to himself. I am inclined in this case to think that such a weighing is irrational. Given his life-plans which we are assuming are those of the average person, his interests and commitments already undertaken, I think it is safe to predict that we can find inconsistencies in his calculations at some point. I am assuming, that this is not a man who for some conscious or unconscious reasons is trying to injure himself nor is he a man who just likes to "live dangerously." I am assuming that he is like us in all the relevant respects but just puts an enormously high negative value on inconvenience—one which does not seem comprehensible or reasonable.

It is always possible, of course to assimilate this person to creatures like myself. I, also, neglect to fasten my seat belt and I concede such behavior is not rational but not because I weigh the inconvenience differently from those who fasten the belts. It is just that having made (roughly) the same calculation as everybody else I ignore it in my actions. [Note: a much better case of weakness of the will than those usually given in ethics texts.] A plausible explanation for this deplorable habit is that although I know in some intellectual sense what the probabilities and risks are I do not fully appreciate them in an emotionally genuine manner.

We have two distinct types of situation in which a man acts in a non-rational fashion. In one case he attaches incorrect weights to some of his values; in the other he neglects to act in accordance with his actual preferences and desires. Clearly there is a stronger and more persuasive argument for paternalism in the latter situation. Here we are really not—by assumption—imposing a good on another person. But why may we not extend our interference to what we might call evaluative delusions? After all in the case of cognitive delusions we are prepared, often, to act against the expressed will of the person involved. If a man believes that when he jumps out the window he will float upwards—Robert Nozick's example—would not we detain him, forcibly if necessary? The reply will be that this man doesn't wish to be injured and if we could convince him that he is mistaken as to the consequences of his action he would not wish to perform the action. But part of what is involved in claiming that a man who doesn't fasten his seat belt is attaching an irrational weight to the inconvenience of fastening it is that if he were to be involved in an accident and severely injured he would look back and admit that the inconvenience wasn't as bad as all that. So there is a sense in which if I could convince him of the consequences of his action he also would not wish to continue his present course of action. Now the notion of consequences being used here is covering a lot of ground. In one case it's being used to indicate what will or can happen as a result of a course of action and in the other it's making a prediction about the future evaluation of the consequences—in the first sense—of a course of action. And whatever the difference between facts and values—whether it be hard and fast or soft and slow—we are genuinely more reluctant to consent to interferences where evaluative differences are the issue. Let me now consider another factor which comes into play in some of these situations which may make an important difference in our willingness to consent to paternalistic restrictions.

Some of the decisions we make are of such a character that they produce changes which are in one or another way irreversible. Situations are created in which it is difficult or impossible to return to anything like the initial stage at which the decision was made. In particular some of these changes will make it impossible to continue to make reasoned choices in the future. I am thinking specifically of decisions which involve taking drugs that are physically or psychologically addictive and those which are destructive of one's mental and physical capacities.

I suggest we think of the imposition of paternalistic interferences in situations of this kind as being a kind of insurance policy which we take out against making decisions which are far-reaching, potentially dangerous and irreversible. Each of these factors is important. Clearly there are many decisions we make that are relatively irreversible. In deciding to learn to play chess I could predict in view of my general interest in games that some portion of my free-time was going to be pre-empted and that it would not be easy to give up the game once I acquired a certain competence. But my whole life-style was not going to be jeopardized in an extreme manner. Further it might be argued that even with addictive drugs such as heroin one's normal life plans would not be seriously interfered with if an inexpensive and adequate supply were readily available. So this type of argument might have a much narrower scope than appears to be the case at first.

A second class of cases concerns decisions which are made under extreme psychological and sociological pressures. I am not thinking here of the making of the decision as being something one is pressured into—e.g. a good reason for making duelling illegal is that unless this is done many people might have to manifest their courage and integrity in ways in which they would rather not do so—but rather of decisions such as that to commit suicide which are usually made at a point where the individual is not thinking clearly and calmly about the nature of his decision. In addition, of course, this comes under the previous heading of all-too-irrevocable decision. Now there are practical steps which a society could take if it wanted to decrease the possibility of suicide—for example not paying social security benefits to the survivors or as religious institutions do, not allowing such persons to be buried with the same status as natural deaths. I think we may count these as interferences with the liberty of persons to attempt suicide and the question is whether they are justifiable.

Using my argument schema the question is whether rational individuals would consent to such limitations. I see no reason for them to consent to an absolute prohibition but I do think it is reasonable for them to agree to some kind of enforced waiting period. Since we are all aware of the possibility of temporary states, such as great fear or depression, that are inimical to the making of well-informed and rational decisions, it would be prudent for all of us if there were some kind of institutional arrangement whereby we were restrained from making a decision which is (all too) irreversible. What this would be like in practice is difficult to envisage and it may be that if no practical arrangements were feasible then we would have to conclude that there should be no restriction at all on this kind of action. But we might have a "cooling off" period, in much the same way that we now require couples who file for divorce to go through a waiting period. Or, more far-fetched, we might imagine a Suicide Board composed of a psychologist and another member picked by the applicant. The Board would be required to meet and talk with the person proposing to take his life, though its approval would not be required.

A third class of decisions—these classes are not supposed to be disjoint—involves dangers which are either not sufficiently understood or appreciated correctly by the persons involved. Let me illustrate, using the example of cigarette smoking, a number of possible cases.

1. A man may not know the facts—e.g., smoking between 1 and 2 packs a day shortens life expectancy 6.2 years, the costs and pain of the illness caused by smoking, etc.
2. A man may know the facts, wish to stop smoking, but not have the requisite willpower.
3. A man may know the facts but not have them play the correct role in his calculation because, say, he discounts the danger psychologically because it is remote in time and/or inflates the attractiveness of other consequences of his decision which he regards as beneficial.

In case 1 what is called for is education, the posting of warnings, etc. In case 2 there is no theoretical problem. We are not imposing a good on someone who rejects it. We are simply using coercion to enable people to carry out their own goals. (Note: There obviously is a difficulty in that only a subclass of the individuals affected wish to be prevented from doing what they are doing.) In case 3 there is a sense in which we are imposing a good on someone since given his current appraisal of the facts he doesn't wish to be restricted. But in another sense we are not imposing a good since what is being claimed—and what must be shown or at least argued for—is that an accurate accounting on his part would lead him to reject his current course of action. Now we all know that such cases exist, that we are prone to disregard dangers that are only possibilities, that immediate pleasures are often magnified and distorted.

If in addition the dangers are severe and far-reaching we could agree to allowing the state a certain degree of power to intervene in such situations. The difficulty is in specifying in advance, even vaguely, the class of cases in which intervention will be legitimate.

A related difficulty is that of drawing a line so that it is not the case that all ultra-hazardous activities are ruled out, e.g., mountain-climbing, bull-fighting, sports-car racing, etc. There are some risks—even very great ones—which a person is entitled to take with his life.

A good deal depends on the nature of the deprivation—e.g., does it prevent the person from engaging in the activity completely or merely limit his participation—and how important to the nature of the activity is the absence of restriction when this is weighed against the role that the activity plays in the life of the person. In the case of automobile seat belts, for example, the restriction is trivial in nature, interferes not at all with the use or enjoyment of the activity, and does, I am assuming, considerably reduce a high risk of serious injury. Whereas, for example, making mountain-climbing illegal prevents completely a person engaging in an activity which may play an important role in his life and his conception of the person he is.

In general the easiest cases to handle are those which can be argued about in the terms which Mill thought to be so important—a concern not just for the happiness or welfare, in some broad sense, of the individual but rather a concern for the autonomy and freedom of the person. I suggest that we would be most likely to consent to paternalism in those instances in which it preserves and enhances for the individual his ability to rationally consider and carry out his own decisions.

I have suggested in this essay a number of types of situations in which it seems plausible that rational men would agree to granting the legislative powers of a society the right to impose restrictions on what Mill calls "self-regarding" conduct. However, rational men knowing something about the resources of ignorance, ill-will and stupidity available to the law-makers of a society—a good case in point is the history of drug legislation in the United States—will be concerned to limit such intervention to a minimum. I suggest in closing two principles designed to achieve this end.

In all cases of paternalistic legislation there must be a heavy and clear burden of proof placed on the authorities to demonstrate the exact nature of the harmful effects (or beneficial consequences) to be avoided (or achieved) and the probability of their occurrence. The burden of proof here is twofold—what lawyers distinguish as the burden of going forward and the burden of persuasion. That the authorities have the burden of going forward means that it is up to them to raise the question and bring forward evidence of the evils to be avoided. Unlike the case of new drugs where the manufacturer must produce some evidence that the drug has been tested and found not harmful, no citizen has to show with respect to self-regarding conduct that it is not harmful or promotes his best interests. In addition the nature and cogency of the evidence for the harmfulness of the course of action must be set at a high level. To paraphrase a formulation of the burden of proof for criminal proceedings—better 10 men ruin themselves than one man be unjustly deprived of liberty.

Finally I suggest a principle of the least restrictive alternative. If there is an alternative way of accomplishing the desired end without restricting liberty then although it may involve great expense, inconvenience, etc., the society must adopt it.

LICENSING PARENTS

Hugh Lafollette

In this essay I shall argue that the state should require all parents to be licensed. My main goal is to demonstrate that the licensing of parents is theoretically desirable, though I shall also argue that a workable and just licensing program actually could be established.

My strategy is simple. After developing the basic rationale for the licensing of parents, I shall consider several objections to the proposal and argue that these objections fail to undermine it. I shall then isolate some striking similarities between this licensing program and our present policies on the adoption of children. If we retain these adoption policies—as we surely should—then, I argue, a general licensing program should also be established. Finally, I shall briefly suggest that the reason many people object to licensing is that they think parents, particularly biological parents, own or have natural sovereignty over their children.

REGULATING POTENTIALLY HARMFUL ACTIVITIES

Our society normally regulates a certain range of activities; it is illegal to perform these activities unless one has received prior permission to do so. We require automobile operators to have licenses. We forbid people from practicing medicine, law, pharmacy, or psychiatry unless they have satisfied certain licensing requirements.

Society's decision to regulate just these activities is not ad hoc. The decision to restrict admission to certain vocations and to forbid some people from driving is based on an eminently plausible, though not often explicitly formulated, rationale. We require drivers to be licensed because driving an auto is an activity which is potentially harmful to others, safe performance of the activity requires a certain competence, and we have a moderately reliable procedure for determining that competence. The potential harm is obvious: incompetent drivers can and do maim and kill people. The best way we have of limiting this harm without sacrificing the benefits of automobile travel is to require that all drivers demonstrate at least minimal competence. We likewise license doctors, lawyers, and psychologists because they perform activities which can harm others. Obviously they must be proficient if they are to perform these activities properly, and we have moderately reliable procedures for determining proficiency.[1] Imagine a world in which everyone could legally drive a car, in which everyone could legally perform surgery, prescribe medications, dispense drugs, or offer legal advice. Such a world would hardly be desirable.

Consequently, any activity that is potentially harmful to others and requires certain demonstrated competence for its safe performance, is subject to regulation—that is, it is theoretically desirable that we regulate it. If we also have a reliable procedure for determining whether someone has the requisite competence, then the action is not only subject to regulation but ought, all things considered, to be regulated.

It is particularly significant that we license these hazardous activities, even though denying a license to someone can severely inconvenience and even harm that person. Furthermore, available competency tests are not 100 percent accurate. Denying someone a driver's license in our society, for example, would inconvenience that person acutely. In effect that person would be prohibited from working, shopping, or visiting in places reachable only by car. Similarly, people denied vocational licenses are inconvenienced, even devastated. We have all heard of individuals who had the "life-long dream" of becoming physicians or lawyers, yet were denied that dream. However, the realization that some people are disappointed or inconvenienced does not diminish our conviction that we must regulate occupations or activities that are potentially dangerous to others. Innocent people must be protected even if it means that others cannot pursue activities they deem highly desirable.

Furthermore, we maintain licensing procedures even though our competency tests are sometimes inaccurate. Some people competent to perform the licensed activity (for example, driving a car) will be unable to demonstrate competence (they freeze up on the driver's test). Others may be incompetent, yet pass the test (they are lucky or certain aspects of competence—for example, the sense of responsibility—are not tested). We recognize clearly—or should recognize clearly—that no test will pick out all and only competent drivers, physicians, lawyers, and so on. Mistakes are inevitable. This does not mean we should forget that innocent people may be harmed by faulty regulatory procedures. In fact, if the procedures are sufficiently faulty, we should cease regulating that activity entirely until more reliable tests are available. I only want to emphasize here that tests need not be perfect. Where moderately reliable tests are available, licensing procedures should be used to protect innocent people from incompetents.[2]

These general criteria for regulatory licensing can certainly be applied to parents. First, parenting is an activity potentially very harmful to children. The potential for harm is apparent: each year more than half a million children are physically abused or neglected by their parents.[3] Many millions more are psychologically abused or neglected—not given love, respect, or a sense of self-worth. The results of this maltreatment are obvious. Abused children bear the physical and psychological scars of maltreatment throughout their lives. Far too often they turn to crime.[4] They are far more likely than others to abuse their own children.[5] Even if these maltreated children never harm anyone, they will probably never be well-adjusted, happy adults. Therefore, parenting clearly satisfies the first criterion of activities subject to regulation.

The second criterion is also incontestably satisfied. A parent must be competent if he is to avoid harming his children; even greater competence is required if he is to do the "job" well. But not everyone has this minimal competence. Many people lack the knowledge needed to rear children adequately. Many others lack the requisite energy, temperament, or stability. Therefore, child-rearing manifestly satisfies both criteria of activities subject to regulation. In fact, I dare say that parenting is a paradigm of such activities since the potential for harm its so great (both in the extent of harm any one person can suffer and in the number of people potentially harmed) and the need for competence is so evident. Consequently, there is good reason to believe that all parents should be licensed. The only ways to avoid this conclusion are to deny the need for licensing *any* potentially harmful activity; to deny that I have identified the standard criteria of activities which should be regulated; to deny that parenting satisfies the standard criteria; to show that even though parenting satisfies the standard criteria there are special reasons why licensing parents is not theoretically desirable; or to show that there is no reliable and just procedure for implementing this program.

While developing my argument for licensing I have already identified the standard criteria for activities that should be regulated, and I have shown that they can properly be applied to parenting. One could deny the legitimacy of regulation by licensing, but in doing so one would condemn not only the regulation of parenting, but also the regulation of drivers, physicians, druggists, and doctors. Furthermore, regulation of hazardous activities appears to be a fundamental task of any stable society.

Thus only two objections remain. In the next section I shall see if there are any special reasons why licensing parents is not theoretically desirable. Then, in the following section, I shall examine several practical objections designed to demonstrate that even if licensing were theoretically desirable, it could not be justly implemented.

THEORETICAL OBJECTIONS TO LICENSING

Licensing is unacceptable, someone might say, since people have a right to have children, just as they have rights to free speech and free religious expression. They do not need a license to speak freely or to worship as they wish. Why? Because they have a right to engage in these activities. Similarly, since people have a right to have children, any attempt to license parents would be unjust.

This is an important objection since many people find it plausible, if not self-evident. However, it is not as convincing as it appears. The specific rights appealed to in this analogy are not without limitations. Both slander and human sacrifice are prohibited by law; both could result from the unrestricted exercise of freedom of speech and freedom of religion. Thus, even if people have these rights, they may sometimes be limited in order to protect innocent people. Consequently, even if people had a right to have children, that right might also be limited in order to protect innocent people, in this case children. Secondly, the phrase "right to have children" is ambiguous; hence, it is important to isolate its most plausible meaning in this context. Two possible interpretations are not credible and can be dismissed summarily. It is implausible to claim either that infertile people have rights to be *given* children or that people have rights to intentionally create children biologically without incurring any subsequent responsibility to them.

A third interpretation, however, is more plausible, particularly when coupled with observations about the degree of intrusion into one's life that the licensing scheme represents. On this interpretation people have a right to rear children if they make good-faith efforts to rear procreated children the best way they see fit. One might defend this claim on the ground that licensing would require too much intrusion into the lives of sincere applicants.

Undoubtedly one should be wary of unnecessary governmental intervention into individuals' lives. In this case, though, the intrusion would not often be substantial, and when it is, it would be warranted. Those granted licenses would face merely minor intervention; only those denied licenses would encounter marked intrusion. This encroachment, however, is a necessary side-effect of licensing parents—just as it is for automobile and vocational licensing. In addition, as I shall argue in more detail later, the degree of intrusion arising from a general licensing program would be no more than, and probably less than, the present (and presumably justifiable) encroachment into the lives of people who apply to adopt children. Furthermore, since some people hold unacceptable views about what is best for children (they think children should be abused regularly), people do not automatically have rights to rear children just because they will rear them in a way they deem appropriate.[6]

Consequently, we come to a somewhat weaker interpretation of this right claim: a person has a right to rear children if he meets certain minimal standards of child rearing. Parents must not abuse or neglect their children and must also provide for the basic needs of the children. This claim of right is certainly more credible than the previously canvassed alternatives, though some people might still reject this claim in situations where exercise of the right would lead to negative consequences, for example, to overpopulation. More to the point, though, this conditional right is compatible with licensing. On this interpretation one has a right to have children only if one is not going to abuse or neglect them. Of course the very purpose of licensing is just to determine whether people *are* going to abuse or neglect their children. If the determination is made that someone will maltreat children, then that person is subject to the limitations of the right to have children and can legitimately be denied a parenting license.

In fact, this conditional way of formulating the right to have children provides a model for formulating all alleged rights to engage in hazardous activities. Consider, for example, the right to drive a car. People do not have an unconditional right to drive, although they do have a right to drive if they are competent. Similarly, people do not have an unconditional right to practice medicine; they have a right only if they are demonstrably competent. Hence, denying a driver's or physician's license to someone who has not demonstrated the requisite competence does not deny that person's rights. Likewise, on this model, denying a parenting license to someone who is not competent does not violate that person's rights.

Of course someone might object that the right is conditional on actually being a person who will abuse or neglect children, whereas my proposal only picks out those we can reasonably predict will abuse children. Hence, this conditional right *would* be incompatible with licensing.

There are two ways to interpret this objection and it is important to distinguish these divergent formulations. First, the objection could be a way of questioning our ability to predict reasonably and accurately whether people would maltreat their own children. This is an important practical objection, but I will defer discussion of it until the next section. Second, this objection could be a way of expressing doubt about the moral propriety of the prior restraint licensing requires. A parental licensing program would deny licenses to applicants judged to be incompetent even though they had never maltreated any children. This practice would be in tension with our normal skepticism about the propriety of prior restraint.

Despite this healthy skepticism, we do sometimes use prior restraint. In extreme circumstances we may hospitalize or imprison people judged insane, even though they are not legally guilty of any crime, simply because we predict they are likely to harm others. More typically, though, prior restraint is used only if the restriction is not terribly onerous and the restricted activity is one which could lead easily to serious harm. Most types of licensing (for example, those for doctors, drivers, and druggists) fall into this latter category. They require prior restraint to prevent serious harm, and generally the restraint is minor—though it is important to remember that some individuals will find it oppressive. The same is true of parental licensing. The purpose of licensing is to prevent serious harm to children. Moreover, the prior restraint required by licensing would not be terribly onerous for many people. Certainly the restraint would be far less extensive than the presumably justifiable prior restraint of, say, insane criminals. Criminals preventively detained and mentally ill people forceably hospitalized are denied most basic liberties, while those denied parental licenses would be denied only that one specific opportunity. They could still vote, work for political candidates, speak on controversial topics, and so on. Doubtless some individuals would find the restraint onerous. But when compared to other types of restraint currently practiced, and when judged in light of the severity of harm maltreated children suffer, the restraint appears *relatively* minor.

Furthermore, we could make certain, as we do with most licensing programs, that individuals denied licenses are given the opportunity to reapply easily and repeatedly for a license. Thus, many people correctly denied licenses (because they are incompetent) would choose (perhaps it would be provided) to take counseling or therapy to improve their chances of passing the next test. On the other hand, most of those mistakenly denied licenses would probably be able to demonstrate in a later test that they would be competent parents.

Consequently, even though one needs to be wary of prior restraint, if the potential for harm is great and the restraint is minor relative to the harm we are trying to prevent—as it would be with parental licensing—then such restraint is justified. This objection, like all the theoretical objections reviewed, has failed.

PRACTICAL OBJECTIONS TO LICENSING

I shall now consider five practical objections to licensing. Each objection focuses on the problems or difficulties of implementing this proposal. According to these objections, licensing is (or may be) theoretically desirable; nevertheless, it cannot be efficiently and justly implemented.

The first objection is that there may not be, or we may not be able to discover, adequate criteria of "a good parent." We simply do not have the knowledge, and it is unlikely that we could ever obtain the knowledge, that would enable us to distinguish adequate from inadequate parents.

Clearly there is some force to this objection. It is highly improbable that we can formulate criteria that would distinguish precisely between good and less than good parents. There is too much we do not know about child development and adult psychology. My proposal, however, does not demand that we make these fine distinctions. It does not demand that we license only the best parents; rather it is designed to exclude only the very bad ones.[7] This is not just a semantic difference, but a substantive one. Although we do not have infallible criteria for picking out good parents, we undoubtedly can identify bad ones—those who will abuse or neglect their children. Even though we could have a lively debate about the range of freedom a child should be given or the appropriateness of corporal punishment, we do not wonder if a parent who severely beats or neglects a child is adequate. We know that person isn't. Consequently, we do have reliable and useable criteria for determining who is a bad parent; we have the criteria necessary to make a licensing program work.

The second practical objection to licensing is that there is no reliable way to predict who will maltreat their children. Without an accurate predictive test, licensing would be not only unjust, but also a waste of time. Now I recognize that as a philosopher (and not a psychologist, sociologist, or social worker), I am on shaky ground if I make sweeping claims about the present or future abilities of professionals to produce such predictive tests. Nevertheless, there are some relevant observations I can offer.

Initially, we need to be certain that the demands on predictive tests are not unreasonable. For example, it would be improper to require that tests be 100 percent accurate. Procedures for licensing drivers, physicans, lawyers, druggists, etc., plainly are not 100 percent (or anywhere near 100 percent) accurate. Presumably we recognize these deficiencies yet embrace the procedures anyway. Consequently, it would be imprudent to demand considerably more exacting standards for the tests used in licensing parents.

In addition, from what I can piece together, the practical possibilities for constructing a reliable predictive test are not all that gloomy. Since my proposal does not require that we make fine line distinctions between good and less than good parents, but rather that we weed out those who are potentially very bad, we can use existing tests that claim to isolate relevant predictive characteristics—whether a person is violence-prone, easily frustrated, or unduly self-centered. In fact, researchers at Nashville General Hospital have developed a brief interview questionnaire which seems to have significant predictive value. Based on their data, the researchers identified 20 percent of the interviewees as a "risk group"—those having great potential for serious problems. After one year they found "the incidence of major breakdown in parent-child interaction in the risk group was approximately four to five times as great as in the low risk group."[8] We also know that parents who maltreat children often have certain identifiable experiences, for example, most of them were themselves maltreated as children. Consequently, if we combined our information about these parents with certain psychological test results, we would probably be able to predict with reasonable accuracy which people will maltreat their children.

However, my point is not to argue about the precise reliability of present tests. I cannot say emphatically that we now have accurate predictive tests. Nevertheless, even if such tests are not available, we could undoubtedly develop them. For example, we could begin a longitudinal study in which all potential parents would be required to take a specified battery of tests. Then these parents could be "followed" to discover which ones abused or neglected their children. By correlating test scores with information on maltreatment, a usable, accurate test could be fashioned. Therefore, I do not think that the present unavailability of such tests (if they are unavailable) would count against the legitimacy of licensing parents.

The third practical objection is that even if a reliable test for ascertaining who would be an acceptable parent were available, administrators would unintentionally misuse that test. These unintentional mistakes would clearly harm innocent individuals. Therefore, so the argument goes, this proposal ought to be scrapped. This objection can be dispensed with fairly easily unless one assumes there is some special reason to believe that more mistakes will be made in administering parenting licenses than in other regulatory activities. No matter how reliable our proceedings are, there will always be mistakes.

We may license a physician who, through incompetence, would cause the death of a patient; or we may mistakenly deny a physician's license to someone who would be competent. But the fact that mistakes are made does not and should not lead us to abandon attempts to determine competence. The harm done in these cases could be far worse than the harm of mistakenly denying a person a parenting license. As far as I can tell, there is no reason to believe that more mistakes will be made here than elsewhere.

The fourth proposed practical objection claims that any testing procedure will be intentionally abused. People administering the process will disqualify people they dislike, or people who espouse views they dislike, from rearing children.

The response to this objection is parallel to the response to the previous objection, namely, that there is no reason to believe that the licensing of parents is more likely to be abused than driver's license tests or other regulatory procedures. In addition, individuals can be protected from prejudicial treatment by pursuing appeals available to them. Since the licensing test can be taken on numerous occasions, the likelihood of the applicant's working with different administrative personnel increases and therefore the likelihood decreases that intentional abuse could ultimately stop a qualified person from rearing children. Consequently, since the probability of such abuse is not more than, and may even be less than, the intentional abuse of judicial and other regulatory authority, this objection does not give us any reason to reject the licensing of parents.

The fifth objection is that we could never adequately, reasonably, and fairly enforce such a program. That is, even if we could establish a reasonable and fair way of determining which people would be inadequate parents, it would be difficult, if not impossible, to enforce the program. How would one deal with violators and what could we do with babies so conceived? There are difficult problems here, no doubt, but they are not insurmountable. We might not punish parents at all—we might just remove the children and put them up for adoption. However, even if we are presently uncertain about the precise way to establish a just and effective form of enforcement, I do not see why this should undermine my licensing proposal. If it is important enough to protect children from being maltreated by parents, then surely a reasonable enforcement procedure can be secured. At least we should assume one can be unless someone shows that it cannot.

AN ANALOGY WITH ADOPTION

So far I have argued that parents should be licensed. Undoubtedly many readers find this claim extremely radical. It is revealing to notice, however, that this program is not as radical as it seems. Our moral and legal systems already recognize that not everyone is capable of rearing children well. In fact, well-entrenched laws require adoptive parents to be investigated—in much the same ways and for much the same reasons as in the general licensing program advocated here. For example, we do not allow just anyone to adopt a child; nor do we let someone adopt without first estimating the likelihood of the person's being a good parent. In fact, the adoptive process is far more rigorous than the general licensing procedures I envision. Prior to adoption the candidates must first formally apply to adopt a child. The applicants are then subjected to an exacting home study to determine whether they really want to have children and whether they are capable of caring for and rearing them adequately. No one is allowed to adopt a child until the administrators can reasonably predict that the person will be an adequate parent. The results of these procedures are impressive. Despite the trauma children often face before they are finally adopted, they are five times less likely to be abused than children reared by their biological parents.[9]

Nevertheless we recognize, or should recognize, that these demanding procedures exclude some people who would be adequate parents. The selection criteria may be inadequate; the testing procedures may be somewhat unreliable. We may make mistakes. Probably there is some intentional abuse of the system. Adoption procedures intrude directly in the applicants' lives. Yet we continue the present adoption policies because we think it better to mistakenly deny some people the opportunity to adopt than to let just anyone adopt.

Once these features of our adoption policies are clearly identified, it becomes quite apparent that there are striking parallels between the general licensing program I have advocated and our present adoption system. Both programs have the same aim—protecting children. Both have the same drawbacks and are subject to the same abuses. The only obvious dissimilarity is that the adoption requirements are *more* rigorous than those proposed for the general licensing program. Consequently, if we think it is so important to protect adopted children, even though people who want to adopt are less likely than biological parents to maltreat their children, then we should likewise afford the same protection to children reared by their biological parents.

I suspect, though, that many people will think the cases are not analogous. The cases are relevantly different, someone might retort, because biological parents have a natural affection for their children and the strength of this affection makes it unlikely that parents would maltreat their biologically produced children.

Even if it were generally true that parents have special natural affections for their biological offspring, that does not mean that all parents have enough affection to keep them from maltreating their children. This should be apparent given the number of children abused each year by their biological parents. Therefore, even if there is generally such a bond, that does not explain why we should not have licensing procedures to protect children of parents who do not have a sufficiently strong bond. Consequently, if we continue our practice of regulating the adoption of children, and certainly we should, we are rationally compelled to establish a licensing program for all parents.

However, I am not wedded to a strict form of licensing. It may well be that there are alternative ways of regulating parents which would achieve the desired results—the protection of children—without strictly prohibiting nonlicensed people from rearing children. For example, a system of tax incentives for licensed parents, and protective services scrutiny of nonlicensed parents, might adequately protect children. If it would, I would endorse the less drastic measure. My principal concern is to protect children from maltreatment by parents. I begin by advocating the more strict form of licensing since that is the standard method of regulating hazardous activities.

I have argued that all parents should be licensed by the state. This licensing program is attractive, not because state intrusion is inherently judicious and efficacious, but simply because it seems to be the best way to prevent children from being reared by incompetent parents. Nonetheless, even after considering the previous arguments, many people will find the proposal a useless academic exercise, probably silly, and possibly even morally perverse. But why? Why do most of us find this proposal unpalatable, particularly when the arguments supporting it are good and the objections to it are philosophically flimsy?

I suspect the answer is found in a long-held, deeply ingrained attitude toward children, repeatedly reaffirmed in recent court decisions, and present, at least to some degree, in almost all of us. The belief is that parents own, or at least have natural sovereignty over, their children.[10] It does not matter precisely how this belief is described, since on both views parents legitimately exercise extensive and virtually unlimited control over their children. Others can properly interfere with or criticize parental decisions only in unusual and tightly prescribed circumstances—for example, when parents severely and repeatedly abuse their children. In all other cases, the parents reign supreme.

This belief is abhorrent and needs to be supplanted with a more child-centered view. Why? Briefly put, this attitude has adverse effects on children and on the adults these children will become. Parents who hold this view may well maltreat their children. If these parents happen to treat their children well, it is only because they want to, not because they think their children deserve or have a right to good treatment. Moreover, this belief is manifestly at odds with the conviction that parents should prepare children for life as adults. Children subject to parents who perceive children in this way are likely to be adequately prepared for adulthood. Hence, to prepare children for life as adults and to protect them from maltreatment, this attitude toward children must be dislodged. As I have argued, licensing is a viable way to protect children. Furthermore, it would increase the likelihood that more children will be adequately prepared for life as adults than is now the case.

Notes

1. "When practice of a profession or calling requires special knowledge or skill and intimately affects public health, morals, order or safety, or general welfare, legislature may prescribe reasonable qualifications for persons desiring to pursue such professions or calling and require them to demonstrate possession of such qualifications by examination on subjects with which such profession or calling has to deal as a condition precedent to right to follow that profession or calling." 50 SE 2nd 735 (1949). Also see 199 US 306, 318 (1905) and 123 US 623, 661 (1887).

For helpful comments and criticisms, I am indebted to Jeffrey Gold, Chris Hackler, James Rachels, and especially to William Aiken, George Graham, and the Editors of the journal. A somewhat different version of this essay will appear in the Proceeding of the Loyola University (Chicago) Symposium, *Justice for the Child within the Family Context*.

Thanks are due to the directors of the symposium for kind permission to publish the essay in *Philosophy & Public Affairs*.

2. What counts as a moderately reliable test for these purposes will vary from circumstance to circumstance. For example, if the activity could cause a relatively small amount of harm, yet regulating that activity would place extensive constraints on people regulated, then any tests should be extremely accurate. On the other hand, if the activity could be exceedingly harmful but the constraints on the regulated person are minor, then the test can be considerably less reliable.
3. The statistics on the incidence of child abuse vary. Probably the most recent detailed study (Saad Nagi, *Child Maltreatment in the United States*, New York: Columbia University Press, 1977) suggests that between 400,000 and 1,000,000 children are abused or neglected each year. Other experts claim the incidence is considerably higher.
4. According to the National Committee for the Prevention of Child Abuse, more than 80 percent of incarcerated criminals were, as children, abused by their parents. In addition, a study in the *Journal of the American Medical Association* 168, no. 3:1755–1758, reported that first-degree murderers from middle-class homes and who have "no history of addiction to drugs, alcoholism, organic disease of the brain, or epilepsy" were frequently found to have been subject to "remorseless physical brutality at the hands of the parents."
5. "A review of the literature points out that abusive parents were raised in the same style that they have recreated in the pattern of rearing children. ... An individual who was raised by parents who used physical force to train their children and who grew up in a violent household has had as a role model the use of force and violence as a means of family problem solving." R. J. Gelles, "Child Abuse as Psychopathology—a Sociological Critique and Reformulation," *American Journal of Orthopsychiatry* 43, no. 4 (1973): 618–619.
6. Some people might question if any parents actually believe they should beat their children. However, that does appear to be the sincere view of many abusing parents. See, for example, case descriptions in *A Silent Tragedy* by Peter and Judith DeCourcy (Sherman Oaks, CA.: Alfred Publishing Co., 1973).

7. I suppose I might be for licensing only good parents if I knew there were reasonable criteria and some plausible way of deciding if a potential parent satisfied these criteria. However, since I don't think we have those criteria or that method, nor can I seriously envision that we will discover those criteria and that method, I haven't seriously entertained the stronger proposal.
8. The research gathered by Altemeir was reported by Ray Helfer in "Review of the Concepts and a Sampling of the Research Relating to Screening for the Potential to Abuse and/or Neglect One's Child." Helfer's paper was presented at a workshop sponsored by the National Committee for the Prevention of Child Abuse, 3–6 December 1978.
9. According to a study published by the Child Welfare League of America, at least 51 percent of the adopted children had suffered, prior to adoption, more than minimal emotional deprivation. See *A Follow-up Study of Adoptions: Post Placement Functioning of Adoption Families*, Elizabeth A. Lawder et al., New York 1969.

   According to a study by David Gil (*Violence Against Children*, Cambridge: Harvard University Press, 1970) only 4 percent of abused children were abused by adoptive parents. Since at least 2 percent of the children in the United States are adopted (*Encyclopedia of Social Work*, National Association of Social Workers, New York, 1977), that means the rate of abuse by biological parents is five times that of adoptive parents.
10. We can see this belief in a court case chronicled by DeCourcy and DeCourcy in *A Silent Tragedy*. The judge ruled that three children, severely and regularly beaten, burned, and cut by their father, should be placed back with their father since he was only "trying to do what is right." If the court did not adopt this belief would it even be tempted to so excuse such abusive behavior? This attitude also emerges in the all-too-frequent court rulings (see S. Katz, *When Parents Fail*, Boston: Beacon Press, 1971) giving custody of children back to their biological parents even though the parents had abandoned them for years, and even though the children expressed a strong desire to stay with foster parents.

    In "The Child, the Law, and the State" (*Children's Rights: Toward the Liberation of the Child*, Leila Berg et al., New York: Praeger Publishers, 1971), Nan Berger persuasively argues that our adoption and foster care laws are comprehensible only if children are regarded as the property of their parents.

SURROGATE MOTHERHOOD AS PRENATAL ADOPTION

Bonnie Steinbock

The recent case of "Baby M" has brought surrogate motherhood to the forefront of American attention. Ultimately, whether we permit or prohibit surrogacy depends on what we take to be good reasons for preventing people from acting as they wish. A growing number of people want to be, or hire, surrogates; are there legitimate reasons to prevent them? Apart from its intrinsic interest, the issue of surrogate motherhood provides us with an opportunity to examine different justifications for limiting individual freedom.

In the first section of this article, I examine the Baby M case and the lessons it offers. In the second section, I examine claims that surrogacy is ethically unacceptable because it is exploitive, inconsistent with human dignity, or

B. Steinbock, "Surrogate Motherhood as Prenatal Adoption," *Law, Medicine, & Health Care*, vol.16, nos. 1 & 2 (Spring-Summer 1988): 44–50.

harmful to the children born of such arrangements. I conclude that these reasons justify restrictions on surrogate contracts, rather than an outright ban.

BABY M

Mary Beth Whitehead, a married mother of two, agreed to be inseminated with the sperm of William Stern and to give up the child to him for a fee of $10,000. The baby (whom Ms. Whitehead named Sara, and the Sterns named Melissa) was born on March 27, 1986. Three days later, Ms. Whitehead took her home from the hospital and turned her over to the Sterns.

Then Ms. Whitehead changed her mind. She went to the Sterns' home, distraught, and pleaded to have the baby temporarily. Afraid that she would kill herself, the Sterns agreed. The next week, Ms. Whitehead informed the Sterns that she had decided to keep the child, and threatened to leave the country if court action was taken.

At that point, the situation deteriorated into a cross between the Keystone Kops and Nazi stormtroopers. Accompanied by five policemen, the Sterns went to the Whitehead residence armed with a court order giving them temporary custody of the child. Ms. Whitehead managed to slip the baby out of a window to her husband, and the following morning the Whiteheads fled with the child to Florida, where Ms. Whitehead's parents lived. During the next three months, the Whiteheads lived in roughly twenty different hotels, motels, and homes to avoid apprehension. From time to time, Ms. Whitehead telephoned Mr. Stern to discuss the matter: he taped these conversations on advice of counsel. Ms. Whitehead threatened to kill herself, to kill the child, and to falsely accuse Mr. Stern of sexually molesting her older daughter.

At the end of July 1986, while Ms. Whitehead was hospitalized with a kidney infection, Florida police raided her mother's home, knocking her down, and seized the child. Baby M was placed in the custody of Mr. Stern, and the Whiteheads returned to New Jersey, where they attempted to regain custody. After a long and emotional court battle, judge Harvey R. Sorkow ruled on March 31, 1987, that the surrogacy contract was valid, and that specific performance was justified in the best interests of the child. Immediately after reading his decision, he called the Sterns into his chambers so that Mr. Stern's wife, Dr. Elizabeth Stern, could legally adopt the child.

This outcome was unexpected and unprecedented. Most commentators had thought that a court would be unlikely to order a reluctant surrogate to give up an infant merely on the basis of a contract.[1] Indeed, if Ms. Whitehead had never surrendered the child to the Sterns, but had simply taken her home and kept her there, the outcome undoubtedly would have been different. It is also likely that Ms. Whitehead's failure to obey the initial custody order angered Judge Sorkow, and affected his decision.

The decision was appealed to the New Jersey Supreme Court, which issued its decision on February 3, 1988. Writing for a unanimous court, Chief Justice Wilentz reversed the lower court's ruling that the surrogacy contract was valid. The court held that a surrogacy contract that provides money for the surrogate mother, and that includes her irrevocable agreement to surrender her child at birth, is invalid and unenforceable. Since the contract was invalid, Ms. Whitehead did not relinquish, nor were there any other grounds for terminating, her parental rights. Therefore, the adoption of Baby M by Dr. Stern was improperly granted, and Ms. Whitehead remains the child's legal mother.

The court further held that the issue of custody is determined solely by the child's best interests, and it agreed with the lower court that it was in Melissa's best interests to remain with the Sterns. However, Ms. Whitehead, as Baby M's legal as well as natural mother, is entitled to have her own interest in visitation considered. The determination of what kind of visitation rights should be granted to her, and under what conditions, was remanded to the trial court.

The distressing details of this case have led many people to reject surrogacy altogether. Do we really want police officers wrenching infants from their mothers' arms, and prolonged custody battles when surrogates find they are unable to surrender their children, as agreed? Advocates of surrogacy say that to reject the practice wholesale, because of one unfortunate instance, is an example of a "hard case" making bad policy. Opponents reply that it is entirely reasonable to focus on the worst potential outcomes when deciding public policy. Everyone can agree on at least one thing: this particular case seems to have been mismanaged from start to finish, and could serve as a manual of how not to arrange a surrogate birth.

First, it is now clear that Mary Beth Whitehead was not a suitable candidate for surrogate motherhood. Her ambivalence about giving up the child was recognized early on, although this information was not passed on to the Sterns.[2] Second, she had contact with the baby after birth, which is usually avoided in "successful" cases. Typically, the adoptive mother is actively involved in the pregnancy, often serving as the pregnant woman's coach in labor. At birth, the baby is given to the adoptive, not the biological mother. The joy of the adoptive parents in holding their child serves both to promote their bonding and to lessen the pain of separation of the biological mother.

At Ms. Whitehead's request, no one at the hospital was aware of the surrogacy arrangement. She and her husband appeared as the proud parents of "Sara Elizabeth Whitehead," the name on her birth certificate. Ms. Whitehead held her baby, nursed her, and took her home from the hospital—just as she would have done in a normal pregnancy and birth. Not surprisingly, she thought of Sara as her child, and she fought with every weapon at her disposal, honorable and dishonorable, to prevent her being taken away. She can hardly be blamed for doing so.[3]

Why did Dr. Stern, who supposedly had a very good relation with Ms. Whitehead before the birth, not act as her labor coach? One possibility is that Ms. Whitehead, ambivalent about giving up her baby, did not want Dr. Stern involved. At her request, the Sterns' visits to the hospital to see the newborn baby were unobtrusive. It is also possible that Dr. Stern was ambivalent about having a child. The original idea of hiring a surrogate was not hers, but her husband's. It was Mr. Stern who felt a "compelling" need to have a child related to him by blood, having lost all his relatives to the Nazis.

Furthermore, Dr. Stern was not infertile, as was stated in the surrogacy agreement. Rather, in 1979 she was diagnosed by two eye specialists as suffering from optic neuritis, which meant that she "probably" had multiple sclerosis. (This was confirmed by all four experts who testified.) Normal conception was ruled out by the Sterns in late 1982, when a medical colleague told Dr. Stern that his wife, a victim of multiple sclerosis, had suffered a temporary paralysis during pregnancy. "We decided the risk wasn't worth it," Mr. Stern said.[4]

Ms. Whitehead's lawyer, Harold J. Cassidy, dismissed the suggestion that Dr. Stern's "mildest case" of multiple sclerosis determined the Sterns' decision to seek a surrogate. He noted that she was not even treated for multiple sclerosis until after the Baby M dispute had started. "It's almost as though it's an afterthought," he said.[5]

Judge Sorkow deemed the decision to avoid conception "medically reasonable and understandable." The Supreme Court did not go so far, noting that Dr. Stern's "anxiety appears to have exceeded the actual risk, which current medical authorities assess as minimal."[6] Nonetheless, the court acknowledged that her anxiety, including fears that pregnancy might precipitate blindness and paraplegia, was "quite real." Certainly, even a woman who wants a child very much may reasonably wish to avoid becoming blind and paralyzed as a result of pregnancy. Yet is it believable that a woman who really wanted a child would decide against pregnancy *solely* on the basis of *someone else's* medical experience? Would she not consult at least one specialist on her *own* medical condition before deciding it wasn't worth the risk? The conclusion that she was at best ambivalent about bearing a child seems irresistible.

This possibility conjures up many people's worst fears about surrogacy: that prosperous women, who do not want to interrupt their careers, will use poor and educationally disadvantaged women to bear their children. I will return shortly to the question of whether this is exploitive. The issue here is psychological: what kind of mother is Dr. Stern likely to be? If she is unwilling to undergo pregnancy, with its discomforts, inconveniences, and risks, will she be willing to make the considerable sacrifices that good parenting requires? Ms. Whitehead's ability to be a good mother was repeatedly questioned during the trial. She was portrayed as immature, untruthful, hysterical, overly identified with her children, and prone to smothering their independence. Even if all this is true—and I think that Ms. Whitehead's inadequacies were exaggerated—Dr. Stern may not be such a prize either. The choice for Baby M may have been between a highly strung, emotional, overinvolved mother, and a remote, detached, even cold one.[7]

The assessment of Ms. Whitehead's ability to be a good mother was biased by the middle-class prejudices of the judge and of the mental health officials who testified. Ms. Whitehead left school at fifteen, and is not conversant with the latest theories on child rearing: she made the egregious error of giving Sara teddy bears to play with, instead of the more "age-appropriate," expert-approved pans and spoons. She proved to be a total failure at patty-cake. If this is evidence of parental inadequacy, we're all in danger of losing our children.

The Supreme Court felt that Ms. Whitehead was "rather harshly judged" and acknowledged the possibility that the trial court was wrong in its initial award of custody. Nevertheless, it affirmed Judge Sorkow's decision to allow the Sterns to retain custody, as being in Melissa's best interests. George Annas disagrees with the "best interests" approach. He points out that Judge Sorkow awarded temporary custody of Baby M to the Sterns in May 1986, without giving the Whiteheads notice or an opportunity to obtain legal representation. That was a serious wrong and injustice to the Whiteheads. To allow the Sterns to keep the child compounds the original unfairness: "justice requires that reasonable consideration be given to returning Baby M to the permanent custody of the Whiteheads."[8]

But a child is not a possession, to be returned to the rightful owner. It is not fairness to all parties that should determine a child's fate, but what is best for her. As Chief Justice Wilentz rightly stated, "The child's interests come first: we will not punish it for judicial errors, assuming any were made."[9]

Subsequent events have substantiated the claim that giving custody to the Sterns was in Melissa's best interests. After losing custody, Ms. Whitehead, whose husband had undergone a vasectomy, became pregnant by another man. She divorced her husband and married Dean R. Gould last November. These developments indicate that the Whiteheads were not able to offer a stable home, although the argument can be made that their marriage might have survived if not for the strains introduced by the court battle and the loss of Baby M. But even if Judge Sorkow had no reason to prefer the Sterns to the Whiteheads back in May 1986, he was still right to give the Sterns custody in March 1987. To take her away then, at nearly eighteen months of age, from the only parents she had ever known would have been disruptive, cruel, and unfair to her.

Annas' preference for a just solution is premised partly on his belief that there *is* no "best interest" solution to this "tragic custody case." I take it that he means that however custody is resolved, Baby M is the loser. Either way, she will be deprived of one parent. However, a best-interests solution is not a perfect solution. It is simply the solution that is on balance best for the child, given the realities of the situation. Applying this standard, Judge Sorkow was right to give the Sterns custody, and the Supreme Court was right to uphold the decision.

The best-interests argument is based on the assumption that Mr. Stern has at least a *prima facie* claim to Baby M. We certainly would not consider allowing a stranger who kidnapped a baby and managed to elude the police for a year to retain custody on the grounds that he was providing a good home to a child who had known no other parent. However, the Baby M case is not analogous. First, Mr. Stern is Baby M's biological father and, as such, has at least some claim to raise her, which no non-parental kidnapper has. Second, Mary Beth Whitehead *agreed* to give him their baby. Unlike the miller's daughter in *Rumpelstiltskin*, the fairy tale to which the Baby M case is sometimes compared, she was not forced into the agreement. Because both Mary Beth Whitehead and Mr. Stern have *prima facie* claims to Baby M, the decision as to who should raise her should be based on her present best interests. Therefore we must, regretfully, tolerate the injustice to Ms. Whitehead, and try to avoid such problems in the future.

It is unfortunate that the court did not decide the issue of visitation on the same basis as custody. By declaring Ms. Whitehead-Gould the legal mother, and maintaining that she is entitled to visitation, the court has prolonged the fight over Baby M. It is hard to see how this can be in her best interests. This is no ordinary divorce case, where the child has a relation with both parents that it is desirable to maintain. As Mr. Stern said at the start of the court hearing to determine visitation, "Melissa has a right to grow and be happy and not be torn between two parents."[10]

The court's decision was well-meaning but internally inconsistent. Out of concern for the best interests of the child, it granted the Sterns custody. At the same time, by holding Ms. Whitehead-Gould to be the legal mother, with visitation rights, it precluded precisely what is most in Melissa's interest, a resolution of the situation. Further, the decision leaves open the distressing possibility that a Baby M situation could happen again. Legislative efforts should be directed toward ensuring that this worst-case scenario never occurs.

SHOULD SURROGACY BE PROHIBITED?

On June 27, 1988, Michigan became the first state to outlaw commercial contracts for women to bear children for others.[11] Yet making a practice illegal does not necessarily make it go away: witness black-market adoption. The legitimate concerns that support a ban on surrogacy might be better served by careful regulation. However, some practices, such as slavery, are ethically unacceptable, regardless of how carefully regulated they are. Let us consider the arguments that surrogacy is intrinsically unacceptable.

Paternalistic Arguments

These arguments against surrogacy take the form of protecting a potential surrogate from a choice she may later regret. As an argument for banning surrogacy, as opposed to providing safeguards to ensure that contracts are freely and knowledgeably undertaken, this is a form of paternalism.

At one time, the characterization of a prohibition as paternalistic was a sufficient reason to reject it. The pendulum has swung back, and many people are willing to accept at least some paternalistic restrictions on freedom. Gerald Dworkin points out that even Mill made one exception to his otherwise absolute rejection of paternalism: he thought that no one should be allowed to sell himself into slavery, because to do so would be to destroy his future autonomy.

This provides a narrow principle to justify some paternalistic interventions. To preserve freedom in the long run, we give up the freedom to make certain choices, those that have results that are "far-reaching, potentially dangerous and irreversible."[12] An example would be a ban on the sale of crack. Virtually everyone who uses crack becomes addicted and, once addicted, a slave to its use. We reasonably and willingly give up our freedom to buy the drug, to protect our ability to make free decisions in the future.

Can a Dworkinian argument be made to rule out surrogacy agreements? Admittedly, the decision to give up a child is permanent, and may have disastrous effects on the surrogate mother. However, many decisions may have long-term, disastrous effects (e.g., postponing childbirth for a career, having an abortion, giving a child up for adoption). Clearly we do not want the state to make decisions for us in all these matters. Dworkin's argument is rightly restricted to paternalistic interferences that protect the individual's autonomy or ability to make decisions in the future. Surrogacy does not involve giving up one's autonomy, which distinguishes it from both the crack and selling-oneself-into-slavery examples. Respect for individual freedom requires us to permit people to make choices they may later regret.

Moral Objections

Four main moral objections to surrogacy were outlined in the Warnock Report.[13]

1. It is inconsistent with human dignity that a woman should use her uterus for financial profit.
2. To deliberately become pregnant with the intention of giving up the child distorts the relationship between mother and child.
3. Surrogacy is degrading because it amounts to child-selling.
4. Since there are some risks attached to pregnancy, no woman ought to be asked to undertake pregnancy for another in order to earn money.[14]

We must all agree that a practice that exploits people or violates human dignity is immoral. However, it is not clear that surrogacy is guilty on either count.

Exploitation The mere fact that pregnancy is *risky* does not make surrogate agreements exploitive, and therefore morally wrong. People often do risky things for money; why should the line be drawn at undergoing pregnancy? The usual response is to compare surrogacy and kidney-selling. The selling of organs is prohibited because of the potential for coercion and exploitation. But why should kidney-selling be viewed as intrinsically coercive? A possible explanation is that no one would do it, unless driven by poverty. The choice is both forced and dangerous, and hence coercive.[15]

The situation is quite different in the case of the race-car driver or stuntman. We do not think that they are *forced* to perform risky activities for money: they freely choose to do so. Unlike selling one's kidneys, these are activities that we can understand (intellectually, anyway) someone choosing to do. Movie stuntmen, for example, often enjoy their work, and derive satisfaction from doing it well. Of course they "do it for the money," in the sense that they would not do it without compensation; few people are willing to work "for free." The element of coercion is missing, however, because they enjoy the job, despite the risks, and could do something else if they chose.

The same is apparently true of most surrogates. "They choose the surrogate role primarily because the fee provides a better economic opportunity than alternative occupations, but also because they enjoy being pregnant and the respect and attention that it draws."[16] Some may derive a feeling of self-worth from an act they regard as highly altruistic: providing a couple with a child they could not otherwise have. If these motives are present, it is far from clear that the surrogate is being exploited. Indeed, it seems objectionally paternalistic to insist that she is.

Human Dignity It may be argued that even if womb-leasing is not necessarily exploitive, it should still be rejected as inconsistent with human dignity. But why? As John Harris points out, hair, blood, and other tissue is often donated or sold; what is so special about the uterus?[17]

Human dignity is more plausibly invoked in the strongest argument against surrogacy, namely, that it is the sale of a child. Children are not property, nor can they be bought or sold.[18] It could be argued that surrogacy is wrong because it is analogous to slavery, and so is inconsistent with human dignity.

However, there are important differences between slavery and a surrogate agreement.[19] The child born of a surrogate is not treated cruelly or deprived of freedom or resold; none of the things that make slavery so awful are part of surrogacy. Still, it may be thought that simply putting a market value on a child is wrong. Human life has intrinsic value; it is literally priceless. Arrangements that ignore this violate our deepest notions of the value of human life. It is profoundly disturbing to hear in a television documentary on surrogacy the boyfriend of a surrogate say, quite candidly, "We're in it for the money."

Judge Sorkow accepted the premise that producing a child for money denigrates human dignity, but he denied that this happens in a surrogate agreement. Ms. Whitehead was not paid for the surrender of the child to the father: she was paid for her willingness to be impregnated and carry Mr. Stern's child to term. The child, once born, is his biological child. "He cannot purchase what is already his."[20]

This is misleading, and not merely because Baby M is as much Ms. Whitehead's child as Mr. Stern's. It is misleading because it glosses over the fact that the surrender of the child was part—indeed, the whole point—of the agreement. If the surrogate were paid merely for being willing to be impregnated and carrying the child to term, then she would fulfill the contract upon giving birth. She could take the money *and* the child. Mr. Stern did not agree to pay Ms. Whitehead merely to *have* his child, but to provide him with a child. The New Jersey Supreme Court held that this violated New Jersey's laws prohibiting the payment or acceptance of money in connection with adoption.

One way to remove the taint of baby-selling would be to limit payment to medical expenses associated with the birth or incurred by the surrogate during pregnancy (as is allowed in many jurisdictions, including New Jersey, in ordinary adoptions).[21] Surrogacy could be seen not as baby-selling, but as a form of adoption. Nowhere did the Supreme Court find any legal prohibition against surrogacy when there is no payment, and when the surrogate has the right to change her mind and keep the child. However, this solution effectively prohibits surrogacy, since few women would become surrogate solely for self-fulfillment or reasons of altruism.

The question, then, is whether we can reconcile paying the surrogate, beyond her medical expenses, with the idea of surrogacy as prenatal adoption. We can do this by separating the terms of the agreement, which include surrendering the infant at birth to the biological father from the justification for payment. The payment should be seen as compensation for the risks, sacrifice, and discomfort the surrogate undergoes during pregnancy. This means that if, through no fault on the part of the surrogate, the baby is stillborn, she should still be paid in full, since she has kept her part of the bargain. (By contrast, in the Stern–Whitehead agreement, Ms. Whitehead was to receive only $1,000 for a stillbirth).[22] If, on the other hand, the surrogate changes her mind and decides to keep the child, she would break the agreement, and would not be entitled to any fee or to compensation for expenses incurred during pregnancy.

The Right of Privacy

Most commentators who invoke the right of privacy do so in support of surrogacy.[23] However, George Annas makes the novel argument that the right to rear a child you have borne is also a privacy right, which cannot be prospectively waived. He says:

> [Judge Sorkow] grudgingly concedes that [Ms. Whitehead] could not prospectively give up her right to have an abortion during pregnancy. ... This would be an intolerable restriction on her liberty and under *Roe v. Wade*, the state has no constitutional authority to enforce a contract that prohibits her from terminating her pregnancy.

But why isn't the same logic applicable to the right to rear a child you have given birth to? Her constitutional rights to rear the child she has given birth to are even stronger since they involve even more intimately, and over a lifetime, her privacy rights to reproduce and rear a child in a family setting.[24]

Absent a compelling state interest (such as protecting a child from unfit parents), it certainly would be an intolerable invasion of privacy for the state to take children from their parents. But Baby M has two parents, both of whom now want her. It is not clear why only people who can give birth (i.e., women) should enjoy the right to rear their children.

Moreover, we do allow women to give their children up for adoption after birth. The state enforces those agreements even if the natural mother, after the prescribed waiting period, changes her mind. Why should the right to rear a child be unwaivable before, but not after, birth? Why should the state have the constitutional authority to uphold postnatal, but not prenatal, adoption agreements? It is not clear why birth should affect the waivability of this right or have the constitutional significance that Annas attributes to it.

Nevertheless, there are sound moral and policy, if not constitutional, reasons to provide a postnatal waiting period in surrogate agreements. As the Baby M case makes painfully clear, the surrogate may underestimate the bond created by gestation and the emotional trauma caused by relinquishing the baby. Compassion requires that we acknowledge these findings, and not deprive a woman of the baby she has carried because, before conception, she underestimated the strength of her feelings for it. Providing a waiting period, as in ordinary postnatal adoptions, will help protect women from making irrevocable mistakes, without banning the practice.

Some may object that this gives too little protection to the prospective adoptive parents. They cannot be sure that the baby is theirs until the waiting period is over. While this is hard on them, a similar burden is placed on other adoptive parents. If the absence of a guarantee serves to discourage people from entering surrogacy agreements, that is not necessarily a bad thing, given all the risks inherent in such contracts. In addition, this requirement would make stricter screening and counseling of surrogates essential, a desirable side-effect.

Harm to Others

Paternalistic and moral objections to surrogacy do not seem to justify an outright ban. What about the effect on the offspring of such contracts? We do not yet have solid data on the effects of being a "surrogate child." Any claim that surrogacy creates psychological problems in the children is purely speculative. But what if we did discover that such children have deep feelings of worthlessness from learning that their natural mothers deliberately created them with the intention of giving them away? Might we ban surrogacy as posing an unacceptable risk of psychological harm to the resulting children?

Feelings of worthlessness are harmful. They can prevent people from living happy, fulfilling lives. However, a surrogate child, even one whose life is miserable because of these feelings, cannot claim to have been harmed by the surrogate agreement. Without the agreement, the child would never have existed. Unless she is willing to say that her life is not worth living because of these feelings, that she would be better off never having been born, she cannot claim to have been harmed by being born of a surrogate mother.[25]

Elsewhere I have argued that children can be *wronged* by being brought into existence, even if they are not, strictly speaking, *harmed*.[26] They are wronged if they are deprived of the minimally decent existence to which all citizens are entitled. We owe it to our children to see that they are not born with such serious impairments that their most basic interests will be doomed in advance. If being born to a surrogate is a handicap of this magnitude, comparable to being born blind or deaf or severely mentally retarded, then surrogacy can be seen as wronging the offspring. This would be a strong reason against permitting such contracts. However, it does not seem likely. Probably the problems arising from surrogacy will be like those faced by adopted children and children whose parents divorce. Such problems are not trivial, but neither are they so serious that the child's very existence can be seen as wrongful.

If surrogate children are neither harmed nor wronged by surrogacy, it may seem that the argument for banning surrogacy on grounds of its harmfulness to the offspring evaporates. After all, if the children themselves have no cause for complaint, how can anyone else claim to reject it on their behalf? Yet it seems extremely counter-intuitive to suggest that the risk of emotional damage to the children born of such arrangements is not even relevant to our deliberations. It seems quite reasonable and proper—even morally obligatory—for policy-makers to think about the possible detrimental effects of new reproductive technologies, and to reject those likely to create physically or emotionally damaged people. The explanation for this must involve the idea that it is wrong to bring people into the world in a harmful condition, even if they are not, strictly speaking, harmed by having been brought into existence.[27] Should evidence emerge that surrogacy produces children with serious psychological problems, that would be a strong reason for banning the practice.

There is some evidence on the effect of surrogacy on the other children of the surrogate mother. One woman reported that her daughter, now seventeen, who was eleven at the time of the surrogate birth, "is still having problems with what I did, and as a result she is still angry with me." She explains: "Nobody told me that a child could bond with a baby while you're still pregnant. I didn't realize then that all the times she listened to his heartbeat and felt his legs kick that she was becoming attached to him."[28]

A less sentimental explanation is possible. It seems likely that her daughter, seeing one child given away, was fearful that the same might be done to her. We can expect anxiety and resentment on the part of children whose mothers give away a brother or sister. The psychological harm to these children is clearly relevant to a determination of whether surrogacy is contrary to public policy. At the same time, it should be remembered that many things, including divorce, remarriage, and even moving to a new neighborhood, create anxiety and resentment in children. We should not use the effect on children as an excuse for banning a practice we find bizarre or offensive.

CONCLUSION

There are many reasons to be extremely cautious of surrogacy. I cannot imagine becoming a surrogate, nor would I advise anyone else to enter into a contract so fraught with peril. But the fact that a practice is risky, foolish, or even morally distasteful is not sufficient reason to outlaw it. It would be better for the state to regulate the practice, and minimize the potential for harm, without infringing on the liberty of citizens.

References

1. See, for example, "Surrogate Motherhood Agreements: Contemporary Legal Aspects of a Biblical Notion," *University of Richmond Law Review*, 16 (1982): 470; "Surrogate Mothers: The Legal Issues," *American Journal of Law & Medicine*, 7 (1981): 338, and Angela Holder, *Legal Issues in Pediatrics and Adolescent Medicine* (New Haven: Yale University Press, 1985), 8: "Where a surrogate mother decides that she does not want to give the baby up for adoption, as has already happened, *it is clear that no court will enforce a contract entered into before the child was born* in which she agreed to surrender her baby for adoption." Emphasis added.

2. Had the Sterns been informed of the psychologist's concerns as to Ms. Whitehead's suitability to be a surrogate, they might have ended the arrangement, costing the Infertility Center its fee. As Chief Justice Wilentz said, "It is apparent that the profit motive got the better of the Infertility Center." In the matter of Baby M, Supreme Court of New Jersey, A-39, at 45.
3. "[W]e think it is expecting something well beyond normal human capabilities to suggest that this mother should have parted with her newly born infant without a struggle. ... We ... cannot conceive of any other case where a perfectly fit mother was expected to surrender her newly born infant, perhaps forever, and was then told she was a bad mother because she did not." Id.: 79.
4. "Father Recalls Surrogate Was 'Perfect,'" *New York Times*, Jan. 6, 1987, B2.
5. Id.
6. In the matter of Baby M, supra note 2, at 8.
7. This possibility was suggested to me by Susan Vermazen.
8. George Annas, "Baby M: Babies (and Justice) for Sale," *Hastings Center Report*, 17, no. 3 (1987): 15.
9. In the matter of Baby M, supra note 2, at 75.
10. "Anger and Anguish at Baby M Visitation Hearing," *New York Times*, March 29, 1988, 17.
11. *New York Times*, June 28, 1988, A20.
12. Gerald Dworkin "Paternalism," in R.A. Wasserstrom, ed., *Morality and the Law* (Belmont, Cal.: Wadsworth, 1971); reprinted in J. Feinberg and H. Gross, eds. *Philosophy of Law*, 3d ed. (Belmont, Cal.: Wadsworth, 1986), 265.
13. M. Warnock, chair, *Report of the Committee of Inquiry into Human Fertilisation and Embryology* (London: Her Majesty's Stationery Office, 1984).
14. As summarized in J. Harris, *The Value of Life* (London: Routledge & Kegan Paul, 1985), 142.
15. For an argument that kidney-selling need not be coercive, see B.A. Brody and H.T. Engelhardt, Jr., *Bioethics: Readings and Cases* (Englewood Cliffs, N.J.: Prentice-Hall, 1987), 331.
16. John Robertson, "Surrogate Mothers: Not So Novel after All," *Hastings Center Report*, 13, no. 5 (1983): 29; citing P. Parker, "Surrogate Mother's Motivations: Initial Findings," *American Journal of Psychiatry*, 140 (1983): 1.
17. Harris, supra note 14, at 144.
18. Several authors note that it is both illegal and contrary to public policy to buy or sell children, and therefore contracts that contemplate this are unenforceable. See B. Cohen, "Surrogate Mothers: Whose Baby Is It?," *American Journal of Law & Medicine*, 10 (1984): 253; "Surrogate Mother Agreements: Contemporary Legal Aspects of a Biblical Notion," *University of Richmond Law Review*, 16 (1982): 469.
19. Robertson makes a similar point, supra note 16, at 33.
20. In re Baby "M," 217 N.J. Super. 372, 525 A.2d 1157 (1987).
21. Cohen, supra note 18. See also Angela Holder, "Surrogate Motherhood: Babies for Fun and Profit," *Law, Medicine & Health Care*, 12 (1984): 115.
22. Annas, supra note 8, at 14.
23. See, for example, Robertson, supra note 16, at 32; and S.R. Gersz, "The Contract in Surrogate Motherhood: A Review of the Issues," *Law, Medicine & Health Care*, 12 (1984): 107.
24. Annas, supra note 8.
25. For discussion of these issues, see D. Parfit, "On Doing the Best for Our Children," in M.D. Bayles, ed., *Ethics and Population* (Cambridge, Mass.: Schenkman, 1976); M.D. Bayles, "Harm to the Unconceived," *Philosophy & Public Affairs*, 5 (1976): 292; J. Glover, *Causing Death and Saving Lives* (Harmondsworth, Eng.: Penguin, 1977), 67; John Robertson, "In Vitro Conception and Harm to the Unborn," *Hastings Center Report*, 8 (1978): 13; J. Feinberg, *Harm to Others* (Oxford: Oxford University Press, 1984), 93.
26. Bonnie Steinbock, "The Logical Case for 'Wrongful Life'," *Hastings Center Report*, 16, no. 2 (1986): 15.
27. For the distinction between being harmed and being in a harmful state, see Feinberg, supra note 25, at 99.
28. "Baby M Case Stirs Feelings of Surrogate Mothers," *New York Times*, March 2, 1987, B1.

THE CASE AGAINST SURROGATE PARENTING

Herbert T. Krimmel

Is it ethical for someone to create a human life with the intention of giving it up? This seems to be the primary question for both surrogate mother arrangements and artificial insemination by donor (AID), since in both situations a person who is providing germinal material does so only upon the assurance that someone else will assume full responsability for the child he or she helps to create.

THE ETHICAL ISSUE

In analyzing the ethics of surrogate mother arrangements, it is helpful to begin by examining the roles the surrogate mother performs. First, she acts as a procreator in providing an ovum to be fertilized. Second, after her ovum has been fertilized by the sperm of the man who wishes to parent the child, she acts as host to the fetus, providing nurture and protection while the newly conceived individual develops.

I see no insurmountable moral objections to the functions the mother performs in this second role as host. Her actions are analogous to those of a foster mother or of a wet-nurse who cares for a child when the natural mother cannot or does not do so. Using a surrogate mother as a host for the fetus when the biological mother cannot bear the child is no more morally objectionable than employing others to help educate, train, or otherwise care for a child. Except in extremes, where the parent relinquishes or delegates responsibilities for a child for trivial reasons, the practice would not seem to raise a serious moral issue.

I would argue, however, that the first role that the surrogate mother performs—providing germinal material to be fertilized—does pose a major ethical problem. The surrogate mother provides her ovum, and enters into a surrogate mother arrangement, with the clear understanding that she is to avoid responsibility for the life she creates. Surrogate mother arrangements are designed to separate in the mind of the surrogate mother the decision to create a child from the decision to have and raise that child. The cause of this dissociation is some other benefit she will receive, most often money. In other words, her desire to create a child is born of some motive other than the desire to be a parent. This separation of the decision to create a child from the decision to parent it is ethically suspect. The child is conceived not because he is wanted by his biological mother, but because he can be useful to someone else. He is conceived in order to be given away.

At their deepest level, surrogate mother arrangements involve a change in motive for creating children: from a desire to have them for their own sake, to a desire to have them because they can provide some other benefit. The surrogate mother creates a child with the intention to abdicate parental responsibilities. Can we view this as ethical? My answer is no. I will explain why by analyzing various situations in which surrogate mother arrangements might be used.

WHY MOTIVE MATTERS

Let's begin with the single parent. A single woman might use AID, or a single man might use a surrogate mother arrangement, if she or he wanted a child but did not want to be burdened with a spouse. Either practice would intentionally deprive the child of a mother or a father. This, I assert, is fundamentally unfair to the child.

Reprinted with permission of the author and the publisher from Hastings Center Report, vol. 13 (October 1983) pp. 35–39.

Those who disagree might point to divorce or to the death of a parent as situations in which a child is deprived of one parent and must rely solely or primarily upon the other. The comparison, however, is inapt. After divorce or the death of a parent, a child may find herself with a single parent due to circumstances that were unfortunate, unintended, and undesired. But when surrogate mother arrangements are used by a single parent, depriving the child of a second parent is one of the intended and desired effects. It is one thing to ask how to make the best of a bad situation when it is thrust upon a person. It is different altogether to ask whether one may intentionally set out to achieve the same result. The morality of identical results (for example, killings) will oftentimes differ depending upon whether the situation is invited by, or involuntarily thrust upon, the actor. Legal distinctions following and based upon this ethical distinction are abundant. The law of self-defense provides a notable example.

Since a woman can get pregnant if she wishes whether or not she is married, and since there is little that society can do to prevent women from creating children even if their intention is to deprive the children of a father, why should we be so concerned about single men using surrogate mother arrangements if they too want a child but not a spouse? To say that women can intentionally plan to be unwed mothers is not to condone the practice. Besides, society will hold the father liable in a paternity action if he can be found and identified, which indicates some social concern that people should not be able to abdicate the responsibilities that they incur in generating children. Otherwise, why do we condemn the proverbial sailor with a pregnant girlfriend in every port?

In many surrogate mother arrangements, of course, the surrogate mother will not be transferring custody of the child to a single man, but to a couple: the child's biological father and a stepmother, his wife. What are the ethics of surrogate mother arrangements when the child is taken into a two-parent family? Again, surrogate mother arrangements and AID pose similar ethical questions: The surrogate mother transfers her parental responsibilities to the wife of the biological father, while with AID the sperm donor relinquishes his interest in the child to the husband of the biological mother. In both cases the child is created with the intention of transferring the responsibility for its care to a new set of parents. The surrogate mother situation is more dramatic than AID since the transfer occurs after the child is born, while in the case of AID the transfer takes place at the time of the insemination. Nevertheless, the ethical point is the same: creating children for the purpose of transferring them. For a surrogate mother the question remains: Is it ethical to create a child for the purpose of transferring it to the wife of the biological father?

At first blush this looks to be little different from the typical adoption, for what is an adoption other than a transfer of responsibility from one set of parents to another? The analogy is misleading, however, for two reasons. First, it is difficult to imagine anyone conceiving children for the purpose of putting them up for adoption. And, if such a bizarre event were to occur, I doubt that we would look upon it with moral approval. Most adoptions arise either because an undesired conception is brought to term, or because the parents wanted to have the child, but find that they are unable to provide for it because of some unfortunate circumstances that develop after conception.

Second, even if surrogate mother arrangements were to be classified as a type of adoption, not all offerings of children for adoption are necessarily moral. For example, would it be moral for parents to offer their three-year-old for adoption because they are bored with the child? Would it be moral for a couple to offer for adoption their newborn female baby because they wanted a boy?

Therefore, even though surrogate mother arrangements may in some superficial ways be likened to adoption, one must still ask whether it is ethical to separate the decision to create children from the desire to have them. I would answer no. The procreator should desire the child for its own sake, and not as a means to attaining some other end. Even though one of the ends may be stated altruistically as an attempt to bring happiness to an infertile couple, the child is still being used by the surrogate. She creates it not because she desires it, but because she desires something from it.

To sanction the use and treatment of human beings as means to the achievement of other goals instead of as ends in themselves is to accept an ethic with a tragic past, and to establish a precedent with a dangerous future. Already the press has reported the decision of one couple to conceive a child for the purpose of using it as a bone marrow donor for its sibling (*Los Angeles Times*, April 17, 1979, p. I-2). And the bioethics literature contains articles seriously considering whether we should clone human beings to serve as an inventory of spare parts for organ transplants and articles that foresee the use of comatose human beings as self-replenishing blood banks and manufacturing plants for human hormones. How far our society is willing to proceed down this road is uncertain, but it is clear that the first step to all these practices is the acceptance of the same principle that the Nazis attempted to use to justify their medical experiments at the Nuremberg War Crimes Trials: that human beings may be used as means to the achievement of other goals, and need not be treated as ends in themselves.

But why, it might be asked, is it so terrible if the surrogate mother does not desire the child for its own sake, when under the proposed surrogate mother arrangements there will be a couple eagerly desiring to have the child and to be its parents? That this argument may not be entirely accurate will be illustrated in the following section, but the basic reply is that creating a child without desiring it fundamentally changes the way we look at children—instead of viewing them as unique individual personalities to be desired in their own right, we may come to view them as commodities or items of manufacture to be desired because of their utility. A recent newspaper account describes the business of an agency that matches surrogate mothers with barren couples as follows:

> Its first product is due for delivery today. Twelve others are on the way and an additional 20 have been ordered. The "company" is Surrogate Mothering Ltd. and the "product" is babies.

The dangers of this view are best illustrated by examining what might go wrong in a surrogate mother arrangement, and most important, by viewing how the various parties to the contract may react to the disappointment.

WHAT MIGHT GO WRONG

Ninety-nine percent of the surrogate mother arrangements may work out just fine; the child will be born normal, and the adopting parents (that is, the biological father and his wife) will want it. But, what happens when, unforeseeably, the child is born deformed? Since many defects cannot be discovered prenatally by amniocentesis or other means, the situation is bound to arise. Similarly, consider what would happen if the biological father were to die before the birth of the child. Or if the "child" turns out to be twins or triplets. Each of these instances poses an inevitable situation where the adopting parents may be unhappy with the prospect of getting the child or children. Although legislation can mandate that the adopting parents take the child or children in whatever condition they come or whatever the situation, provided the surrogate mother has abided by all the contractual provisions of the surrogate mother arrangement, the important point for our discussion is the attitude that the surrogate mother or the adopting parent might have. Consider the example of the deformed child.

When I participated in the Surrogate Parent Foundation's inaugural symposium in November 1981, I was struck by the attitude of both the surrogate mothers and the adopting parents to these problems. The adopting parents worried, "Do we have to take such a child?" And the surrogate mothers said in response, "Well, we don't want to be stuck with it." Clearly, both groups were anxious not be responsible for the "undesirable child" born of the surrogate mother arrangement. What does this portend?

It is human nature that when one pays money, one expects value. Things that one pays for have a way of being seen as commodities. Unavoidable in surrogate mother arrangements are questions such as: "Did I get a good one?" We see similar behavior with respect to the adoption of children: comparatively speaking, there is no shortage of black, Mexican-American, mentally retarded, or older children seeking homes; the shortage is in attractive, intelligent-looking Caucasian babies. Similarly, surrogate mother arrangements involve more than just the desire to have a child. The desire is for a certain type of child.

But, it may be objected, don't all parents voice these same concerns in the normal course of having children? Not exactly. No one doubts or minimizes the pain and disappointment parents feel when they learn that their child is born with some genetic or congenital birth defect. But this is different from the surrogate mother situation, where neither the surrogate mother nor the adopting parents may feel responsible, and both sides may feel that they have a legitimate excuse not to assume responsibility for the child. The surrogate mother might blame the biological father for having "defective sperm," as the adopting parents might blame the surrogate mother for a "defective ovum" or for improper care of the fetus during pregnancy. The adopting parents desire a normal child, not *this* child in any condition, and the surrogate mother doesn't want it in any event. So both sides will feel threatened by the birth of an "undesirable child." Like bruised fruit in the produce bin of a supermarket, this child is likely to become an object of avoidance.

Certainly, in the natural course of having children a mother may doubt whether she wants a child if the father has died before its birth; parents may shy away from a defective infant, or be distressed at the thought of multiple births. Nevertheless, I believe they are more likely to accept these contingencies as a matter of fate. I do not think this is the case with surrogate mother arrangements. After all, in the surrogate mother arrangement the adopting parents can blame someone outside the marital relationship. The surrogate mother has been hosting this child all along, and she is delivering it. It certainly *looks* far more like a commodity than the child that arrives in the natural course within the family unit.

A DANGEROUS AGENDA

Another social problem, which arises out of the first, is the fear that surrogate mother arrangements will fall prey to eugenic concerns. Surrogate mother contracts typically have clauses requiring genetic tests of the fetus and stating that the surrogate mother must have an abortion (or keep the child herself) if the child does not pass these tests.

In the last decade we have witnessed a renaissance of interest in eugenics. This, coupled with advances in biomedical technology, has created a host of abuses and new moral problems. For example, genetic counseling clinics now face a dilemma: amniocentesis, the same procedure that identifies whether a fetus suffers from certain genetic defects, also discloses the sex of a fetus. Genetic counseling clinics have reported that even when the fetus is normal, a disproportionate number of mothers abort female children. Aborting normal fetuses simply because the prospective parents desire children of a certain sex is one result of viewing children as commodities. The recent scandal at the Repository for Germinal Choice, the so-called "Nobel Sperm Bank," provides another chilling example. Their first "customer" was, unbeknownst to the staff, a woman who "had lost custody of two other children because they were abused in an effort to 'make them smart.'" Of course, these and similar evils may occur whether or not surrogate mother arrangements are allowed by law. But to the extent that they promote the view of children as commodities, these arrangements contribute to these problems. There is nothing wrong with striving for betterment, as long as it does not result in intolerance to that which is not perfect. But I fear that the latter attitude will become prevalent.

Sanctioning surrogate mother arrangements can also exert pressures upon the family structure. First, as was noted earlier, there is nothing technically to prevent the use of surrogate mother arrangements by single males desiring to become parents. Indeed, single females can already do this with AID or even without it. But even if legislation were to limit the use of the surrogate mother arrangement to infertile couples, other pressures would occur: namely the intrusion of a third adult into the marital community. I do not think that society is ready to accept either single parenting or quasi-adulterous arrangements as normal.

Another stress on the family structure arises within the family of the surrogate mother. When the child is surrendered to the adopting parents it is removed not only from the surrogate mother, but also from her family. They too have interests to be considered. Do not the siblings of that child have an interest in the fact that their little baby brother has been "given" away? One woman, the mother of a medical student who had often donated sperm for artificial insemination, expressed her feelings to me eloquently. She asked, "I wonder how many grandchildren I have that I have never seen and never been able to hold or cuddle."

Intrafamily tensions can also be expected to result in the family of the adopting parents due to the asymmetry of relationship the adopting parents will have toward the child. The adopting mother has no biological relationship to the child, whereas the adopting father is also the child's biological father. Won't this unequal biological claim on the child be used as a wedge in child-rearing arguments? Can't we imagine the father saying, "Well, he is my son, not yours"? What if the couple eventually gets divorced? Should custody in a subsequent divorce between the adopting mother and the biological father be treated simply as a normal child custody dispute? Or should the biological relationship between father and child weigh more heavily? These questions do not arise in typical adoption situations since both parents are equally unrelated biologically to the child. Indeed, in adoption there is symmetry. The surrogate mother situation is more analogous to second marriages, where the children of one party by a prior marriage are adopted by the new spouse. Since asymmetry in second marriage situations causes problems, we can anticipate similar difficulties arising from surrogate mother arrangements.

There is also the worry that the offspring of a surrogate mother arrangement will be deprived of important information about his or her heritage. This also happens with adopted children or children conceived by AID, who lack information about their biological parents, which could be important to them medically. Another less popularly recognized problem is the danger of half-sibling marriages, where the child of the surrogate mother unwittingly falls in love with a half sister or brother. The only way to avoid these problems is to dispense with the confidentiality of parental records; however, the natural parents may not always want their identity disclosed.

The legalization of surrogate mother arrangements may also put undue pressure upon poor women to use their bodies in this way to support themselves and their families. Analogous problems have arisen in the past with the use of paid blood donors. And occasionally the press reports someone desperate enough to offer to sell an eye or some other organ. I believe that certain things should be viewed as too important to be sold as commodities, and I hope that we have advanced from the time when parents raised children for profitable labor, or found themselves forced to sell their children.

While many of the social dilemmas I have outlined here have their analogies in other present-day occurrences such as divorced families or in adoption, every addition is hurtful. Legalizing surrogate mother arrangements will increase the frequency of these problems, and put more stress on our society's shared moral values.

[CONCLUSION]

An infertile couple might prefer to raise a child with a biological relationship to the husband, rather than to raise an adopted child who has no biological relationship to either the husband or the wife. But does the marginal increase in joy that they might therefore experience outweigh the potential pain that they, or the child conceived in such arrangements, or others might suffer? Does their preference outweigh the social costs and problems that the legalization of surrogate mothering might well engender? I honestly do not know. I don't even know on what hypothetical scale such interests could be weighed and balanced. But even if we could weigh such interests, and even if personal preference outweighed the costs, I still would not be able to say that we could justify achieving those ends by these means; that ethically it would be permissible for a person to create a child, not because she desired it, but because it could be useful to her....

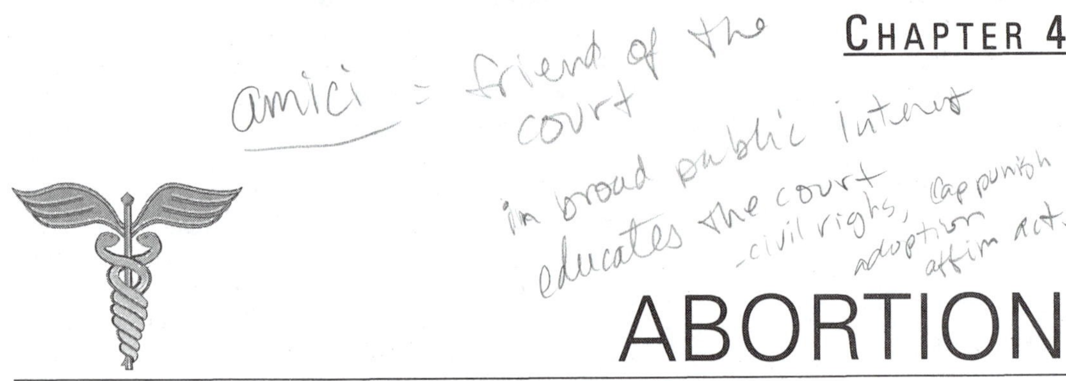

Chapter 4

ABORTION

UNITED STATES SUPREME COURT DECISION

Roe v. Wade

MAJORITY OPINION (DELIVERED BY JUSTICE BLACKMUN)

Three reasons have been advanced to explain historically the enactment of criminal abortion laws in the 19th century and to justify their continued existence.

It has been argued occasionally that these laws were the product of a Victorian social concern to discourage illicit sexual conduct. Texas, however, does not advance this justification in the present case, and it appears that no court or commentator has taken the argument seriously. The appellants and *amici* contend, moreover, that this is not a proper state purpose at all and suggest that, if it were, the Texas statutes are overbroad in protecting it since the law fails to distinguish between married and unwed mothers.

A second reason is concerned with abortion as a medical procedure. When most criminal abortion laws were first enacted, the procedure was a hazardous one for the woman. This was particularly true prior to the development of antisepsis. Antiseptic techniques, of course, were based on discoveries by Lister, Pasteur, and others first announced in 1867, but were not generally accepted and employed until about the turn of the century. Abortion mortality was high. Even after 1900, and perhaps until as late as the development of antibiotics in the 1940s, standard modern techniques such as dilation and curettage were not nearly so safe as they are today. Thus, it has been argued that a state's real concern in enacting a criminal abortion law was to protect the pregnant woman, that is, to restrain her from submitting to a procedure that placed her life in serious jeopardy.

Modern medical techniques have altered this situation. Appellants and various *amici* refer to medical data indicating that abortion in early pregnancy, that is, prior to the end of the first trimester, although not without its risk, is now relatively safe. Mortality rates for women undergoing early abortions, where the procedure

United States Supreme Court, 410 U.S. 113, 93 S.Ct. 705. January 22, 1973.

is legal, appear to be as low as or lower than the rates for normal childbirth. Consequently, any interest of the state in protecting the woman from an inherently hazardous procedure except when it would be equally dangerous for her to forgo it, has largely disappeared. Of course, important state interests in the areas of health and medical standards do remain. The state has a legitimate interest in seeing to it that abortion, like any other medical procedure, is performed under circumstances that insure maximum safety for the patient. This interest obviously extends at least to the performing physician and his staff, to the facilities involved, to the availability of after-care, and to adequate provision for any complication or emergency that might arise. The prevalence of high mortality rates at illegal "abortion mills" strengthens, rather than weakens, the state's interest in regulating the conditions under which abortions are performed. Moreover, the risk to the woman increases as her pregnancy continues. Thus, the state retains a definite interest in protecting the woman's own health and safety when an abortion is proposed at a late stage of pregnancy.

The third reason is the state's interest—some phrase it in terms of duty—in protecting prenatal life. Some of the argument for this justification rests on the theory that a new human life is present from the moment of conception. The state's interest and general obligation to protect life then extends, it is argued, to prenatal life. Only when the life of the pregnant mother herself is at stake, balanced against the life she carries within her, should the interest of the embryo or fetus not prevail. Logically, of course, a legitimate state interest in this area need not stand or fall on acceptance of the belief that life begins at conception or at some other point prior to live birth. In assessing the state's interest, recognition may be given to the less rigid claim that as long as at least potential life is involved, the state may assert interests beyond the protection of the pregnant woman alone.

Parties challenging state abortion laws have sharply disputed in some courts the contention that a purpose of these laws, when enacted, was to protect prenatal life. Pointing to the absence of legislative history to support the contention, they claim that most state laws were designed solely to protect the woman. Because medical advances have lessened this concern, at least with respect to abortion in early pregnancy, they argue that with respect to such abortions the laws can no longer be justified by any state interest. There is some scholarly support for this view of original purpose. The few state courts called upon to interpret their laws in the late 19th and early 20th centuries did focus on the state's interest in protecting the woman's health rather than in preserving the embryo and fetus. Proponents of this view point out that in many states, including Texas, by statute or judicial interpretation, the pregnant woman herself could not be prosecuted for self-abortion or for cooperating in an abortion performed upon her by another. They claim that adoption of the "quickening" distinction through received common law and state statutes tacitly recognizes the greater health hazards inherent in late abortion and impliedly repudiates the theory that life begins at conception.

It is with these interests, and the weight to be attached to them, that this case is concerned.

The Constitution does not explicitly mention any right of privacy. In a line of decisions, however, going back perhaps as far as Union Pacific R. Co. v. Botsford, 141 U.S. 250, 251 (1891), the court has recognized that a right of personal privacy, or a guarantee of certain areas or zones of privacy, does exist under the Constitution. In varying contexts, the court or individual justices have, indeed, found at least the roots of that right in the first amendment, in the fourth and fifth amendments, in the penumbras of the Bill of Rights, in the ninth amendment, or in the concept of liberty guaranteed by the first section of the fourteenth amendment. These decisions make it clear that only personal rights that can be deemed "fundamental" or "implicit" in the concept of ordered liberty are included in this guarantee of personal privacy. They also make it clear that the right has some extension to activities relating to marriage, procreation, contraception, family relationships, and child rearing and education.

This right of privacy, whether it be founded in the fourteenth amendment's concept of personal liberty and restrictions upon state action, as we feel it is, or, as the district court determined, in the ninth amendment's reservation of rights to the people, is broad enough to encompass a woman's decision whether or not to terminate her pregnancy. The detriment that the state would impose upon the pregnant woman by denying this choice altogether is apparent. Specific and direct harm medically diagnosable even in early pregnancy may be involved. Maternity, or additional offspring, may force upon the woman a distressful life and future. Psychological harm may be imminent. Mental and physical health may be taxed by child care. There is also the distress, for all concerned, associated with the unwanted child, and there is the problem of bringing a child into a family already unable, psychologically and otherwise, to care for it. In other cases, as in this one, the additional difficulties and continuing stigma factors the woman and her responsible physician necessarily will consider in consultation.

On the basis of elements such as these, appellant and some *amici* argue that the woman's right is absolute and that she is entitled to terminate her pregnancy at whatever time, in whatever way, and for whatever reason she alone chooses. With this we do not agree. Appellant's arguments that Texas either has no valid interest strong enough to support any limitation upon the woman's sole determination are unpersuasive. The court's decisions recognizing a right of privacy also acknowledge that some state regulation in areas protected by that right is appropriate. As noted above, a state may properly assert important interests in safeguarding health, in maintaining medical standards, and in protecting potential life. At some point in pregnancy, to sustain regulation of the factors that govern the abortion decision. The privacy right involved, therefore, cannot be said to be absolute. In fact, it is not clear to us that the claim asserted by some *amici* that one has an unlimited right to do with one's body as one pleases bears a close relationship to the right of privacy previously articulated in the court's decisions. The court has refused to recognize an unlimited right of this kind in the past.

We, therefore, conclude that the right of personal privacy includes the abortion decision, but that this right is not unqualified and must be considered against important state interests in regulation.

We note that those federal and state courts that have recently considered abortion law challenges have reached the same conclusion. A majority, in addition to the district court in the present case, have held state laws unconstitutional, at least in part, because of vagueness or because of overbreadth and abridgment of rights.

Although the results are divided, most of these courts have agreed that the right of privacy, however based, is broad enough to cover the abortion decision; that the right, nonetheless, is not absolute and is subject to some limitations; and that at some point the state interests as to protection of health, medical standards, and prenatal life, become dominant. We agree with this approach.

Where certain "fundamental rights" are involved, the court has held that regulation limiting these rights may be justified only by a "compelling state interest," and that legislative enactments must be narrowly drawn to express only the legitimate state interests at stake.

In the recent abortion cases, cited above, courts have recognized these principles. Those striking down state laws have generally scrutinized the state's interests in protecting health and potential life, and have concluded that neither interest justified broad limitations on the reasons for which a physician and his pregnant patient might decide that she should have an abortion in the early stages of pregnancy. Courts sustaining state laws have held that the state's determinations to protect health or prenatal life are dominant and constitutionally justifiable.

The district court held that the appellee failed to meet his burden of demonstrating that the Texas statute's infringement upon Roe's rights was necessary to support a compelling state interest, and that, although the appellee presented "several compelling justifications for state presence in the area of abortions," the statutes outstripped these justifications and swept "far beyond any areas of compelling state interest." Appellant and appellee both contest that holding. Appellant, as has been indicated, claims an absolute right that bars any state imposition of criminal penalties in the area. Appellee argues that the state's determination to recognize and protect prenatal life from and after conception constitutes a compelling state interest. As noted above, we do not agree fully with either formulation.

A. The appellee and certain *amici* argue that the fetus is a "person" within the language and meaning of the fourteenth amendment. In support of this, they outline at length and in detail the well-known facts of fetal development. If this suggestion of personhood is established, the appellant's case, of course, collapses, for the fetus' right to life would then be guaranteed specifically by the amendment. The appellant conceded as much on reargument. On the other hand, the appellee conceded on reargument that no case could be cited that holds that a fetus is a person within the meaning of the fourteenth amendment.

The Constitution does not define "person" in so many words. Section 1 of the fourteenth amendment contains three references to "person... " but in nearly all these instances, the use of the word is such that it has application only postnatally. None indicates, with any assurance, that it has any possible prenatal application.

All this, together with our observation, supra, that throughout the major portion of the 19th century prevailing legal abortion practices were far freer than they are today, persuades us that the word "person," as used in the fourteenth amendment, does not include the unborn...

B. The pregnant woman cannot be isolated in her privacy. She carries an embryo and, later, a fetus, if one accepts the medical definitions of the developing young in the human uterus. See Dorland's Illustrated Medical Dictionary 478–479, 547 (24th ed. 1965). The situation therefore is inherently different from marital intimacy, or bedroom possession of obscene material, or marriage, or procreation, or education, with which *Eisenstadt, Griswold, Stanley, Loving, Skinner, Pierce,* and *Meyer* were respectively concerned. As we have intimated above, it is reasonable and appropriate for a state to decide that at some point in time another interest, that of health of the mother or that of potential human life, becomes significantly involved. The woman's privacy is no longer sole and any right of privacy she possesses must be measured accordingly.

Texas urges that, apart from the fourteenth amendment, life begins at conception and is present throughout pregnancy, and that, therefore, the state has a compelling interest in protecting that life from and after conception. We need not resolve the difficult question of when life begins. When those trained in the respective disciplines of medicine, philosophy, and theology are unable to arrive at any consensus, the judiciary, at this point in the development of man's knowledge, is not in a position to speculate as to the answer.

It should be sufficient to note briefly the wide divergence of thinking on this most sensitive and difficult question. There has always been strong support for the view that life does not begin until live birth. This was the belief of the Stoics. It appears to be the predominant, though not the unanimous, attitude of the

Jewish faith. It may be taken to represent also the position of a large segment of the Protestant community, insofar as that can be ascertained; organized groups that have taken a formal position on the abortion issue have generally regarded abortion as a matter for the conscience of the individual and her family. As we have noted, the common law found greater significance in quickening. Physicians and their scientific colleagues have regarded that event with less interest and have tended to focus either upon conception, upon live birth, or upon the interim point at which the fetus becomes "viable," that is, potentially able to live outside the mother's womb, albeit with artificial aid. Viability is usually placed at about seven months (28 weeks) but may occur earlier, even at 24 weeks. The Aristotelian theory of "mediate animation," that held sway throughout the Middle Ages and the Renaissance in Europe, continued to be official Roman Catholic dogma until the 19th century, despite opposition to this "ensoulment" theory from those in the church who would recognize the existence of life from the moment of conception. The latter is now, of course, the official belief of the Catholic church. As one brief *amicus* discloses, this is a view strongly held by many non-Catholics as well, and by many physicians. Substantial problems for precise definition of this view are posed, however, by new embryological data that purport to indicate that conception is a "process" over time, rather than an event, and by new medical techniques implantation of embryos, artificial insemination, and even artificial wombs.

In areas other than criminal abortion, the law has been reluctant to endorse any theory that life, as we recognize it, begins before live birth or to accord legal rights to the unborn except in narrowly defined situations and except when the rights are contingent upon live birth. For example, the traditional rule of tort law denied recovery for prenatal injuries even though the child was born alive. That rule has been changed in almost every jurisdiction. In most states, recovery is said to be permitted only if the fetus was viable, or at least quick, when the injuries were sustained, though few courts have squarely so held. In a recent development, generally opposed by the commentators, some states permit the parents of a stillborn child to maintain an action for wrongful death because of prenatal injuries. Such an action, however, would appear to be one to vindicate the parents' interest and is thus consistent with the view that the fetus, at most, represents only the potentiality of life. Similarly, unborn children have been recognized as acquiring rights or interests by way of inheritance or other devolution of property, and have been represented by guardians ad litem. Perfection of the interests involved, again, has generally been contingent upon live birth. In short, the unborn have never been recognized in the law as persons in the whole sense.

In view of all this, we do not agree that, by adopting one theory of life, Texas may override the rights of the pregnant woman that are at stake. We repeat, however, that the state does have an important and legitimate interest in preserving and protecting the health of the pregnant woman, whether she be a resident of the state or a nonresident who seeks medical consultation and treatment there, and that it has still another important and legitimate interest in protecting the potentiality of human life. These interests are separate and distinct. Each grows in substantiality as the woman approaches term and, at a point during pregnancy, each becomes "compelling."

With respect to the state's important and legitimate interest in the health of the mother, the "compelling" point, in the light of present medical knowledge, is at approximately the end of the first trimester. This is so because of the now-established medical fact, referred to above at 149, that until the end of the first trimester mortality in abortion may be less than mortality in normal childbirth. It follows that, from and after this point, a state may regulate the abortion procedure to the extent that the regulation reasonably relates to the preservation and protection of maternal health. Examples of permissible state regulation in this area are requirements as to the qualifications of the person who is to perform the abortion; as to the licensure of that person; as to the facility in which the procedure is to be performed, that is, whether it must be a hospital or may be a clinic or some other place of less-than-hospital status; as to the licensing of the facility; and the like.

This means, on the other hand, that, for the period of pregnancy prior to this "compelling" point, the attending physician, in consultation with his patient, is free to determine, without regulation by the state, that, in his medical judgment, the patient's pregnancy should be terminated. If that decision is reached, the judgment may be effectuated by an abortion free of interference by the state.

With respect to the state's important and legitimate interest in potential life, the "compelling" point is at viability. This is so because the fetus then presumably has the capability of meaningful life outside the mother's womb. State regulation protective of fetal life after viability thus has both logical and biological justifications. If the state is interested in protecting fetal life after viability, it may go so far as to proscribe abortion during that period, except when it is necessary to preserve the life or health of the mother.

Measured against these standards, art. 1196 of the Texas penal code, in restricting legal abortions to those "procured or attempted by medical advice for the purpose of saving the life of the mother," sweeps too broadly. The statute makes no distinction between abortions performed early in pregnancy and those performed later, and it limits to a single reason, "saving" the mother's life, the legal justification for the procedure. The statute, therefore, cannot survive the constitutional attack made upon it here...

To summarize and to repeat:

1. A state criminal abortion statute of the current Texas type, that excepts from criminality only a lifesaving procedure on behalf of the mother, without regard to pregnancy stage and without recognition of the other interests involved, is violative of the due process clause of the fourteenth amendment.

a. For the stage prior to approximately the end of the first trimester, the abortion decision and its effectuation must be left to the medical judgment of the pregnant woman's attending physician.

b. For the stage subsequent to approximately the end of the first trimester, the state, in promoting its interest in the health of the mother, may, if it chooses, regulate the abortion procedure in ways that are reasonably related to maternal health.

c. For the stage subsequent to viability, the state in promoting its interest in the potentiality of human life may, if it chooses, regulate, and even proscribe, abortion except where it is necessary, in appropriate medical judgment, for the preservation of the life or health of the mother.

2. The state may define the term "physician," as it has been employed in the preceding paragraphs of this part XI of this opinion, to mean only a physician currently licensed by the state, and may proscribe any abortion by a person who is not a physician as so defined. ...

This holding, we feel, is consistent with the relative weights of the respective interests involved, with the lessons and examples of medical and legal history, with the lenity of the common law, and with the demands of the profound problems of the present day. The decision leaves the state free to place increasing restrictions on abortion as the period of pregnancy lengthens, so long as those restrictions are tailored to the recognized state interests. The decision vindicates the right of the physician to administer medical treatment according to his professional judgment up to the points where important state interests provide compelling justifications for intervention. Up to those points, the abortion decision in all its aspects is inherently, and primarily, a medical decision, and basic responsibility for it must rest with the physician. If an individual practitioner abuses the privilege of exercising proper medical judgment, the usual remedies, judicial and intra-professional, are available. ...

DISSENTING OPINION (JUSTICE REHNQUIST)

The court's opinion brings to the decision of this troubling question both extensive historical fact and a wealth of legal scholarship. While the opinion thus commands my respect, I find myself nonetheless in fundamental disagreement with those parts of it that invalidate the Texas statute in question, and therefore dissent.

The court's opinion decides that a state may impose virtually no restriction on the performance of abortions during the first trimester of pregnancy. Our previous decisions indicate that a necessary predicate for such an opinion is a plaintiff who was in her first trimester of pregnancy at some time during the pendency of her lawsuit. While a party may vindicate his own constitutional rights, he may not seek vindication for the rights of others. The court's statement of facts in this case makes clear, however, that the record in no way indicates the presence of such a plaintiff. We know only that plaintiff Roe at the time of filing her complaint was a pregnant woman; for aught that appears in this record, she may have been in her last trimester of pregnancy as of the date the complaint was filed.

Nothing in the court's opinion indicates that Texas might not constitutionally apply its proscription of abortion as written to a woman in that stage of pregnancy. Nonetheless, the court uses her complaint against the Texas statute as a fulcrum for deciding that states may impose virtually no restrictions on medical abortions performed during the first trimester of pregnancy. In deciding such a hypothetical lawsuit, the court departs from the longstanding admonition that it should never "formulate a rule of constitutional law broader than is required by the precise facts to which it is to be applied."

Even if there were a plaintiff in this case capable of litigating the issue which the court decides, I would reach a conclusion opposite to that reached by the court. I have difficulty in concluding, as the court does, that the right of "privacy" is involved in this case. Texas, by the statute here challenged, bars the performance of a medical abortion by a licensed physician on a plaintiff such as Roe. A transaction resulting in an operation such as this is not "private" in the ordinary usage of that word. Nor is the "privacy" in the ordinary usage of that word. Nor is the "privacy" that the court finds here even a distant relative of the freedom from searches and seizures protected by the fourth amendment to the Constitution, which the court has referred to as embodying a right to privacy.

If the court means by the term "privacy" no more than that the claim of a person to be free from unwanted state regulation of consensual transactions may be a form of "liberty" protected by the fourteenth amendment, there is no doubt that similar claims have been upheld in our earlier decisions on the basis of that liberty. I agree with the statement of Mr. Justice Steward in his concurring opinion that the "liberty," against deprivation of which without due process the fourteenth amendment protects, embraces more than the rights found in the Bill of Rights. But that liberty is not guaranteed absolutely against deprivation, only against deprivation without due process of law. The test traditionally applied in the area of social and economic legislation is whether or not a law such as that challenged has a rational relation to a valid state objective. The due process clause of the fourteenth amendment undoubtedly does place a limit, albeit a broad one, on legislative power to enact laws such as this. If the Texas statute were to prohibit an abortion even where the mother's life is in jeopardy, I have little doubt that such a statute would lack a rational relation to a valid state objective under the test stated in Williamson, supra. But the court's sweeping invalidation of any restrictions on abortion during the first trimester is impossible to justify under that standard, and the conscious weighing of competing factors that the court's opinion apparently substitutes for the established test is far more appropriate to a legislative judgment than to a judicial one.

The court eschews the history of the fourteenth amendment in its reliance on the "compelling state interest" test. But the court adds a new wrinkle to this test by transposing it from the legal considerations associated with the equal protection clause of the fourteenth amendment to this case arising under the due process clause of the fourteenth amendment. Unless I misapprehend the consequences of this transplanting of the "compelling state interest test," the court's opinion will accomplish the seemingly impossible feat of leaving this area of the law more confused than it found it.

While the court's opinion quotes from the dissent of Mr. Justice Holmes in Lochner v. New York, 198 U.S. 45, 74 (1905), the result it reaches is more closely attuned to the majority opinion of Mr. Justice Peckham in that case. As in Lochner and similar cases applying substantive due process standards to economic and social welfare legislation, the adoption of the compelling state interest standard will inevitably require the court to examine the legislative policies and pass on the wisdom of these policies in the very process of deciding whether a particular state interest put forward may or may not be "compelling." The decision here to break pregnancy into three distinct terms and to outline the permissible restrictions the state may impose in each one, for example, partakes more of judicial legislation than it does of a determination of the intent of the drafters of the fourteenth amendment.

The fact that a majority of the states reflecting, after all, the majority sentiment in those states, have had restrictions on abortions for at least a century is a strong indication, it seems to me, that the asserted right to an abortion is not "so rooted in the traditions and conscience of our people as to be ranked as fundamental." Even today, when society's views on abortion are changing the very existence of the debate is evidence that the "right to an abortion" is not so universally accepted as the appellant would have us believe.

To reach its result, the court necessarily has had to find within the scope of the fourteenth amendment a right that was apparently completely unknown to the drafters of the amendment. As early as 1821, the first state law dealing directly with abortion was enacted by the Connecticut legislature by the time of the adoption of the fourteenth amendment in 1868, there were at least 36 laws enacted by state or territorial legislatures limiting abortion. While many state have amended or updated their laws, 21 of the laws on the books in 1868 remain in effect today. Indeed,the Texas statute struck down today was, as the majority notes, first enacted in 1857 and "has remained substantially unchanged to the present time."

There apparently was no question concerning the validity of this provision or of any of the other state statutes when the fourteenth amendment was adopted. The only conclusion possible from this history is that the drafters did not intend to have the fourteenth amendment withdraw from the states the power to legislate with respect to this matter.

Even if one were to agree that the case that the court decides were here, and that the enunciation of the substantive constitutional law in the court's opinion were proper, the actual disposition of the case by the court is still difficult to justify. The Texas statute is struck down in toto, even though the court apparently concedes that at later periods of pregnancy Texas might impose these self-same statutory limitations on abortion. My understanding of past practice is that a statute found to be invalid as applied to a particular plaintiff, but not unconstitutional as a whole, is not simply "struck down" but is, instead, declared unconstitutional as applied to the fact situation before the court.

For all of the foregoing reasons, I respectfully dissent.

UNITED STATES SUPREME COURT OPINION IN PLANNED PARENTHOOD OF SOUTHEASTERN PENNSYLVANIA V. CASEY, GOVERNOR OF PENNSYLVANIA

Justices S. O'Connor, A. Kennedy, and D. Souter

I

Liberty finds no refuge in a jurisprudence of doubt. Yet, 19 years after our holding that the Constitution protects a woman's right to terminate her pregnancy in its early stages, Roe v. Wade (1973), that definition of liberty is still questioned. Joining the respondents as amicus curiae, the United States, as it has done in five other cases in the last decade, again asks us to overrule Roe.

At issue ... are five provisions of the Pennsylvania Abortion Control Act of 1982, as amended in 1988 and 1989. ... The Act requires that a woman seeking an abortion give her informed consent prior to the abortion procedure, and specifies that she be provided with certain information at least 24 hours before the abortion is performed. Section 3205. For a minor to obtain an abortion, the Act requires the informed consent of one of her parents, but provides for a judicial bypass option if the minor does not wish to or cannot obtain a parent's consent. Section 3206. Another provision of the Act requires that, unless certain exceptions apply, a married woman seeking an abortion must sign a statement indicating that she has notified her husband of her intended abortion. Section 3209. The Act exempts compliance with these three requirements in the event of a "medical emergency," which is defined in Section 3 of the Act. See Section 3205(a), Section 3206(a), Section 3209(c). In addition to the above provisions regulating the performance of abortions, the Act imposes certain reporting requirements on facilities that provide abortion services.

Before any of these provisions took effect, the petitioners, who are five abortion clinics and one physician representing himself as well as a class of physicians who provide abortion services, brought this suit seeking declaratory and injunctive relief. Each provision was challenged as unconstitutional on its face. The District Court entered a preliminary injunction against the enforcement of the regulations, and, after a 3-day bench trial, held all the provisions at issue here unconstitutional, entering a permanent injunction against Pennsylvania's enforcement of them. The Court of Appeals for the Third Circuit affirmed in part and reversed in part, upholding all of the regulations except for the husband notification requirement... [W]e find it imperative to review once more the principles that define the rights of the woman and the legitimate authority of the State respecting the termination of pregnancies by abortion procedures.

After considering the fundamental constitutional questions resolved by Roe, principles of institutional integrity, and the rule of stare decisis, we are led to conclude this: the essential holding of Roe v. Wade should be retained and once again reaffirmed.

It must be stated at the outset and with clarity that Roe's essential holding, the holding we reaffirm, has three parts. First is a recognition of the right of the woman to choose to have an abortion before viability and to obtain it without undue interference from the State. Before viability, the State's interests are not strong enough to support a prohibition of abortion or the imposition of a substantial obstacle to the woman's effective right to elect the procedure. Second is a confirmation of the State's power to restrict abortions after fetal viability if the law contains exceptions for pregnancies which endanger the woman's life or health. And third is the principle that the State has legitimate interests from the

United States Supreme Court. 505 U.S. 833, 112 S.Ct. 2791. June 29, 1992.

outset of the pregnancy in protecting the health of the woman and the life of the fetus that may become a child. These principles do not contradict one another; and we adhere to each.

II

Constitutional protection of the woman's decision to terminate her pregnancy derives from the Due Process Clause of the Fourteenth Amendment. It declares that no State shall "deprive any person of life, liberty, or property, without due process of law." The controlling word in the cases before us is "liberty."

...It is a promise of the Constitution that there is a realm of personal liberty which the government may not enter. We have vindicated this principle before. Marriage is mentioned nowhere in the Bill of Rights, and interracial marriage was illegal in most States in the 19th century, but the Court was no doubt correct in finding it to be an aspect of liberty protected against state interference by the substantive component of the Due Process Clause. ...

Neither the Bill of Rights nor the specific practices of States at the time of the adoption of the Fourteenth Amendment marks the outer limits of the substantive sphere of liberty which the Fourteenth Amendment protects. ... It is settled now, as it was when the Court heard arguments in Roe v. Wade, that the Constitution places limits on a State's right to interfere with a person's most basic decisions about family and parenthood, as well as bodily integrity.

The inescapable fact is that adjudication of substantive due process claims may call upon the Court in interpreting the Constitution to exercise that same capacity which, by tradition, courts always have exercised: reasoned judgment. ...

III

...No evolution of legal principle has left Roe's doctrinal footings weaker than they were in 1973. No development of constitutional law since the case was decided has implicitly or explicitly left Roe behind as a mere survivor of obsolete constitutional thinking. ...

We have seen how time has overtaken some of Roe's factual assumptions: advances in maternal health care allow for abortions safe to the mother later in pregnancy than was true in 1973, and advances in neonatal care have advanced viability to a point somewhat earlier. But these facts go only to the scheme of time limits on the realization of competing interests, and the divergences from the factual premises of 1973 have no bearing on the validity of Roe's central holding, that viability marks the earliest point at which the State's interest in fetal life is constitutionally adequate to justify a legislative ban on nontherapeutic abortions. The soundness or unsoundness of that constitutional judgment in no sense turns on whether viability occurs at approximately 28 weeks, as was usual at the time of Roe, at 23 to 24 weeks, as it sometimes does today, or at some moment even slightly earlier in pregnancy, as it may if fetal respiratory capacity can somehow be enhanced in the future. Whenever it may occur, the attainment of viability may continue to serve as the critical fact, just as it has done since Roe was decided; which is to say that no change in Roe's factual underpinning has left its central holding obsolete, and none supports an argument for overruling it. ...

The Court's duty in the present case is clear. In 1973, it confronted the already-divisive issue of governmental power to limit personal choice to undergo abortion, for which it provided a new resolution based on the due process guaranteed by the Fourteenth Amendment. Whether or not a new social consensus is developing on that issue, its divisiveness is no less today than in 1973, and pressure to overrule the decision, like pressure to retain it, has grown only more intense. A decision to overrule Roe's essential holding under the existing circumstances would address error, if error there was, at the cost of both profound and unnecessary damage to the Court's legitimacy, and to the Nation's commitment to the rule of law. It is therefore imperative to adhere to the essence of Roe's original decision, and we do so today.

IV

From what we have said so far, it follows that it is a constitutional liberty of the woman to have some freedom to terminate her pregnancy. ... Liberty must not be extinguished for want of a line that is clear. And it falls to us to give some real substance to the woman's liberty to determine whether to carry her pregnancy to full term.

We conclude the line should be drawn at viability, so that, before that time, the woman has a right to choose to terminate her pregnancy. We adhere to this principle for two reasons. First ... is the doctrine of stare decisis. Any judicial act of line-drawing may seem somewhat arbitrary, but Roe was a reasoned statement, elaborated with great care. We have twice reaffirmed it in the face of great opposition. ...

The second reason is that the concept of viability, as we noted in Roe, is the time at which there is a realistic possibility of maintaining and nourishing a life outside the womb, so that the independent existence of the second life can, in reason and all fairness, be the object of state protection that now overrides the rights of the woman. ... We must justify the lines we draw. And there is no line other than viability which is more workable. To be sure, as we have said, there may be some medical developments that affect the precise point of viability, see supra, but this is an imprecision within tolerable limits, given that the medical community and all those who must apply its discoveries will continue to explore the matter. The viability line also has, as a practical matter, an element of fairness. In some broad sense, it might be said that a woman who fails to act before viability has consented to the State's intervention on behalf of the developing child.

The woman's right to terminate her pregnancy before viability is the most central principle of Roe v. Wade. It is a rule of law and a component of liberty we cannot renounce. ...

Yet it must be remembered that Roe v. Wade speaks with clarity in establishing not only the woman's liberty but also the State's "important and legitimate interest in potential life." That portion of the decision in Roe has been given too little acknowledgment and implementation by the Court in its subsequent cases.

Roe established a trimester framework to govern abortion regulations. Under this elaborate but rigid construct, almost no regulation at all is permitted during the first trimester of pregnancy; regulations designed to protect the woman's health, but not to further the State's interest in potential life, are permitted during the second trimester; and, during the third trimester, when the fetus is viable, prohibitions are permitted provided the life or health of the mother is not at stake. Most of our cases since Roe have involved the application of rules derived from the trimester framework.

The trimester framework no doubt was erected to ensure that the woman's right to choose not become so subordinate to the State's interest in promoting fetal life that her choice exists in theory, but not in fact. We do not agree, however, that the trimester approach is necessary to accomplish this objective. A framework of this rigidity was unnecessary, and, in its later interpretation, sometimes contradicted the State's permissible exercise of its powers.

Though the woman has a right to choose to terminate or continue her pregnancy before viability, it does not at all follow that the State is prohibited from taking steps to ensure that this choice is thoughtful and informed. Even in the earliest stages of pregnancy, the State may enact rules and regulations designed to encourage her to know that there are philosophic and social arguments of great weight that can be brought to bear in favor of continuing the pregnancy to full term, and that there are procedures and institutions to allow adoption of unwanted children as well as a certain degree of state assistance if the mother chooses to raise the child herself. ...

...Numerous forms of state regulation might have the incidental effect of increasing the cost or decreasing the availability of medical care, whether for abortion or any other medical procedure. The fact that a law which serves a valid purpose, one not designed to strike at the right itself, has the incidental effect of making it more difficult or more expensive to procure an abortion cannot be enough to invalidate it. Only where state regulation imposes an undue burden on a woman's ability to make this decision does the power of the State reach into the heart of the liberty protected by the Due Process Clause.

...Before viability, Roe and subsequent cases treat all governmental attempts to influence a woman's decision on behalf of the potential life within her as unwarranted. This treatment is, in our judgment, incompatible with the recognition that there is a substantial state interest in potential life throughout pregnancy.

The very notion that the State has a substantial interest in potential life leads to the conclusion that not all regulations must be deemed unwarranted. Not all burdens on the right to decide whether to terminate a pregnancy will be undue. In our view, the undue burden standard is the appropriate means of reconciling the State's interest with the woman's constitutionally protected liberty. ...

...We give this summary:

a. To protect the central right recognized by Roe v. Wade while at the same time accommodating the State's profound interest in potential life, we will employ the undue burden analysis as explained in this opinion. An undue burden exists, and therefore a provision of law is invalid, if its purpose or effect is to place a substantial obstacle in the path of a woman seeking an abortion before the fetus attains viability.

b. We reject the rigid trimester framework of Roe v. Wade. To promote the State's profound interest in potential life, throughout pregnancy, the State may take measures to ensure that the woman's choice is informed, and measures designed to advance this interest will not be invalidated as long as their purpose is to persuade the woman to choose childbirth over abortion. These measures must not be an undue burden on the right.

c. As with any medical procedure, the State may enact regulations to further the health or safety of a woman seeking an abortion. Unnecessary health regulations that have the purpose or effect of presenting a substantial obstacle to a woman seeking an abortion impose an undue burden on the right.

d. Our adoption of the undue burden analysis does not disturb the central holding of Roe v. Wade, and we reaffirm that holding. Regardless of whether exceptions are made for particular circumstances, a State may not prohibit any woman from making the ultimate decision to terminate her pregnancy before viability.

e. We also reaffirm Roe's holding that, "subsequent to viability, the State, in promoting its interest in the potentiality of human life, may, if it chooses, regulate, and even proscribe, abortion except where it is necessary, in appropriate medical judgment, for the preservation of the life or health of the mother."

These principles control our assessment of the Pennsylvania statute, and we now turn to the issue of the validity of its challenged provisions.

V

The Court of Appeals applied what it believed to be the undue burden standard, and upheld each of the provisions except for the husband notification requirement. We agree generally with this conclusion, but refine the undue burden analysis in accordance with the principles articulated above. We now consider the separate statutory sections at issue.

(A)

We [now] consider the informed consent requirement. Section 3205. Except in a medical emergency, the statute requires that at least 24 hours before performing an abortion a physician inform the woman of the nature of the procedure, the health risks of the abortion and of childbirth, and the "probable gestational age of the unborn child." The physician or a qualified nonphysician must inform the woman of the availability of printed materials published by the State describing the fetus and providing information about medical assistance for childbirth, information about child support from the father, and a list of agencies which provide adoption and other services as alternatives to abortion. An abortion may not be performed unless the woman certifies in writing that she has been informed of the availability of these printed materials and has been provided them if she chooses to view them.

Our prior decisions establish that, as with any medical procedure, the State may require a woman to give her written informed consent to an abortion. ...

In *Akron* v. *Akron Center for Reproductive Health, Inc.* (1983) (*Akron I.*) we invalidated an ordinance which required that a woman seeking an abortion be provided by her physician with specific information "designed to influence the woman's informed choice between abortion or childbirth." As we later described the *Akron I* holding in *Thornburgh* v. *American College of Obstetricians and Gynecologists*, there were two purported flaws in the Akron ordinance: the information was designed to dissuade the woman from having an abortion, and the ordinance imposed "a rigid requirement that a specific body of information be given in all cases, irrespective of the particular needs of the patient. ..."

...It cannot be questioned that psychological wellbeing is a facet of health. Nor can it be doubted that most women considering an abortion would deem the impact on the fetus relevant, if not dispositive, to the decision. In attempting to ensure that a woman apprehend the full consequences of her decision, the State furthers the legitimate purpose of reducing the risk that a woman may elect an abortion, only to discover later, with devastating psychological consequences, that her decision was not fully informed. If the information the State requires to be made available to the woman is truthful and not misleading, the requirement may be permissible.

We also see no reason why the State may not require doctors to inform a woman seeking an abortion of the availability of materials relating to the consequences to the fetus, even when those consequences have no direct relation to her health. An example illustrates the point. We would think it constitutional for the State to require that, in order for there to be informed consent to a kidney transplant operation, the recipient must be supplied with information about risks to the donor as well as risks to himself or herself. A requirement that the physician make available information similar to that mandated by the statute here was described in *Thornburgh* as an outright attempt to wedge the Commonwealth's message discouraging abortion into the privacy of the informed consent dialogue between the woman and her physician. We conclude, however, that informed choice need not be defined in such narrow terms that all considerations of the effect on the fetus are made irrelevant. As we have made clear, we depart from the holdings of *Akron I* and *Thornburgh* to the extent that we permit a State to further its legitimate goal of protecting the life of the unborn by enacting legislation aimed at ensuring a decision that is mature and informed, even when, in so doing, the State expresses a preference for childbirth over abortion. In short, requiring that the woman be informed of the availability of information relating to fetal development and the assistance available should she decide to carry the pregnancy to full term is a reasonable measure to ensure an informed choice, one which might cause the woman to choose childbirth over abortion. This requirement cannot be considered a substantial obstacle to obtaining an abortion, and, it follows, there is no undue burden. ...

The Pennsylvania statute also requires us to reconsider the holding in *Akron I* that the State may not require that a physician, as opposed to a qualified assistant, provide information relevant to a woman's informed consent. Since there is no evidence on this record that requiring a doctor to give the information as provided by the statute would amount, in practical terms, to a substantial obstacle to a woman seeking an abortion, we conclude that it is not an undue burden. ...

Our analysis of Pennsylvania's 24-hour waiting period between the provision of the information deemed necessary to informed consent and the performance of an abortion under the undue burden standard requires us to reconsider the premise behind the decision in *Akron I* invalidating a parallel requirement. In *Akron I* we said: Nor are we convinced that the State's legitimate concern that the woman's decision be informed is reasonably served by requiring a 24-hour delay as a matter of course. We consider that conclusion to be wrong. The idea that important decisions will be more informed and deliberate if they follow some period of reflection does not strike us as unreasonable, particularly where the statute directs that important information become part of the background of the decision. The statute, as construed by the Court of Appeals, permits avoidance of the waiting period in the event of a medical emergency, and the record evidence shows that, in the vast majority of cases, a 24-hour delay does not create any appreciable health risk. In theory, at least, the waiting period is a reasonable measure to implement the State's interest in protecting the life of the unborn, a measure that does not amount to an undue burden.

Whether the mandatory 24-hour waiting period is nonetheless invalid because, in practice, it is a substantial obstacle to a woman's choice to terminate her pregnancy is a closer question. The findings of fact by the District Court indicate that, because of the distances many women must travel to reach an abortion provider, the practical effect will often be a delay of much more than a day because the waiting period requires that a woman seeking an abortion make at least two visits to the doctor. The District Court also found that, in many instances, this will increase the exposure of women seeking abortions to "the harassment and hostility of anti-abortion protestors demonstrating outside a clinic." As a result, the District Court found that, for those women who have the fewest financial resources, those who must travel long distances, and those who have difficulty explaining their whereabouts to husbands, employers, or others, the 24-hour waiting period will be "particularly burdensome."

These findings are troubling in some respects, but they do not demonstrate that the waiting period constitutes an undue burden. ...

(B)

Section 3209 of Pennsylvania's abortion law provides, except in cases of medical emergency, that no physician shall perform an abortion on a married woman without receiving a signed statement from the woman that she has notified her spouse that she is about to undergo an abortion. The woman has the option of providing an alternative signed statement certifying that her husband is not the man who impregnated her; that her husband could not be located; that the pregnancy is the result of spousal sexual assault which she has reported; or that the woman believes that notifying her husband will cause him or someone else to inflict bodily injury upon her. A physician who performs an abortion on a married woman without receiving the appropriate signed statement will have his or her license revoked, and is liable to the husband for damages. …

…In well-functioning marriages, spouses discuss important intimate decisions such as whether to bear a child. But there are millions of women in this country who are the victims of regular physical and psychological abuse at the hands of their husbands. Should these women become pregnant, they may have very good reasons for not wishing to inform their husbands of their decision to obtain an abortion. Many may have justifiable fears of physical abuse, but may be no less fearful of the consequences of reporting prior abuse to the Commonwealth of Pennsylvania. Many may have a reasonable fear that notifying their husbands will provoke further instances of child abuse; these women are not exempt from Section 3209's notification requirement. Many may fear devastating forms of psychological abuse from their husbands, including verbal harassment, threats of future violence, the destruction of possessions, physical confinement to the home, the withdrawal of financial support, or the disclosure of the abortion to family and friends. These methods of psychological abuse may act as even more of a deterrent to notification than the possibility of physical violence, but women who are the victims of the abuse are not exempt from Section 3209's notification requirement. And many women who are pregnant as a result of sexual assaults by their husbands will be unable to avail themselves of the exception for spousal sexual assault, because the exception requires that the woman have notified law enforcement authorities within 90 days of the assault, and her husband will be notified of her report once an investigation begins. If anything in this field is certain, it is that victims of spousal sexual assault are extremely reluctant to report the abuse to the government; hence, a great many spousal rape victims will not be exempt from the notification requirement imposed by Section 3209.

(C)

We next consider the parental consent provision. Except in a medical emergency, an unemancipated young woman under 18 may not obtain an abortion unless she and one of her parents (or guardian) provides informed consent as defined above. If neither a parent nor a guardian provides consent, a court may authorize the performance of an abortion upon a determination that the young woman is mature and capable of giving informed consent and has, in fact, given her informed consent, or that an abortion would be in her best interests.

We have been over most of this ground before. Our cases establish, and we reaffirm today, that a State may require a minor seeking an abortion to obtain the consent of a parent or guardian, provided that there is an adequate judicial bypass procedure. Under these precedents, in our view, the one-parent consent requirement and judicial bypass procedure are constitutional.

The only argument made by petitioners respecting this provision and to which our prior decisions do not speak is the contention that the parental consent requirement is invalid because it requires informed parental consent. For the most part, petitioners' argument is a reprise of their argument with respect to the informed consent requirement in general, and we reject it for the reasons given above. Indeed, some of the provisions regarding informed consent have particular force with respect to minors: the waiting period, for example, may provide the parent or parents of a pregnant young woman the opportunity to consult with her in private, and to discuss the consequences of her decision in the context of the values and moral or religious principles of their family.

WHY ABORTION IS IMMORAL

Don Marquis

The view that abortion is, with rare exceptions, seriously immoral has received little support in the recent philosophical literature. No doubt most philosophers affiliated with secular institutions of higher education believe that the anti-abortion position is either a symptom of irrational religious dogma or a conclusion generated by seriously confused philosophical argument. The purpose of this essay is to undermine this general belief. This essay sets out an argument that purports to show, as well as any argument in ethics can show, that abortion is, except possibly in rare cases, seriously immoral, that it is in the same moral category as killing an innocent adult human being. ...

...[A] necessary condition of resolving the abortion controversy is a more theoretical account of the wrongness of killing. After all, if we merely believe, but do not understand, why killing adult human beings such as ourselves is wrong, how could we conceivably show that abortion is either immoral or permissible?

In order to develop such an account, we can start from the following unproblematic assumption concerning our own case: it is wrong to kill *us*. Why is it wrong? Some answers can be easily eliminated. It might be said that what makes killing us wrong is that a killing brutalizes the one who kills. But the brutalization consists of being inured to the performance of an act that is hideously immoral; hence, the brutalization does not explain the immorality. It might be said that what makes killing us wrong is the great loss others would experience due to our absence. Although such hubris is understandable, such an explanation does not account for the wrongness of killing hermits, or those whose lives are relatively independent and whose friends find it easy to make new friends.

A more obvious answer is better. What primarily makes killing wrong is neither its effect on the murderer nor its effect on the victim's friends and relatives, but its effect on the victim. The loss of one's life is one of the greatest losses one can suffer. The loss of one's life deprives one of all the experiences, activities, projects, and enjoyments that would otherwise have constituted one's future. Therefore, killing someone is wrong, primarily because the killing inflicts (one of) the greatest possible losses on the victim. To describe this as the loss of life can be misleading, however. The change in my biological state does not by itself make killing me wrong. The effect of the loss of my biological life is the loss to me of all those activities, projects, experiences, and enjoyments which would otherwise have constituted my future personal life. These activities, projects, experiences, and enjoyments are either valuable for their own sakes or are means to something else that is valuable for its own sake. Some parts of my future are not valued by me now, but will come to be valued by me as I grow older and as my values and capacities change. When I am killed, I am deprived both of what I now value which would have been part of my future personal life, but also what I would come to value. Therefore, when I die, I am deprived of all of the value of my future. Inflicting this loss on me is ultimately what makes killing me wrong. This being the case, it would seem that what makes killing *any* adult human being prima facie seriously wrong is the loss of his or her future.[1]...

The claim that what makes killing wrong is the loss of the victim's future is directly supported by two considerations. In the first place, this theory explains why we regard killing as

Reprinted with permission of the author and the publisher from the *Journal of Philosophy*, vol. 86 (April 1989).

one of the worst of crimes. Killing is especially wrong, because it deprives the victim of more than perhaps any other crime. In the second place, people with AIDS or cancer who know they are dying believe, of course, that dying is a very bad thing for them. They believe that the loss of a future to them that they would otherwise have experienced is what makes their premature death a very bad thing for them. A better theory of the wrongness of killing would require a different natural property associated with killing which better fits with the attitudes of the dying. What could it be?

The view that what makes killing wrong is the loss to the victim of the value of the victim's future gains additional support when some of its implications are examined. In the first place, it is incompatible with the view that it is wrong to kill only beings who are biologically human. It is possible that there exists a different species from another planet whose members have a future like ours. Since having a future like that is what makes killing someone wrong, this theory entails that it would be wrong to kill members of such a species. Hence, this theory is opposed to the claim that only life that is biologically human has great moral worth, a claim which many antiabortionists have seemed to adopt. This opposition, which this theory has in common with personhood theories, seems to be a merit of the theory.

In the second place, the claim that the loss of one's future is the wrong-making feature of one's being killed entails the possibility that the futures of some actual nonhuman mammals on our own planet are sufficiently like ours that it is seriously wrong to kill them also. Whether some animals do have the same right to life as human beings depends on adding to the account of the wrongness of killing some additional account of just what it is about my future or the futures of other adult human beings which makes it wrong to kill us. No such additional account will be offered in this essay. Undoubtedly, the provision of such an account would be a very difficult matter. Undoubtedly, any such account would be quite controversial. Hence, it surely should not reflect badly on this sketch of an elementary theory of the wrongness of killing that it is indeterminate with respect to some very difficult issues regarding animal rights.

In the third place, the claim that the loss of one's future is the wrong-making feature of one's being killed does not entail, as sanctity of human life theories do, that active euthanasia is wrong. Persons who are severely and incurably ill, who face a future of pain and despair, and who wish to die will not have suffered a loss if they are killed. It is, strictly speaking, the value of a human's future which makes killing wrong in this theory. This being so, killing does not necessarily wrong some persons who are sick and dying. Of course, there may be other reasons for a prohibition of active euthanasia, but that is another matter. Sanctity-of-human-life theories seem to hold that active euthanasia is seriously wrong even in an individual case where there seems to be good reason for it independently of public policy considerations. This consequence is most implausible, and it is a plus for the claim that the loss of a future of value is what makes killing wrong that it does not share this consequence.

In the fourth place, the account of the wrongness of killing defended in this essay does straightforwardly entail that it is prima facie seriously wrong to kill children and infants, for we do presume that they have futures of value. Since we do believe that it is wrong to kill defenseless little babies, it is important that a theory of the wrongness of killing easily account for this. Personhood theories of the wrongness of killing, on the other hand, cannot straightforwardly account for the wrongness of killing infants and young children.[2] Hence, such theories must add special ad hoc accounts of the wrongness of killing the young. The plausibility of such ad hoc theories seems to be a function of how desperately one wants such theories to work. The claim that the primary wrong-making feature of a killing is the loss to the victim of the value of its future accounts for the wrongness of killing young children and infants directly; it makes the wrongness of such acts as obvious as we actually think it is. This is a further merit of this theory. Accordingly, it seems that this value of a future-like-ours theory of the wrongness of killing shares strengths of both sanctity-of-life and personhood accounts while avoiding weaknesses of both. In addition, it meshes with a central intuition concerning what makes killing wrong.

The claim that the primary wrong-making feature of a killing is the loss to the victim of the value of its future has obvious consequences for the ethics of abortion. The future of a standard fetus includes a set of experiences, projects, activities, and such which are identical with the futures of adult human beings and are identical with the futures of young children. Since the reason that is sufficient to explain why it is wrong to kill human beings after the time of birth is a reason that also applies to fetuses, it follows that abortion is prima facie seriously morally wrong.

This argument does not rely on the invalid inference that, since it is wrong to kill persons, it is wrong to kill potential persons also. The category that is morally central to this analysis is the category of having a valuable future like ours; it is not the category of personhood. The argument to the conclusion that abortion is prima facie seriously morally wrong proceeded independently of the notion of person or potential person or any equivalent. ...

Of course, this value of a future-like-ours argument, if sound, shows only that abortion is prima facie wrong, not that it is wrong in any and all circumstances. Since the loss of the future to a standard fetus, if killed, is, however, at least as great a loss as the loss of the future to a standard adult human being who is killed, abortion, like ordinary killing, could be justified only by the most compelling reasons. The loss of one's life is almost the greatest misfortune that can happen to one. Presumably abortion could be justified in some circumstances, only if the loss consequent on failing to abort would be at least as great. Accordingly, morally permissible abortions will be rare indeed unless, perhaps, they occur so early in pregnancy that a fetus is not yet definitely an individual. Hence, this argument should be taken as showing that abortion is presumptively very seriously wrong, where the presumption is very strong—as strong as the presumption that killing another adult human being is wrong. ...

In this essay, it has been argued that the correct ethic of the wrongness of killing can be extended to fetal life and used to show that there is a strong presumption that any abortion is morally impermissible. If the ethic of killing adopted here entails, however, that contraception is also seriously immoral, then there would appear to be a difficulty with the analysis of this essay.

But this analysis does not entail that contraception is wrong. Of course, contraception prevents the actualization of a possible future of value. Hence, it follows from the claim that futures of value should be maximized that contraception is prima facie immoral. This obligation to maximize does not exist, however; furthermore, nothing in the ethics of killing in this paper entails that it does. The ethics of killing in this essay would entail that contraception is wrong only if something were denied a human future of value by contraception. Nothing at all is denied such a future by contraception, however.

Candidates for a subject of harm by contraception fall into four categories: (1) some sperm or other, (2) some ovum or other, (3) a sperm and an ovum separately, and (4) a sperm and an ovum together. Assigning the harm to some sperm is utterly arbitrary, for no reason can be given for making a sperm the subject of harm rather than an ovum. Assigning the harm to some ovum is utterly arbitrary, for no reason can be given for making an ovum the subject of harm rather than a sperm. One might attempt to avoid these problems by insisting that contraception deprives both the sperm and the ovum separately of a valuable future like ours. On this alternative, too many futures are lost.

Contraception was supposed to be wrong, because it deprived us of one future of value, not two. One might attempt to avoid this problem by holding that contraception deprives the combination of sperm and ovum of a valuable future like ours. But here the definite article misleads. At the time of contraception, there are hundreds of millions of sperm, one (released) ovum and millions of possible combinations of all of these. There is no actual combination at all. Is the subject of the loss to be a merely possible combination? Which one? This alternative does not yield an actual subject of harm either. Accordingly, the immorality of contraception is not entailed by the loss of a future-like-ours argument simply because there is no nonarbitrarily identifiable subject of the loss in the case of contraception.

The purpose of this essay has been to set out an argument for the serious presumptive wrongness of abortion subject to the assumption that the moral permissibility of abortion stands or falls on the moral status of the fetus. Since a fetus possesses a property, the possession of which in adult human beings is sufficient to make killing an adult human being wrong, abortion is wrong. …

Notes

1. I have been most influenced on this matter by Jonathan Glover, *Causing Death and Saving Lives* (New York: Penguin, 1977), ch. 3; and Robert Young, "What Is So Wrong with Killing People?" *Philosophy*, I.IV, 210 (1979): 515–528.
2. Feinberg, Tooley, Warren, and Engelhardt have all dealt with this problem.

ON THE MORAL AND LEGAL STATUS OF ABORTION

Mary Anne Warren

We will be concerned with both the moral status of abortion, which for our purposes we may define as the act which a woman performs in voluntarily terminating, or allowing another person to terminate, her pregnancy, and the legal status which is appropriate for this act. I will argue that, while it is not possible to produce a satisfactory defense of a woman's right to obtain an abortion without showing that a fetus is not a human being, in the morally relevant sense of that term, we ought not to conclude that the difficulties involved in determining whether or not a fetus is human make it impossible to produce any satisfactory solution to the problem of the moral status of abortion. For it is possible to show that, on the basis of intuitions which we may expect even the opponents of abortion to share, a fetus is not a person, and hence not the sort of entity to which it is proper to ascribe full moral rights.

The question which we must answer in order to produce a satisfactory solution to the problem of the moral status of abortion is this: How are we to define the moral community, the set of beings with full and equal moral rights, such that we can decide whether a human fetus is a member of this community or not? What sort of entity, exactly, has the inalienable rights to life, liberty, and the pursuit of happiness? Jefferson attributed these rights to all *men*, and it may or may not be fair to suggest that he intended to attribute them *only* to men. Perhaps he ought to have attributed them to all human beings. If so, then we arrive, first, at Noonan's problem of defining what makes a being human, and, second, at the equally vital question which Noonan does not consider, namely, What reason is there for identifying the moral community with the set of all human beings, in whatever way we have chosen to define that term?

1. On the Definition of "Human"

One reason why this vital second question is so frequently overlooked in the debate over the moral status of abortion is that the term "human" has two distinct, but not often distinguished, senses. This fact results in a slide of meaning, which serves to conceal the fallaciousness of the traditional argument that since (1) it is wrong to kill innocent human beings, and (2) fetuses are innocent human beings, then (3) it is wrong to kill fetuses. For if "human" is used in the same sense in both (1) and (2) then, whichever of the two senses is meant, one of these premises is question-begging. And if it is used in two different senses then of course the conclusion doesn't follow.

Thus, (1) is a self-evident moral truth,[1] and avoids begging the question about abortion, only if "human being" is used to mean something like "a full-fledged member of the moral community." (It may or may not also be meant to refer exclusively to members of the species *Homo sapiens*.) We may call this the *moral* sense of "human." It is not to be confused with what we will call the *genetic* sense, i.e., the sense in which *any* member of the species is a human being, and no member of any other species could be. If (1) is acceptable only if the moral sense is intended, (2) is non-question-begging only if what is intended is the genetic sense.

In "Deciding Who is Human," Noonan argues for the classification of fetuses with human beings by pointing to the presence of the full genetic code, and the potential capacity for rational thought (p. 135). It is clear that what he needs to show, for his version of the traditional argument to be valid, is that fetuses are human in the moral sense, the sense in which it is analytically true that all human beings have full moral rights. But, in the absence of any argument showing that whatever is genetically human is also morally human, and he gives none, nothing more than genetic humanity can be demonstrated by the presence of the human genetic code. And, as we will see, the *potential* capacity for rational thought can at most show that an entity has the potential for *becoming* human in the moral sense.

2. Defining the Moral Community

Can it be established that genetic humanity is sufficient for moral humanity? I think that there are very good reasons for not defining the moral community in this way. I would like to suggest an alternative way of defining the moral community, which I will argue for only to the extent of explaining why it is, or should be, self-evident. The suggestion is simply that the moral community consists of all and only *people*, rather than all and only human beings;[2] and probably the best way of demonstrating its self-evidence is by considering the concept of personhood, to see what sorts of entity are and are not persons, and what the decision that a being is or is not a person implies about its moral rights.

What characteristics entitle an entity to be considered a person? This is obviously not the place to attempt a complete analysis of the concept of personhood, but we do not need such a fully adequate analysis just to determine whether and why a fetus is or isn't a person. All we need is a rough and approximate list of the most basic criteria of personhood, and some idea of which, or how many, of these an entity must satisfy in order to properly be considered a person.

In searching for such criteria, it is useful to look beyond the set of people with whom we are acquainted, and ask how we would decide whether a totally alien being was a person or not. (For we have no right to assume that genetic humanity is necessary for personhood.) Imagine a space traveler who lands on an unknown planet and encounters a race of beings utterly unlike any he has ever seen or heard of. If he wants to be sure of behaving morally toward these beings, he has to somehow decide whether they are people, and hence have full moral rights, or whether they are the sort of thing which he need not feel guilty about treating as, for example, a source of food.

How should he go about making this decision? If he has some anthropological background, he might look for such things as religion, art, and the manufacturing of tools, weapons, or shelters, since these factors have been used to distinguish our human from our prehuman ancestors, in what seems to be closer to the moral than the genetic sense of "human." And no doubt he would be right to consider the presence of such factors as good evidence that the alien beings were people, and morally human. It would, however, be overly anthropocentric of him to take the absence of these things as adequate evidence that they were not, since we can imagine people who have progressed beyond, or evolved without ever developing, these cultural characteristics.

I suggest that the traits which are most central to the concept of personhood, or humanity in the moral sense, are, very roughly, the following:

1. consciousness (of objects and events external and/or internal to the being), and in particular the capacity to feel pain;
2. reasoning (the *developed* capacity to solve new and relatively complex problem);
3. self-motivated activity (activity which is relatively independent of either genetic or direct external control);
4. the capacity to communicate, by whatever means, messages of an indefinite variety of types, that is, not just with an indefinite number of possible contents, but on indefinitely many possible topics;
5. the presence of self-concepts, and self-awareness, either individual or racial, or both.

Admittedly, there are apt to be a great many problems involved in formulating precise definitions of these criteria, let alone in developing universally valid behavioral criteria for deciding when they apply. But I will assume that both we and our explorer know approximately what (1)–(5) mean, and that he is also able to determine whether or not they apply. How, then, should he use his findings to decide whether or not the alien beings are people? We needn't suppose that an entity must have *all* of these attributes to be properly considered a person; (1) and (2) alone may well be sufficient for personhood, and quite probably (1)–(3) are sufficient. Neither do we need to insist that any one of these criteria is *necessary* for personhood, although once again (1) and (2) look like fairly good candidates for necessary conditions, as does (3), if "activity" is construed so as to include the activity of reasoning.

All we need to claim, to demonstrate that a fetus is not a person, is that any being which satisfies *none* of (1)–(5) is certainly not a person. I consider this claim to be so obvious that I think anyone who denied it, and claimed that a being which satisfied none of (1)–(5) was a person all the same, would thereby demonstrate that he had no notion at all of what a person is—perhaps because he had confused the concept of a person with that of genetic humanity. If the opponents of abortion were to deny the appropriateness of these five criteria, I do not know what further arguments would convince them. We would probably have to admit that our conceptual schemes were indeed irreconcilably different, and that our dispute could not be settled objectively.

I do not expect this to happen, however, since I think that the concept of a person is one which is very nearly universal (to people), and that it is common to both proabortionists and antiabortionists, even though neither group has fully realized the relevance of this concept to the resolution of their dispute. Furthermore, I think that on reflection even the antiabortionists ought to agree not only that (1)–(5) are central to the concept of personhood, but also that it is a part of this concept that all and only people have full moral rights. The concept of a person is in part a moral concept; once we have admitted that *x* is a person we have recognized, even if we have not agreed to respect, *x*'s right to be treated as a member of the moral community. It is true that the claim that *x* is a *human being* is more commonly voiced as part of an appeal to treat *x* decently than is the claim that *x* is a person, but this is either because "human being" is here used in the sense which implies personhood, or because the genetic and moral senses of "human" have been confused.

Now if (1)–(5) are indeed the primary criteria of personhood, then it is clear that genetic humanity is neither necessary nor sufficient for establishing that an entity is a person. Some human beings are not people, and there may well be people who are not human beings. A man or woman whose consciousness has been permanently obliterated but who remains alive is a human being which is no longer a person; defective human beings, with no appreciable mental capacity, are not and presumably never will be people; and a fetus is a human being which is not yet a person, and which therefore cannot coherently be said to have full moral rights. Citizens of the next century should be prepared to recognize highly advanced, self-aware robots or computers, should such be developed, and intelligent inhabitants of other worlds, should such be found, as people in the fullest sense, and to respect their moral rights. But to ascribe full moral rights to an entity which is not a person is as absurd as to ascribe moral obligations and responsibilities to such an entity.

3. Fetal Development and the Right to Life

Two problems arise in the application of these suggestions for the definition of the moral community to the determination of the precise moral status of a human fetus. Given that the paradigm example of a person is a normal adult human being, then (1) How like this paradigm, in particular how far advanced since conception, does a human being need to be before it begins to have a right to life by virtue, not of being fully a person as of yet, but of being *like* a person? and (2) To what extent, if any, does the fact that a fetus has the *potential* for becoming a person endow it with some of the same rights? Each of these questions requires some comment.

In answering the first question, we need not attempt a detailed consideration of the moral rights of organisms which are not developed enough, aware enough, intelligent enough, etc., to be considered people, but which resemble people in some respects. It does seem reasonable to suggest that the more like a person, in the relevant respects, a being is, the stronger is the case for regarding it as having a right to life, and indeed the stronger its right to life is. Thus we ought to take seriously the suggestion that, insofar as "the human individual develops biologically in a continuous fashion … the rights of a human person might develop in the same way."[3] But we must keep in mind that the attributes which are relevant in determining whether or not an entity is enough like a person to be regarded as having some of the same moral rights are no different from those which are relevant to determining whether or not it is fully a person—i.e., are no different from (1)–(5)—and that being genetically human, or having recognizably human facial and other physical features, or detectable brain activity, or the capacity to survive outside the uterus, are simply not among these relevant attributes.

Thus it is clear that even though a seven- or eight-month fetus has features which make it apt to arouse in us almost the same powerful protective instinct as is commonly aroused by a small infant, nevertheless it is not significantly more personlike than is a very small embryo. It is *somewhat* more personlike; it can apparently feel and respond to pain, and it may even have a rudimentary form of consciousness, insofar as its brain is quite active. Nevertheless, it seems safe to say that it is not fully conscious, in the way that an infant of a few months is, and that it cannot reason, or communicate messages of indefinitely many sorts, does not engage in self-motivated activity, and has no self-awareness. Thus, in the *relevant* respects, a fetus, even a fully developed one, is considerably less personlike than is the average mature mammal, indeed the average fish. And I think that a rational person must conclude that if the right to life of a fetus is to be based upon its resemblance to a person, then it cannot be said to have any more right to life than, let us say, a newborn guppy (which also seems to be capable of feeling pain), and that a right of that magnitude could never override a woman's right to obtain an abortion, at any stage of her pregnancy.

There may, of course, be other arguments in favor of placing legal limits upon the stage of pregnancy in which an abortion may be performed. Given the relative safety of the new techniques of artifically inducing labor during the third trimester, the danger to the woman's life or health is no longer such an argument. Neither is the fact that people tend to respond to the thought of abortion in the later stages of pregnancy with emotional repulsion, since mere emotional responses cannot take the place of moral reasoning in determining what ought to be permitted. Nor, finally, is the frequently heard argument that legalizing abortion, especially late in the pregnancy, may erode the level of respect for human life, leading, perhaps, to an increase in unjustified euthanasia and other crimes. For this threat, if it is a threat, can be better met by educating people to the kinds of moral distinctions which we are making here than by limiting access to abortion (which limitation may, in its disregard for the rights of women, be just as damaging to the level of respect for human rights).

Thus, since the fact that even a fully developed fetus is not personlike enough to have any significant right to life on the basis of its personlikeness shows that no legal restrictions upon the stage of pregnancy in which an abortion may be performed can be justified on the grounds that we should protect the rights of the older fetus; and since there is no other apparent justification for such restrictions, we may conclude that they are entirely unjustified. Whether or not it would be *indecent* (whatever that means) for a woman in her seventh month to obtain an abortion just to avoid having to postpone a trip to Europe, it would not, in itself, be *immoral*, and therefore it ought to be permitted.

4. Potential Personhood and the Right to Life

We have seen that a fetus does not resemble a person in any way which can support the claim that it has even some of the same rights. But what about its *potential*, the fact that if nurtured and allowed to develop naturally it will very probably become a person? Doesn't that alone give it at least some right to life? It is hard to deny that the fact that an entity is a potential person is a strong prima facie reason for not destroying it; but we need not conclude from this that a potential person has a right to life, by virtue of that potential. It may be that our feeling that it is better, other things being equal, not to destroy a potential person is better explained by the fact that potential people are still (felt to be) an invaluable resource, not to be lightly squandered. Surely, if every speck of dust were a potential person, we would be much less apt to conclude that every potential person has a right to become actual.

Still, we do not need to insist that a potential person has no right to life whatever. There may well be something immoral, and not just imprudent, about wantonly destroying potential people, when doing so isn't necessary to protect anyone's rights. But even if a potential person does have some prima facie right to life, such a right could not possibly outweigh the right of a woman to obtain an abortion, since the rights of any actual person invariably outweigh those of any potential person, whenever the two conflict. Since this may not be immediately obvious in the case of a human fetus, let us look at another case.

Suppose that our space explorer falls into the hands of an alien culture, whose scientists decide to create a few hundred thousand or more human beings, by breaking his body into its component cells, and using these to create fully developed human beings, with, of course, his genetic code. We may imagine that each of these newly created men will have all of the original man's abilities, skills, knowledge, and so on, and also have an individual self-concept, in short that each of them will be a bona fide (though hardly unique) person. Imagine that the whole project will take only seconds, and that its chances of success are extremely high, and that our explorer knows all of this, and also knows that these people will be treated fairly. I maintain that in such a situation he would have every right to escape if he could, and thus to deprive all of these potential people of their potential lives; for his right to life outweighs all of theirs together, in spite of the fact that they are all genetically human, all innocent, and all have a very high probability of becoming people very soon, if only he refrains from acting.

Indeed, I think he would have a right to escape even if it were not his life which the alien scientists planned to take, but only a year of his freedom, or, indeed, only a day. Nor would he be obligated to stay if he had gotten captured (thus bringing all these people-potentials into existence) because of his own carelessness, or even if he had done so deliberately, knowing the consequences. Regardless of how he got captured, he is not morally obligated to remain in captivity for *any* period of time for the sake of permitting any number of potential people to come into actuality, so great is the margin by which one actual person's right to liberty outweighs whatever right to life even a hundred thousand potential people have. And it seems reasonable to conclude that the rights of a woman will outweigh by a similar margin whatever right to life a fetus may have by virtue of its potential personhood.

Thus, neither a fetus's resemblance to a person, nor its potential for becoming a person provides any basis whatever for the claim that it has any significant right to life. Consequently, a woman's right to protect her health, happiness, freedom, and even her life,[4] by terminating an unwanted pregnancy, will always override whatever right to life it may be appropriate to ascribe to a fetus, even a fully developed one. And thus, in the absence of any overwhelming social need for every possible child, the laws which restrict the right to obtain an abortion, or limit the period of pregnancy during which an abortion may be performed, are a wholly unjustified violation of a woman's most basic moral and constitutional rights.[5]

Notes

1. Of course, the principle that it is (always) wrong to kill innocent human beings is in need of many other modifications, e.g., that it may be permissible to do so to save a greater number of other innocent human beings, but we may safely ignore these complications here.
2. From here on, we will use "human" to mean genetically human, since the moral sense seems closely connected to, and perhaps derived from, the assumption that genetic humanity is sufficient for membership in the moral community.
3. Thomas L. Hayes, "A Biological View," *Commonweal*, 85 (March 17, 1967), 677–78; quoted by Daniel Callahan, in *Abortion, Law, Choice, and Morality* (London: Macmillan & Co., 1970).
4. That is, insofar as the death rate, for the woman, is higher for childbirth than for early abortion.
5. My thanks to the following people, who were kind enough to read and criticize an earlier version of this paper: Herbert Gold, Gene Glass, Anne Lauterbach, Judith Thomson, Mary Mothersill, and Timothy Binkley.

POSTSCRIPT ON INFANTICIDE, FEBRUARY 26, 1982

Mary Anne Warren

One of the most troubling objections to the argument presented in this article is that it may appear to justify not only abortion but infanticide as well. A newborn infant is not a great deal more personlike than a nine-month fetus, and thus it might seem that if late-term abortion is sometimes justified, then infanticide must also be sometimes justified. Yet most people consider that infanticide is a form of murder, and thus never justified.

While it is important to appreciate the emotional force of this objection, its logical force is far less than it may seem at first glance. There are many reasons why infanticide is much more difficult to justify than abortion, even though if my argument is correct neither constitutes the killing of a person. In this country, and in this period of history, the deliberate killing of viable newborns is virtually never justified. This is in part because neonates are so very *close* to being persons that to kill them requires a very strong moral justification—as does the killing of dolphins, whales, chimpanzees, and other highly personlike creatures. It is certainly wrong to kill such beings just for the sake of convenience, or financial profit, or "sport."

Another reason why infanticide is usually wrong, in our society, is that if the newborn's parents do not want it, or are unable to care for it, there are (in most cases) people who are able and eager to adopt it and to provide a good home for it. Many people wait years for the opportunity to adopt a child, and some are unable to do so even though there is every reason to believe that they would be good parents. The needless destruction of a viable infant inevitably deprives some person or persons of a source of great pleasure and satisfaction, perhaps severely impoverishing their lives. Furthermore, even if an infant is considered to be unadoptable (e.g., because of some extremely severe mental or physical handicap) it is still wrong in most cases to kill it. For most of us value the lives of infants, and would prefer to pay taxes to support orphanages and state institutions for the handicapped rather than to allow unwanted infants to be killed. So long as most people feel this way, and so long as our society can afford to provide care for infants which are unwanted or which have special needs that preclude home care, it is wrong to destroy any infant which has a dance of living a reasonably satisfactory life.

If these arguments show that infanticide is wrong, at least in this society, then why don't they also show that late-term abortion is wrong? After all, third trimester fetuses are also highly personlike, and many people value them and would much prefer that they be preserved, even at some cost to themselves. As a potential source of pleasure to some family, a viable fetus is just as valuable as a viable infant. But there is an obvious and crucial difference between the two cases: once the infant is born, its continued life cannot (except, perhaps, in very exceptional cases) pose any serious threat to the woman's life or health, since she is free to put it up for adoption, or, where this is impossible, to place it in a state-supported institution. While she might prefer that it die, rather than being raised by others, it is not clear that such a preference would constitute a right on her part. True, she may suffer greatly from the knowledge that her child will be thrown into the lottery of the adoption system, and that she will be unable to ensure its well-being, or even to know whether it

Reprinted with permission from Mary Anne Warren, from *The Problem of Abortion*, edited by Joel Feinberg (Belmont, CA: Wadsworth, (CA) 1984).

is healthy, happy, doing well in school, etc.; for the law generally does not permit natural parents to remain in contact with their children, once they are adopted by another family. But there are surely better ways of dealing with these problems than by permitting infanticide in such cases. (It might help, for instance, if the natural parents of adopted children could at least receive some information about their progress, without necessarily being informed of the identity of the adopting family.)

In contrast, a pregnant woman's right to protect her own life and health clearly outweighs other people's desire that the fetus be preserved—just as, when a person's life or limb is threatened by some wild animal, and when the threat cannot be removed without killing the animal, the person's right to self-protection outweighs the desires of those who would prefer that the animal not be harmed. Thus, while the moment of birth may not mark any sharp discontinuity in the degree to which an infant possesses a right to life, it does mark the end of the mother's absolute right to determine its fate. Indeed, if and when a late-term abortion could be safely performed without killing the fetus, she would have no absolute right to insist on its death (e.g., if others wish to adopt it or to pay for its care), for the same reason that she does not have a right to insist that a viable infant be killed.

It remains true that according to my argument neither abortion nor the killing of neonates is properly considered a form of murder. Perhaps it is understandable that the law should classify infanticide as murder or homicide, since there is no other existing legal category which adequately or conveniently expresses the force of our society's disapproval of this action. But the moral distinction remains, and it has several important consequences.

In the first place, it implies that when an infant is born into a society which—unlike ours—is so impoverished that it simply cannot care for it adequately without endangering the survival of existing persons, killing it or allowing it to die is not necessarily wrong—provided that there is no *other* society which is willing and able to provide such care. Most human societies, from those at the hunting and gathering stage of economic development to the highly civilized Greeks and Romans, have permitted the practice of infanticide under such unfortunate circumstances, and I would argue that it shows a serious lack of understanding to condemn them as morally backward for this reason alone.

In the second place, the argument implies that when an infant is born with such severe physical anomalies that its life would predictably be a very short and/or very miserable one, even with the most heroic of medical treatment, and where its parents do not choose to bear the often crushing emotional, financial and other burdens attendant upon the artificial prolongation of such a tragic life, it is not morally wrong to cease or withhold treatment, thus allowing the infant a painless death. It is wrong (and sometimes a form of murder) to practice involuntary euthanasia on persons, since they have the right to decide for themselves whether or not they wish to continue to live. But terminally ill neonates cannot make this decision for themselves, and thus it is incumbent upon responsible persons to make the decision for them, as best they can. The mistaken belief that infanticide is always tantamount to murder is responsible for a great deal of unnecessary suffering, not just on the part of infants which are made to endure needlessly prolonged and painful deaths, but also on the part of parents, nurses, and other involved persons, who must watch infants suffering needlessly, helpless to end that suffering in the most humane way.

I am well aware that these conclusions, however modest and reasonable they may seem to some people, strike other people as morally monstrous, and that some people might even prefer to abandon their previous support for women's right to abortion rather than accept a theory which leads to such conclusions about infanticide. But all that these facts show is that abortion is not an isolated moral issue; to fully understand the moral status of abortion we may have to reconsider other moral issues as well, issues not just about infanticide and euthanasia, but also about the moral rights of women and of nonhuman animals. It is a philosopher's task to criticize mistaken beliefs which stand in the way of moral understanding, even when—perhaps especially when—those beliefs are popular and widespread. The belief that moral strictures against killing should apply equally to *all* genetically human entities, and *only* to genetically human entities, is such an error. The overcoming of this error will undoubtedly require long and often painful struggle; but it must be done.

INFANTICIDE AND THE LIBERAL VIEW ON ABORTION

Robert F. Card

I

Mary Anne Warren offers a classic defense of the liberal position in the abortion debate in her piece "On the Moral and Legal Status of Abortion." Warren's main argument consists of offering criteria for personhood which are intuitively plausible, yet exclude fetuses from being persons. A damaging criticism of this approach is that Warren's criteria also seem to commit her to the moral acceptability of infanticide. In a postscript to her original article, Warren denies this implication. While I am not convinced that the reasons Warren identifies for the wrongness of infanticide are compelling, I shall not be concerned to argue this point in particular. Instead, I will closely examine the fit between Warren's original main argument and her postscript reasoning in order to argue that she is mired in a dilemma which requires either that she abandon her liberal view, or accept that infanticide is morally permissible.

Warren presents five traits the possession of which is central to personhood: (1) consciousness, (2) the developed capacity to reason, (3) self-motivated activity, (4) the capacity to communicate an indefinite variety of things, and (5) the presence of a self-concept. Since a fetus does not satisfy these criteria, it is morally acceptable to abort any time during pregnancy. However, a neonate also lacks several of these characteristics [most clearly, (2) and (5)] and therefore is not a person by these criteria. Hence, on this account infanticide seems to be morally permissible until the neonate acquires these traits. Yet this is morally repulsive. In a postscript to her original article, Warren claims that killing infants (or allowing them to die) is not necessarily wrong if the infant is born in an impoverished community where no one can afford to care for it without significant costs to the well-being of existing persons, or if the infant is "defective." Her main point is that it is wrong to kill "normal" infants in a society like ours, given the valuations that most people in society currently hold.

In particular, Warren presents three reasons to ground the moral wrongness of infanticide. First, since neonates are "so very close" to being persons, to kill them requires a very strong moral justification. Second, many persons wish to adopt a healthy newborn, and to be deprived of this may negatively impact their lives. Third, even if the newborn may not be adoptable since it suffers from severe physical or mental challenges, there are many persons who are willing

Reprinted with permission of Blackwell Publishing from *Bioethics*, vol. 14, No. 4, 2000.

to pay taxes to support such children rather than see them killed.

Warren may not be entitled to the first reason, since it appears to be an appeal to the *potentiality* of the neonate. Warren rejects potentiality as a practical concern in the abortion debate, since she thinks that whenever they conflict, the rights of actual persons trump those of potential persons such as neonates. Hence, from Warren's perspective the fact that neonates are "so very close" to personhood cannot itself generate the requirement that a strong moral justification is necessary in order to perform infanticide. If this is correct, then the second and third reasons should be the main ones Warren offers for the wrongness of infanticide.

As Warren recognizes, the reasons she presents may also be used to show that *abortion* is wrong, at least in a society populated with persons who value these fetuses. What I am particularly interested in is Warren's argument for driving a wedge between the wrongness of infanticide and abortion. She attempts to show that even if we accept these reasons, abortion is morally acceptable while infanticide is unacceptable by pointing to a difference between the two cases: "... once the infant is born, its continued life cannot (except, perhaps, in very exceptional cases) pose any serious threat to the woman's life or health, since she is free to put it up for adoption, or, where this is impossible, to place it in a state-suppported institution."

Warren notices rightly that once the fetus is "separated" from the woman, this produces a nontrivial change in the woman's rights regarding what she may acceptably do to it. I will understand the term "abortion" to refer to an ecbolic procedure performed on a pre-viable fetus, which implies that this procedure will result in the death of the fetus. I will understand the term "separation" to refer to an ecbolic procedure which aims at the goal of separating a viable fetus from the mother. For Warren, it is "not clear" that the woman has a right to ask for the death of the newborn once separation has occurred; as she says,

> if and when a late-term abortion could be safely performed without killing the fetus, she would have no absolute right to insist on its death (e.g., if others wish to adopt it or pay for its care), for the same reason that she does not have a right to insist that a viable infant be killed.

Clearly, Warren is correct to both notice this difference between early and late-term abortions, and to acknowledge its significance to the mother-fetus relation. Yet, closer examination of this reasoning will allow us to make several important distinctions which suggest that Warren's argument cannot support the liberal view on abortion. Warren establishes the liberal conclusion that abortion is permissible any time in the course of pregnancy by presenting her main argument (in the original article) that the fetus does not meet the five proposed criteria for personhood. While performing abortion on a (pre-viable) fetus kills it, it does not wrong it according to Warren, since it is not a person (i.e., a human in the moral sense or a full-fledged member of the moral community). The viable fetus does not meet the five criteria either, yet Warren's reasoning in the postscript seems to suggest that once the fetus becomes viable, the rights of the woman *vis à vis* the fetus begin to change—the woman no longer has the (absolute) right to do what will result in the fetus' death.

In particular, Warren's quote above requires that a late-term abortion be possible without killing the fetus. Since I understand "abortion" to imply that the fetus will die, I will refer to this requirement not as "abortion-survivability," but instead as "*separation*-survivability." Separation-survivability actually comes in two forms: *narrow* separation-survivability and *wide* separation-survivability. Narrow separation-survivability only refers to separations accomplished via ecbolic procedures usually reserved for abortion where the fetus in fact survives. Wide separation-survivability is essentially the same category of requirement as viability: it is satisfied if the fetus can be separated from the mother via *any* ecbolic procedure, including means more invasive than those used in standard abortions, e.g., separation via Caesarian section. Warren's quote above refers specifically to narrow separation-survivability, but in the interests of simplicity I will employ the generic term "separation-survivability" from this point onward. Warren's position considers separation-survivability to be a watershed event in determining the rights of the mother *vis à vis* the fetus.

The other important point to notice regarding Warren's postscript argument is that the two acceptable reasons she offers against infanticide concern the value of newborns to *other* people. The newborn does not have any inherent moral interests, but possesses what we might call *solely relational* moral value. Essentially, these two reasons are consequentialist reasons, yet because the newborn lacks any independent moral standing, it does not receive direct moral consideration since in this case there is nothing to consider. On the basis of these consequentialist reasons, however, it may still be wrong to kill the infant because of the effects of this action on possessors of independent moral standing who value the infant.

Considering how these distinctions—between viability and separation-survivability, and between independent moral standing and solely relational moral value—intersect is fruitful. First, on Warren's account, killing something that possesses independent moral standing is worse than killing something that has solely relational moral value. Even supposing that other persons in society had precisely the same intensity of feelings regarding the killing of a being with independent moral standing as they do concerning the killing of a being with solely relational moral value, Warren believes the fact that the former possesses inherent moral interests which are themselves being violated makes the killing of the being with independent moral standing worse. The fact that killing a being with solely relational value is easier to justify than killing a being with independent moral standing makes it more plausible for Warren to maintain that a pregnant woman may kill her fetus rather than undergo any unwanted invasion of her body. Since killing the fetus requires aborting it, on this account the woman retains the right to do what results in its death unless it can be separated and hence born alive, i.e., if it was separation-survivable.

Is this a recognizably liberal position on abortion? Some perspective on this question can be acquired by comparing it with the other main positions in the abortion debate. Supporters of a moderate view on abortion emphasize the importance of some quality acquired during pregnancy such as (e.g.) sentience; they claim that since the fetus acquires independent moral standing during pregnancy, a more weighty moral justification is required for abortion after their favored threshold is surpassed. Warren's position is not a moderate view since she retains the liberal contention that the fetus lacks independent moral status throughout pregnancy. Warren's position is distinct from the conservative view on abortion which only allows killing the fetus to protect the woman's life or health, since for Warren, the fetus can be aborted for any reason after conception (or separated after viability).[1] At first glance, then, Warren's view may seem to be no different from the standard liberal view, if this is understood as follows: "the fetus can be killed any time during pregnancy." On her view, the woman possesses the absolute right to do what results in the death of the fetus until separation-survivability; after that, she loses the absolute right to kill the fetus, but she may end the pregnancy by withdrawing the fetus from her body.[2]

The appearance that Warren actually defends a standard liberal view is shown to be misleading if we consider the following case. Suppose that a woman is pregnant with a fetus that has passed the threshold of separation-survivability, and an unforseen medical condition makes it necessary for the woman to undergo drug therapy or emergency surgery in order to safeguard her health. However, if she does this, suppose that the drugs or surgical procedure will result in the death of the fetus.

It seems that on Warren's view, since the fetus is separation-survivable, one must opt first for separating the mother and fetus, and then proceed to address the mother's medical emergency. However, if delivering the baby before addressing the mother's medical condition would have negative health consequences for the mother, or even result in her death, Warren clearly would not want to agree with this implication.

Warren would likely attempt to dissolve this problem by pointing out that the mother only loses the *absolute* right to do what results in the fetus's death after it becomes separation-survivable; the mother may acceptably put her interests first since, after all, she is a person possessing independent moral standing. Warren does not specify what rights the mother retains after losing her "absolute right" *vis à vis* the fetus, but two obvious candidates are the right to safeguard her health and the right to protect her own life. This response is powerful, yet Warren's own postscript reasoning may prevent her from making this reply for at least two reasons.

First, as discussed above, the first reason Warren presents in the postscript for why infanticide is not morally acceptable gives some weight to the point that fetuses are potential persons. Once Warren distances herself from the categorical claim that the interests of actual persons always trump the interests of potential persons whenever they conflict, it becomes especially uncertain why the interests of *separation-survivable* fetuses could not prevail in at least some instances. Second, and more importantly, in the postscript reasoning Warren has made the fetus's value a function of consequentialist reasons which rely solely upon the valuations of other persons. This means that the decision between safeguarding the health of the mother versus ensuring the life of the separation-survivable fetus is in the hands of the many. It is certainly not unimaginable that the interests of those concerned to protect fetuses, combined with the interests of those who may wish to adopt a healthy child, could outweigh the mother's interests in safeguarding her health or life in some cases. By appealing to such consequentialist reasons, Warren has diluted the importance of the mother's rights to such an extent that the fetus's interests may prevail in the case of the medical emergency. This argument may require not only that the mother "separate" from the fetus before receiving treatment, but in some cases may even require that she carry the child to term (if possible) to avoid irreversible physical and mental damage to the fetus caused by inducing early delivery.[3] It is difficult to see how this line of reasoning could be used to support the liberal view on abortion.

One implication of the foregoing argument is that in order for Warren to keep her liberal defense of abortion from spreading into a defense of infanticide as well, she must base her attempt to drive a wedge between these two things on something besides the value of offspring to other valuers. Otherwise, this attempt will only yield the modified liberal view that fetuses may be separated but not killed whenever they are separation-survivable. To defend the full liberal view while excluding infanticide will require reasons against infanticide that depend upon the offspring having already been born, or more generally, on the possession by the offspring of independent moral standing.

One potential reason which may differentiate fetuses from neonates is that treating newborns as "trial-babies" who can acceptably be killed in the first weeks of life may have negative psychological effects on those children who grow to adulthood. For Warren, there is nothing intrinsically wrong with killing neonate Jerry. The wrongness must derive from how this negatively affects other persons, such as his older brother Tom, who may resent the killing of his baby brother or worry that the same thing could happen to him. This continuing reliance upon consequentialist reasons to escape the problems stemming from infanticide is awkward for Warren, given that her main argument in the original article builds from a very different deontological foundation emphasizing rights and personhood. Further, similar consequentialist reasons are utilized by thinkers such as Peter Singer to establish precisely the conclusion that Warren wishes to avoid, that infanticide on neonates can be morally permissible (even in a society like ours). ...

Notes

1. Would supporters of the conservative view be morally opposed to separation? They may argue that since this person possesses the right to life, it has a right to the use of the mother's body for the full term. This argument assumes that the right to life implies the existence of a right to whatever is necessary for survival, a claim famously interrogated by Judith Thomson, "A Defense of Abortion," *Philosophy and Public Affairs*, 1, 1 (1971) pp. 47–66. More to the point, the use of the mother's body for the full term is (presumably) not necessary for the fetus's survival once it is viable. Hence, conservatives need not necessarily be opposed to separation.
2. Can Warren sensibly think that separation is morally acceptable, even if it entails a serious risk of harm to the fetus? Viability now technically occurs at 22–24 weeks, yet this is no guarantee that the fetus will live: the American College of Obstetrics and Gynecology estimates that fewer than 4% of babies born during weeks twenty-three and twenty-five of the normal forty week gestation period survive. Many of those that to survive will have irreversible physical and mental defects. (On this, see *Intervention and Reflection*, ed. Ronald Munson (Wadsworth, Belmont, 1996, p. 65.) Liberals must think that we have a duty to avoid grave, preventable harm to this (future) person on pain of consistency, since (I should hope) they would be morally appalled if a mother ingested copious amounts of alcohol and drugs while pregnant with a fetus she intends to deliver. If this is plausible, then if a woman has carried a fetus until it is viable and separation threatened great harm to the fetus, it seems that in at least some cases the woman would be obliged to carry the fetus to term.
3. See note 2 above.

ABORTION: A FEMINIST PERSPECTIVE

Susan Sherwin

Because the public debate has been set up as a competition between the rights of women and those of fetuses, feminists have often felt pushed to reject claims of fetal value, in order to protect women's needs. As Kathryn Addelson (1987) has argued, however, viewing abortion in this way "rips it out of the context of women's lives." Other accounts of fetal value are more plausible and less oppressive to women.

On a feminist account fetal development is examined in the context in which it occurs, within women's bodies, rather than in the isolation of imagined abstraction. Fetuses develop in specific pregnancies that occur in the lives of particular women. They are not individuals housed in generic female wombs or full persons at risk only because they are small and subject to the whims of women. Their very existence is relationally defined, reflecting their development within particular women's bodies; that rela-

From *No Longer Patient: Feminist Ethics and Health Care*, by Susan Sherwin, pages 108–114. Reprinted with permission of Temple University Press.

tionship gives those women reason to be concerned about them. Many feminists argue against a perspective that regards the fetus as an independent being and suggest that a more accurate and valuable understanding of pregnancy would involve regarding the pregnant woman "as a biological and social unit" (Rothman 1986, 25).

On this view, fetuses are morally significant, but their status is relational rather than absolute. Unlike other human beings, fetuses do not have any independent existence; their existence is uniquely tied to the support of a specific other. Most nonfeminist accounts have ignored the relational dimension of fetal development and have presumed that the moral status of fetuses could be resolved solely in terms of abstract, metaphysical criteria of personhood as applied to the fetus alone (Tooley 1972; Warren 1973). Throughout much of the nonfeminist literature, commentators argue that some set of properties (such as genetic heritage, moral agency, self-consciousness, language use, or self-determination) will entitle all who possess it to be granted the moral status of persons. They seek some feature by which we can neatly divide the world into moral persons (who are to be valued and protected) and others (who are not entitled to the same group privileges).

This vision, however, misinterprets what is involved in personhood and what is especially valued about persons. Personhood is a social category, not an isolated state. Persons are members of a community, and they should be valued in their concrete, discrete, and different states as specific individuals, not merely as conceptually undifferentiated entities. To be a morally significant category, personhood must involve personality as well as biological integrity. It is not sufficient to consider persons simply as Kantian atoms of rationality, because persons are embodied, conscious beings with particular social histories. Annette Baier has developed a concept of persons as "second persons," which helps explain the sort of social dimension that seems fundamental to any moral notion of personhood:

> A person, perhaps, is best seen as one who was long enough dependent upon other persons to acquire the essential arts of personhood. Persons essentially are *second* persons, who grow up with other persons. … The fact that a person has a life *history*, and that a people collectively have a history depends upon the humbler fact that each person has a childhood in which a cultural heritage is transmitted, ready for adolescent rejection and adult discriminating selection and contribution. Persons come after and before other persons (Baier 1985: 84–5).

Persons, in other words, are members of a social community that shapes and values them, and personhood is a relational concept that must be defined in terms of interactions and relationships with others.

Because humans are fundamentally relational beings, it is important to remember that fetuses are characteristically limited in the "relationships" in which they can "participate"; within those relationships, they can make only the most restricted "contributions." After birth human beings are capable of a much wider range of roles in relationships with a broad variety of partners; that very diversity of possibility and experience leads us to focus on the abstraction of the individual as a constant through all these different relationships. Until birth, however, no such variety is possible, so the fetus must be understood as part of a complex entity that includes the woman who currently sustains the fetus and who will, most likely, be principally responsible for it for many years to come.

A fetus is a unique sort of human entity, then, for it cannot form relationships freely with others, and others cannot readily form relationships with it. A fetus has a primary and particularly intimate sort of "relationship" with the woman in whose womb it develops; connections with any other persons are necessarily indirect and must be mediated through the pregnant woman. The relationship that exists between a woman and her fetus is clearly asymmetrical, because she is the only party to it who is capable of even considering whether the interaction should continue; further, the fetus is wholly dependent on the woman who sustains it, whereas she is quite capable of surviving without it.

Most feminist views of what is valuable about persons reflect the social nature of individual existence. No human, especially no fetus, can exist apart from relationships; efforts to speak of the fetus itself, as if it were not inseparable from the woman in whom it develops, are distorting and dishonest. Fetuses have a unique physical status—within and dependent on particular women. That gives them also a unique social status. However much some might prefer it to be otherwise, no one other than the pregnant woman in question can do anything to support or harm a fetus without doing something to the woman who nurtures it. Because of this inexorable biological reality, the responsibility and privilege of determining a fetus's specific social status and value must rest with the woman carrying it.

Many pregnancies occur to women who place a very high value on the lives of the particular fetuses they carry and choose to see their pregnancies through to term, despite the possible risks and costs involved; it would be wrong of anyone to force such a woman to terminate her pregnancy. Other women, or some of these same women at other times, value other things more highly (for example, their freedom, their health, or previous responsibilities that conflict with those generated by the pregnancies), and so they choose not to continue their pregnancies. The value that women ascribe to individual fetuses varies dramatically from case to case and may well change over the course of any particular pregnancy. The fact that fetal lives can neither be sustained nor destroyed without affecting the women who support them implies that whatever value others may attach to fetuses generally or to specific fetuses individually should not be allowed to outweigh the ranking that is assigned to them by the pregnant women themselves.

No absolute value attaches to fetuses apart from their relational status, which is determined in the context of their particular development. This is not the same, however, as saying that they have no value at all or that they have merely instrumental value, as some liberals suggest. The value that women place on their own fetuses is the sort of value that attaches to an emerging human relationship.

Nevertheless, fetuses are not persons, because they have not developed sufficiently in their capacity for social relationships to be persons in any morally significant sense (that is, they are not yet second persons). In this way they differ from newborns, who immediately begin to develop into persons by virtue of their place as subjects in human relationships; newborns are capable of some forms of communication and response. The moral status of fetuses is determined by the nature of their primary relationship and the value that is created there. Therefore, feminist accounts of abortion emphasize the importance of protecting women's rights to continue or to terminate pregnancies as each sees fit.

THE POLITICS OF ABORTION

Feminist accounts explore the connections between particular social policies and the general patterns of power relationships in our society. With respect to abortion in this framework, Mary Daly observes that "one hundred percent of the bishops who oppose the repeal of antiabortion laws are men and one hundred percent of the people who have abortions are women.... To be comprehended accurately, they [arguments against abortion] must be seen within the context of sexually hierarchical society" (Daly 1973, 106).

Antiabortion activists appeal to arguments about the unconditional value of human life. When we examine their rhetoric more closely, however, we find other ways of interpreting their agenda. In addition to their campaign to criminalize abortion, most abortion opponents condemn all forms of sexual relations outside of heterosexual marriage, and they tend to support patriarchal patterns of dominance within such marriages. Many are distressed that liberal abortion policies support permissive sexuality by allowing women to "get away with" sex outside of marriage. They perceive that ready access to abortion supports women's independence from men.

Although nonfeminist participants in the abortion debates often discount the significance of its broader political dimensions, both feminists and antifeminists consider them crucial. The intensity of the antiabortion movement correlates closely with the increasing strength of feminism in achieving greater equality for women. The original American campaign against abortion can be traced to the middle of the nineteenth century, that is, to the time of the first significant feminist movement in the United States (Luker 1984). Today abortion is widely perceived as supportive of increased freedom and power for women. The campaign against abortion intensified in the 1970s, which was a period of renewed interest in feminism. As Rosalind Petchesky observes, the campaign rested on some powerful symbols: "To feminists and antifeminists alike, it came to represent the image of the 'emancipated woman' in her contemporary identity, focused on her education and work more than on marriage or childbearing; sexually active outside marriage and outside the disciplinary boundaries of the parental family; independently supporting herself and her children; and consciously espousing feminist ideas" (Petchesky 1984, 241). Clearly, much more than the lives of fetuses is at stake in the power struggle over abortion.

When we place abortion in the larger political context, we see that most of the groups active in the struggle to prohibit abortion also support other conservative measures to maintain the forms of dominance that characterize patriarchy (and often class and racial oppression as well). The movement against abortion is led by the Catholic church and other conservative religious institutions, which explicitly endorse not only fetal rights but also male dominance in the home and the church. Most opponents of abortion also oppose virtually all forms of birth control and all forms of sexuality other than monogamous, reproductive sex; usually, they also resist having women assume positions of authority in the dominant public institutions (Luker 1984). Typically, antiabortion activists support conservative economic measures that protect the interests of the privileged classes of society and ignore the needs of the oppressed and disadvantaged (Petchesky 1985). Although they stress their commitment to preserving life, many systematically work to dismantle key social programs that provide life necessities to the underclass. Moreover, some current campaigns against abortion retain elements of the racism that dominated the North American abortian literature in the early years of the twentieth century, wherein abortion was opposed on the grounds that it amounted to racial suicide on the part of whites.

In the eyes of its principal opponents, then, abortion is not an isolated practice; their opposition to abortion is central to a set of social values that runs counter to feminism's objectives. Hence antiabortion activists generally do not offer alternatives to abortion that support feminist interests in overturning the patterns of oppression that confront women. Most deny that there are any legitimate grounds for abortion, short of the need to save a woman's life—and some are not even persuaded by this criterion (Nicholson 1977). They believe that any pregnancy can and should be endured. If the mother is unable or unwilling to care for the child after birth, then they assume that adoption can be easily arranged.

It is doubtful, however, that adoptions are possible for every child whose mother cannot care for it. The world abounds with homeless orphans; even in the industrialized West, where there is a waiting list for adoption of healthy (white) babies, suitable homes cannot always be found for troubled adolescents; inner-city, AIDS babies, or many of the multiply handicapped children whose parents may have tried to care for them but whose marriages broke under the strain.

Furthermore, even if an infant were born healthy and could be readily adopted, we must recognize that surrendering one's child for adoption is an extremely difficult act for most women. The bond that commonly forms between women and their fetuses over the full term of pregnancy is intimate and often intense; many women find that it is not easily broken after birth. Psychologically, for many women adoption is a far more difficult response to unwanted pregnancies than abortion. Therefore, it is misleading to describe pregnancy as merely a nine-month commitment; for most women, seeing a pregnancy through to term involves a lifetime of responsibility and involvement with the resulting child and, in the overwhelming majority of cases, disproportionate burden on the woman through the child-rearing years. An ethics that cares about women would recognize that abortion is often the only acceptable recourse for them.

A DEFENSE OF ABORTION[1]

Judith Jarvis Thomson

Most opposition to abortion relies on the premise that the fetus is a human being, a person, from the moment of conception. The premise is argued for, but, as I think, not well. Take, for example, the most common argument. We are asked to notice that the development of a human being from conception through birth into childhood is continuous; then it is said that to draw a line, to choose a point in this development and say "before this point the thing is not a person, after this point it is a person" is to make an arbitrary choice, a choice for which in the nature of things no good reason can be given. It is concluded that the fetus is, or anyway that we had better say it is, a person from the moment of conception. But this conclusion does not follow. Similar things might be said about the development of an acorn into an oak tree, and it does not follow that acorns are oak trees, or that we had better say they are. Arguments of this form are sometimes called "slippery slope arguments"—the phrase is perhaps self-explanatory—and it is dismaying that opponents of abortion rely on them so heavily and uncritically.

I am inclined to agree, however, that the prospects for "drawing a line" in the development of the fetus look dim. I am inclined to think also that we shall probably have to agree that the fetus has already become a human person well before birth. Indeed, it comes as a surprise when one first learns how early in its life it begins to acquire human characteristics. By the tenth week, for example, it already has a face, arms and legs, fingers and toes; it has internal organs, and brain activity is detectable.[2] On the other hand, I think that the premise is false, that the fetus is not a person from the moment of conception. A newly fertilized ovum, a newly implanted clump of cells, is no more a person than an acorn is an oak tree. But I shall not discuss any of this. For it seems to me to be of great interest to ask what happens if, for the sake of argument, we allow the premise. How, precisely, are we supposed to get from there to the conclusion that abortion is morally impermissible? Opponents of abortion commonly spend most of their time establishing that the fetus is a person, and hardly any time explaining the step from there to the impermissibility of abortion. Perhaps they think the step too simple and obvious to require much comment. Or perhaps instead they are simply being economical in argument. Many of those who defend abortion rely on the premise that the fetus is not a person, but only a bit of tissue that will become a person at birth; and why pay out more arguments than you have to? Whatever the explanation, I suggest that the step they take is neither easy nor obvious, that it calls for closer examination than it is commonly given, and that when we do give it this closer examination we shall feel inclined to reject it.

I propose, then, that we grant that the fetus is a person from the moment of conception. How does the argument go from here? Something like this, I take it. Every person has a right to life. So the fetus has a right to life. No doubt the mother has a right to decide what shall happen in and to her body; everyone would grant that. But surely a person's right to life is stronger and more stringent than the mother's right to decide what happens in and to her body, and so outweighs it. So the fetus may not be killed; an abortion may not be performed.

It sounds plausible. But now let me ask you to imagine this. You wake up in the morning and find yourself back to back in bed with an unconscious violinist. A famous unconscious violinist. He has been found to have a fatal kidney ailment, and the Society of Music Lovers has canvassed all the available medical records and found that you alone have the right blood type to help. They have therefore kidnapped you, and last night the violinist's circulatory system was plugged into yours, so that your kidneys can be used to extract poisons from his blood as well as your own. The director of the hospital now tells you, "Look, we're sorry the Society of Music Lovers did this to you—we would never have permitted it if we had known. But still, they did it, and the violinist now is plugged into you. To unplug you would be to kill him. But never mind, it's only for nine months. By then he will have recovered from his ailment, and can safely be unplugged from you." Is it morally incumbent on you to accede to this situation? No doubt it would be very nice of you if you did, a great kindness. But do you *have* to accede to it? What if it were not nine months, but nine years? Or longer still? What if the director of the hospital says, "Tough luck, I agree, but you've now got to stay in bed, with the violinist plugged into you, for the rest of your life. Because remember this. All persons have a right to life, and violinists are persons. Granted you have a right to decide what happens in and to your body, but a person's right to life outweighs your right to decide what happens in and to your body. So you cannot ever be unplugged from him." I imagine you would regard this as outrageous, which suggests that something really is wrong with that plausible-sounding argument I mentioned a moment ago.

In this case, of course, you were kidnapped; you didn't volunteer for the operation that

Violinist

"Cardiac Condition"

plugged the violinist into your kidneys. Can those who oppose abortion on the ground I mentioned make an exception for a pregnancy due to rape? Certainly. They can say that persons have a right to life only if they didn't come into existence because of rape; or they can say that all persons have a right to life, but that some have less of a right to life than others, in particular, that those who came into existence because of rape have less. But these statements have a rather unpleasant sound. Surely the question of whether you have a right to life at all, or how much of it you have, shouldn't turn on the question of whether or not you are the product of a rape. And in fact the people who oppose abortion on the ground I mentioned do not make this distinction, and hence do not make an exception in case of rape.

Nor do they make an exception for a case in which the mother has to spend the nine months of her pregnancy in bed. They would agree that would be a great pity, and hard on the mother; but all the same, all persons have a right to life, the fetus is a person, and so on. I suspect, in fact, that they would not make an exception for a case in which, miraculously enough, the pregnancy went on for nine years, or even the rest of the mother's life.

Some won't even make an exception for a case in which continuation of the pregnancy is likely to shorten the mother's life; they regard abortion as impermissible even to save the mother's life. Such cases are nowadays very rare, and many opponents of abortion do not accept this extreme view. All the same, it is a good place to begin: a number of points of interest come out in respect to it.

mother's life at risk

1. Let us call the view that abortion is impermissible even to save the mother's life "the extreme view." I want to suggest first that it does not issue from the argument I mentioned earlier without the addition of some fairly powerful premises. Suppose a woman has become pregnant, and now learns that she has a cardiac condition such that she will die if she carries the baby to term. What may be done for her? The fetus, being a person, has a right to life, but as the mother is a person too, so has she a right to life. Presumably they have an equal right to life. How is it supposed to come out that an abortion may not be performed? If mother and child have an equal right to life, shouldn't we perhaps flip a coin? Or should we add to the mother's right to life her right to decide what happens in and to her body, which everybody seems to be ready to grant—the sum of her rights now outweighing the fetus' right to life?

The most familiar argument here is the following. We are told that performing the abortion would be directly killing[3] the child, whereas doing nothing would not be killing the mother, but only letting her die. Moreover, in killing the child, one would be killing an innocent person, for the child has committed no crime, and is not aiming at his mother's death. And then there are a variety of ways in which this might be continued. (1) But as directly killing an innocent person is always and absolutely impermissible, an abortion may not be performed. Or, (2) as directly killing an innocent person is murder, and murder is always and absolutely impermissible, an abortion may not be performed.[4] Or, (3) as one's duty to refrain from directly killing an innocent person is more stringent than one's duty to keep a person from dying, an abortion may not be performed. Or, (4) if one's only options are directly killing an innocent person or letting a person die, one must prefer letting the person die, and thus an abortion may not be performed.[5]

Some people seem to have thought that these are not further premises which must be added if the conclusion is to be reached, but that they follow from the very fact that an innocent person has a right to life.[6] But this seems to me to be a mistake, and perhaps the simplest way to show this is to bring out that while we must certainly grant that innocent persons have a right to life, the theses in (1) through (4) are all false. Take (2), for example. If directly killing an innocent person is murder, and thus is impermissible, then the mother's directly killing

unplug violinist

the innocent person inside her is murder, and thus is impermissible. But it cannot seriously be thought to be murder if the mother performs an abortion on herself to save her life. It cannot seriously be said that she *must* refrain, that she *must* sit passively by and wait for her death. Let us look again at the case of you and the violinist. There you are, in bed with the violinist, and the director of the hospital says to you, "It's all most distressing, and I deeply sympathize, but you see this is putting an additional strain on your kidneys, and you'll be dead within the month. But you *have* to stay where you are all the same. Because unplugging you would be directly killing an innocent violinist, and that's murder, and that's impermissible." If anything in the world is true, it is that you do not commit murder, you do not do what is impermissible, if you reach around to your back and unplug yourself from that violinist to save your life.

The main focus of attention in writings on abortion has been on what a third party may or may not do in answer to a request from a woman for an abortion. This is in a way understandable. Things being as they are, there isn't much a woman can safely do to abort herself. So the question asked is what a third party may do, and what the mother may do, if it is mentioned at all, is deduced, almost as an afterthought, from what it is concluded that third parties may do. But it seems to me that to treat the matter in this way is to refuse to grant to the mother that very status of person which is so firmly insisted on for the fetus. For we cannot simply read off what a person may do from what a third party may do. Suppose you find yourself trapped in a tiny house with a growing child. I mean a very tiny house, and a rapidly growing child—you are already up against the wall of the house and in a few minutes you'll be crushed to death. The child on the other hand won't be crushed to death; if nothing is done to stop him from growing he'll be hurt, but in the end he'll simply burst open the house and walk out a free man. Now I could well understand it if a bystander were to say, "There's nothing we can do for you. We cannot choose between your life and his, we cannot be the ones to decide who is to live, we cannot intervene." But it cannot be concluded that you too can do nothing, that you cannot attack it to save your life. However innocent the child may be, you do not have to wait passively while it crushes you to death. Perhaps a pregnant woman is vaguely felt to have the status of house, to which we don't allow the right of self-defense. But if the woman houses the child, it should be remembered that she is a person who houses it.

I should perhaps stop to say explicitly that I am not claiming that people have a right to do anything whatever to save their lives. I think, rather, that there are drastic limits to the right of self-defense. If someone threatens you with death unless you torture someone else to death, I think you have not the right, even to save your life, to do so. But the case under consideration here is very different. In our case there are only two people involved, one whose life is threatened, and one who threatens it. Both are innocent: the one who is threatened is not threatened because of any fault, the one who threatens does not threaten because of any fault. For this reason we may feel that we bystanders cannot intervene. But the person threatened can.

In sum, a woman surely can defend her life against the threat to it posed by the unborn child, even if doing so involves its death. And this shows not merely that the theses in (1) through (4) are false; it shows also that the extreme view of abortion is false, and so we need not canvass any other possible ways of arriving at it from the argument I mentioned at the outset.

2. The extreme view could of course be weakened to say that while abortion is permissible to save the mother's life, it may not be performed by a third party, but only by the mother herself. But this cannot be right either. For what we have to keep in mind is that the

child growing in a house

mother and the unborn child are not like two tenants in a small house which has, by an unfortunate mistake, been rented to both: the mother *owns* the house. The fact that she does adds to the offensiveness of deducing that the mother can do nothing from the supposition that third parties can do nothing. But it does more than this: it casts a bright light on the supposition that third parties can do nothing. Certainly it lets us see that a third party who says "I cannot choose between you" is fooling himself if he thinks this is impartiality. If Jones has found and fastened on a certain coat, which he needs to keep him from freezing, but which Smith also needs to keep him from freezing, then it is not impartiality that says "I cannot choose between you" when Smith owns the coat. Women have said again and again "This body is *my* body!" and they have reason to feel angry, reason to feel that it has been like shouting into the wind. Smith, after all, is hardly likely to bless us if we say to him, "Of course it's your coat, anybody would grant that it is. But no one may choose between you and Jones who is to have it."

We should really ask what it is that says "no one may choose" in the face of the fact that the body that houses the child is the mother's body. It may be simply a failure to appreciate this fact. But it may be something more interesting, namely the sense that one has a right to refuse to lay hands on people, even where it would be just and fair to do so, even where justice seems to require that somebody do so. Thus justice might call for somebody to get Smith's coat back from Jones, and yet you have a right to refuse to be the one to lay hands on Jones, a right to refuse to do physical violence to him. This, I think, must be granted. But then what should be said is not "no one may choose," but only "*I* cannot choose," and indeed not even this, but "*I* will not *act*," leaving it open that somebody else can or should, and in particular that anyone in a position of authority, with the job of securing people's rights, both can and should. So this is no difficulty. I have not been arguing that any given third party must accede to the mother's request that he perform an abortion to save her life, but only that he may.

I suppose that in some views of human life the mother's body is only on loan to her, the loan not being one which gives her any prior claim to it. One who held this view might well think it impartiality to say "I cannot choose." But I shall simply ignore this possibility. My own view is that if a human being has any just, prior claim to anything at all, he has a just, prior claim to his own body. And perhaps this needn't be argued for here anyway, since, as I mentioned, the arguments against abortion we are looking at do grant that the woman has a right to decide what happens in and to her body.

But although they do grant it, I have tried to show that they do not take seriously what is done in granting it. I suggest the same thing will reappear even more clearly when we turn away from cases in which the mother's life is at stake, and attend, as I propose we now do, to the vastly more common cases in which a woman wants an abortion for some less weighty reason than preserving her own life.

3. Where the mother's life is not at stake, the argument I mentioned at the outset seems to have a much stronger pull. "Everyone has a right to life, so the unborn person has a right to life." And isn't the child's right to life weightier than anything other than the mother's own right to life, which she might put forward as ground for an abortion?

This argument treats the right to life as if it were unproblematic. It is not, and this seems to me to be precisely the source of the mistake.

For we should now, at long last, ask what it comes to, to have a right to life. In some views having a right to life includes having a right to be given at least the bare minimum one needs for continued life. But suppose that what in fact *is* the bare minimum a man needs for continued life is something he has no right at all to be given? If I am sick unto death, and the only thing that will save my life is the touch of Henry Fonda's cool hand on my fevered brow, then all the same, I have no right to be given the touch of Henry Fonda's cool hand on my fevered brow. It would be frightfully nice of him to fly in from the West Coast to provide it. It would be less nice, though no doubt well meant, if my friends flew out to the West Coast and carried Henry Fonda back with them. But I have no right at all against anybody that he should do this for me. Or again, to return to the story I told earlier, the fact that for continued life that violinist needs the continued use of your kidneys does not establish that he has a right to be given the continued use of your kidneys. He certainly has no right against you that *you* should give him continued use of your kidneys. For nobody has any right to use your kidneys unless you give him such a right; and nobody has the right against you that you shall give him this right—if you do allow him to go on using your kidneys, this is a kindness on your part, and not something he can claim from you as his due. Nor has he any right against anybody else that *they* should give him continued use of your kidneys. Certainly he had no right against the Society of Music Lovers that they should plug him into you in the first place. And if you now start to unplug yourself, having learned that you will otherwise have to spend nine years in bed with him, there is nobody in the world who must try to prevent you, in order to see to it that he is given something he has a right to be given.

Some people are rather stricter about the right to life. In their view, it does not include the right to be given anything, but amounts to, and only to, the right not to be killed by anybody. But here a related difficulty arises. If everybody is to refrain from killing that violinist, then everybody must refrain from doing a great many different sorts of things. Everybody must refrain from slitting his throat, everybody must refrain from shooting him—and everybody must refrain from unplugging you from him. But does he have a right against everybody that they shall refrain from unplugging you from him? To refrain from doing this is to allow him to continue to use your kidneys. It could be argued that he has a right against us that *we* should allow him to continue to use your kidneys. That is, while he had no right against us that we should give him the use of your kidneys, it might be argued that he anyway has a right against us that we shall not now intervene and deprive him of the use of your kidneys. I shall come back to third-party interventions later. But certainly the violinist has no right against you that *you* shall allow him to continue to use your kidneys. As I said, if you do allow him to use them, it is a kindness on your part, and not something you owe him.

The difficulty I point to here is not peculiar to the right to life. It reappears in connection with all the other natural rights; and it is something which an adequate account of rights must deal with. For present purposes it is enough just to draw attention to it. But I would stress that I am not arguing that people do not have a right to life—quite to the contrary, it seems to me that the primary control we must place on the acceptability of an account of rights is that it should turn out in that account to be a truth that all persons have a right to life. I am arguing only that having a right to life does not guarantee having either a right to be given the use of or a right to be allowed continued use of another person's body—even if one needs it for life itself. So the right to life will not serve the opponents of abortion in the very simple and clear way in which they seem to have thought it would.

4. There is another way to bring out the difficulty. In the most ordinary sort of case, to deprive someone of what he has a right to is to treat him unjustly. Suppose a boy and his small brother are jointly given a box of chocolates for Christmas. If the older boy takes the box and refuses to give his brother any of the chocolates, he is unjust to him, for the brother has been given a right to half of them. But suppose that, having learned that otherwise it means nine years in bed with that violinist, you unplug yourself from him. You surely are not being unjust to him, for you gave him no right

box of chocolates

to use your kidneys, and no one else can have given him any such right. But we have to notice that in unplugging yourself, you are killing him; and violinists, like everybody else, have a right to life, and thus in the view we were considering just now, the right not to be killed. So here you do what he supposedly has a right you shall not do, but you do not act unjustly to him in doing it.

The emendation which may be made at this point is this: the right to life consists not in the right not to be killed, but rather in the right not to be killed unjustly. This runs a risk of circularity, but never mind: it would enable us to square the fact that the violinist has a right to life with the fact that you do not act unjustly toward him in unplugging yourself, thereby killing him. For if you do not kill him unjustly, you do not violate his right to life, and so it is no wonder you do him no injustice.

But if this emendation is accepted, the gap in the argument against abortion stares us plainly in the face: it is by no means enough to show that the fetus is a person, and to remind us that all persons have a right to life—we need to be shown also that killing the fetus violates its right to life, i.e., that abortion is unjust killing. And is it?

I suppose we may take it as a datum that in a case of pregnancy due to rape the mother has not given the unborn person a right to the use of her body for food and shelter. Indeed, in what pregnancy could it be supposed that the mother has given the unborn person such a right? It is not as if there were unborn persons drifting about the world, to whom a woman who wants a child says "I invite you in."

But it might be argued that there are other ways one can have acquired a right to the use of another person's body than by having been invited to use it by that person. Suppose a woman voluntarily indulges in intercourse, knowing of the chance it will issue in pregnancy, and then she does become pregnant; is she not in part responsible for the presence, in fact the very existence, of the unborn person inside her? No doubt she did not invite it in. But doesn't her partial responsibility for its being there itself give it a right to the use of her body?[7] If so, then her aborting it would be more like the boy's taking away the chocolates, and less like your unplugging yourself from the violinist—doing so would be depriving it of what it does have a right to, and thus would be doing it an injustice.

And then, too, it might be asked whether or not she can kill it even to save her own life: If she voluntarily called it into existence, how can she now kill it, even in self-defense?

The first thing to be said about this is that it is something new. Opponents of abortion have been so concerned to make out the independence of the fetus, in order to establish that it has a right to life, just as its mother does, that they have tended to overlook the possible support they might gain from making out that the fetus is *dependent* on the mother, in order to establish that she has a special kind of responsibility for it, a responsibility that gives it rights against her which are not possessed by any independent person—such as an ailing violinist who is a stranger to her.

On the other hand, this argument would give the unborn person a right to its mother's body only if her pregnancy resulted from a voluntary act, undertaken in full knowledge of the chance a pregnancy might result from it. It would leave out entirely the unborn person whose existence is due to rape. Pending the availability of some further argument, then, we would be left with the conclusion that unborn persons whose existence is due to rape have no right to the use of their mothers' bodies, and thus that aborting them is not depriving them of anything they have a right to and hence is not unjust killing.

And we should also notice that it is not at all plain that this argument really does go even as far as it purports to. For there are cases and cases, and the details make a difference. If the room is stuffy, and I therefore open a window to air it, and a burglar climbs in, it would be absurd to say, "Ah, now he can stay, she's given him a right to the use of her house—for she is partially responsible for his presence there, having voluntarily done what enabled him to get in, in full knowledge that there are such things as burglars, and that burglars burgle." It would be still more absurd to say this if I had had bars installed outside my windows, precisely to prevent burglars from getting in, and a burglar got in only because of a defect in the bars. It remains equally absurd if we imagine it is not a burglar who climbs in, but an innocent person who blunders or falls in. Again, suppose it were like this: people-seeds drift about in the air like pollen, and if you open your windows, one may drift in and take root in your carpets or upholstery. You don't want children, so you fix up your windows with fine mesh screens, the very best you can buy. As can happen, however, and on very, very rare occasions does happen, one of the screens is defective; and a seed drifts in and takes root. Does the person-plant who now develops have a right to the use of your house? Surely not—despite the fact that you voluntarily opened your windows, you knowingly kept carpets and upholstered furniture, and you knew that screens were sometimes defective. Someone may argue that you are responsible for its rooting, that it does have a right to your house, because after all you *could* have lived out your life with bare floors and furniture, or with sealed windows and doors. But this won't do—for by the same token anyone can avoid a pregnancy due to rape by having a hysterectomy, or anyway by never leaving home without a (reliable!) army.

It seems to me that the argument we are looking at can establish at most that there are *some* cases in which the unborn person has a right to the use of its mother's body, and therefore *some* cases in which abortion is unjust killing. There is room for much discussion and argument as to precisely which, if any. But I think we should sidestep this issue and leave it open, for at any rate the argument certainly does not establish that all abortion is unjust killing.

5. There is room for yet another argument here, however. We surely must all grant that there may be cases in which it would be morally indecent to detach a person from your body at the cost of his life. Suppose you learn that what the violinist needs is not nine years of your life, but only one hour: all you need do to save his life is to spend one hour in that bed with him. Suppose also that letting him use your kidneys for that one hour would not affect your health in the slightest. Admittedly you were kidnapped. Admittedly you did not give anyone permission to plug him into you. Nevertheless it seems to me plain you *ought* to allow him to use your kidneys for that hour—it would be indecent to refuse.

Again, suppose pregnancy lasted only an hour, and constituted no threat to life or health. And suppose that a woman becomes pregnant as a result of rape. Admittedly she did not voluntarily do anything to bring about the existence of a child. Admittedly she did nothing at all which would give the unborn person a right to the use of her body. All the same it might well be said, as in the newly emended violinist story, that she *ought* to allow it to remain for that hour—that it would be indecent in her to refuse.

Now some people are inclined to use the term "right" in such a way that it follows from the fact that you ought to allow a person to use your body for the hour he needs, that he has a right to use your body for the hour he needs, even though he has not been given that right by any person or act. They may say that it follows also that if you refuse, you act unjustly toward him. This use of the term is perhaps so common that it cannot be called wrong; nevertheless it seems to me to be an unfortunate loosening of what we would do better to keep a tight rein on. Suppose that box of chocolates I mentioned earlier had not been given to both boys jointly, but was given only to the older boy. There he sits, stolidly eating his way through the box, his small brother watching enviously. Here we are likely to say "You ought not to be so mean. You ought to give your brother some of those chocolates." My own view is that it just does not follow from the truth of this that the brother has any right to any of the chocolates. If the boy refuses to give his brother any, he is greedy, stingy, callous—but not unjust. I suppose that the people I have in mind will say it does follow that the brother has a right to some of the chocolates, and thus that the boy does act unjustly if he refuses to give his brother any. But the effect of saying this is to obscure what we should keep distinct, namely the difference between the boy's refusal in this case and the boy's refusal in the earlier case, in which the box was given to both boys jointly, and in which the small brother thus had what was from any point of view clear title to half.

A further objection to so using the term "right" that from the fact that A ought to do a thing for B, it follows that B has a right against A that A do it for him, is that it is going to make the question of whether or not a man has a right to a thing turn on how easy it is to provide him with it; and this seems not merely unfortunate, but morally unacceptable. Take the case of Henry Fonda again. I said earlier that I had no right to the touch of his cool hand on my fevered brow, even though I needed it to save my life. I said it would be frightfully nice of him to fly in from the West Coast to provide me with it, but that I had no right against him that he should do so. But suppose he isn't on the West Coast. Suppose he has only to walk across the room, place a hand briefly on my brow—and lo, my life is saved. Then surely he ought to do it, it would be indecent to refuse. Is it to be said "Ah, well, it follows that in this case she has a right to the touch of his hand on her brow, and so it would be an injustice in him to refuse"? So that I have a right to it when it is easy for him to provide it, though no right when it's hard? It's rather a shocking idea that anyone's rights should fade away and disappear as it gets harder and harder to accord them to him.

So my own view is that even though you ought to let the violinist use your kidneys for the one hour he needs, we should not conclude that he has a right to do so—we should say that if you refuse, you are, like the boy who owns all the chocolates and will give none away, self-centered and callous, indecent in fact, but not unjust. And similarly, that even supposing a case in which a woman pregnant due to rape ought to allow the unborn person to use her body for the hour he needs, we should not conclude that he has a right to do so; we should conclude that she is self-centered, callous, indecent, but not unjust, if she refuses. The complaints are no less grave; they are just different. However, there is no need to insist on this point. If anyone does wish to deduce "he has a right" from "you ought," then all the same he must surely grant that there are cases in which it is not morally required of you that you allow that violinist to use your kidneys, and in which he does not have a right to use them, and in which you do not do him an injustice if you refuse. And so also for mother and unborn child. Except in such cases as the unborn person has a right to demand it—and we were leaving open the possibility that there may be such cases—nobody is morally *required* to make large sacrifices, of health, of all other interests and concerns, of all other duties and commitments, for nine years, or even for nine months, in order to keep another person alive.

6. We have in fact to distinguish between two kinds of Samaritan: the Good Samaritan and what we might call the Minimally Decent Samaritan. The story of the Good Samaritan, you will remember, goes like this:

> A certain man went down from Jerusalem to Jericho, and fell among thieves, which stripped him of his raiment, and wounded him, and departed, leaving him half dead.
>
> And by chance there came down a certain priest that way; and when he saw him, he passed by on the other side.
>
> And likewise a Levite, when he was at the place, came and looked on him, and passed by on the other side.
>
> But a certain Samaritan, as he journeyed, came where he was; and when he saw him he had compassion on him.
>
> And went to him, and bound up his wounds, pouring in oil and wine, and set him on his own beast, and brought him to an inn, and took care of him.

> And on the morrow, when he departed, he took out two pence, and gave them to the host, and said unto him, "Take care of him; and whatsoever thou spendest more, when I come again, I will repay thee."
>
> (Luke 10:30–35)

The Good Samaritan went out of his way, at some cost to himself, to help one in need of it. We are not told what the options were, that is, whether or not the priest and the Levite could have helped by doing less than the Good Samaritan did, but assuming they could have, then the fact they did nothing at all shows they were not even Minimally Decent Samaritans, not because they were not Samaritans, but because they were not even minimally decent.

These things are a matter of degree, of course, but there is a difference, and it comes out perhaps most clearly in the story of Kitty Genovese, who, as you will remember, was murdered while thirty-eight people watched or listened, and did nothing at all to help her. A Good Samaritan would have rushed out to give direct assistance against the murderer. Or perhaps we had better allow that it would have been a Splendid Samaritan who did this, on the ground that it would have involved a risk of death for himself. But the thirty-eight not only did not do this, they did not even trouble to pick up a phone to call the police. Minimally Decent Samaritanism would call for doing at least that, and their not having done it was monstrous.

After telling the story of the Good Samaritan, Jesus said "Go, and do thou likewise." Perhaps he meant that we are morally required to act as the Good Samaritan did. Perhaps he was urging people to do more than is morally required of them. At all events it seems plain that it was not morally required of any of the thirty-eight that he rush out to give direct assistance at the risk of his own life, and that it is not morally required of anyone that he give long stretches of his life—nine years or nine months—to sustaining the life of a person who has no special right (we were leaving open the possibility of this) to demand it.

Indeed, with one rather striking class of exceptions, no one in any country in the world is *legally* required to do anywhere near as much as this for anyone else. The class of exceptions is obvious. My main concern here is not the state of the law in respect to abortion, but it is worth drawing attention to the fact that in no state in this country is any man compelled by law to be even a Minimally Decent Samaritan to any person; there is no law under which charges could be brought against the thirty-eight who stood by while Kitty Genovese died. By contrast, in most states in this country women are compelled by law to be not merely Minimally Decent Samaritans, but Good Samaritans to unborn persons inside them. This doesn't by itself settle anything one way or the other, because it may well be argued that there should be laws in this country—as there are in many European countries—compelling at least Minimally Decent Samaritanism.[8] But it does show that there is a gross injustice in the existing state of the law. And it shows also that the groups currently working against liberalization of abortion laws, in fact working toward having it declared unconstitutional for a state to permit abortion, had better start working for the adoption of Good Samaritan laws generally, or earn the charge that they are acting in bad faith.

I should think, myself, that Minimally Decent Samaritan laws would be one thing, Good Samaritan laws quite another, and in fact highly improper. But we are not here concerned with the law. What we should ask is not whether anybody should be compelled by law to be a Good Samaritan, but whether we must accede to a situation in which somebody is being compelled—by nature, perhaps—to be a Good Samaritan. We have, in other words, to look now at third-party interventions. I have been arguing that no person is morally required to make large sacrifices to sustain the life of another who has no right to demand them, and this even where the sacrifices do not include life itself; we are not morally required to be Good Samaritans or anyway Very Good Samaritans to one another. But what if a man cannot extricate himself from such a situation? What if he appeals to us to extricate him? It seems to me plain that there are cases in which we can, cases in which a Good Samaritan would extricate him. There you are, you were kidnapped, and nine years in bed with that violinist lie ahead of you. You have your own life to lead. You are sorry, but you simply cannot see giving up so much of your life to the sustaining of his. You cannot extricate yourself, and ask us to do so. I should have thought that—in light of his having no right to the use of your body—it was obvious that we do not have to accede to your being forced to give up so much. We can do what you ask. There is no injustice to the violinist in our doing so.

7. Following the lead of the opponents of abortion, I have throughout been speaking of the fetus merely as a person, and what I have been asking is whether or not the argument we began with, which proceeds only from the fetus' being a person, really does establish its conclusion. I have argued that it does not.

But of course there are arguments and arguments, and it may be said that I have simply fastened on the wrong one. It may be said that what is important is not merely the fact that the fetus is a person, but that it is a person for whom the woman has a special kind of responsibility issuing from the fact that she is its mother. And it might be argued that all my analogies are therefore irrelevant—for you do not have that special kind of responsibility for that violinist, Henry Fonda does not have that special kind of responsibility for me. And our attention might be drawn to the fact that men and women both *are* compelled by law to provide support for their children.

I have in effect dealt (briefly) with this argument in section 4 above; but a (still briefer) recapitulation now may be in order. Surely we do not have any such "special responsibility" for a person unless we have assumed it, explicitly or implicitly. If a set of parents do not try to prevent pregnancy, do not obtain an abortion, and then at the time of birth of the child do not put it out for adoption, but rather take it home with them, then they have assumed responsibility for it, they have given it rights, and they cannot *now* withdraw support from it at the cost of its life because they now find it difficult to go on providing for it. But if they have taken all reasonable precautions against having a child, they do not simply by virtue of their biological relationship to the child who comes into existence have a special responsibility for it. They may wish to assume responsibility for it, or they may not wish to. And I am suggesting that if assuming responsibility for it would require large sacrifices, then they may refuse. A Good Samaritan would not refuse—or anyway, a Splendid Samaritan, if the sacrifices that had to be made were enormous. But then so would a Good Samaritan assume responsibility for that violinist; so would Henry Fonda, if he is a Good Samaritan, fly in from the West Coast and assume responsibility for me.

8. My argument will be found unsatisfactory on two counts by many of those who want to regard abortion as morally permissible. First, while I do argue that abortion is not impermissible, I do not argue that it is always permissible. There may well be cases in which carrying the child to term requires only Minimally Decent Samaritanism of the mother, and this is a standard we must not fall below. I am inclined to think it a merit of my account precisely that it does *not* give a general yes or a general no. It allows for and supports our sense that, for example, a sick and desperately frightened fourteen-year-old schoolgirl, pregnant due to rape, may *of course* choose abortion, and that any law which rules this out is an insane law. And it also allows for and supports our sense that in other cases resort to abortion is even positively indecent. It would be indecent in the woman to request an abortion, and indecent in a doctor to perform it, if she is in her seventh month, and wants the abortion just to avoid the nuisance of postponing a trip abroad. The very fact that the arguments I have been drawing attention to treat all cases of abortion, or even all cases of abortion in which the mother's life is not at stake, as morally on a par ought to have made them suspect at the outset.

Secondly, while I am arguing for the permissibility of abortion in some cases, I am not arguing for the right to secure the death of the unborn child. It is easy to confuse these two things in that up to a certain point in the life of the fetus it is not able to survive outside the mother's body; hence removing it from her body guarantees its death. But they are importantly different. I have argued that you are not morally required to spend nine months in bed, sustaining the life of that violinist; but to say this is by no means to say that if, when you unplug yourself, there is a miracle and he survives, you then have a right to turn round and slit his throat. You may detach yourself even if this costs him his life; you have no right to be guaranteed his death, by some other means, if unplugging yourself does not kill him. There are some people who will feel dissatisfied by this feature of my argument. A woman may be utterly devastated by the thought of a child, a bit of herself, put out for adoption and never seen or heard of again. She may therefore want not merely that the child be detached from her, but more, that it die. Some opponents of abortion are inclined to regard this as beneath contempt—thereby showing insensitivity to what is surely a powerful source of despair. All the same, I agree that the desire for the child's death is not one which anybody may gratify, should it turn out to be possible to detach the child alive.

At this place, however, it should be remembered that we have only been pretending throughout that the fetus is a human being from the moment of conception. A very early abortion is surely not the killing of a person, and so is not dealt with by anything I have said here.

Notes

1. I am very much indebted to James Thomson for discussion, criticism, and many helpful suggestions.
2. Daniel Callahan, *Abortion: Law, Choice and Morality* (New York, 1970), p. 373. This book gives a fascinating survey of the available information on abortion. The Jewish tradition is surveyed in David M. Feldman, *Birth Control in Jewish Law* (New York, 1968), Part 5, the Catholic tradition in John T. Noonan, Jr., "An Almost Absolute Value in History," in *The Morality of Abortion,* ed. John T. Noonan, Jr. (Cambridge, Mass., 1970).
3. The term "direct" in the arguments I refer to is a technical one. Roughly, what is meant by "direct killing" is either killing as an end in itself, or killing as a means to some end, for example, the end of saving someone else's life. See note 6, below, for an example of its use.
4. Cf. *Encyclical Letter of Pope Pius XI on Christian Marriage*, St. Paul Editions (Boston, n.d.), p. 32: "however much we may pity the mother whose health and even life is gravely imperiled in the performance of the duty allotted to her by nature, nevertheless what could ever be a sufficient reason for excusing in any way the direct murder of the innocent? This is precisely what we are dealing with here." Noonan (*The Morality of Abortion*, p. 43) reads this as follows: "What cause can ever avail to excuse in any way the direct killing of the innocent? For it is a question of that."
5. The thesis in (4) is in an interesting way weaker than those in (1), (2), and (3): they rule out abortion even in cases in which both mother *and* child will die if the abortion is not performed. By contrast, one who held the view expressed in (4) could consistently say that one needn't prefer letting two persons die to killing one.
6. Cf. the following passage from Pius XII, *Address to the Italian Catholic Society of Midwives:* "The baby in the maternal breast has the right to life immediately from God.—Hence there is no man, no human authority, no science, no medical, eugenic, social, economic or moral 'indication' which can establish or grant a valid juridical ground for a direct deliberate disposition of an innocent human life, that is a disposition which looks to its destruction either as an end or as a means to another end perhaps in itself not illicit.—The baby, still not born, is a man in the same degree and for the same reason as the mother" (quoted in Noonan, *The Morality of Abortion*, p. 45).

7. The need for a discussion of this argument was brought home to me by members of the Society for Ethical and Legal Philosophy, to whom this paper was originally presented.
8. For a discussion of the difficulties involved, and a survey of the European experience with such laws, see *The Good Samaritan and the Law,* ed. James M. Ratcliffe (New York, 1966).

ABORTION AND THE CONCEPT OF A PERSON

Jane English

The abortion debate rages on. Yet the two most popular positions seem to be clearly mistaken. Conservatives maintain that a human life begins at conception and that therefore abortion must be wrong because it is murder. But not all killings of humans are murders. Most notably, self defense may justify even the killing of an innocent person.

Liberals, on the other hand, are just as mistaken in their argument that since a fetus does not become a person until birth, a woman may do whatever she pleases in and to her own body. First, you cannot do as you please with your own body if it affects other people adversely.[1] Second, if a fetus is not a person, that does not imply that you can do to it anything you wish. Animals, for example, are not persons, yet to kill or torture them for no reason at all is wrong.

At the center of the storm has been the issue of just when it is between ovulation and adulthood that a person appears on the scene. Conservatives draw the line at conception, liberals at birth. In this paper I first examine our concept of a person and conclude that no single criterion can capture the concept of a person and no sharp line can be drawn. Next I argue that if a fetus is a person, abortion is still justifiable in many cases; and if a fetus is not a person, killing it is still wrong in many cases. To a large extent, these two solutions are in agreement. I conclude that our concept of a person cannot and need not bear the weight that the abortion controversy has thrust upon it.

Reprinted from *Canadian Journal of Philosophy*, Vol. 5, No. 2 with permission from University of Calgary Press.

I

The several factions in the abortion argument have drawn battle lines around various proposed criteria for determining what is and what is not a person. For example, Mary Anne Warren[2] lists five features (capacities for reasoning, self-awareness, complex communication, etc.) as her criteria for personhood and argues for the permissibility of abortion because a fetus falls outside this concept. Baruch Brody[3] uses brain waves. Michael Tooley[4] picks having-a-concept-of-self as his criterion and concludes that infanticide and abortion are justifiable, while the killing of adult animals is not. On the other side, Paul Ramsey[5] claims a certain gene structure is the defining characteristic. John Noonan[6] prefers conceived-of-humans and presents counterexamples to various other candidate criteria. For instance, he argues against viability as the criterion because the newborn and infirm would then be non-persons, since they cannot live without the aid of others. He rejects any criterion that calls upon the sorts of sentiments a being can evoke in adults on the grounds that this would allow us to exclude other races as non-persons if we could just view them sufficiently unsentimentally.

These approaches are typical: foes of abortion propose sufficient conditions for personhood which fetuses satisfy, while friends of abortion counter with necessary conditions for personhood which fetuses lack. But these both presuppose that the concept of a person can be captured in a strait jacket of necessary and/or sufficient conditions.[7] Rather, 'person' is a cluster of features, of which rationality, having a self concept and being conceived of humans are only part.

What is typical of persons? Within our concept of a person we include, first, certain biological factors: descended from humans, having a certain genetic make-up, having a head, hands, arms, eyes, capable of locomotion, breathing, eating, sleeping. There are psychological factors: sentience, perception, having a concept of self and of one's own interests and desires, the ability to use tools, the ability to use language or symbol systems, the ability to joke, to be angry, to doubt. There are rationality factors: the ability to reason and draw conclusions, the ability to generalize and to learn from past experience, the ability to sacrifice present interests for greater gains in the future. There are social factors: the ability to work in groups and respond to peer pressures, the ability to recognize and consider as valuable the interests of others, seeing oneself as one among "other minds," the ability to sympathize, encourage, love, the ability to evoke from others the responses of sympathy, encouragement, love, the ability to work with others for mutual advantage. Then there are legal factors: being subject to the law and protected by it, having the ability to sue and enter contracts, being counted in the census, having a name and citizenship, the ability to own property, inherit, and so forth.

Now the point is not that this list is incomplete, or that you can find counterinstances to each of its points. People typically exhibit rationality, for instance, but someone who was irrational would not thereby fail to qualify as a person. On the other hand, something could exhibit the majority of these features and still fail to be a person, as an advanced robot might. There is no single core of necessary and sufficient features which we can draw upon with the assurance that they constitute what really makes a person; there are only features that are more or less typical.

This is not to say that no necessary or sufficient conditions can be given. Being alive is a necessary condition for being a person, and being a U.S. Senator is sufficient. But rather than falling inside a sufficient condition or outside a necessary one, a fetus lies in the penumbra region where our concept of a person is not so simple. For this reason I think a conclusive answer to the question whether a fetus is a person is unattainable.

Here we might note a family of simple fallacies that proceed by stating a necessary condition for personhood and showing that a fetus has that characteristic. This is a form of the fallacy of affirming the consequent. For example, some have mistakenly reasoned from the premise that a fetus is human (after all, it is a human fetus rather than, say, a canine fetus), to the conclusion that it is a human. Adding an equivocation on 'being,' we get the fallacious argument that since a fetus is something both living and human, it is a human being.

Nonetheless, it does seem clear that a fetus has very few of the above family of characteristics, whereas a newborn baby exhibits a much larger proportion of them—and a two-year-old has even more. Note that one traditional antiabortion argument has centered on pointing out the many ways in which a fetus resembles a baby. They emphasize its development ("It already has ten fingers...") without mentioning its dissimilarities to adults (it still has gills and a tail). They also try to evoke the sort of sympathy on our part that we only feel toward other persons ("Never to laugh ... or feel the sunshine?"). This all seems to be a relevant way to argue, since its purpose is to persuade us that a fetus satisfies so many of the important features on the list that it ought to be treated as a person. Also note that a fetus near the time of birth satisfies many more of these factors than a fetus in the early months of development. This could provide reason for making distinctions among the different stages of pregnancy, as the U.S. Supreme Court has done.[8]

Historically, the time at which a person has been said to come into existence has varied widely. Muslims date personhood from fourteen days after conception. Some medievals followed Aristotle in placing ensoulment at forty days after conception for a male fetus and eighty days for a female fetus.[9] In European common law since the Seventeenth Century, abortion was considered the killing of a person only after quickening, the time when a pregnant woman first feels the fetus move on its own. Nor is this variety of opinions surprising. Biologically, a human being develops gradually. We shouldn't expect there to be any specific time or sharp dividing point when a person appears on the scene.

For these reasons I believe our concept of a person is not sharp or decisive enough to bear the weight of a solution to the abortion controversy. To use it to solve that problem is to clarify *obscurum* per *obscurius*.

II

Next let us consider what follows if a fetus is a person after all. Judith Jarvis Thomson's landmark article, "A Defense of Abortion,"[10] correctly points out that some additional argumentation is needed at this point in the conservative argument to bridge the gap between the premise that a fetus is an innocent person and the conclusion that killing it is always wrong. To arrive at this conclusion, we would need the additional premise that killing an innocent person is always wrong. But killing an innocent person is sometimes permissible, most notably in self defense. Some examples may help draw out our intuitions or ordinary judgments about self defense.

Suppose a mad scientist, for instance, hypnotized innocent people to jump out of the bushes and attack innocent passers-by with knives. If you are so attacked, we agree you have a right to kill the attacker in self defense, if killing him is the only way to protect your life or to save yourself from serious injury. It does not seem to matter here that the attacker is not malicious but himself an innocent pawn, for your killing of him is not done in a spirit of retribution but only in self defense.

How severe an injury may you inflict in self defense? In part this depends upon the severity of the injury to be avoided: you may not shoot someone merely to avoid having your clothes torn. This might lead one to the mistaken conclusion that the defense may only equal the threatened injury in severity; that to avoid death you may kill, but to avoid a black eye you may only inflict a black eye or the equivalent. Rather, our laws and customs seem to say that you may create an injury somewhat, but not enormously, greater than the injury to be avoided. To fend off an attack whose outcome would be as serious as rape, a severe beating or the loss of a finger, you may shoot; to avoid having your clothes torn, you may blacken an eye.

Aside from this, the injury you may inflict should only be the minimum necessary to deter or incapacitate the attacker. Even if you know he intends to kill you, you are not justified in shooting him if you could equally well save yourself by the simple expedient of running away. Self defense is for the purpose of avoiding harms rather than equalizing harms.

Some cases of pregnancy present a parallel situation. Though the fetus is itself innocent, it may pose a threat to the pregnant woman's well-being, life prospects or health, mental or physical. If the pregnancy presents a slight threat to her interests, it seems self defense cannot justify abortion. But if the threat is on a par with a serious beating or the loss of a finger, she may kill the fetus that poses such a threat, even if it is an innocent person. If a lesser harm to the fetus could have the same defensive effect, killing it would not be justified. It is unfortunate that the only way to free the woman from the pregnancy entails the death of the fetus (except in very late stages of pregnancy). Thus a self defense model supports Thomson's point that the woman has a right only to be freed from the fetus, not a right to demand its death.[11]

The self defense model is most helpful when we take the pregnant woman's point of view. In the pre-Thomson literature, abortion is often framed as a question for a third party: do you, a doctor, have a right to choose between the life of the woman and that of the fetus? Some have claimed that if you were a passer-by who witnessed a struggle between the innocent hypnotized attacker and his equally innocent victim, you would have no reason to kill either in defense of the other. They have concluded that the self defense model implies that a woman may attempt to abort herself, but that a doctor should not assist her. I think the position of the third party is somewhat more complex. We do feel some inclination to intervene on behalf of the victim rather than the attacker, other things equal. But if both parties are innocent, other factors come into consideration. You would rush to the aid of your husband whether he was attacker or attackee. If a hypnotized famous violinist were attacking a skid row bum, we would try to save the individual who is of more value to society. These considerations would tend to support abortion in some cases.

But suppose you are a frail senior citizen who wishes to avoid being knifed by one of these innocent hypnotics, so you have hired a bodyguard to accompany you. If you are attacked, it is clear we believe that the bodyguard, acting as your agent, has a right to kill the attacker to save you from a serious beating. Your rights of self defense are transferred to your agent. I suggest that we should similarly view the doctor as the pregnant woman's agent in carrying out a defense she is physically incapable of accomplishing herself.

Thanks to modern technology, the cases are rare in which a pregnancy poses as clear a threat to a woman's bodily health as an attacker brandishing a switchblade. How does self defense fare when more subtle, complex and long-range harms are involved?

To consider a somewhat fanciful example, suppose you are a highly trained surgeon when you are kidnapped by the hypnotic attacker. He says he does not intend to harm you but to take you back to the mad scientist who, it turns out, plans to hypnotize you to have a permanent mental block against all your knowledge of medicine. This would automatically destroy your career which would in turn have a serious adverse impact on your family, your personal relationships and your happiness. It seems to me that if the only way you can avoid this outcome is to shoot the innocent attacker, you are justified in so doing. You are defending yourself from a drastic injury to your life prospects. I think it is no exaggeration to claim that unwanted pregnancies (most obviously among teenagers) often have such adverse lifelong consequences as the surgeon's loss of livelihood.

Several parallels arise between various views on abortion and the self defense model. Let's suppose further that these hypnotized attackers only operate at night, so that it is well known that they can be avoided completely by the considerable inconvenience of never leaving your house after dark. One view is that since you could stay home at night, therefore if you go out and are selected by one of these hypnotized people, you have no right to defend yourself. This parallels the view that abstinence is the only acceptable way to avoid pregnancy. Others might hold that you ought to take along some defense such as Mace which will deter the hypnotized person without killing him, but that if this defense fails, you are obliged to submit to the resulting injury, no matter how severe it is. This parallels the view that contraception is all right but abortion is always wrong, even in cases of contraceptive failure.

A third view is that you may kill the hypnotized person only if he will actually kill you, but not if he will only injure you. This is like the position that abortion is permissible only if it is required to save a woman's life. Finally we have the view that it is all right to kill the attacker, even if only to avoid a very slight inconvenience to yourself and even if you knowingly walked down the very street where all these incidents have been taking place without taking along any Mace or protective escort. If we assume that a fetus is a person, this is the analogue of the view that abortion is always justifiable, "on demand."

The self defense model allows us to see an important difference that exists between abortion and infanticide, even if a fetus is a person from conception. Many have argued that the only way to justify abortion without justifying infanticide would be to find some characteristic of personhood that is acquired at birth. Michael Tooley, for one, claims infanticide is justifiable because the really significant characteristics of person are acquired some time after birth. But all such approaches look to characteristics of the developing human and ignore the relation between the fetus and the woman. What if, after birth, the presence of an infant or the need to support it posed a grave threat to the woman's sanity or life prospects? She could escape this threat by the simple expedient of running away. So a solution that does not entail the death of the infant is available. Before birth, such solutions are not available because of the biological dependence of the fetus on the woman. Birth is the crucial point not because of any characteristics the fetus gains, but because after birth the woman can defend herself by a means less drastic than killing the infant. Hence self defense can be used to justify abortion without necessarily thereby justifying infanticide.

III

On the other hand, supposing a fetus is not after all a person, would abortion always be morally permissible? Some opponents of abortion seem worried that if a fetus is not a full-fledged person, then we are justified in treating it in any way at all. However, this does not follow. Non-persons do get some consideration in our moral code, though of course they do not have the same rights as persons have (and in general they do not have moral responsibilities), and though their interests may be overridden by the interests of persons. Still, we cannot just treat them in any way at all.

Treatment of animals is a case in point. It is wrong to torture dogs for fun or to kill wild birds for no reason at all. It is wrong Period, even though dogs and birds do not have the same rights persons do. However, few people think it is wrong to use dogs as experimental animals, causing them considerable suffering in some cases, provided that the resulting research will probably bring discoveries of great benefit to people. And most of us think it all right to kill birds for food or to protect our crops. People's rights are different from the consideration we give to animals, then, for it is wrong to experiment on people, even if others might later benefit a great deal as a result of their suffering. You might volunteer to be a subject, but this would be supererogatory; you certainly have a right to refuse to be a medical guinea pig.

But how do we decide what you may or may not do to non-persons? This is a difficult problem, one for which I believe no adequate account exists. You do not want to say, for instance, that torturing dogs is all right whenever the sum of its effects on people is good—when it doesn't warp the sensibilities of the torturer so much that he mistreats people. If that were the case, it would be all right to torture dogs if you did it in private, or if the torturer lived on a desert island or died soon afterward, so that his actions had no effect on people. This is an inadequate account, because whatever moral consideration animals get, it has to be indefeasible, too. It will have to be a general proscription of certain actions, not merely a weighing of the impact on people on a case-by-case basis.

Rather, we need to distinguish two levels on which consequences of actions can be taken into account in moral reasoning. The traditional objections to Utilitarianism focus on the fact that it operates solely on the first level, taking all the consequences into account in particular cases only. Thus Utilitarianism is open to "desert island" and "lifeboat" counterexamples because these cases are rigged to make the consequences of actions severely limited.

Rawls' theory could be described as a teleological sort of theory, but with teleology operating on a higher level.[12] In choosing the principles to regulate society from the original position, his hypothetical choosers make their decision on the basis of the total consequences of various systems. Furthermore, they are constrained to choose a general set of rules which people can readily learn and apply. An ethical theory must operate by generating a set of sympathies and attitudes toward others which reinforces the functioning of that set of moral principles. Our prohibition against killing people operates by means of certain moral sentiments including sympathy, compassion and guilt. But if these attitudes are to form a coherent set, they carry us further: we tend to perform supererogatory actions, and we tend to feel similar compassion toward person-like non-persons.

It is crucial that psychological facts play a role here. Our psychological constitution makes it the case that for our ethical theory to work, it must prohibit certain treatment of non-persons which are significantly person-like. If our moral rules allowed people to treat some person-like non-persons in ways we do not want people to be treated, this would undermine the system of sympathies and attitudes that makes the ethical system work. For this reason, we would choose in the original position to make mistreatment of some sorts of animals wrong in general (not just wrong in the cases with public impact), even though animals are not themselves parties in the original position. Thus it makes sense that it is those animals whose appearance and behavior are most like those of people that get the most consideration in our moral scheme.

It is because of "coherence of attitudes," I think, that the similarity of a fetus to a baby is very significant. A fetus one week before birth is so much like a newborn baby in our psychological space that we cannot allow any cavalier treatment of the former while expecting full sympathy and nurturative support for the latter. Thus, I think that anti-abortion forces are indeed giving their strongest arguments when they point to the similarities between a fetus and a baby, and when they try to evoke our emotional attachment to and sympathy for the fetus. An early horror story from New York about nurses who were expected to alternate between caring for six-week premature infants and disposing of viable 24-week aborted fetuses is just that—a horror story. These beings are so much alike that no one can be asked to draw a distinction and treat them so very differently.

Remember, however, that in the early weeks after conception, a fetus is not very much unlike a person. It is hard to develop these feelings for a set of genes which doesn't yet have a head, hands, beating heart, response to touch or the ability to move by itself. Thus it seems to me that the alleged "slippery slope" between conception and birth is not so very slippery. In the early stages of pregnancy, abortion can hardly be compared to murder for psychological reasons, but in the latest stages it is psychologically akin to murder.

Another source of similarity is the bodily continuity between fetus and adult. Bodies play a surprisingly central role in our attitudes toward persons. One has only to think of the philosophical literature on how far physical identity suffices for personal identity or Wittgenstein's remark that the best picture of the human soul is the human body. Even after death, when all agree the body is no longer a person, we still observe elaborate customs of respect for the human body; like people who torture dogs, necrophiliacs are not to be trusted with people.[13] So it is appropriate that we show respect to a fetus as the body continuous with the body of a person. This is a degree of resemblance to persons that animals cannot rival.

Michael Tooley also utilizes a parallel with animals. He claims that it is always permissible to drown newborn kittens and draws conclusions about infanticide.[14] But it is only permissible to drown kittens when their survival would cause some hardship. Perhaps it would be a burden to feed and house six more cats or to find other homes for them. The alternative of letting them starve produces even more suffering than the drowning. Since the kittens get their rights secondhand, so to speak, *via* the need for coherence in our attitudes, their interests are often overriden by the interests of full-fledged persons. But if their survival would be no inconvenience to people at all, then it is wrong to drown them, *contra* Tooley.

Tooley's conclusions about abortion are wrong for the same reason. Even if a fetus is not a person, abortion is not always permissible, because of the resemblance of a fetus to a person. I agree with Thomson that it would be wrong for a woman who is seven months pregnant to have an abortion just to avoid having to postpone a trip to Europe. In the early months of pregnancy when the fetus hardly resembles a baby at all, then, abortion is permissible whenever it is in the interests of the pregnant woman or her family. The reasons would only need to outweigh the pain and inconvenience of the abortion itself. In the middle months, when the fetus comes to resemble a person, abortion would be justifiable only when the continuation of the pregnancy or the birth of the child would cause harms—physical, psychological, economic or social—to the woman. In the late months of pregnancy, even on our current assumption that a fetus is not a person, abortion seems to be wrong except to save a woman from significant injury or death.

The Supreme Court has recognized similar gradations in the alleged slippery slope stretching between conception and birth. To this point, the present paper has been a discussion of the moral status of abortion only, not its legal status. In view of the great physical, financial and sometimes psychological costs of abortion, perhaps the legal arrangement most compatible with the proposed moral solution would be the absence of restrictions, that is, so-called abortion "on demand."

So I conclude, first, that application of our concept of a person will not suffice to settle the abortion issue. After all, the biological development of a human being is gradual. Second, whether a fetus is a person or not, abortion is justifiable early in pregnancy to avoid modest harms and seldom justifiable late in pregnancy except to avoid significant injury or death.[15]

Notes

1. We also have paternalistic laws which keep us from harming our own bodies even when no one else is affected. Ironically, anti-abortion laws were originally designed to protect pregnant women from a dangerous but tempting procedure.
2. Mary Anne Warren, "On the Moral and Legal Status of Abortion," *Monist* 57 (1973), p. 55.
3. Baruch Brody, "Fetal Humanity and the Theory of Essentialism," in Robert Baker and Frederick Elliston (eds.), *Philosophy and Sex* (Buffalo, N.Y., 1975).
4. Michael Tooley, "Abortion and Infanticide," *Philosophy and Public Affairs* 2 (1971).
5. Paul Ramsey, "The Morality of Abortion," in James Rachels, ed., *Moral Problems* (New York, 1971).
6. John Noonan, "Abortion and the Catholic Church: a Summary History," *Natural Law Forum* 12 (1967), pp. 125–131.
7. Wittgenstein has argued against the possibility of fifty capturing the concept of a game, *Philosophical Investigations* (New York, 1958), §66–71.
8. Not because the fetus is partly a person and so has some of the rights of persons, but rather because of the rights of person-like non-persons. This I discuss in part III below.
9. Aristotle himself was concerned, however, with the different question of when the soul takes form. For historical data, see Jimmye Kimmey, "How the Abortion Laws Happened," *Ms.* 1 (April, 1973), pp. 48ff and John Noonan, *loc. cit.*
10. J. J. Thomson, "A Defense of Abortion," *Philosophy and Public Affairs* 1 (1971).
11. *Ibid.*, p. 52.
12. John Rawls, *A Theory of Justice* (Cambridge, Mass., 1971), §§ 3–4.

13. On the other hand, if they can be trusted with people, then our moral customs are mistaken. It all depends on the facts of psychology.
14. *Op. cit.*, pp. 40, 60–61.
15. I am deeply indebted to Larry Crocker and Arthur Kuflik for their constructive comments.

ABORTION: A MODERATE VIEW

L. W. Sumner

We can now catalogue the defects of the established views. The common source of these defects lies in their uniform accounts of the moral status of the fetus. These accounts yield three different sorts of awkward implications. First, they require that all abortions be accorded the same moral status regardless of the stage of pregnancy at which they are performed. Thus, liberals must hold that late abortions are as morally innocuous as early ones, and conservatives must hold that early abortions are as morally serious as late ones. Neither view is able to support the common conviction that late abortions are more serious than early ones. Second, these accounts require that all abortions be accorded the same moral status regardless of the reason for which they are performed. Thus, liberals must hold that all abortions are equally innocuous whatever their grounds, and conservatives must hold that all abortions are equally serious whatever their grounds. Neither view is able to support the common conviction that some grounds justify abortion more readily than others. Third, these accounts require that contraception, abortion, and infanticide all be accorded the same moral status. Thus, liberals must hold that all three practices are equally innocuous, while conservatives must hold that they are all equally serious. Neither view is able to support the common conviction that infanticide is more serious than abortion, which is in turn more serious than contraception.

Reprinted with permission of author and Tom Regan from *Health Care Ethics: An Introduction*, Temple University Press.

Awkward results do not constitute a refutation. The constellation of moral issues concerning human reproduction and development is dark and mysterious. It may be that no internally coherent view of abortion will enable us to retain all of our common moral convictions in this landscape. If so, then perhaps the best we can manage is to embrace one of the established views and bring our attitudes (in whatever turns out to be the troublesome area) into line with it. However, results as awkward as these do provide a strong motive to seek an alternative to the established views and thus to explore the logical space between them.

There are various obstacles in the path of developing a moderate view of abortion. For one thing, any such view will lack the appealing simplicity of the established views. Both liberals and conservatives begin by adopting a simple account of the moral status of the fetus and end by supporting a simple abortion policy. A moderate account of the moral status of the fetus and a moderate abortion policy will inevitably be more complex. Further, a moderate account of the moral status of the fetus, whatever its precise shape, will draw a boundary between those fetuses that have moral standing and those that do not. It will then have to show that the location of this boundary is not arbitrary. Finally, a moderate view may seem nothing more than a compromise between the more extreme positions that lacks any independent rationale of its own.

These obstacles may, however, be less formidable than they appear. Although the complexity of a moderate view may render it harder to sell in the marketplace of ideas, it may otherwise be its greatest asset. It should be obvious by now that the moral issues raised by the peculiar nature of the fetus, and its peculiar relationship with its mother, are not simple. It would be surprising therefore if a simple resolution of them were satisfactory. The richer resources of a complex view may enable it to avoid some of the less palatable implications of its simpler rivals. The problem of locating a nonarbitrary threshold is easier to deal with when we recognize that there can be no sharp breakpoint in the course of human development at which moral standing is suddenly acquired. The attempt to define such a breakpoint was the fatal mistake of the naive versions of the liberal and conservative views. If, as seems likely, an acceptable criterion of moral standing is built around some characteristic that is acquired gradually during the normal course of human development, then moral standing will also be acquired gradually during the normal course of human development. In that case, the boundary between those beings that have moral standing and those that do not will be soft and slow rather than hard and fast. The more sophisticated and credible versions of the established views also pick out stages of development rather than precise breakpoints as their thresholds of moral standing; the only innovation of a moderate view is to locate this stage somewhere during pregnancy. The real challenge to a moderate view, therefore, is to show that it can be well grounded, and thus that it is not simply a way of splitting the difference between two equally unattractive options.

Our critique of the established views has equipped us with specifications for the design of a moderate alternative to them. The fundamental flaw of the established views was their adoption of a uniform account of the moral status of the fetus. A moderate view of abortion must therefore be built on a *differential* account of the moral status of the fetus, awarding moral standing to some fetuses and withholding it from others. The further defects of the established views impose three constraints on the shape of such a differential account. It must explain the moral relevance of the gestational age of the fetus at the time of abortion and thus must correlate moral status with level of fetal development. It must also explain the moral relevance, at least at some stages of pregnancy, of the reason for which an abortion is performed. And finally it must preserve the distinction between the moral innocuousness of contraception and the moral seriousness of infanticide. When we combine these specifications, we obtain the rough outline of a moderate view. Such a view will identify the stage of pregnancy during which the fetus gains moral standing. Before that threshold, abortion will be as morally innocuous as contraception and no grounds will be needed to justify it. After the threshold, abortion will be as morally serious as infanticide and some special grounds will be needed to justify it (if it can be justified at this stage at all).

A moderate view is well grounded when it is derivable from an independently plausible criterion of moral standing. It is not difficult to construct a criterion that will yield a threshold somewhere during pregnancy. Let us say that a being is sentient when it has the capacity to experience pleasure and pain and thus the capacity for enjoyment and suffering. Beings that are self-conscious or rational are generally (though perhaps not necessarily) also sentient, but many sentient beings lack both self-consciousness and rationality. A sentience criterion of moral standing thus sets a lower standard than that shared by the established views. Such a criterion will accord moral standing to the mentally handicapped regardless of impairments of their cognitive capacities. It will also accord moral standing to many, perhaps most, nonhuman animals.

The plausibility of a sentience criterion would be partially established by tracing out its implications for moral contexts other than abortion. But it would be considerably enhanced if such a criterion could also be given a deeper grounding. Such a grounding can be supplied by what seems a reasonable conception of the nature of morality. The moral point of view is just one among many evaluative points of view. It appears to be distinguished from the others in two respects: its special concern for the interest, welfare, or well-being of creatures and its requirement of impartiality. Adopting the moral point of view requires in one way or another according equal consideration to the interests of all beings. If this is so, then a being's having an interest to be considered is both necessary and sufficient for its having moral standing. While the notion of interest or welfare is far from transparent, its irreducible core appears to be the capacity for enjoyment and suffering: all and only beings with this capacity have an interest or welfare that the moral point of view requires us to respect. But then it follows easily that sentience is both necessary and sufficient for moral standing.

A criterion of moral standing is well grounded when it is derivable from some independently plausible moral theory. A sentience criterion can be grounded in any member of a class of theories that share the foregoing conception of the nature of morality. Because of the centrality of interest or welfare to that conception, let us call such theories welfare based. A sentience criterion of moral standing can be readily grounded in any welfare-based moral theory. The class of such theories is quite extensive, including everything from varieties of rights theory on the one hand to varieties of utilitarianism on the other. Whatever their conceptual and structural differences, a sentience criterion can be derived from any one of them. The diversity of theoretical resources available to support a sentience criterion is one of its greatest strengths. In addition, a weaker version of such a criterion is also derivable from more eclectic theories that treat the promotion and protection of welfare as one of the basic concerns of morality. Any such theory will yield the result that sentience is sufficient for moral standing, though it may also be necessary, thus providing partial support for a moderate view of abortion. Such a view is entirely unsupported only by moral theories that find no room whatever for the promotion of welfare among the concerns of morality.

When we apply a sentience criterion to the course of human development, it yields the result that the threshold of moral standing is the stage during which the capacity to experience pleasure and pain is first required. This capacity is clearly possessed by a newborn infant (and a full-term fetus) and is clearly not possessed by a pair of gametes (or a newly fertilized ovum). It is therefore acquired during the normal course of gestation. But when? A definite answer awaits a better understanding than we now possess of the development of the fetal nervous system and thus of fetal consciousness. We can, however, venture a provisional answer. It is standard practice to divide the normal course of gestation into three trimesters of thirteen weeks each. It is likely that a fetus is unable to feel pleasure or pain at the beginning of the second trimester and likely that it is able to do so at the end of that trimester. If this is so, then the threshold of sentience, and thus also the threshold of moral standing, occurs sometime during the second trimester.

We can now fill in our earlier sketch of a moderate view of abortion. A fetus acquires moral standing when it acquires sentience, that is to say at some stage in the second trimester of pregnancy. Before that threshold, when the fetus lacks moral standing, the decision to seek an abortion is morally equivalent to the decision to employ contraception; the effect in both cases is to prevent the existence of a being with moral standing. Such decisions are morally innocuous and should be left to the discretion of the parties involved. Thus, the liberal view of abortion, and a permissive abortion policy, are appropriate for early (prethreshold) abortions. After the threshold, when the fetus has moral standing, the decision to seek an abortion is morally equivalent to the decision to commit infanticide; the effect in both cases is to terminate the existence of a being with moral standing. Such decisions are morally serious and should not be left to the discretion of the parties involved (the fetus is now one of the parties involved).

It should follow that the conservative view of abortion and a restrictive abortion policy are appropriate for late (post-threshold) abortions. But this does not follow. Conservatives hold that abortion, because it is homicide, is unjustified on any grounds. This absolute position is indefensible even for post-threshold fetuses with moral standing. Of the four categories of grounds for abortion, neither humanitarian nor socioeconomic grounds will apply to post-threshold abortions, since a permissive policy for the period before the threshold will afford women the opportunity to decide freely whether they wish to continue their pregnancies. Therapeutic grounds will however apply, since serious risks to maternal life or health may materialize after the threshold. If they do, there is no justification for refusing an abortion. A pregnant woman is providing life support for another being that is housed within her body. If continuing to provide that life support will place her own life or health at serious risk, then she cannot justifiably be compelled to do so, even though the fetus has moral standing and will die if deprived of that life support. Seeking an abortion in such circumstances is a legitimate act of self-preservation.

A moderate abortion policy must therefore include a therapeutic ground for post-threshold abortions. It must also include a eugenic ground. Given current technology, some tests for fetal abnormalities can be carried out only in the second trimester. In many cases, therefore, serious abnormalities will be detected only after the fetus has passed the threshold. Circumstantial differences aside, the status of a severely deformed post-threshold fetus is the same as the status of a severely deformed newborn infant. The moral issues concerning the treatment of such newborns are themselves complex, but there appears to be a good case for selective infanticide in some cases. If so, then there is an even better case for late abortion on eugenic grounds, since here we must also reckon in the terrible burden of carrying to term a child that a woman knows to be deformed.

A moderate abortion policy will therefore contain the following ingredients: a time limit that separates early from late abortions, a permissive policy for early abortions, and a policy for late abortions that incorporates both therapeutic and eugenic grounds. This blueprint leaves many smaller questions of design to be settled. The grounds for late abortions must be specified more carefully by determining what is to count as a serious risk to maternal life or health and what is to count as a serious fetal abnormality. While no general formulation of a policy can settle these matters in detail, guidelines can and should be supplied. A policy should also specify the procedure that is to be followed in deciding when a particular case has met these guidelines.

But most of all, a moderate policy must impose a defensible time limit. As we saw earlier, from the moral point of view there can be no question of a sharp breakpoint. Fetal development unfolds gradually and cumulatively, and sentience like all other capacities is acquired slowly and by degrees. Thus we have clear cases of presentient fetuses in the first trimester and clear cases of sentient fetuses in the third trimester. But we also have unclear cases, encompassing many (perhaps most) second-trimester fetuses. From the moral point of view, we can say only that in these cases the moral status of the fetus, and thus the moral status of abortion, is indeterminate. This sort of moral indeterminacy occurs also at later stages of human development, for instance when we are attempting to fix the age of consent or of competence to drink or drive. We do not pretend in these latter cases that the capacity in question is acquired overnight on one's sixteenth or eighteenth birthday, and yet for legal purposes we must draw a sharp and determinate line. Any such line will be somewhat arbitrary, but it is enough if it is drawn within the appropriate threshold stage. So also in the case of a time limit for abortion, it is sufficient if the line for legal purposes is located within the appropriate threshold stage. A time limit anywhere in the second trimester is therefore defensible, at least until we acquire the kind of information about fetal development that will enable us to narrow the threshold stage and thus to locate the time limit with more accuracy.

RATIONALE FOR BANNING ABORTIONS LATE IN PREGNANCY

M. LeRoy Sprang and Mark G. Neerhof

The abortion issue remains in the public eye and the media headlines largely because of a single late-term abortion procedure referred to in the medical literature as intact dilation and extraction (D&X) and in the common vernacular as partial-birth abortion. This article reviews the medical and ethical aspects of this procedure and of late-term abortions in general.

ETHICAL CONSIDERATIONS

Intact D&X (Partial-Birth Abortion) is most commonly performed between 20 and 24 weeks and thereby raises questions of the potential viability of the fetus.

PROFESSIONAL, LEGISLATIVE, AND PUBLIC CONCERNS

An extraordinary medical consensus has emerged that intact D&X is neither necessary nor the safest method for late-term abortion. In addition to American Medical Association (AMA) and ACOG policy statements, Warren Hem, MD, author of *Abortion Practice,* has questioned the efficacy of intact D&X. "I have very serious reservations about this procedure.... You really can't defend it.... I would dispute any statement that this is the safest procedure to use."

Legislative bodies across the United States have decided that intact D&X is not appropriate. In fact, 28 states have approved a ban, and Congress also overwhelmingly voted to ban the procedure with strong bipartisan support.[1]

TERMINATION OF LATE-TERM PREGNANCIES

Many of the medical and ethical issues that pertain to intact D&X also apply to late-term pregnancy termination, defined for the purposes of this articles as termination beyond 20 weeks' gestation. Pregnancy termination at this gestational age can be accomplished either by labor induction or by D&E (dilation and evacuation).

Most clinicians would argue for maintaining the option of late pregnancy termination to save the life of the mother, which is an extraordinarily rare circumstance. Maternal health factors demanding pregnancy termination in the periviable period can almost always be accommodated without sacrificing the fetus and without compromising maternal well-being. The high probability of fetal intact survival beyond the periviable period argues for ending the pregnancy through appropriate delivery. In a similar fashion, the following discussion does not apply to fetuses with anomalies incompatible with prolonged survival. When pregnancy termination is performed for these indications, it should be performed in as humane a fashion as possible. Therefore, intact D&X should not be performed even in these circumstances.

ETHICAL CONSIDERATIONS

The autonomy of the pregnant woman is increasingly counterbalanced by fetal development, the increasing tendency to attribute personhood to the fetus, and the increasing likelihood of independent fetal viability. Fetal development affects maternal autonomy on a inversely sliding scale. As a fetus evolves into an individual capable of survival independent of its mother (and thus personhood), the conditional fetal rights argument gains greater merit.

A second ethical principle concerns beneficence, ie, one individual's obligation to act for the benefit of another. As the fetus matures, the majority of individuals would extend greater and greater beneficence to the fetus. According to Stubblefield, "Inevitably, there must be a gestational age limit for abortion. I would avoid performing abortions after 22 weeks unless the mother's life were endangered or unless the fetus had major malformations so severe as to preclude prolonged survival.... When termination of pregnancy will be undertaken at or after 23 weeks because of serious risk for maternal health, the fetus should be considered as well."[2]

A third ethical principle concerns justice and denotes balancing the rights of distinct individuals. As the fetus develops, more and more people recognize that there are 2 distinct individuals involved. To take a position that would make the value of the fetus depend solely on private choice and on the individual exercise of power fails to understand the importance of communal safeguards against capricious power over life and death.[3]

CONCLUSIONS

Medical professionals have an obligation to thoughtfully consider the medical and ethical issues surrounding pregnancy termination, particularly with respect to intact D&X and late-term abortions. Having done so, we conclude the following: (1) Intact D&X (partial-birth abortion) should not be performed because it is needlessly risky, inhumane, and ethically unacceptable. This procedure is closer to infanticide than it is to abortion. (2) Abortions in the periviable period (currently 23 weeks) and beyond should be considered unethical, unless the fetus has a condition incompatible with prolonged survival or if the mother's life is endangered by the pregnancy. (3) If a maternal medical condition in the periviable period indicates pregnancy termination, the physician should wait, if the medical condition permits, until fetal survival is probable and then proceed with delivery. Such medical decisions must be individualized.

Physicians must preserve their role as healing, compassionate, caring professionals, while recognizing their ethical obligation to care for both the woman and the unborn child. In July 1997, the ACOG Executive Board supplemented its policy on abortion toward this end, stating, "ACOG is opposed to abortion of the healthy fetus that has attained viability in a healthy woman."[4]

We hope that with thoughtful discussions regarding specific issues such as those considered in this article, the opposing forces in the ongoing, stagnant abortion debate will find middle ground on which most can agree. The question is often asked, "But who should decide?" Ultimately, at least in the United States, the public will decide. The results of an August 1997 national poll showed public opinion firmly in the camp of "drawing a line" on abortion rights, with 61% believing that abortion should be legal only under certain circumstances, and 22% defending the legality of abortion under any circumstances.[5] Society will not countenance infanticide. According to Boston University ethicist and health law professor George Annas, JD, MPH, Americans see "a distinction between first trimester and second trimester abortions. The law doesn't, but people do. And rightfully so."[6] He explained that after approximately 20 weeks, the American public sees a baby. The American public's vision of this may be much clearer than that of some of the physicians involved.

References

1. *Status of Bans on "Partial-Birth Abortion" and Other Abortion Methods.* New York, NY: Center for Reproductive Law and Policy; June 29, 1998.
2. Stubblefield PJ. Pregnancy termination. In: Gabbe SG, Niebyl JR, Simpson JL, eds. *Obstetrics, Normal and Problem Pregnancies.* 3rd ed. New York, NY: Churchill Livingston; 1996:1243–1278.
3. Callahan D. The abortion debate: can this chronic public illness be cured? In: Chervenak FA, McCullough LD, eds. *Clin Obstet Gynecol.* 1992;35:783–791.
4. *ACOG Statement of Policy.* Approved by executive board and published in ACOG newsletter; July 1997.
5. Padawer R. "Partial-birth" battle changing public views. *USA Today.* November 17, 1997:17A.
6. Gianellli DM. Medicine adds to debate on late-term abortion. *American Medical News.* March 3, 1997:3, 54–56.

THE CONTINUING NEED FOR LATE ABORTIONS

David A. Grimes

Late abortion is the most controversial aspect of the most divisive social issue of our times.[1] The debate has been strident, confusing, and at times, misleading.[2]

EPIDEMIOLOGY AND TECHNIQUES OF LATE ABORTION

For decades, late induced abortions have been uncommon in the United States. From 1972 through 1992, the proportion of all induced abortions that were performed at 21 or more weeks' gestation ranged from 0.8% to 1.7%.[3] The upper gestational age limit varies by state. However, the claim that many women have elective abortions in the third trimester lacks support. Most reports of abortions at 25 or more weeks' gestation are due to reporting errors or to fetal demise. Between 1979 and 1980, only 3 cases of approximately 70,000 reported induced abortions in Georgia took place at 25 weeks or more. Two procedures were performed for fetal anencephaly, and insufficient information was available for the third.[4] This is believed to be the only published article on this procedure.

Dilation and evacuation (D&E) is the most frequent method used for late abortion in the United States. In 1992, D&E accounted for 86% of all abortions at 21 or more weeks' gestation, whereas labor induction accounted for 14%.[3]

MORBIDITY AND MORTALITY OF LATE ABORTIONS

Compared with labor induction, D&E is preferable in terms of compassion, cost, comfort, and convenience. Negative reactions to second-trimester abortion are directly related to contact with the fetus. Aborting a fetus can be emotionally difficult for women, especially for those who are alone in a hospital in the middle of the night. In contrast, during D&E abortion women have no contact with the fetus. The operation transfers the emotional burden of abortion from women, who have often suffered greatly, to the staff. Dilation and evacuation abortion obviates the need for costly overnight stays in hospital, as is customary with labor induction. Women having D&E abortions are spared a "maxi-labor" followed by a "mini-delivery." Instead of enduring labor, women receive local or general anesthesia for the brief operation. Finally, because D&E abortion takes place on an outpatient basis, women's lives are less disrupted than with hospitalization for 1 or more nights.

CHARACTERISTICS OF WOMEN WHO HAVE LATE ABORTIONS

Women who have late abortions often are disadvantaged. Teenagers, especially those younger than 15 years, and women of minority status disproportionately have late abortions.[3] Many of these patients either do not suspect the pregnancy or attempt to conceal it until the pregnancy becomes evident. Menstrual irregularity is an important risk factor.[5] Women with irregular menses often discover late that they are pregnant. Other risk factors include young age, low educational attainment, having had a sexually transmitted disease, and ambivalence about the decision to abort.[6] Thus, many of the factors associated with late abortions are not easily changed.

Women seeking late abortions are often disadvantaged in other ways, such as lack of knowledge about options, lack of money to pay for the procedure, lack of transportation to a provider, and alcohol or other drug dependence.

Reprinted from *JAMA*, Vol. 280, No. 8 (August 26, 1998), pp. 747–750.

Some young women are unaware of the availability of late abortions. Since enactment of the Hyde Amendment, the federal government has not paid for indigent women to have abortions, and few states subsidize abortion services. Hence, some women need weeks to raise the money to pay for an abortion, which delays the procedure until the second trimester. Of note, states that fund abortions have significantly lower rates of teen pregnancy, low-birth-weight babies, premature births, and births with late or no prenatal care than do other states.

Geography poses yet another barrier: more than 80% of US counties do not have an abortion provider. Providers of late abortion are even more scarce. In 1993, only 13% of US abortion providers offered abortions at 21 weeks, and the cost averaged more than $1000.[7]

INDICATIONS FOR LATE ABORTION

Late abortions are fundamentally important to women's reproductive health.[1] Antenatal fetal diagnosis, such as maternal α-fetoprotein screening and amniocentesis, is predicated on the availability of induced abortion. Although techniques such as chorionic villus sampling and early amniocentesis have allowed earlier diagnosis, by the time results of midtrimester amniocentesis or ultrasound are available, a woman may be beyond 20 weeks' gestation.[8]

Ironically, the availability of late abortion is pronatalist. About 98% of women who undergo genetic screening receive reassuring news.[9] Without the availability of prenatal diagnosis with abortion as an option, many of these women would not have become pregnant or would have aborted all pregnancies that occurred.[8] As noted by Cook,[11] "Macroethical reasons favouring legal abortion in such circumstances rest on the potential to do greater good than harm in the community, and reveal the positive, life-affirming aspects of legally available abortion services."

Illnesses of women and fetal anomalies lead to requests for late abortions. Late abortion can be lifesaving for women with medical disorders aggravated by pregnancy.[12] Conditions such as Eisenmenger syndrome carry a high risk of maternal morbidity and mortality in pregnancy, the latter ranging from 20% to 30%.[13] In recent years, I have performed late abortions for a Kampuchean refugee with craniopagus conjoined twins and a 25-year-old woman with a 9 × 15-cm thoracic aortic aneurysm from newly diagnosed Marfan syndrome. Cancer sometimes makes late abortion necessary. For example, either radical hysterectomy or radiation therapy for cervical cancer before fetal viability involves abortion.

Incest and rape are other compelling indications. Pregnancies resulting from incest among young teenagers or among women with mental handicaps may escape detection until the pregnancy is advanced. Approximately 32,000 pregnancies result from rape each year in the United States; about half of rape victims receive no medical attention, and about one third do not discover the pregnancy until the second trimester.[14]

GESTATIONAL AGE LIMIT FOR ABORTION

The appropriate upper gestational age limit for abortion remains elusive. Most Americans reject absolutist positions on abortion. Absolutist positions are problematic "because no such account can claim final intellectual or moral authority, given the necessarily disputable nature of all accounts of the independent moral status of the fetus."[15]

Instead, most Americans choose the moderate or gradualist view. This holds that the fetus gains increasing human worth as pregnancy advances. "The main difficulty with moderate views of abortion is that they lack the precision of the liberal and the conservative views. Knowledge of fetal development is constantly increasing and no sharp divisions can be drawn between one stage and the next." Given these ambiguities, compassion, tolerance, and judgment are needed to balance the competing interests of fetus, woman, and society.

Some argue that the gestational age limit for abortion should be the point of viability. This is a shifting target, and physicians cannot predict the probability of extrauterine survival for a given fetus. However, few abortion supporters would consider elective abortion after viability morally acceptable, except in rare circumstances in which the fetus has an anomaly incompatible with life.[16] Others[17] claim that neurological development should define the limit: when the fetus becomes sentient, abortion should be impermissible.

Women ultimately determine the status of the fetus. "Thus, before viability, a pregnant woman is free to withhold, confer, or, having once conferred, withdraw the status of being a patient from the fetus." In other words, "for secular gynecologic ethics, the abortion controversy regarding previable fetuses is resolved for physicians by the autonomous decision of the woman regarding her pregnancy and the dependent moral status of the fetus as a patient."[15]

ATTEMPTS TO BAN A LATE ABORTION METHOD

If late abortions were restricted or eliminated, the alternatives that would remain for women would include illegal abortion, adoption, and rearing a child initially unwanted. Studies of women denied abortions have provided important insights.[18] Some women denied abortion seek the procedure elsewhere and succeed; the high rates of reported spontaneous abortion among women in these studies are suspicious. Few women (7%–19%) place their children for adoption.

Children born after their mothers are denied abortion face serious challenges. In a classic study from Scandinavia, these children had a more insecure childhood, more delinquency, more psychiatric care, and more early marriages than did children in a comparison group.[18] Another study found worse school performance, more neurotic symptoms, and more registrations with social welfare authorities.[18] A study from Prague, Czech Republic, found significantly more serious behavior disorders and continued deterioration in school performance. By the time these children had reached their early 20s, they had significantly more job dissatisfaction, fewer friends, and greater dissatisfaction with life in general. Although the findings were not statistically significant, such children also had less education, more criminality, and more registrations for alcohol and other drug problems.[18] Denying requested abortions has adverse consequences that persist at least into early adulthood.

CONCLUSIONS

As noted by Macklin,[19] "The three leading principles of bioethics—respect for persons, beneficence and justice—together provide an ethical mandate for guaranteeing to women throughout the world a legal right to safe abortion." This mandate is especially important for the immature, disadvantaged, and often seriously ill women requesting late abortions in the United States. Regardless of political views on abortion, the scientific evidence is clear and incontrovertible: legal abortion, including late abortion, has been a resounding public health success.

Early abortion is safer, simpler, and less controversial than late abortion. Improving sex education, promoting access to safe and effective contraception, and removing economic and geographic barriers to early abortion can help to reduce the number of late abortions. This is a goal around which there should be broad consensus. Nevertheless, as experience has revealed,[3] the need for late abortion will not disappear. Hence, our continuing responsibility as physicians and as a society is to ensure that these procedures are as safe, comfortable, and compassionate as possible. Women deserve no less from their physicians.

References

1. Rosenfield A. The difficult issue of second-trimester abortion. *N Engl J Med* 1994; 331:324–325.
2. Rich F. Partial-truth abortion. *New York Times*. March 9, 1997:15.
3. Koonin LM, Smith JC, Ramick M, Green CA. Abortion surveillance— United States, 1992. *MMWR Morb Mortal Wkly Rep*. 1996;45(SS-3):1–36.
4. Spitz AM, Lee NC, Grimes DA, Schoenbucher AK, Lavoie M. Third-trimester induced abortion in Georgia, 1979 and 1980. *Am J Public Health*. 1983;73:594–595.
5. Burr WA, Schulz KF. Delayed abortion in an area of easy accessibility. *JAMA*. 1980;244: 44–48.
6. Guilbert E, Marcoux S, Rioux JE. Factors associated with the obtaining of a second-trimester induced abortion. *Can J Public Health*. 1994; 85:402–406.
7. Henshaw SK. Factors hindering access to abortion services. *Fam Plann Perspect*. 1995; 27:54–59, 87.
8. Timothy J, Harris R. Late terminations of pregnancy following second trimester amniocentesis. *Br J Obstet Gynaecol*. 1986;93:343–347.
9. Farmakides G, Bracero L, Marion R, Fleischer A, Schulman H. Pregnancy termination after detection of fetal chromosomal or metabolic abnormalities. *J Perinatol*. 1988;8:101–104.
10. Hewitt J, Coyle PC. Termination of pregnancy limit: 28, 24, or 18 weeks. *Lancet*. 1988; 1:186–187.
11. Cook RJ. Legal abortion: limits and contributions to human life. In: Porter R, O'Connor M, eds. *Abortion: Medical Progress and Social Implications*. London, England: Pitman; 1985: 211–227.
12. Bowers CH, Chervenak JL, Chervenak FA. Late-second-trimester pregnancy termination with dilation and evacuation in critically ill women. *J Reprod Med*. 1989;34:880–883.
13. Gleicher N, Midwall J, Hochberger D, Jaffin H. Eisenmenger's syndrome and pregnancy. *Obstet Gynecol Surv*. 1979;34:721–741.
14. Holmes MM, Resnick HS, Kilpatrick DG, Best CL. Rape-related pregnancy: estimates and descriptive characteristics from a national sample of women. *Am J Obstet Gynecol*. 1996;175: 320–324.
15. McCullough LB, Chervenak FA. *Ethics in Obstetrics and Gynecology*. New York, NY: Oxford University Press; 1994:166–195.
16. Chervenak FA, Farley MA, Walters L, Hobbins JC, Mahoney MJ. When is termination of pregnancy during the third trimester morally justifiable? *N Engl J Med*. 1984;310:501–504.
17. Jones DG. Brain birth and personal identity. *J Med Ethics*. 1989;15:173–178.
18. Dagg PKB. The psychological sequelae of therapeutic abortion: denied and completed. *Am J Psychiatry*. 1991;148:578–585.
19. Macklin R. Abortion controversies: ethics, politics and religion. In: Baird DT, Grimes DA, van Look PFA, eds. *Modern Methods of Inducing Abortion*. Oxford, England: Blackwell Science; 1995:170–189.

UNIT THREE

LIFE, DEATH, AND MEDICAL TECHNOLOGY

CHAPTER 5: ETHICAL ISSUES AT THE END OF LIFE AND CHAPTER 6: GENETICS AND MORALITY

This unit concerns moral questions surrounding the termination of life and creation and modification of life. Chapter 5 examines the ethical questions surrounding euthanasia and physician-assisted suicide. Chapter 6 presents different perspectives on the moral questions stemming from genetics.

Chapter 5 begins with an overview of the legal situation concerning euthanasia by presenting the majority opinion in the United States Supreme Court case of *Cruzan* v. *Director, Missouri Department of Health*. In this case, for the first time the United States Supreme Court judged that individuals have a constitutional right to refuse treatment. Nancy Cruzan was a young woman who suffered severe brain damage as a result of an automobile accident. She entered into a coma and then into a persistent vegetative state, and had a feeding tube inserted into her stomach to provide fluids and nutrition. Her parents requested on Nancy's behalf that the feeding tube be removed so that she may die. The Court argued that competent persons have a right to refuse medical procedures, and that administering fluids and nutrition constitutes medical treatment. Decisions regarding incompetent patients must satisfy a standard of "clear and convincing evidence" that this is what the person would in fact want if he or she could communicate. While this case laid the foundation for patients' rights to refuse treatment, the Court maintained that Ms. Cruzan was incompetent since she was in a persistent vegetative state and that the evidence presented in support of removing her from life support did not meet the standard of "clear and convincing evidence." (In later court proceedings, it was determined with new input from Ms. Cruzan's family and friends that enough evidence existed to authorize the request to remove the feeding tube. On December 26, 1990, Nancy Cruzan died.)

The next grouping of readings looks closely at the moral status of different forms of euthanasia. Throughout the discussion in this unit, the focus will be on voluntary euthanasia, cases in which a competent person asks to die or the family or a representative of an incompetent person requests this on his or her behalf. With regard to Cruzan's case, some may argue that euthanasia is morally acceptable since this is simply "letting her die," not "killing" her. This difference is reflected in the Traditional View since it makes a distinction between "passive" euthanasia, which can be acceptable since this simply allows the patient's underlying medical condition to end their life, and "active" euthanasia, which is never acceptable since this is a form of killing. In James Rachels' classic article "Active and Passive Euthanasia," Rachels interrogates the Traditional View by arguing that the difference between killing and letting die itself holds no moral relevance. Thomas Sullivan responds to Rachels and claims that Rachels has misinterpreted the Traditional View by emphasizing the distinction between killing and letting die. Instead, argues Sullivan, the Traditional View relies on the distinction between *intentional* and *non-intentional* terminations of life, and the cessation of *ordinary* versus *extraordinary* means of treatment. According to Sullivan, the Traditional View states that it is impermissible to intentionally terminate life, and that it is permissible in some cases to terminate extraordinary means of treatment. This view, argues Sullivan, escapes Rachels' criticisms of the Traditional View. In "Voluntary Active Euthanasia," Dan Brock looks very carefully at the possible good and bad consequences that may stem from accepting a policy of voluntary active euthanasia. Brock seems to be a cautious supporter of such a policy, since he argues that the negative consequences often cited as problematic for a policy of voluntary active euthanasia are not in fact as bad as they appear. Daniel Callahan disagrees with Brock by pointing out some of the bad consequences of allowing active euthanasia, which he believes Brock ignores, and by attacking several main arguments in support of a policy of active euthanasia.

When attempting to discern the acceptability of a policy of active euthanasia, one central question concerns the long-term consequences of such a practice. While there is no empirical evidence available for what might happen in the United States, in the Netherlands, a form of active euthanasia has been practiced for several decades. While euthanasia was not legal, beginning in the 1970s the government in Holland made it clear that it would not aggressively pursue legal action against doctors who performed euthanasia. Although there are social and cultural factors that differ between the two nations, the situation in Holland may serve as the best case study available for determining whether a policy of voluntary active euthanasia would lead to a "slippery slope" in which patients were put to death despite their wishes. In "Euthanasia: Normal Medical Practice?," Professors ten Have and Welie discover over one thousand cases of non-voluntary euthanasia—cases in which persons were killed without giving explicit consent, since they were comatose or were incompetent due to medications they were taking. This report is shocking. Recently, Holland has enacted legislation that makes euthanasia legal, given that certain conditions are satisfied, even though there are indications that non-voluntary euthanasia still occurs. These findings lend some weight to the claim that such a policy will lead to a slippery slope and have bad long-term effects.

Finally, the discussion turns to physician-assisted suicide (PAS). In PAS, the patient carries out the final action that brings about death. For instance, the patient may ingest a lethal dosage of pills. David Watts and Timothy Howell argue that while typical arguments against voluntary active euthanasia are forceful, these same arguments are not successful when directed against PAS. Watts and Howell support PAS as long as it involves provision of information (e.g., suggesting a book or web site containing information on how to safely and effectively perform suicide) or means (e.g., writing a prescription for a lethal dosage of medication), but not if it involves direct assistance by the physician.

The next readings are "for and against" selections that address issues closely related to end of life decision-making and which are suitable for in-class debates and small group work. The first for and against reading presents different perspectives on the question of whether or not doctors should participate in PAS. Timothy Quill and Herbert Hendin discuss case studies which suggest some of the benefits and potential dangers of allowing physicians to assist in patient suicide.

The last selections in this chapter focus on medical futility. This issue requires that we look at the moral questions surrounding the termination of medical treatment in a whole new light. While the typical dilemma in euthanasia concerns whether or not a physician should respect a patient's wishes to forgo treatment, the ethical question in cases of medical futility is whether a medical professional who believes a treatment holds no further benefit may acceptably withdraw treatment from a patient who wishes treatment to continue. In their selections, Steven Miles and Felicia Ackerman debate the merits of withholding or continuing treatment in the case of Helga Wanglie, a patient whose family wishes to continue treatment despite the considered opinion of medical professionals.

Chapter 6 begins with a selection in which Laura Purdy argues that it can be morally wrong to have children in cases where a significant risk exists of passing along a serious genetic disease to the child. Purdy builds her case by focusing on Huntington's disease, a disease that has been described by Milton Wexler, a leader in motivating the search for the genetic basis of the disease, as " ... the most terrifying disease on the face of the Earth because its victim is doomed to absolute dementia as terrible as Alzheimer's disease, a loss of physical control akin to muscular dystrophy, and a wasting of the body as bad as the very worst of cancers."[1] Huntington's chorea is a dominant genetic disease, meaning that if a parent possesses the gene for the disease, he or she will contract the disease and there is a 50% chance that the child will inherit the gene. Purdy argues that the greater the danger of serious harm, the stronger the duty to avoid this harm. Since the harm caused by Huntington's disease is so serious, it threatens the moral duty to provide a minimally satisfactory life for our children. For this reason, potential parents at risk for Huntington's have a moral duty either to abort a child who is conceived and possesses the gene for Huntington's, or to not conceive if the parents are opposed to abortion.[2]

Leon Kass provides a number of reasons why adopting an argument similar to Purdy's may be problematic (even though he is not explicitly addressing Purdy). Kass argues that genetic screening is a step in the wrong direction, since it undermines the moral equality of humans and would have terrible effects on "defective" children who are born "accidentally." Using prenatal diagnosis in this way allows parents to decide what kind of humans will be brought into this world, and Kass believes this is not a decision humans ought to be able to make. Related to this, Wertz and Fletcher address the morality of prenatal diagnosis for the purposes of sex selection. They oppose sex selection by discussing and rejecting the main arguments in favor of selecting the sex of the child via prenatal diagnosis (and resorting to abortion if necessary), and offer a number of arguments against sex selection. Their fundamental point is that using prenatal diagnosis to make a decision to continue a pregnancy or to abort a child is morally wrong since it is a form of sexism and sexism is morally wrong.

The discussion then turns to whether genetically modifying humans is morally permissible. In his article, French Anderson supports somatic-cell gene therapy only if it is necessary to treat serious disease, not to provide enhancements or "improved" human characteristics such as increased height or a certain eye color. Ronald Munson and Lawrence Davis defend the moral acceptability of germ-line therapy, those genetic modifications that will affect future generations, as well as somatic-cell therapy, those modifications that will affect only the present generation. Munson and Davis argue that there are no compelling objections to germ-line therapy, and since medicine has a duty to advance itself and to reduce human suffering, germ-line therapy is justified.

One of the most likely ways that the results of the Human Genome Project will affect persons' lives, for better or for worse, concerns how information gathered from genetic testing will be used by insurance companies. If persons are forced to pay higher premiums for health and life insurance based on genetic factors identified by testing, or are denied coverage altogether for these reasons, this will have a significant impact on their lives. Philosopher Thomas Murray argues that insurers should not have any access to genetic information if this is used for the purpose of determining insurance rates and eligibility. Robert Card critically examines Murray's position as well as the position defended by insurers concerning the justice of using genetic information for insurance decision-making, and then defends a moderate position that draws upon John Rawls' (Chapter 1) theory of justice. According to Card, it is unjust in most cases for health insurers to use genetic information to determine health insurance eligibility and rates.

The chapter includes a selection by Dan Brock in which he provides a comprehensive assessment of the benefits and costs associated with cloning. He argues that despite the existence of costs, there are significant benefits of human cloning that suggest that such research should proceed. Finally, a related issue arising in biotechnology concerns the proper use of knowledge gained from genetic research, in particular, the issue of whether genetic researchers should be able to obtain disease gene patents. In his selection Glenn McGee argues that properly framed disease gene patents can be defensible, as long as these are for "methods of discovery" in which researchers figure out how to use genes to make a diagnosis or treat a disease. McGee maintains that this process involves true "work" and that a properly constructed public policy would not slow down research using patented genes. Jon Merz and Mildred Cho respond directly to McGee. They argue that disease genes are not patentable since genetic information is part of nature and one cannot properly patent a product of nature.

CRITICAL THINKING TOOL: SLIPPERY SLOPE ARGUMENTS

A common argument that appears in debates regarding the legalization of euthanasia or the introduction of new genetic technologies is the *slippery slope* argument. In general, when using this strategy, an argument is made against something on the basis that if it is allowed, it will lead to something worse, which in turn leads to something even worse, and, ultimately, to something that is clearly unacceptable. In the moral form of this argument, one draws the conclusion that something clearly morally impermissible results. The basic structure of the argument is as follows (referring to acts or practices as A and B):[3]

1. If we allow A, B will necessarily or very likely follow.
2. B is not morally acceptable.

---

3. Therefore, we must not allow A.

This form of argument can represent a fallacy: as discussed in Chapter 2, if an argument is fallacious, then no matter what subject matter the argument discusses, the argument does not provide sufficient reason for us to believe its conclusion. In particular, an argument fits the pattern of a fallacious slippery slope argument if the connection between A and B is presumed, not proven. If sufficient evidence is presented for this connection, then the argument is not a slippery slope argument. The structure of this argument is in fact Utilitarian (Chapter 1) in nature: it argues that allowing a current policy, while it may seem to be beneficial, will not be best given its future overall consequences. How can we tell when the connection between A and B is sufficiently defended, so that this represents a valid form of argument?

There are two versions of the slippery slope argument, a logical version and an empirical version. The logical form of the argument holds that we are logically committed to B if we allow A. The empirical form says that the effect of allowing A will be that, as a result of social and/or psychological processes, we will also accept B some time in the future. In discussions of social policies, three types of norms are distinguished: those stemming from law, positive morality, and critical morality. *Positive morality* represents the ethical code accepted and currently shared by a society. *Critical morality* represents the ethical principles used to criticize current practices, including principles that stem from present social norms and positive morality.[4] As discussed in Chapter 1 regarding the treatment of cultural ethical relativism, the fact that a social practice is currently accepted does not insulate it from criticism. The focus of our concern is critical morality, the attempt to formulate a set of principles that allow us to reflectively analyze the practices and current norms in medicine.

Can the slippery slope argument be used to construct valid arguments within a critical ethical system? Let's begin with the logical version of the argument, which comes in two forms:

Logical Form #1: there is either no relevant conceptual difference between A and B, or the justification for A also applies to B, and therefore acceptance of A will logically imply acceptance of B.

Logical Form #2: there is a difference between A and B but there is no such difference between A and M, m and n, ... y and z, z and B, and that therefore, allowing A will in the end imply the acceptance of B.[5]

The central difference between these two forms is that form #2 holds that there is a difference between A and B, but that given a social process resulting from allowing A, B will be accepted. Form #1, by contrast, holds that there is no difference between A and B.

Logical Form #1 does have some force in a critical ethical system. This form is based on a requirement of consistency, and a general requirement of consistency is a central feature of moral theories. (For more on this, refer to the Introduction to Unit IV.) Therefore, if it is true that there is no relevant moral difference between A and B and B is clearly morally unacceptable, then we are committed to the claim that A is morally unacceptable.

Logical Form #2 is a different story. We do assume in this form of argument that there is an initial difference between A and B, yet we do not know at what point there fails to be a difference such that we then come to accept B. Fortunately, it is not necessary to resolve this problem to assess this form of argument. The central point is that if we do not know when A and B are sufficiently similar such that the acceptance of B is implied, then we have no conclusive reason against accepting A. There may not be a non-arbitrary point that we can set between A and B for when we have adopted a clearly morally unacceptable policy, but that does not provide any reason to then assume that A itself is morally unacceptable.

To sum up, Logical Form #1 can generate valid arguments in the context of critical morality, while Logical Form #2 does not generate valid arguments in this context. While this does suggest that arguments that have the form of slippery slope arguments do possess some importance for our critical examination of the morality of euthanasia and genetics, this conclusion should be accepted with caution. Making a Logical Form #1 argument as applied to an actual issue such as euthanasia and genetics is very difficult, since to prove that there is no relevant conceptual difference between A and B is often precisely what is at stake! If one begins an argument against abortion by assuming that there is no difference between abortion and the Holocaust perpetrated on Jewish persons by the Nazis, then one can be fairly accused of begging the question (Chapter 2). This initial assumption itself is in need of defense, and this point vitiates even Logical Form #2 arguments as an analytical tool for assessing actual societal policies.

For this reason, the version of the slippery slope argument most often found in medical ethics is the Empirical Form of the argument. This form of the argument assumes that allowing or doing A will ultimately lead to the acceptance of B. While allowing A may not seem bad in itself, B is clearly morally unacceptable from our current point of view. Does the Empirical Form generate valid arguments in the context of a critical ethical system? The Empirical Form assumes that our view of B as a morally unacceptable result is correct. However, this itself is questionable from the perspective of critical morality. Critical moralists realize that views about what is morally acceptable will change as social practices and norms change, and hence, that our intuitions about the moral status of future practices will change as well when we reach that future time. Since critical morality is founded on rational reasons and not intuitions about the wrongness of practices, the empirical form of the argument is of dubious importance unless an explicit connection to a future result that is clearly unacceptable even in future circumstances can be defended. This is a significant burden to meet, but since it is not impossible to satisfy it, the Empirical Form can generate valid arguments in the context of critical morality.

What general conditions must be met before we should accept arguments that have the form of viable slippery slope arguments?[6] First, it must be reasonable to believe that the expected short-term consequences are clear, negative, and probable, and that these follow from the proposed act or policy (A). Second, the long-term consequences must be clear but not inevitable, so that it will be difficult to prevent these consequences, but it is more likely that we can do so by not allowing A if we act now. Third, there must be an alternative that is less susceptible to the slippery slope than the proposed act or policy. It will be helpful to keep these general conditions in mind when assessing arguments that take the form of slippery slope arguments that appear in the readings in this unit.

Let's now look closely at several slippery slope arguments that appear in this unit. One argument (made by Leon Kass) regarding genetic testing claims that if we adopt a policy of genetic testing, this constitutes an attack on the fundamental equality of humans and will lead to an unacceptable program of eugenics. This argument does not seem to equate genetic testing with an unacceptable program of eugenics, and does not suggest that in accepting genetic testing we are logically committed to eugenics. Hence, it appears to be an empirical version of the slippery slope argument. Providing a complete assessment of this argument is beyond the scope of this introduction, but it is worth noting several points made by a few prominent thinkers who have critically examined this matter. One thinker[7] argues that the fear that the Human Genome Project will lead to an oppressive eugenic program in the U.S. is unfounded, since the United States is very different from countries such as Nazi Germany. This perspective stresses the point that reproductive freedom is more easily encroached in dictatorships as compared with democracies, and that in modern democracies, the past abuses of state-run programs are well-known and feared. In addition, those living with disability and illness are politically empowered to a degree not found in the early twentieth century. A comprehensive recent treatment of this issue reaches a similar conclusion.[8] This position maintains that the motivation behind eugenic programs to endow future generations with genes that may improve their lives need not be abandoned if it is pursued justly, and sees no necessary connection between this motivation and wrongdoing. If these points are correct, then arguments based on the sordid history of eugenics do not provide sufficient reason to reject genetic testing and other innovations in reproductive technology.

Another argument that takes the form of a slippery slope argument is the claim that if we adopt a policy of voluntary active euthanasia (A), then this will inevitably lead to a policy that prematurely kills persons despite their wishes (B). This argument is discussed by Daniel Callahan in "When Self-Determination Runs Amok" and in Dan Brock's "Voluntary Active Euthanasia," and this argument also takes the form of an empirical slippery slope argument. Callahan and Brock have opposite opinions on the success of this argument. While Callahan opposes a policy of voluntary active euthanasia since he believes it will have a number of bad effects, Brock argues that it is plausible to think that the good results of such a policy outweigh its bad results.

Is there sufficient reason to believe in a connection between A and B, and are the conditions for accepting a slippery slope argument satisfied in this case? Brock distinguishes between two possible results, a policy of *involuntary* euthanasia, that in which persons who express a wish not to die are euthanized, and a policy of *nonvoluntary* euthanasia, in which persons are euthanized even though their wishes are not clear (perhaps because they are comatose or are incompetent for some other reason). In the selection by ten Have and Welie, they discover over one thousand cases of nonvoluntary euthanasia in the Netherlands. This finding provides substantial evidence for a connection between a policy allowing VAE and a resulting policy that euthanasizes persons despite their wishes. It is important to add, however, that given several major social differences between the Netherlands and other countries such as the United States, the upshot of these findings is not completely clear.

For example, there is socialized, universal health care in the Netherlands. This may suggest that economic motives to reduce the State's healthcare costs are more likely to take precedence over granting a patient the benefit of the doubt. (Conversely, families in the Netherlands do not have economic motivations that may increase the probability of nonvoluntary euthanasia, while this could occur in countries such as the United States that have a (largely) private health care system.) Second, there is a legalistic attitude present in the United States not present in the Netherlands. This provides a system of checks and balances to prevent abuses that is not present in the Netherlands. Finally, the Dutch generally adopt cultural attitudes that are much more permissive than those found in the United States, as exemplified in in their approach to non-prescription (or "recreational") drug regulation. These more permissive attitudes, combined with the other factors, may suggest that the occurrence of a slippery slope towards nonvoluntary euthanasia is not as likely in the United States as it is in European countries that are more similar to Holland. In this case, the first and third conditions for accepting a slippery slope argument appear to be satisfied, yet given that euthanasia has been tolerated in the Netherlands since the 1970s, the second condition may not be met since acting now to discourage VAE may not have a significant effect on the behavior of medical professionals. Even given this point, this slippery slope regarding a slide toward nonvoluntary euthanasia, at least as it applies to countries sufficiently similar to the Netherlands, does possess force.

Notes

1. Quoted in Bishop, J., and Waldholz, M. 1996. *Genome*. (Lincoln: toExcel), p. 31.
2. Of course, the parents may adopt a child or the parent not at risk for Huntington's may serve as a biological parent and the parents may reproduce via reproductive technology (by using donor sperm or ova). Recent developments suggest that pre-implantation screening of the embryo may be possible, which could be used to determine if the child has inherited the gene for Huntington's chorea. However, not implanting an embryo if it possesses the gene may still conflict with some persons' religious or moral beliefs.
3. The discussion in this section is indebted to van der Burg, W. "The Slippery Slope Argument," *Ethics* 102 (October 1991): 42–65.
4. I do not discuss law at this point; in the introduction to Unit IV, the similarities and differences between legal and moral reasoning are brought into focus.
5. *c.f.* van der Burg 1991, p. 44.
6. I follow van der Burg (1991, 61) here.
7. Kevles, D. "Eugenics and the Human Genome Project: Is the Past Prologue?" In *Justice and the Human Genome Project,* ed. Murphy, T. and Lappe, M. (Berkeley: University of California Press, 1994).
8. Buchanan, A., Brock, D., Daniels, N., and Wikler, D. *From Chance to Choice.* (Cambridge: Cambridge University Press, 2000), Chapters 1 and 2.

CHAPTER 5

ETHICAL ISSUES AT THE END OF LIFE

MAJORITY OPINION (DELIVERED BY CHIEF JUSTICE W. REHNQUIST)

Cruzan v. Director, Missouri Department of Health

Petitioner Nancy Beth Cruzan was rendered incompetent as a result of severe injuries sustained during an automobile accident. Co-petitioners Lester and Joyce Cruzan, Nancy's parents and co-guardians, sought a court order directing the withdrawal of their daughter's artificial feeding and hydration equipment after it became apparent that she had virtually no chance of recovering her cognitive faculties. The Supreme Court of Missouri held that because there was no clear and convincing evidence of Nancy's desire to have life-sustaining treatment withdrawn under such circumstances, her parents lacked authority to effectuate such a request. We … now affirm.

On the night of January 11, 1983, Nancy Cruzan lost control of her car as she traveled down Elm Road in Jasper County, Missouri. The vehicle overturned, and Cruzan was discovered lying face down in a ditch without detectable respiratory or cardiac function. Paramedics were able to restore her breathing and heartbeat at the accident site, and she was transported to a hospital in an unconscious state. An attending neurosurgeon diagnosed her as having sustained probable cerebral contusions compounded by significant anoxia (lack of oxygen). The Missouri trial court in this case found that permanent brain damage generally results after 6 minutes in an anoxic state; it was estimated that Cruzan was deprived of oxygen from 12 to 14 minutes. She remained in a coma for approximately three weeks and then progressed to an unconscious state in which she was able to orally ingest some nutrition. In order to ease feeding and further the recovery, surgeons implanted a gastrostomy feeding and hydration tube in Cruzan with the consent of her then husband. Subsequent rehabilitative efforts proved unavailing. She now lies in a Missouri state hospital in what is commonly referred to as a persistent vegetative state: generally, a condition in which a person exhibits motor reflexes but evinces no indications of significant cognitive function.[1] The State of Missouri is bearing the cost of her care.

United States Supreme Court. 110 S.Ct. 2841. June 25, 1990.

After it had become apparent that Nancy Cruzan had virtually no chance of regaining her mental faculties her parents asked hospital employees to terminate the artificial nutrition and hydration procedures. All agree that such a removal would cause her death. The employees refused to honor the request without court approval. The parents then sought and received authorization from the state trial court for termination. The court found that a person in Nancy's condition had a fundamental right under the State and Federal Constitutions to refuse or direct the withdrawal of "death prolonging procedures." The court also found that Nancy's "expressed thoughts at age twenty-five in somewhat serious conversation with a housemate friend that if sick or injured she would not wish to continue her life unless she could live at least halfway normally suggests that given her present condition she would not wish to continue on with her nutrition and hydration."

The Supreme Court of Missouri reversed by a divided vote. The court recognized a right to refuse treatment embodied in the common-law doctrine of informed consent, but expressed skepticism about the application of that doctrine in the circumstances of this case. The court also declined to read a broad right of privacy into the State Constitution which would "support the right of a person to refuse medical treatment in every circumstance," and expressed doubt as to whether such a right existed under the United States Constitution. It then decided that the Missouri Living Will statute (1986) embodied a state policy strongly favoring the preservation of life. The court found that Cruzan's statements to her roommate regarding her desire to live or die under certain conditions were "unreliable for the purpose of determining her intent," and thus insufficient to support the co-guardians' claim to exercise substituted judgment on Nancy's behalf. It rejected the argument that Cruzan's parents were entitled to order the termination of her medical treatment, concluding that "no person can assume that choice for an incompetent in the absence of the formalities required under Missouri's Living Will statutes or the clear and convincing, inherently reliable evidence absent here."...

We granted certiorari to consider the question of whether Cruzan has a right under the United States Constitution which would require the hospital to withdraw life-sustaining treatment from her under these circumstances.

At common law, even the touching of one person by another without consent and without legal justification was a battery. Before the turn of the century, this Court observed that "[n]o right is held more sacred, or is more carefully guarded, by the common law, than the right of every individual to the possession and control of his own person, free from all restraint or interference of others, unless by clear and unquestionable authority of law." This notion of bodily integrity has been embodied in the requirement that informed consent is generally required for medical treatment. Justice Cardozo, while on the Court of Appeals of New York, aptly described this doctrine: "Every human being of adult years and sound mind has a right to determine what shall be done with his own body; and a surgeon who performs an operation without his patient's consent commits an assault, for which he is liable in damages." The informed consent doctrine has become firmly entrenched in American tort law.

The logical corollary of the doctrine of informed consent is that the patient generally possesses the right not to consent, that is, to refuse treatment. Until about 15 years ago and the seminal decision [of the New Jersey Supreme Court] in *re Quinlan* (1976), the number of right-to-refuse-treatment decisions were relatively few. Most of the earlier cases involved patients who refused medical treatment forbidden by their religious beliefs, thus implicating First Amendment rights as well as common law rights of self-determination. More recently, however, with the advance of medical technology capable of sustaining life well past the point where natural forces would have brought certain death in earlier times, cases involving the right to refuse life-sustaining treatment have burgeoned.

In the *Quinlan* case, young Karen Quinlan suffered severe brain damage as the result of anoxia, and entered a persistent vegetative state. Karen's father sought judicial approval to disconnect his daughter's respirator. The New Jersey Supreme Court granted the relief, holding that Karen had a right of privacy grounded in the Federal Constitution to terminate treatment. Recognizing that this right was not absolute, however, the court balanced it against asserted state interests. Noting that the State's interest "weakens and the individual's right to privacy grows as the degree of bodily invasion increases and the prognosis dims," the court concluded that the state interests had to give way in that case. The court also concluded that the "only practical way" to prevent the loss of Karen's privacy right due to her incompetence was to allow her guardian and family to decide "whether she would exercise it in these circumstances."

After *Quinlan*, however, most courts have based a right to refuse treatment either solely on the common law right to informed consent or on both the common law right and a constitutional privacy right...

...State courts have available to them for decision a number of sources state constitutions, statutes, and common law which are not available to us. In this Court, the question is simply and starkly whether the United States Constitution prohibits Missouri from choosing the rule of decision which it did. This is the first case in which we have been squarely presented with the issue of whether the United States Constitution grants what is in common parlance referred to as a "right to die." We follow the judicious counsel ... that in deciding "a question of such magnitude and importance ... it is the [better] part of wisdom not to attempt, by any general statement, to cover every possible phase of the subject."

The Fourteenth Amendment provides that no State shall "deprive any person of life, liberty, or property, without due process of law." The principle that a competent person has a constitutionally protected liberty interest in refusing unwanted medical treatment may be inferred from our prior decisions. In *Jacobson* v. *Massachusetts*, for instance, the Court balanced an individual's liberty interest in declining an unwanted smallpox vaccine against the State's interest in preventing disease...

Just this Term, in the course of holding that a State's procedures for administering antipsychotic medication to prisoners were sufficient to satisfy due process concerns, we recognized that prisoners possess "a significant liberty interest" in avoiding the unwanted administration of antipsychotic drugs under the Due Process Clause of the Fourteenth Amendment. Still other cases support the recognition of a general liberty interest in refusing medical treatment.

But determining that a person has a "liberty interest" under the Due Process Clause does not end the inquiry;[2] "whether respondent's constitutional rights have been violated must be determined by balancing his liberty interests against the relevant state interests."

Petitioners insist that under the general holdings of our cases, the forced administration of life-sustaining medical treatment, and even of artificially delivered food and water essential to life, would implicate a competent person's liberty interest. Although we think the logic of the cases discussed above would embrace such a liberty interest, the dramatic consequences involved in refusal of such treatment would inform the inquiry as to whether the deprivation of that interest is constitutionally permissible. But for purposes of this case, we assume that the United States Constitution would grant a competent person a constitutionally protected right to refuse lifesaving hydration and nutrition.

Petitioners go on to assert that an incompetent person should possess the same right in this respect as is possessed by a competent person. ...

The difficulty with petitioners' claim is that in a sense it begs the question: an incompetent person is not able to make an informed and voluntary choice to exercise a hypothetical right to refuse treatment or any other right. Such a "right" must be exercised for her, if at all, by some sort of surrogate. Here, Missouri has in effect recognized that under certain circumstances a surrogate may act for the patient in electing to have hydration and nutrition withdrawn in such a way as to cause death, but it has established a procedural safeguard to assure that the action of the surrogate conforms as best it may to the wishes expressed by the patient while competent. Missouri requires that evidence of the incompetent's wishes as to the withdrawal of treatment be proved by clear and convincing evidence. The question, then, is whether the United States Constitution forbids the establishment of this procedural requirement by the State. We hold that it does not.

Whether or not Missouri's clear and convincing evidence requirement comports with the United States Constitution depends in part on what interests the State may properly seek to protect in this situation. Missouri relies on its interest in the protection and preservation of human life, and there can be no gainsaying this interest. As a general matter, the States, indeed all civilized nations, demonstrate their commitment to life by treating homicide as serious crime. Moreover, the majority of States in this country have laws imposing criminal penalties on one who assists another to commit suicide. We do not think a State is required to remain neutral in the face of an informed and voluntary decision by a physically able adult to starve to death.

But in the context presented here, a State has more particular interests at stake. The choice between life and death is a deeply personal decision of obvious and overwhelming finality. We believe Missouri may legitimately seek to safeguard the personal element of this choice through the imposition of heightened evidentiary requirements. It cannot be disputed that the Due Process Clause protects an interest in life as well as an interest in refusing life-sustaining medical treatment. Not all incompetent patients will have loved ones available to serve as surrogate decision makers. And even where family members are present, "[t]here will, of course, be some unfortunate situations in which family members will not act to protect a patient." A State is entitled to guard against potential abuses in such situations. Similarly, a State is entitled to consider that a judicial proceeding to make a determination regarding an incompetent's wishes may very well not be an adversarial one, with the added guarantee of accurate fact finding that the adversary process brings with it. Finally, we think a State may properly decline to make judgments about the "quality" of life that a particular individual may enjoy, and simply assert an unqualified interest in the preservation of human life to be weighed against the constitutionally protected interests of the individual.

In our view, Missouri has permissibly sought to advance these interests through the adoption of a "clear and convincing" standard of proof to govern such proceedings. "The function of a standard of proof, as that concept is embodied in the Due Process Clause and in the realm of fact finding, is to 'instruct the fact finder concerning the degree of confidence our society thinks he should have in the correctness of factual conclusions for a particular type of adjudication.'"...

We think it self-evident that the interests at stake in the instant proceedings are more substantial, both on an individual and societal level, than those involved in a run-of-the-mill civil dispute. But not only does the standard of proof reflect the importance of a particular adjudication, it also serves as "a societal judgment about how the risk of error should be distributed between the litigants." The more stringent the burden of proof a party must bear, the more that party bears the risk of an erroneous decision. We believe that Missouri may permissibly place an increased risk of an erroneous decision on those seeking to terminate an incompetent individual's life-sustaining treatment. An erroneous decision not to terminate results in a maintenance of the status quo; the possibility of subsequent developments such as advancements in medical science, the discovery of new evidence regarding the patient's intent, changes in the law, or simply the unexpected death of the patient despite the administration of life-sustaining treatment, at least create the potential that a wrong decision will eventually be corrected or its impact mitigated. An erroneous decision to withdraw life-sustaining treatment, however, is not susceptible of correction....

In sum, we conclude that a State may apply a clear and convincing evidence standard in proceedings where a guardian seeks to discontinue nutrition and hydration of a person diagnosed to be in a persistent vegetative state....

The Supreme Court of Missouri held that in this case the testimony adduced at trial did not amount to clear and convincing proof of the patient's desire to have hydration and nutrition withdrawn. In so doing, it reversed a decision of the Missouri trial court which had found that the evidence "suggest[ed]" Nancy Cruzan would not have desired to continue such measures, but which had not adopted the standard of "clear and convincing evidence" enunciated by the Supreme Court. The testimony adduced at trial consisted primarily of Nancy Cruzan's statements made to a housemate about a year before her accident that she would not want to live should she face life as a "vegetable," and other observations to the same effect. The observations did not deal in terms with withdrawal of medical treatment or of hydration and nutrition. We cannot say that the Supreme Court of Missouri committed constitutional error in reaching the conclusion that it did.[3]

Petitioners alternatively contend that Missouri must accept the "substituted judgment" of close family members even in the absence of substantial proof that their views reflect the views of the patient....

No doubt is engendered by anything in this record but that Nancy Cruzan's mother and father are loving and caring parents. If the State were required by the United States Constitution to repose a right of "substituted judgment" with anyone, the Cruzans would surely qualify. But we do not think the Due Process Clause requires the State to repose judgment on these matters with anyone but the patient herself. Close family members may have a strong feeling, a feeling not at all ignoble or unworthy, but not entirely disinterested, either that they do not wish to witness the continuation of the life of a loved one which they regard as hopeless, meaningless, and even degrading. But there is no automatic assurance that the view of close family members will necessarily be the same as the patient's would have been had she been confronted with the prospect of her situation while competent. All of the reasons previously discussed for allowing Missouri to require clear and convincing evidence of the patient's wishes lead us to conclude that the State may choose to defer only to those wishes, rather than confide the decision to close family members.

The judgment of the Supreme Court of Missouri is *Affirmed.*

Notes

1. The State Supreme Court, adopting much of the trial court's findings, described Nancy Cruzan's medical condition as follows:

   "... In sum, Nancy is diagnosed as in a persistent vegetative state. She is not dead. She is not terminally ill. Medical experts testified that she could live another thirty years."...

2. Although many state courts have held that a right to refuse treatment is encompassed by a generalized constitutional right of privacy, we have never so held. We believe this issue is more properly analyzed in terms of a Fourteenth Amendment liberty interest. See *Bowers* v. *Hardwick* (1986).

3. The clear and convincing standard of proof has been variously defined in this context as "proof sufficient to persuade the trier of fact that the patient held a firm and settled commitment to the termination of life supports under the

circumstances like those presented," and as evidence which "produces in the mind of the trier of fact a firm belief or conviction as to the truth of the allegations sought to be established, evidence so clear, direct and weighty and convincing as to enable [the fact finder] to come to a clear conviction, without hesitancy, of the truth of the precise facts in issue."...

ACTIVE AND PASSIVE EUTHANASIA

James Rachels

The distinction between active and passive euthanasia is thought to be crucial for medical ethics. The idea is that it is permissible, at least in some cases, to withhold treatment and allow a patient to die, but it is never permissible to take any direct action designed to kill the patient. This doctrine seems to be accepted by most doctors, and it is endorsed in a statement adopted by the House of Delegates of the American Medical Association on December 4, 1973:

> The intentional termination of the life of one human being by another—mercy killing—is contrary to that for which the medical profession stands and is contrary to the policy of the American Medical Association.
>
> The cessation of the employment of extraordinary means to prolong the life of the body when there is irrefutable evidence that biological death is imminent is the decision of the patient and/or his immediate family. The advice and judgment of the physician should be freely available to the patient and/or his immediate family.

However, a strong case can be made against this doctrine. In what follows I will set out some of the relevant arguments, and urge doctors to reconsider their views on this matter.

To begin with a familiar type of situation, a patient who is dying of incurable cancer of the throat is in terrible pain, which can no longer be satisfactorily alleviated. He is certain to die within a few days, even if present treatment is continued, but he does not want to go on living for those days since the pain is unbearable. So he asks the doctor for an end to it, and his family joins in the request.

Suppose the doctor agrees to withhold treatment, as the conventional doctrine says he may. The justification for his doing so is that the patient is in terrible agony, and since he is going to die anyway, it would be wrong to prolong his suffering needlessly. But now notice this. If one simply withholds treatment, it may take the patient longer to die, and so he may suffer more than he would if more direct action were taken and a lethal injection given. This fact provides strong reason for thinking that, once the initial decision not to prolong his agony has been made, active euthanasia is actually preferable to passive euthanasia, rather than the reverse. To say otherwise is to endorse the option that leads to more suffering rather than less, and is contrary to the humanitarian impulse that prompts the decision not to prolong his life in the first place.

Part of my point is that the process of being "allowed to die" can be relatively slow and painful, whereas being given a lethal injection is relatively quick and painless. Let me give a different sort of example. In the United States about one in 600 babies is born with Down's syndrome. Most of these babies are otherwise healthy—that is, with only the usual pediatric care, they will proceed to an otherwise normal

Rachels, James. "Active and Passive Euthanasia." From *The New England Journal of Medicine* 292:78–80, 1975.

infancy. Some, however, are born with congenital defects such as intestinal obstructions that require operations if they are to live. Sometimes, the parents and the doctor will decide not to operate, and let the infant die. Anthony Shaw describes what happens then:

> ...When surgery is denied [the doctor] must try to keep the infant from suffering while natural forces sap the baby's life away. As a surgeon whose natural inclination is to use the scalpel to fight off death, standing by and watching a salvageable baby die is the most emotionally exhausting experience I know. It is easy at a conference, in a theoretical discussion, to decide that such infants should be allowed to die. It is altogether different to stand by in the nursery and watch as dehydration and infection wither a tiny being over hours and days. This is a terrible ordeal for me and the hospital staff—much more so than for the parents who never set foot in nursery.*

I can understand why some people are opposed to euthanasia, and insist that such infants must be allowed to live. I think I can also understand why other people favor destroying these babies quickly and painlessly. But why should anyone favor letting "dehydration and infection wither a tiny being over hours and days?" The doctrine that says that a baby may be allowed to dehydrate and wither, but may not be given an injection that would end its life without suffering, seems so patently cruel as to require further refutation. The strong language is not intended to offend, but only to put the point in the clearest possible way.

My second argument is that the conventional doctrine leads to decisions concerning life and death made on irrelevant grounds.

Consider again the case of the infants with Down's syndrome who need operations for congenital defects unrelated to the syndrome to live. Sometimes, there is no operation, and the baby dies, but when there is no such defect, the baby lives on. Now, an operation such as that to remove an intestinal obstruction is not prohibitively difficult. The reason why such operations are not performed in these cases is, clearly, that the child has Down's syndrome and the parents and doctor judge that because of that fact it is better for the child to die.

But notice that this situation is absurd, no matter what view one takes of the lives and potentials of such babies. If the life of such an infant is worth preserving, what does it matter if it needs a simple operation? Or, if one thinks it better that such a baby should not live on, what difference make that it happens to have an unobstructed intestinal tract? In either case, the matter of life and death is being decided on irrelevant grounds. It is the Down's syndrome, and not the intestines, that is the issue. The matter should be decided, if at all, on that basis, and not be allowed to depend on the essentially irrelevant question of whether the intestinal tract is blocked.

What makes this situation possible, of course, is the idea that when there is an intestinal blockage, one can "let the baby die," but when there is no such defect there is nothing that can be done, for one must not "kill" it. The fact that this idea leads to such results as deciding life or death on irrelevant grounds is another good reason why the doctrine should be rejected.

One reason why so many people think that there is an important moral difference between active and passive euthanasia is that they think killing someone is morally worse than letting someone die. But is it? Is killing, in itself, worse than letting die? To investigate this issue, two cases may be considered that are exactly alike except that one involves killing whereas the other involves letting someone die. Then, it can be asked whether this difference makes any difference to the moral assessments. It is important that the cases be exactly alike, except for this one difference, since otherwise one cannot be confident that it is this difference and not some other that accounts for any variation in the assessments of the two cases. So, let us consider this pair of cases:

---

*Shaw A: "Doctor, Do We Have a Choice?" *The New York Times Magazine*, January 30, 1972, p. 54.

In the first, Smith stands to gain a large inheritance if anything should happen to his six-year-old cousin. One evening while the child is taking his bath, Smith sneaks into the bathroom and drowns the child, and then arranges things so that it will look like an accident.

In the second, Jones also stands to gain if anything should happen to his six-year-old cousin. Like Smith, Jones sneaks in planning to drown the child in his bath. However, just as he enters the bathroom Jones sees the child slip and hit his head, and fall face down in the water. Jones is delighted; he stands by, ready to push the child's head back under if it is necessary, but it is not necessary. With only a little thrashing about, the child drowns all by himself, "accidentally," as Jones watches and does nothing.

Now Smith killed the child, whereas Jones "merely" let the child die. That is the only difference between them. Did either man behave better, from a moral point of view? If the difference between killing and letting die were in itself a morally important matter, one should say that Jones's behavior was less reprehensible than Smith's. But does one really want to say that? I think not. In the first place, both men acted from the same motive, personal gain, and both had exactly the same end in view when they acted. It may be inferred from Smith's conduct that he is a bad man, although that judgment may be withdrawn or modified if certain further facts are learned about him—for example, that he is mentally deranged. But would not the very same thing be inferred about Jones from his conduct? And would not the same further considerations also be relevant to any modification of this judgment? Moreover, suppose Jones pleaded, in his own defense, "After all, I didn't do anything except just stand there and watch the child drown. I didn't kill him; I only let him die." Again, if letting die were in itself less bad than killing, this defense should have at least some weight. But it does not. Such a "defense" can only be regarded as a grotesque perversion of moral reasoning. Morally speaking, it is no defense at all.

Now, it may be pointed out, quite properly, that the cases of euthanasia with which doctors are concerned are not like this at all. They do not involve personal gain or the destruction of normal healthy children. Doctors are concerned only with cases in which the patient's life is of no further use to him, or in which the patient's life has become or will soon become a terrible burden. However, the point is the same in these cases: the bare difference between killing and letting die does not, in itself, make a moral difference. If doctor lets a patient die, for humane reasons, he is in the same moral position as if he had given the patient a lethal injection for humane reasons. If his decision was wrong—if, for example, the patient's illness was in fact curable—the decision would be equally regrettable no matter which method was used to carry it out. And if the doctor's decision was the right one, the method used is not in itself important.

The AMA policy statement isolates the crucial issue very well; the crucial issue is "the intentional termination of the life of one human being by another." But after identifying this issue, and forbidding "mercy killing," the statement goes on to deny that the cessation of treatment is the intentional termination of a life. This is where the mistake comes in, for what is the cessation of treatment, in these circumstances, if it is not "the intentional termination of the life of one human being by another?" Of course it is exactly that, and if it were not, there would be no point to it.

Many people will find this judgment hard to accept. One reason, I think, is that it is very easy to conflate the question of whether killing is, in itself, worse than letting die, with the very different question of whether most actual cases of killing are more reprehensible than most actual cases of letting die. Most actual cases of killing are clearly terrible (think, for example, of all the murders reported in the newspapers), and one hears of such cases every day. On the other hand, one hardly ever hears of a case of letting die, except for the actions of doctors who are motivated by humanitarian reasons. So one learns to think of killing in a much worse light than of letting die. But this does not mean that there is something about killing that makes it in itself worse than letting die, for it is not the bare difference between killing and letting die that makes the difference in these cases. Rather, the other factors—the murderer's motive of personal gain, for example, contrasted with the doctor's humanitarian motivation—account for different reactions to the different cases.

I have argued that killing is not in itself any worse than letting die; if my contention is right, it follows that active euthanasia is not any worse than passive euthanasia. What arguments can be given on the other side? The most common, I believe, is the following:

"The important difference between active and passive euthanasia is that, in passive euthanasia, the doctor does not do anything to bring about the patient's death. The doctor does nothing, and the patient dies of whatever ills already afflict him. In active euthanasia, however, the doctor does something to bring about the patient's death: he kills him. The doctor who gives the patient with cancer a lethal injection has himself caused his patient's death; whereas if he merely ceases treatment, the cancer is the cause of the death."

A number of points need to be made here. The first is that it is not exactly correct to say that in passive euthanasia the doctor does nothing, for he does do one thing that is very important: he lets the patient die. "Letting someone die" is certainly different, in some respects, from other types of action—mainly in that it is a kind of action that one may perform by way of not performing certain other actions. For example, one may let a patient die by way of not giving medication, just as one may insult someone by way of not shaking his hand. But for any purpose of moral assessment, it is a type of action nonetheless. The decision to let a patient die is subject to moral appraisal in the same way that a decision to kill him would be subject to moral appraisal: it may be assessed as wise or unwise, compassionate or sadistic, right or wrong. If a doctor deliberately let a patient die who was suffering from a routinely curable illness, the doctor would certainly be to blame for what he had done, just as he would be to blame if he had needlessly killed the patient. Charges against him would then be appropriate. If so, it would be no defense at all for him to insist that he didn't "do anything." He would have done something very serious indeed, for he let his patient die.

Fixing the cause of death may be very important from a legal point of view, for it may determine whether criminal charges are brought against the doctor. But I do not think that this notion can be used to show a moral difference between active and passive euthanasia. The reason why it is considered bad to be the cause of someone's death is that death is regarded as a great evil—and so it is. However, if it has been decided that euthanasia—even passive euthanasia—is desirable in a given case, it has also been decided that in this instance death is no greater an evil than the patient's continued existence. And if this is true, the usual reason for not wanting to be the cause of someone's death simply does not apply.

Finally, doctors may think that all of this is only of academic interest—the sort of thing that philosophers may worry about but that has no practical bearing on their own work. After all, doctors must be concerned about the legal consequences of what they do, and active euthanasia is clearly forbidden by the law. But even so, doctors should also be concerned with the fact that the law is forcing upon them a moral doctrine that may well be indefensible, and has a considerable effect on their practices. Of course, most doctors are not now in the position of being coerced in this matter, for they do not regard themselves as merely going along with what the law requires. Rather, in statements such as the AMA policy statement that I have quoted, they are endorsing this doctrine as a central point of medical ethics. In that statement, active euthanasia is condemned not merely as illegal but as "contrary to that for which the medical profession stands," whereas passive euthanasia is approved. However, the preceding considerations suggest that there is really no moral difference between the two, considered in themselves (there may be important moral differences in some cases in their *consequences*, but, as I pointed out, these differences may make active euthanasia, and not passive euthanasia, the morally preferable option). So, whereas doctors may have to discriminate between active and passive euthanasia to satisfy the law, they should not do any more than that. In particular, they should not give the distinction any added authority and weight by writing it into official statements of medical ethics.

ACTIVE AND PASSIVE EUTHANASIA: AN IMPERTINENT DISTINCTION?

Thomas D. Sullivan

Because of recent advances in medical technology, it is today possible to save or prolong the lives of many persons who in an earlier era would have quickly perished. Unhappily, however, it often is impossible to do so without committing the patient and his or her family to a future filled with sorrows. Modern methods of neuro-surgery can successfully close the opening at the base of the spine of a baby born with severe myelomeningocoele, but do nothing to relieve the paralysis that afflicts it from the waist down or to remedy the patient's incontinence of stool and urine. Antibiotics and skin grafts can spare the life of a victim of severe and massive burns, but fail to eliminate the immobilizing contractions of arms and legs, the extreme pain, and the hideous disfigurement of the face. It is not surprising, therefore, that physicians and moralists in increasing number recommend that assistance should not be given to such patients, and that some have even begun to advocate the deliberate hastening of death by medical means, provided informed consent has been given by the appropriate parties.

The latter recommendation consciously and directly conflicts with what might be called the "traditional" view of the physician's role. The traditional view, as articulated, for example, by the House of Delegates of the American Medical Association in 1973, declared:

> The intentional termination of the life of one human being by another—mercy killing—is contrary to that for which the medical profession stands and is contrary to the policy of the American Medical Association.
>
> The cessation of the employment of extraordinary means to prolong the life of the body when there is irrefutable evidence that biological death is imminent is the decision of the patient and/or his immediate family. The advice and judgment of the physician should be freely available to the patient and/or his immediate family.

Basically this view involves two points: 1) that it is impermissible for the doctor or anyone else to terminate intentionally the life of a patient, but 2) that it is permissible in some cases to cease the employment of "extraordinary means" of preserving life, even though the death of the patient is a foreseeable consequence.

Does this position really make sense? Recent criticism charges that it does not. The heart of the complaint is that the traditional view arbitrarily rules out all cases of intentionally acting to terminate life, but permits what is in fact the moral equivalent, letting patients die. This accusation has been clearly articulated by James Rachels in a widely read article that appeared in a recent issue of the

Reprinted with permission of the author, *The Human Life Review,* 215 Lexington Ave., 4th Floor, New York, NY 10016.

New England Journal of Medicine, entitled "Active and Passive Euthanasia." By "active euthanasia" Rachels seems to mean *doing something* to bring about a patient's death, and by "passive euthanasia," not doing anything, i.e., just letting the patient die. Referring to the A.M.A. statement, Rachels sees the traditional position as always forbidding active euthanasia, but permitting passive euthanasia. Yet, he argues, passive euthanasia may be in some cases morally indistinguishable from active euthanasia, and in other cases even worse. To make his point he asks his readers to consider the case of a Down's syndrome baby with an intestinal obstruction that easily could be remedied through routine surgery. Rachels comments:

> I can understand why some people are opposed to all euthanasia and insist that such infants must be allowed to live. I think I can also understand why other people favor destroying these babies quickly and painlessly. By why should anyone favor letting "dehydration and infection wither a tiny being over hours and days?" The doctrine that says that a baby may be allowed to dehydrate and wither, but may not be given an injection that would end its life without suffering, seems so patently cruel as to require no further refutation.

Rachels' point is that decisions such as the one he describes as "patently cruel" arise out of a misconceived moral distinction between active and passive euthanasia, which in turn rests upon a distinction between killing and letting die that itself has no moral importance.

> One reason why so many people think that there is an important difference between active and passive euthanasia is that they think killing someone is morally worse than letting someone die. But is it? . . . To investigate this issue two cases may be considered that are exactly alike except that one involves killing whereas the other involves letting someone die. Then, it can be asked whether this difference makes any difference to the moral assessments.
>
> In the first, Smith stands to gain a large inheritance if anything should happen to his six-year-old cousin. One evening while the child is taking his bath, Smith sneaks into the bathroom and drowns the child, and then arranges things so that it will look like an accident.
>
> In the second, Jones also stands to gain if anything should happen to his six-year-old cousin. Like Smith, Jones sneaks in planning to drown the child in his bath. However, just as he enters the bathroom Jones sees the child slip and hit his head, and fall face down in the water. Jones is delighted; he stands by, ready to push the child's head back under if it is necessary, but it is not necessary. With only a little thrashing about, the child drowns all by himself, "accidentally," as Jones watches and does nothing.

Rachels observes that Smith killed the child, whereas Jones "merely" let the child die. If there's an important moral distinction between killing and letting die, then, we should say that Jones' behavior from a moral point of view is less reprehensible than Smith's. But while the law might draw some distinctions here, it seems clear that the acts of Jones and Smith are not different in any important way, or, if there is a difference, Jones' action is even worse.

In essence, then, the objection to the position adopted by the A.M.A. of Rachels and those who argue like him is that it endorses a highly questionable moral distinction between killing and letting die, which, if accepted, leads to indefensible medical decisions. Nowhere does Rachels quite come out and say that he favors active euthanasia in some cases, but the implication is clear. Nearly everyone holds that it is sometimes pointless to prolong the process of dying and that in those cases it is morally permissible to let a patient die even though a few hours or days could be salvaged by procedures that would also increase the agonies of the dying. But if it is impossible to defend a general distinction between letting people die and acting to terminate their lives directly, then it would seem that active euthanasia also may be morally permissible.

Now what shall we make of all this? It *is* cruel to stand by and watch a Down's baby die an agonizing death when a simple operation would remove the intestinal obstruction, but to offer the excuse that in failing to operate we didn't *do* anything to bring about death is an example of moral evasiveness comparable to the excuse

Jones would offer for his action of "merely" letting his cousin die. Furthermore, it is true that if someone is trying to bring about the death of another human being, then it makes little difference from the moral point of view if his purpose is achieved by action or by malevolent omission, as in the cases of Jones and Smith.

But if we acknowledge this, are we obliged to give up the traditional view expressed by the A.M.A. statement? Of course not. To begin with, we are hardly obliged to assume the Jones-like role Rachels assigns the defender of the traditional view. We have the option of operating on the Down's baby and saving its life. Rachels mentions that possibility only to hurry past it as if that is not what his opposition would do. But, of course, that is precisely the course of action most defenders of the traditional position would choose.

Secondly, while it may be that the reason some rather confused people give for upholding the traditional view is that they think killing someone is always worse than letting them die, nobody who gives the matter much thought puts it that way. Rather they say that killing someone is clearly morally worse than not killing them, and killing them can be done by acting to bring about their death or by refusing ordinary means to keep them alive in order to bring about the same goal.

What I am suggesting is that Rachels' objections leave the position he sets out to criticize untouched. It is worth noting that the jargon of active and passive euthanasia—and it is jargon—does not appear in the resolution. Nor does the resolution state or imply the distinction Rachels attacks, a distinction that puts a moral premium on overt behavior—moving or not moving one's parts—while totally ignoring the intentions of the agent. That no such distinction is being drawn seems clear from the fact that the A.M.A. resolution speaks approvingly of ceasing to use extra-ordinary means in certain cases, and such withdrawals might easily involve bodily movement, for example unplugging an oxygen machine.

In addition to saddling his opposition with an indefensible distinction it doesn't make, Rachels proceeds to ignore one that it does make—one that is crucial to a just interpretation of the view. Recall the A.M.A. allows the withdrawal of what it calls extraordinary means of preserving life: clearly the contrast here is with ordinary means. Though in its short statement those expressions are not defined, the definition Paul Ramsey refers to as standard in his book, *The Patient as Person,* seems to fit.

> Ordinary means of preserving life are all medicines, treatments, and operations, which offer a reasonable hope of benefit for the patient and which can be obtained and used without excessive expense, pain, and other inconveniences.
>
> Extra-ordinary means of preserving life are all those medicines, treatments, and operations which cannot be obtained without excessive expense, pain, or other inconvenience, or which, if used, would not offer a reasonable hope of benefit.

Now with this distinction in mind, we can see how the traditional view differs from the position Rachels mistakes for it. The traditional view is that the intentional termination of human life is impermissible, irrespective of whether this goal is brought about by action or inaction. Is the action or refraining *aimed at* producing a death? Is the termination of life *sought, chosen or planned?* Is the intention deadly? If so, the act or omission is wrong.

But we all know it is entirely possible that the unwillingness of a physician to use extraordinary means for preserving life may be prompted not by a determination to bring about death, but by other motives. For example, he may realize that further treatment may offer little hope of reversing the dying process and/or be excruciating, as in the case when a massively necrotic bowel condition in a neonate is out of control. The doctor who does what he can to comfort the infant but does not submit it to further treatment or surgery may foresee that the decision will hasten death, but it certainly doesn't follow from that fact that he intends to bring about its death. It is, after all, entirely possible to foresee that something will come about as a result of one's conduct without intending the consequence or side effect. If I drive downtown, I can foresee that I'll wear out my tires a little, but I don't drive downtown with the intention of wearing out my tires. And if I choose to forgo my exercises for a few days, I may think that as a result my physical condition will deteriorate a little, but I don't omit my exercise with a view to running myself down. And if you have to fill a position and select Green, who is better qualified for the post than her rival Brown, you needn't appoint Mrs. Green with the intention of hurting Mr. Brown, though you may foresee that Mr. Brown will feel hurt. And if a country extends its general education programs to its illiterate masses, it is predictable the suicide rate will go up, but even if the public officials are aware of this fact, it doesn't follow that they initiate the program with a view to making the suicide rate go up. In general, then, it is not the case that all the foreseeable consequences and side effects of our conduct are necessarily intended. And it is because the physician's withdrawal of extra-ordinary means can be otherwise motivated than by a desire to bring about the predictable death of the patient that such action cannot categorically be ruled out as wrong.

But the refusal to use ordinary means is an altogether different matter. After all, what is the point of refusing assistance which offers reasonable hope of benefit to the patient without involving excessive pain or other inconvenience? How could it be plausibly maintained that the refusal is not motivated by a desire to bring about the death of the patient? The traditional position, therefore, rules out not only direct actions to bring about death, such as giving a patient a lethal injection, but malevolent omissions as well, such as not providing minimum care for the newborn.

The reason the A.M.A. position sounds so silly when one listens to arguments such as Rachels' is that he slights the distinction between ordinary and extra-ordinary means and then drums on cases where *ordinary* means are refused. The impression is thereby conveyed that the traditional doctrine sanctions omissions that are morally indistinguishable in a substantive way from direct killings, but then incomprehensibly refuses to permit quick and painless termination of life. If the traditional doctrine would approve of Jones' standing by with a grin on his face while his young cousin drowned in a tub, or letting a Down's baby wither and die when ordinary means are available to preserve its life, it would indeed be difficult to see how anyone could defend it. But so to conceive the traditional doctrine is simply to misunderstand it. It is not a doctrine that rests on some supposed distinction between "active" and "passive euthanasia," whatever those words are supposed to mean, nor on a distinction between moving and not moving our bodies. It is simply a prohibition against intentional killing, which includes both direct actions and malevolent omissions.

To summarize—the traditional position represented by the A.M.A. statement is not incoherent. It acknowledges, or more accurately, insists upon the fact that withholding ordinary means to sustain life may be tantamount to killing. The traditional position can be made to appear incoherent only by imposing upon it a crude idea of killing held by none of its more articulate advocates.

Thus the criticism of Rachels and other reformers, misapprehending its target, leaves the traditional position untouched. That position is simply a prohibition of murder. And it is good to remember, as C. S. Lewis once pointed out:

> No man, perhaps, ever at first described to himself the act he was about to do as Murder, or Adultery, or Fraud, or Treachery. . . .and when he hears it so described by other men he is (in a way) sincerely shocked and surprised. Those others "don't understand." If they knew what it had really been like for him, they would not use those crude "stock" names. With a wink or a titter, or a cloud of muddy emotion, the thing has slipped into his will as something not very extraordinary, something of which, rightly understood in all of his peculiar circumstances, he may even feel proud.

I fully realize that there are times when those who have the noble duty to tend the sick and the dying are deeply moved by the sufferings of their patients, especially of the very young and the very old, and desperately wish they could do more than comfort and companion them. Then, perhaps, it seems that universal moral principles are mere abstractions having little to do with the agony of the dying. But of course we do not see best when our eyes are filled with tears.

VOLUNTARY ACTIVE EUTHANASIA

Dan W. Brock

THE CENTRAL ETHICAL ARGUMENT FOR VOLUNTARY ACTIVE EUTHANASIA

The central ethical argument for euthanasia is familiar. It is that the very same two fundamental ethical values supporting the consensus on patient's rights to decide about life-sustaining treatment also support the ethical permissibility of euthanasia. These values are individual self-determination or autonomy and individual well-being. By self-detemination as it bears on euthanasia, I mean people's interest in making important decisions about their lives for themselves according to their own values or conceptions of a good life, and in being left free to act on those decisions. Self-determination is valuable because it permits people to form and live in accordance with their own conception of a good life, at least within the bounds of justice and consistent with others doing so as well. In exercising self-determination people take responsibility for their lives and for the kinds of persons they become. A central aspect of human dignity lies in people's capacity to direct their lives in this way. The value of exercising self-determination presupposes some minimum of decisionmaking capacities or competence, which thus limits the scope of euthanasia supported by self-determination; it cannot justifiably be administered, for example, in cases of serious dementia or treatable clinical depression.

Does the value of individual self-detemination extend to the time and manner of one's death? Most people are very concerned about the nature of the last stage of their lives. This reflects not just a fear of experiencing substantial suffering when dying, but also a desire to retain dignity and control during this last period of life. Death is today increasingly preceded by a long period of significant physical and mental decline, due in part to the technological interventions of modern medicine. Many people adjust to these disabilities and find meaning and value in new activities and ways. Others find the impairments and burdens in the last stage of their lives at some point sufficiently great to make life no longer worth living. For many patients near death, maintaining the quality of one's life, avoiding great suffering, maintaining one's dignity, and insuring that others remember us as we wish them to become of paramount importance and outweigh merely extending one's life. But there is no single, objectively correct answer for everyone as to when, if at all, one's life becomes all things considered a burden and unwanted. If self-determination is a fundamental value, then the great

Reprinted with permission of the author and the publisher from the Hastings Center Report, vol. 22 (March-April 1992), pp. 10–22.

variability among people on this question makes it especially important that individuals control the manner, circumstances, and timing of their dying and death.

The other main value that supports euthanasia is individual well-being. It might seem that individual well-being conflicts with a person's self-determination when the person requests euthanasia. Life itself is commonly taken to be a central good for persons, often valued for its own sake, as well as necessary for pursuit of all other goods within a life. But when a competent patient decides to forgo all further life-sustaining treatment then the patient, either explicitly or implicitly, commonly decides that the best life possible for him or her with treatment is of sufficiently poor quality that it is worse than no further life at all. Life is no longer considered a benefit by the patient, but has now become a burden. The same judgment underlies a request for euthanasia: continued life is seen by the patient as no longer a benefit, but now a burden. Especially in the often severely compromised and debilitated states of many critically ill or dying patients, there is no objective standard, but only the competent patient's judgment of whether continued life is no longer a benefit.

Of course, sometimes there are conditions, such as clinical depression, that call into question whether the patient has made a competent choice, either to forgo life-sustaining treatment or to seek euthanasia, and then the patient's choice need not be evidence that continued life is no longer a benefit for him or her. Just as with decisions about treatment, a determination of incompetence can warrant not honoring the patient's choice; in the case of treatment, we then transfer decisional authority to a surrogate, though in the case of voluntary active euthanasia a determination that the patient is incompetent means that choice is not possible.

The value or right of self-determination does not entitle patients to compel physicians to act contrary to their own moral or professional values. Physicians are moral and professional agents whose own self-determination or integrity should be respected as well. If performing euthanasia became legally permissible, but conflicted with a particular physician's reasonable understanding of his or her moral or professional responsibilities, the care of a patient who requested euthanasia should be transferred to another.

Most opponents do not deny that there are some cases in which the values of patient self-determination and well-being support euthanasia. Instead, they commonly offer two kinds of arguments against it that on their view outweigh or override this support. The first kind of argument is that in any individual case where considerations of the patient's self-determination and well-being do support euthanasia, it is nevertheless always ethically wrong or impermissible. The second kind of argument grants that in some individual cases euthanasia may *not* be ethically wrong, but maintains nonetheless that public and legal policy should never permit it. The first kind of argument focuses on features of any individual case of euthanasia, while the second kind focuses on social or legal policy.

WOULD THE BAD CONSEQUENCES OF EUTHANASIA OUTWEIGH THE GOOD?

The argument against euthanasia at the policy level is stronger than at the level of individual cases, though even here I believe the case is ultimately unpersuasive, or at best indecisive. The policy level is the place where the main issues lie, however, and where moral considerations that might override arguments in favor of euthanasia will be found, if they are found anywhere. It is important to note two kinds of disagreement about the consequences for public policy of permitting euthanasia. First, there is empirical or factual disagreement about what the consequences would be. This disagreement is greatly exacerbated by the lack of firm data on the issue. Second, since on any reasonable assessment there would be both good and bad consequences, there are moral disagreements about the relative importance of different effects. In addition to these two sources of disagreement, there is also no single, well-specified policy proposal for legalizing euthanasia on which policy assessments can focus. But without such specification, and especially without explicit procedures for protecting against well-intentioned misuse and ill-intentioned abuse, the consequences for policy are largely speculative. Despite these difficulties, a preliminary account of the main likely good and bad consequences is possible. This should help clarify where better data or more moral analysis and argument are needed, as well as where policy safeguards must be developed.

Potential Good Consequences of Permitting Euthanasia

What are the likely good consequences? First, if euthanasia were permitted it would be possible to respect the self-determination of competent patients who want it, but now cannot get it because of its illegality. We simply do not know how many such patients and people there are. In the Netherlands, with a population of about 14.5 million (in 1987), estimates in a recent study were that about 1,900 cases of voluntary active euthanasia or physician-assisted suicide occur annually. No straightforward extrapolation to the United States is possible for many reasons, among them, that we do not know how many people here who want euthanasia now get it, despite its illegality. Even with better data on the number of persons who want euthanasia but cannot get it, significant moral disagreement would remain about how much weight should be given to any instance of failure to respect a person's self-determination in this way.

One important factor substantially affecting the number of persons who would seek euthanasia is the extent to which an alternative is available. The widespread acceptance in the law, social policy, and medical practice of the right of a competent patient to forgo life-sustaining treatment suggests that the number of competent persons in the United States who would want euthanasia if it were permitted is probably relatively small.

A second good consequence of making euthanasia legally permissible benefits a much larger group. Polls have shown that a majority of the American public believes that people should have a right to obtain euthanasia if they want it. No doubt the vast majority of those who support this right to euthanasia will never in fact come to want euthanasia for themselves. Nevertheless, making it legally permissible would reassure many people that if they ever do want euthanasia they would be able to obtain it. This reassurance would supplement the broader control over the process of dying given by the right to decide about life-sustaining treatment. Having fire insurance on one's house benefits all who have it, not just those whose houses actually burn down, by reassuring them that in the unlikely event of their house burning down, they will receive the money needed to rebuild it. Likewise, the legalization of euthanasia can be thought of as a kind of insurance policy against being forced to endure a protracted dying process that one has come to find burdensome and unwanted, especially when there is no life-sustaining treatment to forgo. The strong concern about losing control of their care expressed by many people who face serious illness likely to end in death suggests that they give substantial importance to the legalization of euthanasia as a means of maintaining this control.

A third good consequence of the legalization of euthanasia concerns patients whose dying is filled with severe and unrelievable pain or suffering. When there is a life-sustaining treatment that, if forgone, will lead relatively quickly to death, then doing so can bring an end to these patients' suffering without recourse to euthanasia. For patients receiving no such treatment, however, euthanasia may be the only release from their otherwise prolonged suffering and agony. This argument from mercy has always been the strongest argument for euthanasia in those cases to which it applies.

The importance of relieving pain and suffering is less controversial than is the frequency with which patients are forced to undergo untreatable agony that only euthanasia could relieve. If we focus first on suffering caused by physical pain, it is crucial to distinguish pain that *could* be adequately relieved with modern methods of pain control, though it in fact is not, from pain that is relievable only by death. For a variety of reasons, including some physicians' fear of hastening the patient's death, as well as the lack of a publicly accessible means for assessing the amount of the patient's pain, many patients suffer pain that could be, but is not, relieved.

Specialists in pain control, as for example the pain of terminally ill cancer patients, argue that there are very few patients whose pain could not be adequately controlled, though sometimes at the cost of so sedating them that they are effectively unable to interact with other people or their environment. Thus, the argument from mercy in cases of physical pain can probably be met in a large majority of cases by providing adequate measures of pain relief. This should be a high priority, whatever our legal policy on euthanasia—the relief of pain and suffering has long been, quite properly, one of the central goals of medicine. Those cases in which pain could be effectively relieved, but in fact is not, should only count significantly in favor of legalizing euthanasia if all reasonable efforts to change pain management techniques have been tried and have failed.

Dying patients often undergo substantial psychological suffering that is not fully or even principally the result of physical pain. The knowledge about how to relieve this suffering is much more limited than in the case of relieving pain, and efforts to do so are probably more often unsuccessful. If the argument from mercy is extended to patients experiencing great and unrelievable psychological suffering, the numbers of patients to which it applies are much greater.

One last good consequence of legalizing euthanasia is that once death has been accepted, it is often more humane to end life quickly and peacefully, when that is what the patient wants. Such a death will often be seen as better than a more prolonged one. People who suffer a sudden and unexpected death, for example by dying quickly or in their sleep from a heart attack or stroke, are often considered lucky to have died in this way. We care about how we die in part because we care about how others remember us, and we hope they will remember us as we were in "good times" with them and not as we might be when disease has robbed us of our dignity as human beings. As with much in the treatment and care of the dying, people's concerns differ in this respect, but for at least some people, euthanasia will be a more humane death than what they have often experienced with other loved ones and might otherwise expect for themselves.

Some opponents of euthanasia challenge how much importance should be given to any of these good consequences of permitting it, or even whether some would be good consequences at all. But more frequently, opponents cite a number of bad consequences that permitting euthanasia would or could produce, and it is to their assessment that I now turn.

Potential Bad Consequences of Permitting Euthanasia

Some of the arguments against permitting euthanasia are aimed specifically against physicians, while others are aimed against anyone being permitted to perform it. I shall first consider one argument of the former sort. Permitting physicians to perform euthanasia, it is said, would be incompatible with their fundamental moral and professional commitment as healers to care for patients and to protect life. Moreover, if euthanasia by physicians became common, patients would come to fear that a medication was intended not to treat or care, but instead to kill, and would thus lose trust in their physicians. This position was forcefully stated in a paper by Willard Gaylin and his colleagues:

> The very soul of medicine is on trial ... This issue touches medicine at its moral center; if this moral center collapses, if physicians become killers or are even licensed to kill, the profession—and, therewith, each physician—will never again be worthy of trust and respect as healer and comforter and protector of life in all its frailty.

These authors go on to make clear that, while they oppose permitting anyone to perform euthanasia, their special concern is with physicians doing so:

> We call on fellow physicians to say that they will not deliberately kill. We must also say to each of our fellow physicians that we will not tolerate killing of patients and that we shall take disciplinary action against doctors who kill. And we must say to the broader community that if it insists on tolerating or legalizing active euthanasia, it will have to find nonphysicians to do its killing.

If permitting physicians to kill would undermine the very "moral center" of medicine, then almost certainly physicians should not be permitted to perform euthanasia. But how persuasive is this claim? Patients should not fear, as a consequence of permitting *voluntary* active euthanasia, that their physicians will substitute a lethal injection for what patients want and believe is part of their care. If active euthanasia is restricted to cases in which it is truly voluntary, then no patient should fear getting it unless she or he has voluntarily requested it. ... Patients' trust of their physicians could be increased, not eroded, by knowledge that physicians will provide aid in dying when patients seek it.

In spelling out above what I called the positive argument for voluntary active euthanasia, I suggested that two principal values—respecting patients' self-determination and promoting their well-being—underlie the consensus that competent patients, or the surrogates of incompetent patients, are entitled to refuse any life-sustaining treatment and to choose from among available alternative treatments. It is the commitment to these two values in guiding physicians' actions as healers, comforters, and protectors of their patients' lives that should be at the "moral center" of medicine, and these two values support physicians' administering euthanasia when their patients make competent requests for it.

What should not be at that moral center is a commitment to preserving patients' lives as such, without regard to whether those patients' want their lives preserved or judge their preservation a benefit to them. ...

A second bad consequence that some foresee is that permitting euthanasia would weaken society's commitment to provide optimal care for dying patients. We live at a time in which the control of health care costs has become, and is likely to continue to be, the dominant focus of health care policy. If euthanasia is seen as a cheaper alternative to adequate care and treatment, then we might become less scrupulous about providing sometimes costly support and other services to dying patients. Particularly if our society comes to embrace deeper and more explicit rationing of health care, frail, elderly, and dying patients will need to be strong and effective advocates for their own health care and other needs, although they are hardly in a position to do this. We should do nothing to weaken their ability to obtain adequate care and services.

This second worry is difficult to assess because there is little firm evidence about the likelihood of the feared erosion in the care of dying patients. There are at least two reasons, however, for skepticism about this argument. The first is that the same worry could have been directed at recognizing patients' or surrogates' rights to forgo life-sustaining treatment, yet there is no persuasive evidence that recognizing the right to refuse treatment has caused a serious erosion in the quality of care of dying patients. The second reason for skepticism about this worry is that only a very small proportion of deaths would occur from euthanasia if it were permitted. In the Netherlands, where euthanasia under specified circumstances is permitted by the courts, though not authorized by statute, the best estimate of the proportion of overall deaths that result from it is about 2 percent. Thus, the vast majority of critically ill and dying patients will not request it, and so will still have to be cared for by physicians, families, and others. Permitting euthanasia should not diminish people's commitment and concern to maintain and improve the care of these patients. ...

The [third] potential bad consequence of permitting euthanasia has been developed by David Velleman and turns on the subtle point that making a new option or choice available to people can sometimes make them worse off, even if once they have the choice they go on to choose what is best for them. Ordinarily, people's continued existence is viewed by them as given, a fixed condition with which they must cope. Making euthanasia availaible to people as an option denies them the alternative of staying alive by default. If people are offered the option of euthanasia, their continued existence is now a choice for which they can be held responsible and which they can be asked by others to justify. We care, and are right to care, about being able to justify ourselves to others. To the extent that our society is unsympathetic to justifying a severely dependent or impaired existence, a heavy psychological burden of proof may be placed on patients who think their terminal illness or chronic infirmity is not a sufficient reason for dying. Even if they otherwise view their life as worth living, the opinion of others around them that it is not can threaten their reason for living and make euthanasia a rational choice. Thus the existence of the option becomes a subtle pressure to request it.

This argument correctly identifies the reason why offering some patients the option of euthanasia would not benefit them. Velleman takes it not as a reason for opposing all euthanasia, but for restricting it to circumstances where there are "unmistakable and overpowering reasons for persons to want the option of euthanasia, "and for denying the option in all other cases. But there are at least three reasons why such restriction may not be warranted. First, polls and other evidence support that most Americans believe euthanasia should be permitted (though the recent defeat of the referendum to permit it in the state of Washington raises some doubt about this support). Thus, many more people seem to want the choice than would be made worse off by getting it. Second, if giving people the option of ending their life really makes them worse off, then we should not only prohibit euthanasia, but also take back from people the right they now have to decide about life-sustaining treatment. The feared harmful effect should already have occurred from securing people's right to refuse life-sustaining treatment, yet there is no evidence of any such widespread harm or any broad public desire to rescind that right. Third, since there is a wide range of conditions in which reasonable people can and do disagree about whether they would want continued life, it is not possible to restrict the permissibility of euthanasia as narrowly as Velleman suggests without thereby denying it to most persons who would want it; to permit it only in cases in which virtually everyone would want it would be to deny it to most who would want it.

A [fourth] potential bad consequence of making euthanasia legally permissible is that it might weaken the general legal prohibition of homicide. This prohibition is so fundamental to civilized society, it is argued, that we should do nothing that erodes it. If most cases of stopping life support are killing, as I have already argued, then the court cases permitting such killing have already in effect weakened this prohibition. However, neither the courts nor most people have seen these cases as killing and so as challenging the prohibition of homicide. The courts have usually grounded patients' or their surrogates' rights to refuse life-sustaining treatment in rights to privacy, liberty, self-determination, or bodily integrity, not in exceptions to homicide laws.

Legal permission for physicians or others to perform euthanasia could not be grounded in patients' rights to decide about medical treatment. Permitting euthanasia would require qualifying, at least in effect, the legal prohibition against homicide, a prohibition that in general does not allow the consent of the victim to justify or excuse the act. Nevertheless, the very same fundamental basis of the right to decide about life-sustaining treatment—respecting a person's self-determination—does support euthanasia as well. Individual self-determination has long been a well-entrenched and fundamental value in the law, and so extending it to euthanasia would not require appeal to novel legal values or principles. That suicide or attempted suicide is no longer a criminal offense in virtually all states indicates an acceptance of individual self-determination in the taking of one's own life analogous to that required for voluntary active euthanasia. The legal prohibition (in most states) of assisting in suicide and the refusal in the law to accept the consent of the victim as a possible justification of homicide are both arguably a result of difficulties in the legal process of establishing the consent of the victim after the fact. If procedures can be designed that clearly establish the voluntariness of the person's request for euthanasia, it would under those procedures represent a carefully circumscribed qualification on the legal prohibition of homicide. Nevertheless, some remaining worries about this weakening can be captured in the final potential bad consequence, to which I will now turn.

This final potential bad consequence is the central concern of many opponents of euthanasia and, I believe, is the most serious objection to a legal policy permitting it. According to this "slippery slope" worry, although active euthanasia may be morally permissible in cases in which it is unequivocally voluntary and the patient finds his or her condition unbearable, a legal policy, permitting euthanasia would inevitably lead to active euthanasia being performed in many other cases in which it would be morally wrong. To prevent those other wrongful cases of euthanasia we should not permit even morally justified performance of it.

Slippery slope arguments of this form are problematic and difficult to evaluate. From one perspective, they are the last refuge of conservative defenders of the status quo. When all the opponent's objections to the wrongness of euthanasia itself have been met, the opponent then shifts ground and acknowledges both that it is not in itself wrong and that a legal policy which resulted only in its being performed would not be bad. Nevertheless, the opponent maintains, it should still not be permitted because doing so would result in its being performed in other cases in which it is not voluntary and would be wrong. In this argument's most extreme form, permitting euthanasia is the first and fateful step down the slippery slope to Nazism. Once on the slope we will be unable to get off.

Now it cannot be denied that it is *possible* that permitting euthanasia could have these fateful consequences, but that cannot be enough to warrant prohibiting it if it is otherwise justified. A similar *possible* slippery slope worry could have been raised to securing competent patients' rights to decide about life support, but recent history shows such a worry would have been unfounded. It must be relevant how likely it is that we will end with horrendous consequences and an unjustified practice of euthanasia. How *likely* and *widespread* would the abuses and unwarranted extensions of permitting it be? By abuses, I mean the performance of euthanasia that fails to satisfy the conditions required for voluntary active euthanasia, for example, if the patient has been subtly pressured to accept it. By unwarranted extensions of policy. I mean later changes in legal policy to permit not just voluntary euthanasia, but also euthanasia in cases in which, for example, it need not be fully voluntary. Opponents of voluntary euthanasia on slippery slope grounds have not provided the data or evidence neccessary turn their speculative concerns into well-grounded likelihoods.

It is at least clear, however, that both the character and likelihood of abuses of a legal policy permitting euthanasia depend in significant part on the procedures put in place to protect against them. I will not try to detail fully what such procedures might be, but will just give some examples of what they might include:

1. The patient should be provided with all relevant information about his or her medical condition, current prognosis, available alternative treatments, and the prognosis of each.
2. Procedures should ensure that the patient's request for euthanasia is stable or enduring (a brief waiting period could be required) and fully voluntary (an advocate for the patient might be appointed to ensure this).
3. All reasonable alternatives must have been explored for improving the patient's quality of life and relieving any pain or suffering.
4. A psychiatric evaluation should ensure that the patient's request is not the result of a treatable psychological impairment such as depression.

These examples of procedural safeguards are all designed to ensure that the patient's choice is fully informed, voluntary, and competent, and so a true exercise of self-determination. Other proposals for euthanasia would restrict its permissibility further—for example, to the terminally ill—a restriction that cannot be supported by self-determination. Such additional restrictions might, however, be justified by concern for limiting potential harms from abuse. At the same time, it is important not to impose procedural or substantive safeguards so restrictive as to make euthanasia impermissible or practically infeasible in a wide range of justified cases.

These examples of procedural safeguards make clear that it is possible to substantially reduce, though not to eliminate, the potential for abuse of a policy permitting voluntary active euthanasia. Any legalization of the practice should be accompanied by a well-considered set of procedural safeguards together with an ongoing evaluation of its use. Introducing euthanasia into only a few states could be a form of carefully limited and controlled social experiment that would give us evidence about the benefits and harms of the practice. Even then firm and uncontroversial data may remain elusive, as the continuing controversy over what has taken place in the Netherlands in recent years indicates.

The Slip into Nonvoluntary Active Euthanasia

While I believe slippery slope worries can largely be limited by making necessary distinctions both in principle and in practice, one slippery slope concern is legitimate. There is reason to expect that legalization of voluntary active euthanasia might soon be followed by strong pressure to legalize some nonvoluntary euthanasia of incompetent patients unable to express their own wishes. Respecting a person's self-determination and recognizing that continued life is not always of value to a person can support not only voluntary active euthanasia, but some nonvoluntary euthanasia as well. These are the same values that ground competent patients' right to refuse life-sustaining treatment. Recent history here is instructive. In the medical ethics literature, in the courts since Quinlan, and in norms of medical practice, that right has been extended to incompetent patients and exercised by a surrogate who is to decide as the patient would have decided in the circumstances if competent. It has been held unreasonable to continue life-sustaining treatment that the patient would not have wanted just because the patient now lacks the capacity to tell us that. Life-sustaining treatment for incompetent patients is today frequently forgone on the basis of a surrogate's decision, or less frequently on the basis of an advance directive executed by the patient while still competent. The very same logic that has extended the right to refuse life-sustaining treatment from a competent patient to the surrogate of an incompetent patient (acting with or without a formal advance directive from the patient) may well extend the scope of active euthanasia. The argument will be, Why continue to force unwanted life on patients just because they have now lost the capacity to request euthanasia from us?

A related phenomenon may reinforce this slippery slope concern. In the Netherlands, what the courts have sanctioned has been clearly restricted to voluntary euthanasia. In itself, this serves as some evidence that permitting it need *not* lead to permitting the nonvoluntary variety. There is some indication, however, that for many Dutch physicians euthanasia is no longer viewed as a special action, set apart from their usual practice and restricted only to competent persons. Instead, it is seen as one end of a spectrum of caring for dying patients. When viewed in this way it will be difficult to deny euthanasia to a patient for whom it is seen as the best or most appropriate form of care simply because that patient is now incompetent and cannot request it.

Even if voluntary active euthanasia should slip into nonvoluntary active euthanasia, with surrogates acting for incompetent patients, the ethical evaluation is more complex than many opponents of euthanasia allow. Just as in the case of surrogates' decisions to forgo life-sustaining treatment for incompetent patients, so also surrogates' decisions to request euthanasia or incompetent persons would often accurately reflect what the incompetent person would have wanted and would deny the person nothing that he or she would have considered worth having. Making nonvoluntary active euthanasia legally permissible, however, would greatly enlarge the number of patients on whom it might be performed and substantially enlarge the potential for misuse and abuse. As noted above, frail and debilitated elderly people, often demented or otherwise incompetent and thereby unable to defend and assert their own interests, may be especially vulnerable to unwanted euthanasia.

For some people, this risk is more than sufficient reason to oppose the legalization of voluntary euthanasia. But while we should in general be cautious about inferring much from the experience in the Netherlands to what our own experience in the United States might be, there may be one important lesson that we can learn from them. One commentator has noted that in the Netherlands families of incompetent patients have less authority than do families in the United States to act as surrogates for incompetent patients in making decisions to forgo life-sustaining treatment. From the Dutch perspective, it may be we in the United States who are *already* on the slippery slope in haying given surrogates broad authority to forgo life-sustaining treatment for incompetent persons. In this view, the more important moral divide, and the more important with regard to potential for abuse, is not between forgoing life-sustaining treatment and euthanasia, but instead between voluntary and nonvoluntary performance of either. If this is correct, then the more important issue is ensuring the appropriate principles and procedural safeguards for the exercise of decisionmaking authority by surrogates for incompetent persons in *all* decisions at the end of life. This may be the correct response to slippery slope worries about euthanasia.

I have cited both good and bad consequences that have been thought likely from a policy change permitting voluntary active euthanasia, and have tried to evaluate their likelihood and relative importance. Nevertheless, as I noted earlier, reasonable disagreement remains both about the consequences of permitting euthanasia and about which of these consequences are more important. The depth and strength of public and professional debate about whether, all things considered, permitting euthanasia would be desirable or undesirable reflects these disagreements. While my own view is that the balance of considerations supports permitting the practice, my principal purpose here has been to clarify the main issues.

THE ROLE OF PHYSICIANS

If euthanasia is made legally permissible, should physicians take part in it? Should only physicians be permitted to perform it, as is the case in the Netherlands? In discussing whether euthanasia is incompatible with medicine's commitment to curing, caring for, and comforting patients, I argued that it is not at odds with a proper understanding of the aims of medicine, and so need not undermine patients' trust in their physicians. If that argument is correct, then physicians probably should not be prohibited, either by law or by professional norms, from taking part in a legally permissible practice of euthanasia (nor, of course, should they be compelled to do so if their personal or professional scruples forbid it). Most physicians in the Netherlands appear not to understand euthanasia to be incompatible with their professional commitments.

Sometimes patients who would be able to end their lives on their own nevertheless seek the assistance of physicians. Physician involvement in such cases may have important benefits to patients and others beyond simply assuring the use of effective means. Historically, in the United States suicide has carried a strong negative stigma that many today believe unwarranted. Seeking a physician's assistance, or what can almost seem a physician's blessing, may be a way of trying to remove that stigma and show others that the decision for suicide was made with due sriousness and was justified under the circumstances. The physician's involvement provides a kind of social approval, or more accurately helps counter what would otherwise be unwarranted social disapproval.

There are also at least two reasons for restricting the practice of euthanasia to physicians only. First, physicians would inevitably be involved in some of the important procedural safeguards necessary to a defensible practice, such as seeing to it that the patient is well-informed about his or her condition, prognosis, and possible treatments, and ensuring that all reasonable means have been taken to improve the quality of the patient's life. Second, and probably more important, one necessary protection against abuse of the practice is to limit the persons given authority to perform it, so that they can be held accountable for their exercise of that authority. Physicians, whose training and professional norms give some assurance that they would perform euthanasia responsibly, are an appropriate group of persons to whom the practice may be restricted.

WHEN SELF-DETERMINATION RUNS AMOK

Daniel Callahan

The euthanasia debate is not just another moral debate, one in a long list of arguments in our pluralistic society. It is profoundly emblematic of three important turning points in Western thought. The first is that of the legitimate conditions under which one person can kill another. The acceptance of voluntary active euthanasia would morally sanction what can only be called "consenting adult killing." By that term I mean the killing of one person by another in the name of their mutual right to be killer and killed if they freely agree to play those roles. This turn flies in the face of a long-standing effort to limit the circumstances under which one person can take the life of another, from efforts to control the free flow of guns and arms, to abolish capital punishment, and to more tightly control warfare. Euthanasia would add a whole new category of

Reprinted with permission of the author and the publisher from the *Hastings Center Report*, vol. 22 (March-April 1992), pp. 52–55.

killing to a society that already has too many excuses to indulge itself in that way.

The second turning point lies in the meaning and limits of self-determination. The acceptance of euthanasia would sanction a view of autonomy holding that individuals may, in the name of their own private, idiosyncratic view of the good life, call upon others, including such institutions as medicine, to help them pursue that life, even at the risk of harm to the common good. This works against the idea that the meaning and scope of our own right to lead our own lives must be conditioned by and be compatible with, the good of the community, which is more than an aggregate of self-directing individuals.

The third turning point is to be found in the claim being made upon medicine: it should be prepared to make its skills available to individuals to help them achieve their private vision of the good life. This puts medicine in the business of promoting the individualistic pursuit of general human happiness and well-being. It would overturn the traditional belief that medicine should limit its domain to promoting and preserving human health, redirecting it instead to the relief of that suffering which stems from life itself, not merely from a sick body.

I believe that, at each of these three turning points, proponent of euthanasia push us in the wrong direction. Arguments in favor of euthanasia fall into four general categories, which I will take up in turn: (1) the moral claim of individual self-determination and well-being; (2) the moral irrelevance of the difference between killing and allowing to die; (3) the supposed paucity of evidence to show likely harmful consequences of legalized euthanasia; and (4) the compatibility of euthanasia and medical practice.

SELF-DETERMINATION

Central to most arguments for euthanasia is the principle of self-determination. People are presumed to have an interest in deciding for themselves, according to their own beliefs about what makes life good, how they will conduct their lives. That is an important value, but the question in the euthanasia context is, What does it mean and how far should it extend? If it were a question of suicide, where a person takes her own life without assistance from another, that principle might be pertinent, at least for debate. But euthanasia is not that limited a matter. The self-determination in that case can only be effected by the moral and physical assistance of another. Euthanasia is thus no longer a matter only of self-determination, but of a mutual, social decision between two people, the one to be killed and the other to do the killing.

How are we to make the moral move from my right of self-determination to some doctor's right to kill me—from *my* right to *his* right? Where does the doctor's moral warrant to kill come from? Ought doctors to be able to kill anyone they want as long as permission is given by competent persons? Is our right to life just like a piece of property, to be given away or alienated if the price (happiness, relief of suffering) is right? And then to be destroyed with our permission once alienated?

In answer to all those questions, I will say this: I have yet to hear a plausible argument why it should be permissible for us to put this kind of power in the hands of another, whether a doctor or anyone else. The idea that we can waive our right to life, and then give to another the power to take that life, requires a justification yet to be provided by anyone.

Slavery was long ago outlawed on the ground that one person should not have the right to own another, even with the other's permission. Why? Because it is a fundamental moral wrong for one person to give over his life and fate to another, whatever the good consequences, and no less a wrong for another person to have that kind of total, final power. Like slavery, dueling was long ago banned on similar grounds: even free, competent individuals should not have the power to kill each other, whatever their motives, whatever the circumstances. Consenting adult killing, like consenting adult slavery or degradation, is a strange route to human dignity.

There is another problem as well. If doctors, once sanctioned to carry out euthanasia, are to be themselves responsible moral agents—not simply hired hands with lethal injections at the ready—then, they must have their own *independent* moral grounds to kill those who request such services. What do I mean? As those who favor euthanasia are quick to point out, some people want it because their life has become so burdensome it no longer seems worth living.

The doctor will have a difficulty at this point. The degree and intensity to which people suffer from their diseases and their dying, and whether they find life more of a burden than a benefit, has very little directly to do with the nature or extent of their actual physical condition. Three people can have the same condition, but only one will find the suffering unbearable. People suffer, but suffering is as much a function of the values of individuals as it is of the physical causes of that suffering. Inevitably in that circumstance, the doctor will in effect be treating the patient's values. To be responsible, the doctor would have to share those values. The doctor would have to decide, on her own, whether the patient's life was "no longer worth living."

But how could a doctor possibly know that or make such a judgment? Just because the patient said so? I raise this question because, while in Holland at the euthanasia conference reported by Maurice de Wachter ... the doctors present agreed that there is no objective way of measuring or judging the claims of patients that their suffering is unbearable. And if it is difficult to measure suffering, how much more difficult to determine the value of a patient's statement that her life is not worth living?

However one might want to answer such questions, the very need to ask them, to inquire into the physician's responsibility and grounds for medical and moral judgment, points out the social nature of the decision. Euthanasia is not a private matter of self-determination. It is an act that requires two people to make it possible, and a complicit society to make it acceptable.

KILLING AND ALLOWING TO DIE

Against common opinion, the argument is sometimes made that there is no moral difference between stopping life-sustaining treatment and more active forms of killing, such as lethal injection. Instead I would contend that the notion that there is no morally significant difference between omission and commission is just wrong. Consider in its broad implications what the eradication of the distinction implies: that death from disease has been banished, leaving only the actions of physicians in terminating treatment as the cause of death. Biology, which used to bring about death, has apparently been displaced by human agency. Doctors have finally, I suppose, thus genuinely become gods, now doing what nature and the deities once did.

What is the mistake here? It lies in confusing causality and culpability, and in failing to note the way in which human societies have overlaid natural causes with moral rules and interpretations. Causality (by which I mean the direct physical causes of death) and culpability (by which I mean our attribution of moral responsibility to human actions) are confused under three circumstances.

They are confused, first, when the action of a physician in stopping treatment of a patient with an underlying lethal disease is construed as *causing* death. On the contrary, the physician's omission can only bring about a death on the condition that the patient's disease will kill him in the absence of treatment. We may hold the physician morally responsible for the death, if we have morally judged such actions wrongful omissions. But it confuses reality and moral judgment to see an omitted action as having the same causal status as one that directly kills. A lethal injection will kill both a healthy person and a sick person. A physician's omitted treatment will have no effect on a healthy person. Turn off the machine on me, a healthy person, and nothing will happen. It will only, in contrast, bring the life of a sick person to an end because of an underlying fatal disease.

Causality and culpability are confused, second, when we fail to note that judgments of moral responsibility and culpability are human constructs. By that I mean that we human beings, after moral reflection, have decided to call some actions right or wrong, and to devise moral rules to deal with them. When physicians could do nothing to stop death, they were not held responsible for it. When, with medical progress, they began to have some power over death—but only its timing and circumstances, not its ultimate inevitability—moral rules devised to set forth their obligations. Natural causes of death were not thereby banished. They were, instead, overlaid with a medical ethics designed to determine moral culpability in deploying medical power.

To confuse the judgments of this ethics with the physical causes of death—which is the connotation of the word *kill*—is to confuse nature and human action. People will, one way or another, die of some disease; death will have dominion over all of us. To say that a doctor "kills" a patient by allowing this to happen should only be understood as a moral judgment about the licitness of his omission, nothing more. We can, as a fashion of speech only, talk about a doctor *killing* a patient by omitting treatment he should have provided. It is a fashion of speech precisely because it is the underlying disease that brings death when treatment is omitted; that is its cause, not the physician's omission. It is a misuse of the word *killing* to use it when a doctor stops a treatment he believes will no longer benefit the patient—when, that is, he steps aside to allow an eventually inevitable death to occur now rather than later. The only deaths that human beings invented are those that come from direct killing—when, with a lethal injection, we both cause death and are morally responsible for it. In the case of omissions, we do not cause death even if we may be judged morally responsible for it.

This difference between causality and culpability also helps us see why a doctor who has omitted a treatment he should have provided has "killed" that patient while another doctor—performing precisely the same act of omission on another patient in different circumstances—does not kill her, but only allows her to die. The difference is that we have come, by moral convention and conviction, to classify unauthorized or illegitimate omissions as acts of "killing." We call them "killing" in the expanded sense of the term: a culpable action that permits the real cause of death, the underlying disease, to proceed to its lethal conclusion. By contrast, the doctor who, at the patient's request, omits or terminates unwanted treatment does not kill at all. Her underlying disease, not his action, is the physical cause of death; and we have agreed to consider actions of that kind to be morally licit. He thus can truly be said to have "allowed" her to die.

If we fail to maintain the distinction between killing and allowing to die, moreover, there are some disturbing possibilities. The first would be to confirm many physicians in their already too powerful belief that, when patients die or when physicians stop treatment because of the futility of continuing it, they are somehow both morally and physically responsible for the deaths that follow. That notion needs to be abolished, not strengthened. It needlessly and wrongly burdens the physician, to whom should not be attributed the powers of the gods. The second possibility would be that, in every case where a doctor judges medical treatment no longer effective in prolonging life, a quick and direct killing of the patient would be seen as the next, most reasonable step, on grounds of both humaneness and economics. I do not see how that logic could easily be rejected.

CALCULATING THE CONSEQUENCES

When concerns about the adverse social consequences of permitting euthanasia are raised, its advocates tend to dismiss them as unfounded and overly speculative. On the contrary, recent data about the Dutch experience suggests that such concerns are right on target. From my own discussions in Holland, and from the articles on that subject in this issue and elsewhere, I believe we can now fully see most of the *likely* consequences of legal euthanasia.

Three consequences seem almost certain, in this or any other country: the inevitability of some abuse of the law; the difficulty of precisely writing, and then enforcing, the law; and the inherent slipperiness of the moral reasons for legalizing euthanasia in the first place.

Why is abuse inevitable? One reason is that almost all laws on delicate, controversial matters are to some extent abused. This happens because not everyone will agree with the law as written and will bend it, or ignore it, if they can get away with it. From explicit admissions to me by Dutch proponents of euthanasia, and from the corroborating information provided by the Remmelink Report and the outside studies of Carlos Gomez and John Keown, I am convinced that in the Netherlands there are a substantial number of cases of nonvoluntary euthanasia, that is, euthanasia undertaken without the explicit permission of the person being killed. The other reason abuse is inevitable is that the law is likely to have a low enforcement priority in the criminal justice system. Like other laws of similar status, unless there is an unrelenting and harsh willingness to pursue abuse, violations will ordinarily be tolerated. The worst thing to me about my experience in Holland was the casual, seemingly indifferent attitude toward abuse. I think that would happen everywhere.

Why would it be hard to precisely write, and then enforce, the law? The Dutch speak about the requirement of "unbearable" suffering, but admit that such a term is just about indefinable, a highly subjective matter admitting of no objective standards. A requirement for outside opinion is nice, but it is easy to find complaisant colleagues. A requirement that a medical condition be "terminal" will run aground on the notorious difficulties of knowing when an illness is actually terminal.

Apart from those technical problems there is a more profound worry: I see no way, even in principle, to write or enforce a meaningful law that can guarantee effective procedural safeguards. The reason is obvious yet almost always overlooked. The euthanasia transaction will ordinarily take place within the boundaries of the private and confidential doctor-patient relationship. No one can possibly know what takes place in that context unless the doctor chooses to reveal it. In Holland, less than 10 percent of the physicians report their acts of euthanasia and do so with almost complete legal impunity. There is no reason why the situation should be any better elsewhere. Doctors will have their own reasons for keeping euthanasia secret, and some patients will have no less a motive for wanting it concealed.

I would mention, finally, that the moral logic of the motives for euthanasia contain within them the ingredients of abuse. The two standard motives for euthanasia and assisted suicide are said to be our right of self-determination, and our claim upon the mercy of others, especially, doctors, to relieve our suffering. These two motives are typically spliced together and presented as a single justification. Yet if they are considered independently—and there is no inherent reason why they must be linked—they reveal serious problems. It is said that a competent, adult person should have a right to euthanasia for the relief of suffering. But why must the person be suffering? Does not that stipulation already compromise the principle of self-determination? How can self-determination have any limits? Whatever the person's motives may be, why are they not sufficient?

Consider next the person who is suffering but not competent, who is perhaps demented or mentally retarded. The standard argument would deny euthanasia to that person. But why? If a person is suffering but not competent, then it would seem grossly unfair to deny relief solely on the grounds of incompetence. Are the incompetent less entitled to relief from suffering than the competent? Will it only be affluent, middle-class people, mentally fit and savvy about working the medical system, who can qualify? Do the incompetent suffer less because of their incompetence?

Considered from these angles, there are no good moral reasons to limit euthanasia once the principle of taking life for that purpose has been legitimated. If we really believe in self-determination, then any competent person should have a right to be killed by a doctor for any reason that suits him. If we believe in the relief of suffering, then it seems cruel and capricious to deny it to the incompetent. There is, in short, no reasonable or logical stopping point once the turn has been made down the road to euthanasia, which could soon turn into a convenient and commodious expressway.

EUTHANASIA AND MEDICAL PRACTICE

A fourth kind of argument one often hears both in the Netherlands and in this country is that euthanasia and assisted suicide are perfectly compatible with the aims of medicine. I would note at the very outset that a physician who participates in another person's suicide already abuses medicine. Apart from depression (the main statistical cause of suicide), people commit suicide because they find life empty, oppressive, or meaningless. Their judgment is a judgment about the value of continued life, not only about health (even if they are sick). Are doctors now to be given the right to make judgments about the kinds of life worth living and to give their blessing to suicide for those they judge wanting? What conceivable competence, technical or moral, could doctors claim to play such a role? Are we to medicalize suicide, turning judgments about its worth and value into one more clinical issue? Yes, those are rhetorical questions.

Yet they bring us to the core of the problem of euthanasia and medicine. The great temptation of modern medicine, not always resisted, is to move beyond the promotion and preservation of health into the boundless realm of general human happiness and well-being. The root problem of illness and mortality is both medical and philosophical or religious. "Why must I die?" can be asked as a technical, biological question or as a question about the meaning of life. When medicine tries to respond to the latter, which it is always under pressure to do, it moves beyond its proper role.

It is not medicine's place to lift from us the burden of that suffering which turns on the meaning we assign to the decay of the body and its eventual death. It is not medicine's place to determine when lives are not worth living or when the burden of life is too great to be borne. Doctors have no conceivable way of evaluating such claims on the part of patients, and they should have no right to act in response to them. Medicine should try to relieve human suffering, but only that suffering which is brought on by illness and dying as biological phenomena, not that suffering which comes from anguish or despair at the human condition.

Doctors ought to relieve those forms of suffering that medically accompany serious illness and the threat of death. They should relieve pain, do what they can to allay anxiety and uncertainty, and be a comforting presence. As sensitive human beings, doctors should be prepared to respond to patients who ask why they must die, or die in pain. But here the doctor and the patient are at the same level. The doctor may have no better an answer to those old questions than anyone else; and certainly no special insight from his training as a physician. It would be terrible for physicians to forget this, and to think that in a swift, lethal injection, medicine has found its own answer to the riddle of life. It would be a false answer given by the wrong people. It would be no less a false answer for patients. They should neither ask medicine to put its own vocation at risk to serve their private interests, nor think that the answer to suffering is to be killed by another. The problem is precisely that, too often in human history, killing has seemed the quick, efficient way to put aside that which burdens us. It rarely helps, and too often simply adds to one evil still another. That is what I believe euthanasia would accomplish. It is self-determination run amok.

EUTHANASIA: NORMAL MEDICAL PRACTICE?

Henk A.M.J. ten Have, and Jos V. M. Welie

Since the 1973 Leeuwarden trial of a doctor who killed a patient requesting euthanasia, public debate on euthanasia in the Netherlands has become more intense. Despite the fact that, legally, active euthanasia is a criminal offense, physicians are quite open about practicing it. For example, in 1983 several general practitioners published case reports in influential Dutch medical journals. However, the overall incidence of active euthanasia in medical practice was unknown; estimates varied between 2,000 and 20,000 cases a year.

In the 1970s and 1980s a pattern of jurisprudence developed that reflected a considerable judicial lenience toward physicians practicing euthanasia under strict conditions. At least three conditions have been repeatedly referred to in court decisions and bills: (1) the patient's voluntary and persistent request; (2) the hopeless situation of the patient; (3) consultation of a colleague.

Early in 1989 two legislative proposals were submitted to Parliament pertaining to the practice of euthanasia but could not be discussed, as shortly afterwards the Cabinet resigned. In November 1989 the government (a coalition of the Christian Democratic Party and the Socialist Party) announced its intention to suspend political debate on legislation in order to obtain an empirical understanding of the frequency and nature of euthanasia in medical practice. In January 1990 a new committee consisting of three lawyers and three physicians was established by the Ministers of Justice and Public Health to investigate medical practices regarding decisions at the end of life. In September 1991 the committee published its report, followed by new legislative proposals issued by the government on 8 November 1991 and scheduled to be discussed in Parliament about May 1992.

These developments suggest that the current debate in the Netherlands has shifted from the level of medical-ethical arguments, justifying or opposing euthanasia within the doctor-patient relationship, to the socioethical and political problem of whether and how to regulate or legalize the actual practice of euthanasia, given newly accumulated empirical data. Medical-ethical view-points regarding euthanasia in clinical practice have been moved to the background.

In this contribution, we will discuss the present state of the debate, first through an analysis of research into the practice of euthanasia and then through a moral evaluation of its political and legal implications.

RESEARCH INTO THE PRACTICE OF EUTHANASIA

In the fall of 1991 the results of two empirical studies on euthanasia were published. Van der Wal and his associates reported on the results of an exploratory, descriptive, retrospective study of morbidity, age, and sex of patients whose family doctors helped them to die; the study also tried to assess the level of suffering these patients experienced. More infuential was the report of the Committee on the Study of Medical Practice concerning Euthanasia (also called the Remmelink Committee after its president, attorney general of the Supreme Court J. Remmelink). The task of this committee was not to advise the government about legalizing euthanasia, but to investigate the current practice in the Netherlands.

Reprinted with permission of the author and the publisher from the *Hastings Center Report*, vol. 22 (March-April 1992), pp. 34–38.

Some 130,000 people die in the Netherlands each year. In some 49,000 of these instances physicians have to decide whether to continue life support, withhold treatment, increase the dose of morphine to provide adequate pain relief, even at a potentially lethal level, assist in suicide, or actually kill the patient. Although the committee was asked to investigate only the medical practice of terminating life, it decided to look into the whole field, that is, "all situations in which physicians make decisions that aim (also) at ending suffering by hastening the end of the patient's life or in which the probability of a hastening of the end of life must be taken into account."

To obtain data concerning such medical practices, the Institute of Public Health and Social Medicine of the Erasmus University of Rotterdam was requested to undertake an empirical research project. The research group decided (1) to initiate a retrospective study by interviewing a random population of some 400 physicians; (2) to verify the true cause of death of a random sample of some 8,500 recent deaths; (3) to undertake a prospective study in which the 400 interviewed physicians were asked to provide information anonymously about the true cause of death of each of their patients dying in the next six months; and (4) to interview a number of physicians with different specialties to eliminate the possibility, left open by the three previous studies, that particular specialties attract a much higher incidence of euthanasia.

It was found that assisted suicide was relatively uncommon, occurring only some 400 times a year. Euthanasia, defined as "any action that intentionally ends the life of someone else, on the request of that person," is practiced some 2,300 times, or in 5 percent of those 49,000 cases. Since every year some 9,000 patients request euthanasia asking that it be performed within a few weeks—primarily patients suffering severely from cancer but virtually all mentally competent—physicians grant such wishes in less than half of the number of cases. Euthanasia has the highest incidence among family physicians/general practitioners, whereas physicians in nursing homes commit euthanasia relatively seldom.

The results of the study by Van der Wal and colleagues provide some insight into the context of euthanasia decisions, although in their publications no distinction is made between euthanasia (defined as the Remmelink Committee defines it) and assisted suicide. Data were gathered through an anonymous questionnaire in a random sample of family practitioners as well as through an analysis of police reports involving family doctors practicing euthanasia in the province of North Holland (in 1986–89). In 85 percent of these cases the patients suffered from malignant neoplasm; a high percentage of patients had AIDS or multiple sclerosis. In approximately 20 percent, a secondary, usually chronic disease had been diagnosed. Among patients under the age of thirty and over eighty-five euthanasia or assisted suicide was relatively rare.

Van der Wal also examined the nature and extent of the physical and emotional suffering of patients culminating in a request for euthanasia or assisted suicide. Questionnaires were sent to a random sample of family practitioners asking them to rate twenty-four aspects of suffering as well as to assess the life expectancy of the patient they most recently euthanized. According to the respondents, 90 percent of these patients showed severe physical suffering and 71 percent severe emotional suffering. "General weakness or tiredness," "dependence or being in need of help," "loss of dignity," and "pain" were the most frequently identified aspects of suffering. In 63 percent of the cases, life expectancy at the moment of execution of the request was estimated as less than two weeks; in 10 percent it was more than three months.

INTERPRETATION OF THE DATA

In the media, one of the early conclusions drawn from the research reports was that euthanasia apparently was not as frequent as had been assumed by both protagonists and antagonists.

This conclusion is not necessarily false, but upon careful consideration of the data presented in the Remmelink Report itself, it turns out to be rather meaningless. Medical decisions aimed at ending human life are more nuanced and heterogeneous than reflected in the definition. Many physicians do not interpret or classify their actions as euthanasia, even when those actions fall strictly under the range of the definition employed in the report (and common in the Netherlands). Consequently, the figure of 2,300 is not at all a specific or representative indicator of medical decisions leading to patients' death. The report clearly shows that other forms of intentional hastening of death are common practice in the Netherlands, yet fully escape professional, judicial, and social scrutiny.

The empirical data reveal that in 6 percent of the total number of 22,500 cases in which pain medication with a possible lethal effect was administered, hastening death was the very purpose of the administration, and in as many as 30 percent it was at least one of the purposes. Including these figures would increase the incidence of euthanasia to some 8,100 cases.

There also seem to be about 1,000 patients whose death was caused or hastened by physicians without any such request at all. These are patients who no longer were competent to make decisions, yet apparently suffered severely. Notice that these cases do not involve withholding or withdrawing medically futile treatments, since such treatments always have to be withdrawn. Nonetheless, the committee felt that these 1,000 cases are not morally troublesome; moreover, they should be considered "providing assistance to the dying." Nonvoluntary euthanasia was justified because the suffering of those patients had become "unbearable" and life must be considered "given up" according to medical standards. Death would have occurred quickly (usually within a week), if the physician had not acted. Elsewhere, the committee adds that actively ending life when "the vital functions have started failing" is "indisputably normal medical practice."

In some 28 percent of these 1,000 cases, patients had previously expressed the wish to be killed if, for example. the pain ever became unbearable or their situation inhuman. These cases, therefore, can be classified as euthanasia in the strict sense. Yet physicians mentioned "previously uttered request of the patient" as their reason to kill in a mere 17 percent of the cases. The researchers explained this discrepancy by arguing that physicians more often are guided by their own impressions of the patient's unspoken but probable wishes than by explicit oral or written requests. One may wonder whether such "impressions" are always correct. At any rate, a paradox emerges between this kind of reasoning and the very opposite reasoning of a number of courts and legislators to the effect that suffering is a purely subjective phenomenon and that, consequently, only the patient can decide whether his or her suffering has become unbearable. It seems that advocates of euthanasia use the subjective argument when defending the right of the competent patient to opt for euthanasia autonomously, and the impressionist argument when defending the practice of euthanasia on the mentally incompetent patient.

A similar ambiguity is reflected in the research methodology of Van der Wal and colleagues. Diagnoses can best be made by physicians, so there is nothing controversial about classifying diseases of euthanized patients by means of questionnaires mailed to family doctors. However, the assessment of patients' suffering is another matter: it is problematic to ask a physician to assess the depth as well as the nature of his patient's suffering—all the more so in retrospect when the physician has already performed euthanasia on his patient. Quite predictably these physicians claim the condition of 90 percent of the patients was characterized by severe physical suffering. Furthermore, dividing suffering into twenty-four "aspects" is highly problematic, since the relationship between suffering and pain, "dependence," "nausea," "thirst," "constipation," "itch" is variable and subjective. The researchers seem to assume that the individual nature of suffering can be objectified by collecting a multitude of subjective opinions. But even then the data only provide an idea of what *doctors* think about the nature of suffering in their patients. The conclusion that the majority of euthanized patients experience severe physical and emotional suffering is not warranted. It can merely be concluded that the doctors in retrospect think this about their patients, but it is hardly an unexpected finding that euthanizing phycians justify their actions in precisely such terms.

The Remmelink Committee furthermore found that in 45 percent of the 1,000 nonvoluntary euthanasia cases, treatment of pain was no longer adequate to relieve the patient's suffering. However, the impossibility of treating the pain adequately was the reason for killing the patient in only 30 percent of the cases. The remaining 70 percent were killed for different reasons, such as: (1) low quality of life; (2) no prospect of improvement; (3) all forms of medical treatment had become futile; (4) all treatment was withdrawn but the patient did not die; or (5) one should not postpone death. In one-third of the cases, the fact that family and friends no longer could bear the situation played a role in the decisionmaking and indeed one respondent even indicated that economic considerations such as shortage of beds played a role. One may wonder how the committee's judgment that from a medical standpoint these patients were correctly "given up" should be understood. Certainly, such actions are not "indisputably" normal medical practice.

Finally, the Remmelink Report mentions one more category that merits attention: the 20,000 cases in which physicians withhold or withdraw treatment neither because the patient so requests, nor becase the treatment is futile, but because only limited benefit is to be expected and there are other reasons to withdraw or withhold. Looking at these "other reasons," we find that in 16 percent of the nonvoluntary withholdings or withdrawings, hastening death was the point of the decision and in another 19 percent hastening death was one of the reasons. Again, given the definitions of the committee itself, in which intention is the keyword, the cases, at least those where death is the primary point, must be considered nonvoluntary euthanasia, which would imply an increase from 1,000 to 4,200 or even 8,000 such cases. ...

FINAL COMMENTS

Although the outcome of the current debate is still unclear, the results of the empirical studies raise fundamental questions concerning euthanasia and medical practice. In the 1970s the "euthanasia movement" in the Netherlands began as a protest against the power of contemporary medicine to alienate individuals from their own dying. Instead of counterbalancing that power and enhancing the individual's autonomy and control over his or her own life, it seems that social acceptance of euthanasia is resulting in physicians' acquiring even more power over the life and death of their patients. As the Remmelink Report shows, in most cases of ending human life, it is the physician who decides that it is appropriate to hasten death. Furthermore, it is quite remarkable how easily the morally most important cautionary standard established by jurisprudence—the patient's voluntary and persistent request—is brushed aside in the report. The motion adopted by the General Assembly of the Dutch Society of Health Law, published in the *Hastings Center Report* in late 1988, as well as various letters to the editor, repudiate the statement that doctors who terminate the life of patients without request remain unpunished. The latest empirical data prove exactly the opposite.

ASSISTED SUICIDE IS NOT VOLUNTARY ACTIVE EUTHANASIA

David T. Watts and Timothy Howell

Ongoing developments highlight some of the confusion emerging from discussions of voluntary active euthanasia (V.A.E.) and assisted suicide. A significant source of confusion has been the tendency to join these concepts or even to consider them synonymous. For example, the AGS Position Statement on V.A.E. and a recent article by Teno and Lynn in the *Journal of the American Geriatrics Society* both reject easing restrictions on V.A.E. and assisted suicide while making arguments *only* against euthanasia. The National Hospice Organization also opposes euthanasia and assisted suicide, but it, too, appears to blur the distinction between them in stating that "euthanasia encompasses ... in some settings, physician-assisted suicide." Others appear to use the terms euthanasia and and assisted suicide synonymously in arguing against both.

In contrast, the AMA Ethics and Health Policy Counsel argues against physician-assisted suicide and distinguishes this from euthanasia. The AMA Council on Ethical and Judicial Affairs also acknowledges there is "an ethically relevant distinction between euthanasia and assisted suicide that makes assisted suicide a more attractive option." Yet it then goes on to assert that "the ethical concerns about physician-assisted suicide are similar to those of euthanasia since both are essentially interventions intended to cause death."

In order to weigh and appreciate the merits of the different arguments for and against V.A.E. and physician-assisted suicide, it is critical that appropriate distinctions be made. For example, we believe the arguments made in the references cited above and by others against euthanasia are telling. However, we find that these same arguments are substantially weaker when used against assisted suicide. And while we agree with the AMA Council on Ethical and Judicial Affairs that an ethically relevant distinction exists between euthanasia and assisted suicide, we think it is important to distinguish further between different forms of assisted suicide. Only by doing so can we begin to sort out some of the apparent confusion in attitudes toward these issues. We caution our readers that the literature on this topic, while growing, remains preliminary, with little empirical research yet completed. Our arguments, however, are philosophical in nature and do not ultimately stand or fall on empirical data.

Reprinted with permission of Blackwell Publishing from the *Journal of the American Geriatrics Society* (1992), vol. 40, pp. 1043–1046.

DEFINITIONS

Voluntary active euthanasia: Administration of medications or other interventions intended to cause death at a patient's request.

Assisted suicide: Provision of information, means, or direct assistance by which a patient may take his or her own life. Assisted suicide involves several possible levels of assistance: *providing information*, for example, may mean providing toxicological information or describing techniques by which someone may commit suicide; *providing the means* can involve written prescriptions for lethal amounts of medication; *supervising or directly aiding* includes inserting an intravenous line and instructing on starting a lethal infusion.

These levels of assistance have very different implications. Providing only information or means allows individuals to retain the greatest degree of control in choosing the time and mode of their deaths. Physician participation is only indirect. This type of limited assistance is exemplified by the widely reported case of Dr. Timothy Quill, who prescribed a lethal quantity of barbiturates at the request of one of his patients who had leukemia. By contrast, supervising or directly aiding is the type of physician involvement characterizing the case of Dr. Jack Kevorkian and Janet Adkins. Adkins was a 54-year-old woman with a diagnosis of Alzheimer-type dementia who sought Kevorkian's assistance in ending her life. Dr. Kevorkian inserted an intravenous catheter and instructed Mrs. Adkins on activating a lethal infusion of potassium following barbiturate sedation, a process personally monitored by Kevorkian. This form of assisted suicide carries significant potential for physician influence or control of the process, and from it there is only a relatively short step to physician initiation (i.e., active euthanasia). We therefore reject physician-supervised suicide for the arguments commonly made against V.A.E., namely, that legalization would have serious adverse consequences, including potential abuse of vulnerable persons, mistrust of physicians, and diminished availability of supportive services for the dying. We find each of these arguments, however, insufficient when applied to more limited forms of physician-assisted suicide (i.e., providing information or means).

WILL ASSISTED SUICIDE LEAD TO ABUSE OF VULNERABLE PERSONS?

A major concern is that some patients will request euthanasia or assisted suicide out of convenience to others. It is certainly possible that a patient's desire to avoid being a burden could lead to such a request. With euthanasia, there is danger that a patient's request might find too ready acceptance. With assisted suicide, however, the ultimate decision, and the ultimate action, are the patient's, not the physician's. This places an important check and balance on physician initiation or patient acquiescence in euthanasia. As the AMA Council on Ethical and Judicial Affairs acknowledges, a greater level of patient autonomy is afforded by physician-assisted suicide than by euthanasia.

Culturally or socially mediated requests for assisted suicide would remain a significant concern. Patients might also request aid in suicide out of fear, pain, ambivalence, or depression. The requirement that patients commit the ultimate act themselves cannot alone provide a sufficient safeguard. It would be incumbent on physicians to determine, insofar as possible, that requests for assisted suicide were not unduly influenced and that reversible conditions were optimally treated. As to how physicians might respond to such requests, data froth the Netherlands indicate that about 75% of euthanasia requests in that country are refused. It is our impression that most requests for assisted suicide, therefore, appear to represent opportunities for improved symptom control. We believe most serious requests would likely come from patients experiencing distressing symptoms of terminal illness. By opening the door for counseling or treatment of reversible conditions, requests for assisted suicide might actually lead to averting some suicides which would have otherwise occurred.

Another concern regarding euthanasia is that it could come to be accepted without valid consent and that such a practice would more likely affect the frail and impoverished. The Remmelink Commission's investigation of euthanasia in the Netherlands appeared to justify such concerns in estimating that Dutch physicians may have performed 1,000 acts of involuntary euthanasia involving incompetent individuals. But while euthanasia opens up the possibility of invalid consent, with assisted suicide consent is integral to the process. Because the choice of action clearly rests with the individual, there is substantially less likelihood for the abuse of assisted suicide as a societal vehicle for cost containment. And there is little basis for assuming that requests for assisted suicide would come primarily from frail and impoverished persons. Prolonged debilitation inherent in many illnesses is familiar to an increasing number of patients, family members, and health professionals. Such illnesses represent a greater financial threat to the middle- and upper-middle class, since the poor and disenfranchised have less to spend down to indigency. Thus, we suspect requests to assisted suicide might actually be more common from the educated, affluent, and outspoken.

Patients diagnosed with terminal or debilitating conditions are often vulnerable. We agree that such patients might request assisted suicide out of fear of pain, suffering, or isolation, and that too ready acceptance of such requests could be disastrous. Yet, we believe that patients' interests can be safeguarded by requirements for persistent, competent requests as well as thorough assessments for conditions, such as clinical depression, which could be reversed, treated, or ameliorated. Foley recently outlined an approach to the suicidal cancer patient. We share her view that many such patients' requests to terminate life are altered by the availability of expert, continuing hospice services. We concur with Foley and others in calling for the wider availability of such services, so that requests for assisted suicide arising from pain, depression, or other distressing symptoms can be reduced to a minimum.

WOULD ASSISTED SUICIDE UNDERMINE TRUST BETWEEN PATIENTS AND PHYSICIANS?

The cardinal distinction between V.A.E. and assisted suicide is that V.A.E. is killing by physicians, while suicide is self-killing. Prohibiting both euthanasia and physician-supervised suicide (i.e., with direct physician involvement) should diminish worries that patients might have about physicians wrongly administering lethal medicine. At present, physician-patient trust is compromised by widespread concern that physicians try too hard to keep dying patients alive. The very strength of the physician-patient relationship has been cited as a justification for physician involvement in assisted suicide.

A number of ethicists have expressed concern that both euthanasia and assisted suicide, if legalized, would have a negative impact on the way society perceives the role of physicians. Limited forms of assisted suicide, however, have been viewed more positively. Public and professional attitudes appear to be evolving on this issue. A 1990 Gallup poll found that 66% of respondents believed someone in great pain, with "no hope of improvement," had the moral right to commit suicide; in 1975 the figure was 41%. A panel of distinguished physicians has stated that it is not immoral for a physician to assist in the rational suicide of a terminally ill person. The recent publication of a book on techniques of committing or assisting suicide evoked wide interest and significant support for the right of people to take control of their dying. For a significant segment of society, physician involvement in assisted suicide may be welcomed, not feared. Furthermore, while relatively few might be likely to seek assistance with suicide if stricken with a debilitating illness; a substantial number might take solace knowing they could request such assistance.

There is another argument raised against V.A.E. that we believe also falters when used to object to assisted suicide. It has been maintained that prohibiting euthanasia forces physicians to focus on the humane care of dying patients, including meticulous attention to their symptoms. This argument implies that physicians find it easier to relieve the suffering of dying patients by ending their lives rather than attempting the difficult task of palliating their symptoms. But for some patients, the suffering may not be amenable to even the most expert palliation. Even in such instances, some argue that limited forms of assisted suicide should be prohibited on the grounds that not to forbid them would open the door for more generalized, less stringent applications of assisted suicide.

To us, this "slippery slope" argument seems to imply that the moral integrity of the medical profession must be maintained, even if at the cost of prolonged, unnecessary suffering by at least some dying patients. We believe such a posture is itself inhumane and not acceptable. It contradicts a fundamental principle that is an essential ingredient of physician-patient trust: that patient comfort should be a primary goal of the physician in the face of incurable illness. Furthermore, by allowing limited physician involvement in assisted suicide, physicians can respect both the principle of caring that guides them and the patients for whom caring alone is insufficient. We concede that there is another alternative: terminally ill patients who cannot avoid pain while awake may be given continuous anesthetic levels of medication. But this is exactly the sort of dying process we believe many in our society want to avoid.

WILL ASSISTED SUICIDE AND EUTHANASIA WEAKEN SOCIETAL RESOLVE TO INCREASE RESOURCES ALLOCATED TO CARE OF THE DYING?

This argument assumes that V.A.E. and assisted suicide would both be widely practiced, and that their very availability would decrease tangible concern for those not choosing euthanasia or suicide. However, euthanasia is rarely requested even by terminal cancer patients. In the Netherlands, euthanasia accounts for less than 2% of all deaths. These data suggest that even if assisted suicide were available to those with intractable pain or distressing terminal conditions, it would likely be an option chosen by relatively few. With assisted suicide limited to relatively few cases, this argument collapses. For with only a few requesting assisted suicide, the vast number of patients with debilitating illnesses would be undiminished, and their numbers should remain sufficient to motivate societal concern for their needs. Furthermore, to withhold assisted suicide from the few making serious, valid requests would be to subordinate needlessly the interests of these few to those of the many. Compounding their tragedy would be the fact that these individuals could not even benefit from any increase in therapeutic resources prompted by their suffering, insofar as their conditions, are, by definition, not able to be ameliorated.

CONCLUSION

We have argued that assisted suicide and voluntary active euthanasia are different and that each has differing implications for medical practice and society. Further discussion should consider the merits and disadvantages of each, a process enhanced by contrasting them. We have further argued that different forms of assisted suicide can be distinguished both clinically and philosophically. Although some may argue that all forms of assisted suicide are fundamentally the same, we believe the differences can be contrasted as starkly as a written prescription and a suicide machine.

We do not advocate ready acceptance of requests for suicide, nor do we wish to romanticize the concept of rational suicide. In some situations, however, where severe debilitating illness cannot be reversed, suicide may represent a rational choice. If this is the case, then physician assistance could make the process more humane. Along with other geriatricians, we often face dilemmas involving the management of chronic illnesses in late life. We believe we can best serve our patients, and preserve their trust, by respecting their desire for autonomy, dignity, and quality, not only of life, but of dying.

DEATH AND DIGNITY: A CASE OF INDIVIDUALIZED DECISION MAKING

Timothy E. Quill

Diane was feeling tired and had a rash. A common scenario, though there was something subliminally worrisome that prompted me to check her blood count. Her hematocrit was 22, and the white-cell count was 4.3 with some metamyelocytes and unusual white cells. I wanted it to be viral, trying to deny what was staring me in the face. Perhaps in a repeated count it would disappear. I called Diane and told her it might be more serious than I had initially thought—that the test needed to be repeated and that if she felt worse, we might have to move quickly. When she pressed for the possibilities, I reluctantly opened the door to leukemia. Hearing the word seemed to make it exist. "Oh, shit!" she said. "Don't tell me that." Oh, shit! I thought, I wish I didn't have to.

Diane was no ordinary person (although no one I have ever come to know has been really ordinary). She was raised in an alcoholic family and had felt alone for much of her life. She had vaginal cancer as a young woman. Through much of her adult life, she had struggled with depression and her own alcoholism. I had come to know, respect, and admire her over the previous eight years as she confronted these problems and gradually overcame them. She was an incredibly clear, at times brutally honest, thinker and communicator. As she took control of her life, she developed a strong sense of independence and confidence. In the previous 3½ years, her hard work had paid off. She was completely abstinent from alcohol, she had established much deeper connections with her husband, college-age son, and several friends, and her business and her artistic work were blossoming. She felt she was really living fully for the first time.

Not surprisingly, the repeated blood count was abnormal, and detailed examination of the peripheral-blood smear showed myelocytes. I advised her to come into the hospital, explaining that we needed to do a bone marrow biopsy and make some decisions relatively rapidly. She came to the hospital knowing what we would find. She was terrified, angry, and sad. Although we knew the odds, we both clung to the thread of possibility that it might be something else.

The bone marrow confirmed the worst: acute myelomonocytic leukemia. In the face of this tragedy, we looked for signs of hope. This is an area of medicine in which technological intervention has been successful, with cures 25 percent of the time—long-term cures. As I probed the costs of these cures, I heard about induction chemotherapy (three weeks in the hospital, prolonged neutropenia, probable infectious complications, and hair loss; 75 percent of patients respond, 25 percent do not). For the survivors, this is followed by consolidation chemotherapy (with similar side effects; another 25 percent die, for a net survival of 50 percent). Those still alive, to have a reasonable chance of long-term survival, then need bone marrow transplantation (hospitalization for two months and whole-body irradiation, with complete killing of the bone marrow, infectious complications, and the possibility for graft-versus-host disease—with a survival of approximately 50 percent, or 25 percent of the original group). Though hematologists may argue over the exact percentages, they don't argue about the outcome of no treatment—certain death in days, weeks, or at most a few months.

Quill, Timothy E. "Death and Dignity: A Case of Individualized Decision Making" from *The New England Journal of Medicine* 324:691–694.

Believing that delay was dangerous, our oncologist broke the news to Diane and began making plans to insert a Hickman catheter and begin induction chemotherapy that afternoon. When I saw her shortly thereafter, she was enraged at his presumption that she would want treatment, and devastated by the finality of the diagnosis. All she wanted to do was go home and be with her family. She had no further questions about treatment and in fact had decided that she wanted none. Together we lamented her tragedy and the unfairness of life. Before she left, I felt the need to be sure that she and her husband understood that there was some risk in delay, that the problem was not going to go away, and that we needed to keep considering the options over the next several days. We agreed to meet in two days.

She returned in two days with her husband and son. They had talked extensively about the problem and the options. She remained very clear about her wish not to undergo chemotherapy and to live whatever time she had left outside the hospital. As we explored her thinking further, it became clear that she was convinced she would die during the period of treatment and would suffer unspeakably in the process (from hospitalization, from lack of control over her body, from the side effects of chemotherapy, and from pain and anguish). Although I could offer support and my best effort to minimize her suffering if she chose treatment, there was no way I could say any of this would not occur. In fact, the last four patients with acute leukemia at our hospital had died very painful deaths in the hospital during various stages of treatment (a fact I did not share with her). Her family wished she would choose treatment but sadly accepted her decision. She articulated very clearly that it was she who would be experiencing all the side effects of treatment and that odds of 25 percent were not good enough for her to undergo so toxic a course of therapy, given her expectations of chemotherapy and hospitalization and the absence of a closely matched bone marrow donor. I had her repeat her understanding of the treatment, the odds, and what to expect if there were no treatment. I clarified a few misunderstandings, but she had a remarkable grasp of the options and implications.

I have been a longtime advocate of active, informed patient choice of treatment or nontreatment, and of a patient's right to die with as much control and dignity as possible. Yet there was something about her giving up a 25 percent chance of long-term survival in favor of almost certain death that disturbed me. I had seen Diane fight and use her considerable inner resources to overcome alcoholism and depression, and I half expected her to change her mind over the next week. Since the window of time in which effective treatment can be initiated is rather narrow, we met several times that week. We obtained a second hematology consultation and talked at length about the meaning and implications of treatment and nontreatment. She talked to a psychologist she had seen in the past. I gradually understood the decision from her perspective and became convinced that it was the right decision for her. We arranged for home hospice care (although at that time Diane felt reasonably well, was active, and looked healthy), left the door open for her to change her mind, and tried to anticipate how to keep her comfortable in the time she had left.

Just as I was adjusting to her decision, she opened up another area that would stretch me profoundly. It was extraordinarily important to Diane to maintain control of herself and her own dignity during the time remaining to her. When this was no longer possible, she clearly wanted to die. As a former director of a hospice program, I know how to use pain medicines to keep patients comfortable and lessen suffering. I explained the philosophy of comfort care, which I strongly believe in. Although Diane understood and appreciated this, she had known of people lingering in what was called relative comfort, and she wanted no part of it. When the time came, she wanted to take her life in the least painful way possible. Knowing of her desire for independence and her decision to stay in control, I thought this request made perfect sense. I acknowledged and explored this wish but also thought that it was out of the realm of currently accepted medical practice and that it was more than I could offer or promise. In our discussion, it became clear that preoccupation with her fear of a lingering death would interfere with Diane's getting the most out of the time she had left until she found a safe way to ensure her death. I feared the effects of a violent death on her family, the consequences of an ineffective suicide that would leave her lingering in precisely the state she dreaded so much, and the possibility that a family member would be forced to assist her, with all the legal and personal repercussions that would follow. She discussed this at length with her family. They believed that they should respect her choice. With this in mind, I told Diane that information was available from the Hemlock Society that might be helpful to her.

A week later she phoned me with a request for barbiturates for sleep. Since I knew that this was an essential ingredient in a Hemlock Society suicide, I asked her to come to the office to talk things over. She was more than willing to protect me by participating in a superficial conversation about her insomnia, but it was important to me to know how she planned to use the drugs and to be sure that she was not in despair or overwhelmed in a way that might color her judgment. In our discussion, it was apparent that she was having trouble sleeping, but it was also evident that the security of having enough barbiturates available to commit suicide when and if the time came would leave her secure enough to live fully and concentrate on the present. It was clear that she was not despondent and that in fact she was making deep, personal connections with her family and close friends. I made sure that she knew how to use the barbiturates for sleep, and also that she knew the amount needed to commit suicide. We agreed to meet regularly, and she promised to meet with me before taking her life, to ensure that all other avenues had been exhausted. I wrote the prescription with an uneasy feeling about the boundaries I was exploring—spiritual, legal, professional, and personal. Yet I also felt strongly that I was setting her free to get the most out of the time she had left, and to maintain dignity and control on her own terms until her death.

The next several months were very intense and important for Diane. Her son stayed home from college, and they were able to be with one another and say much that had not been said earlier. Her husband did his work at home so that he and Diane could spend more time together. She spent time with her closest friends. I had her come into the hospital for a conference with our residents, at which she illustrated in a most profound and personal way the importance of informed decision making, the right to refuse treatment, and the extraordinarily personal effects of illness and interaction with the medical system. There were emotional and physical hardships as well. She had periods of intense sadness and anger. Several times she became very weak, but she received transfusions as an outpatient and responded with marked improvement of symptoms. She had two serious infections that responded surprisingly well to empirical courses of oral antibiotics. After three tumultuous months, there were two weeks of relative calm and well-being, and fantasies of a miracle began to surface.

Unfortunately, we had no miracle. Bone pain, weakness, fatigue, and fevers began to dominate her life. Although the hospice workers, family members, and I tried our best to minimize the suffering and promote comfort, it was clear that the end was approaching. Diane's immediate future held what she feared the most—increasing discomfort, dependence, and hard choices between pain and sedation. She called up her closest friends and asked them to come over to say goodbye, telling them that she would be leaving soon. As we had agreed, she let me know as well. When we met, it was clear that she knew what she was doing, that she was sad and frightened to be leaving, but that she would be even more terrified to stay and suffer. In our tearful goodbye, she promised a reunion in the future at her favorite spot on the edge of Lake Geneva, with dragons swimming in the sunset.

Two days later her husband called to say that Diane had died. She had said her final goodbyes to her husband and son that morning, and asked them to leave her alone for an hour. After an hour, which must have seemed an eternity, they found her on the couch, lying very still and covered by her favorite shawl. There was no sign of struggle. She seemed to be at peace. They called me for advice about how to proceed. When I arrived at their house, Diane indeed seemed peaceful. Her husband and son were quiet. We talked about what a remarkable person she had been. They seemed to have no doubts about the course she had chosen or about their cooperation, although the unfairness of her illness and the finality of her death were overwhelming to us all.

I called the medical examiner to inform him that a hospice patient had died. When asked about the cause of death, I said, "acute leukemia." He said that was fine and that we should call a funeral director. Although acute leukemia was the truth, it was not the whole story. Yet any mention of suicide would have given rise to a police investigation and probably brought the arrival of an ambulance crew for resuscitation. Diane would have become a "coroner's case," and the decision to perform an autopsy would have been made at the discretion of the medical examiner. The family or I could have been subject to criminal prosecution, and I to professional review, for our roles in support of Diane's choices. Although I truly believe that the family and I gave her the best care possible, allowing her to define her limits and directions as much as possible, I am not sure the law, society, or the medical profession would agree. So I said "acute leukemia" to protect all of us, to protect Diane from an invasion into her past and her body, and to continue to shield society from the knowledge of the degree of suffering that people often undergo in the process of dying. Suffering can be lessened to some extent, but in no way eliminated or made benign, by the careful intervention of a competent, caring physician, given current social constraints.

Diane taught me about the range of help I can provide if I know people well and if I allow them to say what they really want. She taught me about life, death, and honesty and about taking charge and facing tragedy squarely when it strikes. She taught me that I can take small risks for people that I really know and care about. Although I did not assist in her suicide directly, I helped indirectly to make it possible, successful, and relatively painless. Although I know we have measures to help control pain and lessen suffering, to think that people do not suffer in the process of dying is an illusion. Prolonged dying can occasionally be peaceful, but more often the role of the physician and family is limited to lessening but not eliminating severe suffering.

I wonder how many families and physicians secretly help patients over the edge into death in the face of such severe suffering. I wonder how many severely ill or dying patients secretly take their lives, dying alone in despair. I wonder whether the image of Diane's final aloneness will persist in the minds of her family, or if they will remember more the intense, meaningful months they had together before she died. I wonder whether Diane struggled in that last hour, and whether the Hemlock Society's way of death by suicide is the most benign. I wonder why Diane, who gave so much to so many of us, had to be alone for the last hour of her life. I wonder whether I will see Diane again, on the shore of Lake Geneva at sunset, with dragons swimming on the horizon.

SELLING DEATH AND DIGNITY

Herbert Hendin

Dying is hard to market. Voters, many repelled by the image of doctors giving their patients lethal injections, rejected euthanasia initiatives in Washington and California. Learning from these defeats, Oregon sponsors of a similar measure limited it to assisted suicide, while still casting the patient in the role familiar from euthanasia advertising: the noble individualist fighting to exercise the right to die.

Although both assisted suicide and euthanasia have been presented as empowering patients by giving them control over their death, assisted suicide has been seen as protecting against potential medical abuse since the final act is in the patient's hands. Yet opponents see little protection in assisted suicide: people who are helpless or seriously ill are vulnerable to influence or coercion by physicians or relatives who can achieve the same ends with or without direct action.[1] How could advocates counteract not only images of lethal physicians but images of grasping relatives, eager to be rid of a burden or to gain an inheritance by coercing death?

Supporters of assisted suicide and euthanasia have found the ultimate marketing technique to promote the normalization of assisted suicide and euthanasia: the presentation of a case history designed to show how necessary assisted suicide or euthanasia was in that particular instance. Such cases may rely either on nightmarish images of unnecessarily prolonged dying or on predictions of severe disability. The instance in which it is felt that most would agree it was desirable to end life is represented as typical. Those who participate in the death (the relatives, the euthanasia advocates, the physician) are celebrated as enhancing the dignity of the patient, who is usually presented as a heroic, fully independent figure.

How much truth is there in this advertising? Does this accurately describe what happens? Even in cases advocates believe best illustrate the desirability of legalizing assisted suicide or euthanasia, there is ample room to question whether the death administered in fact realizes the patient's wishes and meets his or her needs. Advocates' desire to dramatize these model cases, moreover, requires that they be presented in some detail—and this creates the opportunity to see the discrepancy between theory and practice with regard to assisted suicide and euthanasia.

DEATH ON REQUEST

The ultimate attempt to normalize euthanasia in the Netherlands and make it seem an ordinary part of everyday life was the showing in the fall of 1994 on Dutch television of *Death on Request*,[2] a film of a patient being put to death by euthanasia. Maarten Nederhurst, who created the film, found an agreeable patient and doctor by contacting the Dutch Voluntary Euthanasia Society.

The patient, Cees van Wendel, had been diagnosed as having amyotrophic lateral scelerosis in June 1993; he expressed his wish for euthanasia a month later. Severe muscular weakness confined him to a wheel chair; his speech was barely audible.

Almost 700,000 people saw the first showing of the film in the Netherlands. Subsequently, the right to show the film has been acquired by countries throughout the world. *Prime Time Live* excerpted and showed a representative

Reprinted with permission of the author and publisher from *Hastings Center Report*, Vol. 25, (May–June 1995), pp. 19–23.

segment to American viewers with a voiceover in English. Sam Donaldson introduced the program saying that it took no sides on the issue but added, "It is a story of courage and love."[3] Only for the most gullible viewer.

In point of fact, the doctor, Wilfred von Oijen, is the film's most significant person. He is the manager who can make "everything"—even death—happen. He is presented as someone who has accepted the burden of all phases of experience. The patient is nearly invisible.

The film opens with a chilly scene in winter—trees are bare of leaves, it is cold, wet, inhospitable—not a bad time to die. In an undershirt in his bathroom, the doctor combs his hair getting ready for just another day. His encounters will include treating a child of about ten months, a pregnant woman and a baby, and bringing death to Cees. The purpose of the film is to. include euthanasia both as part of his daily burden as a doctor and as the natural course of events.

In the two house calls van Oijen makes to Cees, of most interest is the tension between the film's professed message—that all want release from illness, the patient most of all—and the message conveyed by what is actually filmed. The relationship depicted is between van Oijen and Antoinette, the patient's wife, who has called the doctor and clearly wants her husband to die.

The wife appears repulsed by her husband's illness, never touching him during their conversation and never permitting Cees to answer any question the doctor asks directly. She "translates" for him, although Cees is at this point in his illness intelligible, able to communicate verbally, but slowly, and able to type out messages on his computer. The doctor asks him if he wants euthanasia, but his wife replies. When Cees begins to cry, the doctor moves sympathetically toward him to touch his arm, but his wife tells the doctor to move away and says it is better to let him cry alone. During his weeping she continues to talk to the doctor. The doctor at no time asks to speak to Cees alone; neither does he ask if anything would make it easier for him to communicate or if additional help in his care would make him want to live.

Virtually the entire film is set up to avoid confronting any of the patient's feelings or how the relationship with his wife affects his agreeing to die. Cees is never seen alone. Van Oijen is obliged to obtain a second opinion from a consultant. The consultant, who appears well known to the doctor, also makes no attempt to communicate with Cees alone, and he too permits the wife to answer all the questions put to Cees. When the consultant asks the pro forma question if Cees is sure he wants to go ahead, Antoinette answers for him. The consultant seems uncomfortable, asks a few more questions, and leaves. The consultation takes practically no time at all. The pharmacist who supplies the lethal medication—one shot to put Cees to sleep and another to help him die—seems only another player in this carefully orchestrated event.

Antoinette visits the doctor to ask where "we stand." She wants the euthanasia over with. Cees has set several dates, but keeps moving them back. Now he has settled on his birthday, and they arrange for van Oijen to do it at eight o'clock after Cees celebrates by drinking a glass of port. Cees makes a joke that sleeping is a little death but this time his sleep will be a lot of death. Van Oijen tries to laugh warmly. Antoinette keeps her distance from the two and remarks that the day has gone slowly and it seemed eight o'clock would never come.

Antoinette helps Cees into bed in preparation for van Oijen to administer the first shot. Van Oijen smiles, gives the injection, and explains the medication will take a while to put Cees into a deep sleep. No one says goodbye. Only after the shot has put Cees to sleep does Antoinette murmur something to her husband. She then moves into the other room with the doctor to permit Cees to sink into a deeper sleep. After a few minutes, they return. When the doctor wants to place Cees in a more comfortable position, she withdraws again. After the second shot is administered, Antoinette and van Oijen sit next to the bed, both holding the arm that has received the injections. Antoinette asks if this was good, presumably wanting to know if it was "good" to kill Cees. Van Oijen reassures her. They leave Cees alone very quickly. On the way into the next room, Antoinette takes a note Cees wrote to her about their relationship and what it meant to him and reads it to the doctor. She seems to want to convey to him that they in fact once had a relationship.

From the beginning, the loneliness and isolation of the husband haunts the film. Only because he is treated from the start as an object does his death seem inevitable. One leaves the film feeling that death with dignity requires more than effective management; it requires being accorded personhood even though one's speech is slurred or one needs to point to letters on a board or communicate through writing on one's computer. Throughout the film, Cees's wife denies him such personhood, as does the doctor, who never questions her control over all of the patient's communication and even the doctor's communication with Cees. The doctor and wife took away Cees's personhood before ALS had claimed it.

A GOOD DEATH FOR LOUISE

An article featured on the cover of the *New York Times Magazine* in the fall of 1993 also used a case description to try to prove the value of assisted suicide to an American audience.[4] The article described the assisted suicide of Louise, a Seattle woman whose death was arranged by her doctor and the Reverend Ralph Mero, head of Compassion in Dying, a group that champions legalizing assisted suicide. Members of the group counsel the terminally ill, offer advice on lethal doses, convince cautious doctors to become involved, and are present during the death. Mero and his followers do not provide the means for suicide (the patients obtain such help from their doctors) and claim not to encourage the patients to seek suicide.

Mero arranged for a *Times* reporter to interview Louise in the last weeks of her life, offering Louise's death as an illustration of the beneficial effects of the organization's work. Yet the account serves equally to illustrate how assisted suicide made both life and death miserable for Louise.

Louise, who was referred to Mero by her doctor, had been ill with an unnamed, degenerative neurological disease. The reporter tells us that "Louise had mentioned suicide periodically during her six years of illness, but the subject came into sudden focus in May during a somber visit to her doctor's office." As Louise recounted it, "I really wasn't having any different symptoms, I just knew something had changed. I looked the doctor right in the eye and said, 'I'm starting to die.' And she said, 'I've had the same impression for a couple of days.'" An MRI scan confirmed that the frontal lobes of Louise's brain had begun to deteriorate, a sign that led her doctor to warn Louise that her life would most likely be measured in months, perhaps weeks. Louise said her doctor explained that "she didn't want to scare me ... she just wanted to be honest. She told me that once the disease becomes active, it progresses very fast, that I would become mentally incapacitated and wouldn't be myself, couldn't care for myself anymore. She would have to look into hospice care, or the hospital, or some other facility where I would stay until I died."

We are told that Louise did not hesitate with her answer. "I can't do that... I don't want that." The reporter continues, "Her doctor, Louise thought, looked both sad and relieved. 'I know, I know,' the doctor said. 'But it has to come from you.'" Louise makes sure that they are both talking about suicide and says, "That's what I'd like to do, go for as long as I can and then end it."

What has happened between Louise and her doctor? The doctor's quick affirmation that Louise is starting to die, even before the MRI scan confirms her decline, is disturbing. She prefaces a grim description of Louise's prognosis with assurance that she does not want to scare her. The doctor's relief when Louise indicates that she is choosing suicide gives us some feeling about her attitudes toward patients in Louise's condition.

As the account continues, the doctor indicates that she would be willing to help, had recently helped another patient whom Louise knew, and said she would prescribe enough barbiturates to kill Louise. To avoid legal trouble, she would not be there when Louise committed suicide. They exchanged several hugs and Louise went home. The doctor called Compassion in Dying for advice. The reporter quotes the doctor as saying about contacting Mero, "I was ecstatic to find someone who's doing what he's doing ... I loved the fact that there were guidelines."

On the phone, Mero advises the doctor on the medication to prescribe and then visits Louise, suggesting that he is prepared to help Louise die before knowing or even meeting her or in any way determining whether she meets any guidelines. When he does meet Louise, she asks him at once if he will help her with her suicide and be there when she does it and she is almost tearfully grateful when he says yes. He repeats many times that it has to be her choice. Louise affirms that it is, saying that all she wants "these next few weeks is to live as peacefully as possible." Louise seems concerned with being close to others during her final time and with spending what is left of her life in an environment of loving leave-taking.

The doctor is concerned that Louise's judgment might soon become impaired: "The question is, at what point is her will going to be affected, and, if suicide is what she wants, does she have the right to do it when she still has the will?" The doctor, like Mero, says she does not want to influence the patient, but worries that Louise might not act in time. "If she loses her mind and doesn't do this, she's going into the hospital. But the last thing I want to do is pressure her to do this."

Yet the closeness before dying that Louise seemed to want is lost in the flurry of activity and planning for her death as each of those involved with her dying pursues his or her own requirements. At a subsequent meeting of Mero and Louise, with Louise's mother and her doctor also present, Mero gives Louise a checklist in which he reviews steps to be taken during the suicide, from the food to be eaten to how the doctor would call the medical examiner.

The doctor indicates she will be out of town for the next week, but that she has told her partner of Louise's plans. "You don't have to wait for me to get back," she tells Louise, hinting, the reporter tells us, that it might be a good idea not to wait. The doctor was more direct when alone with Louise's mother, telling her that she was afraid Louise might not be coherent enough to act if she waited past the coming weekend.

The doctor and Mero discuss how pointed they can be with Louise, wanting her to make an informed decision without frightening her into acting sooner than she was ready. They hoped "she would read between the lines." Mero assures the reporter that he always wants to err on the side of caution. Nonetheless, a few days after the meeting, Mero called the reporter in New York, asking her to come to Seattle as soon as possible. He knew she was planning to come the following week, but he warned her not to wait that long.

The reporter leaves immediately for Seattle and finds Louise in a debilitated condition. She is in pain, getting weaker, and speaks of wanting to end her life while she can still be in control. She says she is almost ready, but not quite.

She needs about a week, mainly to relax and be with her mother.

The reporter blurted out, "Your doctor feels that if you don't act by this weekend you may not be able to." Her words are met with a "wrenching silence" and Louise, looking sharply at her mother, indicates that she hadn't been told that. Her mother says gently that is what the doctor had told her. Louise looks terrified and her mother tells her it's OK to be afraid. "I'm not afraid. I just feel as if everyone is ganging up on me, pressuring me," Louise said, "I just want some time."

Louise's mother was growing less certain that Louise would actually take her own life. When she tried to ask her directly, Louise replied, "I feel like it's all we ever talk about." A friend who had agreed to be with Louise during the suicide is also uncomfortable with Louise's ambivalence but is inclined to attribute her irritability and uncertainty to her mental decline. When Louise indicates that she would wait for Mero to return from a trip and ask his opinion on her holding on for a few days, the friend indicates that this was a bad idea since the change in her mood might be missed by someone like Mero who did not know her well.

Like many people in extreme situations, Louise has expressed two conflicting wishes—to live and to die—and found support only for the latter. The anxiety of her doctor, Mero, her mother, and her friend that Louise might change her mind or lose her "will" may originate in their desire to honor Louise's wishes, or even in their own view of what kind of life is worth living, but eventually overrides the emotions Louise is clearly feeling and comes to affect what happens more than Louise's will. Although those around her act in the name of supporting Louise's autonomy, Louise begins to lose her own death.

Despite predictions, Louise makes it through the weekend. Over the next days she speaks with Mero by phone, but he tells the reporter he kept the conversations short because he was uncomfortable with her growing dependence on his opinion. Nevertheless, after a few such conversations, the contents of which are not revealed, Louise indicated she was ready; that evening Mero came and the assisted suicide was performed. A detailed description of the death scene provides the beginning, the end, and the drama of the published story. Louise did not die immediately but lingered for seven hours. Had she not died from the pills, Mero subsequently implied to the reporter, he would have used a plastic bag to suffocate her, although this violates the Compassion in Dying guidelines.

Everyone—Mero, the friend, the mother, the doctor, and the reporter—all became part of a network pressuring Louise to stick to her decision and to do so in a timely manner. The death was virtually clocked by their anxiety that she might want to live. Mero and the doctor influence the feelings of the mother and the friend so that the issue is not their warm leave-taking and the affection they have had for Louise, but whether they can get her to die according to the time requirements of Mero, the doctor (who probably cannot stay away indefinitely), the reporter (who has her own deadlines), and the disease, which turns out to be on a more flexible schedule than previously thought. Louise is explicit that the doctor, mother, friend, and reporter have become instruments of pressure in moving her along. Mero appears to act more subtly and indirectly through his effect on the others involved with Louise.

Without a death there is, of course, no story, and Mero and the reporter have a stake in the story, although Mero has criticized Jack Kevorkian to the reporter for wanting publicity. The doctor develops a time frame for Louise; her own past troubling experience with a patient who was a friend seems to color the doctor's need to have things over with quickly and in her absence if possible. Louise is clearly frustrated by not having someone to talk to who has no stake in persuading her.

Individually and collectively those involved engender a terror in Louise with which she must struggle alone, while they reassure each other that they are gratifying her last wishes. The end of her life does not seem like death with dignity; nor is there much compassion conveyed in the way Louise was helped to die. Compassion is not an easy emotion to express in the context of an imminent loss. It requires that we look beyond our own pain to convey the power and meaning of all that has gone before in our life with another. Although the mother, friend, and physician may have acted out of good intentions in assisting the suicide, none appears to have honored Louise's need for a "peaceful" parting. None seems to have been able to accept the difficult emotions involved in loving someone who is dying and knowing there is little one can do but convey love and respect for the life that has been lived. The effort to deal with the discomfort of Louise's situation seems to drive the others to "do something" to eliminate the situation.

Watching someone die can be intolerably painful for those who care for the patient. Their wish to have it over with quickly is understandable. Their feeling can become a form of pressure on the patient and must be separated from what the patient actually wants. The patient who wants to live until the end but senses his family cannot tolerate watching him die is familiar to those who care for the terminally ill. Once those close to the patient decide to assist in the suicide, their desire to have it over with can make the pressure put on the patient many times greater. The mood of those assisting is reflected in Macbeth's famous line, "If it were done when tis done, then 'twere well it were done quickly."

Certainly assisted *suicide*—the fact that she took the lethal medication herself—offered no protection to Louise. Short of actually murdering her, it is hard to see how her doctor, Mero, her mother, her friend, and the reporter could have done more to rush her toward death. Case vignettes limited to one or two paragraphs describing the patient's medical symptoms, and leaving out the social context in which euthanasia is being considered, obscure such complex—and often subtle—pressures on patients' "autonomous" decisions to seek death.

EMPOWERMENT FOR WHOM?

Our culture supports the feeling that we should not tolerate situations we cannot control. "Death," Arnold Toynbee has said, "is un-American." The physician who feels a sense of failure and helplessness in the face of incurable disease, or the relative who cannot bear the emotions of loss and separation, finds in assisted suicide and euthanasia an illusion of mastery over the disease and the accompanying feelings of helplessness. Determining when death will occur becomes a way of dealing with frustration.

In the selling of assisted suicide and euthanasia words like "empowerment" and "dignity" are associated only with the choice for dying. But who is being empowered? The more one knows about individual cases, the more apparent it becomes that needs other than those of the patient often prevail. "Empowerment" flows toward the relatives, the doctor who offers a speedy way out if he cannot offer a cure, or the activists who have found in death a cause that gives meaning to their lives. The patient, who may have said she wants to die in the hope of receiving emotional reassurance that all around her want her to live, may find that like Louise she has set in motion a process whose momentum she cannot control. If death with dignity is to be a fact and not a selling slogan, surely what is required is a loving parting that acknowledges the value of the life lived and affirms its continuing meaning.

Euthanasia advocates try to use the individual case to demonstrate that there are some cases of rational or justifiable assisted suicide or euthanasia. If they can demonstrate that there are some such cases, they believe that would justify legalizing euthanasia.

Their argument recalls Abraham's approach in persuading God not to go ahead with his intention to destroy everyone in Sodom. Abraham asks if it would be right for God to destroy Sodom if there were fifty who were righteous within the city. When God agrees to spare Sodom if there were fifty who were righteous, Abraham asks what about forty-five, gradually reduces the number to ten, and gets God to spare the city for the time being for the sake of the ten.

Abraham, however, is arguing in favor of saving life; we want him to succeed and are relieved that he does. Euthanasia advocates are arguing that if there are ten cases where euthanasia might be appropriate, we should legalize a practice that is likely to kill thousands inappropriately.

The appeal of assisted suicide and euthanasia is a symptom of our failure to develop a better response to death and the fear of intolerable pain or artificial prolongation of life. The United States needs a national commission to explore and develop a consensus on the care and treatment of the seriously or terminally ill—a scientific commission similar to the President's Commission that in 1983 gave us guidelines about forgoing life-sustaining treatment with dying patients. Work of a wider scope needs to be done now. There is a great deal of evidence that doctors are not sufficiently trained in relieving pain and other symptoms in the terminally ill. Hospice care is in its infancy. We have not yet educated the public as to the choices they have in refusing or terminating treatment nor has the medical profession learned how best to avoid setting in motion the technology that only prolongs a painful process of dying. And we have not devoted enough time in our medical schools or hospitals to educating future physicians about coming to terms with the painful truth that there will be patients they will not be able to save but whose needs they must address.

How we deal with illness, age, and decline says a great deal about who and what we are, both as individuals and as a society. We should not buy into the view of those who are engulfed by fear of death or by suicidal despair that death is the preferred solution to the problems of illness, age, and depression. We would be encouraging the worst tendencies of depressed patients, most of whom can be helped to overcome their condition. By rushing to "normalize" euthanasia as a medical option along with accepting or refusing treatment, we are inevitably laying the groundwork for a culture that will not only turn euthanasia into a "cure" for depression but may prove to exert a coercion to die on patients when they are most vulnerable. Death ought to be hard to sell.

References

1. Yale Kamisar, "Physician-Assisted Suicide: The Last Bridge to Active Voluntary Euthanasia," in *Examining Euthanasia*, ed. John Keown (Cambridge: Cambridge University Press, in press); Yale Kamisar, "Are Laws against Assisted Suicide Unconstitutional?" *Hastings Center Report* 23, no. 3 (1993): 33–41; Herbert Hendin, "Seduced by Death: Doctors, Patients and the Dutch Cure," *Issues in Law and Medicine* 10, no. 2 (1994): 123–68; Carlos Gomez, *Regulating Death: Euthanasia and the Case of the Netherlands* (New York: Free Press, 1991).
2. "Death on Request," Ikon Television Network, 1994.
3. "Death on Request," *Prime Time Live*, 8 December 1994.
4. Lisa Belken, "There's No Simple Suicide," *New York Times Magazine*, 14 November 1993.

INFORMED DEMAND FOR "NON-BENEFICIAL" MEDICAL TREATMENT

Steven H. Miles

An 85-year-old woman was taken from a nursing home to Hennepin County Medical Center on January 1, 1990, for emergency treatment of dyspnea from chronic bronchiectasis. The patient, Mrs. Helga Wanglie, required emergency intubation and was placed on a respirator. She occasionally acknowledged discomfort and recognized her family but could not communicate clearly. In May, after attempts to wean her from the respirator failed, she was discharged to a chronic care hospital. One week later, her heart stopped during a weaning attempt; she was resuscitated and taken to another hospital for intensive care. She remained unconscious, and a physician suggested that it would be appropriate to consider withdrawing life support. In response, the family transferred her back to the medical center on May 31. Two weeks later, physicians concluded that she was in a persistent vegetative state. She was maintained on a respirator, with repeated courses of antibiotics, frequent airway suctioning, tube feedings, an air flotation bed, and biochemical monitoring.

In June and July of 1990, physicians suggested that life-sustaining treatment be withdrawn since it was not benefiting the patient. Her husband, daughter, and son insisted on continued treatment. They stated their view that physicians should not play God, that the patient would not be better off dead, that removing life support showed moral decay in our civilization, and that a miracle could occur. Her husband told a physician that his wife had never stated her preferences concerning life-sustaining treatment. He believed that the cardiac arrest would not have occurred if she had not been transferred from Hennepin County Medical Center in May. The family reluctantly accepted a do-not-resuscitate order based on the improbability of Mrs. Wanglie's surviving a cardiac arrest. In June, an ethics committee consultant recommended continued counseling for the family. The family declined counseling, including the counsel of their own pastor, and in late July asked that the respirator not be discussed again. In August, nurses expressed their consensus that continued life support did not seem appropriate, and I, as the newly appointed ethics consultant, counseled them.

In October 1990, a new attending physician consulted with specialists and confirmed the permanence of the patient's cerebral and pulmonary conditions. He concluded that she was at the end of her life and that the respirator was "non-beneficial," in that it could not heal her lungs, palliate her suffering, or enable this unconscious and permanently respirator-dependent woman to experience the benefit of the life afforded by respirator support. Because the respirator could prolong life, it was not characterized as "futile."[1] In November, the physician, with my concurrence, told the family that he was not willing to continue to prescribe the respirator. The husband, an attorney, rejected proposals to transfer the patient to another facility or to seek a court order mandating this unusual treatment. The hospital told the family that it would ask a court to decide whether members of its staff were obliged to continue treatment. A second conference two weeks later, after the family had hired an attorney, confirmed these positions, and the husband asserted that the patient had consistently said she wanted respirator support for such a condition.

In December, the medical director and hospital administrator asked the Hennepin County Board of Commissioners (the medical center's board of directors) to allow the hospital to go to court to resolve the dispute. In January, the county board gave permission by a

---

Miles, Steven H. "Informed Demand for 'Non-Beneficial' Medical Treatment." From *The New England Journal of Medicine* 325:512–515.

4-to-3 vote. Neither the hospital nor the county had a financial interest in terminating treatment. Medicare largely financed the $200,000 for the first hospitalization at Hennepin County; a private insurer would pay the $500,000 bill for the second. From February through May of 1991, the family and its attorney unsuccessfully searched for another health care facility that would admit Mrs. Wanglie. Facilities with empty beds cited her poor potential for rehabilitation.

The hospital chose a two-step legal procedure, first asking for the appointment of an independent conservator to decide whether the respirator was beneficial to the patient and second, if the conservator found it was not, for a second hearing on whether it was obliged to provide the respirator. The husband cross-filed, requesting to be appointed conservator. After a hearing in late May, the trial court on July 1, 1991, appointed the husband, as best able to represent the patient's interests. It noted that no request to stop treatment had been made and declined to speculate on the legality of such an order.[2] The hospital said that it would continue to provide the respirator in the light of continuing uncertainty about its legal obligation to provide it. Three days later, despite aggressive care, the patient died of multisystem organ failure resulting from septicemia. The family declined an autopsy and stated that the patient had received excellent care.

DISCUSSION

This sad story illustrates the problem of what to do when a family demands medical treatment that the attending physician concludes cannot benefit the patient. Only 600 elderly people are treated with respirators for more than six months in the United States each year.[3] Presumably, most of these people are actually or potentially conscious. It is common practice to discontinue the use of a respirator before death when it can no longer benefit a patient.[4,5]

We do not know Mrs. Wanglie's treatment preferences. A large majority of elderly people prefer not to receive prolonged respirator support for irreversible unconsciousness.[6] Studies show that an older person's designated family proxy overestimates that person's preference for life-sustaining treatment in a hypothetical coma.[7–9] The implications of this research for clinical decision making have not been cogently analyzed.

A patient's request for a treatment does not necessarily oblige a provider or the health care system. Patients may not demand that physicians injure them (for example, by mutilation), or provide plausible but inappropriate therapies (for example, amphetamines for weight reduction), or therapies that have no value (such as laetrile for cancer). Physicians are not obliged to violate their personal moral views on medical care so long as patients' rights are served. Minnesota's Living Will law says that physicians are "legally bound to act consistently within my wishes within limits of reasonable medical practice" in acting on requests and refusals of treatment.[10] Minnesota's Bill of Patients' Rights says that patients "have the right to appropriate medical ... care based on individual needs ... [which is] limited where the service is not reimbursable."[11] Mrs. Wanglie also had aortic insufficiency. Had this condition worsened, a surgeon's refusal to perform a life-prolonging valve replacement as medically inappropriate would hardly occasion public controversy. As the Minneapolis *Star Tribune* said in an editorial on the eve of the trial,

> The hospital's plea is born of realism, not hubris.... It advances the claim that physicians should not be slaves to technology—any more than patients should be its prisoners. They should be free to deliver, and act on, an honest and time-honored message: "Sorry, there's nothing more we can do."[12]

Disputes between physicians and patients about treatment plans are often handled by transferring patients to the care of other providers. In this case, every provider contacted by the hospital or the family refused to treat this patient with a respirator. These refusals occurred before and after this case became a matter of public controversy and despite the availability of third-party reimbursement. We believe they represent a medical consensus that respirator support is inappropriate in such a case.

The handling of this case is compatible with current practices regarding informed consent, respect for patients' autonomy, and the right to health care. Doctors should inform patients of all medically reasonable treatments, even those available from other providers. Patients can refuse any prescribed treatment or choose among any medical alternatives that physicians are willing to prescribe. Respect for autonomy does not empower patients to oblige physicians to prescribe treatments in ways that are fruitless or inappropriate. Previous "right to die" cases address the different situation of a patient's right to choose to be free of a prescribed therapy. This case is more about the nature of the patient's entitlement to treatment than about the patient's choice in using that entitlement.

The proposal that this family's preference for this unusual and costly treatment, which is commonly regarded as inappropriate, establishes a right to such treatment is ironic, given that preference does not create a right to other needed, efficacious, and widely desired treatments in the United States. We could not afford a universal health care system based on patients' demands. Such a system would irrationally allocate health care to socially powerful people with strong preferences for immediate treatment to the disadvantage of those with less power or less immediate needs.

After the conclusion was reached that the respirator was not benefiting the patient, the decision to seek a review of the duty to provide it was based on an ethic of "stewardship." Even though the insurer played no part in this case, physicians' discretion to prescribe requires responsible handling of requests for inappropriate treatment. Physicians exercise this stewardship by counseling against or denying such treatment or by submitting such requests to external review. This stewardship is not aimed at protecting the assets of insurance companies but rests on fairness to people who have pooled their resources to insure their collective access to appropriate health care. Several citizens complained to Hennepin County Medical Center that Mrs. Wanglie was receiving expensive treatment paid for by people who had not consented to underwrite a level of medical care whose appropriateness was defined by family demands.

Procedures for addressing this kind of dispute are at an early stage of development. Though the American Medical Association[13] and the Society of Critical Care Medicine[14] also support some decisions to withhold requested treatment, the medical center's reasoning most closely follows the guidelines of the American Thoracic Society.[15] The statements of these professional organizations do not clarify when or how a physician may legally withdraw or withhold demanded life-sustaining treatments. The request for a conservator to review the medical conclusion before considering the medical obligation was often misconstrued as implying that the husband was incompetent or ill motivated. The medical center intended to emphasize the desirability of an independent review of its medical conclusion before its obligation to provide the respirator was reviewed by the court. I believe that the grieving husband was simply mistaken about whether the respirator was benefiting his wife. A direct request to remove the respirator seems to center procedural oversight on the soundness of the medical decision making rather than on the nature of the patient's need. Clearly, the gravity of these decisions merits openness, due process, and meticulous accountability. The relative merits of various procedures need further study.

Ultimately, procedures for addressing requests for futile, marginally effective, or inappropriate therapies require a statutory framework, case law, professional standards, a social consensus, and the exercise of professional responsibility. Appropriate ends for medicine are defined by public and professional consensus. Laws can, and do, say that patients may choose only among medically appropriate options, but legislatures are ill suited to define medical appropriateness. Similarly, health-facility policies on this issue will be difficult to design and will focus on due process rather than on specific clinical situations. Public or private payers will ration according to cost and overall efficacy, a rationing that will become more onerous as therapies are misapplied in individual cases. I believe there is a social consensus that intensive care for a person as "overmastered" by disease as this woman was is inappropriate.

Each case must be evaluated individually. In this case, the husband's request seemed entirely inconsistent with what medical care could do for his wife, the standards of the community, and his fair share of resources that many people pooled for their collective medical care. This case is about limits to what can be achieved at the end of life.

References

1. Tomlinson T, Brody H. Futility and the ethics of resuscitation. *JAMA* 1990; 264;1276–80.
2. In re Helga Wanglie, Fourth Judicial District (Dist. Ct., Probate Ct. Div.) PX-91-283. Minnesota, Hennepin County.
3. Office of Technology Assessment Task Force. Life-sustaining technologies and the elderly. Washington. D.C.: Government Printing Office, 1987.
4. Smedira NG, Evans BH, Grais LS, et al. Withholding and withdrawal of life support from the critically ill. *N Engl J Med* 1990; 322:309–15.
5. Lantos JD, Singer PA, Walker RM, et al. The illusion of futility in clinical practice. *Am J Med* 1989; 87:81–4.
6. Emanuel LL, Barry MJ, Stoeckle JD, Ettelson LM, Emanuel EJ. Advance directives for medical care—a case for greater use. *N Engl J Med* 1991; 324:889–95.
7. Zweibel NR, Cassel CK. Treatment choices at the end of life: a comparison of decisions by older patients and their physician-selected proxies. *Gerontologist* 1989; 29:615–21.
8. Tomlinson T, Howe K, Notman M, Rossmiller D. An empirical study of proxy consent for elderly persons. *Gerontologist* 1990; 30:54–64.
9. Danis M, Southerland LI, Garrett JM, et al. A prospective study of advance directives for life-sustaining care. *N Engl J Med* 1991; 324:882–8.
10. Minnesota Statutes. Adult Health Care Decisions Act. 145b.04.
11. Minnesota Statutes. Patients and residents of health care facilities; Bill of rights. 144.651:Subd. 6.
12. Helga Wanglie's life. *Minneapolis Star Tribune.* May 26, 1991:18A.
13. Council on Ethical and Judicial Affairs. American Medical Associalion. Guidelines for the appropriate use of do-not-resuscitate orders. *JAMA* 1991; 265:1868–71.
14. Task Force on Ethics of the Society of Critical Care Medicine. Consensus report on the ethics of forgoing life-sustaining treatments in the critically ill. *Crit Care Med* 1990; 18:1435–9.
15. American Thoracic Society. Withholding and withdrawing life-sustaining therapy. *Am Rev Respir Dis* (in press).

THE SIGNIFICANCE OF A WISH

Felicia Ackerman

The case of Helga Wanglie should be seen in the general context of conflicts that can arise over whether a patient should be maintained on life-support systems. Well-publicized conflicts of this sort usually involve an institution seeking to prolong the life of a patient diagnosed as terminally ill and/or permanently comatose, versus a family that claims, with varying degrees of substantiation, that the patient would not have wanted to be kept alive under these circumstances. But other sorts of conflicts about prolonging life also occur. Patients who have indicated a desire to stay alive may face opposition from family or medical staff who think these patients' lives are not worth prolonging. Such cases can go badly for patients, who may have difficulty getting their preferences even believed, let alone respected.[1]

Reprinted with permission of the author and publisher from *Hastings Center Report*, Vol. 19 (July–August 1991), pp. 27–29.

Helga Wanglie's case is not as clear cut. But in view of the fact that keeping her on a respirator will prolong her life, that there is more reason to believe she would have wanted this than to believe she would not have wanted it, that medical diagnoses of irreversible unconsciousness are not infallible, and that her private health insurance plan has not objected to paying for her respirator support and in fact has publicly taken the position that cost should not be a factor in treatment decisions, I believe HCMC should continue to maintain Mrs. Wanglie on a respirator. This respirator support is medically and economically feasible, and it serves a recognized medical goal—that of prolonging life and allowing a chance at a possible, albeit highly unlikely, return to consciousness.

THE SIGNIFICANCE OF MEDICAL EXPERTISE

Dr. Steven Miles, ethics consultant at HCMC, has argued that continued respirator support is "medically inappropriate" for Mrs. Wanglie. The argument is based on a criterion of medical appropriateness that allows doctors to prescribe respirators for any of three purposes: to allow healing, to alleviate suffering, and to enable otherwise disabled persons to continue to enjoy life. Since keeping Mrs. Wanglie on a respirator serves none of these ends, it is argued, such treatment is medically inappropriate.

But just what does "medically inappropriate" mean here? A clear case of medical inappropriateness would be an attempt to cure cancer with laetrile, since medicine has presumably shown that laetrile cannot cure cancer. Moreover, since laetrile's clinical ineffectiveness is a technical medical fact about which doctors are supposed to have professional expertise, it is professionally appropriate for doctors to refuse to grant a patient's request to have laetrile prescribed for cancer. But HCMC's disagreement with Mrs. Wanglie's family is not a technical dispute about a matter where doctors can be presumed to have greater expertise than laymen. The parties to the dispute do not disagree about whether maintaining Mrs. Wanglie on a respirator is likely to prolong her life; they disagree about whether her life is worth prolonging. This is not a medical question, but a question of values. Hence the term "medically inappropriate," with its implication of the relevance of technical medical expertise, is itself inappropriate in this context. It is as presumptuous and *ethically* inappropriate for doctors to suppose that their professional expertise qualifies them to know what kind of life is worth prolonging as it would be for meteorologists to suppose their professional expertise qualifies them to know what kind of destination is worth a long drive in the rain.

It has also been argued that continued respirator support does not serve Mrs. Wanglie's interests since a permanently unconscious person cannot "enjoy any realization of the quality of life."[2] Yet were this approach to be applied consistently, it would undermine the idea frequently advanced in other life-support cases that it is in the interests of the irreversibly comatose to be "allowed" to die "with dignity." Such people are not suffering or even conscious, so how can death benefit them or serve their interests? The obvious reply in both cases is that there is a sense in which it is in a permanently comatose person's interests to have his or her previous wishes and values respected. And there is some evidence that Mrs. Wanglie would want to be kept alive.

But why suppose doctors are any more obliged to serve this want than they would be to help gratify some nonmedical desire such as a desire to be remembered in a certain way? An obvious answer is that prolonging life is a medical function, as is allowing a possible return to consciousness. Medical diagnoses of irreversible coma are not infallible, as the recent case of Carrie Coons clearly demonstrates. The court order to remove her feeding tube, requested by her family, was rescinded after Mrs. Coons regained consciousness following five and a half months in what was diagnosed as an irreversible vegetative state.[3] Such cases cast additional light on the claim that respirator support is medically inappropriate and not in Mrs. Wanglie's interests. When the alternative is death, the question of whether going for a long-shot chance of recovering consciousness is worth it is quite obviously a question of values, rather than a technical medical question doctors are especially professionally qualified to decide.

THE SIGNIFICANCE OF QUALITY OF LIFE

Medical ethicists who take into account the possibility that seemingly irreversibly comatose patients might regain consciousness have offered further general arguments against maintaining such patients on life-support systems. One such argument relies on the fact that "the few patients who have recovered consciousness after a prolonged period of unconsciousness were severely disabled,"[4] with disabilities including blindness, inability to speak, permanent distortion of limbs, and paralysis. Since many blind, mute, and/or paralyzed people seem to find their lives well worth living, however, the assumption that disability is a fate worse than death seems highly questionable. Moreover, when the patient's views on the matter are unknown, maintaining him on a respirator to give him a chance to regain consciousness and then decide whether to continue his disabled existence seems preferable to denying him even the possibility of a choice by deciding in advance that he would be better off dead. Keeping alive someone who would want to die and "allowing" to die someone who would want a chance of regained consciousness are not parallel wrongs. While both obviously go against the patient's values, only the latter has the additional flaw of doing this in a way that could actually affect his conscious experience.

The other argument asserts that since long-term treatment imposes emotional and often financial burdens on the comatose patient's family and most patients, before losing consciousness, place a high value on their families' welfare, presumably these patients would rather die than be a burden to their loved ones.[5] Though very popular nowadays, this latter sort of argument is cruel because it attributes extreme self-abnegation to those unable to speak for themselves. It is also biased because it assumes great sacrificial love on the part of the patient, but not the family. Why not argue instead that a loving family will not want to deny a beloved member a last chance at regained consciousness and hence that it is *not* in the interest of the patient's loved ones to withdraw life supports? Mrs. Wanglie's family clearly wants her kept alive.[6]

THE SIGNIFICANCE OF A GESTURE

Mrs. Wanglie's family claims that she would want to be kept alive. Yet Dr. Cranford suggests that her family at first denied having previously discussed the matter with her, and that it was only after the HCMC committed itself to going to court that the family claimed Mrs. Wanglie had said she would want to be kept alive. Dr. Miles mentions that during the months when she was on a respirator before becoming unconscious, Mrs. Wanglie at times pulled at her respirator tubing.

I agree that Mrs. Wanglie's views are less than certain. Yet for reasons given above and also because death is irrevocable, there should be a presumption in favor of life when a patient's views are unclear or unknown. Pulling at a respirator tube is obviously insufficient evidence of even a fleeting desire to die; it may simply be a semi-automatic attempt to relieve discomfort, like pulling away in a dentist's chair even when one has an overriding desire that the dental work be performed. Basically, although the circumstances of the family's claim about Mrs. Wanglie's statement of her views make the claim questionable, it is their word against nobody's. No one claims that she ever said she would prefer *not* to be kept alive, despite her months of conscious existence on a respirator.

It has also been argued that we should not allow patients to demand medically inappropriate care when the costs of that care are borne by others who have not consented to do so. I have already discussed the question of medical appropriateness. And a private health plan is paying for Mrs. Wanglie's care, a plan whose officials have publicly stated that cost should not be a factor in treatment decisions. The pool of subscribers to the plan, whose premiums are what indirectly subsidize Mrs. Wanglie's care, have, by being members of this plan, committed themselves to a practice of medicine that does not take cost into account. It would be unfair to make cost a factor in Mrs. Wanglie's treatment decision now. Public statements by health insurance plan officials are expected to be taken into account by consumers selecting health insurance and must not be reneged upon. Mrs. Wanglie's insurer is not seeking to renege. Instead, it is her *doctors* who have decided that her life is not worth prolonging.

Moreover, to say it would be the underlying disease rather than the act of removing the respirator that would cause Helga Wanglie's death is not helpful. If Mrs. Wanglie is, as the HCMC staff claims, irreversibly respirator-dependent, then saying that removing the respirator would cause her death is just as logical as saying that withdrawing a rope from a drowning man would cause his death, even if his death is to be "attributed" to his drowning. If the person in either case has an interest in living, one violates his interest by withdrawing the necessary means. This is what HCMC is seeking court permission to do to Mrs. Wanglie.

References

1. For example, consider the case of seventy-eight-year-old Earl Spring, whose mental deterioration did not prevent him from saying that he did not want to die. The statement of this preference was not considered conclusive reason to keep him on dialysis over his family's objections. Similarly, the *New York Times Magazine* recently described the situation of a severely disabled, elderly woman whose explicit advance directive that she wanted everything possible done to keep her alive was apparently ignored by both her husband and the hospital's ethics committee (K. Bouton, "Painful Decisions: The Role of the Medical Ethicist," 5 August 1990).
2. This argument comes from an unpublished letter from Dr. Steven Miles, made available to me by the *Hastings Center Report* at his request.
3. The Coons case was widely reported in newspapers. For example, see C. De Mare, "'Hopeless' Hospital Patient, 86, Comes Out of Coma," *Albany Times Union*, 12 April 1989. Additional cases of this sort are cited in President's Commission for the Study of Ethical Problems in Medicine and Biomedical and Behavioral Research, *Deciding to Forgo Life-Sustaining Treatment* (Washington, D.C.: U.S. Government Printing Office, 1983).
4. President's Commission, *Deciding to Forgo Life-Sustaining Treatment* p. 182.
5. President's Commission, *Deciding to Forgo Life-Sustaining Treatment*, p. 183.
6. I have given this sort of argument in a letter to the *New York Times*, 4 November 1987, as well as in a short story about terminal illness, "The Forecasting Game," in *Prize Stories 1990: The O. Henry Awards*, ed. W. Abrahams (New York: Doubleday, 1990), pp. 315–35, and in an op-ed "No Thanks, I Don't Want to Die with Dignity," *Providence Journal-Bulletin*, 19 April 1990 (reprinted in other newspapers under various different titles).

GENETICS AND MORALITY

CAN HAVING CHILDREN BE IMMORAL?

L. M. Purdy

I INTRODUCTION

Suppose you know that there is a fifty percent chance you have Huntington's chorea, even though you are still free of symptoms, and that if you do have it, each of your children has a fifty percent chance of having it also.

Should you now have children?

There is always some possibility that a pregnancy will result in a diseased or handicapped child. But certain persons run a higher than average risk of producing such a child. Genetic counselors are increasingly able to calculate the probability that certain problems will occur; this means that more people can find out whether they are in danger of creating unhealthy offspring *before* the birth of a child.

Since this kind of knowledge is available, we ought to use it wisely. I want in this paper to defend the thesis that it is wrong to reproduce when we know there is a high risk of transmitting a serious disease or defect. My argument for this claim is in three parts. The first is that we should try to provide every child with a normal opportunity for health; the second is that in the course of doing this it is not wrong to prevent possible children from existing. The third is that this duty may require us to refrain from childbearing.

One methodological point must be made. I am investigating a problem in biomedical ethics: this is a philosophical enterprise. But the conclusion has practical importance since individuals do face the choice I examine. This raises a question; what relation ought the outcome of this inquiry bear to social policy? It may be held that a person's reproductive life should not be interfered with. Perhaps this is a reasonable position, but it does not follow from it that it is never wrong for an individual to have children or that we should not try to determine when this is the case. All that does follow is that we may not coerce persons with regard to childbearing. Evaluation of this last claim is a separate issue which cannot be handled here.

Reprinted with permission of Rowman & Littlefield Publishers from *Genetics Now*, ed. by John L. Buckley (University Press of America, 1978).

I want to deal with this issue concretely. The reason for this is that, otherwise, discussion is apt to be vague and inconclusive. An additional reason is that it will serve to make us appreciate the magnitude of the difficulties faced by diseased or handicapped individuals. Thus it will be helpful to consider a specific disease. For this purpose I have chosen Huntington's chorea.

II HUNTINGTON'S CHOREA: COURSE AND RISK

Let us now look at Huntington's chorea. First we will consider the course of the disease, then its inheritance pattern.

The symptoms of Huntington's chorea usually begin between the ages of thirty and fifty, but young children can also be affected. It happens this way:

> Onset is insidious. Personality changes (obstinacy, moodiness, lack of initiative) frequently antedate or accompany the involuntary choreic movements. These usually appear first in the face, neck, and arms, and are jerky, irregular, and stretching in character. Contractions of the facial muscles result in grimaces; those of the respiratory muscles, lips, and tongue lead to hesitating, explosive speech. Irregular movements of the trunk are present; the gait is shuffling and dancing. Tendon reflexes are increased … some patients display a fatuous euphoria; others are spiteful, irascible, destructive, and violent. Paranoid reactions are common. Poverty of thought and impairment of attention, memory, and judgment occur. As the disease progresses, walking becomes impossible, swallowing difficult, and dementia profound. Suicide is not uncommon.

The illness lasts about fifteen years, terminating in death.

Who gets Huntington's chorea? It is an autosomal dominant disease; this means it is caused by a single mutant gene located on a non-sex chromosome. It is passed from one generation to the next via affected individuals. When one has the disease, whether one has symptoms and thus knows one has it or not, there is a 50% chance that each child will have it also. If one has escaped it then there is no risk to one's children.

How serious is this risk? For geneticists, a ten percent risk is high. But not every high risk is unacceptable: this depends on what is at stake.

There are two separate evaluations in any judgment about a given risk. The first measures the gravity of the worst possible result; the second perceives a given risk as great or small. As for the first, in medicine as elsewhere, people may regard the same result quite differently:

> … The subjective attitude to the disease or lesion itself may be quite at variance with what informed medical opinion may regard as a realistic appraisal. Relatively minor limb defects with cosmetic overtones are examples here. On the other hand, some patients regard with equanimity genetic lesions which are of major medical importance.

For devastating diseases like Huntington's chorea, this part of the judgment should be unproblematic: no one could want a loved one to suffer so.

There may be considerable disagreement, however, about whether a given probability is big or little. Individuals vary a good deal in their attitude toward this aspect of risk. This suggests that it would be difficult to define the "right" attitude to a particular risk in many circumstances. Nevertheless, there are good grounds for arguing in favor of a conservative approach here. For it is reasonable to take special precautions to avoid very bad consequences, even if the risk is small. But the possible consequences here *are* very bad: a child who may inherit Huntington's chorea is a child with a much larger than average chance of being subjected to severe and prolonged suffering. Even if the child does not have the disease, it may anticipate and fear it, and anticipating an evil, as we all know, may be worse than experiencing it. In addition, if a parent loses the gamble, his child will suffer the consequences. But it is one thing to take a high risk for oneself; to submit someone else to it without his consent is another.

I think that these points indicate that the morality of procreation in situations like this demands further study. I propose to do this by looking first at the position of the possible child, then at that of the potential parent.

III REPRODUCTION: THE POSSIBLE CHILD'S POSITION

The first task in treating the problem from the child's point of view is to find a way of referring to possible future offspring without seeming to confer some sort of morally significant existence upon them. I will call children who might be born in the future but who are not now conceived "possible" children, offspring, individuals, or persons. I stipulate that this term implies nothing about their moral standing.

The second task is to decide what claims about children or possible children are relevant to the morality of childbearing in the circumstances being considered. There are, I think, two such claims. One is that we ought to provide every child with at least a normal opportunity for a good life. The other is that we do not harm possible children if we prevent them from existing. Let us consider both these matters in turn.

A. Opportunity for a Good Life

Accepting the claim that we ought to try to provide for every child a normal opportunity for a good life involves two basic problems: justification and practical application.

Justification of the claim could be derived fairly straightforwardly from either utilitarian or contractarian theories of justice, I think, although a proper discussion would be too lengthy to include here. Of prime importance in any such discussion would be the judgment that to neglect this duty would be to create unnecessary unhappiness or unfair disadvantage for some persons.

The attempt to apply the claim that we should try to provide a normal opportunity for a good life leads to a couple of difficulties. One is knowing what it requires of us. Another is defining "normal opportunity." Let us tackle the latter problem first.

Conceptions of "normal opportunity" vary among societies and also within them: *de rigueur* in some circles are private music lessons and trips to Europe, while in others providing eight years of schooling is a major sacrifice. But there is no need to consider this complication since we are here concerned only with health as a prerequisite for normal opportunity. Thus we can retreat to the more limited claim that every parent should try to ensure normal health for his child. It might be thought that even this moderate claim is unsatisfactory since in some places debilitating conditions are the norm. One could circumvent this objection by saying that parents ought to try to provide for their children health normal for that culture, even though it may be inadequate if measured by some outside standard. This conservative position would still justify efforts to avoid the birth of children at risk for Huntington's chorea and other serious genetic diseases.

But then what does this stand require of us: is sacrifice entailed by the duty to try to provide normal health for our children? The most plausible answer seems to be that as the danger of serious disability increases, the greater the sacrifice demanded of the potential parent. This means it would be more justifiable to recommend that an individual refrain from childbearing if he risks passing on spina bifida than if he risks passing on webbed feet. Working out all the details of such a schema would clearly be a difficult matter; I do not think it would be impossible to set up workable guidelines, though.

Assuming a rough theoretical framework of this sort, the next question we must ask is whether Huntington's chorea substantially impairs an individual's opportunity for a good life.

People appear to have different opinions about the plight of such persons. Optimists argue that a child born into a family afflicted with Huntington's chorea has a reasonable chance of living a satisfactory life. After all, there is a fifty percent chance it will escape the disease even if a parent has already manifested it, and a still greater chance if this is not so. Even if it does have the illness, it will probably enjoy thirty years of healthy life before symptoms appear; and, perhaps, it may not find the disease destructive. Optimists can list diseased or handicapped persons who have lived fruitful lives. They can also find individuals who seem genuinely glad to be alive. One is Rick Donohue, a sufferer from the Joseph family disease: "You know, if my mom hadn't had me, I wouldn't be here for the life I have had. So there is a good possibility I will have children." Optimists therefore conclude that it would be a shame if these persons had not lived.

Pessimists concede these truths, but they take a less sanguine view of them. They think a fifty percent risk of serious disease like Huntington's chorea appallingly high. They suspect that a child born into an afflicted family is liable to spend its youth in dreadful anticipation and fear of the disease. They expect that the disease, if it appears, will be perceived as a tragic and painful end to a blighted life. They point out that Rick Donohue is still young and has not yet experienced the full horror of his sickness.

Empirical research is clearly needed to resolve this dispute: we need much more information about the psychology and life history of sufferers and potential sufferers. Until we have it we cannot know whether the optimist or the pessimist has a better case; definitive judgment must therefore be suspended. In the meantime, however, common sense suggests that the pessimist has the edge.

If some diseased persons do turn out to have a worse than average life there appears to be a case against further childbearing in afflicted families. To support this claim two more judgments are necessary, however. The first is that it is not wrong to refrain from childbearing. The second is that asking individuals to so refrain is less of a sacrifice than might be thought. I will examine each of these judgments.

B. The Morality of Preventing the Birth of Possible Persons

Before going on to look at reasons why it would not be wrong to prevent the birth of possible persons, let me try to clarify the picture a bit. To understand the claim it must be kept in mind that we are considering a prospective situation here, not a retrospective one: we are trying to rank the desirability of various alternative future states of affairs. One possible future state is this: a world where nobody is at risk for Huntington's chorea except as a result of random mutation. This state has been achieved by sons and daughters of persons afflicted with Huntington's chorea ceasing to reproduce. This means that an indeterminate number of children who might have been born were not born. These possible children can be divided into two categories: those who would have been miserable and those who would have lived good lives. To prevent the existence of members of the first category it was necessary to prevent the existence of all. Whether or not this is a good state of affairs depends on the morality of the means and the end. The end, preventing the existence of miserable beings, is surely good; I will argue that preventing the birth of possible persons is not intrinsically wrong. Hence this state of affairs is a morally good one.

Why then is it not in itself wrong to prevent the birth of possible persons? It is not wrong because there seems to be no reason to believe that possible individuals are either deprived or injured if they do not exist. They are not deprived because to be deprived in a morally significant sense one must be able to have experiences. But possible persons do not exist. Since they do not exist, they cannot have experiences. Another way to make this point is to say that each of us might not have been born, although most of us are glad we were. But this does not mean that it makes sense to say that we would have been deprived of something had we not been born. For if we had not been born, we would not exist, and there would be nobody to be deprived of anything. To assert the contrary is to imagine that we are looking at a world in which we do not exist. But this is not the way it would be: there would be nobody to look.

The contention that it is wrong to prevent possible persons from existing because they have a right to exist appears to be equally baseless. The most fundamental objection to this view is that there is no reason to ascribe rights to entities which do not exist. It is one thing to say that as-yet-nonexistent persons will have certain rights if and when they exist: this claim is plausible if made with an eye toward preserving social and environmental goods. But what justification could there be for the claim that nonexistent beings have a right to exist?

Even if one conceded that there was a presumption in favor of letting some nonexistent beings exist, stronger claims could surely override it. For one thing, it would be unfair not to recognize the prior claim of already existing children who are not being properly cared for. One might also argue that it is simply wrong to prevent persons who might have existed from doing so. But this implies that contraception and population control are also wrong.

It is therefore reasonable to maintain that because possible persons have no right to exist, they are not injured if not created. Even if they had that right, it could rather easily be overridden by counterclaims. Hence, since possible persons are neither deprived nor injured if not conceived, it is not wrong to prevent their existence.

C. Conclusion of Part III

At the beginning of Part III I said that two claims are relevant to the morality of childbearing in the circumstances being considered. The first is that we ought to provide every child with at least a normal opportunity for a good life. The second is that we do not deprive or injure possible persons if we prevent their existence.

I suggested that the first claim could be derived from currently accepted theories of justice: a healthy body is generally necessary for happiness and it is also a prerequisite for a fair chance at a good life in our competitive world. Thus it is right to try to ensure that each child is healthy.

I argued, with regard to the second claim, that we do not deprive or injure possible persons if we fail to create them. They cannot be deprived of anything because they do not exist and hence cannot have experiences. They cannot be injured because only an entity with a right to exist could be injured if prevented from existing, but there are no good grounds for believing that they are such entities.

From the conjunction of these two claims I conclude that it is right to try to ensure that a child is healthy even if by doing so we preclude the existence of certain possible persons. Thus it is right for individuals to prevent the birth of children at risk for Huntington's chorea by avoiding parenthood. The next question is whether it is seriously wrong not to avoid parenthood.

IV REPRODUCTION: THE POTENTIAL PARENT'S SITUATION

I have so far argued that if choreics live substantially worse lives than average, then it is right for afflicted families to cease reproduction. But this conflicts with the generally recognized freedom to procreate and so it does not automatically follow that family members ought not to have children. How can we decide whether the duty to try to provide normal health for one's child should take precedence over the right to reproduce?

This is essentially the same question I asked earlier: how much must one sacrifice to try to ensure that one's offspring is healthy? In answer to this I suggested that the greater the danger of serious disability, the more justifiable considerable sacrifice is.

Now asking someone who wants a child to refrain from procreation seems to be asking for a large sacrifice. It may, in fact, appear to be too large to demand of anyone. Yet I think it can be shown that it is not as great as it initially seems.

Why do people want children? There are probably many reasons, but I suspect that the following include some of the most common. One set of reasons has to do with the gratification to be derived from a happy family life—love, companionship, watching a child grow, helping mold it into a good person, sharing its pains and triumphs. Another set of reasons centers about the parents as individuals—validation of their place within a genetically continuous family line, the conception of children as a source of immortality, being surrounded by replicas of themselves.

Are there alternative ways of satisfying these desires? Adoption or technological means provide ways to satisfy most of the desires pertaining to family life without passing on specific genetic defects. Artificial insemination by donor is already available; implantation of donor ova is likely within a few years. Still another option will exist if cloning becomes a reality. In the meantime, we might permit women to conceive and bear babies for those who do not want to do so themselves. But the desire to extend the genetic line, the desire for immortality, and the desire for children that physically resemble one cannot be met by these methods.

Many individuals probably feel these latter desires strongly. This creates a genuine conflict for persons at risk for transmitting serious genetic diseases like Huntington's chorea. The situation seems especially unfair because, unlike normal people, through no fault of their own, doing something they badly want to do may greatly harm others.

But if my common sense assumption that they are in grave danger of harming others is true, then it is imperative to scrutinize their options carefully. On the one hand, they can have children: they satisfy their desires but risk eventual crippling illness and death for their offspring. On the other, they can remain childless or seek nonstandard ways of creating a family: they have some unfulfilled desires, but they avoid risking harm to their children.

I think it is clear which of these two alternatives is best. For the desires which must remain unsatisfied if they forgo normal procreation are less than admirable. To see the genetic line continued entails a sinister legacy of illness and death; the desire for immortality cannot really be satisfied by reproduction anyway; and the desire for children that physically resemble one is narcissistic and its fulfillment cannot be guaranteed even by normal reproduction. Hence the only defence of these desires is that people do in fact feel them.

Now, I am inclined to accept William James' dictum regarding desires: "Take any demand, however slight, which any creature, however weak, may make. Ought it not, for its own sole sake be satisfied? If not, prove why not." Thus I judge a world where more desires are satisfied to be better than one in which fewer are. But not all desires should be regarded as legitimate, since, as James suggests, there may be good reasons why these ought to be disregarded. The fact that their fulfillment will seriously harm others is surely such a reason. And I believe that the circumstances I have described are a clear example of the sort of case where a desire must be judged illegitimate, at least until it can be shown that sufferers from serious genetic diseases like Huntington's chorea do not live considerably worse than average lives. Therefore, I think it is wrong for individuals in this predicament to reproduce.

V CONCLUSION

Let me recapitulate. At the beginning of this paper I asked whether it is wrong for those who risk transmitting severe genetic disease like Huntington's chorea to have "blood" children. Some despair of reaching an answer to this question. But I think such pessimism is not wholly warranted, and that if generally accepted would lead to much unnecessary harm. It is

Need Empirical Research

true that in many cases it is difficult to know what ought to be done. But this does not mean that we should throw up our hands and espouse a completely laissez-fare approach: philosophers can help by probing the central issues and trying to find guidelines for action.

Naturally there is no way to derive an answer to this kind of problem by deductive argument from self-evident premises, for it must depend on a complicated interplay of facts and moral judgments. My preliminary exploration of Huntington's chorea is of this nature. In the course of the discussion I suggested that, if it is true that sufferers live substantially worse lives than do normal persons, those who might transmit it should not have children. This conclusion is supported by the judgments that we ought to try to provide for every child a normal opportunity for a good life, that possible individuals are not harmed if not conceived, and that it is sometimes less justifiable for persons to exercise their right to procreate than one might think.

I want to stress, in conclusion, that my argument is incomplete. To investigate fully even a single disease, like Huntington's chorea, empirical research on the lives of members of afflicted families is necessary. Then, after developing further the themes touched upon here, evaluation of the probable consequences of different policies on society and on future generations is needed. Until the results of a complete study are available, my argument could serve best as a reason for persons at risk for transmitting Huntington's chorea and similar diseases to put off having children. Perhaps this paper will stimulate such inquiry.

IMPLICATIONS OF PRENATAL DIAGNOSIS FOR THE HUMAN RIGHT TO LIFE

Leon R. Kass

It is especially fitting on this occasion to begin by acknowledging how privileged I feel and how pleased I am to be a participant in this symposium. I suspect that I am not alone among the assembled in considering myself fortunate to be here. For I was conceived after antibiotics yet before amniocentesis, late enough to have benefited from medicine's ability to prevent and control fatal infectious diseases, yet early enough to have escaped from medicine's ability to prevent me from living to suffer from my genetic diseases. To be sure, my genetic vices are, as far as I know them, rather modest, taken individually—myopia, asthma and other allergies, bilateral forefoot adduction, bowleggedness, loquaciousness, and pessimism, plus some four to eight as yet undiagnosed recessive lethal genes in the heterozygous condition—but, taken together, and if diagnosable prenatally, I might never have made it.

Just as I am happy to be here, so am I unhappy with what I shall have to say. Little did I realize when I first conceived the topic, "Implications of Prenatal Diagnosis for the Human Right to Life," what a painful and difficult labor it would lead to. More than once while this paper was gestating, I considered obtaining permission to abort it, on the grounds that, by prenatal diagnosis, I knew it to be defective. My lawyer told me that I was legally in the clear, but my conscience reminded me that I had made a commitment to deliver myself of this paper, flawed or not. Next time, I shall practice better contraception.

Any discussion of the ethical issues of genetic counseling and prenatal diagnosis is

Reprinted with permission of the author and Kluwer Academic/Plenum Publishers from *Human Genetics*, ed. Bruce Hilton (1973), pp. 185–87, 188–92.

unavoidably haunted by a ghost called the morality of abortion. This ghost I shall not vex. More precisely, I shall not vex the reader by telling ghost stories. However, I would be neither surprised nor disappointed if my discussion of an admittedly related matter, the ethics of aborting the genetically defective, summons that hovering spirit to the reader's mind. For the morality of abortion is a matter not easily laid to rest, recent efforts to do so notwithstanding. A vote by the legislature of the State of New York can indeed legitimatize the disposal of fetuses, but not of the moral questions. But though the questions remain, there is likely to be little new that can be said about them, and certainly not by me.

Yet before leaving the general question of abortion, let me pause to drop some anchors for the discussion that follows. Despite great differences of opinion both as to what to think and how to reason about abortion, nearly everyone agrees that abortion is a moral issue.[1] What does this mean? Formally, it means that a woman seeking or refusing an abortion can expect to be asked to justify her action. And we can expect that she should be able to give reasons for her choice other than "I like it" or "I don't like it." Substantively, it means that, in the absence of good reasons for intervention, there is some presumption in favor of allowing the pregnancy to continue once it has begun. A common way of expressing this presumption is to say that "the fetus has a right to continued life."[2] In this context, disagreement concerning the moral permissibility of abortion concerns what rights (or interests or needs), and whose, override (take precedence over, or outweigh) this fetal "right." Even most of the "opponents" of abortion agree that the mother's right to live takes precedence, and that abortion to save her life is permissible, perhaps obligatory. Some believe that a woman's right to determine the number and spacing of her children takes precedence, while yet others argue that the need to curb population growth is, at least at this time, overriding.

Hopefully, this brief analysis of what it means to say that abortion is a moral issue is sufficient to establish two points. First, that the fetus is a living thing with some moral claim on us not to do it violence, and therefore, second, that justification must be given for destroying it.

Turning now from the general questions of the ethics of abortion, I wish to focus on the special ethical issues raised by the abortion of "defective" fetuses (so-called "abortion for fetal indications"). I shall consider only the cleanest cases, those cases where well-characterized genetic diseases are diagnosed with a high degree of certainty by means of amniocentesis, in order to sidestep the added moral dilemmas posed when the diagnosis is suspected or possible, but unconfirmed. However, many of the questions I shall discuss could also be raised about cases where genetic analysis gives only a statistical prediction about the genotype of the fetus, and also about cases where the defect has an infectious or chemical rather than a genetic cause (e.g., rubella, thalidomide).

My first and possibly most difficult task is to show that there is anything left to discuss once we have agreed not to discuss the morality of abortion in general. There is a sense in which abortion for genetic defect is, after abortion to save the life of the mother, perhaps the most defensible kind of abortion. Certainly, it is a serious and not a frivolous reason for abortion, defended by its proponents in sober and rational speech—unlike justifications based upon the false notion that a fetus is a mere part of a woman's body, to be used and abused at her pleasure. Standing behind genetic abortion are serious and well-intentioned people, with reasonable ends in view: the prevention of genetic diseases, the elimination of suffering in families, the preservation of precious financial and medical resources, the protection of our genetic heritage. No profiteers, no sex-ploiters, no racists. No arguments about the connection of abortion with promiscuity and licentiousness, no perjured testimony about the mental health of the mother, no arguments about the seriousness of the population problem. In short, clear objective data, a worthy cause, decent men and women. If abortion, what better reason for it?

Yet if genetic abortion is but a happily wagging tail on the dog of abortion, it is simultaneously the nose of a camel protruding under a rather different tent. Precisely because the quality of the fetus is central to the decision to abort, the practice of genetic abortion has implications which go beyond those raised by abortion in general. What may be at stake here is the belief in the radical moral equality of all human beings, the belief that all human beings possess equally and independent of merit certain fundamental rights, one among which is, of course, the right to life.

To be sure, the belief that fundamental human rights belong equally to all human beings has been but an ideal, never realized, often ignored, sometimes shamelessly. Yet it has been perhaps the most powerful moral idea at work in the world for at least two centuries. It is this idea and ideal that animates most of the current political and social criticism around the globe. It is ironic that we should acquire the power to detect and eliminate the genetically unequal at a time when we have finally succeeded in removing much of the stigma and disgrace previously attached to victims of congenital illness, in providing them with improved care and support, and in preventing, by means of education, feelings of guilt on the part of their parents. One might even wonder whether the development of amniocentesis and prenatal diagnosis may represent a backlash against these same humanitarian and egalitarian tendencies in the practice of medicine, which, by helping to sustain to the age of reproduction persons with genetic disease has itself contributed to the increasing incidence of genetic disease, and with it, to increased pressures for genetic screening, genetic counseling, and genetic abortion.

No doubt our humanitarian and egalitarian principles and practices have caused us some new difficulties, but if we mean to waken or turn our backs on them, we should do so consciously and thoughtfully. If, as I believe, the idea and practice of genetic abortion points in that direction, we should make ourselves aware of it. …

GENETIC ABORTION AND THE LIVING DEFECTIVE

The practice of abortion of the genetically defective will no doubt affect our view of and our behavoir toward those abnormals who escape the net of detection and abortion. A child with Down's syndrome or with hemophilia or with muscular dystrophy born at a time when most of his (potential) fellow sufferers were destroyed prenatally is liable to be looked upon by the community as one unfit to be alive, as a second-class (or even lower) human type. He may be seen as a person who need not have been, and who would not have been, if only someone had gotten to him in time.

The parents of such children are also likely to treat them differently, especially if the mother would have wished but failed to get an amniocentesis because of ignorance, poverty, or distance from the testing station, or if the prenatal diagnosis was in error. In such cases, parents are especially likely to resent the child. They may be disinclined to give it the kind of care they might have before the advent of amniocentesis and genetic abortion, rationalizing that a second-class specimen is not entitled to first-class treatment. If pressed to do so, say by physicians, the parents might refuse, and the courts may become involved. This has already begun to happen.

In Maryland, parents of a child with Down's syndrome refused permission to have the child operated on for an intestinal obstruction present at birth. The physicians and the hospital sought an injunction to require the parents to allow surgery. The judge ruled in favor of the parents, despite what I understand to be the weight of precedent to the contrary, on the grounds that the child was Mongoloid; that is, had the child been "normal," the decision would have gone the other way. Although the decision was not appealed to and hence not affirmed by a higher court, we can see through the prism of this case the possibility that the new powers of human genetics will strip the blindfold from the lady of justice and will make official the dangerous doctrine that some men are more equal than others.

The abnormal child may also feel resentful. A child with Down's syndrome or Tay-Sachs disease will probably never know or care, but what about a child with hemophilia or with Turner's syndrome? In the past decade, with medical knowledge and power over the prenatal child increasing and with parental authority over the postnatal child decreasing, we have seen the appearance of a new type of legal action, suits for wrongful life. Children have brought suit against their parents (and others) seeking to recover damages for physical and social handicaps inextricably tied to their birth (e.g., congenital deformities, congenital syphilis, illegitimacy). In some of the American cases, the courts have recognized the justice of the child's claim (that he was injured due to parental negligence), although they have so far refused to award damages, due to policy considerations. In other countries, e.g., in Germany, judgments with compensation have gone for the plaintiffs. With the spread of amniocentesis and genetic abortion, we can only expect such cases to increase. And here it will be the soft-hearted rather than the hard-hearted judges who will establish the doctrine of second-class human beings, out of compassion for the mutants who escaped the traps set out for them.

It may be argued that I am dealing with a problem which, even if it is real, will affect very few people. It may be suggested that very few will escape the traps once we have set them properly and widely, once people are informed about amniocentesis, once the power to detect prenatally grows to its full capacity, and once our "superstitious" opposition to abortion dies out or is extirpated. But in order even to come close to this vision of success, amniocentesis will have to become part of every pregnancy—either by making it mandatory, like the test for syphilis, or by making it "routine medical practice," like the Pap smear. Leaving aside the other problems with universal amniocentesis, we could expect that the problem for the few who escape is likely to be even worse precisely because they will be few.

The point, however, should be generalized. How will we come to view and act toward the many "abnormals" that will remain among us—the retarded, the crippled, the senile, the deformed, and the true mutants—once we embark on a program to root out genetic abnormality? For it must be remembered that we shall always have abnormals—some who escape detection or whose disease is undetectable *in utero*, others as a result of new mutations, birth injuries, accidents, maltreatment, or disease—who will require our care and protection. The existence of "defectives" cannot be fully prevented, not even by totalitarian breeding and weeding programs. Is it not likely that our principle with respect to these people will change from "We try harder" to "Why accept second best?" The idea of "the unwanted because abnormal child" may become a self-fulfilling prophecy, whose consequences may be worse than those of the abnormality itself.

GENETIC AND OTHER DEFECTIVES

The mention of other abnormals points to a second danger of the practice of genetic abortion. Genetic abortion may come to be seen not so much as the prevention of genetic disease, but as the prevention of birth of defective or abnormal children—and, in a way, understandably so. For in the case of what other diseases does preventive medicine consist in the elimination of the patient-at-risk? Moreover, the very language used to discuss genetic disease leads us to the easy but wrong conclusion that the afflicted fetus or person is rather than has a disease. True, one is partly defined by his genotype, but only partly. A person is more than his disease. And yet we slide easily from the language of possession to the language of identity, from "He has hemophilia" to "He is a hemophiliac," from "She has diabetes" through "She is diabetic" to "She is a diabetic," from "The fetus has Down's syndrome" to "The fetus is a Down's." This way of speaking supports the belief that it is defective persons (or potential persons) that are being eliminated, rather than diseases.

If this is so, then it becomes simply accidental that the defect has a genetic cause. Surely, it is only because of the high regard for medicine and science, and for the accuracy of genetic diagnosis, that genotypic defectives are likely to be the first to go. But once the principle, "Defectives should not be born," is established, grounds other than cytological and biochemical may very well be sought. Even ignoring racialists and others equally misguided—of course, they cannot be ignored—we should know that there are social scientists, for example, who believe that one can predict with a high degree of accuracy how a child will turn out from a careful, systematic study of the socio-economic and psychodynamic environment into which he is born and in which he grows up. They might press for the prevention of socio-psychological disease, even of "criminality," by means of prenatal environmental diagnosis and abortion. I have heard rumor that a crude, unscientific form of eliminating potential "phenotypic defectives" is already being practiced in some cities, in that submission to abortion is allegedly being made a condition for the receipt of welfare payments. "Defectives should not be born" is a principle without limits. We can ill-afford to have it established.

Up to this point, I have been discussing the possible implications of the practice of genetic abortion for our belief in and adherence to the idea that, at least in fundamental human matters such as life and liberty, all men are to be considered as equals, that for these matters we should ignore as irrelevant the real qualitative differences amongst men, however important these differences may be for other purposes. Those who are concerned about abortion fear that the permissible time of eliminating the unwanted will be moved forward along the time continuum, against newborns, infants, and children. Similarly, I suggest that we should be concerned lest the attack on gross genetic inequality in fetuses be advanced along the continuum of quality and into the later stages of life.

I am not engaged in predicting the future; I am not saying that amniocentesis and genetic abortion will lead down the road to Nazi Germany. Rather, I am suggesting that the principles underlying genetic abortion simultaneously justify many further steps down that road. The point was very well made by Abraham Lincoln (1854):

> "If A can prove, however conclusively, that he may, of right, enslave B—Why may not B snatch the same argument and prove equally, that he may enslave A?
>
> "You say A is white, and B is black. It is color, then; the lighter having the right to enslave the darker? Take care. By this rule, you are to be slave to the first man you meet with a fairer skin than your own.
>
> "You do not mean color exactly? You mean the whites are intellectually the superiors of the blacks, and, therefore have the right to enslave them? Take care again. By this rule, you are to be slave to the first man you meet with an intellect superior to your own.
>
> "But, say you, it is a question of interest; and, if you can make it your interest, you have the right to enslave another. Very well. And if he can make it his interest, he has the right to enslave you."

Perhaps I have exaggerated the dangers; perhaps we will not abandon our inexplicable preference for generous humanitarianism over consistency. But we should indeed be cautious and move slowly as we give serious consideration to the question "What price the perfect baby?"[3]...

Notes

1. This strikes me as by far the most important inference to be drawn from the fact that men in different times and cultures have answered the abortion question differently. Seen in this light, the differing and changing answers themselves suggest that it is a question not easily put under, at least not for very long.

2. Other ways include: one should not do violence to living or growing things; life is sacred; respect nature; fetal life has value; refrain from taking innocent life; protect and preserve life. As some have pointed out, the terms chosen are of different weight, and would require reasons of different weight to tip the balance in favor of abortion. My choice of the "rights" terminology is not meant to beg the questions of whether such rights really exist, or of where they come from. However, the notion of a "fetal right to life" presents only a little more difficulty in this regard than does the notion of a "human right to life," since the former noes not depend on a claim that the human fetus is already "human." In my sense of the terms "right" and "life," we might even say that a dog or a fetal dog has a "right to life," and that it would be cruel and immoral for a man to go around performing abortions even on dogs for no good reason.
3. For a discussion of the possible biological rather than moral price of attempts to prevent the birth of defective children see Neel (1970) and Motulsky, Fraser, and Felsenstein (1971).

FATAL KNOWLEDGE? PRENATAL DIAGNOSIS AND SEX SELECTION

Dorothy C. Wertz and John C. Fletcher

Examining the ethical arguments on sex selection through prenatal diagnosis and their implications for social policy is now an urgent task for three reasons: (1) Recent data suggest that physicians in the U.S. and some other nations may comply with prenatal requests for sex selection, (2) advances in genetic knowledge, such as international projects to map the human genome, beg a question whether sex selection is a precedent for direct genetic "tinkering" with human characteristics having little or nothing to do with disease, and (3) preconceptual sex determination may become scientifically reliable in the future. Unfortunately, no studies exist on how often patients actually ask for sex selection by prenatal diagnosis or what physicians actually do in practice. Such studies may be impossible to carry out because patients may mask their real intent. Those who do make direct requests for sex selection tend to be in extreme or unusual situations. Some examples:

Case 1. A couple with four healthy daughters desire a son. They request prenatal diagnosis solely to learn the fetus's sex, in the absence of any medical indications. They tell the doctor that if the fetus is a female they will abort it. Further, they say that if the doctor will not grant their request for prenatal diagnosis they will have an abortion rather than risk having a fifth girl.

Case 2. A couple with three sons in their late teens think their family is completed, but the woman finds herself unexpectedly pregnant at age forty-two. She has always wanted a daughter. Still, the couple is ambivalent; though they are not eager for a fourth child, they are tempted by the possibility of continuing the pregnancy long enough to have prenatal diagnosis, which is medically indicated at the woman's age, finding out the fetus's sex, and then making their decision about abortion.

Case 3. An immigrant woman from an Asian nation where sons are strongly preferred requests prenatal diagnosis for fetal sexing. She already has three daughters and says her husband will divorce her, send her home, and "throw her on the dung heap" if she has another.

Reprinted with permission of the author and the publisher from the *Hastings Center Report*, vol. 19 (May–June 1989), pp. 21–27.

By revealing fetal sex, prenatal diagnosis presents prospective parents with a new and troubling possibility: choosing their children's sex through selective abortion. In contrast to past practice, today doctors are much more willing to comply with such requests. When presented with Case 1, 62 percent in a 1985 survey of 295 United States geneticists said that they would either perform prenatal diagnosis for this couple (34%) or would refer them to someone who would perform it (28%). When asked why, most phrased their answers in terms of respect for patients' autonomy and rights of choice. Many regarded sex choice as a logical extension of parents' rights to control the number, timing, spacing, and quality of their offspring. Others said that as long as abortion is available on demand, it should not be denied for specific purposes. Some clearly regarded themselves as technicians who provided services nonjudgmentally; what patients subsequently did with the information was not their business. Few were swayed by the couple's stated intention to abort if they could not discover the fetus's sex. Most considered this a bluff, or at least not a matter of moral concern for the physician.

Geneticists in some other Western nations are not far behind the United States in willingness to permit prenatal sex selection. Sizeable percents in Hungary (60%), Canada (47%), Sweden (38%), Israel (33%), Brazil (30%), Greece (29%), and the United Kingdom (24%) would either perform prenatal diagnosis for this couple or refer. Hungarian geneticists took the threat of abortion seriously; all who would perform prenatal diagnosis said that they were doing so solely to give the fetus at least a 50 percent chance of survival. Elsewhere patterns of moral reasoning were similar to those in the United States. Few (less than 4%) in any Western nation mentioned social issues such as the place of women in society, maintaining a balanced sex ratio, or limiting the population.

Three other studies, with very different populations and purposes, have asked questions about sex choice and prenatal diagnosis. In 1972–73, only 1 percent of 448 MD/PhDs in genetics polled by Sorenson, most of whom were researchers, said they would "approve the use of amniocentesis to determine the sex of the fetus to satisfy parental curiosity." At the time, clinical genetics, where patients are seen in counseling, was a small enterprise, amniocentesis was unproven and considered risky, and Sorenson's question itself suggested frivolity. In 1975, Fraser and Pressor learned that among 149 clinically oriented genetic counselors, 15 percent would recommend amniocentesis for sex selection or refer in general, while 28 percent indicated they would do so in response to a case where a well-informed couple with one girl wanted to be sure that their final child was a son. In 1988, Evans surveyed members of the Society for Perinatal Obstetricians about selective termination of multiple fetuses, and included a question on their views of abortion for sex choice. Evans found that of the 308 respondents, 10.3 percent agreed that this was morally acceptable in the first trimester of pregnancy and 5.3 percent in the second trimester. Due to differences in method, direct comparison of our study with the Sorenson and Evans surveys is not advisable. Our findings are, however, comparable to those of Fraser and Pressor. Their sample was also clinical, and their study also called for response to a hypothetical case. Apparently, attitudes of clinical geneticists about sex selection are even more tolerant today than in 1975.

What explains this changing moral appraisal of sex selection? In the background is a popular desire for the perfect, tailor-made child, a desire to which medicine has contributed by offering the possibility of control over more and more aspects of pregnancy and birth. For some, control over the child's sex seems a logical extension of other kinds of control and respect for reproductive freedom. Further, the consumer movement in the United States has forced doctors to be more open with patients. Many doctors now regard injecting their moral beliefs into the doctor-patient relationship as paternalistic.

Geneticists are in a peculiarly sensitive position, because giving advice or withholding services leaves them open to accusations of practicing eugenics or acting as the gatekeepers to life. The new fields of medical genetics and genetic counseling that developed after World War II stressed "nondirectiveness," support for patients' decisions, whatever these decisions were, and refusal to "tell patients what to do." Today the stance of nondirectiveness (ethical neutrality) in genetic counseling is ubiquitous. A stated practice of nondirectiveness makes it difficult for some practitioners to refuse a service without appearing judgmental. Nevertheless, few desire to remove all moral values from the doctor-patient relationship. There is something distinctly unnerving in the idea of a doctor as pure technician.

THE ETHICS OF SEX SELECTION

Sex selection through prenatal diagnosis asks us to decide upon the limits to reproductive choice. Mary Anne Warren and other feminist authors have considered some central moral arguments on sex selection.

Warren observes that even in a nonsexist society there would remain a natural desire for a child of one's own sex. This desire is not sexism, but a desire for companionship with which most of us sympathize. Meeting this desire is perhaps the strongest argument for sex selection (except to make a prenatal diagnosis of a sex-linked genetic disease, for example, before there was an exact way to diagnose hemophilia or Duchenne's muscular dystrophy by using DNA techniques). We discuss the companionship motive below.

Warren also examines three claims: first, that sex choice would enhance quality of life more for a child of the "wanted" sex than a child of the "unwanted" sex, second, would provide better quality of life for the family that has the "balance" it desires, and third, a better quality of life for the mother, because she will undergo fewer births to have the desired number of children of each sex. Each of these arguments, however, is premised upon the existence of a sexist society. The perception of "better quality of life" would not be comprehensible except against the background of preferential treatment of one sex (usually the male). To practice sex selection for these reasons, Warren maintains, serves not only to perpetuate a sexist society but further would not, in the context of a sexist society, lead to the desired results.

Warren claims, moreover, that there is no evidence that sex selection would result in a better quality of family life; in fact, there are several ways in which it could worsen it. Sex selection could encourage favored treatment of a child whose sex was deliberately selected by parents and result in neglect of existing children whose sex was determined by nature. Sex selection also may occasion marital conflict about family composition, and, in societies where women possess little power, foreclose their only chance to have a girl.

In addition, improved quality of life for women by sex choice is an illusion. Warren argues on consequentialist grounds that (assuming persons would act on their preferences, if they could) in most societies, sex selection would tend to be used against women. Even in the U.S., where most couples desire to have one child of each sex, there are preferences for boys. Even if the selection were in favor of girls, however, the fact remains that sex selection is inherently sexist because it is premised upon a belief in sexual inequality. We agree with Warren's conclusion that there appear to be no valid arguments for sex selection on the basis of "quality of life."

Another argument to justify sex selection is that it would help to limit the population. Families would not have six girls to have their desired son, for example. But there is no evidence that population trends result from a desire to have sons. Rather, most families try to have the number of children that seems most economically advantageous. If they could select sex, and if one sex presented an economic advantage over the other, some families might actually have more children than they would have had in the absence of sex selection.

The most convincing moral arguments against sex choice, however, would refute the "desire for companionship" argument described above, and show that sex choice would be wrong (except perhaps in one very limited case), based on violations of equality, even were preconceptual methods available. Additional arguments are that sex selection may be held to undermine the most important moral reason that justifies prenatal diagnosis—the prevention of serious and untreatable genetic disease, increase morally unjustifiable abortions and thereby threaten reproductive freedom, and pose a precedent for the abuse of genetic knowledge and preconceptual sex determination in the future.

EQUALITY AND JUSTICE

The President's Commission recommended that geneticists reject sex selection because it violates the principle of equality between females and males. However, the Commission did not provide moral arguments to support its position.

Can reasons be offered for sex preferences that are defensible in terms of serious tests of rationality? Michael Bayles has examined the concerns one might advance for sex preference, including replacing oneself biologically; carrying on the family name; rights of inheritance; pleasures associated with one or the other sex (the "desire for companionship"); or jobs that require either males or females.

Bayles rejects each reason, although he is not responsible for all of the reasoning we present here. The sex of one child does not make her or him anymore "my" child than one of the other sex; genetically, parents contribute equally to each child. Women can carry on the family name. They do so increasingly in the United States by retaining their maiden names, hyphenating their last names, or using the husband's family name only in society's private sector. In almost all nations, males and females are now more equal in the capacity to inherit the estates of parents or others. Any normal pleasure that can be enjoyed with a child of one sex such as sports, vacations, hobbies, games, art, and literature can be enjoyed with a child of the other sex. Few jobs exist that women cannot perform as well as or better than men when performance is the criterion for evaluation. Our analysis does not diminish the power of biologically or culturally based sex preferences, but the desire itself cannot directly be acted upon, especially in deliberate choices about sex selection, without a prior admission that it is irrational to do so.

There may be one real exception to the moral case against sex selection when parents want to reduce the harms of sexism and also desire to balance their family in gender. Suppose a future in which a proven, safe, and inexpensive method of preconceptual sex determination exists. Further, suppose that like most Americans you would use natural sex determination with your first child. Whatever the gender of your first child, by prior agreement with your spouse, for subsequent births you want to use sex determination to balance your family.

We find no moral reasons to condemn the desire to balance gender in families, especially if used by parents who want their children to respect sex-based differences and to learn fairness to the opposite sex by practicing it at home. No intrinsic link exists between sexism and the desire for a balanced family. However, there may be serious considerations against sex determination based on potentially harmful consequences. In a society that condemns abortion for sex choice, wide use of preconceptual sex determination could increase the need to ascertain in pregnancy that the "right gender" was indeed selected, with abortion as an option. Parents with a very strong motive to determine the sex of a second or third child would probably not always accept physicians' claims that methods for sex determination are effective. Secondly, preconceptual sex selection could contribute to gender stereotyping before birth and perpetuate sexism in society. Finally, sex determination could harm the parents themselves. If, after sex determination, a child is born with serious health problems, parents could all too readily blame themselves for contributing to *this* child's suffering by having determined his or her origin in a special way.

Thus, though the desire for balance might be beneficially used by parents in this one instance, we believe that most parents would prefer to limit reproductive freedom to avoid possibly harmful consequences of sex predetermination, even under the best of motives.

MISUSE OF PRENATAL DIAGNOSIS

Societal arguments against using prenatal diagnosis for sex selection include the possibility of unbalancing the sex ratio, diminishing the status of women (assuming that sex preference would be for males), and unbalancing the birth order if, for example, most families acted upon their preference for first-born boys. There is, of course, no real proof that any of these things would happen in Western societies. Although families in Western nations may state sex or birth order preferences when answering a survey, these preferences are slight. It is doubtful that many would go to the length of having trial pregnancies and abortions for the purpose of tailoring their families to fit their survey responses. Unbalancing sex ratios through prenatal diagnosis alone seems a very remote possiblity. Preconceptual sex selection—at present not a reliable option—may be a greater danger.

Use of prenatal diagnosis may also contravene the principle of distributive justice, however. The provision of this service for sex selection is a misuse of costly medical resources. In rural and remote sections of the U.S. prenatal diagnosis is still a scarce resource; and the majority of women for whom prenatal diagnosis is medically indicated on the basis of age (over 35) do not receive it. The use of costly, limited medical resources for nonmedical purposes as long as there are women with medical-genetic indications who need this service, and who cannot afford it, is contrary to our beliefs in fairness.

But suppose there were an abundance of prenatal diagnostic sevices, and public funds or insurance reimbursement to provide unlimited procedures to all who request them. What then? Already some communities in the United States are rapidly approaching the situation where prenatal diagnosis is no longer a "scarce" resource. Under these conditions, some doctors would hesitate to withhold it from almost anyone who asks. Risks to the fetus are now considered so minimal, at least for amniocentesis and chorionic villus sampling, that for many doctors they are not an argument for withholding the service, provided that the parents are informed.

A stronger reason to oppose sex selection by prenatal diagnosis is that, whenever it is done, it undermines the major moral reason that justifies prenatal diagnosis and selective abortion—the prevention of serious and untreatable genetic disease. Gender is not a disease. Prenatal diagnosis for a nonmedical reason makes a mockery of medical ethics. …

KNOWLEDGE AS TEMPTATION

The moral and social arguments seem to weigh heavily against performing prenatal diagnosis solely for sex selection. Direct requests for this information, however, are likely to be few in Western nations. Instead, most moral problems will evolve from the knowledge about sex that is incidental to prenatal diagnosis performed for other purposes. Our second case is likely to be most representative of couples in the United States. This couple is clearly eligible for prenatal diagnosis because of the increased risk of chromosomal abnormalities after age thirty-five. Before prenatal diagnosis was widely available, they could have simply had an abortion. Now they face the tempting possibility of waiting, having prenatal diagnosis for chromosome abnormalities (as early as the eighth week if they use chorionic villus sampling), finding out the fetus's sex, and then making their decision. Three instances known to one of us followed this scenario. In all three, the desired sex was female. In one case, the couple had three boys and the husband wanted no more children. When the wife unexpectedly became pregnant, he threatened to leave her. She wanted the child, whatever the sex, but also wanted to preserve the family. Finally they struck a bargain: if the fetus were female, she would carry it to term, otherwise she would abort. It was a girl, and she continued the pregnancy. In a second case, the family had four sons and severe financial hardships. They did not want a fifth child, but said that they would "try harder" if it were a girl. This couple did not take abortion lightly. When prenatal diagnosis revealed a boy and they had the abortion, they spent a long time holding the fetus afterward and grieving. In the third case, the couple had two teen-aged sons and the wife was tempted to continue her unexpected pregnancy long enough to find out if the fetus was female. Her husband convinced her that sex choice was immoral, and she subsequently had an abortion without learning the fetus's sex. Several years later she believes that this decision, though morally correct, was "wrong" for her, and regrets her lost opportunity of perhaps having a girl.

Some parents may welcome the possibility of making such decisions, but for many it is an unwanted, agonizing choice. They are faced with a decision that may cause moral agony, not so much because they make the "wrong" choice, but because the choice exsists. In William Styron's novel, *Sophie's Choice*, Sophie is forced to decide which of her two children to send to the gas chamber. Her subsequent nightmare is not that she chose the wrong child, but that *she* had to make the *choice*. The possibility of sex selection presents parents with a similar moral nightmare. Most would not seek to have prenatal diagnosis solely for sex selection, but their eligibility for the procedure on other grounds presents a temptation. ...

SOME POSSIBLE SOLUTIONS

... Why not simply withhold information about sex, rather than withholding prenatal diagnosis? This would seem a logical solution to the problem. Sex is not a disease, and it would probably be legal for doctors to withhold the information about gender as clinically irrelevant. This alternative has not yet been put to a legal test. Withholding information of any kind, however, is a very sensitive moral issue. Patients in the United States have become used to asking for full disclosure, and ethicists have tried to educate professionals to convey the "whole truth" to competent patients. Withholding information puts control into the hands of doctors, not patients, and sets a precedent for a resurgence of medical paternalism.

Yet doctors do withhold some types of nonmedical information routinely. In our survey, 96 percent of geneticists said they would not tell a woman's husband that he is not the biological father of her child. Instead, most (83%) would tell the woman alone, so that she could use the information to plan the rest of her reproductive life, and let her decide whether to tell her husband. The decision to withhold information from the husband in the interests of protecting family unity is analogous to withholding other types of "incidental" information learned from genetic testing. ...

PROFESSIONAL RESPONSIBILITY

We hold that a very strong normative case exists against sex selection that transcends cultural boundaries, especially based on claims of equal worth of both sexes and justice in social life. Because of studies that trace the evolution of more openness in physicians' attitudes about sex choice, we believe that it is important that the medical profession take a stand now against sex selection. A posture of ethical neutrality on this issue could lead to unfortunate precedents in moral thinking about future uses of genetic knowledge and preconceptual sex determination. Such neutrality undermines the morality that supports prenatal diagnosis and may encourage legal attacks on morally justified reproductive choices, such as genetic services themselves or abortions to prevent a serious and untreatable genetic disorder. To protect more important reproductive choices, the profession will have to abandon its nonjudgmental stance and offer moral guidance. To fail to do so may encourage third parties, courts, or governments to intervene.

GENETICS AND HUMAN MALLEABILITY

W. French Anderson

Just how much can, and should we change human nature ... by genetic engineering? Our response to that hinges on the answers to three further questions: (1) What *can* we do now? Or more precisely, what *are* we doing now in the area of human genetic engineering? (2) What *will* we be able to do? In other words, what technical advances are we likely to achieve over the next five to ten years? (3) What *should* we do? I will argue that a line can be drawn and should be drawn to use gene transfer only for the treatment of serious disease, and not for any other purpose. Gene transfer should never be undertaken in an attempt to enhance or "improve" human beings.

WHAT CAN WE DO?

In 1980 John Fletcher and I published a paper in the *New England Journal of Medicine* in which we delineated what would be necessary before it would be ethical to carry out human gene therapy. As with any other new therapeutic procedure, the fundamental principle is that it should be determined in advance that the probable benefits outweigh the probable risks. We analyzed the risk-benefit determination for somatic cell gene therapy and proposed three questions that need to have been answered from prior animal experimentation: Can the new gene be inserted stably into the correct target cells? Will the new gene be expressed (that is, function) in the cells at an appropriate level? Will the new gene harm the cell or the animal? These criteria are very similar to those required before use of any new therapeutic procedure, surgical operation, or drug. They simply require that the new treatment should get to the area of disease, correct it, and do more good than harm.

A great deal of scientific progress has occurred in the nine years since that paper was published. The technology does now exist for inserting genes into some types of target cells. The procedure being used is called "retroviral-mediated gene transfer." In brief, a disabled murine retrovirus serves as a delivery vehicle for transporting a gene into a population of cells that have been removed from a patient. The gene-engineered cells are then returned to the patient. ...

Reprinted with permission of the author and of the publisher from *Hastings Center Report*, vol. 20 (January/February 1990), pp. 21–24.

WHAT WILL WE BE ABLE TO DO?

Many genetic diseases that are caused by a defect in a single gene should be treatable, such as ADA deficiency (a severe immune deficiency disease of children), sickle cell anemia, hemophilia, and Gaucher disease. Some types of cancer, viral diseases such as AIDS, and some forms of cardiovascular disease are targets for treatment by gene therapy. In addition, germline gene therapy, that is, the insertion of a gene into the reproductive cells of a patient, will probably be technically possible in the foreseeable future. My position on the ethics of germline gene therapy is published elsewhere.

But successful somatic cell gene therapy also opens the door for enhancement genetic engineering, that is, for supplying a specific characteristic that individuals might want for themselves (somatic cell engineering) or their children (germ-line engineering) which would not involve the treatment of a disease. The most obvious example at the moment would be the insertion of a growth hormone gene into a normal child in the hope that this would make the child grow larger. Should parents be allowed to choose (if the science should ever make it possible) whatever useful characteristics they wish for their children?

WHAT SHOULD WE DO?

A line can and should be drawn between somatic cell gene therapy and enhancement genetic engineering. Our society has repeatedly demonstrated that it can draw a line in biomedical research when necessary. The Belmont Report illustrates how guidelines were formulated to delineate ethical from unethical clinical research and to distinguish clinical research from clinical practice. Our responsibility is to determine how and where to draw lines with respect to genetic engineering.

Somatic cell gene therapy for the treatment of severe disease is considered ethical because it can be supported by the fundamental moral principle of beneficence: It would relieve human suffering. Gene therapy would be, therefore, a moral good. Under what circumstances would human genetic engineering not be a moral good? In the broadest sense, when it detracts from, rather than contributes to, the dignity of man. Whether viewed from a theological perspective or a secular humanist one, the justification for drawing a line is founded on the argument that, beyond the line, human values that our society considers important for the dignity of man would be significantly threatened.

Somatic cell enhancement engineering would threaten important human values in two ways: It could be medically hazardous, in that the risks could exceed the potential benefits and the procedure therefore cause harm. And it would be morally precarious, in that it would require moral decisions our society is not now prepared to make, and it could lead to an increase in inequality and discriminatory practices.

Medicine is a very inexact science. We understand roughly how a simple gene works and that there are many thousands of housekeeping genes, that is, genes that do the job of running a cell. We predict that there are genes which make regulatory messages that are involved in the overall control and regulation of the many housekeeping genes. Yet we have only limited understanding of how a body organ develops into the size and shape it does. We know many things about how the central nervous system works—for example, we are beginning to comprehend how molecules are involved in electric circuits, in memory storage, in transmission of signals. But we are a long way from understanding thought and consciousness. And we are even further from understanding the spiritual side of our existence.

Even though we do not understand how a thinking, loving, interacting organism can be derived from its molecules, we are approaching the time when we can change some of those molecules. Might there be genes that influence the brain's organization or structure or metabolism or circuitry in some way so as to allow abstract thinking, contemplation of good and evil, fear of death, awe of a "God"? What if in our innocent attempts to improve our genetic make-up we alter one or more of those genes? Could we test for the alteration? Certainly not at present. If we caused a problem that would affect the individual or his or her offspring, could we repair the damage? Certainly not at present. Every parent who has several children knows that some babies accept and give more affection than others, in the same environment. Do genes control this? What if these genes were accidentally altered? How would we even know if such a gene were altered?

My concern is that, at this point in the development of our culture's scientific expertise, we might be like the young boy who loves to take things apart. He is bright enough to disassemble a watch, and maybe even bright enough to get it back together again so that it works. But what if he tries to "improve" it? Maybe put on bigger hands so that the time can be read more easily. But if the hands are too heavy for the mechanism, the watch will run slowly, erratically, or not at all. The boy can understand what is visible, but he cannot comprehend the precise engineering calculations that determined exactly how strong each spring should be, why the gears interact in the ways that they do, etc. Attempts on his part to improve the watch will probably only harm it. We are now able to provide a new gene so that a property involved in a human life would be changed, for example, a growth hormone gene. If we were to do so simply because we could, I fear we would be like that young boy who changed the watch's hands. We, too, do not really understand what makes the object we are tinkering with tick.

In summary, it could be harmful to insert a gene into humans. In somatic cell gene therapy for an already existing disease the potential benefits could outweigh the risks. In enhancement engineering, however, the risks would be greater while the benefits would be considerably less clear.

Yet even aside from the medical risks, somatic cell enhancement engineering should not be performed because it would be morally precarious. Let us assume that there were no medical risks at all from somatic cell enhancement engineering. There would still be reasons for objecting to this procedure. To illustrate, let us consider some examples. What if a human gene were cloned that could produce a brain chemical resulting in markedly increased memory capacity in monkeys after gene transfer? Should a person be allowed to receive such a gene on request? Should a pubescent adolescent whose parents are both five feet tall be provided with a growth hormone gene on request? Should a worker who is continually exposed to an industrial toxin receive a gene to give him resistance on his or his employer's request?

These scenarios suggest three problems that would be difficult to resolve: What genes should be provided; who should receive a gene; and, how to prevent discrimination against individuals who do or do not receive a gene.

We allow that it would be ethically appropriate to use somatic cell gene therapy for treatment of serious disease. But what distinguishes a serious disease from a "minor" disease from cultural "discomfort"? What is suffering? What is significant suffering? Does the absence of growth hormone that results in a growth limitation to two feet in height represent a genetic disease? What about a limitation to a height of four feet, to five feet? Each observer might draw the lines between serious disease, minor disease, and genetic variation differently. But all can agree that there are extreme cases that produce significant suffering and premature death. Here then is where an initial line should be drawn for determining what genes should be provided: treatment of serious disease.

If the position is established that only patients suffering from serious diseases are candidates for gene insertion, then the issues of patient selection are no different than in other medical situations: the determination is based on medical need within a supply and demand framework. But if the use of gene transfer extends to allow a normal individual to acquire, for example, a memory-enhancing gene, profound problems would result. On what basis is the decision made to allow one individual to receive the gene but not another? Should it go to those best able to benefit society (the smartest already?) To those most in need (those with low intelligence? But how low? Will enhancing memory help a mentally retarded child?)? To those chosen by a lottery? To those who can afford to pay? As long as our society lacks a significant consensus about these answers, the best way to make equitable decisions in this case should be to base them on the seriousness of the objective medical need, rather than on the personal wishes or resources of an individual.

Discrimination can occur in many forms. If individuals are carriers of a disease (for example, sickle cell anemia), would they be pressured to be treated? Would they have difficulty in obtaining health insurance unless they agreed to be treated? These are ethical issues raised also by genetic screening and by the Human Genome project. But the concerns would become even more troublesome if there were the possibility for "correction" by the use of human genetic engineering.

Finally, we must face the issue of eugenics, the attempt to make hereditary "improvements." The abuse of power that societies have historically demonstrated in the pursuit of eugenic goals is well documented. Might we slide into a new age of eugenic thinking by starting with small "improvements"? It would be difficult, if not impossible, to determine where to draw a line once enhancement engineering had begun. Therefore, gene transfer should be used only for the treatment of serious disease and not for putative improvements.

Our society is comfortable with the use of genetic engineering to treat individuals with serious disease. On medical and ethical grounds we should draw a line excluding any form of enhancement engineering. We should not step over the line that delineates treatment from enhancement.

GERM-LINE GENE THERAPY AND THE MEDICAL IMPERATIVE

Ronald Munson and Lawrence H. Davis

Gene therapy refers to the use of recombinant DNA techniques to treat diseases involving missing or impaired genes. It is still in the experimental stages with only a handful of patients at the National Institutes of Health currently undergoing the therapy. Within this decade, however, two types of gene therapy—gene augmentation and gene modification—are likely to become established modes of treatment (see Verma 1990). Gene augmentation, in which a normal copy of a gene is inserted into a cell to direct the synthesis of a protein that would normally be produced by the missing or defective gene, is the only approach so far attempted in humans. Gene modification, in which an impaired gene is corrected by splicing in a gene at a specific location in the cellular DNA but not otherwise altering the cell's genome, has been demonstrated in several mammalian species. Gene surgery, which involves excising an impaired gene and replacing it with a normal copy, remains a distant—although real—possibility.

Munson, R., and L. Davis. "Germ-Line Gene Therapy and the Medical Imperative." *Kennedy Institute of Ethics Journal* 2:2 (1992): 137–158. © The Johns Hopkins University Press. Reprinted with permission of The Johns Hopkins University Press.

Although even the experimental use of gene therapy is recent, its possibilities have been discussed extensively for more than a decade, and critics have raised a number of objections to it or some aspect of it (President's Commission 1982; OTA 1984; Nichols 1988; Walters 1991). NIH committees overseeing the research and many other observers now approve of somatic cell therapy as long as safeguards needed in any experimental procedure are followed and protocols pass appropriate review. No similar consensus has been reached, however, regarding the application of gene therapy to cells in the germ line—ova, sperm, and cells that give rise to them. This is partly because of the enormous technical difficulties facing germ-line gene therapy. But it is also because germ-line gene therapy strikes many as involving especially difficult moral issues. In this paper we examine the most important of these. We argue that none presents an insurmountable moral obstacle to germ-line gene therapy. To the contrary, we will argue that medicine has a positive duty to proceed with its development.

THE LIMITS AND POSSIBILITIES OF SOMATIC CELL AND GERM-LINE THERAPY

Gene therapy is likely to have the most impact in treating diseases caused by single gene defects, especially autosomal recessive disorders (Nichols 1988; Anderson 1990; Holtzman 1989). This accounts for many conditions, including sickle-cell disease, Tay-Sachs disease, phenylketonuria, and cystic fibrosis. The hundreds of diseases caused by chromosomal disorders (e.g., Down Syndrome) or by an interaction between genes and the environment during fetal development (e.g., neural tube defects) are not obvious prospects. But the estimated 4,000 monogenic diseases cause 7 percent of neonatal deaths, affect 1 percent of newborns, and are responsible for almost 10 percent of childhood deaths. About half of these diseases cause early death, and almost three-quarters of the rest produce severe impairments that make ordinary life virtually impossible (Nichols 1988, p. 9).

The thrust of efforts to find ways to treat these diseases so far has involved somatic cell therapy. Hence, even if the therapy can treat or eliminate a disease from an individual who has inherited a faulty gene, it will do nothing to alter the probability that the person's offspring will inherit the same defective gene. For example, someone with Huntington's disease has a 50–50 chance of passing on the gene causing the disease. Even if somatic cell therapy could eliminate the way the gene is expressed, the 50–50 chance of passing it on would remain.

Alteration of germ-line cells might change this. For dominant conditions, the aim would be to remove the defective gene from a person's gametes (ova or sperm cells) or their precursors, and replace it with one that would function normally. For recessive conditions, it might suffice to insert a gene that would function normally. Or instead of this "gametocyte therapy," the cells of an already-conceived pre-embryo might be similarly treated ("pre-embryo transformation"). Success of either of these forms of germ-line gene therapy would mean that neither the individuals resulting from treated gametes or pre-embryo, nor their progeny, would inherit the disorder (Fowler et al. 1989).

If germ-line gene therapy were possible, practical, and widely employed, hundreds of genetic diseases might be eliminated from families. In each case, it would be possible for the disease to occur again through mutation, but the risk would be no greater than in the population at large, and the total number of cases needing somatic cell or other therapy would be greatly reduced. Horrible diseases like Lesch-Nyhan, PKU, and Tay-Sachs would simply disappear as a nightmarish heritage in certain family lines. ... We would reach the goal described over a decade ago by Joseph Fletcher:

> The ultimate goal of [gene therapy] is not to ameliorate the ills of patients prenatally or postnatally, but to start people off healthy and free

of disease through the practice of medicine preconceptively.... It aims to control people's initial genetic design and constitution—their genotypes—by gene surgery and by genetic design. (1974, p. 56)

MORAL OBJECTIONS TO GERM-LINE GENE THERAPY

Against Fletcher's vision, some argue that there is a morally relevant distinction between somatic and germ-line therapy, and that germ-line therapy is a morally unacceptable means of achieving the goal of eradicating genetic disease.

But what wrong can be alleged about germ-line therapy? Its distinguishing feature is its impact on future generations. (In some cases, somatic cell therapy can also have an effect on future generations, but this is not the aim of the treatment—see Lappé 1991, pp. 623f., 627, 629f.) Somehow, this feature has led to a widespread feeling that the procedure is morally questionable. However, the moral doubts are often only hinted at in a rhetorical fashion and are not carefully articulated. Part of what we want to do here is to state those doubts as clearly and persuasively as we can so that we can lay them to rest definitively.

We think all the doubts about germ-line therapy express the single basic worry that it is illegitimate "tampering." The three lines of objection that have played important roles in the public debate see this as tampering with the rights of individuals, with the social order, and with the order of nature itself. We will present and examine each of these in turn, emphasizing the third. In no case will we find an insurmountable moral barrier to the development and use of germ-line therapy.

1. Germ-Line Therapy and Individual Rights

The Parliamentary Assembly of the Council of Europe (1982b) refers to a person's right to a genome that has not been "tampered" with:

> [The Assembly r]ecommends that the Committee of Ministers: ...
>
> ... provide for explicit recognition in the European Convention on Human Rights of the right to a genetic inheritance which has not been artificially interfered with, except in accordance with certain principles which are recognised as being fully compatible with respect for human rights (as, for example, in the field of therapeutic applications) ...

The basis for this alleged right is none too clear, even if we do not question (as many would) the very idea of a right possessed by as-yet-unconceived individuals. Prior to the passage quoted, the recommendation invokes the "rights to life and to human dignity protected by Articles 2 and 3 of the European Convention on Human Rights," and claims that these "imply" the right to a pristine genetic inheritance. We fail to see the "implication." For philosophers like Kant, human dignity is equated with our dignity as rational beings, and not with the whole of our biological nature as homo sapiens. Thus as rational beings, we are ends in ourselves, and have a right not to be treated as mere means to the ends of others (Kant [1785] 1959, p. 47). This may entail that others ought not to interfere (unjustifiably) with our pursuit of our own legitimate ends. It does not entail that others ought not to have interfered with our chances to have been conceived, say, with genes for hazel eye color. ...

Less dramatically, germ-line therapy involves "tampering" with a person's body, so it may easily infringe on several genuine and important individual rights. Yet all forms of gene therapy—indeed, all forms of therapy—can be viewed as doing this. For example, procedures like coronary-artery bypass surgery could violate a person's autonomy and right not to be subjected to harm or to the risk of harm. We offer protection against such violation and legitimate the "tampering" by requiring the individual's "informed consent." Perhaps this would suffice for germ-line therapy as well.

A critic might object that this is a bad analogy because germ-line therapy can affect the descendants of the recipient, too. As many writers have emphasized, this feature makes it impossible to secure the informed consent of all the individuals affected (see, for example, Fletcher 1983; Lappé 1991).

This is undeniably true. However we are aware of no persuasive reasons for thinking that non-existent potential progeny or members of future generations have (as yet) any autonomy that could be tampered with. So there is nothing to protect by requiring their "informed consent." Thus, we see no point in lamenting the impossibility of our obtaining it.

We are less certain about whether those in this group of potential offspring and descendants have the right not to be harmed or subjected to risk of harm. But we are certain that insofar as they have such rights—or, more simply, insofar as we are obligated not to subject them to harm or (extra) risk of harm—neither the rights nor the obligations are absolute.

Some may claim that even if these rights and obligations are not absolute, they still are strong enough so that in practice, germ-line gene therapy would rarely if ever be permissible. This seems implied by the "Declaration of Inuyama" adopted by the Council for International Organizations of Medical Sciences (CIOMS 1991): "There would have to be confidence that, when treatment affecting future generations is undertaken, descendants of those so treated would still agree with the decision generations later."

Similarly, Berger and Gert (1991, p. 679) would limit germ-line therapy to "cases in which the benefits to the person receiving the initial treatment is [sic] so great that it outweighs the risks not only for him but also for all of his descendants" since "the genetic make-up of an unlimited number of people" is affected. We cannot confidently predict what the conditions of life or people's values will be generations from now, so we cannot confidently predict our remote descendants' agreement with our decisions, nor can we judge precisely about benefits and risks to infinitely many of our descendants, so germ-line gene therapy would rarely if ever meet the requirements set by these statements.

But these statements are too strong. The first seems unduly influenced by the idea of informed consent, which we have already argued is irrelevant in this context. And the second views our actions as more momentous than they probably are. We should bear in mind that a remote future generation may be able to reverse a genetic change we introduce that turns out disadvantageous (Moseley 1991, p. 644). And as several authors have pointed out, we regularly make decisions that we know will affect future generations—including the very decision to have children—without acknowledging requirements as strong as these (Moseley 1991, pp. 642f.; Lappé 1991, p. 631; and cf. Zimmerman 1991, p. 597). It is implausible that this practice is wrong, even if we have not been as responsible as we should be in our actions (including reproduction) affecting future generations. ...

Whatever exactly the rights of offspring and descendants, the promise of good enough consequences—say, the eradication of Lesch-Nyhan disease—could outweigh a sufficiently uncertain threat of harm and justify "tampering" with those rights.

If germ-line therapy involves illegitimate tampering, it is not illegitimate tampering with the rights of those directly affected or their descendants. ...

2. Germ-Line Therapy as "Playing God"

The novel feature of germ-line therapy is that by it we modify the very genetic structure that as-yet-unconceived individuals are to have. This seems both more serious and potentially more sinister than any other medical therapies or public health measures. An individual's genetic structure, after all, determines the kind of being an individual will be, apart from and prior to the influence of both the biological and social environment. It determines whether the creature that develops is a bird or a beaver, a horse or a human. Hence, changing the genetic makeup of germ cells is tampering with the very order of nature. In the popular phrase, it is "playing God."

As rhetorically effective as this phrase may be in encouraging a negative attitude toward germ-line therapy, it is not at all clear just what is wrong with "playing God" in this particular way. Three attempts to explain are worth considering. (See also the President's Commission's 1982 report, *Splicing Life*, pp. 53–60.)

a. Germ-Line Therapy as a Prelude to Eugenics Some argue that what begins as genetic "tampering" aimed at obliterating disease will lead to positive eugenics—"tampering" aimed at improving our children and the whole of humanity. As our understanding of the genetic basis of socially desirable traits like musical talent, mathematical insight, and athletic skill increases, we will be able to engineer human beings to meet our specifications. But trying to do this would be wrong (apart from the questions of fair distribution already mentioned) because, as Paul Ramsey (1970, p. 124) puts it, "Man [is not] wise enough to make himself a successful self-modifying system or wise enough to begin doctoring the species." (See also Anderson 1989.)

At least two problems weaken the force of this objection. First, the objection is only to genetic modification in the service of positive eugenics. Even if Ramsey is right about our lacking the wisdom to turn ourselves into a "self-modifying system," it does not follow that there is anything intrinsically wrong with employing germ-line therapy to eliminate diseases. And as for the worry that negative eugenics will lead to positive eugenics, we may note that the potential for practicing positive eugenics has been with us at least since the time we recognized that there is a connection between the traits of offspring and those of their parents. We have resisted virtually all efforts and proposals to make use of selective breeding to shape the human species to satisfy an articulated ideal (Ludmerer 1972). Perhaps our experience with attempts at eugenics fits the description that Mauron and Thévoz give of the whole history of bioethical issues:

> [T]he slippery slope really looks more like a ramshackle staircase: once in a while, we trip down a few steps. This makes us wake up, take stock of ethical shortcomings and climb up the stairs by appropriate measures such as societal regulation. (1991, p. 658)

While it is true that germ-line engineering offers an easier and more effective way to exert control over the human gene pool, we have no reason to suppose that just because we possessed the technology we would employ it. It is simply not true that as a society we have always done whatever it is possible to do. ...

Our second problem for Ramsey, then, is that it is not obvious that we lack the wisdom to "doctor" ourselves in the manner indicated. In truth, we do not yet know whether we have it or not. After we have had experience modifying the genome of other organisms and predicting the outcome, when we have learned the possible drawbacks and the chances of success in modifications performed on humans, then perhaps we can judge our wisdom. We can imagine ways of making ourselves better than we are now, but the unanswered questions concern how much and what kinds of risk we will be willing to take and what sort of price we will be willing to pay to improve ourselves. These questions cannot be answered usefully in a vacuum. (For other discussion of the acceptability of positive eugenics, see Mauron and Thévoz 1991, pp. 651–52.)

b. Germ-Line Therapy and Unpredictable Losses Even if gene therapy remains confined to therapeutic applications, some raise the question "whether something important may be lost as disease genes are eliminated" (Cavalieri 1983, p. 473). On one interpretation, this worry is illustrated by the following sort of case. Suppose we are successful in eliminating sickle-cell disease from the human population by removing the disease causing gene and substituting a gene producing normal red blood cells. As it happens, those with sickle-cell trait (i.e., those who are heterozygous for the gene) are more resistant to falciparum malaria. Hence, if we eliminated the gene, we would also be eliminating the potential benefits its possession bestows.

The objection takes it for granted that eliminating this potential benefit would be obviously wrong. Yet what it fails to consider is that, since we know about the connection between sickle-cell disease and resistance to malaria, we might decide that eliminating a lethal disease like sickle-cell is worth the loss of a relative immunity to malaria. This would be a reasonable decision, especially since we have effective ways of controlling and treating malaria, but lack adequate treatments for sickle-cell disease.

However, a critic might ask, "How many other connections might there be between diseases and important biological capacities that we don't even realize we have but would be lost forever if we rushed to eradicate the diseases by germ-line therapy?" It would be better not to "tamper" with something whose full significance we cannot hope to appreciate in advance.

Critics who invoke the hazard of an unforeseen disaster cannot be satisfied completely. No one can guarantee that an unexpected hazard might not result from germ-line gene therapy. However, we are not totally ignorant of the nature of genes and of the evolutionary process, and there is no reason to fear that germ-line therapy is more likely to produce an unanticipated disaster than is somatic cell therapy or any other use of recombinant DNA technology. These matters must be assessed in individual cases on the basis of acquired knowledge and experience. When the potential benefits of germ-line therapy are considered, rejecting its use on the basis of potential but unknown hazards is not justifiable. ...

MEDICINE AND THE THERAPEUTIC IMPERATIVE

We wish now to go beyond the moral legitimacy of this therapy and argue—still on the assumptions noted—that medicine itself has a prima facie duty to pursue and employ germ-line gene therapy. Sometimes, a certain course of action is morally right, although no one has an obligation to take it. For example, it would be right for physicians to work one day a month without fees in community clinics, but they have no moral duty to do so, either individually or collectively. However, in contrast, we want to claim that members of the medical professions would be collectively derelict if research aimed at the therapeutic use of germ-line gene therapy were neglected without good reason.

We should stress that our claim is only for the existence of a collective obligation, a duty falling on medicine as an enterprise. Very likely, if we are right and our assumptions are correct, then this collective obligation will entail some individual obligations on specific persons or groups of persons. But without a detailed examination of the structure, membership, and existing practices of the medical enterprise, these individual obligations cannot be determined. For a somewhat parallel example, suppose it were argued that the American people had a collective obligation to provide shelter for its homeless; exactly which members of the "American people" had precisely which specific obligations toward this end would be a matter for a wholly different argument, depending on the structure and existing practices of our governmental and other bodies, and many other factors. We shall not attempt this "wholly different argument" for the case of medicine, and so shall not say how the collective obligation differentially affects physicians, medical researchers, public health officials, and others affiliated with the medical enterprise. Our interest is rather in the prima facie duty itself, and its basis in the nature of medicine.

Many assume unreflectively that medicine is a science, and many also think that science is "value-neutral" in some sense. These views may lead one to conclude that "medicine" cannot have any duty at all, prima facie or actual. At most, individual physicians or researchers have obligations to heal or develop therapies because of general moral principles, such as beneficence. (The arguments of Zimmerman (1991, p. 591) and Fletcher and Anderson (1992) may be read this way.) We believe that medicine itself has an obligation.

We escape the reasoning of the preceding paragraph by denying that medicine is a science. (For a detailed defense of this position, see Munson 1981.) We begin our argument by contrasting medicine with science in the respect most relevant here, the idea of what it is most concerned with. …

Medicine, like science, pursues knowledge, but not in a disinterested way. Indeed, it is antithetical to the character of medicine as an enterprise to seek knowledge as an inherent or self-justifying good. Medicine's concern with knowledge is unequivocally instrumental or conditional. Medicine is joined so closely with science in inquiry and experiment, because it is by means of scientific understanding that medicine can most effectively secure its end of promoting human health.

Not all aspects of medicine involve the basic theories and concepts of the natural sciences. Clinical medicine, in particular, involves complicated human interactions, and part of the "art" of medicine involves "taking care" of patients without the guidance of established theories and proven rules. Nevertheless, science is one of contemporary medicine's major means of working to promote the welfare of patients as a population.

An enterprise is successful when it achieves its aims. Loosely speaking, science does its job when it provides persuasive reasons for accepting empirical theories about the nature and character of the world. The success of medicine cannot be judged by any comparable epistemic criterion. Rather, the basic standard of evaluation must be practical or instrumental success with respect to its specific aim.

In seeking to meet health needs, medicine can be described as a quest for control over the factors affecting health. Understanding (knowledge) is important to medicine because it leads to control. Yet where understanding is lacking, medicine will seek control by relying on low-level empirical rules validated by practical success.

A consequence of medicine's aim of meeting health needs is that medicine possesses a therapeutic obligation imposed by its own character. That is, basic to medicine as an enterprise is the prima facie duty to treat those who are ill in ways that will help them achieve the degree of health of which they are capable.

Treatment by drugs or surgery, diet or exercise, is one way in which medicine exercises control over disease, but the therapeutic obligation can also be regarded as involving an obligation to prevent the occurrence of disease. Although the success of a treatment might be most dramatic, preventing a disease altogether might be seen as the most effective form of control. Medicine aims at promoting human health by exercising control over disease, and since elimination is the most effective form of control, elimination of disease is the ultimate aim of medicine.

The eradication of smallpox from the world's population exemplifies the realization of this aim in a particular instance. The elimination of the disease was announced by the World Health Organization in 1979, and certainly the disappearance of the disease is to be preferred over all forms of therapy, no matter how effective. To our knowledge, no one argued that it would be morally wrong to eradicate smallpox through vaccination and other public health measures.

What is true of infectious diseases like smallpox is, of course, also true of genetic diseases. Somatic cell therapy promises to become a valuable means of controlling them and minimizing the suffering they cause. Once again, however, complete control would go beyond prevention or effective treatment in individual cases.

Germ-line gene therapy offers us the chance to rid ourselves completely (except for new mutations) of many serious genetic diseases for which there is no effective treatment. Given medicine's aim of seeing to the health of people and its instrumental character, it is this ideal that medicine is obligated to pursue. Social circumstances (such as a lack of resources to conduct research) and unavoidable difficulties (such as not being able to solve the technical problems of safely and effectively altering sex cells) may make the road leading to germ-line gene therapy a long one. Nevertheless, the prima facie duty to pursue this ideal remains.

CONCLUSION

The more than 4,000 genetic diseases involving a defect in a single gene cause thousands of deaths, an incalculable amount of suffering, and staggering economic costs. We have shown that the objections most often raised to germ-line gene therapy are not so persuasive as to stand in the way of using it to treat diseases. And we have shown that the character of medicine imposes on medical professionals a prima facie duty to pursue the development and use of germ-line gene therapy.

The diseases are so serious and the promise of the therapy so great, that it would be wrong to give in to the objections that have been raised to gene therapy. If they are allowed to prevail, then the social and scientific support needed to realize the therapeutic possibilities of gene therapy may never materialize. This outcome would be as wrong and almost as serious as if we had failed to develop and use antibiotics or vaccines.

References

Anderson, W. French. 1989. Human Gene Therapy: Why Draw a Line? *The Journal of Medicine and Philosophy* 14:681–93.

———. 1990. Genetics and Human Malleability. *Hastings Center Report* 20 (1):21–24.

Aslanidis, C., Jansen, G., Amemiya, C., et al. 1992. Cloning of the Essential Myotonic Dystrophy Region and Mapping of the Putative Defect. *Nature* 355:548–49.

Berger, Edward M., and Gert, Bernard M. 1991. Genetic Disorders and the Ethical Status of Germ-line Gene Therapy. *The Journal of Medicine and Philosophy* 16:667–83.

Buxton, J., Shelbourne, P., Davies, J., et al. 1992. Detection of an Unstable Fragment of DNA Specific to Individuals with Myotonic Dystrophy. *Nature* 355:547–48.

Cavalieri, Liebe F. 1983. Testimony at a Hearing before the Subcommittee and Oversight of the Committee on Science and Technology, U.S. House of Representatives, 16–18 November 1982. In *Human Genetic Engineering*, Committee Print No. 170, pp. 470–76. Washington, DC: U.S. Government Printing Office.

Chalmers, Alan. 1990. *Science and Its Fabrication*. Minneapolis: University of Minnesota Press.

CIOMS [Council for International Organizations of Medical Sciences]. 1991. *Human Genome Mapping, Genetic Screening and Gene Therapy: Ethical Issues. Proceedings o f the XXIVth CIOMS Conference: Human Genome Mapping, Genetic Screening and Therapy*, ed. Z. Bankowski and A. M. Capron. Geneva.

Cook-Deegan, Robert Mullan. 1990. Human Gene Therapy and Congress. *Human Gene Therapy* 1:163–70.

Council of Europe, Parliamentary Assembly. 1982a. Report on genetic engineering presented by the Legal Affairs Committee, J.P. Elmquist rapporteur. Document 4832 of the 33rd Ordinary Session, 18 January. Strasbourg, France.

———1982b. Recommendation 934 "On genetic engineering." Strasbourg, France.

———1986. Recommendation 1046 "On the use of human embryos. ..." Strasbourg, France.

———1989. Recommendation 1100 "On the use of human embryos. ..." Strasbourg, France.

Culver, Charles C., and Gert, Bernard M. 1982. *Philosophy in Medicine*. New York: Oxford University Press.

Fletcher, John C. 1983. Moral Problems and Ethical Issues in Prospective Human Gene Therapy. *Virginia Law Review* 69:538–40.

Fletcher, John C., and Anderson, W. French. 1992. Germ-Line Gene Therapy: A New Stage of Debate. *Law, Medicine, and Health Care* 20 (1–2), forthcoming.

Fletcher, Joseph. 1974. *The Ethics of Genetic Control*. New York: Doubleday.

Fowler, Gregory, Juengst, Eric T., and Zimmerman, Burke K. 1989. Germ-line Gene Therapy and the Clinical Ethos of Medical Genetics. *Theoretical Medicine* 10:151–65.

Harley, H. G., Brook, J. D., Rundle, S. A., et al. 1992. Expansion of an Unstable DNA Region and Phenotypic Variation in Myotonic Dystrophy. *Nature* 355:545–46.

Harsanyi, Zsolt. 1983. Testimony at a Hearing before the Subcommittee and. Oversight of the Committee on Science and Technology, U.S. House of Representatives, 16–18 November 1982. In *Human Genetic Engineering*, Committee Print No. 170, pp. 221–33. Washington, DC: U.S. Government Printing Office.

Holtzman, Neil A. 1989. *Proceed with Caution*. Baltimore, MD: The Johns Hopkins University Press.

Kant, Immanuel. [1785] 1959. *Foundations of the Metaphysics of Morals*. Trans. Lewis White Beck. Indianapolis: The Bobbs Merrill Company, Inc.

Kass, Leon. 1972. New Beginnings in Life. In *The New Genetics*, ed. Michael Hamilton, pp. 15–63. Grand Rapids, MI: Eerdmans.

Krimsky, Sheldon. 1990. Human Gene Therapy: Must We Know Where to Stop before We Start? *Human Gene Therapy* 1:171–73.

Lappé, Marc. 1991. Ethical Issues in Manipulating the Human Germ Line. *The Journal of Medicine and Philosophy* 16:621–39.

Laudan, Larry. 1990. Normative Naturalism. *Philosophy of Science* 57:44–59.

Lavitrano, M., Camaiano, A., Fazio, V., et al. 1989. Sperm Cells as Vectors for Introducing Foreign DNA into Eggs: Genetic Transformation of Mice. *Cell* 57:717–23.

Leenen, H. J. J. 1988. Genetic Manipulation with Human Beings. *Medicine and Law* 7:71–79.

Ludmerer, Kenneth M. 1972. *Genetics and American Society: A Historical Appraisal*. Baltimore, MD: The Johns Hopkins University Press.

Mathieu, Deborah. 1991. *Preventing Prenatal Harm: Should the State Intervene?* Dordrecht, Holland: Kluwer Academic Publishers.

Mauron, Alex, and Thévoz, Jean-Marie. 1991. Germ-line Engineering: A Few European Voices. *The Journal of Medicine and Philosophy* 16:649–66.

Moseley, Ray. 1991. Commentary: Maintaining the Somatic/Germ-line Distinction: Some Ethical, Drawbacks. *The Journal of Medicine and Philosophy* 16:641–47.

Munson, Ronald. 1981. Why Medicine Cannot Be a Science. *The Journal of Medicine and Philosophy* 6:183–208.

Munson, Ronald, Albert, Daniel A., and Resnick, Michael D. 1988. *Reasoning in Medicine*. Baltimore: The Johns Hopkins University Press.

Nichols, Eve K. 1988. *Human Gene Therapy*. Cambridge, MA: Harvard University Press.

OTA. 1984. *Human Gene Therapy—A Background Paper*. Washington, DC: Office of Technology Assessment.

President's Commission for the Study of Ethical Problems in Medicine and Biomedical and Behavioral Research. 1982. *Splicing Life: A Report on the Social and Ethical Issues of Genetic Engineering with Human Beings*. Washington, DC: U.S. Government Printing Office.

Purdy, L. M. 1988. Genetic Diseases: Can Having Children Be Immoral? In *Intervention and Reflection: Basic Issues in Medical Ethics*, ed. Ronald Munson, pp. 364–71. Belmont, CA: Wadsworth Publishing Co.

Ramsey, Paul. 1970. *Fabricated Man*. New Haven, CT: Yale University Press.

Rosenberg, Alexander. 1990. Normative Naturalism and the Role of Philosophy. *Philosophy of Science* 57:34–43.

Walters, LeRoy. 1991. Human Gene Therapy: Ethics and Public Policy. *Human Gene Therapy* 2:115–22.

Verma, Inder M. 1990. Gene Therapy. *Scientific American* 172:68–72.

Zimmerman, Burke K. 1991. Human Germ-line Therapy: The Case for Its Development and Use. *The Journal of Medicine and Philosophy* 16:593–612.

GENETICS AND THE MORAL MISSION OF HEALTH INSURANCE

Thomas H. Murray

All men are created equal. So reads one of the United States of America's founding political documents. This stirring affirmation of equality was not meant as a claim that all people are equivalent in all respects. Surely the drafters of the Declaration of Independence and the Constitution were as aware then as we are now of the wondrous variety of humankind. People differ in their appearance, their talents, and their character, among other things, and those differences matter enormously.

The commitment to equality embodied in our political tradition is not a claim that people, in fact, are indistinguishable from one another. Rather it is an assertion that before this government, this system of laws and courts, all persons are to be given equal standing, and all persons must be treated with equal regard.

Human genetics, in contrast, is a *science of inequality*—a study of human particularity and difference. One of the most difficult challenges facing us in the coming flood tide of genetic information is how to assimilate these evidences of human differences without undermining our commitment to political, legal, and moral equality.

The information about human differences pouring forth from the science of human genetics provides us with a multitude of opportunities to treat people differently according to some aspect of their genetic makeup. Deciding which uses of this information are just and which are unjust will require us to reexamine the ethical significance of a wide variety of human differences and the larger social purposes of a variety of institutions, among them health, life, and other forms of insurance.

Health insurance in the United States has moved from a system based mostly on community rating where, in a given community, all people pay comparable rates, to a system where the cost to the purchasers of insurance is based on the expected claims—a risk- or experienced-based system. This movement has significant ethical as well as economic overtones. Community rating was a system that reflected a notion of community responsibility for providing health care for its members, where the qualifying principle was community membership. Other differences, such as preexisting risks, did not count as morally relevant distinctions. Risk- and experience-based systems presume that it is fair to charge different prices, or to refuse to insure people entirely, if they will need expensive health care. Such systems treat predicted need for care as a morally relevant difference among persons that justifies differential access to health insurance, and through it, to health care. But this presumes precisely what is in question: what are good moral reasons for treating people differently with respect to access to health insurance and health care? ...

GENETICS AND DISTRIBUTIVE JUSTICE

Distributive justice, as the term implies, concerns the distribution of social goods or ills: in its simplest formulation it holds that like cases are to be treated alike and unlike cases are to be treated differently. All depends, obviously, on how we fill in the material conditions of this purely formal statement of comparative justice. When we are asking about a particular occasion of just or unjust treatment, the question commonly takes the form, What makes these

Reprinted with permission of the author and publisher from the *Hastings Center Report*, vol. 22 (November-December 1992), pp. 12–17.

cases like or unlike in a morally relevant way? Failure to state a morally relevant reason for treating people differently opens one to the charge that one's action was arbitrary, capricious, and unjust.

Human genetics provides a large and rapidly growing set of differences among persons that may be used to try to justify unequal treatment. For many genetic differences and many distributions of social goods, the moral relevance of the difference seems transparently obvious. Height, for example, is largely determined by genetics. Does it make any sense to say that it was unfair to allow Kareem Abdul Jabaar to play center in the National Basketball Association for many years, but not me, just because he is taller than I am, and our differences in height are genetic, rather than anything we can claim credit for accomplishing? Most people would judge that to be absurd. In this instance a genetic difference—height—constitutes a morally relevant difference that justifies treating people differently. That same difference, however, would not justify treating us differently if, for example, we were accused of a crime, or being judged on our literary accomplishments, or in need of health care. ...

Having health insurance is away to pay for ... treatment—the cost of treating a serious illness can easily exceed an average family's ability to pay for it. Health insurance is, for most people, the means to the end of health care. It is not the good of health care itself. But to the extent that it determines who does and who does not have access to care, and who has the peace of mind that comes with knowing that if care is needed it will be available, access to health insurance is a matter of justice.

GENETIC TESTING: THE CHALLENGE FOR HEALTH INSURANCE

Research in human genetics, such as the Genome Project, is likely to increase dramatically our ability to predict whether individuals are at risk for particular diseases. There are tests currently offered for diseases such as Huntington's, where the presence of the gene assures that the individual will develop the disease if he or she lives long enough. There are tests for carrier status such as cystic fibrosis where two copies of the defective gene—one from each parent—must be inherited in order for symptomatic disease to occur. And there will be tests for diseases of complex etiology such as heart disease, cancer, stroke, lung disease, and the like. For certain relatively rare genes there will be a strong connection between having the gene and having the disease. Yet most of the common killing and disabling diseases are more likely to have a complex variety of causes, including perhaps several genes each of which has some predictive relationship with the disease. These risk-oriented genetic predictors potentially are very interesting to employers and insurers.

Genetic information, in fact, is used now by insurers. There may be considerable genetic information in one's medical record. If your policy is being individually underwritten, that entire record can be copied and shipped to the prospective insurer and that information used to justify increasing the price or denying health insurance altogether. But this begs a prior question: should information about genetic differences be used at all in health insurance?

One argument against paying any special attention to genetic predictors of risk is that insurers already use risk predictors that have genetic components. Coronary artery disease is an example. It is well known that people with higher levels of cholesterol, especially the low-density-lipoprotein component, are at higher risk of coronary artery disease and subsequent heart attacks. It also seems clear that an individual's cholesterol level is at least in part determined by genetics. Variations in individual metabolism can have a substantial impact on a person's cholesterol level, such that two people can be equally virtuous (or careless) in diet and exercise and yet have very different cholesterol levels, and, presumably, very different risks for coronary artery disease and heart attack.

In time it is likely that researchers will discover a number of genes that affect cholesterol metabolism and, presumably, cholesterol level, arterial disease, and the risk of a heart attack. We may be able to construct a genetic profile of an individual's risk of heart disease. Does such a predictive index differ in any ethically significant way from today's cholesterol test, which has not evoked similar objections?

Genetic tests differ from a cholesterol test in that the latter, even if significantly influenced by genetics, is still in some measure under the individual's control. The risk of heart attack is affected by a variety of health-related behaviors including diet, exercise, stress, and smoking. To the extent that people can be held responsible for their behavior, their cholesterol level is something for which they have some responsibility. On the other hand, people cannot be said to be responsible for their genes. An old maxim in ethics is "Ought implies can." You should not be held morally accountable for that which you were powerless to influence.

Genetic tests may also have more direct distributional consequences. Alleles occur in different frequencies in different ethnic groups; it would not be surprising to find that an allele associated with an epidemiologically significant disease such as coronary artery disease was more prevalent in some ethnic groups than in others. Alpha-1 antitrypsin deficiency, associated with lung disease, appears to be more common among people of Scandinavian ancestry. If the group in which the allele occurs more often was not historically a target of discrimination, we might not be particularly concerned. If, however, the allele was more common in a group that continues to suffer discrimination, such as sickle-cell trait in people of African descent, we would have good reason for concern. The mere fact that genetic predictors have the potential to affect differentially ethnic groups that experience discrimination does not uniquely distinguish them from other risk predictors. Hypertension, for example, is more prevalent among Americans of African heritage. But the immediate and direct tie between genetics and ethnicity may make genetic testing a more blatant use of a potentially explosive and discriminatory social classification scheme.

A third response to the claim that we need not worry about genetic risk testing because it is essentially similar to things like cholesterol testing is to question the premise that people know about the genetic component of cholesterol. Discussions of cholesterol in the media emphasize the things people can do to lower it. Reminders that cholesterol level is also significantly affected by genetics appear less frequently, and it may well be that most people are unaware that cholesterol level has a substantial genetic component. If people did understand that, perhaps they would be less tolerant of the widespread use of cholesterol testing to determine insurance eligibility, precisely because it was to that extent outside of individuals' control.

There is yet another possibility: that the central notion underlying commercial health insurance underwriting—the greater the likelihood of illness, the more one should pay for coverage—is morally unsound.

ACTUARIAL FAIRNESS

Insurers take a particular view of fairness: actuarial fairness. Actuarial fairness claims that "policyholders with the same expected risk of loss should be treated equally. ... An insurance company has the responsibility to treat all its policyholders fairly by establishing premiums at a level consistent with the risk represented by each individual policyholder." This definition of fairness begs the question: Why should we count differences in risk of disease as an ethically relevant justification for treating people differently in their access to health insurance and health care?

Actuarial fairness does have a realm of application in which it seems reasonable. Call it the Lloyds of London model: if two oil tanker companies ask to have their cargoes and vessels insured, one for a trip up the Atlantic to a U.S.

port, the other for a voyage through the Arabian Gulf during the height of the war in Kuwait and Iraq, the owner of the first ship would cry foul if she were charged the same extraordinarily high rate as the owner of the second. Most of us, I suspect, would agree that charging the two owners the same rate would be unfair. What makes it so?

For one thing, the two ships are exposed to vastly different risks, and it seems only fair to charge them accordingly. (The process of assessing risks is called underwriting.) Furthermore, the risks were assumed voluntarily. Third, the goal of both owners is profit, and it seems reasonable to ask them to bear the expense of voluntarily assumed risks. We could also ask how commercial insurance divides up the world. In this hypothetical it divides it into those who prefer prudent business ventures and those willing to take great risks. That does not seem to be an objectionable way to parse the world for the purpose of insuring oil tankers.

In practice, insurers do not behave as if actuarial fairness were an iron-clad moral rule. Valid predictors may not be used for a variety of reasons, typically having to do with other notions of fairness—for example, not discriminating on the basis of race, sex, class, or locale, even though these characteristics are related to the likelihood of insurance claims. Deborah Stone, who has studied insurance practices for HIV infection, dismisses the idea of actuarial fairness and argues instead that:

> insurability is the set of policy decisions by insurers about whom to accept. It is not a trait, but a concept of *membership*. ... Treated as a scientific fact about individuals, the notion of insurability disguises fundamentally political decisions about membership in a community of mutual responsibility.

UNDERWRITING AND THE SOCIAL PURPOSES OF INSURANCE

The threat genetic testing poses to the future of insurance for health-related risks—including health, life, and disability insurance—compels us to reexamine the social purposes served by insurance. Two points are obvious: first, that different types of insurance can have different purposes; and second, that the purpose of a particular form of insurance must be understood within its social context.

Life insurance, for example, is meant to provide financial security for one's dependents in the event that one dies. In the contemporary United States we must evaluate the role of such insurance in the context of a not particularly generous social welfare system that would otherwise leave the surviving dependents of a deceased breadwinner in very poor financial condition. The typical purchaser is an individual with one or more dependents who are unlikely to become financially independent in the immediate future. The benefits from life insurance are intended to tide survivors over until they can become financially self-sufficient, or live out their lives decently; they are not meant to provide windfalls to friends of the deceased. To the extent that life insurance is perceived as serving a need rather than being merely a commodity, we are likely to regard it as something that ought to be available to all. Our public policies toward life insurance suggest we view it otherwise, however. We prohibit certain actuarially valid distinctions such as ethnicity in setting life insurance rates. But we do not require that all persons, whatever their age, employment, or health, be permitted to buy life insurance at identical prices or at all. In consequence, the financial dependents of a person unable to obtain life insurance may suffer devastating changes in their life prospects if the principal earner dies.

Does the Lloyds of London model fit health care? Despite the current enthusiasm for tying voluntary behavior to health, most illness and disability is neither chosen nor in any sense "deserved," distinguishing it from the risks of shipping oil in a war zone. Neither is the goal of health care for those who seek it profit. Daniels argues that "justice requires that we protect *fair equality of opportunity* for individuals in a society." Reasonable access to health care in the contemporary United States is a necessary condition for fair equality of opportunity to pursue other goods that life affords. The social purpose of health insurance, understood in this way, is to provide access to the health care that people need to have a fair opportunity in life.

Lastly, how does underwriting in health insurance divide the world? It sets off the well from the ill and those likely to become ill. For insurers, the concept of actuarial fairness provides a rationale for charging much higher rates or declining to insure persons with a substantial possibility of illness or disability, reasoning that such persons should bear the costs associated with their particular risks. Persons at risk could find it difficult to obtain insurance at affordable rates, or at all. ...

IMPLICATIONS FOR POLICY

The era of predictive genetic testing coincides with a period of grave public concern about health care. ... There is little doubt that the current ragged system of private and public programs, with its many holes and frayed edges, must be changed. The conviction that health care ought to be available to those who need it seems to be widely shared. That conviction, together with a growing sense that the current patchwork is failing, may be strong enough to overcome the citizenry's hesitations about government inefficiency. Indeed, it seems likely that private health insurance would not have survived this long if not for government intervention. Tax subsidies for employer-sponsored health insurance programs amounted to $39.5 billion in 1991. In addition, we provide direct government coverage for the health needs of people that commercial insurers want to avoid: Medicare, for those much more likely to need health care; and Medicaid, for some of those unable to pay for their own insurance.

Public programs such as Medicare and Medicaid tell us something important about our moral convictions on health care. They suggest that we are not content to allow the old and the poor simply to languish without access to care. Had we not passed such legislation, we well might have overturned or radically restructured the existing system of commercial health insurance decades ago.

There are good reasons to doubt that actuarial fairness is an adequate description of genuine fairness in health insurance. It may be a sufficient principle for commercial insurance against losses of ships at sea, but even a brief inquiry into the social purpose of health insurance suggests that apportioning by risks, as actuarial fairness dictates, fails to accomplish the primary social goals of health insurance. Genetic tests, like other predictors of the need for health care, are not good reasons for treating people differently with respect to access to health insurance.

GENETIC INFORMATION, HEALTH INSURANCE, AND RAWLSIAN JUSTICE

Robert F. Card

I

Philosophical questions arising from the Human Genome Project are not completely novel: they raise traditional issues in social and political philosophy as well as pressing questions in medical ethics, since properly addressing these questions is central to building a just society. The question I shall focus on in this paper is the following: does using genetic information for decisions about insurance coverage and insurance premiums constitute a form of morally unacceptable *discrimination*? In order to answer this question, we must address the larger issue of whether the use of genetic information bases decisions upon an arbitrary and unjust basis, and to do this, we must invoke moral and social/political philosophy.

I will argue that using genetic information to determine insurance premiums and eligibility is an unjust practice by applying a Rawlsian theory of justice to this issue. We will begin by looking at two arguments for positions on opposite ends of the continuum on this issue.

II

Insurance company advocates present two main arguments in support of their claim to *full disclosure* to all genetic information (I understand genetic information to be, minimally, the results of tests on DNA and RNA, and related gene testing.) These arguments appear, for instance, in the American Council of Life Insurance and Health Insurance Association of America's (ACLI-HIAA) Task Force on Genetic Testing (1991). First, they argue that it is only fair to treat those with significant genetic risks differently, since if this is not done, healthier policyholders are unfairly "taxed" by policyholders with less favorable genetic prospects. Second, insurance companies argue that there should be full disclosure of genetic test results since individuals who possess detailed knowledge of their genetic inheritance could use this private information to engage in "adverse selection" to exploit insurance companies. Essentially, adverse selection occurs when a person who possesses a high risk for genetic disease purchases extra health insurance in light of this guarded information, and when those who have low risks for serious genetic disease minimize their coverage on this basis. The claim is that if the consumer acts on information not available to insurance companies, this is unfair since it would have a devastating effect on insurance markets.

On the opposite side of the debate, philosopher Thomas Murray (1992) believes that the insurers' argument is fundamentally mistaken, and argues that insurance companies should have *no access* to genetic information. He supports his position by arguing that the model of actuarial fairness upon which insurance is based is not fair when applied in this context, since it can result in an unjust form of "double-jeopardy." For instance, LDL cholesterol levels are used as a determinant for risk of heart disease, yet one's LDL cholesterol is partly determined by genetics. Two persons who are equally careful with respect to diet and exercise can have significantly different chances for heart disease. Utilizing test results for genetic disorders that are out of one's control will add to the existing unfairness already experienced by those who have come up short in the genetic lottery. Murray's conclusion is that the model of actuarial fairness *is* fair with respect to voluntarily assumed, risky behavior, but is not fair when used in the insurance industry, since much of the risk associated with illness is not voluntarily assumed.

I think that the guiding ideas in Murray's discussion point in the right direction, yet he does not explicitly provide a solid philosophical foundation for these ideas. In addition, I do not believe these guiding ideas imply that insurance companies can *never* underwrite on the basis of genetic information. First, I will briefly criticize both the insurers' and Murray's position, and then develop the guiding ideas just suggested.

III

The insurers' position is burdened with a number of serious difficulties. To clarify, their claim could simply include *full disclosure of genetic test results on tests by ordered by the patient*, or could suggest *mandatory testing requirements* for insurance eligibility. If insurance companies wish to support mandatory genetic testing, the fact that persons have an average of five recessive genes for genetic disease would seem to suggest that all persons are bad risks (Munson 1996, Chapter 7). At the very least, insurance rates would likely increase making insurance unaffordable to many more persons.

In addition, exacting economic costs on the basis of genetic risk is analogous to punishing persons before they commit a crime. Even if we could accurately predict who was more likely to have (e.g.) criminal tendencies, this would not justify incarcerating them or otherwise punishing them before they had broken the law. Since genetic risk is a probabilistic concept, only if one believes in a strict form of genetic determinism would the imposition of such economic penalties by insurance companies be justified. However, given the importance of environmental influences, belief in such genetic determinism is unfounded (Kitcher 1996, Sober 2000). This is obvious enough: a predisposition to heart disease does not ultimately control how one's life will go, since a person with this predisposition could escape the disease by making intelligent choices with regard to exercise and diet or could simply die in an auto accident.

If insurance companies instead lay claim to results from genetic tests ordered by the patient, it is unclear why they are entitled to *full disclosure* of such test results. Insurers attempt to justify this belief by appealing to the possibility of adverse selection, yet a simple example illustrates that the possibility of adverse selection does not support a claim to full disclosure. A person with a family history of Huntington's disease may order a genetic test for herself, or for her fetus via amniocentesis, only out of an interest in this disease. Even if we suppose that the mother's test is negative, genetic tests may uncover other unfortunate aspects of her genetics inheritance. If the test is administered to the fetus and is negative, other genetic risk factors for the fetus could be revealed. If full disclosure includes revealing these other unfortunate aspects, then full disclosure may lead to increased premiums when the insurance company learns of these other genetic risk factors. However, if only the negative test results regarding the gene for Huntington's are disclosed to the patient by the genetic counselor, it is unjust to increase this person's insurance premiums on the basis of other factors which are discovered, since she has no *knowledge* of these other genetic risk factors. Only those troubling aspects of one's genetic inheritance which one *knows* can be used to engage in adverse selection.

Murray's argument has difficulties as well. Murray's general principle is that if one's genetic risk factors and medical condition are not in that person's control, then it is not fair to economically penalize that person for these factors. Call this the *Control Principle*. I find this principle compelling. The main problem with Murray's application of this principle, though, is that it does not properly acknowledge the phenomena of adverse selection. While insurance companies make too much of adverse selection, Murray's position does not take the possibility of adverse selection seriously enough. If insurance companies can never have access to genetic information, then if consumers are aware of certain genetic risk factors and act on the basis of this asymmetric information, this unfairly puts insurance companies in peril.

What is the precise reason why we should adopt this principle? The next task will be to develop and qualify the Control Principle; I will do this by grounding its philosophical foundations in a Rawlsian theory of justice.

IV

On John Rawls' social/political theory, the vision of a just society is one which is governed by principles that persons choose from an impartial standpoint. Impartiality is attained by adopting a frame of mind, called the Original Position, in which we are put behind a veil of ignorance which deprives us of many crucial facts about ourselves (eg., social position, natural assets and abilities, intelligence, strength, particular conception of the good life, etc.). The goal in the Original Position is for the representatives to come to agreement on the principles of justice. One may think that since the representatives know so little about themselves, it would be impossible for them to arrive at such an agreement.

To address this concern, Rawls introduces the notion of "primary goods," those goods which every rational person is presumed to want whatever else he or she wants. To decide which conception of justice is most to their advantage, the representatives assume that they prefer more rather than less primary goods, since these are useful in advancing all rational plans of life. Primary goods fall into two basic types: social primary goods and natural primary goods (1971, 62). Examples of social primary goods include basic rights and liberties, powers and opportunities, income and wealth, and the social bases of self-respect. Other primary goods such as health, vigor, intelligence, and imagination are considered to be natural primary goods.

Earlier, we addressed the "adverse selection" argument. The Rawlsian position will address the objection that policyholders with less favorable genetic prospects unjustly "tax" their more fortunate policyholders, and will help us to locate a defensible moderate position between the two extremes of the insurers' argument and Murray's position. There are four main points which need to be examined to develop a Rawlsian approach to controlling genetic information in relation to health insurance.

1. The social purpose of health insurance is intimately tied to the fact that health is a natural primary good.

Adequate health is necessary for fulfilling every person's goals. It is undeniable that one's genetic makeup affects one's health in some ways, even if we avoid belief in genetic determinism. Health is a particularly interesting natural primary good since while it cannot itself be literally distributed by the basic structure of society, the necessary conditions of good health can (such as competent medical care, pharmaceuticals, etc.). The possession of this natural good is tied much more closely to the level of social primary goods enjoyed than the other natural primary goods (vigor, intelligence, and imagination). On a Rawlsian theory, citizens are to be given an equal *index* of primary goods, meaning that they are given the *all-purpose means* to actually utilize their liberties in order to frame and pursue what they value in life.

2. In the Original Position, representatives would not approve a principle which disadvantages those with unfavorable genetic prospects.

We can gain insight regarding this point if we understand Rawls' principles of justice. There are two principles which Rawls believes the parties in the Original Position will ratify, (1) the Liberty Principle and (2) the Difference Principle, and these are as follows:

> (1) Each person is to have an equal right to the most extensive total system of equal basic liberties compatible with a similar system of liberties for all, and (2) social and economic inequalities are to be arranged so that they are both: (a) to the greatest benefit of the least advantaged, consistent with the just savings principle, and (b) are attached to offices and positions open to all under conditions of fair equality of opportunity (1971, 302).

Principle (1) is given priority over (2), and part (b) of the second principle is prior to part (a), which is called the *Difference Principle.*

Rawls reasons that the parties in the Original Position will be very conservative in their decisions, given the constraints on information imposed on them. This suggests they will not support institutional policies regarding health insurance which economically favor persons with better genetic prospects, just as they will not support polices which favor men over women, or Caucasians over African-Americans. The reason is simple: each representative is assumed to be self-interested, and by supporting such a policy one may be hurting oneself, since he or she may be a member of the disfavored class. A Rawlsian theory should explicitly exclude knowledge of one's genetic makeup as well, since such information undermines the assumption that the representatives in the Original Position will choose from an impartial perspective in which persons are represented as equals. Genetic advantage and disadvantage is a natural asset which affects the relative bargaining position of persons, and therefore should not be known by the parties to ensure that the decision in the Original Position is fair.

3. Adopting a principle which economically penalizes those with unfavorable genetic prospects undermines the primary good of self-respect, and hence does not recognize persons as free and equal citizens.

Rawls (1971, 440) believes that self-respect is perhaps the most important primary good. This is the case since on a Rawlsian view, a person is happy if she is in the process of successfully executing a rational plan of life under favorable conditions, and possessing self-respect is necessary for having such a plan. Without it one will not feel that her plans are worthwhile and will lack the confidence to believe that these plans are attainable. Since having a rational plan of life is crucial for happiness and self-respect makes viable rational plans possible, self-respect is an all-important primary good.

Some (Kass 1973) argue that using genetic information to make distinctions between persons constitutes an attack on human dignity and will create a genetic underclass. The true worry here is that a whole class of persons will internalize negative judgments regarding their potential, and will see themselves as incapable of fulfilling their rational plans of life because of their genetic makeup. Persons who have self-respect will rationally wish to live only in a society in which they are treated as free and equal citizens. Supporting a policy which allows the use of genetic information for health insurance purposes contradicts the public recognition of persons as equal citizens and sacrifices fair equality of opportunity, thereby undermining self-respect, and hence is not allowable in a just society.

4. The Rawlsian "Control Principle" does not support using genetic information to determine health insurance premiums and eligibility.

The Rawlsian Control Principle says that in a just society, principles determining or affecting the distribution of primary goods should not be based upon factors that are not within citizens' control. This principle is implicit in Rawls' theory, and it must be qualified. Rawls' clearest discussion bearing on the Control Principle occurs when he discusses how differential natural assets are handled on his theory of justice as fairness. Rawls directly criticizes conceptions of equality on which "... the strength of men's claims is directly influenced by the distribution of natural abilities, and therefore by contingencies that are arbitrary from the moral point of view" (1971, 510–511). For Rawls, the special advantages a person receives by using their natural assets are to be governed by the Difference Principle.

Rawls clearly rejects views of political equality on which persons may reap the benefits of their natural talents without any questions of fairness arising. These persons have not done anything to allow them the full benefits which result from the exercise of these capacities. A corollary to this principle suggests that for Rawls, questions of fairness would arise if persons who were disadvantaged with regard to natural abilities were economically penalized. The reason for this is that the factors which are used to determine the economic disadvantages are not in their control; they have done nothing to deserve these penalties. I suggest that one's genetic makeup is a plausible example of a natural talent in the sense in which Rawls uses this term. It is the ultimate inherent or natural asset of the body, and on a Rawlsian theory of justice, the benefits which accrue to individuals with fortunate genetic prospects would be distributed through the basic structure of society in accordance with the Difference Principle. Redistributing these benefits would allow individuals with less fortunate genetic prospects to avoid economic penalties arising from higher insurance premiums.

In a just society, the desire for low insurance premiums does not trump the principles which determine or affect a fair distribution of primary goods. This is especially true when the distribution of the primary good is affected by accidents of natural endowment, and hence are out of persons' control, as is the case with one's genetic makeup. For this reason, the objection that less healthy policyholders unjustly "tax" healthier policyholders fails.

One may object that given the argument in this paper, it also follows that health insurers cannot use family history in determining eligibility and premiums, and this is an absurd implication since it places unfair burdens on insurers. There are two things to consider in response. First, does this implication follow? Second, if so, is this implication absurd?

To address the first question, I will simply accept that the similarities between using the results of genetic testing on DNA and RNA and family history are sufficiently compelling. Hence, I accept for the sake of argument that use of family history is prohibited in a fair process of insurance decision-making.

Is this implication absurd? It may seem absurd since it violates common practice. However, we are engaged in a normative enterprise which can question familiar practices; for instance, as discussed earlier, the common use of LDL cholesterol levels in insurance decisions is not above moral scrutiny. I maintain that the use of family history is even more unfair than utilizing the results of genetic testing on the insured person, since using family history is like utilizing a secondhand report on one's genes. It is analogous to using circumstantial evidence, while genetic testing is analogous to using an eyewitness report. While genetic testing of the individual is a more accurate predictor than family history, as I have argued, its use is severely limited in a just society. Especially given the fact that many genetic risk factors for disease are transmitted from parent to child via recessive genes, family history is an even more unreliable indicator of unfavorable genetic prospects and the risk of actual illness, and hence results in unfair decisions regarding health insurance eligibility and premiums.

If family history and genetic testing cannot be used, then what *can* be used to determine eligibility and premiums? If insurance companies must charge everyone the same premiums, without being able to use actuarial methods to properly price risk, one could object that this is unfair to insurance companies. On my view, it need not be the case that insurance companies charge every person the same premiums in a just society. According to the argument contained in this paper, they could in principle modify premiums on the basis of factors that are within a person's control. These factors include engaging in risky behaviors (e.g., smoking cigarettes) or not engaging in healthy behaviors (e.g., not regularly exercising). These points rebut the objection that my position places unfair restrictions on insurance companies.

To sum up, a Rawlsian position on the use of genetic information for health insurance purposes is a moderate position that avoids the problems associated with both of the extreme positions. It avoids the difficulties stemming from adverse selection by allowing genetic information to be used in determining eligibility and insurance premiums only when the individual has specific knowledge of a significant genetic risk factor, say, by being given this information from a counselor after having a genetic test performed. It does not support the claim that information should be subject to *full disclosure* to insurance companies, nor that it should *never* be disclosed. This conclusion is plausible given a proper understanding of adequate health as a natural primary good, health insurance as a necessary means for protecting and implementing persons' rational plans of life, and the lack of control that persons have over their genetic prospects.

Bibliography

American Council of Life Insurance and Health Insurance Association of America (ACLI-HIAA) 1991. Report of the ALCI-HIAA Task Force on Genetic Testing. In Levine 1999, 208–214.

Buchanan, A., Brock, D., Daniels, N., and Wikler, D. 2000. *From Chance to Choice.* (Cambridge: Cambridge University Press).

Kass, L. 1973. "Implications of Prenatal Diagnosis for the Right to Life." Reprinted in Mappes and DeGrazia 1996, pp. 488–492.

Kitcher, P. 1996. *The Lives to Come.* (New York: Touchstone/Simon and Schuster).

Levine, C. (ed.) 1999. *Taking Sides: Clashing Views on Controversial Bioethical Issues.* Eighth Edition. (Guilford, CT: Dushkin/McGraw-Hill).

Mappes, T., and DeGrazia, D. 1996. *Biomedical Ethics.* (New York: McGraw-Hill).

Munson, R. 1996. *Intervention and Reflection: Basic Issues in Medical Ethics.* Fifth Edition. (Belmont, CA: Wadsworth Publishing).

Murray 1992. "Genetics and the Moral Mission of Health Insurance." *Hastings Center Report.* (November/December), 215–220. Reprinted in Levine 1999.

Rawls 1971. *A Theory of Justice.* (Cambridge: Belknap Press).

Sober, E. 2000. "The Meaning of Genetic Causation." Appendix One in Buchanan, A., Brock, D., Daniels, N., and Wikler, D. 2000.

HUMAN CLONING AND THE CHALLENGE OF REGULATION

John A. Robertson

The birth of Dolly, the sheep cloned from a mammary cell of an adult ewe, has initiated a public debate about human cloning. Although cloning of humans may never be clinically feasible, discussion of the ethical, legal, and social issues raised is important. Cloning is just one of several techniques potentially available to select, control, or alter the genome of offspring.[1–3] The development of such technology poses an important social challenge: how to ensure that the technology is used to enhance, rather than limit, individual freedom and welfare.

A key ethical question is whether a responsible couple, interested in rearing healthy offspring biologically related to them, might ethically choose to use cloning (or other genetic-selection techniques) for that purpose. The answer should take into account the benefits sought through the use of the techniques and any potential harm to offspring or to other interests.

The most likely uses of cloning would be far removed from the bizarre or horrific scenarios that initially dominated media coverage.[4] Theoretically, cloning would enable rich or powerful persons to clone themselves several times over, and commercial entrepreneurs might hire women to bear clones of sports or entertainment celebrities to be sold to others to rear. But current reproductive techniques can also be abused, and existing laws against selling children would apply to those created by cloning.

There is no reason to think that the ability to clone humans will cause many people to turn to cloning when other methods of reproduction would enable them to have healthy children. Cloning a human being by somatic-cell nuclear transfer, for example, would require a consenting person as a source of DNA, eggs to be enucleated and then fused with the DNA, a

---

Robertson, John A. "Human Cloning and the Challenge of Regulation." From *The New England Journal of Medicine,* 339:119–122, 1998.

woman who would carry and deliver the child, and a person or couple to raise the child. Given this reality, cloning is most likely to be sought by couples who, because of infertility, a high risk of severe genetic disease, or other factors, cannot or do not wish to conceive a child.

Several plausible scenarios can be imagined. Rather than use sperm, egg, or embryo from anonymous donors, couples who are infertile as a result of gametic insufficiency might choose to clone one of the partners. If the husband were the source of the DNA and the wife provided the egg that received the nuclear transfer and then gestated the fetus, they would have a child biologically related to each of them and would not need to rely on anonymous gamete or embryo donation. Of course, many infertile couples might still prefer gamete or embryo donation or adoption. But there is nothing inherently wrong in wishing to be biologically related to one's children, even when this goal cannot be achieved through sexual reproduction.

A second plausible application would be for a couple at high risk of having offspring with a genetic disease.[5] Couples in this situation must now choose whether to risk the birth of an affected child, to undergo prenatal or preimplantation diagnosis and abortion or the discarding of embryos, to accept gamete donation, to seek adoption, or to remain childless. If cloning were available, however, some couples, in line with prevailing concepts of kinship, family, and parenting, might strongly prefer to clone one of themselves or another family member. Alternatively, if they already had a healthy child, they might choose to use cloning to create a later-born twin of that child. In the more distant future, it is even possible that the child whose DNA was replicated would not have been born healthy but would have been made healthy by gene therapy after birth.

A third application relates to obtaining tissue or organs for transplantation. A child who needed an organ or tissue transplant might lack a medically suitable donor. Couples in this situation have sometimes conceived a child coitally in the hope that he or she would have the correct tissue type to serve, for example, as a bone marrow donor for an older sibling.[6–7] If the child's disease was not genetic, a couple might prefer to clone the affected child to be sure that the tissue would match.

It might eventually be possible to procure suitable tissue or organs by cloning the source DNA only to the point at which stem cells or other material might be obtained for transplantation, thus avoiding the need to bring a child into the world for the sake of obtaining tissue.[8] Cloning a person's cells up to the embryo stage might provide a source of stem cells or tissue for the person cloned. Cloning might also be used to enable a couple to clone a dead or dying child so as to have that child live on in some closely related form, to obtain sufficient numbers of embryos for transfer and pregnancy, or to eliminate mitochondrial disease.[5]

Most, if not all, of the potential uses of cloning are controversial, usually because of the explicit copying of the genome. As the National Bioethics Advisory Commission noted, in addition to concern about physical safety and eugenics, somatic-cell cloning raises issues of the individuality, autonomy, objectification, and kinship of the resulting children.[5] In other instances, such as the production of embryos to serve as tissue banks, the ethical issue is the sacrifice of embryos created solely for that purpose.

Given the wide leeway now granted couples to use assisted reproduction and prenatal genetic selection in forming families, cloning should not be rejected in all circumstances as unethical or illegitimate. The manipulation of embryos and the use of gamete donors and surrogates are increasingly common. Most fetuses conceived in the United States and Western Europe are now screened for genetic or chromosomal anomalies. Before conception, screening to identify carriers of genetic diseases is widespread.[9] Such practices also deviate from conventional notions of reproduction, kinship, and medical treatment of infertility, yet they are widely accepted.

Despite the similarity of cloning to current practices, however, the dissimilarities should not be overlooked. The aim of most other forms of assisted reproduction is the birth of a child who is a descendant of at least one member of the couple, not an identical twin. Most genetic selection acts negatively to identify and screen out unwanted traits such as genetic disease, not positively to choose or replicate the genome as in somatic-cell cloning.[3] It is not clear, however, why a child's relation to his or her rearing parents must always be that of sexually reproduced descendant when such a relationship is not possible because of infertility or other factors. Indeed, in gamete donation and adoption, although sexual reproduction is involved, a full descendant relation between the child and both rearing parents is lacking. Nor should the difference between negative and positive means of selecting children determine the ethical or social acceptability of cloning or other techniques. In both situations, a deliberate choice is made so that a child is born with one genome rather than another or is not born at all.

Is cloning sufficiently similar to current assisted-reproduction and genetic-selection practices to be treated similarly as a presumptively protected exercise of family or reproductive liberty?[10] Couples who request cloning in the situations I have described are seeking to rear healthy children with whom they will have a genetic or biologic tie, just as couples who conceive their children sexually do. Whether described as "replication" or as "reproduction," the resort to cloning is similar enough in purpose and effects to other reproduction and genetic-selection practices that it should be treated similarly. Therefore, a couple should be free to choose cloning unless there are compelling reasons for thinking that this would create harm that the other procedures would not cause.[10]

The concern of the National Bioethics Advisory Commission about the welfare of the clone reflects two types of fear. The first is that a child with the same nuclear DNA as another person, who is thus that person's later-born identical twin, will be so severely harmed by the identity of nuclear DNA between them that it is morally preferable, if not obligatory, that the child not be born at all.[5] In this the case the fear is that the later-born twin will lack individuality or the freedom to create his or her own identity because of confusion or expectations caused by having the same DNA as another person.[5,11]

This claim does not withstand the close scrutiny that should precede interference with a couple's freedom to bear and rear biologically related children.[10] Having the same genome as another person is not in itself harmful, as widespread experience with monozygotic twins shows. Being a twin does not deny either twin his or her individuality or freedom, and twins often have a special intimacy or closeness that few non-twin siblings can experience.[12] There is no reason to think that being a later-born identical twin resulting from cloning would change the overall assessment of being a twin.

Differences in mitochondria and the uterine and childhood environment will undercut problems of similarity and minimize the risk of overidentification with the first twin. A clone of Smith may look like Smith, but he or she will not be Smith and will lack many of Smith's phenotypic characteristics. The effects of having similar DNA will also depend on the length of time before the second twin is born, on whether the twins are raised together, on whether they are informed that they are genetic twins, on whether other people are so informed, on the beliefs that the rearing parents have about genetic influence on behavior, and on other factors. Haying a previously born twin might in some circumstances also prove to be a source of support or intimacy for the later-born child.

The risk that parents or the child will overly identify the child with the DNA source also seems surmountable. Would the child invariably be expected to match the phenotypic characteristics of the DNA source, thus denying the second twin an "open future" and the freedom to develop his or her own identity?[5,11,13] In response to this question, one must ask whether couples who choose to clone offspring are more likely to want a child who is a mere replica of the DNA source or a child who is unique and valued for more than his or her genes. Couples may use cloning in order to ensure that the biologic child they rear is healthy, to maintain a family connection in the face of gametic infertility, or to obtain matched tissue for transplantation and yet still be responsibly committed to the welfare of their child, including his or her separate identity and interests and right to develop as he or she chooses.

The second type of fear is that parents who choose their child's genome through somatic-cell cloning will view the child as a commodity or an object to serve their own ends.[5] We do not view children born through coital or assisted reproduction as "mere means" just because people reproduce in order to have company in old age, to fulfill what they see as God's will, to prove their virility, to have heirs, to save a relationship, or to serve other selfish purposes.[14] What counts is how a child is treated after birth. Self-interested motives for having children do not prevent parents from loving children for themselves once they are born.

The use of cloning to form families in the situations I have described, though closely related to currrent assisted-reproduction and genetic-selection practices, does offer unique variations. The novelty of the relation—cloning in lieu of sperm donation, for example, produces a later-born identical twin raised by the older twin and his spouse—will create special psychological and social challenges. Can these challenges be successfully met, so that cloning produces net good for families and society? Given the largely positive experience with assisted-reproduction techniques that initially appeared frightening, cautious optimism is justified. We should be able to develop procedures and guidelines for cloning that will allow us to obtain its benefits while minimizing its problems and dangers.

In the light of these considerations, I would argue that a ban on privately funded cloning research is unjustified and likely to hamper important types of research.[8] A permanent ban on the cloning of human beings, as advocated by the Council of Europe and proposed in Congress, is also unjustified.[15,16] A more limited ban—whether for 5 years, as proposed by the National Bioethics Advisory Commission and enacted in California, or for 10 years, as in the bill of Senator Dianne Feinstein (D-Calif.) and Senator Edward M. Kennedy (D-Mass.) that is now before Congress—is also open to question.[5,17,18] Given the early state of cloning science and the widely shared view that the transfer of cloned embryos to the uterus before the safety and efficacy of the procedure has been established is unethical, few responsible physicians are likely to offer human cloning in the near future.[5] Nor are profit-motivated entrepreneurs, such as Richard Seed, likely to have many customers for their cloning services until the safety of the procedure is demonstrated.[19] A ban on human cloning for a limited period would thus serve largely symbolic purposes. Symbolic legislation, however, often has substantial costs.[20,21] A government-imposed prohibition on privately funded cloning, even for a limited period, should not be enacted unless there is a compelling need. Such a need has not been demonstrated.

Rather than seek to prohibit all uses of human cloning, we should focus our attention on ensuring that cloning is done well. No physician or couple should embark on cloning without careful thought about the novel relational issues and child-rearing responsibilities that will ensue. We need regulations or guidelines to ensure safety and efficacy, fully informed consent and counseling for the couple, the consent of any person who may provide DNA, guarantees of parental rights and duties, and a limit on the number of clones from any single source.[10] It may also be important to restrict cloning to situations where there is a strong likelihood that the couple or individual initiating the procedure will also rear the resulting child. This principle will encourage a stable parenting situation and minimize the chance that cloning entrepreneurs will create clones to be sold to others.[22] As our experience grows, some restrictions on who may serve as a source of DNA for cloning (for example, a ban on cloning one's parents) may also be defensible.[10]

Cloning is important because it is the first of several positive means of genetic selection that may be sought by families seeking to have and rear healthy, biologically related offspring. In the future, mitochondrial transplantation, germ-line gene therapy, genetic enhancement, and other forms of prenatal genetic alteration may be possible.[3, 23, 24] With each new technique, as with cloning, the key question will be whether it serves important health, reproductive, or family needs and whether its benefits outweigh any likely harm. Cloning illustrates the principle that when legitimate uses of a technique are likely, regulatory policy should avoid prohibition and focus on ensuring that the technique is used responsibly for the good of those directly involved. As genetic knowledge continues to grow, the challenge of regulation will occupy us for some time to come.

References

1. Silver, L.M. *Remaking Eden: Cloning and Beyond in a Brave New World*. New York: Avon Books, 1997.
2. Walters, L., Palmer, J.G. *The Ethics of Human Gene Therapy*. New York: Oxford University Press, 1997.
3. Robertson, J.A. "Genetic selection of offspring characteristics." *Boston Univ Law Rev* 1996;76: 421–82.
4. Begley, S. "Can we clone humans?" *Newsweek*. March 10, 1997: 53–60.
5. Cloning human beings: report and recommendations of the National Bioethics Advisory Commission. Rockville, Md.: National Bioethics Advisory Commission, June 1997.
6. Robertson, J.A. *Children of Choice: Freedom and the New Reproductive Technologies*. Princeton, N.J.: Princeton University Press, 1994.
7. Kearney, W., Caplan, A.L. "Parity for the donation of bone marrow: ethical and policy considerations." In: Blank, R.H., Bonnicksen, A.L., eds. *Emerging Issues in Biomedical Policy: An Annual Review*. Vol. 1. New York: Columbia University Press, 1992: 262–85.
8. Kassirer, J.P., Rosenthal, N.A. "Should human cloning research be off limits?" *N Engl J Med* 1998; 338:905–6.
9. Holtzman, N.A. *Proceed with Caution: Predicting Genetic Risks in the Recombinant DNA Era*. Baltimore: Johns Hopkins University Press, 1989.
10. Robertson, J.A. "Liberty, identity, and human cloning." *Texas Law Rev* 1998; 77:1371–456.
11. Davis, D.S. "What's wrong with cloning?" *Jurimetrics* 1997; 38:83–9.
12. Segal, N.L. "Behavioral aspects of intergenerational human cloning: what twins tell us." *Jurimetrics* 1997; 38:57–68.
13. Jonas, H. *Philosophical Essays: From Ancient Creed to Technological Man*. Englewood Cliffs, N.J.: Prentice-Hall, 1974: 161.
14. Heyd, D. *Genethics: Moral Issues in the Creation of People*. Berkeley: University of California Press, 1992.
15. Council of Europe. Draft additional protocol to the Convention on Human Rights and Biomedicine on the prohibition of cloning human beings with explanatory report and Parliamentary Assembly opinion (adopted September 22, 1997). XXXVI International Legal Materials 1415 (1997).
16. Human Cloning Prohibition Act, H. R. 923, S.1601 (March 5, 1997).
17. Act of Oct. 4, 1997, ch. 688, 1997 Cal. Legis. Serv. 3790 (West, WESTLAW through 1997 Sess.).
18. Prohibition on Cloning of Human Beings Act, S. 1602, 105th Cong. (1998).
19. Stolberg, S.G. "A small spark ignites debate on laws on cloning humans." *New York Times*. January 19, 1998: A1.
20. Gusfield, J. *Symbolic Crusade: Status Politics and the American Temperance Movement*. Urbana: University of Illinois Press, 1963.

21. Wolf, S.M. "Ban cloning? Why NBAC is wrong." *Hastings Cent Rep* 1997; 27(5):12.
22. Wilson, J.Q. "The paradox of cloning." *The Weekly Standard*. May 26, 1997: 23–7.
23. Zhang, J., Grifo, J., Blaszczyk, A. et al. "In vitro maturation of human preovulatory oocytes reconstructed by germinal vesicle transfer." *Fertil Steril* 1997; 68: Suppl:Sl. abstract.
24. Bonnicksen, A.L. "Transplanting nuclei between human eggs: implications for germ-line genetics." *Politics and the Life Sciences*. March 1998: 3–10.

WHY WE SHOULD BAN HUMAN CLONING

George J. Annas

In February the U.S. Senate voted 54 to 42 against bringing an anticloning bill directly to the floor for a vote.[1] During the debate, more than 16 scientific and medical organizations, including the American Society of Reproductive Medicine and the Federation of American Societies for Experimental Biology, and 27 Nobel prize–winning scientists, agreed that there should be a moratorium on the creation of a human being by somatic nuclear transplants. What the groups objected to was legislation that went beyond this prohibition to include cloning human cells, genes, and tissues. An alternative proposal was introduced by Senator Edward M. Kennedy (D-Mass.) and Senator Dianne Feinstein (D-Calif) and modeled on a 1997 proposal by President Bill Clinton and his National Bioethics Advisory Commission. It would, in line with the views of all of these scientific groups, outlaw attempts to produce a child but permit all other forms of cloning research.[2, 3] Because the issue is intimately involved with research with embryos and abortion politics, in many ways the congressional debates over human cloning are a replay of past debates on fetal-tissue transplants[4] and research using human embryos.[5] Nonetheless, the virtually unanimous scientific consensus on the advisability of a legislative ban or voluntary moratorium on the attempt to create a human child by cloning justifies deeper discussion of the issue than it has received so far.

It has been more than a year since embryologist Ian Wilmut and his colleagues announced to the world that they had cloned a sheep.[6] No one has yet duplicated their work, raising serious questions about whether Dolly the sheep was cloned from a stem cell or a fetal cell, rather than a fully differentiated cell.[7] For my purposes, the success or failure of Wilmut's experiment is not the issue. Public attention to somatic-cell nuclear cloning presents an opportunity to consider the broader issues of public regulation of human research and the meaning of human reproduction.

CLONING AND IMAGINATION

In the 1970s, human cloning was a centerpiece issue in bioethical debates in the United States.[8, 9] In 1978, a House committee held a hearing on human cloning in response to the publication of David Rorvik's *In His Image: The Cloning of a Man*.[10] All the scientists who testified assured the committee that the supposed account of the cloning of a human being was fictional and that the techniques described in the book could not work. The chief point the scientists wanted to make, however, was that they did not want any laws enacted that might affect their research.

Annas, George J. "Why We Should Ban Human Cloning." From *The New England Journal of Medicine*, 339:122–125, 1998.

In the words of one, "There is no need for any form of regulation, and it could only in the long run have a harmful effect."[11] The book was an elaborate fable, but it presented a valuable opportunity to discuss the ethical implications of cloning. The failure to see it as a fable was a failure of imagination. We normally do not look to novels for scientific knowledge, but they provide more: insights into life itself.[12]

This failure of imagination has been witnessed repeatedly, most recently in 1997, when President Clinton asked the National Bioethics Advisory Commission to make recommendations about human cloning. Although acknowledging in their report that human cloning has always seemed the stuff of science fiction rather than science, the group did not commission any background papers on how fiction informs the debate. Even a cursory reading of books like Aldous Huxley's *Brave New World*, Ira Levin's *The Boys from Brazil*, and Fay Weldon's *The Cloning of Joanna May*, for example, would have saved much time and needless debate. Literary treatments of cloning inform us that cloning is an evolutionary dead end that can only replicate what already exists but cannot improve it; that exact replication of a human is not possible; that cloning is not inherently about infertile couples or twins, but about a technique that can produce an indefinite number of genetic duplicates; that clones must be accorded the same human rights as persons that we grant any other human; and that personal identity, human dignity, and parental responsibility are at the core of the debate about human cloning.

We might also have gained a better appreciation of our responsibilities to our children had we examined fiction more closely. The reporter who described Wilmut as "Dolly's laboratory father,"[13] for example, probably could not have done a better job of conjuring up images of Mary Shelley's *Frankenstein* if he had tried. Frankenstein was also his creature's father and god; the creature told him, "I ought to be thy Adam." As in the case of Dolly, the "spark of life" was infused into the creature by an electric current. Shelley's great novel explores virtually all the noncommercial elements of today's debate.

The naming of the world's first cloned mammal also has great significance. The sole survivor of 277 cloned embryos (or "fused couplets"), the clone could have been named after its sequence in this group (for example, C-137), but this would only have emphasized its character as a laboratory product. In stark contrast, the name Dolly (provided for the public and not used in the scientific report in *Nature*, in which she is identified as 6LL3) suggests a unique individual. Victor Frankenstein, of course, never named his creature, thereby repudiating any parental responsibility. The creature himself evolved into a monster when he was rejected not only by Frankenstein, but by society as well. Naming the world's first mammal clone Dolly was meant to distance her from the Frankenstein myth both by making her something she is not (a doll) and by accepting "parental" responsibility for her.

Unlike Shelley's world, the future envisioned in Huxley's *Brave New World*, in which all humans are created by cloning through embryo splitting and conditioned to join a specified worker group, was always unlikely. There are much more efficient ways of creating killers or terrorists (or even soldiers and workers) than through cloning. Physical and psychological conditioning can turn teenagers into terrorists in a matter of months, so there is no need to wait 18 to 20 years for the clones to grow up and be trained themselves. Cloning has no real military or paramilitary uses. Even clones of Adolf Hitler would have been very different people because they would have grown up in a radically altered world environment.

CLONING AND REPRODUCTION

Even though virtually all scientists oppose it, a minority of free-marketers and bioethicists have suggested that there might nonetheless be some good reasons to clone a human. But virtually all these suggestions themselves expose the central problem of cloning: the devaluing of persons by depriving them of their uniqueness. One common example suggested is cloning a dying or recently deceased child if this is what the grieving parents want. A fictional cover story in the March 1998 issue of *Wired*, for example, tells the story of the world's first clone.[14] She is cloned from the DNA of a dead two-week-old infant, who died from a mitochondrial defect that is later "cured" by cloning with an enucleated donor egg. The closer one gets to the embryo stage, the more cloning a child looks like the much less problematic method of cloning by "twinning" or embryo splitting. And proponents of cloning tend to want to "naturalize" and "normalize" asexual replication by arguing that it is just like having "natural" twins.

Embryo splitting might be justified if only a few embryos could be produced by an infertile couple and all were implanted at the same time (since this does not involve replicating an existing and known genome). But scenarios of cloning by nuclear transfer have involved older children, and the only reason to clone an existing human is to create a genetic replica. Using the bodies of children to replicate them encourages all of us to devalue children and treat them as interchangeable commodities. For example, thanks to cloning, the death of a child need no longer be a singular human tragedy but, rather, can be an opportunity to try to replicate the no longer priceless (or irreplaceable) dead child. No one should have such dominion over a child (even a dead or dying child) as to use his or her genes to create the child's child.

Cloning would also radically alter what it means to be human by replicating a living or dead human being asexually to produce a person with a single genetic parent. The danger is that through human cloning we will lose something vital to our humanity, the uniqueness (and therefore the value and dignity) of every human. Cloning represents the height of genetic reductionism and genetic determinism.

Population geneticist R.C. Lewontin has challenged my position that the first human clone would also be the first human with a single genetic parent by arguing that, instead, "a child by cloning has a full set of chromosomes like anyone else, half of which were derived from a mother and half from a father. It happens that these chromosomes were passed through another individual, the cloning donor, on the way to the child. That donor is certainly not the child's 'parent' in any biological sense, but simply an earlier offspring of the original parents."[15] Lewontin takes genetic reductionism to perhaps its logical extreme. People become no more than containers of their parents' genes, and their parents have the right to treat them not as individual human beings, but rather as human embryos—entities that can be split and replicated at their whim without any consideration of the child's choice or welfare. Children (even adult children), according to Lewontin's view, have no say in whether they are replicated or not, because it is their parents, not they, who are reproducing. This radical redefinition of reproduction and parenthood, and the denial of the choice to procreate or not, turns out to be an even stronger argument against cloning children than its biologic novelty. Of course, we could require the consent of adults to be cloned—but why should we, if they are not becoming parents?

Related human rights and human dignity would also prohibit using cloned children as organ sources for their father or mother original. Nor is there any constitutional right to be cloned in the United States that is triggered by marriage to someone with whom an adult cannot reproduce sexually, because there is no tradition of asexual replication and because permitting asexual replication is not necessary to safeguard any existing concept of ordered liberty (rights fundamental to ordered liberty are the rights the Supreme Court sees as essential to individual liberty in our society).

Although it is possible to imagine some scenarios in which cloning could be used for the treatment of infertility, the use of cloning simply provides parents another choice for choice's sake, not out of necessity. Moreover, in a fundamental sense, cloning cannot be a treatment for infertility. This replication technique changes the very concept of infertility itself, since all humans have somatic cells that could be used for asexual replication and therefore no one would be unable to replicate himself or herself asexually. In vitro fertilization, on the other hand, simply provides a technological way for otherwise infertile humans to reproduce sexually.

John Robertson argues that adults have a right to procreate in any way they can, and that the interests of the children cannot be taken into account because the resulting children cannot be harmed (since without cloning the children would not exist at all).[16] But this argument amounts to a tautology. It applies equally to everyone alive; none of us would exist had it not been for the precise and unpredictable time when the father's sperm and the mother's egg met. This biologic fact, however, does not justify a conclusion that our parents had no obligations to us as their future children. If it did, it would be equally acceptable, from the child's perspective, to be gestated in a great ape, or even a cow, or to be composed of a mixture of ape genes and human genes.

The primary reason for banning the cloning of living or dead humans was articulated by the philosopher Hans Jonas in the early 1970s. He correctly noted that it does not matter that creating an exact duplicate of an existing person is impossible. What matters is that the person is chosen to be cloned because of some characteristic or characteristics he or she possesses (which, it is hoped, would also be possessed by the genetic copy or clone). Jonas argued that cloning is always a crime against the clone, the crime of depriving the clone of his or her "existential right to certain subjective terms of being"—particularly, the "right to ignorance" of facts about his or her origin that are likely to be "paralyzing for the spontaneity of becoming himself" or herself.[17] This advance knowledge of what another has or has not accomplished with the clone's genome destroys the clone's "condition for authentic growth" in seeking to answer the fundamental question of all beings, "Who am I?" Jonas continues: "The ethical command here entering the enlarged stage of our powers is: never to violate the right to that ignorance which is a condition of authentic action; or: to respect the right of each human life to find its own way and be a surprise to itself."[17]

Jonas is correct. His rationale, of course, applies only to a "delayed genetic twin" or "serial twin" created from an existing human, not to genetically identical twins born at the same time, including those created by cloning with use of embryo splitting. Even if one does not agree with him, however, it is hypocritical to argue that a cloning technique that limits the liberty and choices of the resulting child or children can be justified on the grounds that cloning expands the liberty and choices of would-be cloners.[18]

MORATORIUMS AND BANS ON HUMAN CLONING

Members of the National Bioethics Advisory Commission could not agree on much, but they did conclude that any current attempt to clone a human being should be prohibited by basic ethical principles that ban putting human subjects at substantial risk without their informed consent. But danger itself will not prevent scientists and physicians from performing first-of-their-kind experiments—from implanting a baboon's heart in a human baby to using a permanent artificial heart in an adult—and cloning techniques may be both safer and more efficient in the future. We must identify a mechanism that can both prevent premature experimentation and permit reasonable experimentation when the facts change.

The mechanism I favor is a broad-based regulatory agency to oversee human experimentation in the areas of genetic engineering, research with human embryos, xenografts, artificial organs, and other potentially dangerous boundary-crossing experiments.[19] Any such national regulatory agency must be composed almost exclusively of nonresearchers and nonphysicians so it can reflect public values, not parochial concerns. Currently, the operative American ethic seems to be that if any possible case can be imagined in which a new technology might be useful, it should not be prohibited, no matter what harm might result. One of the most important procedural steps Congress should take in setting up a federal agency to regulate human experimentation would be to put the burden of proof on those who propose to undertake novel experiments (including cloning) that risk harm and call deeply held social values into question.

This shift in the burden of proof is critical if society is to have an influence over science.[20] Without it, social control is not possible. This model applies the precautionary principle of international environmental law to cloning and other potentially harmful biomedical experiments involving humans. The principle requires governments to protect the public health and the environment from realistic threats of irreversible harm or catastrophic consequences even in the absence of clear evidence of harm.[21] Under this principle, proponents of human cloning would have the burden of proving that there was some compelling contravailing need to benefit either current or future generations before such an experiment was permitted (for example, if the entire species were to become sterile). Thus, regulators would not have the burden of proving that there was some compelling reason not to approve it. This regulatory scheme would depend on at least a de facto, if not a de jure, ban or moratorium on such experiments and a mechanism such as my proposed regulatory agency that could lift the ban. The suggestion that the Food and Drug Administration (FDA) can substitute for such an agency is fanciful. The FDA has no jurisdiction over either the practice of medicine or human replication and is far too narrowly constituted to represent the public in this area. Some see human cloning as inevitable and uncontrollable.[22, 23] Control will be difficult, and it will ultimately require close international cooperation. But this is no reason not to try—any more than a recognition that controlling terrorism or biologic weapons is difficult and uncertain justifies making no attempt at control.

On the recommendation of the National Bioethics Advisory Commission, the White House sent proposed anticloning legislation to Congress in June 1997. The Clinton proposal receded into obscurity until early 1998, when a Chicago physicist, Richard Seed, made national news by announcing that he intended to raise funds to clone a human. Because Seed acted like a prototypical "mad scientist," his proposal was greeted with almost universal condemnation.[24] Like the 1978 Rorvik hoax, however, it provided another opportunity for public discussion of cloning and prompted a more refined version of the Clinton proposal: the Feinstein–Kennedy bill. We can (and should) take advantage of this opportunity to distinguish the cloning of cells and tissues from the cloning of human beings by somatic nuclear transplantation[25] and to permit the former while prohibiting the latter. We should also take the opportunity to fill in the regulatory lacuna that permits any individual scientist to act first and consider the human consequences later, and we should use the controversy over cloning as an opportunity to begin an international dialogue on human experimentation.

References

1. U.S. Senate. 144 Cong. Rec. S561-S580, S607-S608 (1998).
2. S. 1611 (Feinstein–Kennedy Prohibition on Cloning of Human Beings Act of 1998).
3. Cloning human beings: report and recommendations of the National Bioethics Advisory Commission. Rockville, Md.: National Bioethics Advisory Commission, June 1997.
4. Annas, G.J., Elias, S. "The politics of transplantation of human fetal tissue." *N Engl J Med* 1989; 320:1079–82.
5. Annas, G.J., Caplan, A., Elias, S. "The politics of human embryo research—avoiding ethical gridlock." *N Engl J Med* 1996; 334:1329–32.

6. Wilmut, I., Schnieke, A.E., McWhir, J., Kind, A.J., Campbell, K.H. "Viable offspring derived from fetal and adult mammalian cells." *Nature* 1997; 385:810–3.
7. Butler, D. "Dolly researcher plans further experiments after challenges." *Nature* 1998; 391:825–6.
8. Lederberg, J. "Experimental genetics and human evolution." *Am Naturalist* 1966; 100:519–31.
9. Watson, J.D. "Moving toward the clonal man." *Atlantic Monthly*. May 1971:50–3.
10. Rorvik, D.M. *In His Image: The Cloning of a Man*. Philadelphia: J.B. Lippincott, 1978.
11. Development in cell biology and genetics, cloning. Hearings before the Subcommittee on Health and the Environment of the Committee on Interstate and Foreign Commerce of the U.S. House of Representatives, 95th Congress, 2d Session, May 31, 1978.
12. Chomsky, N. *Language and Problems of Knowledge: The Managua Lectures*. Cambridge, Mass.: MIT Press, 1988.
13. Montalbano, W. "Cloned sheep is star, but not sole project, at institute." *Los Angeles Times*. February 25, 1997:A7.
14. Kadrey, R. "Carbon copy: meet the first human clone." *Wired*. March 1998:146–50.
15. Lewontin, R.C. "Confusion over cloning." *New York Review of Books*. October 23, 1997:20–3.
16. Robertson, J.A. *Children of Choice: Freedom and the New Reproductive Technologies*. Princeton, N.J.: Princeton University Press; 1994: 169.
17. Jonas, H. *Philosophical Essays: From Ancient Creed to Technological Man*. Englewood Cliffs N.J.: Prentice-Hall, 1974:162–3.
18. Annas, G.J. *Some Choice: Law, Medicine and the Market*. New York: Oxford University Press, 1998:14–5.
19. Annas, G.J. "Regulatory models for human embryo cloning: The free market professional guidelines, and government restrictions." *Kennedy Inst Ethics J* 1994; 4:235–49.
20. Hearings before the U.S. Senate Subcommittee on Public Health and Safety, 105th Congress, 1st Session, March 12, 1997. (Or see: http://www-busph.bu.edu/depts/lw/clonetest.htm.)
21. Cross, F.B. "Paradoxical perils of the precautionary principle." *Washington Lee Law Rev* 1996; 53:851–925.
22. Kolata, G.B. *Clone: The Road to Dolly, and the Path Ahead*. New York: W. Morrow, 1998.
23. Silver, L.M. *Remaking Eden: Cloning and Beyond in a Brave New World*. New York: Avon Books, 1997.
24. Knox, R.A. "A Chicagoan plans to offer cloning of humans." *Boston Globe*. January 7, 1998:A3.
25. Kassirer, J.P., Rosenthal, N.A. "Should human cloning research be off limits?" *N Engl J Med* 1998; 338:905–6.

CLONING HUMAN BEINGS: AN ASSESSMENT OF THE ETHICAL ISSUES PRO AND CON

Dan W. Brock

The world of science and the public at large were both shocked and fascinated by the announcement in the journal *Nature* by Ian Wilmut and his colleagues that they had successfully cloned a sheep from a single cell of an adult sheep (Wilmut, 1997). But many were troubled or apparently even horrified at the prospect that cloning of adult humans by the same process might be possible as well. The response of most scientific and political leaders to the prospect of human cloning, indeed of Dr. Wilmut as well, was of immediate and strong condemnation.

From "Cloning Human Beings: An Assessment of the Ethical Issues Pro and Con." From *Clones and Clones*, ed. Nussbaum, M., and Sunstein, C. (New York: W. W. Norton & Co., 1988), pp. 141–64.

A few more cautious voices were heard both suggesting some possible benefits from the use of human cloning in limited circumstances and questioning its too quick prohibition, but they were a clear minority. A striking feature of these early responses was that their strength and intensity seemed far to outrun the arguments and reasons offered in support of them—they seemed often to be "gut level" emotional reactions rather than considered reflections on the issues. Such reactions should not be simply dismissed, both because they may point us to important considerations otherwise missed and not easily articulated, and because they often have a major impact on public policy. But the *formation of public policy should not ignore the moral reasons and arguments that bear on the practice of human cloning*—these must be articulated in order to understand and inform people's more immediate emotional responses. This essay is an effort to articulate, and to evaluate critically, the main moral considerations and arguments for and against human cloning. Though many people's religious beliefs inform their views on human cloning, and it is often difficult to separate religious from secular positions, I shall restrict myself to arguments and reasons that can be given a clear secular formulation.

On each side of the issue there are two distinct kinds of moral arguments brought forward. On the one hand, some opponents claim that human cloning would violate fundamental moral or human rights, while some proponents argue that its prohibition would violate such rights. While moral and even human rights need not be understood as absolute, they do place moral restrictions on permissible actions that an appeal to a mere balance of benefits over harms cannot justify overriding; for example, the rights of human subjects in research must be respected even if the result is that some potentially beneficial research is more difficult or cannot be done. On the other hand, both opponents and proponents also cite the likely harms and benefits, both to individuals and to society, of the practice. I shall begin with the arguments in support of permitting human cloning, although with no implication that it is the stronger or weaker position.

MORAL ARGUMENTS IN SUPPORT OF HUMAN CLONING

Is There a Moral Right to Use Human Cloning?

What moral right might protect at least some access to the use of human cloning? A commitment to individual liberty, such as defended by J. S. Mill, requires that individuals be left free to use human cloning if they so choose and if their doing so does not cause significant harms to others, but liberty is too broad in scope to be an uncontroversial moral right (Mill, 1859; Rhodes, 1995). Human cloning is a means of reproduction (in the most literal sense) and so the most plausible moral right at stake in its use is a right to reproductive freedom or procreative liberty (Robertson, 1994a; Brock, 1994), understood to include both the choice not to reproduce, for example, by means of contraception or abortion, and also the right to reproduce.

The right to reproductive freedom is properly understood to include the right to use various assisted reproductive technologies (ARTs), such as in vitro fertilization (IVF), oocyte donation, and so forth. The reproductive right relevant to human cloning is a negative right, that is, a right to use ARTs without interference by the government or others when made available by a willing provider. The choice of an assisted means of reproduction should be protected by reproductive freedom even when it is not the only means for individuals to reproduce, just as the choice among different means of preventing conception is protected by reproductive freedom. However, the case for permitting the use of a particular means of reproduction is strongest when it is necessary for particular individuals to be able to procreate at all, or to do so without great burdens or harms to themselves or others. In some cases human cloning could be the only means for individuals to procreate while retaining a biological tie to their child, but in other cases different means of procreating might also be possible.

It could be argued that human cloning is not covered by the right to reproductive freedom because whereas current ARTs and practices covered by that right are remedies for inabilities to reproduce sexually, human cloning is an entirely new means of reproduction; indeed, its critics see it as more a means of manufacturing humans than of reproduction. Human cloning is a different means of reproduction than sexual reproduction, but it is a means that can serve individuals' interest in reproducing. If it is not protected by the moral right to reproductive freedom, I believe that must be not because it is a new means of reproducing, but instead because it has other objectionable or harmful features; I shall evaluate these other ethical objections to it later.

When individuals have alternative means of procreating, human cloning typically would be chosen because it replicates a particular individual's genome. The reproductive interest in question then is not simply reproduction itself, but a more specific interest in choosing what kind of children to have. The right to reproductive freedom is usually understood to cover at least some choice about the kind of children one will have. Some individuals choose reproductive partners in the hope of producing offspring with desirable traits. Genetic testing of fetuses or preimplantation embryos for genetic disease or abnormality is done to avoid having a child with those diseases or abnormalities. Respect for individual self-determination, which is one of the grounds of a moral right to reproductive freedom, includes respecting individuals' choices about whether to have a child with a condition that will place severe burdens on them, and cause severe burdens to the child itself.

The less a reproductive choice is primarily the determination of one's own life, but primarily the determination of the nature of another, as in the case of human cloning, the more moral weight the interests of that other person, that is the cloned child, should have in decisions that determine its nature (Annas, 1994). But even then parents are typically accorded substantial, but not unlimited, discretion in shaping the persons their children will become, for example, through education and other child-rearing decisions. Even if not part of reproductive freedom, the right to raise one's children as one sees fit, within limits mostly determined by the interests of the children, is also a right to determine within limits what kinds of persons one's children will become. This right includes not just preventing certain diseases or harms to children, but selecting and shaping desirable features and traits in one's children. The use of human cloning is one way to exercise that right.

Public policy and the law now permit prospective parents to conceive, or to carry a conception to term, when there is a significant risk or even certainty that the child will suffer from a serious genetic disease. Even when others think the risk or certainty of genetic disease makes it morally wrong to conceive, or to carry a fetus to term, the parents' right to reproductive freedom permits them to do so. Most possible harms to a cloned child are less serious than the genetic harms with which parents can now permit their offspring to be conceived or born.

I conclude that there is good reason to accept that a right to reproductive freedom presumptively includes both a right to select the means of reproduction, as well as a right to determine what kind of children to have, by use of human cloning. However, the specific reproductive interest of determining what kind of children to have is less weighty than are other reproductive interests and choices whose impact falls more directly and exclusively on the parents rather than the child. Even if a moral right to reproductive freedom protects the use of human cloning, that does not settle the moral issue about human cloning, since there may be other moral rights in conflict with this right, or serious enough harms from human cloning to override the right to use it; this right can be thought of as establishing a serious moral presumption supporting access to human cloning.

What Individual or Social Benefits Might Human Cloning Produce?

Largely Individual Benefits The literature on human cloning by nuclear transfer or by embryo splitting contains a few examples of circumstances in which individuals might have good reasons to want to use human cloning. However, human cloning seems not to be the unique answer to any great or pressing human need and its benefits appear to be limited at most. What are the principal possible benefits of human cloning that might give individuals good reasons to want to use it?

1. Human cloning would be a new means to relieve the infertility some persons now experience. Human cloning would allow women who have no ova or men who have no sperm to produce an offspring that is biologically related to them (Eisenberg, 1976; Robertson, 1994b, 1997; LaBar, 1984). Embryos might also be cloned, by either nuclear transfer or embryo splitting, in order to increase the number of embryos for implantation and improve the chances of successful conception (NABER, 1994). The benefits from human cloning to relieve infertility are greater the more persons there are who cannot overcome their infertility by any other means acceptable to them. I do not know of data on this point, but the numbers who would use cloning for this reason are probably not large.

The large number of children throughout the world possibly available for adoption represents an alternative solution to infertility only if we are prepared to discount as illegitimate the strong desire of many persons, fertile and infertile, for the experience of pregnancy and for having and raising a child biologically related to them. While not important to all infertile (or fertile) individuals, it is important to many and is respected and met through other forms of assisted reproduction that maintain a biological connection when that is possible; that desire does not become illegitimate simply because human cloning would be the best or only means of overcoming an individual's infertility.

2. Human cloning would enable couples in which one party risks transmitting a serious hereditary disease to an offspring to reproduce without doing so (Robertson, 1994b). By using donor sperm or egg donation, such hereditary risks can generally be avoided now without the use of human cloning. These procedures may be unacceptable to some couples, however, or at least considered less desirable than human cloning because they introduce a third party's genes into their reproduction instead of giving their offspring only the genes of one of them. Thus, in some cases human cloning could be a reasonable means of preventing genetically transmitted harms to offspring. Here too, we do not know how many persons would want to use human cloning instead of other means of avoiding the risk of genetic transmission of a disease or of accepting the risk of transmitting the disease, but the numbers again are probably not large.

3. Human cloning to make a later twin would enable a person to obtain needed organs or tissues for transplantation (Robertson, 1994b, 1997; Kahn, 1989; Harris, 1992). Human cloning would solve the problem of finding a transplant donor whose organ or tissue is an acceptable match and would eliminate, or drastically reduce, the risk of transplant rejection by the host. The availability of human cloning for this purpose would amount to a form of insurance to enable treatment of certain kinds of medical conditions. Of course, sometimes the medical need would be too urgent to permit waiting for the cloning, gestation, and development that is necessary before tissues or organs can be obtained for transplantation. In other cases, taking an organ also needed by the later twin, such as a heart or a liver, would be impermissible because it would violate the later twin's rights.

Such a practice can be criticized on the ground that it treats the later twin not as a person valued and loved for his or her own sake, as an end in itself in Kantian terms, but simply as a means for benefiting another. This criticism assumes, however, that only thus one motive defines the reproduction and the relation of the person to his or her later twin. The well-known case some years ago in California of the Ayalas, who conceived in the hopes of obtaining a source for a bone marrow transplant for their teenage daughter suffering from leukemia, illustrates the mistake in this assumption. They argued that whether or not the child they conceived turned out to be a possible donor for their daughter, they would value and love the child for itself, and treat it as they would treat any other member of their family. That one reason they wanted it, as a possible means to saving their daughter's life, did not preclude their also loving and valuing it for its own sake; in Kantian terms, it was treated as a possible means to saving their daughter, but not *solely as a means*, which is what the Kantian view proscribes.

Indeed, when people have children, whether by sexual means or with the aid of ARTs, their motives and reasons for doing so are typically many and complex, and include reasons less laudable than obtaining lifesaving medical treatment, such as having someone who needs them, enabling them to live on their own, qualifying for government benefit programs, and so forth. While these are not admirable motives for having children and may not bode well for the child's upbringing and future, public policy does not assess prospective parents' motives and reasons for procreating as a condition of their doing so.

4. Human cloning would enable individuals to clone someone who had special meaning to them, such as a child who had died (Robertson, 1994b). There is no denying that if human cloning were available, some individuals would want to use it for this purpose, but their desire usually would be based on a deep confusion. Cloning such a child would not replace the child the parents had loved and lost, but would only create a different child with the same genes. The child they loved and lost was a unique individual who had been shaped by his or her environment and choices, not just his or her genes, and more importantly who had experienced a particular relationship with them. Even if the later cloned child could not only have the same genes but also be subjected to the same environment, which of course is impossible, it would remain a different child than the one they had loved and lost because it would share a different history with them (Thomas, 1974). Cloning the lost child might help the parents accept and move on from their loss, but another already existing sibling or a new child that was not a clone might do this equally well; indeed, it might do so better since the appearance of the cloned later twin would be a constant reminder of the child they had lost. Nevertheless, if human cloning enabled some individuals to clone a person who had special meaning to them and doing so gave them deep satisfaction, that would be a benefit to them even if their reasons for wanting to do so, and the satisfaction they in turn received, were based on a confusion.

Largely Social Benefits

5. Human cloning would enable the duplication of individuals of great talent, genius, character, or other exemplary qualities. Unlike the first four reasons for human cloning which appeal to benefits to specific individuals, this reason looks to benefits to the broader society from being able to replicate extraordinary individuals—a Mozart, Einstein, Gandhi, or Schweitzer (Lederberg, 1966; McKinnell, 1979). Much of the appeal of this reason, like much support and opposition to human cloning, rests largely on a confused and false assumption of genetic determinism, that is, that one's genes fully determine what one will become, do, and accomplish. What made Mozart, Einstein, Gandhi, and Schweitzer the extraordinary individuals they were was the confluence of their particular genetic endowments with the environments in which they were raised and lived and the particular historical moments they in different ways seized. Cloning them would produce individuals with the same genetic inheritances (nuclear transfer does not even produce 100 percent genetic identity, although for the sake of exploring the moral issues I have followed the common assumption that it does), but it is not possible to replicate their environments or the historical contexts in which they lived and their greatness flourished. We do not know the degree or specific respects in which any individual's greatness depended on "nature" or "nurture," but we do know that it always depends on an interaction of them both. Cloning could not even replicate individuals' extraordinary capabilities, much less their accomplishments, because these too are the product of their inherited genes and their environments, not of their genes alone.

None of this is to deny that Mozart's and Einstein's extraordinary musical and intellectual capabilities, nor even Gandhi's and Schweitzer's extraordinary moral greatness, were produced in part by their unique genetic inheritances. Cloning them might well produce individuals with exceptional capacities, but we simply do not know how close their clones would be in capacities or accomplishments to the great individuals from whom they were cloned. Even so, the hope for exceptional, even if less and different, accomplishment from cloning such extraordinary individuals might be a reasonable ground for doing so.

Worries here about abuse, however, surface quickly. Whose standards of greatness would be used to select individuals to be cloned? Who would control use of human cloning technology for the benefit of society or mankind at large? Particular groups, segments of society, or governments might use the technology for their own benefit, under the cover of benefiting society or even mankind at large.

6. Human cloning and research on human cloning might make possible important advances in scientific knowledge, for example, about human development (Walters, 1982; Smith, 1983). While important potential advances in scientific or medical knowledge from human cloning or human cloning research have frequently been cited, there are at least three reasons for caution about such claims. First, there is always considerable uncertainty about the nature and importance of the new scientific or medical knowledge to which a dramatic new technology like human cloning will lead; the road to new knowledge is never mapped in advance and takes many unexpected turns. Second, we do not know what new knowledge from human cloning or human cloning research could also be gained by other means that do not have the problematic moral features to which its opponents object. Third, what human cloning research would be compatible with ethical and legal requirements for the use of human subjects in research is complex, controversial, and largely unexplored. Creating human clones solely for the purpose of research would be to use them solely for the benefit of others without their consent, and so unethical. But if and when human cloning was established to be safe and effective, then new scientific knowledge might be obtained from its use for legitimate, nonresearch reasons.

Although there is considerable uncertainty concerning most of human cloning's possible individual and social benefits that I have discussed, and although no doubt it could have other benefits or uses that we cannot yet envisage, I believe it is reasonable to conclude at this time that human cloning does not seem to promise great benefits or uniquely to meet great human needs. Nevertheless, despite these limited benefits, a moral case can be made that freedom to use human cloning is protected by the important moral right to reproductive freedom. I shall turn now to what moral rights might be violated, or harms produced, by research on or use of human cloning.

MORAL ARGUMENTS AGAINST HUMAN CLONING

Would the Use of Human Cloning Violate Important Moral Rights?

Many of the immediate condemnations of any possible human cloning following Wilmut's cloning of Dolly claimed that it would violate moral or human rights, but it was usually not specified precisely, or often even at all, what rights would be violated (WHO, 1997). I shall consider two possible candidates for such a right: a right to have a unique identity and a right to ignorance about one's future or to an open future. Claims that cloning denies individuals a unique identity are common, but I shall argue that even if there is a right to a unique identity, it could not be violated by human cloning. The right to ignorance or to an open future has only been explicitly defended, to my knowledge, by two commentators, and in the context of human cloning, only by Hans Jonas; it supports a more promising, but in my view ultimately unsuccessful, argument that human cloning would violate an important moral or human right.

Is there a moral or human right to a unique identity, and if so would it be violated by human cloning? For human cloning to violate a right to a unique identity, the relevant sense of identity would have to be genetic identity, that is, a right to a unique unrepeated genome. This would be violated by human cloning, but is there any such right? It might be thought that cases of identical twins show there is no such right because no one claims that the moral or human rights of the twins have been violated. However, this consideration is not conclusive (Kass, 1985; NABER, 1994). Only human actions can violate others' rights; outcomes that would constitute a rights violation if deliberately caused by human action are not a rights violation if a result of natural causes. If Arthur deliberately strikes Barry on the head so hard as to cause his death, he violates Barry's right not to be killed; if lightning strikes Cheryl, causing her death, her right not to be killed has not been violated. Thus, the case of twins does not show that there could not be a right to a unique genetic identity.

What is the sense of identity that might plausibly be what each person has a right to have uniquely, that constitutes the special uniqueness of each individual (Macklin 1994; Chadwick 1982)? Even with the same genes, homozygous twins are numerically distinct and not identical, so what is intended must be the various properties and characteristics that make each individual qualitatively unique and different from others. Does having the same genome as another person undermine that unique qualitative identity? Only on the crudest genetic determinism, according to which an individual's genes completely and decisively determine everything else about the individual, all his or her other nongenetic features and properties, together with the entire history or biography that constitutes his or her life. But there is no reason whatever to believe that kind of genetic determinism. Even with the same genes, differences in genetically identical twins' psychological and personal characteristics develop over time together with differences in their life histories, personal relationships, and life choices; sharing an identical genome does not prevent twins from developing distinct and unique personal identities of their own.

We need not pursue whether there is a moral or human right to a unique identity—no such right is found among typical accounts and enumerations of moral or human rights—because even if there is such a right, sharing a genome with another individual as a result of human cloning would not violate it. The idea of the uniqueness, or unique identity, of each person historically predates the development of modern genetics. A unique genome thus could not be the ground of this long-standing belief in the unique human identity of each person.

I turn now to whether human cloning would violate what Hans Jonas called a right to ignorance, or what Joel Feinberg called a right to an open future (Jonas, 1974; Feinberg, 1980). Jonas argued that human cloning in which there is a substantial time gap between the beginning of the lives of the earlier and later twin is fundamentally different from the simultaneous beginning of the lives of homozygous twins that occur in nature. Although contemporaneous twins begin their lives with the same genetic inheritance, they do so at the same time, and so in ignorance of what the other who shares the same genome will by his or her choices make of his or her life.

A later twin created by human cloning, Jonas argues, knows, or at least believes she knows, too much about herself. For there is already in the world another person, her earlier twin, who from the same genetic starting point has made the life choices that are still in the later twin's future. It will seem that her life has already been lived and played out by another, that her fate is already determined; she will lose the sense of human possibility in freely and spontaneously creating her own future and authentic self. It is tyrannical, Jonas claims, for the earlier twin to try to determine another's fate in this way.

Jonas's objection can be interpreted so as not to assume either a false genetic determinism, or a belief in it. A later twin might grant that he is not determined to follow in his earlier twin's footsteps, but nevertheless the earlier twin's life might always haunt him, standing as an undue influence on his life, and shaping it in ways to which others' lives are not vulnerable. But the force of the objection still seems to rest on the false assumption that having the same genome as his earlier twin unduly restricts his freedom to create a different life and self than the earlier twin's. Moreover, a family environment also importantly shapes children's development, but there is no force to the claim of a younger sibling that the existence of an older sibling raised in that same family is an undue influence on the younger sibling's freedom to make his own life for himself in that environment. Indeed, the younger twin or sibling might gain the benefit of being able to learn from the older twin's or sibling's mistakes.

A closely related argument can be derived from what Joel Feinberg has called a child's right to an open future. This requires that others raising a child not to close off the future possibilities that the child would otherwise have as to eliminate a reasonable range of opportunities for the child autonomously to construct his or her own life. One way this right might be violated is to create a later twin who will believe her future has already been set for her by the choices made and the life lived by her earlier twin.

The central difficulty in these appeals to a right either to ignorance or to an open future is that the right is not violated merely because the later twin is likely to *believe* that his future is already determined, when that belief is clearly false and supported only by the crudest genetic determinism. If we know the later twin will falsely believe that his open future has been taken from him as a result of being cloned, even though in reality it has not, then we know that cloning will cause the twin psychological distress, but not that it will violate his right. Jonas's right to ignorance, and Feinberg's right of a child to an open future, are not violated by human cloning, though they do point to psychological harms that a later twin may be likely to experience and that I will take up later.

Neither a moral or human right to a unique identity, nor one to ignorance and an open future, would be violated by human cloning. There may be other moral or human rights that human cloning would violate, but I do not know what they might be. I turn now to consideration of the harms that human cloning might produce.

What Individual or Social Harms Might Human Cloning Produce?

There are many possible individual or social harms that have been posited by one or another commentator and I shall only try to cover the more plausible and significant of them.

Largely Individual Harms

1. Human cloning would produce psychological distress and harm in the later twin. No doubt knowing the path in life taken by one's earlier twin might often have several bad psychological effects (Callahan, 1993; LaBar, 1984; Macklin, 1994; McCormick, 1993; Studdard, 1978; Rainer, 1978; Verhey, 1994). The later twin might feel, even if mistakenly, that her fate has already been substantially laid out, and so have difficulty freely and spontaneously taking responsibility for and making her own fate and life. The later twin's experience or sense of autonomy and freedom might be substantially diminished, even if in actual fact they are diminished much less than it seems to her. She might have a diminished sense of her own uniqueness and individuality, even if once again these are in fact diminished little or not at all by having an earlier twin with the same genome. If the later twin is the clone of a particularly exemplary individual, perhaps with some special capabilities and accomplishments, she might experience excessive pressure to reach the very high standards of ability and accomplishment of the earlier twin (Rainer, 1978). These various psychological effects might take a heavy toll on the later twin and be serious burdens to her.

While psychological harms of these kinds from human cloning are certainly possible, and perhaps even likely in some cases, they remain at this point only speculative since we have no experience with human cloning and the creation of earlier and later twins. Nevertheless, if experience with human cloning confirmed that serious and unavoidable psychological harms typically occurred to the later twin, that would be a serious moral reason to avoid the practice. Intuitively at least, psychological burdens and harms seem more likely and more serious for a person who is only one of many identical later twins cloned from one original source, so that the clone might run into another identical twin around every street corner. This prospect could be a good reason to place sharp limits on the number of twins that could be cloned from any one source.

One argument has been used by several commentators to undermine the apparent significance of potential psychological harms to a later twin (Chadwick, 1982; Robertson, 1994b, 1997; Macklin, 1994). The point derives from a general problem, called the nonidentity problem, posed by the philosopher Derek Parfit, although not originally directed to human cloning (Parfit, 1984). Here is the argument. Even if all these psychological burdens from human cloning could not be avoided for any later twin, they are not harms to the twin, and so not reasons not to clone the twin. That is because the only way for the twin to avoid the harms is never to be cloned, and so never to exist at all. But these psychological burdens, hard though they might be, are not so bad as to make the twin's life, all things considered, not worth living. So the later twin is not harmed by being given a life even with these psychological burdens, since the alternative of never existing at all is arguably worse—he or she never has a worthwhile life—but certainly not better for the twin. And if the later twin is not harmed by having been created with these unavoidable burdens, then how could he or she be wronged by having been created with them? And if the later twin is not wronged, then why is any wrong being done by human cloning? This argument has considerable potential import, for if it is sound it will undermine the apparent moral importance of any bad consequence of human cloning to the later twin that is not so serious as to make the twin's life, all things considered, not worth living.

I defended elsewhere the position regarding the general case of genetically transmitted handicaps, that if one could have a *different* child without comparable burdens (for the case of cloning, by using a different method of reproduction which did not result in a later twin), there is as strong a moral reason to do so as there would be not to cause similar burdens to an already existing child (Brock, 1995). Choosing to create the later twin with serious psychological burdens instead of a different person who would be free of them, without weighty overriding reasons for choosing the former, would be morally irresponsible or wrong, even if doing so does not harm or wrong the later twin who could only exist with the burdens. These issues are too detailed and complex to pursue here and the nonidentity problem remains controversial and not fully resolved, but at the least, the argument for disregarding the psychological burdens to the later twin because he or she could not exist without them is controversial, and in my view mistaken. Such psychological harms, as I shall continue to call them, are speculative, but they should not be disregarded because of the nonidentity problem.

2. Human cloning procedures would carry unacceptable risks to the clone. There is no doubt that attempts to clone a human being at the present time would carry unacceptable risks to the clone. Further research on the procedure with animals, as well as research to establish its safety and effectiveness for humans, is clearly necessary before it would be ethical to use the procedure on humans. One risk to the clone is the failure to implant, grow, and develop successfully, but this would involve the embryo's death or destruction long before most people or the law consider it to be a person with moral or legal protections of its life.

Other risks to the clone are that the procedure in some way goes wrong, or unanticipated harms come to the clone; for example, Harold Varmus, director of the National Institutes of Health, raised the concern that a cell many years old from which a person is cloned could have accumulated genetic mutations during its years in another adult that could give the resulting clone a predisposition to cancer or other diseases of aging (Weiss, 1997). Risks to an ovum donor (if any), a nucleus donor, and a woman who receives the embryo for implantation would likely be ethically acceptable with the informed consent of the involved parties.

I believe it is too soon to say whether unavoidable risks to the clone would make human cloning forever unethical. At a minimum, further research is needed to better define the potential risks to humans. But we should not insist on a standard that requires risks to be lower than those we accept in sexual reproduction, or in other forms of ART.

Largely Social Harms

3. Human cloning would lessen the worth of individuals and diminish respect for human life. Unelaborated claims to this effect were common in the media after the announcement of the cloning of Dolly. Ruth Macklin explored and criticized the claim that human cloning would diminish the value we place on, and our respect for, human life because it would lead to persons being viewed as replaceable (Macklin, 1994). As I have argued concerning a right to a unique identity, only on a confused and indefensible notion of human identity is a person's identity determined solely by his or her genes, and so no individual could be fully replaced by a later clone possessing the same genes. Ordinary people recognize this clearly. For example, parents of a child dying of a fatal disease would find it insensitive and ludicrous to be told they should not grieve for their coming loss because it is possible to replace him by cloning him; it is *their child who is dying* whom they love and value, and that child and his importance to them is not replaceable by a cloned later twin. Even if they would also come to love and value a later twin as much as they now love and value their child who is dying, that would be to love and value that *different child* for its own sake, not as a replacement for the child they lost. Our relations of love and friendship are with distinct, historically situated individuals with whom over time we have shared experiences and our lives, and whose loss to us can never be replaced.

A different version of this worry is that human cloning would result in persons' worth or value seeming diminished because we would come to see persons as able to be manufactured or "handmade." This demystification of the creation of human life would reduce our appreciation and awe of human life and of its natural creation. It would be a mistake, however, to conclude that a person created by human cloning is of less value or is less worthy of respect than one created by sexual reproduction. At least outside of some religious contexts, it is the nature of a being, not how it is created, that is the source of its value and makes it worthy of respect. For many people, gaining a scientific understanding of the truly extraordinary complexity of human reproduction and development increases, instead of decreases, their awe of the process and its product.

A more subtle route by which the value we place on each individual human life might be diminished could come from the use of human cloning with the aim of creating a child with a particular genome, either the genome of another individual especially meaningful to those doing the cloning or an individual with exceptional talents, abilities, and accomplishments. The child then comes to be objectified, valued only as an object and for its genome, or at least for its genome's expected phenotypic expression, and no longer recognized as having the intrinsic equal moral value of all persons, simply as persons. For the moral value and respect due all persons to come to be seen as resting only on the instrumental value of individuals and of their particular qualities to others would be to fundamentally change the moral status properly accorded to persons. Individuals would lose their moral standing as full and equal members of the moral community, replaced by the different instrumental value each has to others.

Such a change in the equal moral value and worth accorded to persons should be avoided at all costs, but it is far from clear that such a change would result from permitting human cloning. Parents, for example, are quite capable of distinguishing their children's intrinsic value, just as individual persons, from their instrumental value based on their particular qualities or properties. The equal moral value and respect due all persons simply as persons is not incompatible with the different instrumental value of different individuals; Einstein and an untalented physics graduate student have vastly different value as scientists, but share and are entitled to equal moral value and respect as persons. It is a confused mistake to conflate these two kinds of value and respect. If making a large number of clones from one original person would be more likely to foster it, that would be a further reason to limit the number of clones that could be made from one individual.

4. Human cloning might be used by commercial interests for financial gain. Both opponents and proponents of human cloning agree that cloned embryos should not be able to be bought and sold. In a science fiction frame of mind, one can imagine commercial interests offering genetically certified and guaranteed embryos for sale, perhaps offering a catalogue of different embryos cloned from individuals with a variety of talents, capacities, and other desirable properties. This would be a fundamental violation of the equal moral respect and dignity owed to all persons, treating them instead as objects to be differentially valued, bought, and sold in the marketplace. Even if embryos are not yet persons at the time they would be purchased or sold, they would be being valued, bought, and sold for the persons they will become. The moral consensus against any commercial market in embryos, cloned or otherwise, should be enforced by law whatever the public policy ultimately is on human cloning.

5. Human cloning might be used by governments or other groups for immoral and exploitative purposes. In *Brave New World*, Aldous Huxley imagined cloning individuals who have been engineered with limited abilities and conditioned to do, and to be happy doing, the menial work that society needed done (Huxley, 1932). Selection and control in the creation of people was exercised not in the interests of the persons created, but in the interests of the society and at the expense of the persons created; nor did it serve individuals' interests in reproduction and parenting. Any use of human cloning for such purposes would exploit the clones solely as means for the benefit of others, and would violate the equal moral respect and dignity they are owed as full moral persons. If human cloning is permitted to go forward, it should be with regulations that would clearly prohibit such immoral exploitation.

Fiction contains even more disturbing or bizarre uses of human cloning, such as Mengele's creation of many clones of Hitler in Ira Levin's *The Boys from Brazil* (Levin, 1976), Woody Allen's science fiction cinematic spoof *Sleeper* in which a dictator's only remaining part, his nose, must be destroyed to keep it from being cloned, and the contemporary science fiction film *Blade Runner*. These nightmare scenarios may be quite improbable, but their impact should not be underestimated on public concern with technologies like human cloning. Regulation of human cloning must assure the public that even such far-fetched abuses will not take place.

CONCLUSION

Human cloning has until now received little serious and careful ethical attention because it was typically dismissed as science fiction, and it stirs deep, but difficult to articulate, uneasiness and even revulsion in many people. Any ethical assessment of human cloning at this point must be tentative and provisional. Fortunately, the science and technology of human cloning are not yet in hand, and so a public and professional debate is possible without the need for a hasty, precipitate policy response.

The ethical pros and cons of human cloning, as I see them at this time, are sufficiently balanced and uncertain that there is not an ethically decisive case either for or against permitting it or doing it. Access to human cloning can plausibly be brought within a moral right to reproductive freedom, but its potential legitimate uses appear few and do not promise substantial benefits. It is not a central component of the moral right to reproductive freedom and it does not uniquely serve any major or pressing individual or social needs. On the other hand, contrary to the pronouncements of many of its opponents, human cloning seems not to be a violation of moral or human rights. But it does risk some significant individual or social harms, although most are based on common public confusions about genetic determinism, human identity, and the effects of human cloning. Because most potential harms feared from human cloning remain speculative, they seem insufficient to warrant at this time a complete legal prohibition of either research on or later use of human cloning, if and when its safety and efficacy are established. Legitimate moral concerns about the use and effects of human cloning, however, underline the need for careful public oversight of research on its development, together with a wider public and professional debate and review before cloning is used on human beings.

References

Annas, G. J. (1994). "Regulatory Models for Human Embryo Cloning: The Free Market, Professional Guidelines, and Government Restrictions." *Kennedy Institute of Ethics Journal* 4, 3:235–249.

Brock, D. W. (1994). "Reproductive Freedom: Its Nature, Bases and Limits," in *Health Care Ethics: Critical Issues for Health Professionals*, eds. D. Thomasma and J. Monagle. Gaithersbrug, MD: Aspen Publishers.

Brock, D. W. (1995). "The Non-Identity Problem and Genetic Harm." *Bioethics* 9:269–275.

Callahan, D. (1993). "Perspective on Cloning: A Threat to Individual Uniqueness." *Los Angeles Times*, November 12, 1993: B7.

Chadwick, R. F. (1982). "Cloning." *Philosophy* 57: 201–209.

Eisenberg, L. (1976). "The Outcome as Cause: Predestination and Human Cloning." *The Journal of Medicine and Philosophy* 1:318–331.

Feinberg, J. (1980). "The Child's Right to an Open Future," in *Whose Child? Children's Rights, Parental Authority, and State Power*, eds. W. Aiken and H. LaFollette. Totowa, NJ: Rowman and Littlefield.

Harris, J. (1992). *Wonderwoman and Superman: The Ethics of Biotechnology.* Oxford: Oxford University Press.

Huxley, A. (1932). *Brave New World*. London: Chalto and Winders.

Jonas, H. (1974). *Philosophical Essays: From Ancient Creed to Technological Man*. Englewood Cliffs, NJ: Prentice-Hall.

Kahn, C. (1989). "Can We Achieve Immortality?" *Free Inquiry* 9:14–18.

Kass, L. (1985). *Toward a More Natural Science*. New York: The Free Press.

LaBar, M. (1984)."The Pros and Cons of Human Cloning." *Thought* 57:318–333.

Lederberg, J. (1966). "Experimental Genetics and Human Evolution." *The American Naturalist* 100:519–531.

Levin, I. (1976). *The Boys from Brazil*. New York: Random House.

Macklin, R. (1994). "Splitting Embryos on the Slippery Slope: Ethics and Public Policy." *Kennedy Institute of Ethics Journal* 4:209–226.

McCormick, R. (1993). "Should We Clone Humans?" *Christian Century* 110:1148–1149.

McKinnell, R. (1979). *Cloning: A Biologist Reports*. Minneapolis, MN: University of Minnesota Press.

Mill, J. S. (1859). *On Liberty*. Indianapolis, IN: Bobbs-Merrill Publishing.

NABER (National Advisory Board on Ethics in Reproduction) (1994). "Report on Human Cloning Through Embryo Splitting: An Amber Light." *Kennedy Institute of Ethics Journal* 4:251–282.

Parfit, D. (1984). *Reasons and Persons*. Oxford: Oxford University Press.

Rainer, J. D. (1978). "Commentary." *Man and Medicine: The Journal of Values and Ethics in Health Care* 3:115–117.

Rhodes, R. (1995). "Clones, Harms, and Rights." *Cambridge Quarterly of Healthcare Ethics* 4: 285–290.

Robertson, J. A. (1994a). *Children of Choice: Freedom and the New Reproductive Technologies*. Princeton, NJ: Princeton University Press.

Robertson, J. A. (1994b). "The Question of Human Cloning." *Hastings Center Report* 24:6–14.

Robertson, J. A. (1997). "A Ban on Cloning and Cloning Research is Unjustified." Testimony Presented to the National Bioethics Advisory Commission, March 1997.

Smith, G. P. (1983). "Intimations of Immortality: Clones, Cyrons and the Law." *University of New South Wales Law Journal* 6:119–132.

Studdard, A. (t 978). "The Lone Clone." *Man and Medicine: The Journal of Values and Ethics in Health Care* 3:109–114.

Thomas, L. (1974). "Notes of a Biology Watcher: On Cloning a Human Being." *New England Journal of Medicine* 291:1296–1297.

Verhey, A. D. (1994). "Cloning: Revisiting an Old Debate." *Kennedy Institute of Ethics Journal* 4:227–234.

Walters, W. A. W. (1982). "Cloning, Ectogenesis, and Hybrids: Things to Come?" in *Test-Tube Babies*, eds. W. A. W. Walters and P Singer. Melbourne: Oxford University Press.

Weiss, R. (1997). "Cloning Suddenly Has Government's Attention." *International Herald Tribune*, March 7, 1997.

WHO (World Health Organization Press Office). (March 11, 1997). "WHO Director General Condemns Human Cloning." World Health Organization, Geneva, Switzerland.

Wilmut, I., et al. (1997). "Viable Offspring Derived from Fetal and Adult Mammalian Cells." *Nature* 385:810–813.

This essay is a shorter version of a paper prepared for the National Bioethics Advisory Commission.

I want to acknowledge with gratitude the invaluable help of my research assistant, Insoo Hyun, on this paper. He not only made it possible to complete the paper on the National Bioethics Advisory Commission's tight schedule, but also improved it with a number of insightful substantive suggestions.

GENE PATENTS CAN BE ETHICAL

Glenn McGee

When one examines the emerging debate about genetic patenting, it becomes clear that those who oppose so-called "gene patents" misunderstand genetics or apply inappropriate moral and jurisprudential theory. In this brief essay I examine some arguments against gene patents of the "methods for detection" variety, and conclude that patents on methods for detecting the presence of a genetic correlation with disease-related (and other) phenotypes can be appropriate, and that with several precautions the U.S. Patent and Trademark Office should continue granting patent protection to investigators who generate genetic disease diagnostic innovations.

There are two arguments against gene patents. The first is that genetic information is a part of nature, and one ought not, indeed cannot, patent nature. Patents allow long-term control of new and innovative processes to be secured by inventors. You have to figure out how to do something in order to receive a patent, and the process you create must have utility. Critics charge that finding a gene is not innovative. Arthur Caplan and Jon Merz, for example, compare the identification of disease genes to the land rush. The basic tools utilized in the multimillion dollar laboratories that identify genes, they point out, are themselves covered by patent protection, and render the search for genes similar to using conventional means to find new territory. Caplan and Merz contend that although the scientists who identified some forms of a gene that correlate with breast cancer are entitled to claim their discovery, discovering new land is not the same thing as owning a process. Put another way, the telescope is indeed an innovative instrument, and someone can indeed patent the technologies involved in telescopes, but it is another thing entirely to point your innovative telescope up at the heavens and begin claiming each new star as a product of technological innovation, thus protecting the process of looking at each new star. The point is well taken. The discoverer of Pluto has not invented a process, no matter how much utility might be claimed from finding and using the discovery of Pluto. If we follow this line of analysis with genes, locating new genes is a matter of sailing into new territory with old boats, so the correct mode of protection for the "finders" of new genes would be something other than patents, akin to land use or water rights laws.

However, it seems to me that opponents of the patenting of disease genes erroneously assume that the U.S. Patent and Trademark Office, and the courts that enforce patent claims, can be a final arbiter for some arcane, metaphysical distinction between "discoveries of nature" and useful technologies made by humans. Opponents of patents for "methods of detecting" a relationship between genes and disease assert that such patents are improper because they involve no "reworking" of a gene from its "natural form," and are thus attempts to patent nature. Opponents of disease-related gene patents argue that genes are natural phenomena discovered using previously patented devices. Merz, Cho, Robertson, and Leonard, for example, write that "the discovery that a particular DNA sequence at a specific locus or that different forms of a gene are associated with a disease does not qualify that scientific knowledge as patentable subject matter because no human alteration of an existing organism or naturally occurring entity is involved ... [and] because it is merely an observation of a state of

Reprinted with the permission of Cambridge University Press from *Cambridge Quarterly of Healthcare Ethics* (1998) Vol. 7, No. 4, pp. 417–421.

nature or 'nature's "handiwork.'" But is it so clear? It seems to me that while disease genes are in one sense discoverable by conventional means, their utility and indeed their meaning as a commercial object is not discovered but rather invented. Investigators who patent alleles for, or even a gene *for* susceptibility to cancer can legitimately claim a patent for "methods for detecting" a relationship between a particular bit of DNA and some phenotype. The job of the U.S. Patent and Trademark Office is to evaluate whether the patent claims a novel method for detecting a particular relationship between the DNA of a person and some phenotype for a particular purpose (e.g., diagnosing the presence of possibility of future disease states). Methods patents do not patent disease genes per se, but instead the process of making use of that DNA in diagnosis.

There is a subtle distinction to be made between "observing DNA" and constructing a DNA-based product for diagnosis of some disease or phenotype, much too subtle to be captured in any obvious way by the blunt rules about patentable subject matter, let alone by the intent of our Constitutional founders. Nonetheless the distinction is real, and goes right to the heart of what patents are supposed to do. Disease gene patents are more an innovation of scientists than a discovery. That we sometimes tend to believe otherwise is to some extent a product of *genetic essentialism*, our cultural belief that genes are a simple, self-evident library of data present in everyone and responsible for all aspects of human embodiment and disease. If we begin with the idea that genes are a simple code to be read or stumbled upon, we miss the immensely difficult epidemiological task of clarifying otherwise diffuse relationships between particular environments and genes, and between particular groups and genes. If I find a strange tree in the Vermont forest, take a clipping back to my lab, discover that eating the tree cures a disease, and file a patent application for the tree itself, or for very broad uses of the tree, the U.S. Patent and Trademark Office is likely to reject my application. However, if I take a clipping and purify, package, intensify, or in other ways make a product *derived* from that clipping, the U.S. Patent and Trademark Office may grant me a patent alongside the thousands of other medical device or pharmaceutical patents. It was obvious to the Office that cDNA, express sequence tags (ESTs), and RNA that has been "purified" in some way merited patent issuance. What must be answered is whether the process of describing disease-related genes is like examining a "natural form" (like the regular clipping from the tree), or like changing nature to serve a novel purpose (like making a special tea from my clipping).

There is little hope of demonstrating that a disease-related gene mutation is natural, out there to be discovered and possessed of a priori identity. Disease genes are identified in the application by their phenotypic products, when some bits of DNA can be put to explanatory use for some diagnostic purpose. But this is true also of Nebraska. Nebraska is a state only when we say it is. Its geography, climate, and flora are identifiable only after we establish the boundaries for some other purpose. We do not patent Nebraska. Patents for disease-related gene mutations and genes are by contrast useful when the innovation involved in creating some genetic diagnosis product is useful, novel, and nonobvious. While finding a new gene requires no new or novel piece of equipment, and involves no "purification" by probes or other "artificial" tools, the work of identifying the group of people possessed of a phenotype, the specific methods by which mutations are associated with a particular phenotype, and the methods for putting the epidemiological evidence to specific work in making a diagnosis, are clearly synthetic and novel and are not themselves natural phenomena. Having a phenotype, like having a disease, is in part a matter of social and scientific convention about which states of human life possess relevant or important differences meriting medical intervention or classification. We sometimes forget that even when a gene is highly correlated with a particular disease, that doesn't make the disease "genetic." Finding DNA is a discovery. Correlating it with human life for the purpose of creating a diagnostic process is innovation.

Thus not to allow disease-related gene work patent protection seems misguided. If making an extract of my tree clipping can be classed as innovative and patentable, why should we allow genetic essentialism to persuade us that the line between discovering nature and making technology is unblurred for work involving genetic diagnosis? It is in fact a blurry line, and the best we can hope for is to limit the use of patenting to cases where it clearly protects the making of particular diagnostic tests and elements of viral vectors for gene therapy. The U.S. Patent and Trademark Office does not have special access to the heavens, and to expect that they will treat all disease-related gene mutations and genes as "purely natural" phenomena is to ask them to buy in to a particularly intractable element of genetic essentialism: the claim that genes are natural things, things "in themselves." So far the patent office has wisely refused to endorse this analysis, opting instead to patent genes or alleles when they are employed in a novel product even if that product is tied directly to embodied human biology.

Think about the matter in intellectual rather than simple physical terms and things seem clearer. When the anthropologist begins to observe a new community, her work is quite clearly that of the observer, and her work products are most clearly associated with existing and well-recognized anthropological methods. She may publish initial findings about the community but she will not yet be doing synthetic work. She is pointing a telescope into the heavens, cataloguing a new star. As her work proceeds, though, she will increasingly develop new ways of understanding the community and new modes for gathering data. Much of her new data will take on new forms and be published in different ways, e.g., as personal reports from her slow, partial assimilation into the culture. Let us imagine that she is now approached by a U.S. soft drink company for advice in understanding this new market. Using her synthetic work, she may develop for them a scheme for interpreting the wishes of the community, using an instrument that will tell who will want to buy soda on the basis of signs and signals otherwise uninterpretable. The U.S. Patent and Trademark Office will be receptive to her intellectual patent application for the methods for detecting such receptiveness, even though she began with simple and well-understood methods for gathering knowledge. Her late turn to identify a way of thinking about the community for the purpose of "diagnosing" its interest in soda is novel and patentable. My point by analogy is that the teams working on genetic diagnosis are entitled to the same protection for whatever diagnostic utility they derive. However Faustian is the anthropologist's appropriation of her early project, it would be essentialism to insist that she is merely patenting a priori natural facts. She, and the patent applicants for gene patents, should be able to request patent protection for innovative scholarly work that mutates and culminates in novel products.

It seems to me no one would care much about the preceding debate were it not for the second argument against gene patents, which holds that gene patents create a "toll bridge" barring research using patented genes. Opponents of gene patents hold that a researcher who wants to study some chromosome may not be able to look at human genetic information without paying the people who "found" it. This argument is more important because is suggests that genetic patents will clog up the works of genetic research, creating an anticompetitive environment in which genetic tests will not be developed if researchers in the early stages of work on common diseases will not be able to afford to pay the tolls necessary for start-up research.

However, correctly framed and issued disease-related gene patents will in no way preclude access to genetic material by the thousands of laboratories in high schools, colleges, and of course medical sciences departments that are conducting research in molecular and cellular engineering without using the device actually patented by the patentee. Infringement of the patent occurs when other organizations put the innovation per se to use, and the actual innovation is put to use only when the method for detecting the allele's or gene's correlation with the particular phenotype is applied to a patient. The critical issue is that the patent office be very clear about what it is that the patent claims about the disease or phenotype being diagnosed. A clear patent application is a good one if and only if it identifies a well-studied body of epidemiological data about the effectiveness of use of particular genetic information in finding disposition to, or physiologic evidence of, some phenotype. Companies should not be able to throw up a flag as they identify each new chunk of the genome: there must be utility, and only that useful device is patentable.

In the final analysis, none of us wants to sell Yellowstone, the stars in the sky, or our bodies. The effort to diagnose genetic correlation with disease creates new kinds of information for particular purposes. It is not, as some opponents of genetic patenting would have it, an effort to own the "code of codes" or to lock up investigation of genetic disease.

DISEASE GENES ARE NOT PATENTABLE: A REBUTTAL OF MCGEE

Jon F. Merz and Mildred K. Cho

Dr. McGee presents a cogent argument for the patentability of the diagnosis of gene forms that are found to be associated with disease or other phenotypic manifestations. We're convinced he's wrong. An analogy will help explain why.

Some years ago, in the Black Forest, people hunted down the elusive truffle, that culinary delight, with pigs learned in the art of rooting around in, you guessed it, tree roots. People and pigs had been collaborating in the search for truffles for thousands of years. Among the truffles collected in the forest, none was as highly prized—or as rare—as the White Truffle. It would reward its finder with 10 times the price of other truffles at market. But the White Truffle was much more elusive than other truffles, and a day in the forest would yield an average 1 White Truffle for every 100 regular truffles.

Reprinted with permission of Cambridge University Press from *Cambridge Quarterly of Healthcare Ethics* (1998), Vol. 7, No. 4, pp. 425–427.

After 20 years of truffle trifles (and meticulous notekeeping), one Franz Statistiner did make an interesting (and, as we shall see, valuable) observation: 9 of every 10 White Truffles that he had gathered over the years were found on the roots of red oak trees, and, overall, 20% of truffles found on red oaks were White!

Franz contemplated keeping his finding secret and simply targeting his pigs on their daily jaunts to search only red oaks, thereby increasing his yield of White Truffles. He was worried, however, that other truffle hunters would soon note his success in the market and figure out his secret. Instead, he went to a patent lawyer.

A good patent lawyer. She wrote and got an imaginary patent with the following claims:

> I Claim:
>
> 1. A method of detecting an increased chance of having White Truffles under a tree comprising directly or indirectly:
>   detecting whether or not a tree is a Red Oak Tree;

and observing whether or not the tree is more likely to have White Truffles growing under it, wherein Red Oak Trees have an increased likelihood of having White Truffles thereunder.

2. The method of claim 1, wherein said detecting step comprises looking for trees having at least one Red Oak Tree Leaf growing thereon.

Franz then was able to collect royalties from all other hunters who focused their search on red oak trees, making him wildly wealthy. Franz bought the forest.

Sound reasonable? Dr. McGee apparently agrees with us: neither the discovery nor the act of looking at red oak trees for the purpose of diagnosing the increased likelihood of finding White Truffles is patentable subject matter. What has been discovered is a mere phenomenon of nature, an (as yet unexplained) association between an observation of a particular type of tree in the forest and the empirical fact that such trees have a "natural" propensity for White Truffles. It is no more than an observation of a thing and the mental step of understanding the informational value of that thing.

The truffle patent is not only analogous to a disease gene patent, but has been craftily drafted directly from U.S. Patent No. 5,508,167, entitled Methods of Screening for Alzheimer's Disease, which reads:

What is claimed is:

1. A method of detecting if a subject is at increased risk of developing late onset Alzheimer's disease (AD) comprising directly or indirectly:

   detecting the presence or absence of an apolipoprotein E type 4 isoform (ApoE4) in the subject;

   and

   observing whether or not the subject is at increased risk of developing late onset AD by observing if the presence of ApoE4 is or is not detected, wherein the presence of ApoE4 indicates said subject is at increased risk of developing late onset AD.

This invention, Dr. McGee and the U.S. Patent and Trademark Office agree, is patentable. What differs? The act of "detecting" in the truffle patent requires one's eyes and knowledge of any unique characteristics of the red oak tree, such as the leaf specified in claim 2. Detecting in the AD patent requires use of PCR, Southern analysis, sequencing, or one of numerous other previously established means of looking at the chemical structure known as DNA. Each entails steps that are obvious to anyone skilled in the pertinent art. The act of looking at trees or genes, respectively, comprises normal knowledge and skill of those trained in their respective arts. Any one device or method for looking might itself be a patentable innovation (such as a microscope, telescope, or PCR), but the special protections afforded by patenting should not be extended to all specific acts of looking.

What else differs? The "invention" underlying the truffle patent is the association of red oak trees with an increased chance of finding White Truffles thereunder. The "invention" underlying the AD patent is the association of a particular allele with an increased chance of disease occurrence. Both are empirical observations; both are simply epidemiologic discoveries about (albeit within our current understanding of) naturally occurring phenomena.

Dr. McGee's argument is based on two false premises. The first is that the difficulty and effort involved in making a discovery, the "immensely difficult epidemiological task of purifying otherwise diffuse relationships between particular environments and genes, and between particular groups and genes," make the discovery patentable.

Everyone agrees that a basic scientific or statistical discovery, regardless of how difficult it was to make or how much effort and money went into it, is not patentable subject matter. As the U.S. Supreme Court stated in a case in which it invalidated claims for a mixture of bacteria, "[P]atents cannot issue for the discovery of the phenomena of nature. ... The qualities of these bacteria, like the heat of the sun, electricity, or the qualities of metals, are part of the storehouse of knowledge of all men. They are manifestations of laws of nature, free to all men and reserved exclusively to none." The Supreme Court more recently reiterated that "[t]he laws of nature, physical phenomena, and abstract ideas have been held not patentable. ... Thus a new mineral discovered in the earth or a new plant found in the wild is not patentable subject matter. Likewise, Einstein could not patent his celebrated law that $E = mc^2$; nor could Newton have patented the law of gravity." The work Einstein and Newton put into these discoveries was synthetic and novel, but their genius and remarkable efforts do not make their observations of associations between physical entities patentable.

Furthermore, the fact that several research groups independently clone and sequence genes associated with diseases, often within weeks of each other, suggests that the effort is not that innovative to those skilled in the arts. If the entire coding sequence of the human genome is sequenced at the end of the Human Genome Project, it will become even less of an effort to correlate the presence of sequences with disease. At some point, by Dr. McGee's argument, associations between genes and diseases will not be patentable because of the ease—a simple computer search—of finding these (as well as far more complex multigene and gene-environment) relationships. To say that these associations are patentable is "genetic exceptionalism": allowing oneself to be unduly dazzled, nay, mesmerized, by the novelty of biotechnology compared to other technologies. It is genetic exceptionalism to say that finding associations between red oak trees and White Truffles using the well-established method of shoveling is not patentable, but that finding associations between a gene and a disease using well-established methods of mapping, cloning, and sequencing genes, and of identifying people with mutations is patentable.

Dr. McGee's second false premise is that he predicates patentability on the usefulness of the discovery. However, market potential is not a necessary, much less a satisfactory, condition to determining whether something comprises patentable subject matter. It is simply irrelevant. Gold and diamonds, while valuable, are not patentable subject matter, regardless of who first discovered them or how difficult those discoveries were. McGee's arguments show how easy it is to segue from an inquiry about whether something is patentable subject matter to questions about whether that something satisfies the tests for patentability; that is, it must be new, useful, and nonobvious. Under U.S. patent law, however, these are separate issues, and confounding them muddles the underlying question.

Arguing that correlating discoveries with "human life for the purpose of creating a diagnostic process is innovation" as does McGee sets us on a slippery slope that would wreak havoc with healthcare. By this argument, tests used in performing physical examinations (including asking patients questions, feeling their thyroid glands, and listening to their lungs and heart with stethoscopes) as methods of detecting abnormalities should be patentable. Many of the methods used in routine physicals took years of clinical observations and effort, resulted from a synthetic and creative process, and are undoubtedly useful. Yet are they patentable?

At bottom, the "detection" involved in the truffle and disease gene patents itself is not patentable. Everyone is free to look at those things—be they trees or genes—that exist independent of the ingenuity, innovation, and manufacture of humans. The fact that someone discovers a reason for looking does not change that basic premise. The scientific reason itself is not patentable, and it does not render the act of looking in the specific case patentable.

Independent of the foregoing, we believe there are substantive arguments against disease gene patenting based not on patentability of the subject matter but on public policy and ethics. As we have asserted elsewhere, the risks to patient health and access to care, to physician-patient relations, and to the biomedical research enterprise far outweigh the possible benefits that could be attributed to disease gene patents. While we believe the courts should invalidate these broad diagnosis methods patents under the product of nature doctrine, we firmly believe that the unethical patenting practices reflected in these patents should be more firmly enjoined by the medical profession and by healthcare institutions. Unfortunately, the ethical proscriptions have been emasculated by financial pressures, by increasing commercialism of academic medicine, and by profiteering. The profession must clean up its act, or Congress may intervene.

Because of perceived abuse of patents of surgical methods, Congress enacted a law in late 1996 that holds physicians not liable for infringement of "pure process" patent. That law does not apply to "biotechnology patents" (perhaps reflecting Congress's love affair with things biotechnic, and perhaps reflecting the acknowledged assistance of the biotechnology industry in drafting the law), and does not protect laboratories approved under the Clinical Laboratories Improvement Act. That law was a stopgap against more drastic legislation prohibiting medical process patents; if methods patenting continues to burgeon (and diagnostics comprises the largest share of biotechnology patents being issued), Congress should expand the law's protections. Already, the human chorionic gonadotropin patent, a similarly broad diagnostic patent, has led to the abandonment of prenatal testing that had been the standard of care. This is simply unacceptable. These patents are contrary to good medical practice, and must be prohibited.

UNIT FOUR

HIV, AIDS, AND THE PROVIDER/PATIENT RELATIONSHIP

CHAPTER 7: ETHICS AND HIV/AIDS AND CHAPTER 8: THE RELATIONSHIP BETWEEN MEDICAL PROFESSIONALS AND PATIENTS

Chapter 7 contains readings that discuss the moral dilemmas that surround the identification and treatment of HIV/AIDS. Many issues that arise correspond with those discussed in Chapter 8, which concerns the physician/patient relationship, since to ask questions such as whether a physician has a moral obligation to treat an HIV-positive patient is to inquire about the type of relationship the physician has to his or her patient.

Edmund Pellegrino and John Arras both discuss the question, "Do physicians have a duty to place themselves at risk in order to help their patients?" This question is addressed specifically with regard to treating HIV-positive patients. Pellegrino stresses the distinction between an occupation and a profession, and argues that since physicians are part of a profession, they have moral obligations that diverge from their self-interested motivations. Arras also argues in support of a duty to treat on the part of physicians. Arras analyzes different approaches to grounding a duty to treat, and he rejects a voluntary model and a social contract model. He argues that the appropriate model emphasizes being a virtuous physician, a role that includes taking risks as part of the job.

The next group of readings discusses the topic of confidentiality, in particular, when and if medical professionals are under a duty to disclose a patient's medical status if it is believed that this patient poses a threat to another person. In the Majority Opinion of the California Supreme Court case of *Tarasoff* v. *University of California Regents*, Judge Tobriner addresses a case in which an estranged boyfriend, Prosenjit Poddar, told his psychological therapist that he intended to kill his former girlfriend, Tatiana Tarasoff. Two months after this admission, Poddar killed Tarasoff. Judge Tobriner argued that the psychologist did have a duty of care toward Tarasoff, which implies that the psychologist had a duty to inform her, her parents, or the police of this threat, a duty that was not satisfied. The basis of this duty concerns the foreseeability of the harm coming to a specifiable individual (Tarasoff), the special professional context within which Poddar made this admission, and the fact that the psychologist did predict that Poddar would in fact kill Tarasoff. In a dissenting opinion, Judge Clark argues that the costs of establishing a professional duty to warn others at risk will outweigh its benefits, since compromising patient confidentiality will also undermine effective patient treatment. Morton Winston addresses the issue of confidentiality specifically within the context of HIV and AIDS. Winston argues that there is no absolute duty for medical professionals to keep patient information confidential. He suggests two principles, the Harm Principle and the Vulnerability Principle, to establish the boundaries of when the duty of confidentiality can be overridden, and provides several examples of cases to fill out his approach. The issue of confidentiality as it applies specifically to HIV/AIDS is brought into focus in the selection "Please Don't Tell!" In this piece, Len Fleck and Marcia Angell offer differing perspectives on a case study in which a man wishes not to tell his sister of his HIV-positive status, even though she will be providing some medical care for him and hence may be at some risk of exposure.

The last group of readings addresses the question of whether there is a moral duty to test and treat HIV-positive pregnant women with medications that can significantly reduce the chance that their children will become infected. An important study revealed that pregnant women who took the anti-viral drug zidovudine during the last two trimesters of pregnancy and received it intravenously during the birthing process could reduce the chance of infecting their child with HIV by approximately 66%. The Working Group on HIV Testing of Pregnant Women and Newborns concludes that pregnant women should be informed of the option to be tested and receive zidovudine treatment, but they are opposed to mandatory testing and treatment. The Working Group rejects reducing "vertical transmission," the transmission of disease from mother to child during pregnancy, as a viable goal since this will undermine reproductive freedom and further stigmatize women from oppressed social groups who are HIV-positive.

Ronald Bayer agrees with the conclusion of the Working Group that mandatory testing of mothers is not justified, and argues that mandatory treatment of HIV-positive women is not acceptable since this violates their autonomy and does not secure informed consent from these women. In this case, minimizing the child's chances for contracting disease requires also treating the pregnant woman, yet treating the child *in utero* poses risks to the pregnant woman. For instance, beginning a course of zidovudine during pregnancy may not be necessary for the woman's health if she is in the early stages of HIV infection. However, once this treatment is started, if it is stopped after the birth, this increases the chance that the HIV virus can mutate and become drug-resistant when the woman needs treatment. If the treatment is continued after the birth of the child even though it is not strictly speaking necessary, this then reduces the number of years this woman can expect to live since most persons become resistant to these drugs over time. The readings in this chapter demonstrate that the moral issues stemming from the testing and treatment of HIV/AIDS are complex.

Chapter 8 begins with Ruth Macklin's discussion of whether a Jehovah's Witness may justifiably refuse a blood transfusion for religious reasons. Macklin examines two reasons why Jehovah's Witnesses should not be forcibly transfused: an appeal to freedom of religion and to autonomy to make life-shaping choices. She also discusses several bases for arguing that such persons should be forcibly treated, reasons that stem from paternalistic arguments and the rights of physicians to do what correct medical practice dictates. Macklin argues that it is morally justifiable to administer such blood transfusions to incompetent patients and to minor children even over the religious objections of their parents. Macklin does not think that paternalistic arguments for forcible transfusions are successful when applied to competent adult patients, though she weighs this finding against the point that physicians have the right to do what is accepted as standard medical practice. This would seem to imply that a basis exists for forcible transfusions on competent adults in some cases, or at least that physicians may refuse to perform surgeries in which a blood transfusion is likely needed and a patient refuses to consent to the blood transfusion. Mark Sheldon provides a counterpoint to Macklin's position in his selection, "Ethical Issues in the Forced Transfusion of Jehovah's Witness Children." After reviewing the legal framework in the United States for dealing with this controversy, Sheldon argues that such parents should have the right to refuse blood transfusions for their children. Jehovah's Witness parents cannot be said to be harming their children, since such parents are simply placing their children's spiritual interest in obtaining eternal life over their worldly interests.

In "Opinion in *Canterbury* v. *Spence,*" Judge Robinson addresses a case in which a young man, John Canterbury, becomes paraplegic after a surgical procedure. Canterbury's physician, Dr. Spence, did not advise his patient that the surgery carried a 1% risk of paraplegia, since he was concerned that this would deter Canterbury from undergoing the surgery and this would not be in the patient's best interest. Judge Robinson argues that Dr. Spence was not justified in withholding this information from Canterbury, since this information is material to the patient making an informed decision. This decision, then, suggests a general principle for when a physician has met the conditions necessary for having secured informed consent. Howard Brody examines and rejects several different standards for informed consent, and defends a "transparency" standard in which the patient is informed when it is true that the doctor's basic thinking has been made clear. Revealing one's basic thinking requires the doctor to point out what factors are most salient in his or her decision, to engage in conversation, and to answer questions to the patient's satisfaction. This argument is interesting since Brody's standard may conflict with Judge Robinson's finding that Dr. Spence did not secure informed consent from Canterbury, if it is assumed that the 1% chance of paraplegia was not part of Spence's basic thinking.

Another issue bearing on the relationship between medical professionals and patients concerns how to determine when a patient is competent to offer informed consent. Allen Buchanan and Dan Brock set forth three different standards for determining patient competence, and settle upon a standard that bases competence on the process of reasoning that led up to the patient's decision. Buchanan and Brock believe that no one standard of competence is appropriate for all decisions and discuss the circumstances in which each standard is most appropriate. Tom Tomlinson discusses an important objection to Buchanan and Brock's account, that it is more likely to demand an assessment of a person's competence when she refuses treatment, even if the person's competence would not have been called into question if treatment had been accepted. This seems arbitrary since the patient's presumed status will change without anything about the patient changing, such as his level of understanding, mental capacities, or medical condition. Tomlinson argues that Buchanan and Brock confuse the need for a variable standard of evidence for competence with a variable standard of competence itself. His main point is that if one makes an unusual decision to refuse treatment, we should not then say they need to be "more competent" for us to respect that decision as compared with a decision to accept treatment. Instead, all we need is stronger evidence that this is a decision made by a person that can truly be capable of making well-informed decisions, since the stakes are higher in cases of refused treatment.

The final issue discussed under the umbrella of the physician/patient relationship concerns truth-telling. Roger Higgs believes that telling patients the truth about their condition is of primary importance, though he recognizes rare exceptions to this general principle. Howard Brody addresses the topic of truth-telling with an emphasis on preserving the patient's hope when revealing an unpromising medical prognosis. Brody argues that telling patients the truth is compatible with preserving hope, since it is more difficult to take away hope than commonly recognized.

CRITICAL THINKING TOOL: LEGAL REASONING AND MORAL REASONING

In Chapter 2, we discussed the distinction between descriptive and normative statements. In essence, descriptive statements focus on what *is* the case, while normative statements focus on what *ought to be* the case. Needless to say, these two types of statements are distinct, since the way things are is often not the way things ought to be. Normative statements are the focus in moral philosophy, since ethical philosophers are concerned with examining the arguments for and against claims that we morally ought or ought not do certain things. We also discussed the naturalistic fallacy in Chapter 2, which highlighted the logical error of assuming that because something is the case, then it ought to be that way. It is simply mistaken to directly move from a claim about the way things are to a claim about the way things ought to be.

This section provides a critical discussion of the methods of legal reasoning and moral reasoning. Recalling the naturalistic fallacy frames an important issue relating to these two types of reasoning that concerns the proper place of appeals to tradition/authority. As Julie Van Camp[1] notes, one major difference between legal reasoning and philosophical reasoning (and moral reasoning in particular) is that in the law, appeals to precedent are an essential element. This is captured in the expression "*stare decisis*," which means "to stand on the decision." Simply put, the vast majority of arguments in support of a defensible legal holding refer to previous decisions in the law, or precedents. Of course, over time the law changes, and in such cases one must argue why the previous precedents are no longer applicable or valid in supporting a different holding. Yet in critical philosophical or moral reasoning, direct appeals to authority or the way things have been are rejected as providing in themselves a sound basis for an argument. There is something of a tension, then, between the legal decisions that have influenced moral debates in medical ethics and the perspective of critical thinking that asks us to examine the arguments on their face. Several of the main bioethical issues discussed in this chapter's readings relate especially closely to important legal precedents, and hence we will examine these two forms of reasoning in this section.

To begin, the fact that X is a law is a descriptive matter; one can simply ask, "Is using a radar detection device in one's automobile legally prohibited or not in this state?" However, laws may or may not possess moral force. Laws against murder seem to either draw from or contribute to the moral prohibition on murder. However, laws against speeding (assuming one is otherwise driving carefully and in an unimpaired state) do not necessarily ground a claim that speeding is morally wrong. Yet laws could still possess some degree of normative force, even if they are properly categorized as descriptive statements. The true proposition that "Humans are capable of feeling pain" is a descriptive statement, yet it also offers support for the moral claim "Do not cause human beings unnecessary pain." Particular laws may possess normative force even if they do not in themselves possess moral force, since, as distinguished law scholar H.L.A. Hart[2] notes, there are non-moral uses of *ought*: "... given appropriate contexts, 'ought,' 'must,' and 'should' may be used when it is patent that nothing moral is at stake. You ought to, you should, you must change your wet clothes."

There are two possible questions one may ask when critically discussing the similarities and differences between law and morality. The first question concerns whether the concepts of law and morality are analytically linked. It seems simple enough to point out that an action can be immoral and not illegal, such as telling a lie about one's personal life (assuming one is not under oath in a court of law), and that an action can be illegal and not immoral, such as failing to file one's tax forms in triplicate in accordance with a local statute. The deeper query here asks whether a morally questionable law can in fact be a legitimate law. One can puzzle over a law, for instance, present in Nazi Germany in which making derogatory statements about the Third Reich was illegal and mandated a severe punishment (including death). While this is an interesting philosophical question, the focus of this section is not on this issue, but instead on the differing characteristics of legal and moral reasoning.

While these features are somewhat contentious, there are several general characteristics of moral judgments worth discussing. When one engages in moral reasoning and makes a moral judgment that "X is morally right," then one is committed to the claim that all things *relevantly similar* to X are morally right. This is the characteristic of *universalizability* in moral reasoning. This characteristic admits of several different interpretations. On the weak interpretation, if I judge X to be right, then I must judge all actions relevantly similar to X to be right. This is simply a minimal claim regarding consistency: if no morally relevant differences exist between cases X1 and X2, I must judge X1 and X2 as both morally right or wrong. On the strong interpretation, if I believe that X is morally right, then everyone must make the same moral judgment regarding X. On this conception, there is only one correct moral judgment that applies to any moral situation or action. These two different interpretations differ in that the former applies simply within one person while the latter applies across judgers. Universalizability is held to be a characteristic of moral judgments by those who support the moral theories of Utilitarianism and Kantianism.

Second, there is the characteristic of *action-guidingness*. The main idea is that it is part of the nature of moral judgments that they are a recommendation for one's behavior, and if one fails to be moved to action, then one has failed in some way. This characteristic is highlighted particularly by those who emphasize that ethics is a practical enterprise. Aretaic theorists who follow in the footsteps of Aristotle would especially emphasize this characteristic. Finally, some theorists subscribe to what is called a *publicity condition* on moral judging. This condition states that when engaging in ethical reasoning, one's moral judgment must be considered a piece of public advice to all. Supporters of this feature maintain that a moral judgment cannot properly be made in support of an action if its moral status is kept secret or is not in principle knowable to all persons. This condition may gain force if we think that morality is essentially *social* in nature—its purpose is to guide public policy and for all to know its tenets. Most notably, deontological thinker John Rawls (discussed in Chapter 1) supports the idea that proper moral reasoning must meet such a publicity condition.

Legal reasoning, by contrast, consists in a process that has differing characteristics. As already mentioned, legal reasoning is based on precedent. This requires that one first research a case and locate previous court cases that address the same issue. Then, one must seek out precedents in other cases that have strong similarities to the case under consideration. The principle of "*stare decisis*" inevitably involves the use of analogical reasoning (discussed in Chapter 2). One must find cases analogous to the case under scrutiny that have favorable precedents that have survived legal scrutiny. The structure of the argument is that the decision from the earlier case applies to the present case since the two cases are relevantly similar. For this reason, we should draw a legal conclusion similar to the one suggested by the previous precedents. It is worth noting that legal reasoning is not exclusively based on precedents; if that were true, novel cases could not be adjudicated. For instance, developing technologies often pose new legal challenges. In some cases, these challenges can be assimilated to settled law relating to other analogous types of cases. For example, in debates regarding the status of surrogacy contracts (see Chapter 3), the relevant issues were discussed in terms of laws concerning the adoption of children. In this way, surrogacy was subsumed under previous laws, and could be viewed as a form of "prenatal adoption."

Previous decisions are also rethought as well, and such holdings do not represent an appeal to analogical reasoning or precedents. In some cases, opinions of the dissenting judges (called *dissenting opinions*) are included as part of the holding. These are referred to as the *minority opinion*, in contrast with the *majority opinion*, which represents the actual legal holding or conclusion in the case. Dissenting opinions can be very important, even though they are not in fact part of the legal conclusion established in a case. For example, in *Roe* v. *Wade* (1973) (see Chapter 4) Justice William Rehnquist registered a forceful dissent. If one looks to the decision reached in the U.S. Supreme Court case *Planned Parenthood of Southeastern Pa.* v. *Casey* (1992) (see Chapter 4), many elements of that decision are foreshadowed in Rehnquist's dissent nearly twenty years earlier. While legal reasoning relies on appeals to precedent, the making of law is a dynamic process as well.

Let's now apply some of these points in a critical analysis of issues discussed in Chapters 7 and 8. In Chapter 7, one central moral issue concerns the confidentiality of patients' medical information. Typically, respect for patient privacy prohibits sharing patients' medical information unless they give consent for its disclosure. However, in the majority opinion in the California State Supreme Court of *Tarasoff* v.

University of California Regents, it was determined that there is a duty on the part of medical professionals to violate patient confidentiality and to warn identifiable third parties who may be in danger. In the Tarasoff case, an estranged boyfriend (Poddar) told his therapist that he intended to kill his former girlfriend (Tarasoff). Poddar's therapist recommended that he be detained for psychological evaluation, but his superior did not agree. When Poddar seemed rational, he was released on the basis of his promise to stay away from his former girlfriend. Two months later, Poddar killed Tarasoff. Neither the psychologists nor the police notified Tarasoff, and the Court found that in not doing so they acted with reckless disregard for her safety.

This majority opinion, delivered by Judge Tobriner, established a "duty to warn" that was questioned in a dissenting opinion by Judge Clark, who argued that the costs of establishing a duty to warn will outweigh its benefits. Judge Clark maintained that if patient confidentiality is compromised, then adequate treatment will be as well. In particular, Clark offers the following reasons against violating confidentiality and establishing a "duty to warn." First, Clark reasons that without strict confidentiality, many patients may not seek treatment for mental illness, since there is a stigma associated with having such a disease. Second, confidentiality is necessary for getting patients to fully disclose as part of their treatment. If patients are concerned about whether the content of their psychological sessions will be revealed to others, they may not "open up" and this may hinder their treatment. Third, Clark points out that it will be very difficult to accurately predict whether a person who says something questionable in a psychological session will in fact harm another through violent action.

In later legal decisions, this holding has been seen as applicable to the question of whether a medical professional has a "duty to warn" identifiable persons who may be at risk of contracting HIV. In particular, in a case where a patient tests seropositive, does a medical professional have a duty to contact persons who may have been sexually active with the HIV-positive person? While the law concerning this issue is still evolving, Lawrence Gostin[3] points out that there have already been cases in which a medical professional has been found liable for failure to inform persons of the risk of HIV infection. The question that truly needs to be explored, however, is whether the situation with respect to individuals at risk of violence from persons suffering from mental illness, upon which the *Tarasoff* opinion is based, is truly analogous to cases of possible harm stemming from sexual activity with a person who has been confirmed as HIV-positive.

There are several possible dissimilarities between the two cases that may not allow the reasoning in *Tarasoff* to apply neatly to the case of HIV.[4] First, while Poddar's action of killing Tarasoff was clearly a moral violation of Tárasoff, is the same equally true in an HIV-related case? It is unclear whether this is in fact true, assuming that the sexual activity between the two persons was consensual. Another factor that may make a difference is whether the person who tested HIV-positive knew or had any reason to strongly suspect that he was HIV-positive. In a case in which one engages in unprotected sexual activity with another and does not disclose his HIV-positive status, from a moral perspective we may consider this comparable to the moral wrongness of murder. However, if the person who ultimately tested seropositive did not know he had the virus, then it is much more unclear whether this behavior is comparable to murder. A second and related dissimilarity is that Tarasoff was in no position to defend herself from the harm resulting from Poddar's actions. The same is not true in an HIV-related case, since it is reasonable to think that partners who voluntarily engage in consensual sexual activity bear some responsibility to gain knowledge about their partner's sexual history and/or take the necessary precautions to minimize the chances of contracting HIV/AIDS. Given these dissimilarities, at the very least, the *Tarasoff* case is not clearly analogous to cases of a possible "duty to warn" with respect to HIV-infection. Hence, it is unclear whether the precedent in *Tarasoff* should in fact be applied to HIV cases.

In Chapter 8, one of the main moral issues concerns the question of whether parents may refuse medical treatment for their children on religious grounds. In particular, the controversy surrounds adults who, on the basis of their Christian beliefs as Jehovah's Witnesses, refuse blood transfusions since they believe this is in accord with the Bible. It is important to note that Jehovah's Witnesses accept all other forms of medical treatments, and while some states have passed laws that recognize spiritual treatment as an acceptable form of health care for children, critics think this decision constitutes child abuse and child neglect. The general precedent, as discussed by Macklin, is that competent adults can refuse treatment on the basis of religious beliefs, while incompetent adults or minors can be transfused even over the demands of family members to the contrary. In his selection contained in this chapter, Mark Sheldon points out that the case which set the precedent, *Prince* v. *Massachusetts* (1944), was not a case dealing with medical treatment at all. Jehovah's Witnesses are required by their religion to spread their faith, and this case examined whether a woman who had a nine-year-old child with her on the street selling Jehovah's Witness magazines violated child labor laws. In his article, Sheldon questions the fit between the court decisions which followed upholding *Prince* and the precedent involving the forcible transfusion of minors, arguing that it is unclear whether parents who refuse blood transfusions harm their children. In his argument, Sheldon takes a strategy similar to the criticism deployed above concerning the application of *Tarasoff* to HIV cases.

The precedent stemming from the *Prince* decision, which was applied to the issue of forcible blood transfusions for minors, also has implications for the moral issues surrounding HIV/AIDS. One moral issue in Chapter 7, as discussed in the articles by the Working Group and Bayer, concerns the question of whether pregnant women should be tested (and perhaps forcibly treated) for HIV as a way to reduce the probability of transmission of HIV to the fetus. An important study revealed that if pregnant women received HIV-treatment drugs (AZT/ZDV) for the last two trimesters of pregnancy and during birthing, this reduced the transmission rate of HIV to the fetus by 66%. While both the Working Group and Bayer oppose even mandatory HIV testing for pregnant women, the *Prince* precedent raises some puzzles concerning the moral issues involved in HIV treatment. In the discussion of his position opposing mandatory testing and the setting of the reduction of vertical (mother–fetus) HIV-transmission as a goal, Bayer specifically mentions the Jehovah's Witness case. Bayer seems to think that adults can refuse treatment, even if it is lifesaving, and this fits with the *Prince* precedent as applied to the forcible blood transfusion case. Yet, if one supports the *Prince* precedent in such cases, it is clear that forcible medical treatments on children, even over the religious objections of their parents, are sometimes acceptable if there is a grave risk of harm or loss of life. But a very similar risk of harm applies in the case of an HIV-positive fetus! In the HIV case, however, in order to offer medical treatment to the child *in utero*, we must also treat the mother as well. Even if the mother does not wish for the child to undergo the course of HIV-treatment drugs, if we support the *Prince* precedent, then it would seem that we must (or at least could) engage in forcible medical treatment on the mother as well. This is a conclusion that is difficult for most persons to accept, since it undercuts the ideal of patient autonomy.

There is at least one potential difference between the two cases that may allow one to favor forcible blood transfusions on minors while not supporting forcible medical treatment on HIV-positive pregnant women for their child while *in utero*. There are tangible risks to pregnant women who undergo the course of AZT/ZDV during the last two trimesters of pregnancy and birthing to minimize the chance of vertical transmission. HIV-positive persons who begin antiviral treatments should continue them, otherwise there is the possibility that the virus may mutate and become drug-resistant. The current strategy for addressing HIV is to allow a seropositive individual's immune system to keep the virus in check as long as possible, which then delays the usage of AZT/ZDV and tends to extend the infected person's life expectancy. However, if a pregnant woman were forcibly treated with HIV drugs, then this would open her up to serious risks if she stopped using the drugs and may decrease her life expectancy. These risks do not befall the parents of children who receive forcible blood transfusions, and hence, this represents an important difference between the two cases.

Finally, it is worth noting that there are other options besides forcible medical treatment in both cases. In the Jehovah's Witness case, alternative treatment methods can be used. These include using nonblood replacement fluids, surgical techniques that reduce the need for blood products, and, recently, methods of capturing and "recycling" the patient's own blood during surgery. These methods do not violate the beliefs of Jehovah's Witnesses. In the HIV case, the child contracts HIV from the birthing process by coming into contact with bodily fluids and blood from the mother. Childbirth methods which minimize this contact, including most recently bloodless Cesarean sections, allow the possibility of minimizing the risk of vertical transmission without the associated dangers of HIV drug treatment for the mother.

This section provides a critical treatment of the concepts of moral reasoning and legal reasoning, and offers an analysis of several key legal precedents that apply to the moral issues addressed in this unit. At the very least, the preceding discussion suggests that one cannot simply "read off" the morality of a course of action by referring to an associated legal holding.

Notes

1. *Ethical Issues in the Courts*, Preface. (Belmont, CA: Wadsworth Publishing, 2001).
2. "Legal and Moral Obligation," in A.I. Melden, *Essays in Moral Philosophy* (Seattle: Washington University Press), p. 83.
3. Lawrence O. Gostin, "Confidentiality vs. the Duty to Warn: Ethical and Legal Dilemmas in the HIV Epidemic," *JIAPAC*, September 1995.
4. The discussion in this paragraph is indebted to Donald C. Ainslie, "Questioning Bioethics: AIDS, Sexual Ethics, and the Duty to Warn," *Hastings Center Report* 29, No. 5 (1999): 26–35.

CHAPTER 7

ETHICS AND HIV/AIDS

ALTRUISM, SELF-INTEREST, AND MEDICAL ETHICS

Edmund D. Pellegrino

Nothing more exposes a physician's true ethics than the way he or she balances his or her own interests against those of the patient. Whether the physician is refusing to care for patients with the acquired immunodeficiency syndrome (AIDS) for fear of contagion (the subject Zuger and Miles discuss in this issue of *JAMA*) or withdrawing from emergency department service for fear of malpractice suits, striking for better pay or fees, or earning a gatekeeper's bonus by blocking access to medical care, the question raised is the same. Does medicine entail effacement of the physician's self-interests—even to the point of personal and financial risk? Is some degree of altruism a moral obligation, or is nonmaleficence the limit of the physician's mandatory beneficence? How far does physician advocacy go? What does the concept of physician as advocate mean?

Reprinted from *JAMA*, Vol. 258, No. 14 (October 9, 1987), pp. 1939–40.

...[A]lthough the question is not new, the historic and ethical precedents are inconsistent. Even now, with respect to caring for AIDS patients, the guidelines are confusing. Item VI of the current American Medical Association Principles affirms the physician's right to choose whom to treat. The Ethical and Judicial Council acknowledges the tradition to treat but permits "alternate arrangements" for physicians emotionally unable to comply. On the other hand, the American College of Physicians and the Infectious Disease Society of America are unequivocal about the physician's duty to treat.

These inconsistencies cannot be resolved without a more explicit choice between two fundamentally opposed conceptions of medicine itself. One conception calls for self-effacement by the physician, while the other accommodates physician self-interest. Not to choose between these two is to reinforce the cynics, discourage the conscientious, and undermine the moral credibility of our whole enterprise. Some of us would argue that there is a right answer, but that a wrong answer is more honest than no answer at all.

The arguments of those who defend refusals to care for AIDS patients are several: AIDS was not in the social contract when they entered medicine, obligations to self and family override obligations to patients, physicians who contract AIDS are permanently lost to society and their patients, treating patients when one is fearful or hostile only compromises their care, some physicians are emotionally unable to cope, and house staff carry an unfair share of the risks.

Leaving aside the fact that the risks of contagion are disproportionate to the fear, these arguments are cogent only if we accept the conception of medicine that undergirds them, ie, medicine is an occupation like any other, and the physician has the same "rights" as the businessman or the craftsman. Medical knowledge belongs to the physician to be dispensed in the marketplace on terms set by its owner. Being ill and in need of care is no different from needing any other service or commodity. Competence and avoidance of harm are all that can legitimately be demanded of physicians. ...

There are at least three things specific to medicine that impose an obligation of effacement of self-interest on the physician and that distinguish medicine from business and most other careers or forms of livelihood.

First is the nature of illness itself. The sick person is in a uniquely dependent, anxious, vulnerable, and exploitable state. Patients must bare their weakness, compromise their dignity, and reveal intimacies of body and mind. The predicament forces them to trust the physician in a relationship of relative powerlessness. Moreover, physicians invite that trust when offering to put knowledge at the service of the sick. A medical need in itself constitutes a moral claim on those equipped to help.

Second, the knowledge the physician offers is not proprietary. It is acquired through the privilege of a medical education. Society sanctions certain invasions of privacy such as dissecting the human body, participating in the care of the sick, or experimenting with human subjects. The student is permitted access to the world's medical knowledge, much of it gained by observation and experiment on generations of sick persons. All of this, and even financial subsidization for medical education, is permitted for one purpose—that society have an uninterrupted supply of trained medical personnel.

The physician's knowledge, therefore, is not individually owned and ought not be used primarily for personal gain, prestige, or power. Rather, the profession holds this knowledge in trust for the good of the sick. Those who enter the profession are automatically parties to a collective covenant—one that cannot be interpreted unilaterally.

Finally, this covenant is publicly acknowledged when the physician takes an oath at graduation. This—not the degree—is the graduate's formal entry into the profession. The oath—whichever one is taken—is a public promise that the new physician understands the gravity of this calling and promises to be competent and to use that competence in the interests of the sick. Some degree of effacement of self-interest is thus present in every medical oath. That is what makes medicine truly a profession.

These three things—the nature of illness, the nonproprietary character of medical knowledge, and the oath of fidelity to the patients' interests—generate strong moral obligations. To refuse to care for AIDS patients, even if the danger were much greater than it is, is to abnegate what is essential to being a physician. The physician is no more free to flee from danger in performance of his or her duties than the fireman, the policeman, or the soldier. To be sure, society and the profession have complementary obligations to reduce the risks and distribute the obligation fairly. However, physicians and other health professionals cannot avoid the obligation to make their knowledge available to all who need it.

Two divergent conceptions of medicine oppose each other in medical ethics today. One entails self-effacement, the other rejects it. What the AIDS epidemic and, in their own ways, the commercialization of medicine have done is to force an explicit choice. To make that choice, we need something we do not yet have—a moral philosophy of medicine, something that goes beyond professional codes, or the analysis of ethical puzzles. What is called for is a return to the normative quest of classic ethics—the quest for what it is to be a good physician and for what kind of person the physician should be.

AIDS AND THE DUTY TO TREAT

John D. Arras

Do physicians, by virtue of their role as health care professionals, have a duty to treat HIV-infected patients? Must they subject themselves to the very small, but nonetheless terrifying, risk of becoming infected themselves in order to live up to the ethical demands of their calling? For most physicians toiling in the front lines against AIDS, this is a new and totally unanticipated moral question that has yet to receive a clear and satisfying answer.

The current generation of physicians has experienced very little exposure to serious occupational risk. Well protected by antiseptic techniques and antibiotics for a period of roughly thirty years, doctors in developed countries have come to believe (with some justification) that they are exempt from the riskier aspects of medicine that had claimed the lives of so many of their predecessors. Prior to this *pax antibiotica*, risk and fear accompanied physicians daily, especially during the all-too-frequent periods of plague and virulent infectious disease. For many, if not most, of these physicians, to be a doctor *meant* that one was willing to take personal risks for the benefit of patients. One entered the profession with a keen appreciation of the hazards. By abruptly dispelling this perception of relative safety, AIDS has compelled today's physicians to reopen the traditional inquiry into the moral relationship between hazard and professional duty.

AIDS has likewise highlighted the limits of most contemporary bioethical inquiries into the physician-patient relationship. In their singleminded campaign against the excesses of medical paternalism, most bioethicists have been content merely to refute physicians' claims to moral expertise and special prerogatives based upon their Hippocratic duty to benefit the patient. In undermining this claim, bioethicists have completely ignored the question of whether physicians might still have special *responsibilities* as healers.

Moreover, the bioethicists' favorite metaphor for describing the physician-patient relationship, the contract between free and equal moral agents, has further obscured the issue of physicians' obligations to place themselves at risk in the service of their patients. By stressing voluntary nature of the physician-patient "contract," bioethicists have inadvertently reinforced the notion that physicians, as free moral agents, have a perfect right to choose whomever they wish to serve. This claim to contractual freedom, enshrined in the 1957 AMA Code of Ethics, likewise fails to address the question of whether physicians have a special duty to enter into contracts with hazardous patients.

Although there are many ways in which physicians can fail to discharge their putative duty to care for HIV-infected patients, ranging from outright refusal to foot-dragging, I shall focus on the central problem of categorical refusal to treat due to fear of infection. Do all physicians have an ethical duty to treat HIV-infected patients in spite of the risk, or can physicians fully discharge

Reprinted with permission of the author and the publisher from *Hastings Center Report*, Vol. 18 (April/May 1988) Special Supplement, pp. 10–14, 16–18.

their moral duty to such persons by referring them to other physicians who are willing and capable of treating them? In short, is voluntarism an ethically acceptable basis for medical practice in the age of AIDS?

PROTECTING THE VULNERABLE: INDIVIDUAL RIGHTS AND PROFESSIONAL OBLIGATIONS

One promising starting point for our inquiry is to focus on the medical need of HIV-infected patients. These persons harbor a potentially lethal virus and may already be manifesting symptoms of ARC (AIDS Related Complex) or AIDS. They may require treatment of AIDS related conditions—such as Kaposi's sarcoma and pneumocystis pneumonia—or they may incidentally have other health problems requiring attention, such as kidney failure, heart defects, or dental problems. Although the diagnosis of HIV disease renders their plight particularly poignant, these patients resemble all patients with serious illnesses insofar as they are sick, vulnerable, and needy.

One compelling, though still contested, response to such health needs is to claim that they establish either an individual right to health care or at least a social duty to provide it. This approach holds that because of the pivotal importance of health needs, including those needs created by AIDS, each person either infected with the virus or manifesting symptoms has a claim, grounded in justice, to the provision of needed health care.

The obvious drawback of this approach for our purposes is that it entirely avoids the question of physicians' individual or collective responsibility for HIV-infected patients. Whether we accept the language of individual rights or the language of societal obligation, the duty to provide care could be interpreted to fall squarely upon society through the vehicle of government, not on physicians as individuals or as a professional group. A voluntaristic system, with special incentives for those willing to treat, is compatible with this kind of societal duty.

A closely related argument makes use of the notion of a social contract between society and the medical profession. In exchange for the performance of a vital public service—that is, ministering to the needs of the sick and vulnerable—physicians as a group are granted monopolistic privileges over the practice of medicine. By seeking and receiving such a benefit, physicians incur a corresponding obligation founded on the notion of reciprocity. If physicians are granted a monopoly over medical practice and then refuse to treat certain patients who are perhaps the most vulnerable members of society, who else will treat them? Just as the police have a duty to protect defenseless citizens based on their monopoly over the legitimate use of force, so physicians have a duty to treat those in medical need, even in the face of some personal risk.

By establishing some sort of duty to treat, the social contract approach thus improves upon the right-to-health-care argument, but we must concede immediately that it locates the duty not on the shoulders of each and every physician, but rather at the level of the medical profession. Since the parties to this contract are society and the profession, the social contract cannot generate, at least in the first instance, the kind of responsibility that goes through the profession to each individual member. So long as society's vital interest in caring for the vulnerable is secured, the social contract is upheld, no matter what the response of individual physicians.

This is where the analogy between physicians and the police breaks down. Whereas both groups have a professional monopoly on providing a vital public service, as well as the corresponding professional duty to provide it, individual police officers are also expected to take risks in the course of their ordinary duties. Whether they like it or not, they have to go down that dark alley where danger lurks. The reason for this disparity in the terms of these two social contracts is that police officers cannot usually delegate their risky business to others. Except for medical emergencies and personnel at public hospitals—the two obvious exceptions to the social contract's inattention to individual performance—physicians can usually refer undesirable or especially hazardous cases to others.

The sort of duty to treat generated by the social contract strategy is thus clearly compatible, at least in theory, with a voluntaristic system. Indeed, some might argue that such a voluntaristic system provides an optimal solution to the problem of AIDS: the patients get respectful care from physicians who really wish to provide it; unwilling doctors are freed from professional or legal coercion; and willing physicians are rewarded either by their own virtue or by incentives. In theory, everyone's needs and interests are thus secured by the social contract under conditions of maximal freedom of choice.

In practice, however, there is reason to believe that such a voluntaristic system might prove to be either unstable or inadequate. In the first place, such systems might place unfair demands upon those physicians who are willing to treat HIV-infected patients. If the majority of hospital-based physicians exempt themselves from the care of such patients, thereby dumping the burden upon a willing few, the resulting division of labor might easily be perceived as being grossly unfair. Those who undertook the nearly exclusive care of AIDS patients would thereby expose themselves to higher risk of both psychological burnout and eventual infection. In response to this perception, recalcitrant physicians might well agree to treat their fair share of AIDS patients so that the burden might be more or less equally distributed among the staff. Even so, it must be conceded that this shift from voluntarism to egalitarianism would be attributable, not to any putative individual duty to patients, but rather to a perceived duty to treat one's *colleagues* fairly.

An individualized duty to treat HIV-infected patients might nevertheless be empirically derived from the social contract if we could demonstrate that a voluntaristic system failed to perform according to the terms of the contract. Indeed, if it could be shown that voluntaristic systems tended to harm HIV-infected patients or failed to meet their needs, then the social contract could consistently call for the imposition of a duty to treat upon each and every doctor.

Demonstrating likely harms to HIV-infected patients under a purely voluntaristic system is not difficult First, refusing to treat a person because he or she has AIDS or HIV infection ordinarily constitutes an insult of monumental proportions. The prospective patient is stigmatized and made to feel like an outcast. In itself this amounts to a significant injury.

Secondly, the delays inherent in any system of widespread referrals might themselves cause significant harms. If patients suffering from severe or painful maladies are refused care by a physician or clinic and referred elsewhere, their conditions may well be exacerbated by the time they find someone willing and able to treat them.

But perhaps the most obvious and serious problem with any voluntaristic system is that it would in all probability lead to lack of access and to substandard care. The dental profession provides an interesting case in point. A recent informal poll of the 4,100 member Chicago Dental Society revealed only three dentists, all from the same clinic, who were willing to accept new AIDS referrals.

Even if a voluntaristic system were able to produce enough willing physicians to solve the problem of access, the quality of the care received would remain an open question. Although it is possible (but not likely) that such a system could find the right incentives to achieve acceptable levels of quality, the history of our treatment of poor, stigmatized, and unpopular groups indicates that AIDS patients, like the insane and criminals, will most likely receive inadequate and substandard care. In either case, if the system were unable to secure either access or quality, the social contract through the conditions of licensure would justify the imposition of an individualized duty to treat.

An individual duty to treat can thus be empirically derived from the collective duty ascribed to the profession, and this duty can justifiably be imposed by the state in conformity with the social contract. Perhaps this is enough to get the job done, and perhaps in the long run that is what matters most to AIDS patients; but it is certainly not the stuff on which legends of professional virtue are based. In order to ground the sort of individualized and unmediated duty to treat patients—despite substantial hazard—that we associate with the historical tradition of medicine, we have to shift our focus from the specific task of meeting social needs to understanding traditional conceptions of the virtuous physician.

CONCEPTIONS OF PROFESSIONAL VIRTUE

In general, virtue-based accounts of the physician-patient relationship depend upon both a specific conception of the goal or good of the medical art and an account of the virtues (for example, competence, courage, fidelity) necessary to attain that good. In contrast to the more standard bioethical methodologies that attempt to marshall rules and principles toward the resolution of specific quandaries or dilemmas, virtue ethics is more concerned with articulating the character and role-specific duties of the good physician. There are two different approaches to virtue ethics that speak to the issue of physicians' duty to treat. One relies on a rather abstract end-means relationship; the other attempts to ground the notion of the virtuous physician in an analysis of the commitments endorsed by the profession historically. ...

MORAL TRADITION AND MEDICAL VIRTUE

[The latter] approach relies, not on the nature or essence of medicine *sub specie aeternitatis*, but rather on the notion of a moral tradition embedded in the on-going history of the profession. Proponents of this view would agree with Alasdair MacIntyre's claim that we cannot answer the question "What am I to do?" without first answering the prior question "Of what story or stories do I find myself a part?" They would then proceed to tell a story, to relate a history, of a profession that has incorporated a willingness to take risks for the benefit of patients as a constitutive element in physicians' self-understanding. Over time, this account would explain, the profession elevated the ideal of steadfast devotion to the well being of patients to the status of a fundamental duty, a definitive element inherent in the very role of physician. According to this story, physicians, if queried about their commitment to accept risk in the line of duty, would simply respond, "This is who we are; this is what we do. Those who fail to treat are cowards and not true physicians."

1. The Problem of Evidence

Incredibly, however, this is a history that has yet to be written. Apart from two pertinent articles that adopt contradictory positions, there are no focused, comprehensive, historical studies of physicians' duty to treat. This is obviously a major problem for the virtue-based approach, since it attempts to ground the duty to treat in the historical practice and traditional self-understandings of physicians. In the absence of a reliable historical record, the status of the virtue-based duty is problematical.

To be sure, there is some historical evidence attesting to the existence of a self-perceived duty. Darrel M. Amundsen notes, for example, that as early as the 14th century, flight in the face of plague was regarded, both by physicians and the public at large, as a dereliction of duty and a shameful thing. Although many physicians did, in fact, flee the plague, Amundsen contends that a standard of behavior had emerged according to which their retreat would be harshly judged. In support of this view, he quotes Guy de Chauliac, the Pope's physician at Avignon, who ruefully declared, "And I, to avoid infamy, dared not absent myself but with continual fear preserved myself as best I could."

Another important example of self-sacrificial behavior motivated by medical duty is provided by Benjamin Rush during the great yellow fever epidemic at Philadelphia in 1793. Although Rush's extraordinary devotion to patients during the epidemic has become the stuff of legend—as opposed, sadly, to the efficacy of his violent treatments—it is crucial to note that his courage was perceived by himself and others as required by duty. His acts were courageous, not because they went beyond the call of duty, but rather because he did his duty when others might be sorely tempted to flee from it.

In spite of this "oral tradition" attesting to a duty to treat, we still lack rigorous historical studies that would establish an unbroken chain of professional duty stretching from the advent of the Black Death in Europe to modern times. Moreover, it is noteworthy that the only medical historian who has attempted to focus on this vast stretch of time has come to a very different conclusion. According to Daniel Fox, the history of medicine is marked, not so much by an unbroken tradition of risk taking for patients, as by a tradition of negotiation between civic leaders and the medical profession to provide for the needs of patients during epidemics. In short, Fox claims that voluntarism, rather than any individualized professional duty to treat, has been the historical norm.

2. The Burden of Proof

Notwithstanding the absence of hard historical data on the duty to treat throughout the past six centuries, two salient facts suggest that the burden of proof should lie with those who would deny the existence of this duty. First, the persistence of an oral tradition or "folk wisdom" among physicians attesting to a duty to take risks for patients tells us a good deal about how physicians have traditionally understood their professional role. This sort of narrative tradition can still speak powerfully to us even if it does not meet the exacting standards of contemporary historiography.

Second, even if historians eventually demonstrate that voluntarism, rather than individual duty, best describes the behavior and beliefs of most physicians from the Middle Ages to the 20th century, they will most likely have to concede that, from the latter half of the 19th century onwards, tales of heroism eclipse accounts of flight as a sense of individual duty became indisputably rooted in the medical conscience. Even Zuger and Miles, who eventually conclude that the duty to treat cannot be firmly grounded in the vast canvass of medical history, admit that from the 1850s onwards "it becomes far more difficult to find recorded instances of physicians' reluctance to accept the risks that epidemics entailed for them. The stories of the cholera pandemics of the 19th century, the plague in the Orient, the influenza pandemic of 1918, polio in the 1950s, are largely ones of medical heroism."

This firm understanding of the physician's duty was explicitly recognized as early as 1847 in the first code of ethics of the American Medical Association, which stated that "...when pestilence prevails, it is their duty to face the danger, and to continue their labors for the alleviation of the suffering, even at the jeopardy of their own lives." Language to this effect remained in the Code until 1957, when it was dropped on account of medicine's (ultimately provisional) conquest of pestilential diseases. Following a prolonged period of indecision on the physician's duty to treat HIV-infected patients, the A.M.A. in November 1987 unambiguously reaffirmed the duty to treat in the face of risk. Although such codes are by no means infallible guides to the moral sensibilities of physicians, they at least provide good evidence of a profession's considered ethical judgments and of its own sense of identity.

Thus, although the historical record is woefully incomplete and physicians' track record is markedly inconsistent, our recent history reveals a very strong professional commitment to place the needs of the patient first, even at the risk of one's own health or life. This historical understanding, based perhaps more on *story* than on *historiography*, is aptly captured in Arnold Relman's claim that "the risk of contracting the patient's disease is one of the risks that is inherent in the profession of medicine. Physicians who are not willing to accept that risk...ought not to be in the practice of medicine." ...

AIDS AND THE DUTY TO TREAT

Can or should the traditional duty to treat be extended to include HIV-infected patients? To answer this question, we must ask additional questions about the nature of the risks posed by AIDS to physicians. What exactly is the risk of transmission through occupational exposure? And, how should this risk be evaluated?

What Is the Risk? Since physicians do not usually have sex or share needles with their patients, the most likely routes of transmission are needle-stick accidents and blood splashing. In contrast to the risk of acquiring hepatitis B through an errant needlestick, the risk of HIV infection from similar accidents is very small—probably no more than one per every 200 incidents. Even this low level of risk can be essentially eliminated for many physicians by scrupulous attention to established infection-control recommendations.

This is not to say that there is no risk at all. By February 1988, at least eight health care workers had acquired HIV infection through occupational exposure, and those who go on to develop full-blown AIDS will almost certainly die. Moreover, some physicians may be at higher risk for HIV infection. Surgeons, obstetricians and emergency room personnel, for example, appear to be disproportionately vulnerable to needle sticks and exposure to blood. Significantly, however, existing studies do not indicate a higher rate of occupational HIV transmission among these "high blood profile" specialties.

Evaluating the Risk of AIDS In addition to the task of scientifically estimating their actual exposure to risk, physicians must also evaluate this risk. Is it worth running? At first glance, this would appear to be an easy question for a historically based virtue ethics, since the objective risk of death from occupational exposure to HIV simply pales in comparison with the risks run by previous generations of physicians. But we must recall that the threshold separating duty from supererogation depends upon culturally relative definitions of reasonable or acceptable risks. What if risks that were acceptable thirty, sixty, or one hundred years ago are no longer deemed reasonable by physicians and the society at large?

Conditions certainly have changed, and these changes are responsible for much of our current perplexity regarding the limits of the duty to treat. Perhaps most importantly, the world (or at least the industrialized, affluent part of it) is now a much safer place. Prior to the development of antibiotics, antisepsis, and vaccines, the entire population of the world might be said to have constituted a gigantic "high risk group" for early death from pestilence and other killer diseases. Life for most people, including physicians, was on average much shorter than it is today.

Thus, to a 19th century physician, death from yellow fever would no doubt have seemed a tragic but not extraordinary possibility. By contrast, present day physicians fully expect to live a long life; they no longer believe that anyone, especially themselves, should die from an infectious disease.

Notwithstanding this displacement of the threshold of supererogation, today's medical profession appears to be extending its historical commitment to encompass those who suffer from HIV and AIDS. As the A.M.A. policy statement recently made clear, "that tradition must be maintained. ... A physician may not ethically refuse to treat a patient whose condition is within the physician's current realm of competence solely because the patient is seropositive." Although some physicians have privately or publicly engaged in categorical refusals to care for HIV-infected patients, they appear to constitute, in the words of Surgeon General Koop, "a fearful and irrational minority." To be sure, many physicians, especially the younger ones who bear most of the burden of caring for AIDS patients, tread a narrow path like Guy de Chauliac between fear of AIDS and fear of infamy; but very few are driven by fear to renounce the care of AIDS patients altogether.

Thus, while our altered perceptions of relative risk may help to account for resistance to treating AIDS patients, it appears that the medical profession has collectively decided, albeit with a significant amount of internal dissent, to view most occupational exposures to HIV disease as at least comparable to other risks inherent in the practice of medicine—that is, as "acceptable risks."

Notwithstanding this consensus on the basic issue, a significant number of physicians, especially those who are no longer subjected to the discipline of internship and residency programs, have come to the conclusion that for them the risk is not worth running, even if they concur with the CDC's low estimates. How can this be explained?

The answer lies, at least in part, in the way some of these physicians perceive those afflicted with HIV disease. In refusing to deal with such patients, many physicians seem not merely to be saying, "Why should I risk my life?" but rather, "Why should I risk my life for the likes of homosexuals and intravenous drug abusers?" In other words, these physicians want to know why they must incur even small risks of serious harm for the benefit of morally suspect groups. It is one thing, they say, to risk one's life for an "innocent" child afflicted with AIDS through no fault of his own, but it is quite another thing to expose oneself to risks for patients who have "brought it upon themselves" through behaviors that are either illegal, immoral, or both.

This attempt to turn the HIV-infected person into a complete Other by means of distancing and devaluation is often supplemented by a simultaneous movement of imaginative identification. As he evaluates the risks, the physician places himself in the shoes of the AIDS patient, but instead of achieving sympathy, this act of identification often yields only horror. The physician must contemplate not only the risk of death, however small, but also the risk of dying as people often die of AIDS in our society—that is, as outcasts, as stigmatized objects of fascination and disgust.

The appropriate societal response to a reluctance to treat based on this kind of fear should be a renewed effort to extend compassion and humane services to *all* AIDS sufferers. The fear of stigmatization is real and a matter of legitimate concern. Although it does not justify categorical refusals to treat, such fear is not a shameful response to societal intolerance. If physicians are to be expected to put their lives on the line, the least society can do is to treat them and their families with gratitude and the utmost respect if they become infected.

But as for those physicians who refuse to treat because they do not deem the lives and health of homosexuals and drug addicts to be worth the slightest exposure to risk, it would seem that they violate an even more basic duty traditionally espoused by the medical profession: the duty to treat all patients with respect for their human dignity, irrespective of considerations of their personal attributes, their social or economic status, or the nature of their disease. ...

TARASOFF V. REGENTS OF THE UNIVERSITY OF CALIFORNIA

Majority Opinion (delivered by Justice Tobriner)

On October 27, 1969, Prosenjit Poddar killed Tatiana Tarasoff. Plaintiffs, Tatiana's parents, allege that two months earlier Poddar confided his intention to kill Tatiana to Dr. Lawrence Moore, a psychologist employed by the Cowell Memorial Hospital at the University of California at Berkeley. They allege that on Moore's request, the campus police briefly detained Poddar, but released him when he appeared rational. They further claim that Dr. Harvey Powelson, Moore's superior, then directed that no further action be taken to detain Poddar. No one warned plaintiffs of Tatiana's peril. ...

California Supreme Court, 131 California Reporter 14, July 1, 1976. Reprinted with permission of Thomson West.

We shall explain that defendant therapists cannot escape liability merely because Tatiana herself was not their patient. When a therapist determines, or pursuant to the standards of his profession should determine, that his patient presents a serious danger of violence to another, he incurs an obligation to use reasonable care to protect the intended victim against such danger. The discharge of this duty may require the therapist to take one or more of various steps, depending upon the nature of the case. Thus it may call for him to warn the intended victim or others likely to apprise the victim of the danger, to notify the police, or to take whatever other steps are reasonably necessary under the circumstances. ...

Plaintiffs' first cause of action, entitled "Failure to Detain a Dangerous Patient," alleges that on August 20, 1969, Poddar was a voluntary outpatient receiving therapy at Cowell Memorial Hospital. Poddar informed Moore, his therapist, that he was going to kill an unnamed girl, readily identifiable as Tatiana, when she returned home from spending the summer in Brazil. Moore, with the concurrence of Dr. Gold, who had initially examined Poddar, and Dr. Yandell, assistant to the director of the department of psychiatry, decided that Poddar should be committed for observation in a mental hospital. Moore orally notified Officers Atkinson and Teel of the campus police that he would request commitment. He then sent a letter to Police Chief William Beall requesting the assistance of the police department in securing Poddar's confinement.

Officers Atkinson, Brownrigg, and Halleran took Poddar into custody, but, satisfied that Poddar was rational, released him on his promise to stay away from Tatiana. Powelson, director of the department of psychiatry at Cowell Memorial Hospital, then asked the police to return Moore's letter, directed that all copies of the letter and notes that Moore had taken as therapist be destroyed, and "ordered no action to place Prosenjit Poddar in 72-hour treatment and evaluation facility."

Plaintiffs' second cause of action, entitled "Failure to Warn On a Dangerous Patient," incorporates the allegations of the first cause of action, but adds the assertion that defendants negligently permitted Poddar to be released from police custody without "notifying the parents of Tatiana Tarasoff that their daughter was in grave danger from Posenjit Poddar." Poddar persuaded Tatiana's brother to share an apartment with him near Tatiana's residence; shortly after her return from Brazil, Poddar went to her residence and killed her.

Plaintiffs' third cause of action, entitled "Abandonment of a Dangerous Patient," seeks $10,000 punitive damages against defendant Powelson. Incorporating the crucial allegations of the first cause of action, plaintiffs charge that Powelson "did the things herein alleged with intent to abandon a dangerous patient, and said acts were done maliciously and oppressively."

Plaintiffs' fourth cause of action, for "Breach of Primary Duty to Patient and the Public," states essentially the same allegations as the first cause of action, but seeks to characterize defendants' conduct as a breach of duty to safeguard their patient and the public. Since such conclusory labels add nothing to the factual allegations of the complaint, the first and fourth causes of action are legally indistinguishable. ...

... We direct our attention ... to the issue of whether plaintiffs' second cause of action can be amended to state a basis for recovery.

PLAINTIFFS CAN STATE A CAUSE OF ACTION AGAINST DEFENDANT THERAPISTS FOR NEGLIGENT FAILURE TO PROTECT TATIANA

The second cause of action can be amended to allege that Tatiana's death proximately resulted from defendants' negligent failure to warn Tatiana or others likely to apprise her of her danger. Plaintiffs contend that as amended, such allegations of negligence and proximate causation, with resulting damages, establish a cause of action. Defendants, however, contend that in the circumstances of the present case they owed no duty of care to Tatiana or her parents and that, in the absence of duty, they were free to act in careless disregard of Tatiana's life and safety.

In analyzing this issue, we bear in mind that legal duties are not discoverable facts of nature, but merely conclusory expressions that, in cases of a particular type, liability should be imposed for damage done. ... "The assertion that liability must ... be denied because defendant bears no 'duty' to plaintiff" 'begs the essential question—whether the plaintiff's interests are entitled to legal protection against the defendant's conduct. ... [Duty] is not sacrosanct in itself, but only an expression of the sum total of those considerations of policy which lead the law to say that the particular plaintiff is entitled to protection.

In the landmark case of *Rowland* v. *Christian* (1968), Justice Peters recognized that liability should be imposed "for injury occasioned to another by his want of ordinary care or skill" as expressed in section 1714 of the Civil Code. Thus, Justice Peters, quoting from *Heaven* v. *Pender* (1883) stated: "'whenever one person is by circumstances placed in such a position with regard to another ... that if he did not use ordinary care and skill in his own conduct ... he would cause danger of injury to the person or property of the other, a duty arises to use ordinary care and skill to avoid such danger.'"

We depart from "this fundamental principle" only upon the "balancing of a number of considerations"; major ones "are the foreseeability of harm to the plaintiff, the degree of certainty that the plaintiff suffered injury, the closeness of the connection between the defendant's conduct and the injury suffered, the moral blame attached to the defendant's conduct, the policy of preventing future harm, the extent of the burden to the defendant and consequences to the community of imposing a duty to exercise care with resulting liability for breach, and the availability, cost and prevalence of insurance for the risk involved."

The most important of these considerations in establishing duty is foreseeability. As a general principle, a defendant owes a duty of care to all persons who are foreseeably endangered by his conduct, with respect to all risks which make the conduct unreasonably dangerous. As we shall explain, however, when the avoidance of foreseeable harm requires a defendant to control the conduct of another person, or to warn of such conduct, the common law has traditionally imposed liability only if the defendant bears some special relationship to the dangerous person or to the potential victim. Since the relationship between a therapist and his patient satisfies this requirement, we need not here decide whether foreseeability alone is sufficient to create a duty to exercise reasonable care to protect a potential victim of another's conduct.

Although, as we have stated above, under the common law, as a general rule, one person owed no duty to control the conduct of another nor to warn those endangered by such conduct, the courts have carved out an exception to this rule in cases in which the defendant stands in some special relationship to either the person whose conduct needs to be controlled or in a relationship to the foreseeable victim of that conduct. Applying this exception to the present case, we note that a relationship of defendant therapists to either Tatiana or Poddar will suffice to establish a duty of care; as explained in section 315 of the Restatement Second of Torts, a duty of care may arise from either "(a) a special relation ... between the actor and the third person which imposes a duty upon the actor to control the third person's conduct, or (b) a special relation ... between the actor and the other which gives to the other a right of protection."

Although plaintiffs' pleadings assert no special relation between Tatiana and defendant therapists, they establish as between Poddar and defendant therapists the special relation that arises between a patient and his doctor or psychotherapist. Such a relationship may support affirmative duties for the benefit of third persons. Thus, for example, a hospital must exercise reasonable care to control the behavior of a patient which may endanger other persons. A doctor must also warn a patient if the patient's condition or medication renders certain conduct, such as driving a car, dangerous to others.

Although the California decisions that recognize this duty have involved cases in which the defendant stood in a special relationship both to the victim and to the person whose conduct created the danger, we do not think that the duty should logically be constricted to such situations. Decisions of other jurisdictions hold that the single relationship of a doctor to his patient is sufficient to support the duty to exercise reasonable care to protect others against dangers emanating from the patient's illness. The courts hold that a doctor is liable to persons infected by his patient if he negligently fails to diagnose a contagious disease or, having diagnosed the illness, fails to warn members of the patient's family.

Since it involved a dangerous mental patient, the decision in *Merchants Nat. Bank & Trust Co. of Fargo* v. *United States* comes closer to the issue. The Veterans Administration arranged for the patient to work on a local farm, but did not inform the farmer of the man's background. The farmer consequently permitted the patient to come and go freely during nonworking hours; the patient borrowed a car, drove to his wife's residence and killed her. Notwithstanding the lack of any "special relationship" between the Veterans Administration and the wife, the court found the Veterans Administration liable for the wrongful death of the wife.

In their summary of the relevant rulings Fleming and Maximov conclude that the "case law should dispel any notion that to impose on the therapists a duty to take precautions for the safety of persons threatened by a patient, where due care so requires, is in any way opposed to contemporary ground rules on the duty relationship. On the contrary, there now seems to be sufficient authority to support the conclusion that by entering into a doctor-patient relationship the therapist becomes sufficiently involved to assume some responsibility for the safety, not only of the patient himself, but also of any third person whom the doctor knows to be threatened by the patient."

Defendants contend, however, that imposition of a duty to exercise reasonable care to protect third persons is unworkable because therapists cannot accurately predict whether or not a patient will resort to violence. In support of this argument amicus representing the American Psychiatric Association and other professional societies cites numerous articles which indicate that therapists, in the present state of the art, are unable reliably to predict violent acts; their forecasts, amicus claims, tend consistently to overpredict violence, and indeed are more often wrong than right. Since predictions of violence are often erroneous, amicus concludes, the courts should not render rulings that predicate the liability of therapists upon the validity of such predictions.

The role of the psychiatrist, who is indeed a practitioner of medicine, and that of the psychologist who performs an allied function, are like that of the physician who must conform to the standards of the profession and who must often make diagnoses and predictions based upon such evaluations. Thus the judgment of the therapist in diagnosing emotional disorders and in predicting whether a patient presents a serious danger of violence is comparable to the judgment which doctors and professionals must regularly render under accepted rules of responsibility.

We recognize the difficulty that a therapist encounters in attempting to forecast whether a patient presents a serious danger of violence. Obviously, we do not require that the therapist, in making that determination, render a perfect performance; the therapist need only exercise "that reasonable degree of skill, knowledge, and care ordinarily possessed and exercised by members of [that professional specialty] under similar circumstances." Within the broad range of reasonable practice and treatment in which professional opinion and judgment may differ, the therapist is free to exercise his or her own best judgment without liability; proof, aided by hindsight, that he or she judged wrongly is insufficient to establish negligence.

In the instant case, however, the pleadings do not raise any question as to failure of defendant therapists to predict that Poddar presented a serious danger of violence. On the contrary, the present complaints allege that defendant therapists did in fact predict that Poddar would kill, but were negligent in failing to warn.

Amicus contends, however, that even when a therapist does in fact predict that a patient poses a serious danger of violence to others, the therapist should be absolved of any responsibility for failing to act to protect the potential victim. In our view, however, once a therapist does in fact determine, or under applicable professional standards reasonably should have determined, that a patient poses a serious danger of violence to others, he bears a duty to exercise reasonable care to protect the foreseeable victim of that danger. While the discharge of this duty of due care will necessarily vary with the facts of each case, in each instance the adequacy of the therapist's conduct must be measured against the traditional negligence standard of the rendition of reasonable care under the circumstances. As explained in Fleming and Maximov, The Patient or His Victim: The Therapist's Dilemma (1974) "... the ultimate question of resolving the tension between the conflicting interests of patient and potential victim is one of social policy, not professional expertise. ... In sum, the therapist owes a legal duty not only to his patient, but also to his patient's would-be victim and is subject in both respects to scrutiny by judge and jury. ..."

The risk that unnecessary warnings may be given is a reasonable price to pay for the lives of possible victims that may be saved. We would hesitate to hold that the therapist who is aware that his patient expects to attempt to assassinate the President of the United States would not be obligated to warn the authorities because the therapist cannot predict with accuracy that his patient will commit the crime.

Defendants further argue that free and open communication is essential to psychotherapy; that "Unless a patient ... is assured that ... information [revealed by him] can and will be held in utmost confidence, he will be reluctant to make the full disclosure upon which diagnosis and treatment ... depends." The giving of a warning, defendants contend, constitutes a breach of trust which entails the revelation of confidential communications.

We recognize the public interest in supporting effective treatment of mental illness and in protecting the rights of patients to privacy, and the consequent public importance of safeguarding the confidential character of psychotherapeutic communication. Against this interest, however, we must weigh the public interest in safety from violent assault. The Legislature has undertaken the difficult task of balancing the countervailing concerns. In Evidence Code section 1014, it established a broad rule of privilege to protect confidential communications between patient and psychotherapist. In Evidence Code section 1024, the Legislature created a specific and limited exception to the psychotherapist-patient privilege: "There is no privilege ... if the psychotherapist has reasonable cause to believe that the patient is in such mental or emotional condition as to be dangerous to himself or to the person or property of another and that disclosure of the communication is necessary to prevent the threatened danger."

We realize that the open and confidential character of psychotherapeutic dialogue encourages patients to express threats of violence, few of which are ever executed. Certainly a therapist should not be encouraged routinely to reveal such threats; such disclosures could seriously disrupt the patient's relationship with his therapist and with the persons threatened. To the contrary, the therapist's obligations to his patient require that he not disclose a confidence unless such disclosure is necessary to avert danger to others, and even then that he do so discreetly, and in a fashion that would preserve the privacy of his patient to the fullest extent compatible with the prevention of the threatened danger.

The revelation of a communication under the above circumstances is not a breach of trust or a violation of professional ethics; as stated in the Principles of Medical Ethics of the American Medical Association (1957), section 9: "A physician may not reveal the confidence entrusted to him in the course of medical attendance ... *unless he is required to do so by law or unless it becomes necessary in order to protect the welfare of the individual or of the community.*" (Italics added.) We conclude that the public policy favoring protection of the confidential character of patient-psychotherapist communications must yield to the extent to which disclosure is essential to avert danger to others. The protective privilege ends where the public peril begins.

Our current crowded and computerized society compels the interdependence of its members. In this risk-infested society we can hardly tolerate the further exposure to danger that would result from a concealed knowledge of the therapist that his patient was lethal. If the exercise of reasonable care to protect the threatened victim requires the therapist to warn the endangered party or those who can reasonably be expected to notify him, we see no sufficient societal interest that would protect and justify concealment. The containment of such risks lies in the public interest. For the foregoing reasons, we find that plaintiffs' complaints can be amended to state a cause of action against defendants Moore, Powelson, Gold, and Yandell and against the Regents as their employer, for breach of a duty to exercise reasonable care to protect Tatiana. ...

DISSENTING OPINION (DELIVERED BY JUSTICE CLARK)

Until today's majority opinion, both legal and medical authorities have agreed that confidentiality is essential to effectively treat the mentally ill, and that imposing a duty on doctors to disclose patient threats to potential victims would greatly impair treatment.

Further, recognizing that effective treatment and society's safety are necessarily intertwined, the Legislature has already decided effective and confidential treatment is preferred over imposition of a duty to warn.

The issue whether effective treatment for the mentally ill should be sacrificed to a system of warnings is, in my opinion, properly one for the Legislature, and we are bound by its judgment. Moreover, even in the absence of clear legislative direction, we must reach the same conclusion because imposing the majority's new duty is certain to result in a net increase in violence ...

Common Law Analysis

Entirely apart from the statutory provisions, the same result must be reached upon considering both general tort principles and the public policies favoring effective treatment, reduction of violence, and justified commitment.

Generally, a person owes no duty to control the conduct of another. Exceptions are recognized only in limited situations where (1) a special relationship exists between the defendant and injured party, or (2) a special relationship exists between defendant and the active wrongdoer, imposing a duty on defendant to control the wrongdoer's conduct. The majority does not contend the first exception is appropriate to this case.

Policy generally determines duty. Principal policy considerations include foreseeability of harm, certainty of the plaintiff's injury, proximity of the defendant's conduct to the plaintiff's injury, moral blame attributable to defendant's conduct, prevention of future harm, burden on the defendant, and consequences to the community.

Overwhelming policy considerations weigh against imposing a duty on psychotherapists to warn a potential victim against harm. While offering virtually no benefit to society, such a duty will frustrate psychiatric treatment, invade fundamental patient rights and increase violence.

The importance of psychiatric treatment and its need for confidentiality have been recognized by this court. "It is clearly recognized that the very practice of psychiatry vitally depends upon the reputation in the community that the psychiatrist will not tell." (Slovenko, Psychiatry and a Second Look at the Medical Privilege (1960) 6 Wayne L.Rev. 175, 188.)

Assurance of confidentiality is important for three reasons.

Deterrence From Treatment First, without substantial assurance of confidentiality, those requiring treatment will be deterred from seeking assistance. It remains an unfortunate fact in our society that people seeking psychiatric guidance tend to become stigmatized. Apprehension of such stigma—apparently increased by the propensity of people considering treatment to see themselves in the worst possible light—creates a well-recognized reluctance to seek aid. This reluctance is alleviated by the psychiatrist's assurance of confidentiality.

Full Disclosure Second, the guarantee of confidentiality is essential in eliciting the full disclosure necessary for effective treatment. The psychiatric patient approaches treatment with conscious and unconscious inhibitions against revealing his innermost thoughts. "Every person, however well-motivated, has to overcome resistances to therapeutic exploration. These resistances seek support from every possible source and the possibility of disclosure would easily be employed in the service of resistance." (Goldstein & Katz, supra, 36 Conn.Bar J. 175, 179; see also, 118 Am.J.Psych. 734, 735.) Until a patient can trust his psychiatrist not to violate their confidential relationship, "the unconscious psychological control mechanism of repression will prevent the recall of past experiences." (Butler, Psychotherapy and Griswold: Is Confidentiality a Privilege or a Right? (1971) 3 Conn.L.Rev. 599, 604.)

Successful Treatment Third, even if the patient fully discloses his thoughts, assurance that the confidential relationship will not be breached is necessary to maintain his trust in his psychiatrist—the very means by which treatment is effected. "[T]he essence of much psychotherapy is the contribution of trust in the external world and ultimately in the self, modelled upon the trusting relationship established during therapy." (Dawidoff, The Malpractice of Psychiatrists, 1966 Duke L.J. 696, 704.) Patients will be helped only if they can form a trusting relationship with the psychiatrist. All authorities appear to agree that if the trust relationship cannot be developed because of collusive communication between the psychiatrist and others, treatment will be frustrated.

Given the importance of confidentiality to the practice of psychiatry, it becomes clear the duty to warn imposed by the majority will cripple the use and effectiveness of psychiatry. Many people, potentially violent—yet susceptible to treatment—will be deterred from seeking it; those seeking it will be inhibited from making revelations necessary to effective treatment; and, forcing the psychiatrist to violate the patient's trust will destroy the interpersonal relationship by which treatment is effected.

Violence and Civil Commitment By imposing a duty to warn, the majority contributes to the danger to society of violence by the mentally ill and greatly increases the risk of civil commitment—the total deprivation of liberty—of those who should not be confined. The impairment of treatment and risk of improper commitment resulting from the new duty to warn will not be limited to a few patients but will extend to a large number of the mentally ill. Although under existing psychiatric procedures only a relatively few receiving treatment will ever present a risk of violence, the number making threats is huge, and it is the latter group—not just the former—whose treatment will be impaired and whose risk of commitment will be increased.

Both the legal and psychiatric communities recognize that the process of determining potential violence in a patient is far from exact, being fraught with complexity and uncertainty.[1] In fact, precision has not even been attained in predicting who of those having already committed violent acts will again become violent, a task recognized to be of much simpler proportions.

This predictive uncertainty means that the number of disclosures will necessarily be large. As noted above, psychiatric patients are encouraged to discuss all thoughts of violence, and they often express such thoughts. However, unlike this court, the psychiatrist does not enjoy the benefit of overwhelming hindsight in seeing which few, if any, of his patients will ultimately become violent. Now, confronted by the majority's new duty, the psychiatrist must instantaneously calculate potential violence from each patient on each visit. The difficulties researchers have encountered in accurately predicting violence will be heightened for the practicing psychiatrist dealing for brief periods in his office with heretofore nonviolent patients. And, given the decision not to warn or commit must always be made at the psychiatrist's civil peril, one can expect most doubts will be resolved in favor of the psychiatrist protecting himself.

Neither alternative open to the psychiatrist seeking to protect himself is in the public interest. The warning itself is an impairment of the psychiatrist's ability to treat, depriving many patients of adequate treatment. It is to be expected that after disclosing their threats, a significant number of patients, who would not become violent if treated according to existing practices, will engage in violent conduct as a result of unsuccessful treatment. In short, the majority's duty to warn will not only impair treatment of many who would never become violent but worse, will result in a net increase in violence.[2]

The second alternative open to the psychiatrist is to commit his patient rather than to warn. Even in the absence of threat of civil liability, the doubts of psychiatrists as to the seriousness of patient threats have led psychiatrists to overcommit to mental institutions. This overcommitment has been authoritatively documented in both legal and psychiatric studies. This practice is so prevalent that it has been estimated that "as many as twenty harmless persons are incarcerated for every one who will commit a violent act." (Steadman & Cocozza, Stimulus/Response: We Can't Predict Who Is Dangerous (Jan. 1975) 8 Psych. Today 32, 35.)

Given the incentive to commit created by the majority's duty, this already serious situation will be worsened. ...

Notes

1. A shocking illustration of psychotherapists' inability to predict dangerousness ... is cited and discussed in Ennis, *Prisoners of Psychiatry: Mental Patients, Psychiatrists, and the Law* (1972): "In a well-known study, psychiatrists predicted that 989 persons were so dangerous that they could not be kept even in civil mental hospitals, but would have to be kept in maximum security hospitals run by the Department of Corrections. Then, because of a United States Supreme Court decision, those persons were transferred to civil hospitals. After a year, the Department of Mental Hygiene reported that one-fifth of them had been discharged to the community, and over half had agreed to remain as voluntary patients. During the year, only 7 of the 989 committed or threatened any act that was sufficiently dangerous to require retransfer to the maximum security hospital. Seven correct predictions out of almost a thousand is not a very impressive record.

   Other studies, and there are many, have reached the same conclusion: psychiatrists simply cannot predict dangerous behavior." (Id., at p. 227)

2. The majority concedes that psychotherapeutic dialogue often results in the patient expressing threats of violence that are rarely executed. The practical problem, of course, lies in ascertaining which threats from which patients will be carried out. As to this problem, the majority is silent. They do, however, caution that a therapist certainly "should not be encouraged routinely to reveal such threats; such disclosures could

seriously disrupt the patient's relationship with his therapist and with the persons threatened."

Thus, in effect, the majority informs the therapists that they must accurately predict dangerousness—a task recognized as extremely difficult—or face crushing civil liability. The majority's reliance on the traditional standard of care for professionals that "therapist need only exercise 'that reasonable degree of skill, knowledge, and care ordinarily possessed and exercised by members of [that professional specialty] under similar circumstances'" is seriously misplaced. This standard of care assumes that, to a large extent, the subject matter of the specialty is ascertainable. One clearly ascertainable element in the psychiatric field is that the therapist cannot accurately predict dangerousness, which, in turn, means that the standard is inappropriate for lack of a relevant criterion by which to judge the therapist's decision. The inappropriateness of the standard the majority would have us use is made patent when consideration is given to studies, by several eminent authorities, indicating that "[t]he chances of a second psychiatrist agreeing with the diagnosis of a first psychiatrist are barely better than 50-50; or stated differently, there is about as much chance that a different expert would come to some different conclusion as there is that the other would agree.'" (Ennis & Litwack, *Psychiatry and the Presumption of Expertise: Flipping Coins in the Courtroom*, supra, 62 Cal.L.Rev. 693, 701, quoting, Ziskin, *Coping With Psychiatric and Psychological Testimony*, p. 126.) The majority's attempt to apply a normative scheme to a profession which must be concerned with problems that balk at standardization is clearly erroneous.

In any event, an ascertainable standard would not serve to limit psychiatrist disclosure of threats with the resulting impairment of treatment. However compassionate, the psychiatrist hearing the threat remains faced with potential crushing civil liability for a mistaken evaluation of his patient and will be forced to resolve even the slightest doubt in favor of disclosure or commitment.

AIDS, CONFIDENTIALITY, AND THE RIGHT TO KNOW

Morton E. Winston

In June of 1987, a young woman who was nine months pregnant was shot with an arrow fired from a hunting bow on a Baltimore street by a man who was engaged in an argument with another person. Emergency workers from the city fire fighting unit were called to the scene, administered resuscitation to the profusely bleeding woman and took her to a local hospital where she died shortly afterwards. Her child, delivered by emergency Caesarian section, died the next day.

This tragedy would have been quickly forgotten as yet another incident of random urban violence if it had not been later learned that the woman was infected with the AIDS virus. A nurse at the hospital decided on her own initiative that the rescue workers who had brought the woman to the emergency room should be informed that they had been exposed to HIV-infected blood and contacted them directly. Several days after this story hit the newspapers two state legislators introduced a bill adding AIDS to the list of diseases that hospitals would be required to inform workers about. A hospital spokeswoman was quoted in the newspaper as opposing the proposed legislation on the grounds that it would violate patient confidentiality, and that, "People taking care of patients should assume that everyone is a potential

From *Public Affairs Quarterly*, Vol. 2, No. 2 (April 1998). Reprinted with permission of *Public Affairs Quarterly*.

AIDS patient and take precautions. The burden is on you to take care of yourself."[1]

This case, and others like it, raises difficult and weighty ethical and public policy issues. What are the limits of medical confidentiality? Who, if anyone, has a right to know that they may have been exposed to AIDS or other dangerous infectious diseases? Whose responsibility is it to inform the sexual contacts of AIDS patients or others who may have been exposed to the infection? Can public health policies be framed which will effectively prevent the spread of the epidemic while also protecting the civil and human rights of its victims?

I. THE LIMITS OF CONFIDENTIALITY

The rule of medical confidentiality enjoins physicians, nurses, and health care workers from revealing to third parties information about a patient obtained in the course of medical treatment. The rule protecting a patient's secrets is firmly entrenched in medical practice, in medical education, and receives explicit mention in all major medical oaths and codes of medical ethics. Sissela Bok has argued that the ethical justification for confidentiality rests on four arguments.[2]

The first and most powerful justification for the rule of confidentiality derives from the individual's right, flowing from autonomy, to control personal information and to protect privacy. The right of individuals to control access to sensitive information about themselves is particularly important in cases where revelation of such information would subject the individual to invidious discrimination, deprivation of rights, or physical or emotional harm. Since persons who are HIV-infected or who have AIDS or ARC (AIDS-Related Complex), are often subjected to discrimination, loss of employment, refusal of housing and insurance, many physicians believe that the confidentiality of HIV antibody test results and diagnoses of AIDS should be safeguarded under all circumstances. Since many infected persons and AIDS patients are members of groups which have traditionally been subject to discrimination or social disapproval—homosexuals, drug users, or prostitutes—the protection of confidentiality of patients who belong to these groups is especially indicated.

The second and third arguments for confidentiality concern the special moral relationship which exists between physicians and their patients. Medical practice requires that patients reveal intimate personal secrets to their physicians, and that physicians live up to the trust that is required on the part of patients to reveal such information; to fail to do so would violate the physician's duty of fidelity. Additionally, since medical practice is normally conducted under a tacit promise of confidentiality, physicians would violate this expectation by revealing their patients' secrets.

The fourth argument for confidentiality is based on utilitarian or broadly pragmatic considerations. Without a guarantee of confidentiality, potential patients in need of medical care would be deterred from seeking medical assistance from fear that sensitive personal information will be revealed to third parties thereby exposing the individual to the risk of unjust discrimination or other harm. Many physicians who work with AIDS patients find such pragmatic arguments particularly compelling, believing, perhaps correctly, that breaches of medical confidentiality concerning antibody status or a diagnosis of AIDS, would have a "chilling effect" preventing people in high-risk groups from seeking voluntary antibody testing and counselling. Since programs of education designed to encourage voluntary testing and voluntary behavior change are widely believed to be the only effective and ethically acceptable means to curtail the spread of the AIDS epidemic, measures which mandate testing for members of certain groups, and which permit disclosure of test results to third parties, are viewed as inimical to the medical communities' effort to control and treat this disease.[3]

Together, these four arguments present a compelling rationale for treating confidentiality as sacrosanct, particularly in the context of AIDS, and according to Bok, help to "explain the ritualistic tone in which the duty of preserving secrets is repeatedly set forth in professional oaths and codes of ethics."[4] But, she continues,

> Not only does this rationale point to links with the most fundamental grounds of autonomy and relationship and trust and help; it also serves as a rationalization that helps deflect ethical inquiry. The very self-evidence that it claims can then expand beyond its legitimate applications. Confidentiality, like all secrecy, can then cover up for and in turn lead to a great deal of error, injury, pathology, and abuse.[5]

Bok believes that confidentiality is at best a prima facie obligation, one that while generally justified, can be overridden in certain situations by more compelling moral obligations. Among the situations which license breaches of confidentiality Bok cites are: cases involving a minor child or incompetent patient who would be harmed if sensitive information were not disclosed to a parent or guardian, cases involving threats of violence against identifiable third parties, cases involving contagious sexually transmitted diseases, and other cases where identifiable third parties would be harmed or placed at risk unknowingly by failure to disclose information known to a physician obtained through therapeutic communication.

In general, personal autonomy, and the derivative right of individuals to control personal information, is limited by the "Harm Principle" [HP], which requires moral agents to refrain from acts and omissions which would foreseeably result in preventable wrongful harm to innocent others. Bok argues that when HP (or a related ethical principle which I will discuss shortly) comes into play, "the prima facie premises supporting confidentiality are overriden, " ...[6] If this argument is correct, then the strict observance of confidentiality cannot be ethically justified in all cases, and physicians and nurses who invoke the rule of confidentiality in order to justify their not disclosing information concerning threats or risks to innocent third parties, may be guilty of negligence.

Before accepting this conclusion, however, it is necessary that we clarify the force of HP in the context of the ethics of AIDS, and refine the analysis of the conditions under which breaches of confidentiality pertaining to a patient's antibody status or a diagnosis of AIDS may be ethically justifiable.

II. VULNERABILITY, DISEASE CONTROL, AND DISCRIMINATION

Defenders of HP typically hold that all moral agents have a general moral obligation with respect to all moral patients to (a) avoid harm, (b) prevent or protect against harm, and (c) remove harm. One problem with HP is that not all acts and omissions which result in harm to others appear to be wrong. For instance, if I buy the last pint of Haagen-Daz coffee ice cream in the store, then I have, in some sense, harmed the next customer who wants to buy this good. Similarly, if one baseball team defeats another, then they have harmed the other team. But neither of these cases represent *wrongful* harms. Why then are some harms wrongful and others not?

Robert Goodin has recently developed a theory which provides at least a partial answer to this question. According to Goodin, the duty to protect against harm tends to arise most strongly in contexts in which someone is specially dependent on others or in some way specially vulnerable to their choices and actions.[7] He dubs this the Vulnerability Principle [VP]. Vulnerability, implying risk or susceptibility to harm, should be understood in a relational sense: being vulnerable to another is a condition which involves both a relative inability of the vulnerable party to protect themselves from harm or risk, and a correlative ability of another individual to act (or refrain from actions) which would foreseeably place the vulnerable party in a position of harm or risk or remove them from such a position.

No one is completely invulnerable, and we are all to some extent dependent on the choices and actions of others. However, where there exists a rough parity of power among the parties to protect their own interests, VP does not apply. It only applies in cases where one party is *specially* vulnerable, the parties are unequal in their powers or abilities to protect their own interests, or where an inequality in knowledge or power gives one party an unfair advantage over the other.

The Vulnerability Principle is related to the Harm Principle in giving a more precise analysis of the circumstances in which a strict duty to protect others arises. For example, under HP it might be thought that individuals, qua moral agents, have a duty to insure that persons be inoculated against contagious, preventable diseases, such as polio. However, while we have no strong obligations under HP to ensure that other adults have been inoculated, we *do* have a strong general obligation under VP to see to it that all young children are inoculated, and I have a special duty as a parent to see that my own children are inoculated. Children, as a class, are especially vulnerable and lack the ability to protect themselves. Being a parent *intensifies* the duty to prevent harm to children, by focussing the duty to protect the vulnerable on individuals who are specially responsible for the care of children. For other adults, on the other hand, I have no strong duty to protect, since I may generally assume that mature moral agents have both the ability and the responsibility to protect themselves.[8]

Viewed in this light, the remarks quoted earlier by the hospital spokeswoman take on new meaning and relevance. She argued that it is the responsibility of health care workers to protect themselves by taking appropriate infection control measures in situations in which they may be exposed to blood infected with HIV. This argument might be a good one if people who occupy these professional roles are trained in such measures and are equipped to use them when appropriate. If they were so equipped, then in the Baltimore case, the nurse who later informed the rescue workers of the patient's antibody status was *not* specially responsible to prevent harm; the paramedics were responsible for their own safety.

The main problem with this argument is that it is not always possible to assume that emergency workers and others who provide direct care to AIDS patients or HIV-infected individuals are properly trained and equipped in infection control, nor, even if they are, that it is always feasible for them to employ these procedures in emergency situations. The scene of an emergency is not a controlled environment, and while emergency and public safety workers make take precautions such as wearing gloves and masks, these measures can be rendered ineffective, say, if a glove is torn and the worker cut while wrestling someone from a mass of twisted metal that was a car. While *post hoc* notification of the antibody status of people whom public safety workers have handled may not prevent them from contracting infection, it can alert them to the need to be tested, and thus can prevent them from spreading the infection (if they are in fact infected) to others, e.g. their spouses.

Health care workers, public safety workers, paramedics, and others who come into direct contact with blood which may be infected with the AIDS virus represent a class of persons for whom the Vulnerability Principle suggests a special "duty to protect" is appropriate. It is appropriate in these cases because such workers are routinely exposed to blood in the course of their professional activities, and exposure to infected blood is one way in which people can become infected with the AIDS virus. Such workers could protect themselves by simply refusing to handle anyone whom they suspected of harboring the infection. Doing this, however, would mean violating their professional responsibility to provide care. Hence, morally, they can only protect themselves by reducing their risk of exposure, in this case, by employing infection control measures and being careful. In this respect, health care workers, whether they work inside or outside of the hospital, are in a relevantly different moral situation than ordinary people who are not routinely exposed to blood and who have no special duty to provide care, and this makes them specially vulnerable. It thus appears that the nurse who informed the emergency workers of their risk of exposure did the right thing in informing them, since in doing so she was discharging a duty to protect the vulnerable.[9]

But do similar conclusions follow with respect to "ordinary" persons who need not expose themselves to infection in the course of their professional activities? Consider the case in which a patient who is known to have a positive antibody status informs his physician that he does not intend to break off having sexual relations and that he will not tell his fiancée that he is infected with the AIDS virus.[10]

In this case, we have a known, unsuspecting party, the fiancée, who will be placed at risk by failure to discharge a duty to protect. The fiancée is vulnerable in this case to the infected patient, since it is primarily *his* actions or omissions which place her at risk. According HP + VP, the patient has a strong special responsibility to protect those with whom he has or will have sexual relations against infection. There are a number of ways in which he can discharge this duty. For instance, he can break off the relationship, abstain from sexual intercourse, practice "safe sex," or he can inform his fiancée of his antibody status. This last option protects the fiancée by alerting her to the need to protect herself. But does the physician in this case also have a special responsibility to protect the fiancée?

She does, in this case, if she has good reason to believe that her patient will not discharge his responsibility to protect his fiancée or inform her of his positive antibody status. Since the physician possesses the information which would alert her patient's fiancée to a special need to protect herself, and the only other person who has this information will not reveal it, the fiancée is specially dependent upon the physician's choices and actions. Were she to fail to attempt to persuade her patient to reveal the information, or if he still refused to do so, to see to it that the patient's fiancée was informed, she would be acting in complicity with a patient who was violating his duty to prevent harm, and so would also be acting unethically under the Vulnerability Principle.

It thus appears that the rule of confidentiality protecting a patient's HIV antibody status cannot be regarded as absolute. There are several sorts of cases where HP + VP override the rule of confidentiality. However, finding there are justified exceptions to a generally justified rule of practice does not allow for unrestricted disclosure of antibody status to all and sundry. The basic question which must be answered in considering revealing confidential information concerning a patient's HIV antibody status is: *Is the individual to be notified someone who is specially vulnerable? That is, are they someone who faces a significant risk of exposure to the infection, and, will revealing confidential information to them assist them in reducing this risk to themselves or others?*

Answering this question is not always going to be easy, and applying HP + VP, and balancing its claims against those of confidentiality will require an extraordinary degree of moral sensitivity and discretion. Because the rule of confidentiality describes a valid prima facie moral responsibility of physicians, the burden of proof must always fall on those who would violate it in order to accommodate the claims of an opposing ethical principle. Perhaps this is why physicians tend to assume that if the rule of confidentiality is not absolute, it might as well be treated as such. Physicians, nurses, and others who are privy to information about patients' antibody status, by and large, are likely to lack the relevant degree of ethical sensitivity to discriminate the cases in which confidentiality can be justifiably violated from those where it cannot. So if we must err, the argument goes, it is better to err on the side of confidentiality.

Aside from underestimating the moral sensitivity of members of these professional groups, this argument fails to take into account that there are two ways of erring—one can err by wrongfully disclosing confidential information to those who have no right to know it, and one can err by failing to disclose confidential information to those who do have a right to know it. The harms that can result from errors of the first kind are often significant, and sometimes irreparable. But so are the harms that result from errors of the second kind. While the burden of proof should be placed on those who would breach the prima facie rule of confidentiality, it is should sometimes be possible for persons to satisfy this burden and act in accordance with HP + VP without moral fault.

The strength of conviction with which many physicians in the forefront of AIDS research and treatment argue for the protection of confidentiality can be explained partly by recognizing that they view themselves as having a special responsibility to prevent harm to AIDS patients. The harm which they seek to prevent, however, is not only harm to their patient's health. It is also social harm caused by discrimination that these physicians are trying to prevent. This is yet a different application of HP + VP in the context of AIDS which merits close attention.

As was noted earlier, the particular strength of the pragmatic argument for confidentiality in the context of AIDS, derives from the fact that, because of the public hysteria about AIDS, HIV infected persons or those with AIDS or ARC are likely to be subjected to invidious discrimination in housing, employment, access to insurance and other sevices, should the information that they are AIDS patients or are HIV-infected become widely known. These are clearly wrongful harms, but whose responsibility is it to prevent such harms? Generally speaking, preventing the harms which arise from injustice and disregard of civil and human rights is the proper responsibility of public officials. However, at present, only a few municipalities, San Francisco, New York City, and Washington, D.C. have enacted AIDS anti-discrimination legislation, and recently, the Reagan Administration has taken the position that it is not a Federal responsibility to do so.[11]

Because the efforts of public officials to pass and enforce effective AIDS anti-discrimination measures have been lackadaisical, many physicians feel that they have inherited the responsibility to protect their patients against the social harms caused by discrimination, and have acted on that conviction in the only way readily available to them, by insisting that the rule of confidentiality be strictly observed with respect to persons infected with HIV. Confidentiality of HIV antibody test results and diagnoses of AIDS is currently seen as the only effective barrier against unjust discrimination.

By relying exclusively on a guarantee of absolute confidentiality to protect people with AIDS from discrimination, we acknowledge the problem of harm caused by discrimination but do not effectively address it. The passage of anti-discrimination standards applying to HIV-infected persons, people with AIDS, ARC, and members of groups who are perceived as being infected, should be the first priority of all those who are concerned to prevent the spread of this disease. Such measures are justified not only on the grounds of human dignity, and human rights, but because in the context of the AIDS epidemic, they will also tend to function as effective public health measures by removing (or diminishing) one reason which deters persons at risk from seeking testing and counselling. Medical personnel and public health authorities who take the position that confidentiality is absolute in order to shield their patients from discrimination, will increasingly find themselves in the uncomfortable position of being accomplices to the irresponsible behavior of known noncompliant positives. What is needed, then, is a finely drawn public policy that includes strong and effective anti-discrimination standards, a public education program which encourages individual and professional responsibility, and a set of clear effective guidelines for public health authorities concerning when and to whom confidential information necessary for disease control and the protection of those at risk may be revealed.

III. WHO HAS A RIGHT TO KNOW?

The Vulnerability Principle suggests that breaches of confidentiality may be justified in cases where the following conditions obtain:

(1) there is an identifiable person or an identifiable group of people who are "at risk" of contracting AIDS from a known carrier, (2) the carrier has not or will not disclose his/her antibody status to those persons whom he/she has placed or will place at risk, and (3) the identity of the carrier and his/her antibody status is known to a physician, nurse, health care worker, public health authority, or another person privileged to this information. It is justifiable, under these circumstances, to reveal information which might enable others to identify an AIDS patient or HIV-infected person. Revelation of confidential information is justified under this rule by the fact that others are vulnerable to infection, or may be unknowingly infecting others, and the information to be revealed may serve as an effective means of protecting those at risk.

The phrase "at risk" is most significant since not everyone who comes into contact with AIDS patients and HIV-infected persons will be placed at risk. Those persons who are most at risk are sexual partners of persons who are infected, persons who are exposed to an infected person's blood, and the fetuses of infected women.[12] Because these are the only documented means of transmitting the disease, it is relatively easy in the case of AIDS to identify those individuals who are specially vulnerable, and to distinguish them from others who are not. In particular, persons who will at most have "casual contact" with the patient are not specially vulnerable.[13] Discrimination in housing or employment is, therefore, not justifiable since AIDS cannot be transmitted by merely working in the same office or living in the same house as an HIV-infected person. On the other hand, it is known that AIDS can be transmitted by sexual contact or by blood or blood products. Fears of contagion via these routes are not irrational, and public policies should address ways of preventing the further spread of the disease.

A policy option which has been suggested is mandatory HIV antibody testing for everyone, or for everyone in certain risk groups, or for people applying for marriage licenses, or as a preemployment screen. However, mandatory testing programs are fraught with ethical problems and, in general, are neither cost-effective nor just.[14] HIV testing should remain voluntary, but, if it is voluntary, and the onus of informing the sexual contacts of those who test positive is also voluntary, then some HIV-infected individuals will not be tested, and of those who are tested and are found to be positive, some will not inform their sexual partners.

A more justifiable policy would be to keep testing voluntary, but to urge those who test positive to disclose their antibody status to their known sexual contacts, or if they do not wish to or will not do this themselves, to ask them to supply the names of their partners so that notification of those at risk can proceed by other means. A number of states have instituted such programs of voluntary partner notification.[15] The ethical rationale supporting such measures derives a "right to know" another person's HIV antibody status from HP + VP, the fact that sexual transmission of HIV has been documented, and the assumption that notification will enable those who may have been exposed to the infection to protect themselves, and, if they are already infected, to protect others.

The main problem with reliance on voluntary personal disclosure is that there is no way to check to see whether or not the infected person has indeed complied and informed all of their contacts. Another way to carry out partner notification is to have the carrier voluntarily reveal the names of their sexual and drug contacts to physicians or nurses who will then personally notify partners. This method of contacting those at risk is preferable on two grounds: it may be emotionally easier for some people to have partner notification handled by third parties, and secondly, there is a way of checking to see that all identified sexual contacts have been notified.

The main problem with this proposal is that it places primary care providers in an uncomfortable "dual role." Instead of leaving this matter to the discretion of direct health care providers, procedures should be devised whereby physicians, nurses and other primary care personnel can avoid "dual roles" as caregivers and public health officers. One way to do this is to establish a special office in the state public health administration and to have public health authorities notify persons known to be at risk. Physicians and nurses can confidentially report cases of HIV infection to this office, and public health officials can make the determination as to whether notification of partners is warranted in accordance with the Vulnerability Principle. Patients should always be informed that this is being done, and should sign a form releasing the information needed to notify contacts. Notification taking this form would not have to indicate the source of the information, a private physician or clinic, and this might help allay fears about a "chilling effect" on a particular physician's AIDS practice. The notification of contacts should also attempt to protect the identity of the carrier. In making a partner notification, personnel in the public health office can simply state that they have reason to believe that a person may have been exposed to HIV and to urge that they report for testing and counselling.

This method will work with respect to known positives who voluntarily comply, but can anything be done about those who refuse to reveal the names of their contacts, or reveal only some of them?

Noncompliance in supplying names of sexual or IV drug partners should not be associated with sanctions such as fines or short prison terms; we cannot extort or coerce this kind of information, and such measures will tend to discourage some persons from seeking testing and counselling. The appropriate response to this kind of noncompliance should be a warning that more active means of contract tracing which involve greater risk of disclosure or invasion of privacy, such as surveillance and investigation, may be employed. In extreme cases, e.g. where known carriers continue to engage in practices likely to infect others, e.g. prostitution, stronger remedies and sanctions, e.g. civil commitment, quarantine, or arrest, may be justified.

Some may argue that such programs of partner notification and limited contract tracing are unwise on the grounds that they will tend to deter individuals from being tested in the first place. The reply is that such programs will not deter individuals who are socially responsible and are willing to take steps to protect themselves and others from HIV infection, and it will tend to increase compliance with voluntary disease control measures among identified HIV-infected members of risk groups who are reluctant to accept their social responsibilities. However, such programs have little chance of success unless they are coupled with strong federal anti-discrimination policies which are strictly enforced.[16] Such measures would function analogously to infection control measures in reducing or removing the risk of harm caused by discrimination, thereby enabling people to act more responsibly.

Even so, programs of voluntary partner notification and limited contact tracing for sexual and IV drug partners of known noncompliant positives will not prevent the infection from being transmitted. It is estimated that there are 1.5 million people in the United States currently infected with the virus and therefore capable of transmitting it. The overwhelming majority of those infected do not know that they are infected. Thus, the onus of responsibility for protecting people who are "at risk" rests primarily with those persons who engage in high risk behaviors, and only secondarily with other persons who have knowledge of infection or infectiousness such as health care providers and public health authorities. In some other cases, for instance, cases of pediatric AIDS, parents and classroom teachers will also have a "right to know" because they will be the ones responsible for the care and protection of minors. However, except in these cases, i.e. in cases where another individual should have knowledge of HIV infection in order to protect themselves or specially vulnerable others from risk of infection, there is no generalized "right to know." Confidentiality should be protected in all other cases.[17]

Notes

1. *The Baltimore Sun* June 11, 1987, p. D1.
2. Sissela Bok, *Secrets: On the Ethics of Concealment and Revelation* (New York: Vintage Books, 1983); Chapter IX.
3. Sheldon Landesman presents this argument compellingly: "Any legally or socially sanctioned act that breaches confidentiality or imposes additional burdens (such as job loss or cancellation of insurance) acts as a disincentive to voluntary testing. Thus if all physicians were legally required to report HIV-positive persons to a health department or to inform sexual partners at risk from the HIV-positive person, no one would come forward for testing. This is especially true if the physician is known to treat many patients with AIDS and HIV infection. The public knowledge that such a physician has violated confidentiality would result (indeed, has resulted in several cases) in a sharp decline of potentially infected persons seeking counselling and testing. Consequently, a growing number of persons would remain ignorant of their infectiousness as would their sexual partners," *The Hastings Center Report*, Vol. 17, (1987), p. 25.
4. Bok, *Op. Cit.*, p. 123.
5. *Ibid.*
6. *Ibid.*, pp. 129–130. In a note at the end of this passage Bok concedes that the fourth premise involves important "line-drawing" problems which may vary among cases, a point that I will address shortly in the context of AIDS prevention and treatment.
7. Robert E. Goodin, *Protecting the Vulnerable: A Reanalysis of Our Social Responsibilities* (Chicago: The University of Chicago Press, 1985).
8. It follows on this view that I also have a responsibility to protect myself, or my future selves, from such preventable harms. Cf. M. E. Winston, "Responsibility to Oneself," unpublished paper presented at the American Philosophical Association, Pacific Division Meetings, March 27, 1987.
9. In fact, the fire fighters who provided emergency care to the wounded Baltimore woman were not wearing gloves. In this particular case a further reason for condoning the nurse's action might be found in the fact that the patient died. Is it possible to violate confidentiality when the person whose secret is revealed is dead? The pragmatic justifications for the rule of confidentiality would still apply in such cases, but it is a moot question as to whether the deceased individual themselves can be harmed or wronged by revealing confidential information. See Joan Callahan, "Harming the Dead," *Ethics*, Vol. 97 (1987), pp. 341–352.
10. Cf. "AIDS and a Duty to Protect," *The Hastings Center Report*, Vol. 17, (1987), pp. 22–23.
11. *The New York Times*, September 21, 1987, p. A1.
12. The Centers for Disease Control lists persons belonging to certain groups or who engage in certain types of behavior as having "high risk" of contracting HIV, and these include: homosexual/bisexual males, IV drug users, persons born in countries where heterosexual transmission is prevalent (e.g. Haiti and Central African countries), hemophiliacs, male and female prostitutes, sexual partners of members of high-risk groups, infants born to women in high-risk groups, and persons receiving blood transfusions before 1985 when screening for HIV began. [CDC. Additional Recommendations to Reduce Sexual and Drug Abuse-Related Transmission of Human T-Lymphotropic Virus Type III/Lymphadenopathy-Associated Virus. MMWR 1986 March 14; 152–155.] It is important to note that not everyone belonging to these groups is "at risk." Certain behaviors in certain contexts place individuals at risk, and other behaviors can reduce or remove these risks.
13. In an epidemiological study by Friedland, et. al of the family members of 39 AIDS patients it was found that there were no instances of horizontal transmission of HIV to family members living in the same household. [Friedland, G. H.,

Saltzman, B. R., Rogers, M. S., Kahl, P. A, Lesser, M. L., Mayers, M. M., and Klein, R. S., "Lack of transmission of HTLV-III/LAV infection to household contacts of patients with AIDS or AIDS-related complex with oral candidiasis," *New England Journal of Medicine*. Vol. 314 (1986), pp. 344–349.] Additionally, there is no known risk of transmission of HIV in settings such as offices, schools, factories, or by personal services workers, such as beauticians and barbers or food service workers. [CDG. Recommendations for preventing transmission of infection with T-lymphotropic virus type III/lymphadenopathy-associated virus in the workplace. MMWR 1985, vol. 34, no. 45, pp. 682–695.]

14. See Kenneth R. Howe, "Why Mandatory Screening for AIDS Is a Very Bad Idea." In Christine Pierce and Donald VanDeVeer (Eds.), *AIDS: Ethics and Public Policy* (Belmont: Wadsworth Publishing Co., 1988), pp. 140–149.
15. In Maryland, the Governor's Task Force on AIDS has recently recommended that, "Health care providers should strongly encourage HIV-infected patients to speak directly to and refer their own sexual and needle-sharing contacts for counselling and medical evaluation. There are instances, however, when these professionals may be *obligated* to notify persons *known* to have had significant exposures to HIV infection. In such cases, the duty to notify is a matter of good medical practice and supercedes the need to maintain confidentiality." *AIDS and Maryland: Policy Guidelines and Recommendations*, report of the Governor's Task Force on Acquired Immune Deficiency Syndrome. December 1986.
16. Cf. Larry Gostin, "Time for Federal Laws on AIDS Discrimination," Letter to the Editor, *The New York Times*, October 1, 1987.
17. I am indebted to David Newell and to an anonymous reviewer for helpful comments on this paper.

PLEASE DON'T TELL!: A CASE ABOUT HIV AND CONFIDENTIALITY

With Commentaries by Leonard Fleck and Marcia Angell

The patient, Carlos R., was a twenty-one year old Hispanic male who had suffered gunshot wounds to the abdomen in gang violence. He was uninsured. His stay in the hospital was somewhat shorter than might have been expected, but otherwise unremarkable. It was felt that he could safely complete his recovery at home. Carlos admitted to his attending physician that he was HIV-positive, which was confirmed.

At discharge the attending physician recommended a daily home nursing visit for wound care. However, Medicaid would not fund this nursing visit because a caregiver lived in the home who could adequately provide this care, namely, the patient's twenty-two-year-old sister Consuela, who in fact was willing to accept this burden. Their mother had died almost ten years ago, and Consuela had been a mother to Carlos and their younger sister since then. Carlos had no objection to Consuela's providing this care, but he insisted absolutely that she was not to know his HIV status. He had always been on good terms with Consuela, but she did not know he was actively homosexual. His greatest fear, though, was that his father would learn of his homosexual orientation, which is generally looked upon with great disdain by Hispanics.

Reprinted with permission of the authors and the publisher from *Hastings Center Report*, Vol. 21 (November/December 1991), pp. 39–40.

Would Carlo's physician be morally justified in breaching patient confidentiality on the grounds that he had a "duty to warn"?

COMMENTARY BY LEONARD FLECK

If there were a home health nurse to care for this patient, presumably there would be no reason to breach confidentiality since the expectation would be that she would follow universal precautions. Of course, universal precautions could be explained to the patient's sister. In an ideal world this would seem to be a satisfactory response that protects both Carlos's rights and Consuela's welfare. But the world is not ideal.

We know that health professionals, who surely ought to have the knowledge that would motivate them to take universal precautions seriously, often fail to take just such precautions. It is easy to imagine that Consuela could be equally casual or careless, especially when she had not been specifically warned that her brother was HIV-infected. Given this possibility, does the physician have a duty to warn that would justify breaching confidentiality? I shall argue that he may not breach confidentiality but he must be reasonably attentive to Consuela's safety. Ordinarily the conditions that must be met to invoke a duty to warn are: (1) an imminent threat of serious and irreversible harm, (2) no alternative to averting that threat other than this breach of confidentiality, and (3) proportionality between the harm averted by this breach of confidentiality and the harm associated with such a breach. In my judgment, none of these conditions are satisfactorily met.

No one doubts that becoming HIV-infected represents a serious and irreversible harm. But, in reality, is that threat imminent enough to justify breaching confidentiality? If we were talking about two individuals who were going to have sexual intercourse on repeated occasions, then the imminence condition would likely be met. But the patient's sister will be caring for his wound for only a week or two, and wound care does not by itself involve any exchange of body fluids. If we had two-hundred and forty surgeons operating on two-hundred and forty HIV-infected patients, and if each of those surgeons nicked himself while doing surgery, then the likelihood is that only one of them would become HIV-infected. Using this as a reference point, the likelihood of this young woman seroconverting if her intact skin comes into contact with the blood of this patient is very remote at best.

Moreover in this instance there are alternatives. A frank and serious discussion with Consuela about the need for universal precautions, plus monitored, thorough training in correct wound care, fulfills what I would regard as a reasonable duty to warn in these circumstances. Similar instructions ought to be given to Carlos so that he can monitor her performance. He can be reminded that this is a small price for protecting his confidentiality as well as his sister's health. It might also be necessary to provide gloves and other such equipment required to observe universal precautions.

We can imagine easily enough that there might be a lapse in conscientiousness on Consuela's part, that she might come into contact with his blood. But even if this were to happen, the likelihood of her seroconverting is remote at best. This is where proportionality between the harm averted by the breach and the harm associated with it comes in. For if confidentiality were breached and she were informed of his HIV status, this would likely have very serious consequences for Carlos. As a layperson with no professional duty to preserve confidentiality herself, Consuela might inform other family members, which could lead to his being ostracized from the family. And even if she kept the information confidential, she might be too afraid to provide the care for Carlos, who might then end up with no one to care for him.

The right to confidentiality is a right that can be freely waived. The physician could engage Carlos in a frank moral discussion aimed at persuading him that the reasonable and decent thing to do is to inform his sister of his HIV status. Perhaps the physician offers assurances that she would be able to keep that information in strict confidence. The patient agrees. Then what happens? It is easy to imagine that Consuela balks at caring for her brother, for fear of infection.

Medicaid would still refuse to pay for home nursing care because a caregiver would still be in the home, albeit a terrified caregiver. Consuela's response may not be rational, but it is certainly possible. If she were to react in this way it would be an easy "out" to say that it was Carlos who freely agreed to the release of the confidential information so now he'll just have to live with those consequences. But the matter is really more complex than that. At the very least the physician would have to apprise Carlos of the fact that his sister might divulge his HIV status to some number of other individuals. But if the physician impresses this possibility on Carlos vividly enough, Carlos might be even more reluctant to self-disclose his HIV status to Consuela. In that case the physician is morally obligated to respect that confidentiality.

COMMENTARY BY MARCIA ANGELL

It would be wrong, I believe, to ask this young woman to undertake the nursing care of her brother and not inform her that he is HIV-infected.

The claim of a patient that a doctor hold his secrets in confidence is strong but not absolute. It can be overridden by stronger, competing claims. For example, a doctor would not agree to hold in confidence a diagnosis of rubella, if the patient were planning to be in the presence of a pregnant woman without warning her. Similarly, a doctor would be justified in acting on knowledge that a patient planned to commit a crime. Confidentiality should, of course, be honored when the secret is entirely personal, that is, when it could have no substantial impact on anyone else. On the other hand, when it would pose a major threat to others, the claim of confidentiality must be overridden. Difficulties arise when the competing claims are nearly equal in moral weight.

In this scenario, does Consuela have any claims on the doctor? I believe she does, and that her claims are very compelling. They stem, first, from her right to have information she might consider relevant to her decision to act as her brother's nurse, and, second, from the health care system's obligation to warn of a possible risk to her health. I would like to focus first on whether Consuela has a right to information apart from the question of whether there is in fact an appreciable risk. I believe that she has such a right, for three reasons.

First, there is an element of deception in *not* informing Consuela that her brother is HIV infected. Most people in her situation would want to know if their "patient" were HIV-infected and would presume that they would be told if that were the case. (I suspect that a private nurse hired in a similar situation would expect to be told—and that she would be.) At some level, perhaps unconsciously, Consuela would assume that Carlos did not have HIV infection because no one said that he did. Thus, in keeping Carlos's secret, the doctor implicitly deceives Consuela—not a net moral gain, I think.

Second, Consuela has been impressed to provide nursing care in part because the health system is using her to avoid providing a service it would otherwise be responsible for. This fact, I believe, gives the health care system an additional obligation to her, which includes giving her all the information that might bear on her decision to accept this responsibility. It might be argued that the information about her brother's HIV infection is not relevant, but it is patronizing to make this assumption. She may for any number of reasons, quite apart from the risk of transmission, find it important to know that he is HIV-infected.

Finally, I can't help feeling that this young woman has already been exploited by her family and that the health care system should not collude in doing so again. We are told that since she was twelve, she has acted as "mother" to a brother only one year younger, presumably simply because she is female, since she is no more a mother than he is. Now she is being asked to be a nurse, as well as a mother, again presumably because she is female. In this context, concerns about the sensibilities of the father or about Carlos's fear of them are not very compelling, particularly when they are buttressed by stereotypes about Hispanic families. Furthermore, both his father and his sister will almost certainly learn the truth eventually.

What about the risk of transmission from Carlos to Consuela? Many would—wrongly, I believe—base their arguments solely on this question. Insofar as they did, they would have very little to go on. The truth is that no one knows what the risk would be to Consuela. To my knowledge, there have been no studies that would yield data on the point. Most likely the risk would be extremely small, particularly if there were no blood or pus in the wound, but it would be speculative to say how small. We do know that Consuela has no experience with universal precautions and could not be expected to use them diligently with her brother unless she had some sense of why she might be doing so. In any case, the doctor has no right to decide for this young woman that she should assume a risk, even if he believes it would be remote. That is for her to decide. The only judgment he has a right to make is whether *she* might consider the information that her brother is HIV-infected to be relevant to her decision to nurse him, and I think it is reasonable to assume she might.

There is, I believe, only one ethical way out of this dilemma. The doctor should strongly encourage Carlos to tell his sister that he is HIV-infected or offer to do it for him. She could be asked not to tell their father, and I would see no problem with this. I would have no hesitation in appealing to the fact that Carlos already owes Consuela a great deal. If Carlos insisted that his sister not be told, the doctor should see to it that his nursing needs are met in some other way. In sum, then, I believe the doctor should pass the dilemma to the patient: Carlos can decide to accept Consuela's generosity in return for which he must tell her he is HIV infected (or ask the doctor to tell her)—or he can decide not to tell her and do without her nursing care.

HIV INFECTION, PREGNANT WOMEN, AND NEWBORNS

A POLICY PROPOSAL FOR INFORMATION AND TESTING

Working Group on HIV Testing of Pregnant Women and Newborns

Among the many tragic dimensions of the human immunodeficiency virus (HIV) epidemic as it moves into the 1990s is the growing number of infected women, infants, and children. Women now constitute approximately 10% of the acquired immunodeficiency syndrome (AIDS) cases thus far reported to the Centers for Disease Control. Most of these women are of reproductive age. The US Public Health Service has projected that there will be approximately 3000 cases of pediatric AIDS by the end of 1991. In most of these cases, infants

Reprinted from *JAMA*, Vol. 264, No. 18 (November 14, 1990), pp. 2416–20.

will have acquired the infection through vertical transmission from their mothers.

As the public health impact of HIV infection in women and children has increased, so has interest in screening pregnant women and newborns for evidence of HIV infection. Currently, however, knowing that a pregnant woman is seropositive does not necessarily indicate that her fetus is or will be affected. Human immunodeficiency virus testing of the newborn reveals only the presence or absence of maternal antibodies and thus establishes if mothers are infected, not if the infants themselves are infected. It is currently estimated that in the United States about 30% of HIV-positive mothers transmit HIV to their newborn infants.

Whether among pregnant women or newborns, HIV disproportionately affects disadvantaged women and children of color, adds yet another layer of complexity to the policy problem of who should be screened. Currently, the Centers for Disease Control reports that over 70% of women with AIDS in the United States are African-American or Hispanic. The mode of transmission in most of these cases is intravenous drug use or sexual intercourse with an intravenous drug user.

Screening of pregnant women and newborns raises profound moral, legal, and policy issues. To date, no national professional association or committee has called for the mandatory screening of either pregnant women or newborns, although arguments favoring mandatory policies have appeared in the literature. ... Numerous national groups have advocated offering testing to either all pregnant women or all "high-risk" pregnant women. In addition, some organizations and commentators have called for directive counseling to discourage HIV-infected women from becoming pregnant or bearing children.

This article presents a detailed 10-point program of policy recommendations for both pregnant women and newborns, and develops its rationale through the examination of potential objections and criticisms.

POLICY RECOMMENDATIONS

We advocate a policy of informing all pregnant women and new mothers about the epidemic of HIV infection and the availability of HIV testing. Although screening of either pregnant women or newborns is not the central focus of our policy, because we defend a consent requirement for testing, our position can be interpreted as a policy of voluntary screening. In our view, a policy of mandatory screening either for pregnant women or for newborns is not justified in the current situation on traditional public health criteria or other grounds. Moreover, we reject implementation of counseling and screening policies that interfere with women's reproductive freedom or that result in the unfair stigmatization of vulnerable social groups. Our specific policy recommendations are as follows:

1. All pregnant women and new mothers should be informed about HIV infection and the availability of HIV testing for themselves and their newborns. Informing of pregnant women should take place at the time of registration for prenatal care. ... (Ideally, all women should be informed about the HIV epidemic and HIV testing in advance of pregnancy, as part of preconception care. In addition, it may shortly be advisable, either because an intrapartum intervention becomes available or because it becomes desirable to manage third trimester HIV-positive women differently, to discuss HIV testing again late in pregnancy.)

2. The information to be presented to pregnant women and new mothers may be provided through printed or audiovisual materials. However, in communities with a significant degree of HIV infection or drug use, a personal discussion is of particular importance and should be conducted. Whatever method is selected, the information disclosed should cover the same topics and content and should be presented in a manner and language that is meaningful and understandable to the women served.

3. The information conveyed under recommendations 1 and 2 does not substitute for either pretest or posttest counseling. All women who express an interest in HIV testing for themselves or their newborns should receive personal pretest counseling; those tested should receive personal posttest counseling.

4. Both prenatal and newborn testing are to be voluntary, with a requirement of informed consent or parental consent. Consent for testing should be solicited only after pretest counseling.

5. The involvement of state and local health departments is essential to the successful implementation of this policy. Health departments should assume responsibility for developing and updating the educational materials referred to above, assuring the availability of materials in several languages, providing protocols and training for pretest and posttest counseling, and developing evaluation mechanisms to assume the proper conduct of the program. (State government may seek regulatory or legislative means to mandate the obligations of providers of prenatal and newborn care to inform pregnant women and new mothers about the HIV epidemic and the availability of HIV testing. Alternatively, jurisdictions may choose not to mandate these obligations by regulation or legislation unless mechanisms for guiding professional conduct fail, over a reasonable period of time, to ensure adoption of the practice.)

6. Health departments should also establish standards for laboratory procedures, including a requirement that all positive tests be confirmed on an independently drawn, second blood specimen prior to communicating results to the pregnant woman or new mother.

7. Every effort should be made to secure specialized medical interventions for the management of HIV infection, appropriate social services and supports, intensive primary care and abortion services (where requested by pregnant women) for all women and infants identified as HIV positive as a result of prenatal or newborn testing. All women should be informed of any difficulties in obtaining these interventions or services for themselves or their newborns. Specific obstacles to treatment or services should be discussed during pretest counseling with any woman interested in HIV testing for herself or her newborn.

8. Once it is established whether or not infants born to mothers who are HIV positive are infected with HIV, any medical or other records including information about HIV test results should be corrected to verify either that the infant has been diagnosed as infected or that the infant is not HIV-infected.

9. To assure recommendation 7, regional networks of referral services for HIV-positive women and their infants should be established. Each network should assist health care providers with the medical management and counseling of HIV-positive women and their infants, and should offer supportive social services directly to pregnant women and new mothers.

10. Existing laws regarding medical confidentiality and antidiscrimination protections should be strengthened and specifically extended to persons with HIV infection to combat the harmful consequences associated with unavoidable disclosures or public identification of HIV status. The variation between state confidentiality and antidiscrimination protections should be replaced by a uniform, national policy.

MAJOR OBJECTIONS TO POLICY RECOMMENDATIONS

Our position is subject to several powerful criticisms or objections, both from the perspective of those who favor an aggressive screening policy and from those who have serious reservations about the propriety of any type of maternal or neonatal screening or testing.

Why Pregnant Women?

Why do we need a public policy on HIV screening of pregnant women? The justification for our policy proposals reflects the importance of four goals: (1) to advance the national campaign to educate the public about HIV disease and how it can be prevented; (2) to enhance the current and future reproductive choices of women; (3) to identify women and newborns who can benefit from medical advances in the clinical management of HIV infection; and (4) to allow proper obstetrical treatment of women infected with HIV. ...

With the exception of our fourth goal, the goals of our policy are not specific to pregnant women. Goals 2 and 3 apply to all sexually active women, and goal 1 to all persons. Nonetheless, we have focused on pregnant women in this project for several reasons. First, the issue of vertical transmission has put pregnant women into the policy spotlight. In the near future, interventions may be available to reduce the rate of vertical transmission. We were motivated to head off policy directives that viewed pregnant women as mere vessels for the unborn or vectors of disease by developing policies respectful of the reproductive rights and interests of pregnant women. Second, we believe that primary medical care is a desirable setting for educating individuals about HIV disease and the availability of HIV testing. For many women pregnancy is the only time when they have access to comprehensive primary care services. Among women who do not receive prenatal care—which often is the situation for women who are at particular risk for HIV disease—the postpartum hospital stay is, unfortunately, often the only opportunity afforded health care providers to discuss HIV infection and to attempt referral to appropriate medical services. ...

Is Not a "Targeted" Program More Appropriate?

As noted earlier, HIV infection in women and children is a highly focal epidemic. It occurs disproportionately in poor women and children of color living in the inner cities of a few metropolitan areas. Would it not be more appropriate to target information and screening resources where there is the highest concentration of infection?

We reject a "targeted" policy for several reasons. Basing the offering of testing to pregnant women on an assessment of individual risk factors has been shown to be inefficient for both hepatitis and HIV infection. As a result, targeting would need to be based on proxies for individual risk such as sociodemographic criteria. Targeting by sociodemographic criteria is, however, invidiously discriminatory on its face. Unlike certain genetic conditions, there is no biological basis for targeting HIV programs by ethnicity. Although our program only calls for informing women about the HIV epidemic and the availability of voluntary testing, the targeting of this program to only poor women of color would send the false and dangerous message that, among women, only persons of this racial and ethnic description are at risk for HIV infection. Moreover, it labels all such women—the overwhelming majority of whom are not and never will be infected—as sources of contagion. The fact that groups identified as "carrying the virus" for AIDS suffer discrimination, social prejudice, and hardship has been well documented with regard to gay men. Poor women and children of color already suffer these burdens disproportionately. Thus, to add the stigma of AIDS contagion to poor women of color is to further harm a group of persons who are already unfairly disadvantaged.

Targeting based on community prevalence rates, rather than sociodemographic criteria, is also morally problematic. Substantial efficiency is not likely to occur unless "high prevalence areas" are narrowly defined. The more narrow this definition is, the greater the potential that community prevalence rates become merely thinly veiled proxies for ethnicity and poverty. Targeting by prevalence rates would also place an inappropriate burden on women in "low prevalence areas" who have risk factors for HIV infection and for whom testing may be beneficial. In the absence of a policy such as we propose, these women may be unaware either of being at increased risk or of how to obtain testing. Certain women, such as migrant workers, might be particularly ill served.

There are also public health arguments against targeting. As noted previously, targeting may serve to create or reinforce in women who are outside the targeted group the dangerous view that they are invulnerable to HIV. Targeting thus could undermine the public health objective of universal adoption of safer sex and drug use practices. In addition, informing women about the HIV epidemic is of value in all areas of the country. There is some reason to suspect that the current epidemiological pattern of HIV infection among women and children may be shifting (Tim Donders, MD, HIV Seroepidemiology Branch, oral communication, May 1990). An informed public is our best defense against today's low-prevalence community becoming tomorrow's newest area of outbreak. Of particular concern are communities with significant drug use problems but as yet no significant HIV infection.

It might be argued that in rejecting targeting we have failed to understand what justice requires in the case of poor and minority women. Specifically, in this instance, justice may require not equal treatment but the provision of greater benefits to the worst-off members of society. Targeting, because it is more efficient, would presumably provide greater benefits to the women in the program. In order for this claim to be substantiated, however, it would first have to be established that the benefits of a targeted program to poor women of color outweigh the harms of stigma and labeling discussed earlier. Given our nation's unfortunate history with regard to the treatment of minorities, women, and the poor, it is not surprising that some read in a policy of targeting not a desire to do good, but an agenda of genocide. ...

CONCLUSION

In the face of the complex issues and uncertainties that surround HIV infection and diagnosis in pregnant women and infants, any policy proposal is likely to be controversial and in some respects unsatisfactory. We have presented the 10 core elements of a policy that we believe represents the best compromise of competing interests and social goals. This policy is sensitive to the current medical and social facts; we examine the implications of anticipated future developments on our recommendations elsewhere.

We do not expect our policy recommendations to have any immediate or isolated effect on HIV transmission rates. It is unrealistic to expect any program of information about HIV infection and the availability of testing to, by itselly, affect transmission rates, let alone a program directed at women, given the history of inequality of power and the legacy of sexual subordination that all too often still characterize relations between men and women in our society. We do believe, however, that educational programs can make a difference. With regard to smoking, it has been established that while individual educational efforts were largely ineffective, the cumulative impact of multiple educational efforts in a sustained national antismoking campaign dramatically altered cultural values and reduced the prevalence of smoking. It is to be hoped that, over time, our nation will have a similar experience with HIV infection.

Nevertheless, a comprehensive policy response to controlling the HIV epidemic requires a broader focus than we have adopted herein. Human immunodeficiency virus disease in women and children is a disease of families and, as noted above, is intimately connected to relations between men and women. Any comprehensive policy must address the needs and interests of men as well women and must address the root of the problem of HIV infection in women—drug dependency and the poverty and social isolation that make the use of drugs attractive. Without adequate drug rehabilitation services and social policies and programs that can empower both disadvantaged women and men to break the cycle of poverty that links them to drug use, policies of public information and the availability of HIV testing cannot be expected to significantly affect the pace of the HIV epidemic.

ETHICAL CHALLENGES POSED BY ZIDOVUDINE TREATMENT TO REDUCE VERTICAL TRANSMISSION OF HIV

Ronald Bayer

In February 1994 the Data and Safety Monitoring Board of the National Institute of Allergy and Infectious Diseases recommended the interruption of a clinical trial designed to determine whether the administration of zidovudine to pregnant women infected with the human immunodeficiency virus (HIV) and to their newborns could reduce the rate of vertical viral transmission. Given the responsibilities of the Data and Safety Monitoring Board, there was no alternative. The difference in the rate of transmission between those receiving zidovudine and those receiving placebo was statistically significant ($P = 0.00006$). Women who received zidovudin had a transmission rate of 8.3 percent, as compared with 25.5 percent among those who received placebo—a reduction in the risk of transmission of 67.5 percent. The results of this trial (known as Protocol 076) appear in this issue of the *Journal.*

Many questions remain unanswered. Most critically, will the administration of zidovudine to pregnant women and their newborns pose a risk to the 70 to 80 percent of children who, though born to infected women, would not themselves have been infected? Is there some risk that the use of zidovudine during pregnancy will diminish the effectiveness of the drug when the woman's own clinical course would suggest the advisability of antiretroviral treatment?

Nevertheless, in the otherwise bleak clinical picture that has surrounded AIDS, especially since the report last year that early use of zidovudine in HIV infection had no apparent effect on clinical outcome, these findings represent very good news. In the clinical alert issued by the National Institutes of Health on February 20, 1994, the prospect of a "substantial potential benefit" was juxtaposed with the possibility of "unknown long-term risks."

The prospect of such benefit has led many clinicians to argue that the case for testing pregnant women for HIV infection is stronger than ever. Nevertheless, many advocates for patients with AIDS and proponents of women's rights have expressed skepticism about the claims made on behalf of zidovudine treatment during pregnancy. Some have charged that an effort to modify current practice on the basis of the new finding would constitute "malpractice." Driving such skepticism has been the fear that the new clinical findings would be used to override the privacy rights of pregnant women at risk for HIV, the vast majority of whom are poor black or Hispanic women.

These fears and the extent to which the new findings have produced anxiety instead of elation must be understood in the context of a history of efforts to impose treatment, even invasive procedures, on pregnant women in the interests of the offspring, and of national surveys that indicate that the vast majority of physicians favor mandatory screening of pregnant women. Mandatory screening usually refers to testing whose results can be linked to a particular woman in the absence of her consent and despite her express refusal. Most pertinently, the reaction to Protocol 076 was shaped by the fierce and widely reported debate in New York over mandatory screening of newborns for HIV. That debate and its outcome shed light on the important similarities and differences in ethics and politics between

---

Bayer, R., "Ethical Challenges Posed by Zidovudine Treatment to Reduce Vertical Transmission of HIV." From *The New England Journal of Medicine* 331:1223–25.

screening newborns and screening pregnant women.

In 1993 the New York state legislature considered, but ultimately rejected, a proposal by a legislator, long a defender of the reproductive rights of women, to end the mandatory blinded serologic surveillance of newborns and to replace it with a system of mandatory screening of newborns for the purposes of case finding. Opponents of blinded surveillance were appalled that it could determine how many but not which babies carried maternal antibody to HIV. Yet it was the very fact that no child or mother could be identified that had, for many, rendered such surveillance without consent ethically acceptable. On the other hand, others believed that the prospects for early clinical intervention in infected infants required that each baby who could benefit from such care receive it. To them, the right of the child to treatment was held to be more compelling than the mother's claim to privacy. Among those supporting the bill for mandatory unblinded testing of newborns were two of the three state branches of the American Academy of Pediatrics and *The New York Times*, which termed the concern about maternal privacy in this instance "theological."

Undergirding the position of those who supported mandatory unblinded screening of newborns was the ethical principle that the state had a special responsibility to protect the medical interests of the child, even when such protection necessitated, in rare instances, overriding parental refusal. This principle has long been reflected in, for example, the well-established practice of providing blood transfusions to the children of Jehovah's Witnesses despite parental objection. Even more relevant is the practice of mandatory or quasimandatory testing of newborns for a host of inborn metabolic conditions.

Much of the opposition to mandatory unblinded testing of newborns centered on the principle that no woman should ever be compelled to undergo testing for HIV. Since the mandatory testing of newborns in fact entailed the mandatory identification of infection in their mothers, the proposed policy was deemed ethically and politically unacceptable. More important than this principle for the outcome of the debate was the fact that despite advances in the management of HIV disease, early treatment could do little to affect fundamentally the life expectancy of HIV-infected children. If it were possible to save the lives of such children or to extend them dramatically, the weight of ethical argument as well as the political picture would undoubtedly change. In my view, the case for unblinded screening and treatment of newborns does not yet outweigh the privacy claims of the mother.

But if the prospect of radical improvement in the welfare of children could justify mandatory screening of newborns, why have there been so few calls for the mandatory unblinded testing of pregnant women in the light of the results of Protocol 076? Not surprisingly, intense opposition to mandatory screening during pregnancy for case-finding purposes has come from the proponents of privacy who also opposed compulsory newborn testing on principled grounds. But advocates of mandatory screening of newborns have also been loath to embrace compulsory testing of pregnant women. Why has this been so? The answer lies in the difference between the status of newborns and the status of adults. Mandatory screening of children could become justifiable if therapeutic interventions could substantially extend the lives of infected children, because treatment, regardless of parental objections, would be imperative. By contrast, the mandatory screening of pregnant women is objectionable because mandatory treatment of competent adults is virtually never acceptable. Although some states require the screening of all pregnant women for hepatitis and syphilis, in general the principle of informed consent guarantees that adults have a right to refuse care, even lifesaving care. This is so even when others view the refusal of treatment as foolish or irresponsible. In view of the remaining uncertainties about the long-term consequences of zidovudine treatment during pregnancy for both the mother and her offspring, the principle of consent to both screening and treatment is even more relevant.

There are also matters of practical concern. The pragmatic aspects alone of the treatment regimen defined in Protocol 076 make the prospect of therapy without the full cooperation of infected pregnant women difficult to contemplate. Even if one sought to mandate the use of an intravenous dose of zidovudine during delivery, how could one enforce a daily regimen of five doses of zidovudine during the second and third trimesters of pregnancy? Would anything short of incarceration make such treatment possible?

Thus, both ethics and practicality dictate the rejection of compulsory treatment of pregnant women. What is needed are strong efforts to persuade women to be tested for HIV and to encourage those who are infected to undergo zidovudine treatment after being fully informed of the benefits and the uncertain, but remote, prospects of long-term negative consequences. That is precisely the conclusion reached by the Public Health Service task force convened to consider the implications of Protocol 076.

If mandatory unblinded screening and treatment of pregnant women cannot be justified, ensuring access to zidovudine treatment for pregnant women does raise important issues of a different order. Obstetricians must be encouraged to offer HIV testing to pregnant women—especially those who live in communities where the seroprevalence of the virus is high. Making that possible will require considering whether the sometimes elaborate requirements for extensive counseling before testing, mandated by law in some states, are compatible with the new clinical prospects. This issue is especially relevant in the overburdened obstetrical services of America's inner cities. Making testing routine while preserving the right of informed consent will be a great challenge.

More important, no recommendation for HIV testing would be ethical if access to the needed therapy and support was not ensured. Given the failure of the American health care system to guarantee access to health care, given that too many women at risk for HIV receivc either no perinatal care or inadequate care, and given the poverty of the overwhelming majority of women who are infected, it is by no means certain that the scientific breakthrough represented by Protocol 076 will evoke the necessary social response.

No comment on the importance of the finding that zidovudine may radically reduce the rate of HIV transmission from infected women to their babies should fail to note that this major therapeutic achievement will have little or no effect on women in developing nations, where the toll of pediatric AIDS is most severe. Whether the wealthy nations of the world will be able and willing to make zidovudine available to the poorest nations will determine the course of the global epidemiology of pediatric AIDS. It will also tell us much about the extent to which our capacity for compassion can match our capacity for scientific progress.

THE RELATIONSHIP BETWEEN MEDICAL PROFESSIONALS AND PATIENTS

CONSENT, COERCION, AND CONFLICTS OF RIGHTS

Ruth Macklin

Cases of conflict of rights are not infrequent in law and morality. A range of cases that has gained increasing prominence recently centers around the autonomy of persons and their right to make decisions in matters affecting their own life and death. This paper will focus on a particular case of conflict of rights: the case of Jehovah's Witnesses who refuse blood transfusions for religious reasons and the question of whether or not there exists a right to compel medical treatment. The Jehovah's Witnesses who refuse blood transfusions do not do so because they want to die; in most cases, however, they appear to believe that they will die if their blood is not transfused. Members of this sect are acting on what is generally believed to be a constitutionally guaranteed right: freedom of religion, which is said to include not only freedom of religious belief, but also the right to act on such beliefs.

This study will examine a cluster of moral issues surrounding the Jehovah's Witness case. Some pertain to minor children of Jehovah's Witness parents, while others concern adult Witnesses who refuse treatment for themselves. The focus will be on the case as a moral one rather than a legal one, although arguments employed in some of the legal cases will be invoked. This is an issue at the intersection of law and morality—one in which the courts themselves have rendered conflicting decisions and have looked to moral principles for guidance. As is usually the case in ethics, whatever the courts may have decided does not settle the moral dispute, but the arguments and issues invoked in legal disputes often mirror the ethical dimensions of the case. The conflict—in both law and morals—arises out of a religious prohibition

Macklin, R. "Consent, Coercion, and Conflicts of Rights." *Perspectives in Biology and Medicine*, 20:3, (1977), 360–371.

against blood transfusions, a prohibition that rests on an interpretation of certain scriptural passages by the Jehovah's Witness sect.

The Witnesses' prohibition of blood transfusions derives from an interpretation of several Old Testament passages, chief among which is the following from Lev. 17:10–14:

> And whatsoever man there be of the house of Israel or of the strangers that sojourn among you, that eateth any manner of blood; I will even set my face against that soul that eateth blood, and will cut him off from among his people.
>
> ...
>
> Therefore I said unto the children of Israel, no soul of you shall eat blood, neither shall any stranger that sojourneth among you eat blood. And whatsoever man there be of the children of Israel, or of the strangers that sojourn among you, which hunteth and catcheth any beast or fowl that may be eaten; he shall even pour out the blood thereof, and cover it with dust. For it is the life of all flesh; the blood of it is for the life thereof: therefore I said unto the children of Israel, ye shall eat the blood of no manner of flesh; for the life of all flesh is the blood thereof: whosoever eateth it shall be cut off.[1]

The question immediately arises, On what basis do the Jehovah's Witnesses construe intravenous blood transfusions as an instance of eating blood? Witnesses sometimes claim that the prohibition against transfusions arises out of a literal interpretation of the relevant biblical passages, but the interpretation in question seems anything but "literal." One explanation for this is as follows: "Since they have been prohibited by the Bible from eating blood, they steadfastly proclaim that intravenous transfusion has no bearing on the matter, as it basically makes no difference whether the blood enters by the vein or by the alimentary tract. In their widely quoted reference *Blood, Medicine, and the Law of God* they constantly refer to the medical printed matter which early in the 20th century declared that blood transfusions are nothing more than a source of nutrition by a shorter route than ordinary" [1, p. 539]. Whether based on a literal interpretation of the Bible or not, the Witnesses' prohibition against transfusions extends not only to whole blood, but also to any blood derivative, such as plasma and albumin (blood substitutes are, however, quite acceptable) [1, p. 539].

This brief account of the basis of the religious prohibition has not yet addressed the moral issues involved; but for the sake of completeness, let us note two additional features of the Jehovah's Witness view—features that bear directly on the moral conflict.

The first point concerns the Witnesses' belief about the consequences of violating the prohibition: Receiving blood transfusions is an unpardonable sin resulting in withdrawal of the opportunity to attain eternal life [2]. In particular, the transgression is punishable by being "cut off": "Since the Witnesses do not believe in eternal damnation, to be 'cut off' signifies losing one's opportunity to qualify for resurrection" [3, p. 75]. A second, related feature of the Witnesses' belief system is their view that man's life on earth is not important: "They fervently believe that they are only passing through and that the faithful who have not been corrupted nor polluted will attain eternal life in Heaven" [1, p. 539]. This belief is important in the structure of a moral argument that pits the value of preservation of life on earth against other values, for example, presumed eternal life in Heaven. Put another way, the Witnesses can argue that the duty to preserve or prolong human life is always overridden by their perceived duty to God, so in a case of conflict duty to God dictates the right course of action.

THE ADULT JEHOVAH'S WITNESS PATIENT

Freedom to exercise one's religious beliefs is one important aspect of the moral and legal issues involved in these cases. But in addition to this specific constitutionally guaranteed right, there are other rights and moral values that would be relevant even if religious freedom were not at issue. Even in cases that do not involve religious freedom at all, the question of the right to compel medical treatment against a patient's wishes raises some knotty moral problems. The Jehovah's Witness case may prove instructive for the range of cases in which religious freedom is not at issue.

Just which rights or values are involved in the adult Jehovah's Witness case, and how do they conflict? We shall return later to the right to act on one's religious beliefs, but first let us look at other moral concepts that enter into Witnesses' moral defense. Chief among these is the notion of autonomy. Does the patient in a medical setting have the autonomy that we normally accord persons simply by virtue of their being human? Or does one's status as a *patient* deprive him of a measure of autonomy normally accorded him as a nonpatient *person*? Many medical practitioners tend to argue for decreased autonomy of patients, while some religious ethicists, a number of moral philosophers, and a small number of physicians defend autonomous decision making on the part of patients. So one clearly identifiable moral issue concerns the autonomy of a person who becomes a patient. Does he or she have the right to make decisions about the details of medical treatment and about whether some treatments are to be undertaken at all? One may defend the Witnesses' right to refuse blood transfusions by appealing to the autonomy of the patient qua person solely on moral grounds, without even invoking First Amendment freedoms (i.e., freedom of religion).

The right of autonomous decision making on the part of the patient is in direct conflict with a right claimed on behalf of the treating physician: the "professional" right (duty, perhaps) of a doctor to do what correct medical practice dictates. As one writer notes: "In our society, medical treatment is a right which is guaranteed to every citizen, regardless of his religious tenets. But it is also the physician's inherent, albeit uncodified, right not to have constraints applied to a therapeutic program, which he regards as necessary for the patient's welfare or survival" [3, p. 73]. Unlike other sorts of cases involving refusal of medical treatment on religious grounds (notably, Christian Scientists' refusal to accept any medical treatment), Jehovah's Witnesses are opposed only to one specific treatment regimen: transfusion of whole blood or blood fractions. As a result, Witnesses visit doctors, voluntarily enter hospitals, and submit themselves to the usual range of treatments, with the singular exception of accepting transfusions. The question arises, then, Does the physician have a duty to do everything for a patient that is dictated by accepted medical practice? In a court case in 1965 (*United States* v. *George*, 33 LW2518), the court argued that "the patient voluntarily submitted himself to and insisted on medical treatment. At the same time, he sought to dictate a course of treatment to his physician which amounted to malpractice. The court held that under these circumstances, a physician cannot be required to ignore the mandates of his own conscience, even in the name of the exercise of religious freedom. A patient can knowingly refuse treatment but he cannot demand mistreatment" [3, p. 78].

The right or duty of a physician, as described here, does seem to be in direct conflict with both (1) the religious freedom of the Jehovah's Witness patient and (2) the autonomy of the patient as a person, or his right to decide on matters affecting his own life and death. The worth of human life and the duty to preserve it are usually viewed as paramount moral values in our culture. Since those arguing in favor of the right to compel medical treatment will invoke this important value in their defense, and moral dilemma has no clear solution.

It is worth noting briefly several additional moral issues involved in the adult Jehovah's Witness case. One is the issue of informed consent. Because of the refusal of Jehovah's Witnesses to grant consent to transfuse themselves or their relatives (including minor children), physicians may not (morally or legally) act contrary to the patient's wishes. But a court order may be obtained authorizing the physician to transfuse the patient. What, then, is the status of the requirement for "informed consent" in medical matters if the patient's publicly expressed wishes can be overridden by a doctor who obtains a court order? A second relevant moral issue concerns the competency of the Jehovah's Witness patient to make the decision about transfusion at the time that decision needs to be made. Is a semicomatose person competent to make decisions? Is a person in excruciating pain competent? A person suffering from mild shock? Surely, an unconscious person is not. In this last case, and perhaps the preceding ones as well, someone other than the patient must make the decision to refuse transfusion for him. Perhaps the patient, with death as the consequence of refusing treatment, would abandon his religious tenet in favor of the desire to live. Ought a family member decide for the patient, when the patient is unable to decide for himself? There is, obviously, no easy solution to these moral dilemmas. Arguments that rest on sound moral principles can be constructed to support either view, and such arguments have been embodied in several legal cases in the past few years. We shall return to these considerations in the final section, but first we turn to the overlapping, yet somewhat different set of issues concerning minor children of Jehovah's Witnesses.

TRANSFUSING MINOR CHILDREN OF JEHOVAH'S WITNESSES

The moral principles involved in the case of minor children of Jehovah's Witnesses differ in some important respects from principles that enter into the case of adult Witnesses who refuse transfusions for themselves. It is worth noting that all legal cases in which the transfusion of minor children was at issue were decided in favor of transfusing the child, against the religious objections of the parents. In these cases, the arguments given by the courts are a mixture of citation of legal statutes and precedents and appeal to moral principles. In one case in Ohio the court argued as follows:

> [W]hile [parents] may, under certain circumstances, deprive [their child] of his liberty or his property, under no circumstances, with or without religious sanction, may they deprive him of his life! [4, p. 131]

In this and other legal decisions, the religious right of the parents is seen as secondary to the right to life and health on the part of the child. ...

It might be argued that Jehovah's Witness parents, in refusing permission for blood to be given to their child, are acting in accordance with their perceived duty to God, as dictated by their religion, and that this duty to God overrides whatever secular duties they may have to preserve the life and health of their child. Here it can only be replied that when an action done in accordance with perceived duties to God results in the likelihood of harm or death to another person (whether child or adult), then the duties to preserve life here on earth take precedence. The duties of a physician are to preserve and prolong life and to alleviate suffering. These duties are not in the least mitigated by considerations of God's will, the possibility of life after death, or a view that God at some later time rewards those who suffer here on earth. Freedom of religion does not include the right to act in a manner that will result in harm or death to others.

If the parents refuse to grant permission for blood to be given to their child when failure to give blood will result in death or severe harm to the child, their prima facie right to retain control over their child no longer exists. Whatever the parents' reasons for refusing to allow blood to be given, and whether the parents believe that the child will survive or not, the case sufficiently resembles that of child neglect (in respect to harm to the child); in the absence of fulfillment of their primary duties, it is morally justifiable to take control of the child away from parents and administer blood transfusions against the parents' wishes and contrary to their religious convictions.

RIGHTS AND THE CONFLICT OF RIGHTS

It is evident that the case of the adult Jehovah's Witness who refuses blood transfusions for himself is a good deal more complicated than that of minor children of Jehovah's Witness parents. The arguments—both moral and legal—in the case of children rest largely on the moral belief that no one has the right or authority to make life-threatening decisions for persons unable to make those decisions for themselves. If this analysis is sound, it supplies a principle for dealing with the case of the adult patient who is not in a position to state his wishes at the time the treatment is medically required. This principle is avowedly paternalistic but is intended to be applied in those cases where a measure of paternalism seems morally justifiable. To the extent that a person is unable or not fully competent to decide for himself at the time transfusion is needed, it seems appropriate for medical personnel to decide in favor of life-saving treatment. Whatever a person may have claimed prior to an emergency in which death is imminent, and regardless of what relatives may claim on his behalf, it is morally wrong for others to act in a manner that will probably result in his death.

The task of ascertaining a person's competence to make decisions for himself presents a myriad of problems, some of them moral, some epistemological, and some conceptual. These problems are no different, in principle, from the difficulty of ascertaining the competency of retarded persons, the mentally ill, aged senile persons, and others. This is not to suggest that no difficulty exists but, rather, that similar problems arise in many other sorts of cases where competency needs to be ascertained for moral or legal or practical reasons.

There are several recent court cases dealing with adult Jehovah's Witness patients. In some of these cases the court refused the request to transfuse the patient; in others, the court decided that transfusion was warranted, despite the religious objections. The case of *John F. Kennedy Memorial Hospital* v. *Heston* was one of those in which transfusion was ordered, contrary to the patient's religious convictions. But it is important to note that the patient was deemed incompetent to make the decision for herself at the time transfusion was needed. The judge who delivered the court's opinion stated:

> Delores Heston, age 22 and unmarried, was severely injured in an automobile accident. She was taken to the plaintiff hospital where it was determined that she would expire unless operated upon for a ruptured spleen and that if operated upon she would expire unless whole blood was administered. ... Miss Heston insists she expressed her refusal to accept blood, but the evidence indicates she was in shock on admittance to the hospital and in the judgment of the attending physicians and nurses was then or soon became disoriented and incoherent. Her mother remained adamant in her opposition to a transfusion, and signed a release of liability for the hospital and medical personnel. Miss Heston did not execute a release; presumably she could not. Her father could not be located. [5, p. 671]

This case, then, fits the principle suggested above: To the extent that a person is unable or not fully competent to decide for himself at the time transfusion is needed, it seems appropriate for medical personnel to decide in favor of life-saving treatment.

In another case, *In re Osborne*, the court decided against transfusion. But here it was ascertained that the patient was not impaired in his ability to make judgments, that he "understood the consequences of his decision, and had with full understanding executed a statement refusing the recommended transfusion and releasing the hospital from liability" [6, p. 373]. This decision might be defended, in a moral argument, by appealing to the notion of the autonomy of persons; the legal defense rests, however, on the constitutionally guaranteed freedom of religion. A footnote in the court's opinion in *Osborne* says: "No case has come to light where refusal of medical care was based on individual choice absent religious convictions." But whether based on the moral concept of autonomy, or on the legal and moral right to act on one's religious beliefs, the right of a person (whose competency has been ascertained) to refuse medical treatment must be viewed as a viable moral alternative. Such a right rests on the precept of individual liberty that protects persons of sound mind against paternalistic interference by others.

CONCLUSION

It seems apparent that the only justification that can be offered for the coercive act of administering a blood transfusion without a person's consent and against his will is a paternalistic one. I follow that characterization of paternalism put forth by Gerald Dworkin: "the interference with a person's liberty of action justified by reasons referring exclusively to the welfare, good, happiness, needs, interests or values of the person being coerced" [7, p. 65]. Now a person's life is involved in his welfare or good in the extreme—so much so, it might be argued, that it is not on a par with other things that contribute to one's welfare. Indeed, the existence of life is a necessary condition for there being any welfare, happiness, needs, interests, or values at all. Still, interference with a person's (presumably rational) decision to end his life or allow it to end presupposes a belief on the part of the interferer that he knows what is best for the person. This would, in fact, be the case if a Jehovah's Witness patient believed that he would not die if he were not transfused in cases where informed medical opinion predicts the reverse. But the Witness who accepts the high probability of his own death and still refuses transfusion does not disagree concerning matters of empirical fact with those who wish to interfere on his behalf. Dworkin identifies this as a value conflict, a case in which "a value such as health—or indeed life—may be overridden by competing values. Thus the problem with the Christian Scientist and blood transfusions. It may be more important for him to reject 'impure substances' than to go on living" [7, p. 78].[2] But Dworkin is wrong if he construes this as solely a question of conflict in values, and he is also mistaken in identifying one of the competing values as rejection of "impure substances." It is, rather, eternal life over against mortal life that the Jehovah's Witness is weighing, and rather than risk being "cut off" he opts to allow his mortal life to terminate.

It would appear, then, that beliefs about metaphysical matters of fact—as well as competing values—are involved in the Jehovah's Witness's decision. That such beliefs may be mistaken or ill founded is not sufficient warrant for paternalistic interference, unless it can be shown that persons who entertain such beliefs are irrational. But it would fly in the face of long-standing traditions and practices—especially in America—to deem persons irrational solely on the basis of religious convictions that differ from our own. If, however, the Witnesses are not to be judged irrational by virtue of their religious belief system, then the one clearly acceptable ground for paternalistic intervention is pulled out from under. Medical practitioners are sometimes criticized for acting in a paternalistic manner toward patients, so it is not surprising to see physicians advocate a course of action that overrides a patient's expressed wishes. But if the patient is deemed competent or rational (by whatever practical criteria are employed or ought to be adopted), then there is no warrant for interfering with his decisions, even those that affect his continued existence. Unless all decisions to end one's life (or allow it to terminate) are viewed as *ex hypothesi* irrational, interference with a person's liberty to choose in favor of what he believes to take precedence over continued mortal existence is an act of unjustified paternalism. Paternalism may be considered justifiable in cases where the agent is incompetent to make informed or rational judgments about his own welfare. The Jehovah's Witness who refuses a blood transfusion may be *mistaken* about what is in his long-range welfare, but he is not incompetent to make judgments based on his belief system. It is only if we decide that his particular set of religious beliefs constitutes good evidence for his overall irrationality that we are justified in interfering paternalistically with his liberty. While I am personally inclined to view such religious belief systems as irrational (because they are not warranted on the evidence), I do not thereby deem their proponents irrational *in a general sense* for holding such beliefs. And this, it seems, is the correct way of looking at the case of adult Jehovah's Witnesses who are deemed mentally competent (according to the usual medical criteria) and yet who refuse blood transfusions. Only if we are prepared to accept paternalistic interference with the liberty of (otherwise) rational or competent adults in similar cases are we justified in transfusing these patients against their expressed wishes.

We cannot let the matter rest here, however, because of the problems this solution would pose for medical practice. It has been argued above that the physician has a "right not to have constraints applied to a therapeutic program, which he regards as necessary for the patient's welfare or survival"; and one court opinion stated that "a physician cannot be required to ignore the mandates of his own conscience, even in the name of the exercise of religious freedom. A patient can knowingly refuse treatment, but he cannot demand mistreatment." Jehovah's Witnesses who present themselves for treatment and who are judged rational or competent to give or withhold consent should be given the option of either (*a*) being treated in accordance with the dictates of accepted medical practice, including blood transfusion if necessary; or (*b*) refusing in advance any treatment in which transfusion is normally a necessary component or is likely to be required in the case at hand. Presenting these options to the patient preserves his decision-making autonomy while not requiring the physician to embark on a treatment that amounts to malpractice.

If it is objected that this proposed solution violates the precepts of accepted medical practice, I can only reply that those precepts embody a measure of paternalism that is unjustifiable when judged against a principle of individual liberty that mandates autonomy of decision making for rational adult persons. Moreover, the precepts of accepted medical practice have been known to change, varying with the introduction of new medical technology, transformations in social consciousness, and other alterations in the status quo. Not all patients who can be treated vigorously are so treated; one aspect of current debates focuses on the moral dilemmas surrounding patient autonomy—the sorts of problems addressed in this paper. Consistent with the decision-making autonomy accorded a patient who is deemed rational enough to offer informed consent is the right of a physician to refuse to be dictated to in matters of medical competence. Once treatment is undertaken, the judgment that a blood transfusion is necessary would seem to be a judgment requiring medical competence. The decision to undertake treatment at all in such cases is not a purely medical matter but might well be decided by a patient who has full knowledge of the consequences yet who insists nonetheless on what amounts to partial treatment or mistreatment by attending physicians.

I have argued that the autonomy of patients, as rational persons, ought to be respected. But this autonomy implies a responsibility for one's decisions—a responsibility that entails acceptance of the consequences. And these consequences include the right of physicians to reject a treatment regimen proposed by the patient, which is contrary to sound medical practice. If, faced with this consequence, some Jehovah's Witnesses opt for treatment with transfusion rather than no treatment at all, so much the better for such cases of conflict of rights. Those Witnesses who remain steadfast in their refusal to accept transfusions are exercising their right of autonomous decision making in matters concerning their own welfare—in the words of Justice Louis Brandeis, "the right to be let alone." In a judicial opinion rendered in a case involving a Jehovah's Witness who refused transfusion, Justice Warren Burger recalled Brandeis's view as follows: "Nothing in [his] utterance suggests that Justice Brandeis thought an individual possessed these rights only as to *sensible* beliefs, *valid* thoughts, *reasonable* emotions, or *well-founded* sensations. I suggest he intended to include a great many foolish, unreasonable, and even absurd ideas which do not conform, such as refusing medical treatment even at great risk" [8]. The risks are indeed great in the cases we have been discussing. But the sorts of risks to health or life a person may take, in the interest of something he considers worth the risk, appear to know no bounds. If an adult agent is rational and competent to make decisions, the risks are his to take.

References

1. I. G. Thomas, R. W. Edmark, and T. W. Jones. *Am. Surg.*, 34:538, 1968.
2. W. T. Fitts, Jr., and M. J. Orloff. *Surg. Gynecol. Obstet.*, 180:502, 1959.
3. D. C. Schechter, *Am. J. Surg.*, 116:73, 1968.
4. *In re* Clark, 185 N.E. 2d 128, 1962.
5. John F. Kennedy Memorial Hospital *v.* Heston, 279 A. 2d 670, 1971.
6. *In re* Osborne, 294 A. 2d 372, 1972.
7. G. Dworkin. *Monist*, 56:64, 1972.
8. Application of President and Directors of Georgetown College, 331 F. 2n 1010 (D.C. Cir.), 1964.

Notes

1. Other passages commonly cited in this connection are Genesis 9:4 ("Only the flesh with its soul—its blood—you must not eat"), Genesis 9:5, and Acts 15:28–29.
2. Dworkin is apparently confusing Christian Scientists and Jehovah's Witnesses, since he elsewhere [7, p. 68] mentions Christian Scientists in connection with blood transfusions—a connection in which Jehovah's Witnesses are unique in their rejection of this medical procedure and no other.

ETHICAL ISSUES IN THE FORCED TRANSFUSION OF JEHOVAH'S WITNESS CHILDREN

Mark Sheldon

INTRODUCTION

The purpose of this article is to discuss the issue of forced blood transfusion for Jehovah's Witness children, particularly in cases where the lack of a transfusion will result in the child's death. The discussion will consist of several parts. First, background concerning the beliefs of Jehovah's Witness will be provided. This will be followed by a description of the legal framework within which the state, through the courts, has established the legitimacy of forced blood transfusion. Then, arguments developed in the ethics literature supporting such intervention will be reviewed and critically evaluated. It will

Reprinted by permission of Elsevier Science from *The Journal of Emergency Medicine*, Vol. 14, 1996, pp. 251–57.

be established that the basis upon which the state takes such action has not been defended well in the existing ethics literature. The final section of the paper will consist of observations and recommendations. The paper, with some misgiving, will conclude that it is right for the state to take temporary custody of a child of Jehovah's Witnesses in order to force the child to undergo a blood transfusion.

BELIEFS OF JEHOVAH'S WITNESSES

Jehovah's Witnesses are Christians who believe the Bible is the Word of God in its entirety. Their name is taken from a statement that appears in the book of Isaiah: "Ye are my witnesses, saith Jehovah" (Isa. 43:10). Beginning as a nondenominational Bible study group in 1879 near Pittsburgh, led by Charles T. Russell, the group grew quickly and spread across the country. By 1881, the group formed the Watch Tower Bible and Tract Society. By 1909, the society had grown into an international organization with headquarters in Brooklyn, New York. Since witnessing to God through preaching was their main activity, Witnesses were among the first to engage in radio broadcasting. These efforts eventually gave way, during the 1930s, to house-to-house visits and street-corner preaching. Presently, there are estimated to be approximately 2.2 million Jehovah's Witnesses in more than 200 countries around the world, with about 554,000 Witnesses in the United States.[1]

As a group, Jehovah's Witnesses have faced numerous challenges. In the 1930s and 1940s, when their right to make home visitations was challenged, the courts affirmed their right to freedom of speech. Jehovah's Witnesses comply with most modern medical and surgical procedures, and a number of Witnesses are physicians and surgeons.[2] They do not smoke, use recreational drugs, or have abortions. They view life as sacred. Why, then, do Witnesses appear to contradict this commitment to the idea that life is sacred, and reject blood transfusions at critical moments when it is a matter of life and death? In their pamphlet, *Jehovah's Witnesses and the Question of Blood,*[3] they make the following statement:

> The issue of blood for Jehovah's Witnesses ... involves the most fundamental principles on which they as Christians base their lives. Their relationship with their creator and God is at stake.

The seriousness of the question of blood for Witnesses can be compared to the seriousness of idolatry for Jews. ...

It is the Acts of Apostles, in particular, which serves most centrally as the basis for the rejection of blood transfusions. After listing those things from which believers should abstain, it reads: "... from which if ye keep yourselves, ye shall do well" (Acts 15:28–29).

Therefore, Jehovah's Witnesses take literally the numerous passages which proscribe the consumption of blood. They believe that the violation of this proscription will result in loss of eternal life. Witnesses do not reject this world. To the contrary, they value and seek bodily health. Still, they do not think "physical life is limited to this present, temporal existence."[4] They believe that it is wrong to contrast "physical life" with "eternal life." Rather, Witnesses believe that God will, in the future, destroy life on earth, ending both personal life and conscious spiritual life. Eventually, they believe, God will resurrect the bodies of the faithful, and a limited number "will reign with God in heaven, while the remainder will live a life without end on a renewed earth."[4] They believe that life in the future, therefore, will be physical, earthly, and eternal.

THE LEGAL FRAMEWORK

When adults are concerned, the courts generally have determined that the competent adult Jehovah's Witness, who has no dependent minor children, has a right to refuse blood transfusion.[5] When children are concerned, however, the situation is very different. Interestingly enough, the decision that appears to have set the major precedent, *Prince* v. *Massachusetts* (1944), was not a case dealing with medical treatment, but with child labor laws.[5] An aunt, who was the legal custodian of a 9-year-old, had the child on the street with her selling Jehovah's Witness magazines. Although this was in violation of child labor laws, the defense claimed that Jehovah's Witnesses were required by their religion to spread the gospel. The little girl indicated that she wanted to sell the magazines to avoid eternal damnation. Defense, therefore, claimed that this was a violation of her right to freedom of religious belief. In response, the Supreme Court ruled that the state has authority as *parens patriae* to act in the interest of the child's well being, and that, on this basis, parental control can be restricted. While this particular decision had nothing to do with transfusion, the court[6] reached this conclusion:

> Neither the rights of religion nor the right of parenthood are beyond limitation ... Parents may be free to make martyrs of themselves, but they are not free to make martyrs of their children before they have reached the age when they can make that choice for themselves.

A series of court decisions followed upholding *Prince*, but also dealing with the legitimacy of state intervention in matters that do or do not involve life-or-death situations. Again, it is interesting to note that *Prince* did not involve a life-and-death situation.[5]

WITNESSES' VIEWS REGARDING CHILDREN

In their pamphlet, *Jehovah's Witnesses and the Question of Blood*,[3] the Witnesses make the following statement:

> Jehovah's Witnesses are sure that obeying the directions from their Creator is for their lasting good.

The Witnesses then make the point that their refusal of blood transfusion cannot rightfully be construed either as suicide or as an exercise of the right to die, but it must be seen as respect for God's word.[3]

In addressing the issue of children, Witnesses[3] make the following argument:

> Likely the aspect of this matter that is most highly charged with emotion involves the treating of children. All of us realize that children need care and protection. God-fearing parents particularly appreciate this. They deeply love their children and keenly feel their God-given responsibility to care for them and make decisions for their lasting welfare.—Ephesians 6:14.
>
> Society, too, recognizes parental responsibility, acknowledging that parents are the ones primarily authorized to provide for and decide for their children. Logically, religious beliefs in the family have a bearing on this. Children are certainly benefited if their parents' religion stresses the need to care for them. That is so with Jehovah's Witnesses, who in no way want to neglect their children. They recognize it as their God-given obligation to provide food, clothing, shelter and health care for them. Moreover, a genuine appreciation of the need to provide for one's children also requires inculcating in them morality and regard for what is right.

Witnesses indicate that they are fully aware of the significance of their refusal of blood transfusion for their children. However, they state that they do this out of devotion to God and out of love for their children. They claim that they cherish their children and are concerned for their children's future welfare. They do not believe that their actions should be construed as neglect. Rather, they believe that they probably are better parents than many parents in the larger society. They point to society's toleration for loose parenting, which leads to children growing up without respect for life, morality, or themselves. They hold up as examples the early Christian families who died at the hands of the Romans as model. Further, Witnesses claim to have evidence that as their children grow, they made the same choices that their parents previously made for them.

The aspect of the quote that should be emphasized is that Jehovah's Witness parents perceive themselves as acting in their children's best interest. They do not want their children to be "cut off" from the possibility of obtaining eternal life. They do not believe that it is in any way appropriate to describe their actions as involving neglect or disregard for their children. It is true, of course, that their belief that they may he better parents than others does not provide support for their right to deny blood transfusion to their children. Also, it is not clear what evidence they have to support their claim that their children will, when grown, reach the same decision as they have. But it seems clear that to describe their actions as neglectful is problematic.

THE ETHICS LITERATURE

Uniformly, the ethics literature expresses the view that it is right for the state to take temporary custody of a child to force it to undergo a blood transfusion in cases 1) when the lack of transfusion will lead to the child's death and 2) when the child is too young to give assent. However, I also believe that the basis upon which the state takes such action is not well defended in the existing ethics literature. This section consists of a review of representative arguments supporting state intervention, along with criticism of these arguments.

In 1977, Ruth Macklin[7] wrote, in an article still much referred to and often anthologized, the following:

> It might be argued that Jehovah's Witness parents, in refusing permission for blood to be given to their child, are acting in accordance with their perceived duty to God, as dictated by their religion, and that this duty to God overrides whatever secular duties they may have to preserve the life and health of their child.

Macklin[8] criticized this belief:

> Here it can only be replied that when an action done in accordance with perceived duties to God results in the likelihood of harm or death to another person (whether child or adult), then the duties to preserve life here on earth take precedence. The duties of a physician are to preserve and prolong life and to alleviate suffering. ... Freedom of religion does not include the right to act in a manner that will result in harm or death to another.

A few points in response to Macklin's argument are in order. The first and fundamental question is: from whose perspective is "harm" being defined? Second, she identifies "harm" with "death." These are not necessarily the same. She[7] states:

> If the parents refuse to grant permission for blood to be given to their child when failure to give blood will result in death or severe harm ... their prima facie right to retain control over their child no longer exists ... the case [at this point] sufficiently resembles that of child neglect [in respect to harm to the child]. ... in the absence of fulfillment of their duties, it is mortally justifiable to take control of the child away from the parent.

From Macklin's point of view, the act "sufficiently resembles child neglect." However, on what basis is this determined to be child neglect? This is only possible to claim if the religious perspective of the parents is set aside. What makes this move acceptable? The vague comment "sufficiently resembles child neglect" does not seem to provide such a basis.

Another interesting discussion of this issue appears in a 1983 article[8] that appeared in *Hospital Progress*. The article states: "The basic ethical principle involved is beneficence: One is obliged to do whatever good one reasonably can for another person."[8] The argument is different from Macklin's in that duty is seen positively (doing good) rather than negatively (avoiding harm). The article indicates a certain concern for the family and recognizes that it is "especially dangerous today, when society tends increasingly to allow the state to take over parents' functions."[8] However, it makes the following point:[8]

> When the person is a minor, the obligation of beneficence falls primarily on the parents. When the parents for whatever reasons, even sincerely held religious beliefs, fall in this regard, then society, usually through its legal processes, must step in and provide for the child's good. Certain members of society, such as physicians or hospital administrators, are in a position to detect parental failure in these matters and therefore have a moral obligation to call the child's plight to civil authorities' attention.

Two comments are necessary. The first is that the use of the language "parental failure" is heavily condemnatory, and not clearly appropriate. Second, while there may not be a problem, as there was above, in defining "harm," there is the problem of defining "good."

Another document that addresses the issue of state intervention is "Religious Exemptions From Child Abuse Statutes," produced by the Committee on Bioethics of the American Academy of Pediatrics in 1988.[9] This document is essentially a recommendation to change child abuse and neglect statutes that exempt parents on the basis of religious freedom.

Again, as in the Macklin article, the problem exists concerning the fact that whether harm is present depends on the perspective from which it is identified. Also, what truly constitutes the "welfare" of the child is a matter of perspective.

Another representative approach in the ethics literature appears in an article by Gary Benfield, MD, published in *Legal Aspects of Medical Practice*.[10] He attempts, he points out, to address the human side of the issue, and he does, one can argue, make a sincere effort to try to understand the feelings of the Jehovah's Witness parents. He describes one of his cases that involved a young Rh-positive mother who gave birth to an Rh-positive male. He quotes[10] the mother:

> Three days after the birth of our son, we were told that on the very day of his birth he was taken from us, by a simple dial of the phone, and given blood ... You have touched the very depth of my being. The pain I felt is the same pain had I been told of my son's death ... I realize it is difficult to understand how two people claiming to love their child are willing to let that child die. We as Jehovah's Witnesses believe in that promised kingdom of God's as a real ruling power, and when that kingdom that we all pray for does come to this earth, our son will be given back to us. We would just have to wait a little longer to watch him grow and to give him all the love we stored up for him in our hearts over the last few months ... Jehovah's Witnesses do not reject blood for their children due to lack of love ... If we violate God's law on blood and the child dies, we have endangered his opportunity for everlasting life in God's new world.

Benfield's comments, in response to the mother's statement, are interesting and revealing. He remarks that after he considered all the options, he chose the one that "would best benefit my innocent patient,"[10] a description which seems to impute something negative and possibly exploitative to the mother's relationship with the child. Second, he explains the basis for his choice. This consists of him asking himself, "Can I live with this decision?"[10] His answer is, "Yes." One can argue, however, that there is a problem in resolving an ethical dilemma on this basis. Such a criterion allows for anything that human beings "can live with." It is probably the case that Benfield is a sensitive and caring person, but this is a dangerous way to proceed. Presumably (this comment is not meant to reflect on Benfield but on the methodology he employs to resolve ethical dilemmas), Nazi doctors could "live with" their decisions.

Benfeld[10] continues:

> The parents felt that, by giving blood, I would compromise their son's chances for everlasting life. I disagreed. I felt that Jehovah, a loving God, would welcome their child in "God's new world" were he to die having received blood or not. Who was right?

In this passage, Benfield ventures beyond the basis justifying intervention expressed in the ethics literature quoted above. He does not focus on the issue of "harm" or "good" or "welfare." Instead, he is engaged in theological debate. This, of course, prompts a question concerning the expertise a physician must have in order to engage in such commentary, to make a judgment concerning the validity of another's religious belief. The question is not what Benfield does, but why. What legitimately entitles him to force a transfusion on the child? A claim to possess a more valid religious insight than the mother is not available to him simply by virtue of being a physician. Nothing about being a physician provides a basis for his conviction that he understands better than the mother does how God works. In addition, she does not make a decision on the basis of what she "can live with." She acts on the basis of scripture. For her, this is not a matter of speculation or theological debate. She acts in a way that is prescribed for her by her religious tradition.

OBSERVATIONS AND CONCLUSIONS

The following observations and conclusions should be viewed as preliminary thoughts in response to the issues raised in this article. They are preliminary in the sense that more discussion is warranted.

1. The criticism of the ethics literature, contained in this paper, does not imply that there is no basis for the existence of statutes concerned with child abuse and neglect. This is a different question. The state, on this issue, appropriately takes guidance from scientists (psychiatrists and psychologist) who do studies, determine consequences, and measure pain and adverse reaction related to abuse and neglect. The state can develop expertise in this area and can claim knowledge of what constitutes child welfare, benefit, best interest, and harm. But where the issue is ultimately spiritual and where obtaining eternal life is the objective, it is clear that the state can make no claim to any sort of knowledge. Undergoing a blood transfusion may, in fact, cut off one from obtaining eternal life, and the state simply does not have the expertise and knowledge that would enable it to judge the merits of such a claim.
2. Given this lack of expertise in such ultimate questions, the state, it seems to me, must accede that all talk of harm, benefit, best interest, and martyrdom amounts to what appears to be rhetoric and not argument. Jehovah's Witness parents, in refusing blood transfusion, cannot be said to be truly harming or neglecting their children. It is simply not the case that knowledge, which would make such a judgment legitimate, is available. That refusing a transfusion is harmful can certainly be believed, and one can argue that such is the case, but it cannot be known. Therefore, the state, in taking temporary guardianship to transfuse the child, cannot be said, with certainty, to be doing this for the child's welfare. It is simply not known whether this is the case.

What, therefore, makes it legitimate to order transfusions for the children of Jehovah's Witness? The most defensible argument is that the state's weakness is also its strength. That is, while the state does not know truly what is in the child's best interest, neither does anyone else. What the parents believe is in the child's best interest may be mistaken. Given that no one knows what is in the child's best interest, the role of the state is to ensure that children ultimately become adults, able to decide, independently, what is in their own best interest. It is not even that the state assumes that it knows it to be in the child's best interest to become an adult. It may not be. It is simply that no one knows what is in the child's best interest, and the responsibility of the state is to make certain that persons who make decisions which are irrevocable do so when they are competent. A source of disquiet is that many people believe, with good reason, that parents know what is in their child's best interest. This is a belief that is not easily dismissed. And, in fact, it is not dismissed here. Ideally, the family is a very significant moral institution. More than any other institution in society, the family, properly focused, values human beings simply because they *are*, not because of any use to which they can be put. And, for this reason, it is probably in a child's best interest (and society's best interest, as well) that the family be maintained to the extent that it is, as a unit, consistent with this objective of such nurturance. . . .

References

1. Mead, F. S. Handbook of denominations in the United States. Nashville: Abingdon Press; 1980;148.

2. Dixon, J. L., Smalley, M. G. Jehovah's Witnesses: the surgical/ethical challenge. *JAMA*, 1981; 246(27):2471–2.
3. Jehovah's Witnesses and the question of blood. Brooklyn, NY: Watchtower Bible and Tract Society: 1977.
4. Studdard, P. A., Greene, J. Y. Jehovah's Witnesses and blood transfusion: toward the resolution of a conflict of conscience. *Ala J Med Sci*. 1986; 23(4):455.
5. Hirsh, H. L., Phifer, H. The interface of medicine, religion, and the law: religious objections to medical treatment. *Med. Law*. 1985; 4(2): 121–39.
6. *Prince* v. *Massachusetts*.
7. Mucklin, R. Consent, coercion and conflict of rights. *Perspect Biol Med*. 1977; 20(365):365–6.
8. Editorial. May a Catholic hospital allow blondless surgery for children? *Hosp Prog*. 1983; 64(9):58,60.
9. Committee on Bioethics of the American Academy of Pediatrics. Religious exemptions from child abuse states. *Pediatrics*. 1988: 81(1): 169–71.
10. Benfield, D. G. Giving blood to the critically ill newborn of Jehovah's Witness parents: the human side of the issue. *Leg Aspects Med Pract*. 1978; 6(6):19–22.

OPINION IN *CANTERBURY V. SPENCE*

Judge Spotswood W. Robinson III

Suits charging failure by a physician adequately to disclose the risks and alternatives of proposed treatment are not innovations in American law. They date back a good half-century, and in the last decade they have multiplied rapidly. There is, nonetheless, disagreement among the courts and the commentators on many major questions, and there is no precedent of our own directly in point. For the tools enabling resolution of the issues on this appeal, we are forced to begin at first principles.

The root premise is the concept, fundamental in American jurisprudence, that "every human being of adult years and sound mind has a right to determine what shall be done with his own body. ..." True consent to what happens to one's self is the informed exercise of a choice, and that entails an opportunity to evaluate knowledgeably the options available and the risks attendant upon each. The average patient has little or no understanding of the medical arts, and ordinarily has only his physician to whom he can look for enlightenment with which to reach an intelligent decision. From these almost axiomatic considerations springs the need, and in turn the requirement, of a reasonable divulgence by physician to patient to make such a decision possible.

A physician is under a duty to treat his patient skillfully but proficiency in diagnosis and therapy is not the full measure of his responsibility. The cases demonstrate that the physician is under an obligation to communicate specific information to the patient when the exigencies of reasonable care call for it. Due care may require a physician perceiving symptoms of bodily abnormality to alert the patient to the condition. It may call upon the physician confronting an ailment which does not respond to his ministrations to inform the patient thereof. It may command the physician to instruct the patient as to any limitations to be presently observed for his own welfare, and as to any precautionary therapy he should seek in the future.

U.S. Court of Appeals, District of Columbia Circuit; 464 Federal Reporter, 2d, 772. May 19, 1972. Reprinted with permission of Thomson West. Notes omitted.

It may oblige the physician to advise the patient of the need for or desirability of any alternative treatment promising greater benefit than that being pursued. Just as plainly, due care normally demands that the physician warn the patient of any risks to his well-being which contemplated therapy may involve.

The context in which the duty of risk-disclosure arises is invariably the occasion for decision as to whether a particular treatment procedure is to be undertaken. To the physician, whose training enables a self-satisfying evaluation, the answer may seem clear, but it is the prerogative of the patient, not the physician, to determine for himself the direction in which his interests seem to lie. To enable the patient to chart his course understandably, some familiarity with the therapeutic alternatives and their hazards becomes essential.

A reasonable revelation in these respects is not only a necessity but, as we see it, is as much a matter of the physician's duty. It is a duty to warn of the dangers lurking in the proposed treatment, and that is surely a facet of due care. It is, too, a duty to impart information which the patient has every right to expect. The patient's reliance upon the physician is a trust of the kind which traditionally has exacted obligations beyond those associated with armslength transactions. His dependence upon the physician for information affecting his well-being, in terms of contemplated treatment, is well-nigh abject. As earlier noted, long before the instant litigation arose, courts had recognized that the physician had the responsibility of satisfying the vital informational needs of the patient. More recently, we ourselves have found "in the fiducial qualities of [the physician-patient] relationship the physician's duty to reveal to the patient that which in his best interests it is important that he should know." We now find, as a part of the physician's overall obligation to the patient, a similar duty of reasonable disclosure of the choices with respect to proposed therapy and the dangers inherently and potentially involved. ...

Once the circumstances give rise to a duty on the physician's part to inform his patient, the next inquiry is the scope of the disclosure the physician is legally obliged to make. The courts have frequently confronted this problem but no uniform standard defining the adequacy of the divulgence emerges from the decisions. Some have said "full" disclosure, a norm we are unwilling to adopt literally. It seems obviously prohibitive and unrealistic to expect physicians to discuss with their patients every risk of proposed treatment—no matter how small or remote—and generally unnecessary from the patient's viewpoint as well. Indeed, the cases speaking in terms of "full" disclosure appear to envision something less than total disclosure, leaving unanswered the question of just how much.

The larger number of courts, as might be expected, have applied tests framed with reference to prevailing fashion within the medical profession. Some have measured the disclosure by "good medical practice," others by what a reasonable practitioner would have bared under the circumstances, and still others by what medical custom in the community would demand. We have explored this rather considerable body of law but are unprepared to follow it. The duty to disclose, we have reasoned, arises from phenomena apart from medical custom and practice. The latter, we think, should no more establish the scope of the duty than its existence. Any definition of scope in terms purely of a professional standard is at odds with the patient's prerogative to decide on projected therapy himself. That prerogative, we have said, is at the very foundation of the duty to disclose, and both the patient's right to know and the physician's correlative obligation to tell him are diluted to the extent that its compass is dictated by the medical profession.

In our view, the patient's right of self-decision shapes the boundaries of the duty to reveal. That right can be effectively exercised only if the patient possesses enough information to enable an intelligent choice. The scope of the physician's communications to the patient, then, must be measured by the patient's need, and that need is the information material to the decision. Thus the test for determining whether a particular peril must be divulged is its materiality to the patient's decision: all risks potentially affecting the decision must be unmasked. And to safeguard the patient's interest in achieving his own determination on treatment, the law must itself set the standard for adequate disclosure.

Optimally for the patient, exposure of a risk would be mandatory whenever the patient would deem it significant to his decision, either singly or in combination with other risks. Such a requirement, however, would summon the physician to second-guess the patient, whose ideas on materiality could hardly be known to the physician. That would make an undue demand upon medical practitioners, whose conduct, like that of others, is to be measured in terms of reasonableness. Consonantly with orthodox negligence doctrine, the physician's liability for nondisclosure is to be determined on the basis of foresight, not hindsight; no less than any other aspect of negligence, the issue on nondisclosure must be approached from the viewpoint of the reasonableness of the physician's divulgence in terms of what he knows or should know to be the patient's informational needs. If, but only if, the fact-finder can say that the physician's communication was unreasonably inadequate is an imposition of liability legally or morally justified.

Of necessity, the content of the disclosure rests in the first instance with the physician. Ordinarily it is only he who is in position to identify particular dangers; always he must make a judgment, in terms of materiality, as to whether and to what extent revelation to the patient is called for. He cannot know with complete exactitude what the patient would consider important to his decision, but on the basis of his medical training and experience he can sense how the average, reasonable patient expectably would react. Indeed, with knowledge of, or ability to learn, his patient's background and current condition, he is in a position superior to that of most others—attorneys, for example—who are called upon to make judgments on pain of liability in damages for unreasonable miscalculation.

From these considerations we derive the breadth of the disclosure of risks legally to be required. The scope of the standard is not subjective as to either the physician or the patient; it remains objective with due regard for the patient's informational needs and with suitable leeway for the physician's situation. In broad outline, we agree that "[a] risk is thus material when a reasonable person, in what the physician knows or should know to be the patient's position, would be likely to attach significance to the risk or cluster of risks in deciding whether or not to forego the proposed therapy."

The topics importantly demanding a communication of information are the inherent and potential hazards of the proposed treatment, the alternatives to that treatment, if any, and the results likely if the patient remains untreated. The factors contributing significance to the dangerousness of a medical technique are, of course, the incidence of injury and the degree of the harm threatened. A very small chance of death or serious disablement may well be significant; a potential disability which dramatically outweighs the potential benefit of the therapy or the detriments of the existing malady may summon discussion with the patient.

There is no bright line separating the significant from the insignificant; the answer in any case must abide a rule of reason. Some dangers—infection, for example—are inherent in any operation; there is no obligation to communicate those of which persons of average sophistication are aware. Even more clearly, the physician bears no responsibility for discussion of hazards the patient has already discovered, or those having no apparent materiality to patients' decision on therapy. The disclosure doctrine, like others marking lines between permissible and impermissible behavior in medical practice, is in essence a requirement of conduct prudent under the circumstances. Whenever nondisclosure of particular risk information is open to debate by reasonable-minded men, the issue is for the finder of the facts.

Two exceptions to the general rule of disclosure have been noted by the courts. Each is in the nature of a physician's privilege not to disclose, and the reasoning underlying them is appealing. Each, indeed, is but a recognition that, as important as is the patient's right to know, it is greatly outweighed by the magnitudinous circumstances giving rise to the privilege. The first comes into play when the patient is unconscious or otherwise incapable of consenting, and harm from a failure to treat is imminent and outweighs any harm threatened by the proposed treatment. When a genuine emergency of that sort arises, it is settled that the impracticality of conferring with the patient dispenses with need for it. Even in situations of that character the physician should, as current law requires, attempt to secure a relative's consent if possible. But if time is too short to accommodate discussion, obviously the physician should proceed with the treatment.

The second exception obtains when risk-disclosure poses such a threat of detriment to the patient as to become unfeasible or contraindicated from a medical point of view. It is recognized that patients occasionally become so ill or emotionally distraught on disclosure as to foreclose a rational decision, or complicate or hinder the treatment, or perhaps even pose psychological damage to the patient. Where that is so, the cases have generally held that the physician is armed with a privilege to keep the information from the patient, and we think it clear that portents of that type may justify the physician in action he deems medically warranted. The critical inquiry is whether the physician responded to a sound medical judgment that communication of the risk information would present a threat to the patient's well-being.

The physician's privilege to withhold information for therapeutic reasons must be carefully circumscribed, however, for otherwise it might devour the disclosure rule itself. The privilege does not accept the paternalistic notion that the physician may remain silent simply because divulgence might prompt the patient to forgo therapy the physician feels the patient really needs. That attitude presumes instability or perversity for even the normal patient, and runs counter to the foundation principle that the patient should and ordinarily can make the choice for himself. Nor does the privilege contemplate operation save where the patient's reaction to risk information, as reasonably foreseen by the physician, is menacing. And even in a situation of that kind, disclosure to a close relative with a view to securing consent to the proposed treatment may be the only alternative open to the physician. …

TRANSPARENCY: INFORMED CONSENT IN PRIMARY CARE

Howard Brody

While the patient's right to give informed consent to medical treatment is now well-established both in U.S. law and in biomedical ethics, evidence continues to suggest that the concept has been poorly integrated into American medical practice, and that in many instances the needs and desires of patients are not being well met by current policies. It appears that the theory and the practice of informed consent are out of joint in some crucial

Reprinted with permission of the author and publisher from *Hastings Center Report*, Vol. 19 (September/October 1989), pp. 5–9.

ways. This is particularly true for primary care settings, a context typically ignored by medical ethics literature, but where the majority of doctor-patient encounters occur. Indeed, some have suggested that the concept of informed consent is virtually foreign to primary care medicine where benign paternalism appropriately reigns and where respect for patient autonomy is almost completely absent.

It is worth asking whether current legal standards for informed consent tend to resolve the problem or to exacerbate it. I will maintain that accepted legal standards, at least in the form commonly employed by courts, send physicians the wrong message about what is expected of them. An alternative standard that would send physicians the correct message, a conversation standard, is probably unworkable legally. As an alternative, I will propose a transparency standard as a compromise that gives physicians a doable task and allows courts to review appropriately. I must begin, however, by briefly identifying some assumptions crucial to the development of this position even though space precludes complete argumentation and documentation.

CRUCIAL ASSUMPTIONS

Informed consent is a meaningful ethical concept only to the extent that it can be realized and promoted within the ongoing practice of good medicine. This need not imply diminished respect for patient autonomy, for there are excellent reasons to regard respect for patient autonomy as a central feature of good medical care. Informed consent, properly understood, must be considered an essential ingredient of good patient care, and a physician who lacks the skills to inform patients appropriately and obtain proper consent should be viewed as lacking essential medical skills necessary for practice. It is not enough to see informed consent as a nonmedical, legalistic exercise designed to promote patient autonomy, one that interrupts the process of medical care.

However, available empirical evidence strongly suggests that this is precisely how physicians currently view informed consent practices. Informed consent is still seen as bureaucratic legalism rather than as part of patient care. Physicians often deny the existence of realistic treatment alternatives, thereby attenuating the perceived need to inform the patient of meaningful options. While patients may be informed, efforts are seldom made to assess accurately the patient's actual need or desire for information, or what the patient then proceeds to do with the information provided. Physicians typically underestimate patients' desire to be informed and overestimate their desire to be involved in decisionmaking. Physicians may also view informed consent as an empty charade, since they are confident in their abilities to manipulate consent by how they discuss or divulge information.

A third assumption is that there are important differences between the practice of primary care medicine and the tertiary care settings that have been most frequently discussed in the literature on informed consent. The models of informed consent discussed below typically take as the paradigm case something like surgery for breast cancer or the performance of an invasive and risky radiologic procedure. It is assumed that the risks to the patient are significant, and the values placed on alternative forms of treatment are quite weighty. Moreover, it is assumed that the specialist physician performing the procedure probably does a fairly limited number of procedures and thus could be expected to know exhaustively the precise risks, benefits, and alternatives for each.

Primary care medicine, however, fails to fit this model. The primary care physician, instead of performing five or six complicated and risky procedures frequently, may engage in several hundred treatment modalities during an average week of practice. In many cases, risks to the patient are negligible and conflicts over patient values and the goals of treatment or nontreatment are of little consequence. Moreover, in contrast to the tertiary care patient, the typical ambulatory patient is much better able to exercise freedom of choice and somewhat less likely to be intimidated by either the severity of the disease or the expertise of the physician; the opportunities for changing one's mind once treatment has begun are also much greater. Indeed, in primary care, it is much more likely for the full process of informed consent to treatment (such as the beginning and the dose adjustment of an anti-hypertensive medication) to occur over several office visits rather than at one single point in time.

It might be argued that for all these reasons, the stakes are so low in primary care that it is fully appropriate for informed consent to be interpreted only with regard to the specialized or tertiary care setting. I believe that this is quite incorrect for three reasons. First, good primary care medicine ought to embrace respect for patient autonomy, and if patient autonomy is operationalized in informed consent, properly understood, then it ought to be part and parcel of good primary care. Second, the claim that the primary care physician cannot be expected to obtain the patient's informed consent seems to undermine the idea that informed consent could or ought to be part of the daily practice of medicine. Third, primary care encounters are statistically more common than the highly specialized encounters previously used as models for the concept of informed consent.

ACCEPTED LEGAL STANDARDS

Most of the literature on legal approaches to informed consent addresses the tension between the community practice standard and the reasonable patient standard, with the latter seen as the more satisfactory, emerging legal standard. However, neither standard sends the proper message to the physician about what is expected of her to promote patient autonomy effectively and to serve the informational needs of patients in daily practice.

The community practice standard sends the wrong message because it leaves the door open too wide for physician paternalism. The physician is instructed to behave as other physicians in that specialty behave, regardless of how well or how poorly that behavior serves patients' needs. Certainly, behaving the way other physicians behave is a task we might expect physicians to readily accomplish; unfortunately, the standard fails to inform them of the end toward which the task is aimed.

The reasonable patient standard does a much better job of indicating the centrality of respect for patient autonomy and the desired outcome of the informed consent process, which is revealing the information that a reasonable person would need to make an informed and rational decision. This standard is particularly valuable when modified to include the specific informational and decisional needs of a particular patient.

If certain things were true about the relationship between medicine and law in today's society, the reasonable patient standard would provide acceptable guidance to physicians. One feature would be that physicians esteem the law as a positive force in guiding their practice, rather than as a threat to their well-being that must be handled defensively. Another element would be a prospective consideration by the law of what the physician could reasonably have been expected to do in practice, rather than a retrospective review armed with the foreknowledge that some significant patient harm has already occurred.

Unfortunately, given the present legal climate, the physician is much more likely to get a mixed or an undesirable message from the reasonable patient standard. The message the physician hears from the reasonable patient standard is that one must exhaustively lay out all possible risks as well as benefits and alternatives of the proposed procedure. If one remembers to discuss fifty possible risks, and the patient in a particular case suffers the fifty-first, the physician might subsequently be found liable for incomplete disclosure. Since lawsuits are triggered when patients suffer harm, disclosure of risk becomes relatively more important than disclosure of benefits. Moreover, disclosure of information becomes much more critical than effective patient participation in decisionmaking. Physicians consider it more important to document what they said to the patient than to document how the patient used or thought about that information subsequently.

In specialty practice, many of these concerns can be nicely met by detailed written or videotaped consent documents, which can provide the depth of information required while still putting the benefits and alternatives in proper context. This is workable when one engages in a limited number of procedures and can have a complete document or videotape for each. However, this approach is not feasible for primary care, when the number of procedures may be much more numerous and the time available with each patient may be considerably less. Moreover, it is simply not realistic to expect even the best educated of primary care physicians to rattle off at a moment's notice a detailed list of significant risks attached to any of the many drugs and therapeutic modalities they recommend.

This sets informed consent apart from all other aspects of medical practice in a way that I believe is widely perceived by nonpaternalistic primary care physicians, but which is almost never commented upon in the medical ethics literature. To the physician obtaining informed consent, *you never know when you are finished.* When a primary care physician is told to treat a patient for strep throat or to counsel a person suffering a normal grief reaction from the recent death of a relative, the physician has a good sense of what it means to complete the task at hand. When a physician is told to obtain the patient's informed consent for a medical intervention, the impression is quite different. A list of as many possible risks as can be thought of may still omit some significant ones. A list of all the risks that actually have occurred may still not have dealt with the patient's need to know risks in relation to benefits and alternatives. A description of all benefits, risks, and alternatives may not establish whether the patient has understood the information. If the patient says he understands, the physician has to wonder whether he really understands or whether he is simply saying this to be accommodating. As the law currently *appears* to operate (in the perception of the defensively minded physician), there never comes a point at which you can be certain that you have adequately completed your legal as well as your ethical task.

The point is not simply that physicians are paranoid about the law; more fundamentally, physicians are getting a message that informed consent is very different from any other task they are asked to perform in medicine. If physicians conclude that informed consent is therefore not properly part of medicine at all, but is rather a legalistic and bureaucratic hurdle they must overcome at their own peril, blame cannot be attributed to paternalistic attitudes or lack of respect for patient autonomy.

THE CONVERSATION MODEL

A metaphor employed by Jay Katz, informed consent as conversation, provides an approach to respect for patient autonomy that can be readily integrated within primary care practice. Just as the specific needs of an individual patient for information, or the meaning that patient will attach to the information as it is presented, cannot be known in advance, one cannot always tell in advance how a conversation is going to turn out. One must follow the process along and take one's cues from the unfolding conversation itself. Despite the absence of any formal rules for carrying out or completing a conversation on a specific subject, most people have a good intuitive grasp of what it means for a conversation to be finished, what it means to change the subject in the middle of a conversation, and what it means to later reopen a conversation one had thought was completed when something new has just arisen. Thus, the metaphor suggests that informed consent consists not in a formal process carried out strictly by protocol but in a conversation designed to encourage patient participation in all medical decisions to the extent that the patient wishes to be included. The idea of informed consent as physician-patient conversation could, when properly developed, be a useful analytic tool for ethical issues in informed consent, and could also be a powerful educational tool for highlighting the skills and attitudes that a physician needs to successfully integrate this process within patient care.

If primary care physicians understand informed consent as this sort of conversation process, the idea that exact rules cannot be given for its successful management could cease to be a mystery. Physicians would instead be guided to rely on their own intuitions and communication skills, with careful attention to information received from the patient, to determine when an adequate job had been done in the informed consent process. Moreover, physicians would be encouraged to see informed consent as a genuinely mutual and participatory process, instead of being reduced to the one-way disclosure of information. In effect, informed consent could be demystified, and located within the context of the everyday relationships between physician and patient, albeit with a renewed emphasis on patient participation.

Unfortunately, the conversation metaphor does not lend itself to ready translation into a legal standard for determining whether or not the physician has satisfied her basic responsibilities to the patient. There seems to be an inherently subjective element to conversation that makes it ill-suited as a legal standard for review of controversial cases. A conversation in which one participates is by its nature a very different thing from the same conversation described to an outsider. It is hard to imagine how a jury could be instructed to determine in retrospect whether or not a particular conversation was adequate for its purposes. However, without the possibility for legal review, the message that patient autonomy is an important value and that patients have important rights within primary care would seem to be severely undermined. The question then is whether some of the important strengths of the conversation model can be retained in another model that does allow better guidance.

THE TRANSPARENCY STANDARD

I propose the transparency standard as a means to operationalize the best features of the conversation model in medical practice. According to this standard, adequate informed consent is obtained when a reasonably informed patient is allowed to participate in the medical decision to the extent that patient wishes. In turn, "reasonably informed" consists of two features: (1) the physician discloses the basis on which the proposed treatment, or alternative possible treatments, have been chosen; and (2) the patient is allowed to ask questions suggested by the disclosure of the physician's reasoning, and those questions are answered to the patient's satisfaction.

According to the transparency model, the key to reasonable disclosure is not adherence to existing standards of other practitioners, nor is it adherence to a list of risks that a hypothetical reasonable patient would want to know. Instead, disclosure is adequate when the physician's basic thinking has been rendered transparent to the patient. If the physician arrives at a recommended therapeutic or diagnostic intervention only after carefully examining a list of risks and benefits, then rendering the physician's thinking transparent requires that those risks and benefits be detailed for the patient. If the physician's thinking has not followed that route but has reached its conclusion by other considerations, then what needs to be disclosed to the patient is accordingly different. Essentially, the transparency standard requires the physician to engage in the typical patient-management thought process, only to *do it out loud in language understandable to the patient.*

To see how this might work in practice, consider the following as possible general decision-making strategies that might be used by a primary physician:

1. The intervention, in addition to being presumably low-risk, is also routine and automatic. The physician, faced with a case like that presented by the patient, almost always chooses this treatment.
2. The decision is not routine but seems to offer clear benefit with minimal risk.
3. The proposed procedure offers substantial chances for benefit, but also very substantial risks.
4. The proposed intervention offers substantial risks and extremely questionable benefits. Unfortunately, possible alternative courses of action also have high risk and uncertain benefit.

The exact risks entailed by treatment loom much larger in the physician's own thinking in cases 3 and 4 than in cases 1 and 2. The transparency standard would require that physicians at least mention the various risks to patients in scenarios 3 and 4, but would not necessarily require physicians exhaustively to describe risks, unless the patient asked, in scenarios 1 and 2.

The transparency standard seems to offer some considerable advantages for informing physicians what can legitimately be expected of them in the promotion of patient autonomy while carrying out the activities of primary care medicine. We would hope that the well-trained primary care physician generally thinks before acting. On that assumption, the physician can be told exactly when she is finished obtaining informed consent—first, she has to share her thinking with the patient; secondly, she has to encourage and answer questions; and third, she has to discover how participatory he wishes to be and facilitate that level of participation. This seems a much more reasonable task within primary care than an exhaustive listing of often irrelevant risk factors.

There are also considerable advantages for the patient in this approach. The patient retains the right to ask for an exhaustive recital of risks and alternatives. However, the vast majority of patients, in a primary care setting particularly, would wish to supplement a standardized recital of risks and benefits of treatment with some questions like, "Yes, doctor, but what does this really mean for me? What meaning am I supposed to attach to the information that you've just given?" For example, in scenarios 1 and 2, the precise and specific risk probabilities and possibilities are very small considerations in the thinking of the physician, and reciting an exhaustive list of risks would seriously misstate just what the physician was thinking. If the physician did detail a laundry list of risk factors, the patient might very well ask, "Well, doctor, just what should I think about what you have just told me?" and the thoughtful and concerned physician might well reply, "There's certainly a small possibility that one of these bad things will happen to you; but I think the chance is extremely remote and in my own practice I have never seen anything like that occur." The patient is very likely to give much more weight to that statement, putting the risks in perspective, than he is to the listing of risks. And that emphasis corresponds with an understanding of how the physician herself has reached the decision.

The transparency standard should further facilitate and encourage useful questions from patients. If a patient is given a routine list of risks and benefits and then is asked "Do you have any questions?" the response may well be perfunctory and automatic. If the patient is told precisely the grounds on which the physician has made her recommendation, and then asked the same question, the response is much more likely to be individualized and meaningful.

There certainly would be problems in applying the transparency standard in the courtroom, but these do not appear to be materially more difficult than those encountered in applying other standards; moreover, this standard could call attention to more important features in the ethical relationship between physician and patient. Consider the fairly typical case, in which a patient suffers harm from the occurrence of a rare but predictable complication of a procedure, and then claims that he would not have consented had he known about that risk. Under the present "enlightened" court standards, the jury would examine whether a reasonable patient would have needed to know about that risk factor prior to making a decision on the proposed intervention. Under the transparency standard, the question would instead be whether the physician thought about that risk factor as a relevant consideration prior to recommending the course of action to the patient. If the physician did seriously consider that risk factor, but failed to reveal that to the patient, he was in effect making up the patient's mind in advance about what risks were worth accepting. In that situation, the physician could easily be held liable. If, on the other hand, that risk was considered too insignificant to play a role in determining which intervention ought to be performed, the physician may still have rendered his thinking completely transparent to the patient even though that specific risk factor was not mentioned. In this circumstance, the physician would be held to have done an adequate job of disclosing information. A question would still exist as to whether a competent physician ought to have known about that risk factor and ought to have considered it more carefully prior to doing the procedure. But that question raises the issue of negligence, which is where such considerations properly belong, and removes the problem from the context of informed consent. Obviously, the standard of informed consent is misapplied if it is intended by itself to prevent the practice of negligent medicine.

TRANSPARENCY IN MEDICAL PRACTICE

Will adopting a legal standard like transparency change medical practice for the better? Ultimately only empirical research will answer this question. We know almost nothing about the sorts of conversations primary care physicians now have with their patients, or what would happen if these physicians routinely tried harder to share their basic thinking about therapeutic choices. In this setting it is possible to argue that the transparency standard will have deleterious effects. Perhaps the physician's basic thinking will fail to include risk issues that patients, from their perspective, would regard as substantial. Perhaps how physicians think about therapeutic choice will prove to be too idiosyncratic and variable to serve as any sort of standard. Perhaps disclosing basic thinking processes will impede rather than promote optimal patient participation in decisions.

But the transparency standard must be judged, not only against ideal medical practice, but also against the present-day standard and the message it sends to practitioners. I have argued that that message is, "You can protect yourself legally only by guessing all bad outcomes that might occur and warning each patient explicitly that he might suffer any of them." The transparency standard is an attempt to send the message, "You can protect yourself legally by conversing with your patients in a way that promotes their participation in medical decisions, and more specifically by making sure that they see the basic reasoning you used to arrive at the recommended treatment." It seems at least plausible to me that the attempt is worth making.

The reasonable person standard may still be the best way to view informed consent in highly specialized settings where a relatively small number of discrete and potentially risky procedures are the daily order of business. In primary care settings, the best ethical advice we can give physicians is to view informed consent as an ongoing process of conversation designed to maximize patient participation after adequately revealing the key facts. Because the conversation metaphor does not by itself suggest measures for later judicial review, a transparency standard, or something like it, may be a reasonable way to operationalize that concept in primary care practice. Some positive side-effects of this might be more focus on good diagnostic and therapeutic decisionmaking on the physician's part, since it will be understood that the patient will be made aware of what the physician's reasoning process has been like, and better documentation of management decisions in the patient record. If these occur, then it will be clearer that the standard of informed consent has promoted rather than impeded high quality patient care.

STANDARDS OF COMPETENCE

Allen E. Buchanan and Dan W. Brock

DIFFERENT STANDARDS OF COMPETENCE

A number of different standards of competence have been identified and supported in the literature, although statutory and case law provide little help in articulating precise standards. It is neither feasible nor necessary to discuss here all the alternatives that have been proposed. Instead, the range of alternatives will be delineated and the difficulties of the main standards will be examined in order to clarify and defend the decision-relative analysis offered above. More or less stringent standards of competence in effect strike different balances between the values of patient well-being and self-determination.

A. A Minimal Standard of Competence

An example of a minimal standard of competence is that the patient merely be able to express a preference. This standard respects every expressed choice of a patient, and so is not in fact a criterion of *competent* choice at all. It entirely disregards whether defects or mistakes are present in the reasoning process leading to the choice, whether the choice is in accord with the patient's own conception of his or her good, and whether the choice would be harmful to the patient. It thus fails to provide any protection for patient well-being, and it is insensitive to the way the value of self-determination itself varies both with the nature of the decision to be made and with differences in people's capacities to choose in accordance with their conceptions of their own good.

B. An Outcome Standard of Competence

At the other extreme are standards that look solely to the *content* or *outcome* of the decision—for example, the standard that the choice be a reasonable one, or be what other reasonable or rational persons would choose. On this view, failure of the patient's choice to match some such allegedly objective outcome standard of choice entails that it is an incompetent choice. Such a standard maximally protects patient well-being—although only according to the standard's conception of well-being—but fails adequately to respect patient self-determination.

At bottom, a person's interest in self-determination is his or her interest in defining, revising over time, and pursuing his or her own particular conception of the good life. As we noted above of ideal theories of the good for persons, there are serious practical or fallibilist risks associated with any purportedly objective standard for the correct decision—the standard may ignore the patient's own distinctive conception of the good and may constitute enforcement of unjustified ideals or unjustifiably substitute another's conception of what is best for the patient. Moreover, even such a standard's theoretical claim to protect maximally a patient's well-being is only as strong as the objective account of a person's well-being on which the standard rests. Many proponents of ideal theories only assert the ideals and fail even to recognize the need for justifying them, much less proceed to do so.

Although ascertaining the correct or best theory of individual well-being or the good for persons is a complex and controversial task, we argued above that any standard of individual well-being that does not ultimately rest on an individual's own underlying and enduring aims and values is both problematic in theory and subject to intolerable abuse in practice. There may be room in some broad policy decisions or overall theories of justice for more "objective" and interpersonal measures of well-being that fail fully to reflect differences in individuals' own views of their well-being, but we believe there is *much less room* for such purportedly objective measures in the kind of judgments of concern here—judgments about appropriate treatment for an individual patient. Thus, a standard that judges competence by comparing the content of a patient's decision to some objective standard for the correct decision may fail even to protect appropriately a patient's well-being.

C. A Process Standard of Decision-Making Competence

An adequate standard of competence will focus primarily not on the content of the patient's decision but on the *process* of the reasoning that leads up to that decision. There are two central questions for any process standard of competence. First, a process standard must set a level of reasoning required for the patient to be competent. In other words, how well must the patient understand and reason to be competent? How much can understanding be limited or reasoning be defective and still be compatible with competence? The second question often passes without explicit notice by those evaluating competence. How certain must those persons evaluating competence be about how well the patient has understood and reasoned in coming to a decision? This second question is important because it is common in cases of marginal or questionable competence for there to be a significant degree of uncertainty about the patient's reasoning and decision-making process that can never be eliminated.

RELATION OF THE PROCESS STANDARD OF COMPETENCE TO EXPECTED HARMS AND BENEFITS

Because the competence evaluation requires striking a balance between the two values of respecting patients' rights to decide for themselves and protecting them from the harmful consequences of their own choices, it should be clear that no single standard of competence—no single answer to the questions above—can be adequate for all decisions. This is true because (1) the degree of expected harm from choices made at a given level of understanding and reasoning can vary from none to the most serious, including major disability or death, and because (2) the importance or value to the patient of self-determination can vary depending on the choice being made.

There is an important implication of this view that the standard of competence ought to vary in part with the expected harms or benefits to the patient of acting in accordance with the patient's choice—namely, that just because a patient is competent to consent to a treatment, it does *not* follow that the patient is competent to refuse it, and vice versa. For example, consent to a low-risk lifesaving procedure by

an otherwise healthy individual should require only a minimal level of competence, but refusal of that same procedure by such an individual should require the highest level of competence.

Because the appropriate level of competence properly required for a particular decision must be adjusted to the consequences of acting on that decision, no single standard of decision-making competence is adequate. Instead, the level of competence appropriately required for decision making varies along a full range from low/minimal to high/maximal. Table 1 illustrates this variation, with the treatment choices listed used only as examples of any treatment choice with that relative risk/benefit assessment.

The net balance of expected benefits and risks of the patient's choice in comparison with other alternatives will usually be determined by the physician. This assessment should focus on the expected effects of a particular treatment option in forwarding the patient's underlying and enduring aims and values, to the extent that these are known. When the patient's aims and values are not known, the risk/benefit assessment will balance the expected effects of a particular treatment option in achieving the general goals of health care in prolonging life, preventing injury and disability, and relieving suffering as against its risks of harm. The table indicates that the relevant comparison is with other available alternatives, and the degree to which the net benefit/risk balance of the alternative chosen is better or worse than that for optimal alternative treatment options. It should be noted that a choice might properly require only low/minimal competence, even

TABLE 1 *Decision-making competence and patient well-being*

The patient's treatment choice	Other's risk/benefit assessment of that choice in comparison with other alternatives	Level of decision-making competence required	Grounds for believing patient's choice best promotes/protects own well-being
Patient consents to lumbar puncture for presumed meningitis	Net balance substantially better than for possible alternatives	Low/minimal	Principally the benefit/risk assessment made by others
Patient chooses lumpectomy for breast cancer	Net balance roughly comparable to that of other alternatives	Moderate/median	Roughly equally from the benefit/risk assessment made by others and from the patient's decision that the chosen alternative best fits own conception of own good
Patient refuses surgery for simple appendectomy	Net balance substantially worse than for another alternative or alternatives	High/maximal	Principally from patient's decision that the chosen alternative best fits own conception of own good

though its expected risks exceed its expected benefits or it is more generally a high-risk treatment, because all other available alternatives have substantially worse risk/benefit ratios.

Table 1 also indicates, for each level of competence, the relative importance of different *grounds* for believing that a patient's own choice best promotes his or her well-being. This brings out an important point. For *all* patient choices, other people responsible for deciding whether those choices should be respected should have grounds for believing that the choice, if it is to be honored, is reasonably in accord with the patient's well-being (although the choice need not, of course, *maximally* promote the patient's interests). When the patient's level of decision-making competence need be only at the low/minimal level, as in the agreement to a lumbar puncture for presumed meningitis, these grounds derive only minimally from the fact that the patient has chosen the option in question; they principally stem from others' positive assessment of the choice's expected effects on the patient's well-being.

At the other extreme, when the expected effects of the patient's choice for his or her well-being appear to be substantially worse than available alternatives, as in the refusal of a simple appendectomy, the requirement of a high/maximal level of competence provides grounds for relying on the patient's decision as itself establishing that the choice best fits the patient's good (his or her own underlying and enduring aims and values). The highest level of competence should assure that no significant mistakes in the patient's reasoning and decision making are present, and is required to rebut the presumption that the choice is not in fact reasonably related to the patient's interests.

When the expected effects for the patient's well-being of his or her choice are approximately comparable to those of alternatives, as in the choice of a lumpectomy for treatment of breast cancer, a moderate/median level of competence is sufficient to provide reasonable grounds that the choice promotes the patient's good and that her well-being is adequately protected. It is also reasonable to assume that as the level of competence required increases (from minimal to maximal), the instrumental value or importance of respecting the patient's self-determination increases as well, specifically the part of the value of self-determination that rests on the assumption that persons will secure their good when they choose for themselves. As competence increases, other things being equal, the likelihood of this happening increases.

Thus, according to the concept of competence endorsed here, a particular individual's decision-making capacity at a given time may be sufficient for making a decision to refuse a diagnostic procedure when forgoing the procedure does not carry a significant risk, although it would not necessarily be sufficient for refusing a surgical procedure that would correct a life-threatening condition. The greater the risk relative to other alternatives—where risk is a function of the severity of the expected harm and the probability of its occurrence—the greater the level of communication, understanding, and reasoning skills required for competence to make that decision. It is not always true, however, that if a person is competent to make one decision, then he or she is competent to make another decision so long as it involves equal risk. Even if the risk is the same, one decision may be more complex, and hence require a higher level of capacity for understanding options and reasoning about consequences.

In the previous section, we rejected a standard of competence that looks to the content or outcome of the decision in favor of a standard that focuses on the process of the patient's reasoning. This may appear inconsistent with our insistence here that the appropriate level of decision-making capacity required for competence should depend in significant part on the effects for the patient's well-being of accepting his or her choice, since what those effects are clearly depends on the content or outcome of the patient's choice. However, there is no inconsistency. The competence evaluation addresses the process of the patient's reasoning, whereas the degree of defectiveness and limitation of, and uncertainty about, that process that is compatible with competence depends in significant part on the likely harm to the patient's well-being of accepting his or her choice. To the extent that they are known, the effects on the patient's well-being should be evaluated in terms of his or her own underlying and enduring aims and values, or, where these are not known, in terms of the effects on life and health. Thus in our approach there is no use of an "objective" standard for the best or correct decision that is known to be in conflict with the patient's own underlying and enduring aims and values, which was the objectionable feature of a content or outcome standard of competence.

The evaluation of the patient's decision making will seek to assess how well the patient has understood the nature of the proposed treatment and any significant alternatives, the expected benefits and risks and the likelihood of each, the reason for the recommendation, and then whether the patient has made a choice that reasonably conforms to his or her underlying and enduring aims and values. Two broad kinds of defect are then possible; first, "factual" misunderstanding about the nature and likelihood of an outcome, for example from limitations in cognitive understanding resulting from stroke or from impairment of short-term memory resulting from dementia; second, failure of the patient's choice to be based on his or her underlying and enduring aims and values, for example because depression has temporarily distorted them so that the patient "no longer cares" about restoration of the function he or she had valued before becoming depressed.

A crude but perhaps helpful way of characterizing the proper aim of the evaluator of the competence of a seemingly harmful or "bad" patient choice is to think of him or her addressing the patient in this fashion: "Help me try to understand and make sense of your choice. Help me to see whether your choice is reasonable, not in the sense that it is what I or most people would choose, but that it is reasonable for you in light of your underlying and enduring aims and values." This is the proper focus of a *process* standard of competence.

Some may object that misguided paternalists will always be ready to assert that their interference with the patient's choice is "deep down" in accord with what we have called the patient's "underlying and enduring aims and values," or at least with what these would be except for unfortunate distortions. If there is no objective way to determine a person's underlying and enduring aims and values then the worry is that our view will lead to excessive paternalism. We acknowledge that this determination will often be difficult and uncertain, for example in cases like severe chronic depression, leading to genuine and justified uncertainty about the patient's "true" aims and values. But any claims that the aims and values actually expressed by the patient are not his underlying and enduring aims and values should be based on evidence of the distortion of the actual aims and values independent of their mere difference with some other, "better" aims and values. Just as the process standard of competence focuses on the process of the patient's reasoning, so also it requires evidence of a process of distortion of the patient's aims and values to justify evaluating choices by a standard other than the patient's actually expressed aims and values.

WHO DECIDES, AND WHAT?

Tom Tomlinson

The concept of competence [advanced in Buchanan and Brock's book, *Deciding for Others*] shares much with the view that has been dominant since the reports of the President's Commission for the Study of Ethical Problems in Medicine, which, as staff members, Buchanan and Brock helped to write. Competence is decision relative because decisions of different complexities may call on different mental capacities. Adult persons should be presumed competent. Because of the importance of self-determination, the burden of proving a person's incompetence rests on others.

The capacities necessary for making a competent decision start with the capacity for understanding the facts pertinent to the decision at hand, including not only an intellectual grasp of the facts, but the capacity to understand imaginatively what it would feel like to experience the outcomes of the various alternative choices. The capacity for communication is also required, both as a means for others to evaluate understanding and for the person to communicate the preferred choice. Competence also requires capacities for reasoning and deliberation—again, not in the abstract, but for inferring from the facts how the various choices will affect one's values and goals. The last capacity important for competence is the possession of a set of values that is "consistent, stable, and affirmed" as one's own.

Although all of these capacities are matters of degree, competence itself is not a matter of degree, but of threshold. One is either competent to make a given decision at a given time, or one is not. The problem, then, is where to set the threshold.

Buchanan and Brock argue that the threshold is set by balancing the two values that are served by the process of informed consent: the patient's well-being and the patient's self-determination. Although they acknowledge that there are competing standards for defining well-being, they think that all the plausible standards are substantially subjective: that is, a person's well-being must be understood in terms of the hierarchy of values that the person himself or herself affirms. The value of self-determination is partly instrumental because it is more likely to result in choices that enhance well-being as defined in the individual's own terms; and it is partly intrinsic because we often prefer to decide for ourselves, even when we don't think we would make the best decision.

Setting the level of the threshold of competence requires balancing these two values in order to steer between two dangers. Setting the threshold too high will take decision-making authority away from a patient who was competent to exercise it and will compromise the value of self-determination. Setting the threshold too low will permit an incompetent patient to choose unwisely and will compromise the value of protecting the patient's well-being.

Buchanan and Brock observe that anyone who advocates, as they do, a "process standard" that assesses the process of reasoning by which the patient came to a decision, must answer two questions. First, how well must the patient understand and reason to be judged competent, and, second, how certain must the evaluators

Reprinted with permission of the Institue of Medical Humanities, University of Texas Medical Branch, from *Medical Humanities Review*, vol. 5, (July 5, 1991), pp. 73–6.

be that their assessment of the patient's understanding is accurate? When the patient would pay a high price if we are wrong about his or her competence, we will want to be very certain indeed.

They believe that these considerations argue for a sliding-scale standard of competence. When there is a low risk of harm in respecting the patient's choice, a minimal capacity for understanding is sufficient. When there is a high risk of harm, we should require the patient to demonstrate a maximal capacity for understanding.

> [A] particular individual's decision-making capacity at a given time may be sufficient for making a decision to refuse a diagnostic procedure when forgoing the procedure does not carry a significant risk, although it would not necessarily be sufficient for refusing a surgical procedure that would correct a life-threatening condition. The greater the risk relative to other alternatives ... the greater the level of communication, understanding, and reasoning skills required for competence to make that decision.

One implication of this view is that assessing a patient's competence is perfectly defensible when the patient refuses treatment, even if the patient's competence would not have been questioned if treatment had been accepted. Refusal is never in itself sufficient evidence of incompetence.

Does this sliding-scale model provide the most defensible conception of competence? One important set of objections comes from Charles Culver and Bernard Gert, most recently in the *Milbank Quarterly* in 1990. Even though competence, in their view, remains relative to the kind of decision to be made, it is a characteristic of persons, not of any specific decision. This point is illustrated most vividly by considering a counterintuitive consequence of the sliding-scale model: that a patient could be competent to accept treatment, but not competent to reject the very same treatment. In Buchanan and Brock's view, the decision to accept lifesaving and benign treatment is a low-risk decision that requires only a minimal level of understanding to be competent. The decision to reject that treatment, however, is a high-risk decision that requires a high level of understanding to be competent. Therefore, the status of the patient who decides to refuse treatment that he or she had previously accepted could change from competent to incompetent, even though nothing has changed about the patient's level of understanding, medical condition, treatment procedures, or any other fact except the choice itself. For Culver and Gert, competence is the capacity of the patient to understand and appreciate the facts pertaining to a specific kind of decision, a capacity that can be evaluated prior to and independently of the decision finally made and is the same for refusal as for acceptance of treatment. Culver and Gert agree with Buchanan and Brock that deciding whether the patient's choice will be respected requires consideration of the patient's well-being, but they argue that it is done by assessing the rationality of the decision rather than the competence of the decision maker. Even a competent patient's choice can be "seriously irrational"—can threaten serious harm for no good reason. When that is the case, the competent patient's choice should be overruled.

Buchanan and Brock reply at least to earlier versions of this argument by agreeing that competence, in our common-sense notion of it, is a characteristic of persons. But they reject Culver and Gert's conception because it allows a fully competent patient's choice to be overruled for paternalistic reasons. This is a position that breaks too sharply with our ethical and legal traditions, which accord almost absolute decisional authority to the competent patient. This criticism of Culver and Gert is aimed in the right direction but could be much stronger. For them, respect for autonomy drops out altogether as a moral consideration in decisions about respecting refusal of treatment. For Culver and Gert, only the rationality or irrationality of the refusal is relevant to any decision about respecting it, regardless of competence as they understand it. Since rationality is taken to be a characteristic of a decision and in no respect a characteristic of the patient, the rationality of the patient's choice is to be judged without reference to that person's individual values and goals, but instead from a social or more ideal perspective. Respect for the intrinsic worth of individual, idiosyncratic conceptions of the good no longer operates as a brake on paternalistic interventions.

Buchanan and Brock could have avoided Culver and Gert's objection entirely if they hadn't confused the need for a variable standard of *evidence* for competence with a variable standard of *capacity* for competence. Culver and Gert are right in arguing that competence is a characteristic of persons and that the capacities required for competence vary with the complexities of the decision that is pending, not with the risk to the patient's well-being that one decision or another poses. Contrary to Buchanan and Brock, competence itself is not a balancing concept that weighs self-determination against well-being. Nevertheless, the level of risk to the patient's well-being remains relevant to the assessment of competence because it determines what the stakes of an incorrect assessment are and, in turn, how certain we need to be that the patient's decision is in fact a competent one. When the consent is to a lifesaving and benign procedure, it doesn't matter whether we are wrong to judge the patient competent; we will treat the patient in any case. When, however, that patient changes his or her mind and refuses the procedure, it matters a great deal whether we're wrong in judging the patient to be competent and, in the name of self-determination, we permit the refusal to stand. In this circumstance, we rightly demand a much higher degree of evidence for that person's competence, not because the capacities necessary for a competent decision about this treatment have changed, but because our need to be sure about the patient's possession of those capacities has escalated dramatically.

This approach is a third position that incorporates elements of the other two. Competence is a capacity of persons that is independent of consent and refusal and does not weigh self-determination against well-being; and yet the risks to a patient's well-being justify a different approach to evaluating competence when the patient is refusing treatment rather than consenting to it. The irrationality of the patient's choice, judged from a position external to the patient's own hierarchy of values and goals, is no more than a red flag that indicates the need to inquire into the patient's competence more closely; contrary to Culver and Gert, it is not, in itself, a consideration that can be weighed paternalistically against the competent patient's right to self-determination, a right that remains nearly absolute.

After all is said and done, this dispute may in some part be a philosophical tempest in a teapot. The ethically significant question is when an adult's refusal of treatment may be overruled, and on that question it is hard to distinguish between *when it is competent, but irrational* (Culver and Gert) and *when it is irrational, hence difficult to find competent* (Buchanan and Brock). As a practical matter, any of these conceptions would end up treating cases in much the same way. …

ON TELLING PATIENTS THE TRUTH

Roger Higgs

That honesty should be an important issue for debate in medical circles may seem bizarre. Nurses and doctors are usually thought of as model citizens. Outside the immediate field of health care, when a passport is to be signed, a reference given, or a special allowance made by a government welfare agency, a nurse's or doctor's signature is considered a good warrant, and false certification treated as a serious breach of professional conduct. Yet at the focus of medical activity or skill, at the bedside or in the clinic, when patient meets professional there is often doubt. Is the truth being told?

Many who are unfamiliar with illness and its treatment may well be forgiven for wondering if this doubt has not been exaggerated. It is as if laundry men were to discuss the merits of clean clothes, or fishmongers of refrigeration. But those with experience, either as patients or professionals, will immediately recognize the situation. Although openness is increasingly practised, there is still uncertainty in the minds of many doctors or nurses faced with communicating bad news; as for instance when a test shows up an unexpected and probably incurable cancer, or when meeting the gaze of a severely ill child, or answering the questions of a mother in mid-pregnancy whose unborn child is discovered to be badly handicapped. What should be said? There can be few who have not, on occasions such as these, told less than the truth. Certainly the issue is a regular preoccupation of nurses and doctors in training. Why destroy hope? Why create anxiety, or something worse? Isn't it "First, do no harm?"[1]

Reprinted from *Moral Dilemmas in Modern Medicine*, ed. Michael Lockwood (1986); pp. 187–191; 193–202. Reprinted by permission of Oxford University Press.

The concerns of the patient are very different. For many, fear of the unknown is the worst disease of all, and yet direct information seems so hard to obtain. The ward round goes past quickly, unintelligible words are muttered—was I supposed to hear and understand? In the surgery the general practitioner signs his prescription pad and clearly it's time to be gone. Everybody is too busy saving lives to give explanations. It may come as a shock to learn that it is policy, not just pressure of work, that prevents a patient learning the truth about himself. If truth is the first casualty, trust must be the second. "Of course they wouldn't say, especially if things were bad," said the elderly woman just back from out-patients, "they've got that Oath, haven't they?" She had learned to expect from doctors, at the best, silence; at the worst, deception. It was part of the system, an essential ingredient, as old as Hippocrates. However honest a citizen, it was somehow part of the doctor's job not to tell the truth to his patient.

These reactions, from both patient and doctor, are most commonly encountered when there is news to communicate of a relatively insidious and life-threatening disease like cancer. Often a collusion seems to be set up, preventing openness on either side. A 45-year-old woman, married with one son of nine, was diagnosed as having acute myeloid leukaemia, and in spite of the treatment was dying in hospital. In response to enquiries, her practitioner was told that she had asked no questions, and didn't want to know anything. The practice nurse, whom she knew, visited the ward. After half an hour the patient burst into tears, desperate to discuss what was going to happen to her son when she died.

However harrowing these occasions, it is easier to decide what to do when the ultimate outcome is clear. It may be much more difficult to know what to say when the future is less certain, such as in the first episode of what is probably multiple sclerosis, or when a patient is about to undergo a mutilating operation. But even in work outside hospital, where such dramatic problems arise less commonly, whether to tell the truth and how much to tell can still be a regular issue. How much should this patient know about the side effects of his drugs? An elderly man sits weeping in an old people's home, and the healthy but exhausted daughter wants the doctor to tell her father that she's medically unfit to have him back. The single mother wants a certificate to say that she is unwell so that she can stay at home to look after her sick child. A colleague is often drunk on duty, and is making mistakes. A husband with venereal disease wants his wife to be treated without her knowledge. An outraged father demands to know if his teenage daughter has been put on the pill. A mother comes in with a child to have a boil lanced. "Please tell him it won't hurt." A former student writes from abroad needing to complete his professional experience and asks for a reference for a job he didn't do.[2] Whether the issue is large or small, the truth is at stake. What should the response be?

Discussion of the apparently more dramatic situations may provide a good starting point. Recently a small group of medical students, new to clinical experience, were hotly debating what a patient with cancer should be told. One student maintained strongly that the less said to the patient the better. Others disagreed. When asked whether there was any group of patients they could agree should never be told the truth about a life-threatening illness, the students chose children, and agreed that they would not speak openly to children under six. When asked to try to remember what life was like when they were six, one student replied that he remembered how his mother had died when he was that age. Suddenly the student who had advocated non-disclosure became animated. "That's extraordinary. My mother died when I was six too. My father said she'd gone away for a time, but would come back soon. One day he said she was coming home again. My younger sister and I were very excited. We waited at the window upstairs until we saw his car drive up. He got out and helped a woman out of the car. Then we saw. It wasn't mum. I suppose I never forgave him—or her, really."[3]

It is hard to know with whom to sympathize in this sad tale. But its stark simplicity serves to highlight some essential points. First, somehow more clearly than in the examples involving patients, not telling the truth is seen for what it really is. It is, of course, quite possible, and very common in clinical practice, for doctors (or nurses) to engage in deliberate deceit without actually *saying* anything they believe to be false. But, given the special responsibilities of the doctor, and the relationship of trust that exists beween him and his patient, one could hardly argue that this was morally any different from telling outright lies. Surely it is the *intention* that is all important. We may be silent, tactful, or reserved, but if we intend to deceive, what we are doing is tantamount to lying. The debate in ward or surgery is suddenly stood on its head. The question is no longer "Should we tell the truth?" but "What justification is there for telling a lie?" This relates to the second important point, that medical ethics are part of general morality, and not a separate field of their own with their own rules. Unless there are special justifications, health-care professionals are working within the same moral constraints as lay people. A lie is a lie wherever told and whoever tells it.

But do doctors have a special dispensation from the usual principles that guide the conduct of our society? It is widely felt that on occasion they do, and such a dispensation is as necessary to all doctors as freedom from the charge of assault is to a surgeon. But if it is impossible to look after ill patients and always be open and truthful, how can we balance this against the clear need for truthfulness on all other occasions? If deception is like a medicine to be given in certain doses in certain cases, what guidance exists about its administration?

My elderly patient reflected the widely held view that truthtelling, or perhaps withholding, was part of the tradition of medicine enshrined in its oaths and codes. Although the writer of the "Decorum" in the Hippocratic corpus advises physicians of the danger of telling patients about the nature of their illness "... for many patients through this cause have taken a turn for the worse,"[4] the Oath itself is completely silent on this issue. This extraordinary omission is continued through all the more modern codes and declarations. The first mention of veracity as a principle is to be found in the American Medical Association's "Principles of Ethics" of 1980, which states that the physician should "deal honestly with patients and colleagues and strive to expose those physicians deficient in character or competence, or who engage in fraud and deception."[5] Despite the difficulties of the latter injunction, which seems in some way to divert attention from the basic need for honest communication with the patient, here at last is a clear statement. This declaration signally fails, however, to provide the guidance that we might perhaps have expected for the professional facing his or her individual dilemma.

The reticence of these earlier codes is shared, with some important exceptions, by medical writing elsewhere. Until recently most of what had been usefully said could be summed up by the articles of medical writers such as Thomas Percival, Worthington Hooker, Richard Cabot, and Joseph Collins, which show a wide scatter of viewpoints but do at least confront the problems directly.[6] There is, however, one widely quoted statement by Lawrence Henderson, writing in the *New England Journal of Medicine* in 1955.[7] "It is meaningless to speak of telling the truth, the whole truth and nothing but the truth to a patient ... because it is ... a sheer impossibility ... Since telling the truth is impossible, there can be no sharp distinction between what is true and what is false." Unfortunately, Henderson's analysis embodies a major and important error. This feeling of "unknowableness," the "soap in the bath" quality of truth as a concept has fascinated many, and has become a central issue of epistemology (the philosophical theory of knowledge), attracting practical, clever, kind, and thoughtful people away by its siren song. "Truth is a river that is always splitting up into arms that reunite," said Cyril Connolly. "Islanded between the arms, the inhabitants argue for a lifetime as to which is the main river."[8] A superficial understanding of modern physics, with Heisenberg's fascinating uncertainty principle, has helped to confuse medical thinkers further.[9] The more precise our knowledge of the positions of subatomic particles, the less precise, in consequence, must be our knowledge of their velocities and vice versa. If we can never know the whole truth in any situation, what need have we to struggle to think whether to tell or not to tell?

But we must not allow ourselves to be confused, as Henderson was, and as so many others have been, by a failure to distinguish between truth, the abstract concept, of which we shall always have an imperfect grasp, and *telling* the truth, where the intention is all important. Whether or not we can ever fully grasp or express the whole picture, whether we know ultimately what the truth really is, we must speak truthfully, and intend to convey what we understand, or we shall lie. In Sissela Bok's words "The moral question of whether you are lying or not is not *settled* by establishing the truth or falsity of what you say. In order to settle the question, we must know whether you *intend your statement to mislead*."[10]

Most modern thinkers in the field of medical ethics would hold that truthfulness is indeed a central principle of conduct, but that it is capable of coming into conflict with other principles, to which it must occasionally give way. On the other hand, the principle of veracity often receives support from other principles. For instance, it is hard to see how a patient can have autonomy, can make a free choice about matters concerning himself, without some measure of understanding of the facts as they influence the case; and that implies, under normal circumstances, some open, honest discussion with his advisers.

Once the central position of honesty has been established, we still need to examine whether doctors and nurses really do have, as has been suggested, special exemption from being truthful because of the nature of their work, and if so under what circumstances.

It may finally be decided that in a crisis there is no acceptable alternative, as when life is ebbing and truthfulness would bring certain disaster. Alternatively, the moral issue may appear so trivial as not to be worth considering (as, for example, when a doctor is called out at night by a patient who apologizes by saying, "I hope you don't mind me calling you at this time. doctor," and the doctor replies, "No, not at all."). However, occasions of these two types are few, fewer than those in which deliberate deceit would generally be regarded as acceptable in current medical practice, and should regularly be debated "in public" if abuses are to be avoided.[11] To this end it is necessary now to examine critically the arguments commonly used to defend lying to patients.

First comes the argument that it is enormously difficult to put across a technical subject to those with little technical knowledge and understanding, in a situation where so little is predictable. A patient has bowel cancer. With surgery it might be cured, or it might recur. Can the patient understand the effects of treatment? The symptom she is now getting might be due to cancer, there might be secondaries, and they in turn might be suppressible for a long time, or not at all. What future symptoms might occur, how long will she live, how will she die—all these are desperately important questions for the patient, but even for her doctor the answers can only be informed guesses, in an area where uncertainty is so hard to bear.

Yet to say we do not know anything is a lie. As doctors we know a great deal, and *can* make informed guesses or offer likelihoods. The whole truth may be impossible to attain, but truthfulness is not. "I do not know" can be a major piece of honesty. To deprive the patient of honest communication because we cannot know everything is, as we have seen, not only confused thinking but immoral. Thus deprived, the patient cannot plan, he cannot choose. If choice is the crux of morality, it may also, as we have argued elsewhere, be central to health. If he cannot choose, the patient cannot ever be considered to be fully restored to health.[12]

This argument also raises another human failing—to confuse the difficult with the unimportant. Passing information to people who have more restricted background, whether through lack of experience or of understanding, can be extremely difficult and time-consuming, but this is no reason why it should be shunned. Quite the reverse. Like the difficult passages in a piece of music, these tasks should be practiced, studied, and techniques developed so that communication is efficient and effective. For the purposes of informed consent, the patient must be given the information he needs, as a reasonable person, to make a reasoned choice.

The second argument for telling lies to patients is that no patient likes hearing depressing or frightening news. That is certainly true. There must be few who do. But in other walks of life no professional would normally consider it his or her duty to suppress information simply in order to preserve happiness. No accountant, foreseeing bankruptcy in his client's affairs, would chat cheerfully about the Budget or a temporarily reassuring credit account. Yet such suppression of information occurs daily in wards or surgeries throughout the country. Is this what patients themselves want?

In order to find out, a number of studies have been conducted over the past thirty years.[13] In most studies there is a significant minority of patients, perhaps about a fifth, who, if given information, deny having been told. Sometimes this must be pure forgetfulness, sometimes it relates to the lack of skill of the informer, but sometimes with bad or unwelcome news there is an element of what is (perhaps not quite correctly) called "denial." The observer feels that at one level the news has been taken in, but at another its validity or reality has not been accepted. This process has been recognized as a buffer for the mind against the shock of unacceptable news, and often seems to be part of a process leading to its ultimate acceptance.[14] But once this group has been allowed for, most surveys find that, of those who have had or who could have had a diagnosis made of, say, cancer, between two-thirds and three-quarters of those questioned were either glad to have been told, or declared that they would wish to know. Indeed, surveys reveal that most *doctors* would themselves wish to be told the truth, even though (according to earlier studies at least) most of those same doctors said they would not speak openly to their patients—a curious double standard! Thus these surveys have unearthed, at least for the present, a common misunderstanding between doctors and patients, a general preference for openness among patients, and a significant but small group whose wish not to be informed must surely be respected. We return once more to the skill needed to detect such differences in the individual case, and the need for training in such skills.

Why doctors have for so long misunderstood their patients' wishes is perhaps related to the task itself. Doctors don't want to give bad news, just as patients don't want it in abstract, but doctors have the choice of withholding the information, and in so doing protecting themselves from the pain of telling, and from the blame of being the bearer of bad news. In addition it has been suggested that doctors are particularly fearful of death and illness. Montaigne suggested that men have to think about death and be prepared to accept it, and one would think that doctors would get used to death. Yet perhaps this very familiarity has created an obsession that amounts to fear. Just as the police seem over-concerned with violence, and firemen with fire, perhaps doctors have met death in their professional training only as the enemy, never as something to come to terms with, or even as a natural force to be respected and, when the time is ripe, accepted or even welcomed.

Paternalism may be justifiable in the short term, and to "kid" someone, to treat him as a child because he is ill, and perhaps dying, may be very tempting. Yet true respect for that person (adult or child) can only be shown by allowing him allowable choices, by granting him whatever control is left, as weakness gradually undermines his hold on life. If respect is important then at the very least there must be no acceptable or effective alternative to lying in a particular situation if the lie is to be justified.

However, a third argument for lying can be advanced, namely, that truthfulness can actually do harm. "What you don't know can't hurt you" is a phrase in common parlance (though it hardly fits with concepts of presymptomatic screening for preventable disease!). However, it is undeniable that blunt and unfeeling communication of unpleasant truths can cause acute distress, and sometimes long-term disability. The fear that professionals often have of upsetting people, of causing a scene, of making fools of themselves by letting unpleasant emotions flourish, seems to have elevated this argument beyond its natural limits. It is not unusual to find that the fear of creating harm will deter a surgical team from discussing a diagnosis gently with a patient, but not deter it from performing radical and mutilating surgery. Harm is a very personal concept. Most medical schools have, circulating in the refectory, a story about a patient who was informed that he had cancer and then leapt to his death. The intended moral for the medical student is, keep your mouth shut and do no harm. But that may not be the correct lesson to be learned from such cases (which I believe, in any case, to be less numerous than is commonly supposed). The style of telling could have been brutal, with no follow-up or support. It may have been the suggested treatment, not the basic illness, that led the patient to resort to such a desperate measure. Suicide in illness is remarkably rare, but, though tragic, could be seen as a logical response to an overwhelming challenge. No mention is usually made of suicide rates in other circumstances, or the isolation felt by ill and warded patients, or the feelings of anger uncovered when someone takes such precipitate and forbidden action against himself. What these cases do, surely, is argue, not for no telling, but for better telling, for sensitivity and care in determining how much the patient wants to know, explaining carefully in ways the patient can understand, and providing full support and "after-care" as in other treatments.

But even if it is accepted that the short-term effect of telling the truth may sometimes be considerable psychological disturbance, in the long term the balance seems definitely to swing the other way. The effects of lying are dramatically illustrated in "A Case of Obstructed Death?"[15] False information prevented a woman from returning to healthy living after a cancer operation, and robbed her of six months of active life. Also, the long-term effect of lies on the family and, perhaps most importantly, on society, is incalculable. If trust is gradually corroded, "if the wells are poisoned," progress is hard. Mistrust creates lack of communication and increased fear, and this generation has seen just such a fearful myth created around cancer.[16] Just how much harm has been done by this "demonizing" of cancer, preventing people coming to their doctors, or alternatively creating unnecessary attendances on doctors, will probably never be known.

There are doubtless many other reasons why doctors lie to their patients; but these can hardly be used to justify lies, even if we should acknowledge them in passing. Knowledge is power, and certainly doctors, though usually probably for reasons of work-load rather than anything more sinister, like to remain "in control." Health professionals may, like others, wish to protect themselves from confrontation, and may find it easier to coerce or manipulate than to gain permission. There may be a desire to avoid any pressure for change. And there is the constant problem of lack of time.

If the importance of open communication with the patient is accepted, we need to know when to say what. If a patient is going for investigations, it may be possible at that time, before details are known, to have a discussion about whether he would like to know the details. A minor "contract" can be made. "I promise to tell you what I know, if you ask me." Once that time is past, however, it requires skill and sensitivity to assess what a patient wants to know. Allowing the time and opportunity for the patient to ask questions is the most important thing, but one must realize that the patient's apparent question may conceal the one he really wants answered. "Do I have cancer?" may contain the more important questions "How or when will I die?" "Will there be pain?" The doctor will not necessarily be helping by giving an extended pathology lesson. The informer may need to know more: "I don't want to avoid your question, and I promise to answer as truthfully as I can, but first ..." It has been pointed out that in many cases the terminal patient will tell the doctor, not vice versa, if the right opportunities are created and the style and timing is appropriate. Then it is a question of not telling but listening to the truth.[17]

If in spite of all this there still seems to be a need to tell lies, we must be able to justify them. That the person is a child, or "not very bright," will not do. Given the two ends of the spectrum of crisis and triviality, the vast middle range of communication requires honesty, so that autonomy and choice can be maintained. If lies are to be told, there really must be no acceptable alternative. If we break an important moral principle, that principle still retains its force, and its "shadow" has to be acknowledged. As professionals we shall have to ensure that we follow up, that we work through the broken trust or the disillusionment that the lie will bring to the patient, just as we would follow up and work through bad news, a major operation, or a psychiatric "sectioning." This follow-up may also be called for in our relationship with our colleagues if there has been major disagreement about what should be done.

In summary, there are *some* circumstances in which the health professions are probably exempted from society's general requirement for truthfulness. But not telling the truth is usually the same as telling a lie, and a lie requires strong justification. Lying must be a last resort, and we should act as if we were to be called upon to defend the decision in public debate, even if our duty of confidentiality does not allow this in practice. We should always aim to respect the other important principles governing interactions with patients, especially the preservation of the patient's autonomy. When all is said and done, many arguments for individual cases of lying do not hold water. Whether or not knowing the truth is essential to the patient's health, telling the truth is essential to the health of the doctor–patient relationship.

Notes

1. *Primum non nocere*—this is a latinization of a statement which is not directly Hippocratic, but may be derived from the *Epidemics* Book 1 Chapter II: "As to diseases, make a habit of two things—to help, or at least do no harm." *Hippocrates*, 4 Vols. (London: William Heinemann, 1923–31), Vol. I. Translation W. H. S. Jones.
2. Cases collected by the author in his own practice.
3. Case collected by the author.
4. Quoted in Reiser, Dyck, and Curran (eds), *Ethics in Medicine, Historical Perspectives and Contemporary Concerns* (Cambridge, Mass.: MIT Press, 1977).
5. American Medical Association, "Text of the American Medical Association New Principles of Medical Ethics" *American Medical News* (August 1–8 1980), 9.
6. To be found in Reiser *et al.*, op. cit. (see n. 4 above).
7. Lawrence Henderson, "Physician and Patient as a Social System," *New England Journal of Medicine*, 212 (1935).
8. Quoted in W. H. Auden and Louis Kronenberger (eds), *The Faber Book of Aphorisms* (London: Faber, 1962).
9. The uncertainty principle is a consequence of quantum mechanics discovered by Heisenberg in 1927.
10. Sissela Bok, *Lying: Moral Choice in Public and Private Life* (London: Quartet, 1980).
11. John Rawls, *A Theory of Justice* (Cambridge, Mass.: Harvard University Press, Belknap Press, 1971).
12. Op. cit. (see n. 15 above).
13. Summarized well in Robert Veatch, "Truth-telling I" in *Encyclopaedia of Bioethics*, op. cit. (see n. 12 above).
14. The five stages of reacting to bad news, or news of dying, are described in *On Death and Dying* by Elizabeth Kubler-Ross (London: Tavistock, 1970). Not everyone agrees with her model. For another view see a very stimulating article "Therapeutic Uses of Truth" by Michael Simpson in E. Wilkes (ed.), *The Dying Patient* (Lancaster: MTP Press, 1982). "In my model there are only two stages—the stage when you believe in the Kubler-Ross five and the stage when you do not."
15. Roger Higgs, "Truth at the last—A Case of Obstructed Death?", *Journal of Medical Ethics*, 8 (1982), 48–50, and Roger Higgs, "Obstructed Death Revisited," *Journal of Medical Ethics*, 8 (1982), pp. 154–6.
16. Susan Sontag, *Illness as Metaphor* (New York: Farrar, Straus and Giroux, 1978).
17. Cicely Saunders, "Telling Patients," *District Nursing* (now *Queens Nursing Journal*) (September 1963), pp. 149–50, 154.

HOPE

Howard Brody

Those of us who talk about ethical issues in medicine have our spiel on "truth-telling" down pat. We talk about the historical background of the policy of benign deception; about data that show that patients generally suspect the truth anyway; about recent changes in physician behavior in the direction of complete disclosure of unwelcome diagnostic news; and finally, about the important ethical principles of autonomy and individual self-determination. But sooner or later comes the rejoinder, delivered with the air of laying down the trump card: "All of that sounds very good. But how can you possibly justify ever taking away the patient's hope?"

In debates on medical ethics, this question is all too often left unanswered. I believe that there is a satisfactory answer and that it has more to do, as Norman Cousins very correctly pointed out, with the "art of medicine" rather than the ethics of medicine. It is possible to tell the patient his true diagnosis in such a way as to leave him and his family emotionally devastated. It is also possible to prescribe the wrong dose of digoxin or to operate on the left knee for an arthropathy present on the right. We should not confuse botching our jobs with adhering to an erroneous ethical principle.

We know from placebo research how potent the patient's emotions and ideas can be in healing the body. We also know that the physician is placed in a pivotal role to influence the patient's ideas and emotions for better or for worse. Since hope is such a powerful medicine, we ought to manage our therapeutic relationships so as to maximize its effects. But to do so, we ought to have a more precise idea of hope's psychopharmacological properties than is commonly gained from the truth-telling debate.

I would like to offer two rather rash observations about hope in this attempt to advance our understanding. The first is that, while we talk with great facility about the dangers of taking away the patient's hope, I am not sure that we really have the power to do so except in very rare instances.

One does not have to practice medicine for long before one becomes aware of the profound emotional impact that our most innocent, off-handed remarks can have on our patients. As most of us would not have become physicians if we did not have the desire, at some level, to wield power over our fellow creatures, these incidents tend to confirm our satisfying myths of omnipotence. We may forget the much greater numbers of our patients who go on smoking despite our dire warnings, or who always seem to have a few extra penicillin pills in the medicine cabinet despite our firm admonishments to "take the pills four times a day until the prescription is completely gone."

Anecdotes have been told of patients who die of their terminal cancer, firmly convinced that they are in perfect health and that the slides must have been mixed up in the laboratory. I have had an elderly man tell me with great gusto how ten years ago his physicians had told him that he had only six months to live with his prostatic carcinoma. Certainly, anecdotes can be offered to support the opposing view also; but I think that in general hope may be more resilient than we realize. The most callous pronouncement of doom may prompt not despair, but rather an intense commitment to proving that SOB wrong. And, if more sophisticated defense mechanisms fail, denial is not a bad thing to fall back on.

Reprinted from *JAMA*, Vol. 246, No. 13 (September 25, 1981), pp. 1411–1412.

The second rash observation is that it is almost always possible to combine frank and accurate disclosure of the truth with an invigorating infusion of hope. For one thing, in many cases, the actual facts are not as grim as we think, if the patient is motivated to hear the good news along with the bad. We can truthfully tell the patient with terminal cancer, along with, "Statistically I would say that your life span is more likely to be measured in months rather than years," the additional message, "Somehow a few lucky or highly motivated patients seem to beat the odds and live much longer than we expect." The patient, depending on his or her own needs at the time, can choose to hear that the glass is 95% empty or that it is 5% full. …

If we were as good at listening to our patients as we are at telling them things, we would learn that hope is not automatically equated with survival. Hope means different things to different people; and hope means different things to the same person as he moves through different stages of his illness and his emotional reaction to it. The man who last year hoped for a cure for his arthritis may now hope that, on a good day, he can get in nine holes of golf. And, for those unfortunates for whom those who would keep them alive have become truly the "inquisitor" instead of the savior, hope may mean a pain-free and oblivious death.

Giving hope, then, need not consist of, "You really don't have cancer after all," or, "We removed all the cancer surgically and your ten-year survival prognosis is excellent." Giving hope can be: "We will be able to give you medicines to keep you free of pain," or, "You will still be around this weekend to visit with your grandchildren when they come," or, "I will not abandon you." (Which in turn makes us wonder, when patients "lose hope" after being told the truth in a callous, brutal manner, if they are not responding to the unspoken message of the physician's detachment and abandonment rather than to the spoken words.) When we talk to patients and find out what is really worrying them, we can almost always give some realistic assurances.

If we understand the psychopharmacological features of hope in this way, we realize that setting hope-maintaining against truth-telling is to create a false dichotomy. There is no fundamental conflict between our moral duty to preserve hope—to heal our patients with our words and not just with our medicines—and our moral duty to respect our patients as adult human beings who should be given the information they need to make their own free choices about their lives. We as physicians can maintain the demeanor that calms and reassures our patients—the positive sense of "arrogance" described by Franz Ingelfinger—and still take the initiative in disclosing truth. And once we realize that this is possible, we can turn our attention to the real question, which is how to learn and how to teach the skills necessary to do it as well as possible. …

UNIT FIVE

MEDICAL RESEARCH, ALLOCATION, AND JUSTICE

CHAPTER 9: RESEARCH ON HUMAN SUBJECTS AND CHAPTER 10: ALLOCATION OF MEDICAL RESOURCES AND JUSTICE ISSUES IN HEALTH CARE SYSTEMS

Chapter 9 discusses the ethical issues involved with research on human subjects. The chapter begins with several codes (*The Nuremberg Code* and the *Declaration of Helsinki*) which serve as important public policy statements. These statements stress related themes, such as the voluntary and informed consent of the subject, an assessment of the degree of risk to the subjects versus the purported benefits of the research, protections of the subjects' privacy and integrity, and a fair procedure for selecting subjects. In the readings that follow in this chapter, we will further explore these themes.

In his contribution, Arthur Caplan discusses the infamous Tuskegee Syphilis Study in which approximately 400 African-American men who had syphilis were not treated for venereal disease, but were simply monitored to determine the natural progression of the disease. This study continued for 40 years, from 1932 to 1972, even though effective antibiotic treatment with penicillin for syphilis was known to exist in the 1940s. Caplan highlights several important issues in his essay. First, are the data generated by a morally questionable study valid? Second, and more importantly, even if these data are valid, should results from morally questionable studies be cited and used by researchers? Similarly, Paul Ramsey condemns experiments conducted by discussing Willowbrook State School, a home for mentally challenged students in New York. In these experiments, children were left vulnerable to hepatitis, and Ramsey maintains that there was no sound reason for the experiment. In addition, Ramsey argues that the experiments were flawed because other relevant alternatives for treating the hepatitis epidemic were ignored, the personnel of the institution were left vulnerable to hepatitis, and the consent given by the parents of children who participated in the study was morally questionable.

Many of these ethical issues surface in the discussion of how (or whether) randomized clinical trials (RCTs) can be used in a morally appropriate manner. In RCTs, subjects who are members of the control group are known to possess the medical problem under examination, yet are not given the experimental treatment. Samuel Hellman and Deborah Hellman argue that RCTs are morally problematic since they do not allow physicians to satisfy their individualized duty of care to their patients. Physicians who conduct randomized trials, according to Hellman and Hellman, fail to acknowledge the rights of dignity of all of their subjects, since they allow some subjects to experience harms that are intended to benefit society as a whole. Benjamin Freedman responds to the concerns raised by the Hellmans by defending the moral acceptability of RCTs. Freedman argues that for a comparative trial to be ethical, it must begin in, and continue in, a state of *clinical equipoise*. According to Freedman, "...clinical equipoise is a situation in which there exists (or is pending) an honest disagreement in the expert clinical community regarding the comparative merits of two or more forms of treatment for a given condition." Freedman maintains that if this equipoise condition is satisfied throughout the trial, it cannot be said that a subject enrolling in the study is denied a right to treatment, since no medical consensus for or against the appropriate treatment exists. In addition, Freedman challenges the Hellmans' claim that subjects who are part of the control group are used merely as a means, which thereby violates Kant's moral principle (see Chapter 1). He claims that it is clear only that subjects are used as a means, which is not in itself morally objectionable. While Freedman makes clear how the concept of equipoise can be incorporated in a response to concerns about RCTs, he does not elaborate on the concept of equipoise itself. His seminal article "Equipoise and the Ethics of Clinical Research" is included to afford a deeper understanding of this concept.

The focus then moves away from general concerns surrounding RCTs to the particular issues involved in third-world trials of regimens to reduce the transmission of HIV from mother to child. In "The Ethics of Clinical Research in the Third World," Marcia Angell agrees with Freedman that the equipoise requirement must be met for a randomized clinical trial to be morally acceptable. Angell points out, however, that the third-world HIV trials generally included a placebo arm in which subjects do not receive zidovudine (AZT), even though this has been shown to reduce mother-to-infant transmission by approximately 66%. On this basis, Angell suggests that these trials do not meet the equipoise condition. At the end of her article, Angell discusses the question of whether reports of research conducted in an unethical manner should be published, and claims that there has been a retreat from the principles laid out in the Nuremberg Code and the Declaration of Helsinki with respect to clinical trials.

Chapter 10 discusses different perspectives on the justice of allocating scarce medical resources and the moral issues of responsibility and rectification associated with the making of medical errors. In the first selection in the chapter, George Annas critically evaluates several different approaches to allocating transplant organs. Annas argues against a market approach, a method using a selection committee, a lottery system, and the customary system that uses blanket conditions concerning the patient's age or perceived social worth. Annas argues in support of a mixed approach that uses a medical screening, and then allocates organs on a first-come, first-served basis. This approach remains flexible in that it allows individuals in immediate danger of death to "jump" in front of other possible recipients who can survive long enough to wait for another organ.

In "Alcoholics and Liver Transplantation," Cohen, Benjamin, et al., address the specific issue of whether alcoholics should be categorically excluded from receiving liver transplants, given the fact of their alcoholism. They criticize the moral argument supporting exclusion, that alcoholics are morally responsible for their illness due to their chosen personal behavior, by arguing that we do not withhold treatment to other persons who act recklessly or irresponsibly. They criticize the medical argument in support of exclusion, that alcoholic recipients do not fare as well as others, by arguing that in other cases, we allow transplants or other medical procedures even when there is known to be a low probability of survival. They maintain that singling out alcoholics on the basis of these arguments would be arbitrary and unacceptable.

The discussion then turns to the moral issues involved in rationing health care in general. Daniel Callahan argues that rationing health care resources in the United States on the basis of age can be just, since our collective social obligations only involve helping people to live out a natural life span. Our moral obligation is not to provide individuals with any and every form of medical technology that could extend their lives, but only those life-extending technologies necessary for the achievement of a natural life span. Callahan maintains that beyond the point of a natural life span, society should only provide medical means to alleviate suffering. In contrast to Callahan, Norman Daniels argues that the rationing system in place in the United States health care system does not accord with principles of justice. To support this claim, Daniels compares the U.S. system to the British health care system. While the British "say no" to some patients by denying them organ transplants or renal dialysis, the British can appeal to a justice argument when doing so. This is the case since they provide universal access to high-quality healthcare for all their citizens and when a procedure is rationed they make clear which procedures are available for alternative uses. In such a system there must be some limits, and these limits are defined and defended as part of the best overall plan for securing citizens' health and well-being. In the U.S. healthcare system, by contrast, Daniels points out that doctors are given financial incentives to limit care. Such "gatekeeper" bonuses undermine the notion that the doctor serves as the patient's agent, and therefore "saying no" in the United States system is much more difficult since no appeal to the justice of rationing care is available. Marcia Angell raises concerns about rationing that are very similar to those discussed by Daniels. Angell first sketches a brief history of the development of the "third-party payer" system in the U.S. Angell points out that while the doctor's duty should be to meet the healthcare needs of his or her individual patient, today's doctors have been cast into a double role in which they must also make decisions about how to best allocate society's resources. Angell criticizes this development in which doctors also serve as agents of managed care plans by pointing out several serious problems with this role.

The final readings in the chapter address the topic of medical errors. While everyone agrees that medical errors are bad and should be minimized, it is unclear what to do to minimize them and how to respond to those harmed by medical errors. In 1999, the Institute of Medicine (IOM) published a report entitled *To Err Is Human: Building a Safer Health System*. This report suggested that the rate of medical errors in the

United States is surprisingly high, and that the cause of the problem stems from features of the healthcare delivery system, not simply from incompetence or lack of attention on the part of individual medical professionals. The IOM report points to research that suggests that at least 44,000 Americans die each year as a result of medical errors, with some studies indicating that the number may be as high as 98,000. This means that deaths from medical errors represent approximately the fourth-leading to the eighth-leading cause of death in the United States (depending on whether the lower or higher figure is adopted). As the IOM report notes, more people die in a given year as a result of medical errors than from motor vehicle accidents. One scholar has noted that medical errors are responsible for as many deaths as three jumbo jet crashes every two days. Medical errors are the great "silent killer," compared with more newsworthy (but less deadly) events such as airline crashes or automobile accidents.

The remainder of the selections in this chapter address the philosophical and ethical issues brought into focus by the IOM report. Andrew Thurman argues from both an ethical and a legal basis in support of the idea of medical professionals disclosing medical errors. From an ethical perspective, covering up medical errors erodes the trust at the heart of the physician/patient relationship, as well as precludes the possibility of learning from errors. As discussed in Chapters 5 and 8, the doctrine of informed consent is deeply rooted in medical ethics and is central to autonomous decision-making by patients. Thurman points out that since the doctrine of informed consent is also embedded in health care law, failing to disclose medical errors to patients does not adequately allow for informed decision-making, especially concerning continued treatment by particular medical providers. Thurman addresses three frequently cited barriers to informing patients of medical errors, and argues that none of these barriers provides a good reason for failing to disclose. He concludes by briefly discussing a process for disclosing medical errors to patients. This connects closely to the next selection, "Guidelines for Disclosure and Discussion of Conditions and Events with Patients, Families, and Guardians," which is reprinted from the University of Pittsburgh Medical Center Presbyterian Policy and Procedure Manual. This is one example of a policy that serves to clearly define a process for "truth-telling" even when all of the facts following a medical error may not be known.

Finally, Steve Kraman and Ginny Hamm report their experiences in the wake of a policy put into effect at a Veteran's Affairs (VA) Medical Center in Lexington, Kentucky in 1987. In essence, this VA hospital practices a policy of extreme honesty. In the event of an adverse event, after the incident is identified, a fact-finding mission is undertaken to determine whether the standard of care was violated, whether a medical error occurred, and the extent of harm (if any) to the patient.[1] Once consensus is reached concerning the event, assuming that it was determined to be a medical error, the patient or next of kin are contacted and a full disclosure is made. An apology is offered and responsibility for the error is assumed by the hospital. Then, a settlement is discussed with the patient or next of kin, and they are told of the funds available within the VA system. The parties have the choice to go outside the VA system as well, but help is offered to the parties to fill out any necessary paperwork for filing a claim with the VA. Finally, the VA hospital aims to improve the defective systems that contributed to the error. As Kraman and Hamm report, the results of this policy at one particular VA medical center suggest that extreme honesty results in less money being paid out in lawsuits, increases patient satisfaction, and increases the satisfaction of the medical professionals working at the hospital. The debate surrounding the IOM findings on medical errors is one of the newest debates within medical ethics, yet the literature on this topic at this date suggests that ethical, legal, and financial considerations may all point in the same direction toward timely disclosure of medical errors to those affected.

CRITICAL THINKING TOOL: ANALYSIS OF STATISTICS AND STUDIES

It is common for arguments to be based on statistical data or on a study. In this section, we discuss how to analyze statistical arguments as well as pose critical thinking questions about studies, referring to readings from Chapters 9 and 10. The purpose is to offer a more reflective understanding of the arguments and studies discussed in this chapter, which will help you to determine whether a statistical argument or study logically supports its conclusion.

A statistical argument is an inductive argument that attempts to establish its conclusion with a certain probability, not a deductive argument that attempts to establish its claim with certainty (see Chapter 2). In general, there are three main factors we need to determine to assess the acceptability of a statistical study. First, we need to know when the study was taken. Outdated data are often misleading since they do not reflect recent changes or advances. Second, we must know the size of the study. In Chapter 2, we discussed the fallacy of hasty generalization. In this fallacy, the logical error resides in drawing an inference on the basis of unusual cases or on the basis of a single case. If the sample size is too small, such as a sample of one person, then we cannot logically support any inferences relating to a class larger than that consisting of one individual! Finally, we need to determine the diversity of the study. The important point is that the sample population must be representative of the target population. What this means is that the sample population must possess all features of the target population relevant to the property under consideration in the study, and it must possess them in the same proportions as the target population. This does not mean, though, that to be representative a sample must possess the relevant properties in the same proportions as the population in general, as long as the target population is some subset of the general population. This third factor relates to the fallacy of biased statistics, discussed in Chapter 2. In this logical error, the mistake does not derive specifically from the size of the sample population, but instead, from a "mismatch" between the sample and target populations. For example, if one attempted to logically support an inference about the health of American men by studying Olympic athletes from the U.S., this study would be skewed, even if the sample were large enough to logically support other inferences. These fallacies remind us that all three of these factors are important when critically analyzing statistical arguments.

The readings on medical errors in Chapter 10 discuss the problem of medical errors in the wake of the IOM report, *To Err Is Human*. This report, issued in 1999, caused quite a stir given its finding that an exceptionally high rate of medical errors exists in U.S. hospitals. The report refers to two studies, one conducted in Colorado and Utah, and the other conducted in New York. These studies found that adverse events occurred in 2.9 percent and 3.7 percent of hospitalizations, respectively. The report also cites statistics that in Colorado and Utah hospitals, 6.6 percent of adverse events led to death, as compared with 13.6 percent in the hospitals in New York. In both studies, over half of the adverse events were deemed preventable. The IOM report notes that if these results are extrapolated to the over 33.6 million hospital admissions to U.S. hospitals in 1997, the results of the Colorado and Utah study imply that at least 44,000 Americans die each year as a result of medical errors. The results of the New York study suggest that as many as 98,000 may die as a result of medical mistakes.[2] These figures are shockingly high, since little attention has been focused on medical errors, especially given that even the more conservative figure is greater than the annual number of deaths resulting from widely discussed events such as automobile accidents, breast cancer, or AIDS in the Unites States.

What are we to think of these figures? Critically thinking about these statistics suggests a few points. First, there is no reason to think that the studies referred to in the IOM report are flawed with respect to the date, size, or diversity of the studies. They are good studies according to these criteria. The IOM report's figures were widely reported in the public media, given the surprising conclusion that the deaths attributable to medical errors in fact constitute approximately the eighth-leading cause of death to the fourth-leading cause of death, depending on the study used. However, while the 44,000 and 98,000 figures were considered among the central findings of the report, critically analyzing the study suggests that the IOM report may have underestimated the rate of medical error.

This is the case for at least two reasons. First, not all medical errors lead to death. If the 44,000 and 98,000 figures derived from the extrapolation are viewed as suggestive of the rate of U.S. medical errors, this is seriously misleading, since these figures only focus on deaths caused by medical errors. These figures do not include medical errors that result in serious harm to patients, or mistakes that may result in minor harm and go undetected (i.e., mistakes that result in a patient's condition temporarily worsening that are interpreted as a spontaneous downturn). Second, it is reasonable to suspect that at least as many (if not more) errors occur in outpatient settings as in inpatient settings. However, the data discussed in the IOM report refer only to medical errors that occur in hospital admissions and inpatient treatment. If we widen the scope to include this other class of patients, it is almost certainly the case that the number of medical errors that lead to death is significantly higher than that suggested by the IOM figures. And, in addition, there is a large number of medical errors that do not result in death that occur in outpatient settings that also go unrecognized. It is important to emphasize that the foregoing remarks are not intended as a criticism of the IOM report—the statistical data discussed in the report, it is reasonable to think, are legitimate. The point is simply that the target population is possibly larger than expected! The findings suggested by the IOM report are too conservative, and it is reasonable to think that a larger number of medical errors occur than suggested by the report.

In the reading by Kraman and Hamm included in Chapter 10, an approach for addressing and reconciling the harm stemming from medical mistakes is discussed. Kraman and Hamm review a policy of "extreme honesty" put in place at a Veteran's Administration hospital in Lexington, Kentucky, following two large adverse malpractice judgments. These judgments alone resulted in more than one million dollars in payouts by the hospital to those harmed as a result of medical errors. Kraman and Hamm report that the change to the policy of "extreme honesty" has led to a dramatic decrease in payouts resulting from therapeutic or diagnostic mistakes. In particular, the VA paid out an average of only $190,000 per year over seven years. In the seven years after the policy went into effect, only eight claims went to trial, at an estimated cost of $250,000 each in legal fees. Of those, seven were dismissed and the last was won by the hospital. As a result of this policy change, the hospital has realized a multimillion dollar savings in payments and legal fees per year. Kraman and Hamm note that the Department of Veteran Affairs now requires such a policy for all of its facilities.

This "honesty policy" is somewhat similar to the UPMC-PH's "Guidelines for Disclosure and Discussion of Conditions and Events with Patients, Families, and Guardians" (included in Chapter 10). Kraman and Hamm's article may seem to suggest that such an "honesty policy" is a good idea for all hospitals, both in terms of morality as well as in economic terms, but there are several reasons to think that such a conclusion is too broad.[3] The clientele served by VA hospitals is very different from the patients who are served by other hospitals: their patients are veterans who do not elect or cannot elect to receive care at other hospitals. It is possible that these VA patients would be less inclined to sue the hospital for damages resulting from a medical error disclosed by the staff, given the fact that they may have no other options for further care and may simply feel grateful for the medical care they receive. This may distinguish them from typical patients who receive care at public or private hospitals. In addition, this policy has only been tested in one VA hospital. For these reasons, we should be careful in generalizing these conclusions in an attempt to support inferences about other VA hospitals, much less inferences about what might be the best policy at other public or private hospitals.

We have discussed three factors for determining whether a study is a "good" study—that is, whether the study will logically support inferences about a target population. But what questions should we ask to determine whether a study is *morally good*? There are significant ethical questions that underlie the factors we have been using in our discussion of statistical studies. For instance, we have emphasized that it is crucial that the sample be sufficiently large and representative, but the manner in which the subjects are recruited is just as important from the moral point of view. The subjects must be capable of providing voluntary, informed consent, and must have done so prior to participation in the study. Meeting this requirement can be more difficult than it initially appears. For instance, it is common on college campuses for students to be offered the opportunity to participate in experiments conducted by their instructor (often for extra credit or some other incentive). Researchers may find it easier to recruit subjects in this way, since they are drawing from a "captive" audience. Yet, such "convenience" samples raise both methodological and moral problems. If the sample is drawn only from college freshmen who are enrolled in an introductory psychology course, it is not always the case that the results of such studies will be generalizable across a larger population. The representativeness condition may not be satisfied. In addition, are students or other possible subjects in a vulnerable position truly providing voluntary participation? If this is not the case, then the experiment is flawed from an ethical point of view.

There are several important concepts bearing on studies with which you should be familiar. First, a *randomized* clinical trial is one in which subjects are randomly placed in different study groups to determine their response to a treatment or therapy. One group consists of the "treatment" arm of the study, and subjects in this group actually receive the experimental therapy itself. The other group is the "control" group, and members of this group either receive no treatment, or an alternative treatment, to assess the efficacy of the experimental therapy under study. It is well-known that subjects experience a positive change in their perceived health from the very idea of taking a drug or participating in a medical study. This is the *placebo effect*, and it is important for the researchers to tease apart what positive change is due to the therapy or treatment in question, and what change is due simply to the subjects' positive state of mind. To accomplish this task, subjects are often unaware of what arm of the study they occupy. In a *single-blinded* trial, usually the subject (but sometimes the researcher) is unaware of whether or not they are in fact receiving the medical therapy. The power of suggestion plays a role in the perceptions of researchers as well. A researcher who knows that a certain subject is part of the treatment group may be inclined to perceive that subject's progress as more favorable as compared with a subject she knows to occupy the control arm, especially if that subject receives a *placebo*, which is an inert substance such as a sugar pill. To control for this contingency, many studies are *double-blinded* so that both the subjects and the researchers are unaware of the arm of the study occupied by each subject.

Blinded studies raise many complex ethical questions. While the benefits of engaging in blinded studies seem clear, if the subjects do not know what arm of the study they will occupy, it is unclear whether they can truly provide voluntary *informed* consent concerning their participation. In addition, it seems unfair to actively recruit subjects who cannot in fact receive any benefit if they are members of the control arm of the study. This second possible problem is addressed by the concept of equipoise (discussed earlier): randomized, double-blinded clinical trials are ethically acceptable only if the different arms of the study are in clinical equipoise. The equipoise condition is satisfied just in case there is an honest disagreement in the clinical community regarding the comparative merits of the forms of treatment employed. The equipoise condition can be satisfied even if the control arm consists of a placebo or no treatment, so long as there is no consensus among experts about whether the therapy provided is superior to no treatment.

A particular study discussed in Chapter 9 raises these ethical issues in a pointed manner. The case concerns studies performed in the third world that examined the usage of zidovudine (AZT) to reduce the transmission of HIV from mother to child during pregnancy. As discussed earlier, a study known as the AIDS Clinical Trial Group (ACTG) 076 determined in 1994 that the use of zidovudine during pregnancy reduced the rate of transmission from mother to child from 25% to approximately 8%. The ethical controversy discussed in Chapter 9 stems from later studies that are based on the 076 study. As discussed by Bayer (Chapter 7), the 076 protocol is very demanding in that it calls for HIV-positive pregnant women to take five doses of zidovudine during the second and third trimesters of pregnancy, as well as approve of an intravenous dose of zidovudine during delivery. The entire 076 therapy costs more than $1000 per pregnancy, yet this is much too costly for women in third-world nations.[4]

An effective yet less costly alternative was needed. A series of HIV studies were performed in Thailand, the Ivory Coast, and Gambia. For instance, in Thailand 198 pregnant women received a short course of AZT, and 199 women received a placebo from 36 weeks gestation until delivery. Transmission rates were reported to be 9.2% in the AZT group and 18.6 percent in the placebo group.

This study was supported by the United States and eleven other developing nations, and the fact that this study took place was made public in 1997. The ethical acceptability of these later studies are debated to this day. The ethical concerns stem from the claim that the risk/benefit ratio for women in the placebo group makes this experiment unacceptable; the assessment of the risk/benefit ratio is tied to the concept of clinical equipoise. The argument against the trial, then, is that the arms of the study are not in equipoise. This is the case because given the accepted findings of the 076 protocol, there is no genuine disagreement in the clinical community between the effectiveness of AZT treatment on the one hand and no treatment (placebo) on the other. The members of the control group, one may claim, are disadvantaged by virtue of the randomization, and therefore, the experiment is morally unacceptable.

The common response to this argument is that the members of the control group in the Thai experiment were not disadvantaged by the randomization. In fact, one may claim, being a subject in the study was the only likely way that HIV-positive women in Thailand could have the opportunity to receive zidovudine in the first place. The reason for this is that even the short course costs $50 to $80 per pregnancy, yet the average health budget in the countries in which the short course was tested was approximately $10 per person, per year.[5] Hence, this argument states that even though the women in the control group received no direct benefit in the course of participating in the experiment, since this is their "only chance" to receive the medical treatment, it is not correct to say that these women were disadvantaged by the randomization process in the experiment.

This argument and reply does an excellent job of illustrating the type of ethical questions that surround blinded clinical trials. It is important to see that these questions are not simply queries concerning whether the methodology employed in the study will damage its ability to logically support inferences about a target population. Instead, these concerns arise from philosophical questioning and a critical analysis of the ethical features of such studies.

What can be said about this argument and the reply by its opponent? It is (unfortunately) true that for the Thai women who were members of the control group, their participation in the study was their only reasonable opportunity to receive zidovudine. However, it is unclear what real force this point carries in this debate, since there are two concerns that appear to be conflated in the opponent's argument. The fact that the Thai women would not otherwise have any reasonable opportunity to receive AZT treatment raises a justice issue: while such treatment became part of the standard of care for women in the United States following the 076 study, in other parts of the world, persons receive less aggressive health care. The central issue with respect to the ethical status of the short course AZT experiments concerns whether or not the trials met the requirement of clinical equipoise. There was no honest disagreement in the clinical community regarding the comparative merits of treatment with AZT or no treatment with AZT, if the goal is to reduce the transmission of HIV from mother to child during pregnancy. For this reason, the trial does not meet the condition of clinical equipoise, and as such is ethically unacceptable.

Those who maintain that the trials were ethically acceptable wish to relativize the application of the concept of equipoise so that it reflects whether or not the treatment under consideration is part of the standard of care in the community in which the study takes place. One of their main claims is that the long course of AZT was not part of the standard of care in Thailand or the African nations in which the short course studies took place. For this reason, it is claimed that the equipoise condition is not violated and there was no clear agreement in the clinical community concerning the comparative merits or usage of AZT. This conclusion does not follow, however, since the fact that AZT treatment is not part of the standard of care in the third world relates to an issue concerning the *justice* of allocating health care resources—it does not ground any conclusion concerning the equipoise condition. Put in other words, the concept of clinical equipoise concerns (according to Freedman) the "... comparative merits of two or more forms of treatment for a given condition," and does not relate to the probability that a person in a certain community will be able to receive that treatment or whether that treatment is part of the standard of care. This conflates issues about the justice of allocating medical resources with concerns about the comparative efficacy of different treatments. The points about AZT treatment as the local "standard of care" and the satisfaction of the equipoise condition are separable; even if no reasonable disagreement concerning the relative merits of different treatments exists (i.e., the equipoise condition is satisfied), whether a treatment becomes part of the standard of care is a function of additional pragmatic and economic factors. The fact that it was the subjects' only chance to receive AZT therapy is immaterial in establishing that the equipoise condition is satisfied. Since the requirement of clinical equipoise was not met in the short course AZT trials, it is reasonable to conclude that these trials are ethically unacceptable.

Notes

1. The additional details of the procedure not contained in Kraman and Hamm's article are derived from Dr. Steve Kraman's presentation, "Full Disclosure in Risk Management: The Lexington VA Experience," at the Michigan State Medical Society's Fifth Annual Conference on Bioethics, October 6, 2001.
2. The statistics in this paragraph can be found in Kohn, L., Corrigan, J., and Donaldson, M., (eds.) Committee on Quality of Healthcare in America (Institute of Medicine). 1999. *To Err Is Human: Building a Safer Health System.* (Washington, D.C.: National Academy Press), pp. 1–2.
3. I should not be understood as saying that Kraman and Hamm are suggesting this, only that one may think that given the success of this VA hospital's "extreme honesty policy," all other hospitals should follow suit.
4. The discussion here is indebted to Barnbaum, D., and Byron, M. *Research Ethics* (Prentice Hall, 2001), pp. 4–6.
5. Barnbaum and Byron, *Research Ethics* (Prentice Hall, 2001), p. 5.

CHAPTER 9

RESEARCH ON HUMAN SUBJECTS

NUREMBERG CODE

1. The voluntary consent of the human subject is absolutely essential. This means that the person involved should have legal capacity to give consent; should be so situated as to be able to exercise free power of choice, without the intervention of any element of force, fraud, deceit, duress, over-reaching, or other ulterior form of constraint or coercion; and should have sufficient knowledge and comprehension of the elements of the subject matter involved as to enable him to make an understanding and enlightened decision. This latter element requires that before the acceptance of an affirmative decision by the experimental subject there should be made known to him the nature, duration, and purpose of the experiment; the method and means by which it is to be conducted; all inconveniences and hazards reasonably to be expected; and the effects upon his health or person which may possibly come from his participation in the experiment.

   The duty and responsibility for ascertaining the quality of the consent rest upon each individual who initiates, directs or engages in the experiment. It is a personal duty and responsibility which may not be delegated to another with impunity.

2. The experiment should be such as to yield fruitful results for the good of society, unprocurable by other methods or means of study, and not random and unnecessary in nature.

3. The experiment should be so designed and based on the results of animal experimentation and a knowledge of the natural history of the disease or other problem under study that the anticipated results will justify the performance of the experiment.

4. The experiment should be so conducted as to avoid all unnecessary physical and mental suffering and injury.

5. No experiment should be conducted where there is an *a priori* reason to believe that death or disabling injury will occur; except, perhaps, in those experiments where the experimental physicians also serve as subjects.

6. The degree of risk to be taken should never exceed that determined by the humanitarian importance of the problem to be solved by the experiment.

7. Proper preparations should be made and adequate facilities provided to protect the experimental subject against even remote possibilities of injury, disability, or death.
8. The experiment should be conducted only by scientifically qualified persons. The highest degree of skill and care should be required through all stages of the experiment of those who conduct or engage in the experiment.
9. During the course of the experiment the human subject should be at liberty to bring the experiment to an end if he has reached the physical or mental state where continuation of the experiment seems to him to be impossible.
10. During the course of the experiment the scientist in charge must be prepared to terminate the experiment at any stage, if he has probable cause to believe, in the exercise of the good faith, superior skill and careful judgment required of him that a continuation of the experiment is likely to result in injury, disability, or death to the experimental subject.

WORLD MEDICAL ASSOCIATION DECLARATION OF HELSINKI

ETHICAL PRINCIPLES FOR MEDICAL RESEARCH INVOLVING HUMAN SUBJECTS

Adopted by the 18th WMA General Assembly
Helsinki, Finland, June 1964
and amended by the
29th WMA General Assembly, Tokyo, Japan, October 1975
35th WMA General Assembly, Venice, Italy, October 1983
41st WMA General Assembly, Hong Kong, September 1989
48th WMA General Assembly, Somerset West, Republic of South Africa, October 1996
and the
52nd WMA General Assembly, Edinburgh, Scotland, October 2000
Note of Clarification on Paragraph 29 added by the WMA General Assembly, Washington 2002

A. INTRODUCTION

1. The World Medical Association has developed the Declaration of Helsinki as a statement of ethical principles to provide guidance to physicians and other participants in medical research involving human subjects. Medical research involving human subjects includes research on identifiable human material or identifiable data.
2. It is the duty of the physician to promote and safeguard the health of the people. The physician's knowledge and conscience are dedicated to the fulfillment of this duty.

3. The Declaration of Geneva of the World Medical Association binds the physician with the words, "The health of my patient will be my first consideration," and the International Code of Medical Ethics declares that, "A physician shall act only in the patient's interest when providing medical care which might have the effect of weakening the physical and mental condition of the patient."
4. Medical progress is based on research which ultimately must rest in part on experimentation involving human subjects.
5. In medical research on human subjects, considerations related to the well-being of the human subject should take precedence over the interests of science and society.
6. The primary purpose of medical research involving human subjects is to improve prophylactic, diagnostic and therapeutic procedures and the understanding of the aetiology and pathogenesis of disease. Even the best proven prophylactic, diagnostic, and therapeutic methods must continuously be challenged through research for their effectiveness, efficiency, accessibility and quality.
7. In current medical practice and in medical research, most prophylactic, diagnostic and therapeutic procedures involve risks and burdens.
8. Medical research is subject to ethical standards that promote respect for all human beings and protect their health and rights. Some research populations are vulnerable and need special protection. The particular needs of the economically and medically disadvantaged must be recognized. Special attention is also required for those who cannot give or refuse consent for themselves, for those who may be subject to giving consent under duress, for those who will not benefit personally from the research and for those for whom the research is combined with care.
9. Research Investigators should be aware of the ethical, legal and regulatory requirements for research on human subjects in their own countries as well as applicable international requirements. No national ethical, legal or regulatory requirement should be allowed to reduce or eliminate any of the protections for human subjects set forth in this Declaration.

B. BASIC PRINCIPLES FOR ALL MEDICAL RESEARCH

10. It is the duty of the physician in medical research to protect the life, health, privacy, and dignity of the human subject.
11. Medical research involving human subjects must conform to generally accepted scientific principles, be based on a thorough knowledge of the scientific literature, other relevant sources of information, and on adequate laboratory and, where appropriate, animal experimentation.
12. Appropriate caution must be exercised in the conduct of research which may affect the environment, and the welfare of animals used for research must be respected.
13. The design and performance of each experimental procedure involving human subjects should be clearly formulated in an experimental protocol. This protocol should be submitted for consideration, comment, guidance, and where appropriate, approval to a specially appointed ethical review committee, which must be independent of the investigator, the sponsor or any other kind of undue influence. This independent committee should be in conformity with the laws and regulations of the country in which the research experiment is performed. The committee has the right to monitor ongoing trials. The researcher has the obligation to provide monitoring information to the committee, especially any serious adverse events. The

researcher should also submit to the committee, for review, information regarding funding, sponsors, institutional affiliations, other potential conflicts of interest and incentives for subjects.

14. The research protocol should always contain a statement of the ethical considerations involved and should indicate that there is compliance with the principles enunciated in this Declaration.
15. Medical research involving human subjects should be conducted only by scientifically qualified persons and under the supervision of a clinically competent medical person. The responsibility for the human subject must always rest with a medically qualified person and never rest on the subject of the research, even though the subject has given consent.
16. Every medical research project involving human subjects should be preceded by careful assessment of predictable risks and burdens in comparison with foreseeable benefits to the subject or to others. This does not preclude the participation of healthy volunteers in medical research. The design of all studies should be publicly available.
17. Physicians should abstain from engaging in research projects involving human subjects unless they are confident that the risks involved have been adequately assessed and can be satisfactorily managed. Physicians should cease any investigation if the risks are found to outweigh the potential benefits or if there is conclusive proof of positive and beneficial results.
18. Medical research involving human subjects should only be conducted if the importance of the objective outweighs the inherent risks and burdens to the subject. This is especially important when the human subjects are healthy volunteers.
19. Medical research is only justified if there is a reasonable likelihood that the populations in which the research is carried out stand to benefit from the results of the research.
20. The subjects must be volunteers and informed participants in the research project.
21. The right of research subjects to safeguard their integrity must always be respected. Every precaution should be taken to respect the privacy of the subject, the confidentiality of the patient's information and to minimize the impact of the study on the subject's physical and mental integrity and on the personality of the subject.
22. In any research on human beings, each potential subject must be adequately informed of the aims, methods, sources of funding, any possible conflicts of interest, institutional affiliations of the researcher, the anticipated benefits and potential risks of the study and the discomfort it may entail. The subject should be informed of the right to abstain from participation in the study or to withdraw consent to participate at any time without reprisal. After ensuring that the subject has understood the information, the physician should then obtain the subject's freely-given informed consent, preferably in writing. If the consent cannot be obtained in writing, the non-written consent must be formally documented and witnessed.
23. When obtaining informed consent for the research project the physician should be particularly cautious if the subject is in a dependent relationship with the physician or may consent under duress. In that case the informed consent should be obtained by a well-informed physician who is not engaged in the investigation and who is completely independent of this relationship.
24. For a research subject who is legally incompetent, physically or mentally incapable of giving consent or is a legally incompetent minor, the investigator must obtain informed consent from the legally authorized representative in accordance with applicable law. These groups should not be included in research unless the research is necessary to promote the health

of the population represented and this research cannot instead be performed on legally competent persons.

25. When a subject deemed legally incompetent, such as a minor child, is able to give assent to decisions about participation in research, the investigator must obtain that assent in addition to the consent of the legally authorized representative.

26. Research on individuals from whom it is not possible to obtain consent, including proxy or advance consent, should be done only if the physical/mental condition that prevents obtaining informed consent is a necessary characteristic of the research population. The specific reasons for involving research subjects with a condition that renders them unable to give informed consent should be stated in the experimental protocol for consideration and approval of the review committee. The protocol should state that consent to remain in the research should be obtained as soon as possible from the individual or a legally authorized surrogate.

27. Both authors and publishers have ethical obligations. In publication of the results of research, the investigators are obliged to preserve the accuracy of the results. Negative as well as positive results should be published or otherwise publicly available. Sources of funding, institutional affiliations and any possible conflicts of interest should be declared in the publication. Reports of experimentation not in accordance with the principles laid down in this Declaration should not be accepted for publication.

C. ADDITIONAL PRINCIPLES FOR MEDICAL RESEARCH COMBINED WITH MEDICAL CARE

28. The physician may combine medical research with medical care, only to the extent that the research is justified by its potential prophylactic, diagnostic or therapeutic value. When medical research is combined with medical care, additional standards apply to protect the patients who are research subjects.

29. The benefits, risks, burdens and effectiveness of a new method should be tested against those of the best current prophylactic, diagnostic, and therapeutic methods. This does not exclude the use of placebo, or no treatment, in studies where no proven prophylactic, diagnostic or therapeutic method exists.

30. At the conclusion of the study, every patient entered into the study should be assured of access to the best proven prophylactic, diagnostic and therapeutic methods identified by the study.

31. The physician should fully inform the patient which aspects of the care are related to the research. The refusal of a patient to participate in a study must never interfere with the patient-physician relationship.

32. In the treatment of a patient, where proven prophylactic, diagnostic and therapeutic methods do not exist or have been ineffective, the physician, with informed consent from the patient, must be free to use unproven or new prophylactic, diagnostic and therapeutic measures, if in the physician's judgement it offers hope of saving life, re-establishing health or alleviating suffering. Where possible, these measures should be made the object of research, designed to evaluate their safety and efficacy. In all cases, new infomation should be recorded and, where appropriate, published. The other relevant guidelines of this Declaration should be followed.

FOOTNOTE

Note of Clarification on Paragraph 29 of the WMA Declaration of Helsinki

The WMA hereby reaffirms its position that extreme care must be taken in making use of a placebo-controlled trial and that in general this methodology should only be used in the absence of existing proven therapy. However, a placebo-controlled trial may be ethically acceptable, even if proven therapy is available, under the following circumstances:

- Where for compelling and scientifically sound methodological reasons its use is necessary to determine the efficacy or safety of a prophylactic, diagnostic or therapeutic method; or
- Where a prophylactic, diagnostic or therapeutic method is being investigated for a minor condition and the patients who receive placebo will not be subject to any additional risk of serious or irreversible harm.

All other provisions of the Declaration of Helsinki must be adhered to, especially the need for appropriate ethical and scientific review.

WHEN EVIL INTRUDES: THE LEGACY OF THE TUSKEGEE SYPHILIS STUDY

Arthur L. Caplan

This year [1992] marks the twentieth anniversary of the end of the Tuskegee syphilis study, one of the more notorious episodes in the history of human subjects research in the United States. Begun in 1932, the study was purportedly designed to determine the natural history of untreated syphilis in a population of some 400 black men in Tuskegee, Alabama. The research subjects, all of whom had syphilis at the time they were enrolled in the study, were matched against 200 uninfected controls.

Though the subjects had received the standard heavy metals therapy available in 1932, they were denied antibiotic therapy when it became clear in the 1940s that penicillin was a safe and effective treatment for the disease. Subjects were recruited with misleading promises of "special free treatment" (actually spinal taps done without anesthesia to study the neurological effects of syphilis), and were enrolled without their informed consent. Disclosure of the ongoing research in the popular media in 1972 led to the termination of the study and ultimately to the National Research Act of 1974, which mandates institutional review board (IRB) approval of all federally funded proposed research with human subjects.

As final payments are being made under the agreement that settled a class action lawsuit brought on behalf of the subjects of the Tuskegee study, the articles that follow look at different facets of Tuskegee's legacy. Should the results of an immorally conducted study continue to serve as the "gold standard" in our clinical understanding of syphilis? How shall we strike a balance between protecting vulnerable classes of subjects already discriminated against and seeing that minorities are adequately represented in—and reap the benefits of—clinical trials? What lingering meanings does Tuskegee have in the African American community, and how do those meanings affect current efforts

Reprinted with permission of the author and the publisher from *The Hastings Center Report*, Vol. 22, No. 6 (1992), pp. 29–32.

not only to conduct biomedical research, but also to provide effective health care in the community? And finally, what messages do race, or other kinds of difference, carry in our culture?

—Bette-Jean Crigger

Twenty years ago Peter Buxtun, a public health official working for the United States Public Health Service, complained to a reporter for the Associated Press that he was deeply concerned about the morality of an ongoing study being sponsored by the Public Health Service—a study compiling information about the course and effects of syphilis in human beings based upon medical examinations of poor black men in Macon County, Alabama. The men, or more accurately, those still living, had been coming in for annual examinations for forty years. They were not receiving standard therapy for syphilis. In late July of 1972 the *Washington Star* and the *New York Times* ran front-page stories based on Buxtun's concerns about what has been called the longest running "nontherapeutic experiment" on human beings in medical history and "the most notorious case of prolonged and knowing violation of subject's rights"—the Tuskegee study.[1]

Buxtun went public with his ethical concerns after years of complaining to officials from the Centers for Disease Control and the Public Health Service with no apparent effect. His decision to blow the whistle led to a series of sensational congressional hearings chaired by Senator Edward Kennedy in February and March of 1973. Legislators and federal officials expressed outrage over the immorality of a study in which poor, illiterate men had been deceived and given placebo treatment rather than standard therapy so that more could be learned about syphilis. Americans found it hard to believe that the Public Health Service had intentionally and systematically duped men with a disease as serious as syphilis—contagious, disabling, and life-threatening—for more than forty years.

The level of outrage about the Tuskegee study was enormous. One CDC official labeled the experiment akin to "genocide."[2] As a result of public anger over the immorality of the study, Congress created an ad hoc blue ribbon panel to review both the Tuskegee study and the adequacy of existing protections for subjects in all federally sponsored research. Even though the panel did not receive all the information about the study that the government had available,[3] they were still concerned enough about what had taken place to recommend the creation of a national board with the resources to reexamine all aspects of human experimentation in the United States. Congress, in 1974, created the National Commission for the Protection of Human Subjects of Biomedical and Behavioral Research which, in its seventeen reports and numerous appendix volumes, laid the foundation for the ethical requirements that govern the conduct of research on human subjects in the United States to this day.

Syphilis continues to challenge America's and the world's medical, public health, and moral resources. While there are a variety of antibiotics available to treat the disease, it has proven to be a stubborn and resilient foe. The Centers for Disease Control has found steady and alarming increases in the incidence of primary and secondary syphilis over the past decade. It is still a major public health problem in the United States today, especially among young black males.

The rise in the incidence of the disease has ensured that writings about the diagnosis, management, and treatment of syphilis are prominently featured in the professional literature of public health and biomedicine as well as in standard textbooks about venereal and infectious diseases. Ongoing concern about syphilis has led physicians and public health officials to draw upon as much information as they can about the course of the disease. One of the bitter if generally unacknowledged ironies of the Tuskegee study is that, while it now occupies a special place of shame in the annals of human experimentation, its findings are still widely cited by the contemporary biomedical community.

In looking at instances of scientific misconduct and moral malfeasance with respect to research it is quite common to find the position advanced that good science is incompatible with bad ethics. When one wrestles with the horror of the medical abuse of vulnerable human beings it is somewhat comforting to believe that those who engage in such abuse could not produce anything of real value to medicine. Yet the continuing invocation of the findings of the Tuskegee study by those who diagnose, study, or treat syphilis shows that it is sometimes impossible to avoid a confrontation with the question of the ethics of relying on knowledge obtained in the course of immoral research.

The "bad ethics, therefore bad science" argument actually has two distinct components. One part of the argument holds that researchers engaged in obvious immoral conduct with their subjects could not generate useful or valid scientific findings. The second part holds that when the ethical conduct of research is egregiously immoral then any findings obtained ought not to be admitted into the body of scientific knowledge. While it may often be true that it is difficult to trust findings obtained using subjects who were abused or harmed (as was the case in Nazi concentration camp studies),[4] this part of the argument is not always true. Even a cursory glance through the literature of health care reveals that the Tuskegee study was and remains a key source of information about the diagnosis, signs, symptoms, and course of syphilis. No effort has been made to impugn its findings, and the biomedical community has relied upon them for decades.

James Jones, in his landmark book on the Tuskegee study, *Bad Blood*, notes that no researcher involved in the study ever published a single, comprehensive summary of its findings. The absence of such a review paper may have fostered the impression that no substantive findings of any real significance were obtained. But Jones also notes in the appendix to his book that Public Health Service scientists, physicians, and nurses associated with the study published a total of thirteen articles between 1936 and 1973 based solely upon its findings. These papers appeared in a wide variety of peer-reviewed journals, including *Public Health Reports, Milbank Fund Memorial Quarterly, Journal of Chronic Diseases*, and *Archives of Internal Medicine*.

It is a relatively simple matter to establish the importance assigned to the findings of the Tuskegee study by the contemporary biomedical community. The computerization on large data bases of the majority of the world's professional biomedical journals allows searches to be conducted to see which, if any, recent journal articles cite any of the thirteen papers presenting the findings of the Tuskegee study. An initial database search for the period January 1985 to February 1991 produced twenty such citations from a wide spectrum of journals, including American, British, and German publications. The twenty citations make reference to seven of the original thirteen papers.

A visit to any large medical library will also quickly reveal the importance assigned to the findings of the Tuskegee study in recent years. An informal random selection of twenty medical textbooks on sexually transmitted diseases, infectious disease, human sexuality, and public health published after 1984 turned up four books that made explicit reference to the study and cited at least one of the same thirteen articles. Three textbooks were published in the United States, one in England.

The range of journals in which contemporary articles on syphilis, venereal disease, and dementia directly cite the papers reporting the findings of the Tuskegee study is quite large. Direct citations of the Tuskegee study papers appear in articles in the *Journal of Family Practice* (1986), *The Lancet* (1986), *British Heart Journal* (1987), *New England Journal of Medicine* (1987), *Journal of the American Geriatrics Society* (1989), *The American Journal of Medicine* (1989), *American Journal of Public Health* (1989), and *Medical Clinics of North America* (1990), among others.

Nearly all the references in both the periodical literature and the medical textbooks use the Tuskegee study to describe the natural history of the disease. A recent review article on cardiovascular syphilis is typical of the way in which the Tuskegee study and its findings are cited:

> In 1932, the United States Public Health Service initiated the Tuskegee Study to delineate further the natural history of untreated syphilis. A total of 412 men with untreated syphilis and 204 uninfected matched controls were followed prospectively. Vonderlehr (15), reviewing the autopsy material from the first years of the study, noted that only one-fourth of the untreated patients were without evidence of any form of tertiary syphilis after 15 years of infection. Moreover, cardiovascular involvement was the most frequently detected abnormality. Peters (16) analyzed the autopsy data from the first 20 years of the study. He found that 50% of patients who had been infected for 10 years had demonstrable cardiovascular involvement. Of the 40% of syphilitic patients who died during this period, the primary causes of death were cardiovascular or central nervous system syphilis (16). Of the 41% of survivors at 30 years of follow-up, 12% had clinical evidence of late, predominantly cardiovascular syphilis (17). Most of these patients had evidence of cardiovascular syphilis at the 15-year analysis (17). These data ... indicate that ... complications are usually evident 10 to 20 years after primary infection, and cardiovascular syphilis is the predominant cause of demise in those patients who die as a direct result of syphilis.[5]

The reference numbers 15, 16, and 17 in the excerpt are to three of the thirteen papers reporting the findings of the Tuskegee study.

Yet another representative example from the contemporary periodical literature of health care invoking the findings of the Tuskegee study appears in a review of neurosyphilis and dementia:

> Neurosyphilis is rare as a manifestation of syphilis. Tertiary and late latent syphilis have been decreasing in incidence since the 1950s. There have been two studies of untreated syphilis: in the Oslo study neurosyphilis eventually developed in 7% of the patients, and in the Tuskegee study, syphilitic involvement of the cardiovascular system or the central nervous system was the primary cause of death in 30% of the infected patients, with cardiovascular involvement being much more common than neurosyphilis.[6]

Textbook references are quite similar to those that appear in the periodical literature. In giving an overview of the natural course of untreated syphilis one recent text states:

> A prospective study involving 431 black men with seropositive latent syphilis of 3 or more years' duration was undertaken in 1932 (the Tuskegee study, 1932–1962) (16). This study showed that hypertension in syphilitic black men 25–50 years of age was 17 percent more common than in nonsyphilitics. Cardiovascular complications including hypertension were more common than neurologic complications were, and both were increased over control populations. Anatomic evidence of aortitis was found to be 25–35 percent more common in autopsied syphilitics, while evidence of central nervous system syphilis was found in 4 percent of the patients.[7]

Reference number 16 is to one of the thirteen papers in which the Tuskegee findings were presented.

These examples clearly illustrate the continuing importance assigned to the Tuskegee study by those concerned with understanding and treating syphilis. The case for the study's importance could be further bolstered by tracking down secondary and tertiary references to its findings. There can be no disputing the fact that contemporary medicine has accepted the findings as valid and continues to rely on them as a key source of knowledge about the natural history of the disease.

The acceptance of the Tuskegee study findings as valid refutes the argument that bad ethics is always incompatible with valid science, but the question still remains as to whether the data of the Tuskegee study should continue to be utilized. It may make sense in some situations to argue that data obtained by immoral means should not be used purely on ethical grounds. But even if it were wrong to cite data acquired by immoral means there is simply no way to purge the knowledge gained in the Tuskegee study from biomedicine. Too much of what is known about the natural history of syphilis is based upon the study, and that knowledge has become so deeply embedded that it could not be removed.

Still, the view that the study was immoral and therefore worthless has flourished. This is a cause for concern, because the belief that not much of value came from the Tuskegee study allows both medicine and bioethics to avoid examining such troubling questions as how immoral research could be conducted by reputable scientists under the sponsorship of the American government for forty years, how such research could be allowed to continue long after the promulgation of the Nuremberg and Helsinki Codes, and what the moral duties and responsibilities are of those in biomedicine who continue to cite the study's findings today.

While one of the textbooks that discusses the Tuskegee study does make reference to the ethical shadow hanging over the findings,[8] none of the others and none of the articles in the peer-reviewed periodical literature that directly cite the papers based on the study do so. Should the results of the Tuskegee study continue to be invoked in review articles and texts without some accompanying discussion of the manner in which the findings were obtained and the ethical impact that the study had on the subsequent responsibilities of researchers? Given that the study played a crucial role in causing Americans to rethink the ethics of human experimentation, it would seem morally incumbent upon those who discuss its findings in the context of textbooks and review articles to allot some space for a discussion of the ethical problems associated with it.

There are obvious limits to the extent to which anyone writing a scientific paper or book can review the circumstances and conditions under which scientific knowledge was obtained. The history of medicine is replete with examples of research, certainly considered immoral by contemporary standards, that generate findings still widely accepted and cited. Not every article in a scientific journal can be used as a vehicle for educating the reader about the morality of human experimentation.

But there are obvious forums in biomedicine, such as textbooks and review articles, where it makes sense for authors to include some discussion of the ethical circumstances surrounding morally dubious or blatantly immoral research. The obvious immorality of research methods should not blind us to the importance of noting and discussing them. If no place is made for discussions of the morality of studies such as Tuskegee, the research community may become complacent about the importance of its responsibilities toward human subjects at the same time as the public comes to believe that good science cannot emerge from immoral research.

References

1. Stephen B. Thomas and Sandra C. Quinn, "The Tuskegee Syphilis Study, 1932 to 1972: Implications for HIV Education and AIDS Risk Education Programs in the Black Community," *American Journal of Public Health* 81, no. 11 (1991): 1498–1505, at 1501; Ruth Faden and Tom Beauchamp, *A History and Theory of Informed Consent* (New York: Oxford, 1986), p. 165.
2. James H. Jones, *Bad Blood: The Tuskegee Syphilis Experiment* (New York: Free Press, 1981), p. 207.
3. Jay Katz, personal communication, 1991.
4. See Arthur Caplan, ed., *When Medicine Went Mad* (New York: Humana, 1992).
5. J. D. Jackson and J. D. Radolf, "Cardiovascular Syphilis," *The American Journal of Medicine* 87 (October 1989): 428–29.
6. J. A. Rhymes, C. Woodson, R Sparage-Sachs, and C. K. Cassel, "Nonmedical Complications of

Diagnostic Workup for Dementia: University of Chicago Grand Rounds," *Journal of the American Geriatrics Society* 37, no. 12 (1989): 1157–64, at 1160.

7. G. L. Mandell, R G. Douglas, Jr., and J. E. Bennett, eds., *Principles and Practice of Infectious Diseases*, 3rd ed. (New York: Churchill Livingstone, 1990), p. 1797.

8. K. K. Holmes, P. Mardh, P. F. Sparling, and P. J. Wiesner, *Sexually Transmitted Diseases*, 2nd ed. (New York: McGraw-Hill, 1990).

JUDGMENT ON WILLOWBROOK

Paul Ramsey

In 1958 and 1959 the *New England Journal of Medicine* reported a series of experiments performed upon patients and new admittees to the Willowbrook State School, a home for retarded children in Staten Island, New York.[1] These experiments were described as "an attempt to control the high prevalence of infectious hepatitis in an institution for mentally defective patients." The experiments were said to be justified because, under conditions of an existing controlled outbreak of hepatitis in the institution, "knowledge obtained from a series of suitable studies could well lead to its control." In actuality, the experiments were designed to duplicate and confirm the efficacy of gamma globulin in immunization against hepatitis, to develop and improve or improve upon that inoculum, and to learn more about infectious hepatitis in general.

The experiments were justified—doubtless, after a great deal of soul searching—for the following reasons: there was a smoldering epidemic throughout the institution and "it was apparent that most of the patients at Willowbrook were naturally exposed to hepatitis virus"; infectious hepatitis is a much milder disease in children; the strain at Willowbrook was especially mild; only the strain or strains of the virus already disseminated at Willowbrook were used; and only those small and incompetent patients whose parents gave consent were used.

The patient population at Willowbrook was 4478, growing at a rate of one patient a day over a three-year span, or from 10 to 15 new admissions per week. In the first trial the existing population was divided into two groups: one group served as uninoculated controls, and the other group was inoculated with 0.01 ml. of gamma globulin per pound of body weight. Then for a second trial new admittees and those left uninoculated before were again divided: one group served as uninoculated controls and the other was inoculated with 0.06 ml. of gamma globulin per pound of body weight. This proved that Stokes et al. had correctly demonstrated that the larger amount would give significant immunity for up to seven or eight months.[2]

Serious ethical questions may be raised about the trials so far described. No mention is made of any attempt to enlist the adult personnel of the institution, numbering nearly 1,000 including nearly 600 attendants on ward duty, and new additions to the staff, in these studies whose excusing reason was that almost everyone was "naturally" exposed to the Willowbrook virus. Nothing requires that major research into the natural history of hepatitis be first undertaken in children. Experiments have been carried out in the military and with prisoners as subjects. There have been fatalities

From Paul Ramsey *The Patient as a Person*, Yale University Press © 1970. Reprinted with permission of Yale University Press.

from the experiments; but surely in all these cases the consent of the volunteers was as valid or better than the proxy consent of these children's "representatives." There would have been no question of the understanding consent that might have been given by the adult personnel at Willowbrook, if significant benefits were expected from studying that virus.

Second, nothing is said that would warrant withholding an inoculation of some degree of known efficacy from part of the population, or for withholding in the first trial less than the full amount of gamma globulin that had served to immunize in previous tests, except the need to test, confirm, and improve the inoculum. That, of course, was a desirable goal; but it does not seem possible to warrant withholding gamma globulin for the reason that is often said to justify controlled trials, namely, that one procedure is *as likely* to succeed as the other.

Third, nothing is said about attempts to control or defeat the low-grade epidemic at Willowbrook by more ordinary, if more costly and less experimental, procedures. Nor is anything said about admitting no more patients until this goal had been accomplished. This was not a massive urban hospital whose teeming population would have to be turned out into the streets, with resulting dangers to themselves and to public health, in order to sanitize the place. Instead, between 200 and 250 patients were housed in each of 18 buildings over approximately 400 acres in a semirural setting of fields, woods, and well-kept, spacious lawns. Clearly it would have been possible to secure other accommodation for new admissions away from the infection, while eradicating the infection at Willowbrook building by building. This might have cost money, and it would certainly have required astute detective work to discover the source of the infection. The doctors determined that the new patients likely were not carrying the infection upon admission, and that it did not arise from the procedures and routine inoculations given them at the time of admission. Why not go further in the search for the source of the epidemic? If this had been an orphanage for normal children or a floor of private patients, instead of a school for mentally defective children, one wonders whether the doctors would so readily have accepted the hepatitis as a "natural" occurrence and even as an opportunity for study.

The next step was to attempt to induce "passive-active immunity" by feeding the virus to patients already protected by gamma globulin. In this attempt to improve the inoculum, permission was obtained from the parents of children from 5 to 10 years of age newly admitted to Willowbrook, who were then isolated from contact with the rest of the institution. All were inoculated with gamma globulin and then divided into two groups: one served as controls while the other group of new patients were fed the Willowbrook virus, obtained from feces, in doses having 50 percent infectivity, i.e., in concentrations estimated to produce hepatitis with jaundice in half the subjects tested. Then twice the 50 percent infectivity was tried. This proved, among other things, that hepatitis has an "alimentary-tract phase" in which it can be transmitted from one person to another while still "inapparent" in the first person. This, doubtless, is exceedingly important information in learning how to control epidemics of infectious hepatitis. The second of the two articles mentioned above describes studies of the incubation period of the virus and of whether pooled serum remained infectious when aged and frozen. Still the small, mentally defective patients who were deliberately fed infectious hepatitis are described as having suffered mildly in most cases: "The liver became enlarged in the majority, occasionally a week or two before the onset of jaundice. Vomiting and anorexia usually lasted only a few days. Most of the children gained weight during the course of hepatitis."

That mild description of what happened to the children who were fed hepatitis (and who continued to be introduced into the unaltered environment of Willowbrook) is itself alarming, since it is now definitely known that cirrhosis of the liver results from infectious hepatitis more frequently than from excessive consumption of alcohol! Now, or in 1958 and 1959, no one knows what may be other serious consequences of contracting infectious hepatitis. Understanding human volunteers were then and are now needed in the study of this disease, although a South American monkey has now successfully been given a form of hepatitis, and can henceforth serve as our ally in its conquest. But not children who cannot consent knowingly. If Peace Corps workers are regularly given gamma globulin before going abroad as a guard against their contracting hepatitis, and are inoculated at intervals thereafter, it seems that this is the least we should do for mentally defective children before they "go abroad" to Willowbrook or other institutions set up for their care.

Discussions pro and con of the Willowbrook experiments that have come to my attention serve only to reinforce the ethical objections that can be raised against what was done simply from a careful analysis of the original articles reporting the research design and findings. In an address at the 1968 Ross Conference on Pediatric Research, Dr. Saul Krugman raised the question, Should vaccine trials be carried out in adult volunteers before subjecting children to similar tests?[3] He answered this question in the negative. The reason adduced was simply that "a vaccine virus trial may be a more hazardous procedure for adults than for children." Medical researchers, of course, are required to minimize the hazards, but not by moving from consenting to unconsenting subjects. This apology clearly shows that adults and children have become interchangeable in face of the overriding importance of obtaining the research goal. This means that the special moral claims of children for care and protection are forgotten, and especially the claims of children who are most weak and vulnerable. (Krugman's reference to the measles vaccine trials is not to the point.)

The *Medical Tribune* explains that the 16-bed isolation unit set up at Willowbrook served "to protect the study subjects from Willowbrook's other endemic diseases—such as shigellosis, measles, rubella and respiratory and parasitic infections—while exposing them to hepatitis."[4] This presumably compensated for the infection they were given. It is not convincingly shown that the children could by no means, however costly, have been protected from the epidemic of hepatitis. The statement that Willowbrook "had endemic infectious hepatitis and a sufficiently open population so that the disease could never be quieted by exhausting the supply of susceptibles" is at best enigmatic.

Oddly, physicians defending the propriety of the Willowbrook hepatitis project soon begin talking like poorly instructed "natural lawyers"! Dr. Louis Lasagna and Dr. Geoffrey Edsall, for example, find these experiments unobjectionable—both, for the reason stated by Edsall: "the children would apparently incur no greater risk than they were likely to run by nature." In any case, Edsall's examples of parents consenting with a son 17 years of age for him to go to war, and society's agreement with minors that they can drive cars and hurt themselves were entirely beside the point. Dr. David D. Rutstein adheres to a stricter standard in regard to research on infectious hepatitis: "It is not ethical to use human subjects for the growth of a virus for any purpose."[5]

The latter sweeping verdict may depend on knowledge of the effects of viruses on chromasomal difficulties, mongolism, etc., that was not available to the Willowbrook group when their researches were begun thirteen years ago. If so, this is a telling point against appeal to "no discernible risks" as the sole standard applicable to the use of children in medical experimentation. That would lend support to the proposition that we always know that there are unknown and undiscerned risks in the case of an invasion of the fortress of the body—which then can be consented to by an adult in behalf of a child only if it is in the child's behalf medically.

When asked what she told the parents of the subject-children at Willowbrook, Dr. Joan Giles replied, "I explain that there is no vaccine against infectious hepatitis....I also tell them that we can modify the disease with gamma globulin but we can't provide lasting immunity without letting them get the disease."[6] Obviously vaccines giving "lasting immunity" are not the only kinds of vaccine to be used in caring for patients.

Doubtless the studies at Willowbrook resulted in improvement in the vaccine, to the benefit of present and future patients. In September 1966, "a routine program of GG [gamma gobulin] administration to every new patient at Willowbrook" was begun. This cut the incidence of icteric hepatitis 80 to 85 percent. Then follows a significant statement in the *Medical Tribune* article: "A similar reduction in the icteric form of the disease has been accomplished among the employees, who began getting routine GG earlier in the study."[7] Not only did the research team (so far as these reports show) fail to consider and adopt the alternative that new admittees to the staff be asked to become volunteers for an investigation that might improve the vaccine against the strand of infectious hepatitis to which they as well as the children were exposed. Instead, the staff was routinely protected earlier than the inmates were! And, as we have seen, there was evidence from the beginning that gamma gobulin provided at least some protection. A "modification" of the disease was still an inoculum, even if this provided no lasting immunization and had to be repeated. It is axiomatic to medical ethics that a known remedy or protection—even if not perfect or even if the best exact administration of it has not been proved—should not be withheld from individual patients. It seems to a layman that from the beginning various trials at immunization of all new admittees might have been made, and controlled observation made of their different degrees of effectiveness against "nature" at Willowbrook. This would doubtless have been a longer way round, namely, the "anecdotal" method of investigative treatment that comes off second best in comparison with controlled trials. Yet this seems to be the alternative dictated by our received medical ethics, and the only one expressive of minimal care of the primary patients themselves.

Finally, except for one episode the obtaining of parental consent (on the premise that this is ethically valid) seems to have been very well handled. Wards of the state were not used, though by law the administrator at Willowbrook could have signed consent for them. Only new admittees whose parents were available were entered by proxy consent into the project. Explanation was made to groups of these parents, and they were given time to think about it and consult with their own family physicians.[8] Then late in 1964 Willowbrook was closed to all new admissions because of overcrowding. What then happened can most impartially be described in the words of an article defending the Willowbrook project on medical and ethical grounds:

> Parents who applied for their children to get in were sent a form letter over Dr. Hammond's signature saying that there was no space for new admissions and that their name was being put on a waiting list.
>
> But the hepatitis program, occupying its own space in the institution, continued to admit new patients as each new study group began. "Where do you find new admissions except by canvassing the people who have applied for admission?" Dr. Hammond asked.
>
> So a new batch of form letters went out, saying that there were a few vacancies in the hepatitis research unit if the parents cared to consider volunteering their child for that.
>
> In some instances the second form letter apparently was received as closely as a week after the first letter arrived.[9]

Granting—as I do not—the validity of parental consent to research upon children not in their behalf medically, what sort of consent was that? Surely, the duress upon these parents with children so defective as to require institutionalization was far greater than the duress on prisoners given tobacco or paid or promised parole for their cooperation! I grant that the timing of these events was inadvertent. Since, however, ethics is a matter of criticizing institutions and not only of exculpating or making culprits of individual men, the inadvertence does not matter. This is the strongest possible argument for saying that even if parents have the right to consent to submit the children who are directly and continuously in their care to nonbeneficial medical experimentation, this should not be the rule of practice governing institutions set up for their care.

Such use of captive populations of children for purely experimental purposes ought to be made legally impossible. My view is that this should be stopped by legal acknowledgment of the moral invalidity of parental or legal proxy consent for the child to procedures having no relation to a child's own diagnosis or treatment. If this is not done, canons of loyalty require that the rule of practice (by law, or otherwise) be that children in institutions and not directly under the care of parents or relatives should *never* be used in medical investigations having present pain or discomfort and unknown present and future risks to them, and promising future possible benefits only for others.

Notes

1. Robert Ward, Saul Krugman, Joan P. Giles, A. Milton Jacobs, and Oscar Bodansky, "Infectious Hepatitis: Studies of Its Natural History and Prevention," *New England Journal of Medicine* 258, no. 9 (February 27, 1958): 407–16; Saul Krugman, Robert Ward, Joan P. Giles, Oscar Bodansky, and A. Milton Jacobs, "Infectious Hepatitis: Detection of the Virus during the Incubation Period and in Clinically Inapparent Infection," *New England Journal of Medicine* 261, no. 15 (October 8, 1959): 729–34. The following account and unannotated quotations are taken from these articles.
2. J. Stokes, Jr., et al., "Infectious Hepatitis: Length of Protection by Immune Serum Globulin (Gamma Globulin) during Epidemics," *Journal of the American Medical Association* 147 (1951): 714–19. Since the half-life of gamma globulin is three weeks, no one knows exactly why it immunizes for so long a period. The "highly significant protection against hepatitis obtained by the use of gamma globulin," however, had been confirmed as early as 1945 (see Edward B. Grossman, Sloan G. Stewart, and Joseph Stokes, "Post-Transfusion Hepatitis in Battle Casualties," *Journal of the American Medical Association* 129, no. 15 [December 8, 1945]: 991–94). The inoculation *withheld* in the Willowbrook experiments had, therefore, proved valuable.
3. Saul Krugman, "Reflections on Pediatric Clinical Investigations," in *Problems of Drug Evaluation in Infants and Children,* Report of the Fifty-eighth Ross Conference on Pediatric Research, Dorado Beach, Puerto Rico, May 5–7, 1968 (Columbus: Ross Laboratories), pp. 41–42.
4. "Studies with Children Backed on Medical, Ethical Grounds," *Medical Tribune and Medical News* 8, no. 19 (February 20, 1967): 1, 23.
5. *Daedalus*, Spring 1969, pp. 471–72, 529. See also pp. 458, 470–72. Since it is the proper business of an ethicist to uphold the proposition that only retrogression in civility can result from bad moral reasoning and the use of inept examples, however innocent, it is fair to point out the startling comparison between Edsall's "argument" and the statement of Dr. Karl Brandt, plenipotentiary in charge of all medical activities in the Nazi Reich: "Do you think that one can obtain any worth-while, fundamental results without a definite toll of lives? The same goes for technological development. You cannot build a great bridge, a gigantic building—you cannot establish a speed record without deaths!" (quoted by Leo Alexander, "War Crimes: Their Social-Psychological Aspects," *American Journal of Psychiatry* 105, no. 3 [September 1948]: 172). Casualties to progress, or injuries accepted in

setting speed limits, are morally quite different from death or maiming or even only risk, or unknown risks, directly and deliberately imposed upon an unconsenting human being.

6. *Medical Tribune*, February 20, 1967, p. 23.
7. *Medical Tribune*, February 20, 1967, p. 23.
8. Krugman, "Reflections on Pediatric Clinical Investigations," pp. 41–42.
9. *Medical Tribune*, February 20, 1967, p. 25.

OF MICE BUT NOT MEN: PROBLEMS OF THE RANDOMIZED CLINICAL TRIAL

Samuel Hellman and Deborah S. Hellman

As medicine has become increasingly scientific and less accepting of unsupported opinion or proof by anecdote, the randomized controlled clinical trial has become the standard technique for changing diagnostic or therapeutic methods. The use of this technique creates an ethical dilemma.[1,2] Researchers participating in such studies are required to modify their ethical commitments to individual patients and do serious damage to the concept of the physician as a practicing, empathetic professional who is primarily concerned with each patient as an individual. Researchers using a randomized clinical trial can be described as physician-scientists, a term that expresses the tension between the two roles. The physician, by entering into a relationship with an individual patient, assumes certain obligations, including the commitment always to act in the patient's best interests. As Leon Kass has rightly maintained, "the physician must produce unswervingly the virtues of loyalty and fidelity to his patient."[3] Though the ethical requirements of this relationship have been modified by legal obligations to report wounds of a suspicious nature and certain infectious diseases, these obligations in no way conflict with the central ethical obligation to act in the best interests of the patient medically. Instead, certain nonmedical interests of the patient are preempted by other social concerns.

The role of the scientist is quite different. The clinical scientist is concerned with answering questions—i.e., determining the validity of formally constructed hypotheses. Such scientific information, it is presumed, will benefit humanity in general. The clinical scientist's role has been well described by Dr. Anthony Fauci, director of the National Institute of Allergy and Infectious Diseases, who states the goals of the randomized clinical trial in these words: "It's not to deliver therapy. It's to answer a scientific question so that the drug can be available for everybody once you've established safety and efficacy."[4] The demands of such a study can conflict in a number of ways with the physician's duty to minister to patients. The study may create a false dichotomy in the physician's opinions: according to the premise of the randomized clinical trial, the physician may only know or not know whether a proposed course of treatment represents an improvement; no middle position is permitted. What the physician thinks, suspects, believes, or has a hunch about is assigned to the "not knowing" category, because knowing is defined on the basis of an arbitrary but accepted statistical test performed in a randomized clinical

---

Hellman, S. and Hellman, D. S. "Of Mice But Not Men: Problems of the Randomized Clinical Trial." From *The New England Journal of Medicine*, 324:1585–1589, 1991.

trial. Thus, little credence is given to information gained beforehand in other ways or to information accrued during the trial but without the required statistical degree of assurance that a difference is not due to chance. The randomized clinical trial also prevents the treatment technique from being modified on the basis of the growing knowledge of the physicians during their participation in the trial. Moreover, it limits access to the data as they are collected until specific milestones are achieved. This prevents physicians from profiting not only from their individual experience, but also from the collective experience of the other participants.

The randomized clinical trial requires doctors to act simultaneously as physicians and as scientists. This puts them in a difficult and sometimes untenable ethical position. The conflicting moral demands arising from the use of the randomized clinical trial reflect the classic conflict between rights-based moral theories and utilitarian ones. The first of these, which depend on the moral theory of Immanuel Kant (and seen more recently in neo-Kantian philosophers, such as John Rawls[5]), asserts that human beings, by virtue of their unique capacity for rational thought, are bearers of dignity. As such, they ought not to be treated merely as means to an end; rather, they must always be treated as ends in themselves. Utilitarianism, by contrast, defines what is right as the greatest good for the greatest number—that is, as social utility. This view, articulated by Jeremy Bentham and John Stuart Mill, requires that pleasures (understood broadly, to include such pleasures as health and well-being) and pains be added together. The morally correct act is the act that produces the most pleasure and the least pain overall.

A classic objection to the utilitarian position is that according to that theory, the distribution of pleasures and pains is of no moral consequence. This element of the theory severely restricts physicians from being utilitarians, or at least from following the theory's dictates. Physicians must care very deeply about the distribution of pain and pleasure, for they have entered into a relationship with one or a number of individual patients. They cannot be indifferent to whether it is these patients or others that suffer for the general benefit of society. Even though society might gain from the suffering of a few, and even though the doctor might believe that such a benefit is worth a given patient's suffering (i.e., that utilitarianism is right in the particular case), the ethical obligation created by the covenant between doctor and patient requires the doctor to see the interests of the individual patient as primary and compelling. In essence, the doctor–patient relationship requires doctors to see their patients as bearers of rights who cannot be merely used for the greater good of humanity.

As Fauci has suggested,[4] the randomized clinical trial routinely asks physicians to sacrifice the interests of their particular patients for the sake of the study and that of the information that it will make available for the benefit of society. This practice is ethically problematic. Consider first the initial formulation of a trial. In particular, consider the case of a disease for which there is no satisfactory therapy—for example, advanced cancer or the acquired immunodeficiency syndrome (AIDS). A new agent that promises more effectiveness is the subject of the study. The control group must be given either an unsatisfactory treatment or a placebo. Even though the therapeutic value of the new agent is unproved, if physicians think that it has promise, are they acting in the best interests of their patients in allowing them to be randomly assigned to the control group? Is persisting in such an assignment consistent with the specific commitments taken on in the doctor–patient relationship? As a result of interactions with patients with AIDS and their advocates, Merigan[6] recently suggested modifications in the design of clinical trials that attempt to deal with the unsatisfactory treatment given to the control group. The view of such activists has been expressed by Rebecca Pringle Smith of Community Research Initiative in New York: "Even if you have a supply of compliant martyrs, trials must have some ethical validity."[4]

If the physician has no opinion about whether the new treatment is acceptable, then random assignment is ethically acceptable, but such lack of enthusiasm for the new treatment does not augur well for either the patient or the study. Alternatively, the treatment may show promise of beneficial results but also present a risk of undesirable complications. When the physician believes that the severity and likelihood of harm and good are evenly balanced, randomization may be ethically acceptable. If the physician has no preference for either treatment (is in a state of equipoise[7, 8]), then randomization is acceptable. If, however, he or she believes that the new treatment may be either more or less successful or more or less toxic, the use of randomization is not consistent with fidelity to the patient.

The argument usually used to justify randomization is that it provides, in essence, a critique of the usefulness of the physician's beliefs and opinions, those that have not yet been validated by a randomized clinical trial. As the argument goes, these not-yet-validated beliefs are as likely to be wrong as right. Although physicians are ethically required to provide their patients with the best available treatment, there simply is no best treatment yet known.

The reply to this argument takes two forms. First, and most important, even if this view of the reliability of a physician's opinions is accurate, the ethical constraints of an individual doctor's relationship with a particular patient require the doctor to provide individual care. Although physicians must take pains to make clear the speculative nature of their views, they cannot withhold these views from the patient. The patient asks from the doctor both knowledge and judgment. The relationship established between them rightfully allows patients to ask for the judgment of their particular physicians, not merely that of the medical profession in general. Second, it may not be true, in fact, that the not-yet-validated beliefs of physicians are as likely to be wrong as right. The greater certainty obtained with a randomized clinical trial is beneficial, but that does not mean that a lesser degree of certainty is without value. Physicians can acquire knowledge through methods other than the randomized clinical trial. Such knowledge, acquired over time and less formally than is required in a randomized clinical trial, may be of great value to a patient.

Even if it is ethically acceptable to begin a study, one often forms an opinion during its course—especially in studies that are impossible to conduct in a truly double-blinded fashion—that makes it ethically problematic to continue. The inability to remain blinded usually occurs in studies of cancer or AIDS, for example, because the therapy is associated by nature with serious side effects. Trials attempt to restrict the physician's access to the data in order to prevent such unblinding. Such restrictions should make physicians eschew the trial, since their ability to act in the patient's best interests will be limited. Even supporters of randomized clinical trials, such as Merigan, agree that interim findings should be presented to patients to ensure that no one receives what seems an inferior treatment.[6] Once physicians have formed a view about the new treatment, can they continue randomization? If random assignment is stopped, the study may be lost and the participation of the previous patients wasted. However, if physicians continue the randomization when they have a definite opinion about the efficacy of the experimental drug, they are not acting in accordance with the requirements of the doctor–patient relationship. Furthermore, as their opinion becomes more firm, stopping the randomization may not be enough. Physicians may be ethically required to treat the patients formerly placed in the control group with the therapy that now seems probably effective. To do so would be faithful to the obligations created by the doctor-patient relationship, but it would destroy the study.

To resolve this dilemma, one might suggest that the patient has abrogated the rights implicit in a doctor–patient relationship by signing an informed-consent form. We argue that such rights cannot be waived or abrogated. They are inalienable. The right to be treated as an individual deserving the physician's best judgment and care, rather than to be used as a means to determine the best treatment for others, is inherent in every person. This right, based on the concept of dignity, cannot be waived. What of altruism, then? Is it not the patient's right to make a sacrifice for the general good? This question must be considered from both positions—that of the patient and that of the physician. Although patients may decide to waive this right, it is not consistent with the role of a physician to ask that they do so. In asking, the doctor acts as a scientist instead. The physician's role here is to propose what he or she believes is best medically for the specific patient, not to suggest participation in a study from which the patient cannot gain. Because the opportunity to help future patients is of potential value to a patient, some would say physicians should not deny it. Although this point has merit, it offers so many opportunities for abuse that we are extremely uncomfortable about accepting it. The responsibilities of physicians are much clearer; they are to minister to the current patient.

Moreover, even if patients could waive this right, it is questionable whether those with terminal illness would be truly able to give voluntary informed consent. Such patients are extremely dependent on both their physicians and the health care system. Aware of this dependence, physicians must not ask for consent, for in such cases the very asking breaches the doctor–patient relationship. Anxious to please their physicians, patients may have difficulty refusing to participate in the trial the physicians describe. The patients may perceive their refusal as damaging to the relationship, whether or not it is so. Such perceptions of coercion affect the decision. Informed-consent forms are difficult to understand, especially for patients under the stress of serious illness for which there is no satisfactory treatment. The forms are usually lengthy, somewhat legalistic, complicated, and confusing, and they hardly bespeak the compassion expected of the medical profession. It is important to remember that those who have studied the doctor–patient relationship have emphasized its empathetic nature.

> [The] relationship between doctor and patient partakes of a peculiar intimacy. It presupposes on the part of the physician not only knowledge of his fellow men but sympathy. ... This aspect of the practice of medicine has been designated as the art; yet I wonder whether it should not, most properly, be called the essence. [9]

How is such a view of the relationship consonant with random assignment and informed consent? The Physician's Oath of the World Medical Association affirms the primacy of the deontologic view of patients' rights: "Concern for the interests of the subject must always prevail over the interests of science and society." [10]

Furthermore, a single study is often not considered sufficient. Before a new form of therapy is generally accepted, confirmatory trials must be conducted. How can one conduct such trials ethically unless one is convinced that the first trial was in error? The ethical problems we have discussed are only exacerbated when a completed randomized clinical trial indicates that a given treatment is preferable. Even if the physician believes the initial trial was in error, the physician must indicate to the patient the full results of that trial.

The most common reply to the ethical arguments has been that the alternative is to return to the physician's intuition, to anecdotes, or to both as the basis of medical opinion. We all accept the dangers of such a practice. The argument states that we must therefore accept randomized, controlled clinical trials regardless of their ethical problems because of the great social benefit they make possible, and we salve our conscience with the knowledge that informed consent has been given. This returns us to the conflict between patients' rights and social utility. Some would argue that this tension can be resolved by placing a relative value on each. If the patient's right that is being compromised is not a fundamental right and the social gain is very great, then the study might be justified. When the right is fundamental, however, no amount of social gain, or almost none, will justify its sacrifice. Consider, for example, the experiments on humans done by physicians under the Nazi regime. All would agree that these are unacceptable regardless of the value of the scientific information gained. Some people go so far as to say that no use should be made of the results of those experiments because of the clearly unethical manner in which the data were collected. This extreme example may not seem relevant, but we believe that in its hyperbole it clarifies the fallacy of a utilitarian approach to the physician's relationship with the patient. To consider the utilitarian gain is consistent neither with the physician's role nor with the patient's rights.

It is fallacious to suggest that only the randomized clinical trial can provide valid information or that all information acquired by this technique is valid. Such experimental methods are intended to reduce error and bias and therefore reduce the uncertainty of the result. Uncertainty cannot be eliminated, however. The scientific method is based on increasing probabilities and increasingly refined approximations of truth.[11] Although the randomized clinical trial contributes to these ends, it is neither unique nor perfect. Other techniques may also be useful.[12]

Randomized trials often place physicians in the ethically intolerable position of choosing between the good of the patient and that of society. We urge that such situations be avoided and that other techniques of acquiring clinical information be adopted. For example, concerning trials of treatments for AIDS, Byar et al.[13] have said that "some traditional approaches to the clinical-trials process may be unnecessarily rigid and unsuitable for this disease." In this case, AIDS is not what is so different; rather, the difference is in the presence of AIDS activists, articulate spokespersons for the ethical problems created by the application of the randomized clinical trial to terminal illnesses. Such arguments are equally applicable to advanced cancer and other serious illnesses. Byar et al. agree that there are even circumstances in which uncontrolled clinical trials may be justified: when there is no effective treatment to use as a control, when the prognosis is uniformly poor, and when there is a reasonable expectation of benefit without excessive toxicity. These conditions are usually found in clinical trials of advanced cancer.

The purpose of the randomized clinical trial is to avoid the problems of observer bias and patient selection. It seems to us that techniques might be developed to deal with these issues in other ways. Randomized clinical trials deal with them in a cumbersome and heavy-handed manner, by requiring large numbers of patients in the hope that random assignment will balance the heterogeneous distribution of patients into the different groups. By observing known characteristics of patients, such as age and sex, and distributing them equally between groups, it is thought that unknown factors important in determining outcomes will also be distributed equally. Surely, other techniques can be developed to deal with both observer bias and patient selection. Prospective studies without randomization, but with the evaluation of patients by uninvolved third parties, should remove observer bias. Similar methods have been suggested by Royall.[12] Prospective matched-pair analysis, in which patients are treated in a manner consistent with their physician's views, ought to help ensure equivalence between the groups and thus mitigate the effect of patient selection, at least with regard to known covariates. With regard to unknown covariates, the security would rest, as in randomized trials, in the enrollment of large numbers of patients and in confirmatory studies. This method would not pose ethical difficulties, since patients would receive the treatment recommended by their physician. They would be included in the study by independent observers matching patients with respect to known characteristics, a process that would not affect patient care and that could be performed independently any number of times.

This brief discussion of alternatives to randomized clinical trials is sketchy and incomplete. We wish only to point out that there may be satisfactory alternatives, not to describe and evaluate them completely. Even if randomized clinical trials were much better than any alternative, however, the ethical dilemmas they present may put their use at variance with the primary obligations of the physician. In this regard, Angell cautions, "If this commitment to the patient is attenuated, even for so good a cause as benefits to future patients, the implicit assumptions of the doctor–patient relationship are violated."[14] The risk of such attenuation by the randomized trial is great. The AIDS activists have brought this dramatically to the attention of the academic medical community. Techniques appropriate to the laboratory may not be applicable to humans. We must develop and use alternative methods for acquiring clinical knowledge.

References

1. Hellman, S. "Randomized clinical trials and the doctor–patient relationship: an ethical dilemma." *Cancer Clin Trials* 1979; 2:189–93.
2. *Idem*. A doctors dilemma: the doctor–patient relationship in clinical investigation. In: Proceedings of the Fourth National Conference on Human Values and Cancer, New York, March 15–17, 1984. New York: American Cancer Society, 1984:144–6.
3. Kass, L. R. *Toward a More Natural Science: Biology and Human Affairs*. New York: Free Press, 1985:196.
4. Palca, J. "AIDS drug trials enter new age." *Science* 1989; 246:19–21.
5. Rawls, J. *A Theory of Justice*. Cambridge, MA: Belknap Press of Harvard University Press, 1971:183–92, 446–52.
6. Merigan, T.C. "You *can* teach an old dog new tricks—how AIDS trials are pioneering new strategies." *N Engl J Med* 1990; 323:1341–3.
7. Freedman, B. "Equipoise and the ethics of clinical research." *N Engl J Med* 1987; 317:141–5.
8. Singer, P.A., Lantos, J.D., Whitington, P.F., Broelsch, C. E., and Siegler, M. "Equipoise and the ethics of segmental liver transplantation." *Clin Res* 1988; 36:539–45.
9. Longcope, W.T. "Methods and medicine." *Bull Johns Hopkins Hosp* 1932; 50:4–20.
10. "Report on medical ethics." *World Med Assoc Bull* 1949; 1:109, 111.
11. Popper, K. "The problem of induction." In: Miller D, ed. *Popper Selections*. Princeton, NJ: Princeton University Press, 1985:101–17.
12. Royall, R.M. "Ethics and statistics in randomized clinical trials." *Stat Sci* 1991; 6(1):52–62.
13. Byar, D.P., Schoenfeld, D.A., Green, S.B., et al. "Design considerations for AIDS trials." *N Engl J Med* 1990; 323:1343–8.
14. Angell, M. "Patients' preferences in randomized clinical trials." *N Engl J Med* 1984; 310:1385–7.

A RESPONSE TO A PURPORTED ETHICAL DIFFICULTY WITH RANDOMIZED CLINICAL TRIALS INVOLVING CANCER PATIENTS

Benjamin Freedman

In recent years, for a variety of reasons, the mainstay of clinical investigation—the randomized controlled clinical trial (RCT)—has increasingly come under attack. Since Charles Fried's influential monograph, the opponents of controlled trials have claimed the moral high ground. They claim to perceive a conflict between the medical and scientific duties of the physician-investigator, and between the conduct of the trial and a patient's rights. Samuel and Deborah Hellman write, for example, that "the randomized clinical trial routinely asks physicians to sacrifice the interests of their particular patients for the sake of the study and that of the information that it will make available for the benefit of society." Maurie Markman's attraction to this point of view is clear when he writes that "the individual physician's principal ethical responsibility is to the *individual patient* that he or she is treating, and *not* to future patients [emphases in original]." In the interests of returning Markman to the fold, I will concentrate on resolving this central challenge to the ethics of RCTs.

It is unfortunately true that the most common responses from protrialists, by revealing fundamental misunderstandings of basic ethical concepts, do not inspire confidence in the ethics of human research as currently conducted. Proponents of clinical trials will commonly begin their apologia by citing benefits derived from trials—by validating the safety and efficacy of new treatments, and, at least as important, by discrediting accepted forms of treatment. So far so good. But they often go on to argue that there is a need to balance the rights of subjects against the needs of society. By this tactic, the proponents of clinical trials have implicitly morally surrendered, for to admit that something is a right is to admit that it represents a domain of action protected from the claims or interests of other individuals or of society itself. A liberal society has rightly learned to look askance at claims that rights of individuals need to yield to the demands of the collective. Patients' claims, then, because of their nature as rights, supercede the requirements of the collectivity.

Sometimes, indeed, the surrender is explicit. At the conclusion of a symposium on the ethics of research on human subjects, Sir Colin Dollery, a major figure in clinical trials, complained to the speaker: "You assume a dominant role for ethics—I think to the point of arrogance. Ethical judgments will be of little value unless the scientific innovations about which they are made ... are useful." But it is the nature of ethical judgments that they are, indeed, "dominant" as normative or accepted guides to action. One may say, "I know that *X* is the ethical thing to do, but I won't *X*." That expresses no logical contradiction, but simply weakness of will. But it is, by contrast, plainly contradictory to admit that *X* is ethical, yet to deny or doubt that one ought to *X*.

Closer examination and finer distinctions reveal, however, that the conflict between patients' rights and social interests is not at all at issue in controlled clinical trials. There is no need for proponents of clinical trials to concede the moral high ground.

What is the patient right that is compromised by clinical trials? The fear most common to patients who are hesitant about enrolling is that

The Journal of Clinical Ethics, 3, No. 3, Fall 1992: 231–34.

they would not receive the best care, that their right to treatment would be sacrificed in the interests of science. This presumes, of course, that the patient has a right to treatment. Such a right must in reason be grounded in patient need (a patient who is not ill has no right to treatment) and in medical knowledge and capability (a patient with an incurable illness has rights to be cared for, but no right to be cured).

That granted, we need to specify the kind of treatment to which a patient might reasonably claim a right. It was in this connection that I introduced the concept of *clinical equipoise* as critical to understanding the ethics of clinical trials. Clinical equipoise is a situation in which there exists (or is pending) an honest disagreement in the expert clinical community regarding the comparative merits of two or more forms of treatment for a given condition. To be ethical, a controlled clinical trial must begin and be conducted in a continuing state of clinical equipoise–as between the arms of the study—and must, moreover, offer some reasonable hope that the successful conclusion of the trial will disturb equipoise (that is, resolve the controversy in the expert clinical community).

This theory presumes that a right to a specific medical treatment must be grounded in a professional judgment, which is concretized in the term *clinical equipoise.* A patient who has rights to medical treatment has rights restricted to, though not necessarily exhaustive of, those treatments that are understood by the medical community to be appropriate for his condition. A patient may eccentrically claim some good from a physician that is not recognized by the medical community as appropriate treatment. A physician may even grant this claim; but in so doing, he must realize that he has not provided medical treatment itself. Contrariwise, by failing to fulfill this request, the physician has not failed to satisfy the patient's right to medical treatment.

Provided that a comparative trial is ethical, therefore, it begins in a state of clinical equipoise. For that reason, by definition, nobody enrolling in the trial is denied his or her right to medical treatment, for no medical consensus for or against the treatment assignment exists.

(The modern climate requires that I introduce two simple caveats. First, I am ignoring economic and political factors that go into the grounding of a right to treatment. This is easy enough for one in Canada to write, but may be difficult for someone in the United States to read. Second, when speaking of treatment that is recognized to be condition-appropriate by the medical community, I mean to include only those judgments grounded in medical knowledge rather than social judgments. I would hope to avoid the current bioethical muddle over "medical futility," but if my claims need to be translated into terms appropriate to that controversy, "physiological futility" is close but not identical to what I mean by "inappropriate." For simplicity's sake, the best model to have in mind is the common patient demand for antibiotic treatment of an illness diagnosed as viral.)

Two errors are commonly committed in connection with the concept of clinical equipoise. The first mistake is in thinking that clinical equipoise (or its disturbance) relates to a single endpoint of a trial—commonly, efficacy. As a function of expert clinical judgment, clinical equipoise must incorporate all of the many factors that go into favoring one regimen over its competitors. Treatment *A* may be favored over *B* because it is more effective; or, because it is almost as effective, but considerably less toxic, or, because it is easier to administer, allowing, for example, treatment on an outpatient basis; or, because patients are more compliant with it; and so forth.

Just as equipoise may be based upon any one or combination of these or other factors, it may be disturbed in the same way. Markman's second example, which discusses the efficacy of a multidrug combination chemotherapy regimen, seems vulnerable to this objection. Even were the results of trial convincing with regard to the efficacy of this approach, it has not disturbed clinical equipoise in its favor unless other issues, such as toxicity, have been resolved as well. It is well worth pointing out that the endpoints of trials, particularly in cancer treatment, are far too narrow to disturb clinical equipoise in and of themselves, but they are neccessary steps along a seriatim path. For that matter, in ignoring the compendious judgment involved in ascertaining equipoise, some studies spuriously claim that all of their arms are in equipoise on the basis of one variable (such as five-year survival rates), when they are clearly out of equipoise because of other factors (such as differences in pain and disfigurement).

The second mistake occurs in identifying clinical equipoise with an individual physician's point of indifference between two treatments. Citing the article in which I developed the concept and another article applying it, for example, the Hellmans write, "If the physician has no preference for either treatment (is in a state of equipoise), then randomization is acceptable." But an individual physician is not the arbiter of appropriate or acceptable medical practice.

There are numerous occasions outside of clinical trials where outsiders need to determine whether the treatment provided was appropriate to the patient's condition. Regulators, as well as third-party payers—private or governmental—need to answer the question, as do health planners and administrators of health-care facilities. Disciplinary bodies of professional associations, and, most tellingly, courts judging allegations of malpractice, have to ascertain this as well. It is never the case that the judgment of an individual physician concerning whether a treatment is condition-appropriate (that is, whether it belongs within the therapeutic armamentarium) is sufficient. In all of these instances, however varied might be their rules of investigation and procedure, the ultimate question is: Does the expert professional community accept this treatment as appropriate for this condition? Since clinical equipoise and its disturbance apply to putative medical treatments for given conditions, this is a matter that is determined legally, morally and reasonably by that medical community with the recognized relevant expertise.

Markman may have fallen into this error writing repeatedly of the judgment of the treating or enrolling physician (and, in the first page, of the responsibility of "the individual physician") with respect to the clinical trial. There is, however, another way of looking at this. Whereas the status of a putative treatment within the medical armamentarium must be settled by the medical *community*, the application of that judgment *vis-à-vis* a given patient is, of course, the judgment (and the responsibility) of the *individual physician*. This individual clinical judgment must be exercised when enrolling a subject, rather than subjugated to the judgment of those who constructed the trial. Indeed, many studies will list this as a criterion of exclusion: "Those subjects who, in the judgment of the accruing physician, would be put at undue risk by participating."

Another point: the Hellmans write of a physician's duty in treating a patient to employ what he "thinks, suspects, believes, or has a hunch about." This is clearly overstated as duty: why not add to the list the physician's hopes, fantasies, fond but dotty beliefs, and illusions? Yet patients do choose physicians, in part, because of trust in their tacit knowledge and inchoate judgment, and not merely their sapient grasp of the current medical consensus. It would be a disservice to patients for a physician to see his or her role simply as a vehicle for transmitting the wisdom received from the expert medical community in all cases (though when a departure is made, this is done at the legal peril of the doctor!).

But what follows from this inalienable duty of the treating physician? Not as much as the opponents of trials would have us believe. A physician certainly has the right to refuse to participate in a trial that he believes places some participants at a medical disadvantage. Moreover, if he or she is convinced of that, he or she has a *duty* to abstain from participating. But that only speaks to the physician, and does not necessarily affect the patient. What opponents of trials forget is that the patient—the subject—is the ultimate decision maker—in fact, in law, and in ethics. In at least some cases, the fact that there is an open trial for which a patient meets the eligibility criteria needs to be disclosed as one medical alternative, to satisfy ethical norms of informed consent. A physician with convictions that the trial will put subjects at undue risk should inform the prospective subject of that conviction and the reasons for it, and may well recommend to the subject to decline participation. It will then be up to the patient whether to seek enrollment via another physician.

Most commonly at issue, though, is a physician's preference rather than conviction. In such cases, it is perfectly ethical—and becomingly modest—for a physician to participate in a trial, setting aside private misgivings based upon anecdote as overbalanced by the medical literature.

Finally, something should be said about the underlying philosophical buttress on which antitrialists rely. Following Kant, the Hellmans argue that the underlying issue is that persons "ought not to be treated merely as means to an end; rather, they must always be treated as ends in themselves." Clinical trials, however, are designed to yield reliable data and to ground scientifically valid inferences. In that sense, the treatments and examinations that a subject of a clinical trial undergoes are means to a scientific end, rather than interventions done solely for the subject's own benefit.

But the Kantian formulation is notoriously rigoristic, and implausible in the form cited. We treat others as means all the time, in order to achieve ends the others do not share, and are so treated in return. When buying a carton of milk or leaving a message, I am treating the cashier or secretary as means to an end they do not share. Were this unvarnished principle to hold, all but purely altruistic transactions would be ethically deficient. Clinical trials would be in very good (and, indeed, very bad) company. Those who follow the Kantian view are not concerned about treating another as a means, but rather about treating someone in a way that contradicts the other's personhood itself—that is, in a way that denies the fact that the person is not simply a means but is also an end. A paradigm case is when I treat someone in a way that serves my ends but, at the same time, is contrary to the other's best interest. It is true that a subject's participation in a clinical trial serves scientific ends, but what has not been shown is that it is contrary to the best interests of the subject. In cases where the two equipoise conditions are satisfied, this cannot be shown.

However, in some cases we are uncertain about whether an intervention will serve the best interests of the other, and so we ask that person. That is one reason for requiring informed consent to studies. There is another. By obtaining the consent of the other party to treat him as an end to one's own means, in effect, an identity of ends between both parties has been created. Applying this amended Kantian dictum, then, we should ask: Is there anything about clinical trials that necessarily implies that subjects are treated contrary to their personhood? And the answer is, of course, no—provided a proper consent has been obtained.

There remain many hard questions to ask about the ethies of controlled clinical studies. Many talents will be needed to address those questions and to reform current practice. Since those questions will only be asked by those who understand that such studies rest upon a sound ethical foundation, I am hopeful that Markman and others will reconsider their misgivings.

EQUIPOISE AND THE ETHICS OF CLINICAL RESEARCH

Benjamin Freedman

There is widespread agreement that ethics requires that each clinical trial begin with an honest null hypothesis.[1,2] In the simplest model, testing a new treatment B on a defined patient population P for which the current accepted treatment is A, it is necessary that the clinical investigator be in a state of genuine uncertainty regarding the comparative merits of treatments A and B for population P. If a physician knows that these treatments are not equivalent, ethics requires that the superior treatment be recommended. Following Fried, I call this state of uncertainty about the relative merits of A and B "equipoise."[3]

Equipoise is an ethically necessary condition in all cases of clinical research. In trials with several arms, equipoise must exist between all arms of the trial; otherwise the trial design should be modified to exdude the inferior treatment. If equipoise is disturbed during the course of a trial, the trial may need to be terminated and all subjects previously enrolled (as well as other patients within the relevant population) may have to be offered the superior treatment. It has been rigorously argued that a trial with a placebo is ethical only in investigating conditions for which there is no known treatment[2]; this argument reflects a special application of the requirement for equipoise. Although equipoise has commonly been discussed in the special context of the ethics of randomized clinical trials,[4,5] it is important to recognize it as an ethical condition of all controlled clinical trials, whether or not they are randomized, placebo-controlled, or blinded.

Freedman, B. "Equipoise and the Ethics of Clinical Research" from *The New England Journal of Medicine* 317: 141–145, 1987.

The recent increase in attention to the ethics of research with human subjects has highlighted problems associated with equipoise. Yet, as I shall attempt to show, contemporary literature, if anything, minimizes those difficulties. Moreover, there is evidence that concern on the part of investigators about failure to satisfy the requirements for equipoise can doom a trial as a result of the consequent failure to enroll a sufficient number of subjects.

The solutions that have been offered to date fail to resolve these problems in a way that would permit clinical trials to proceed. This paper argues that these problems are predicated on a faulty concept of equipoise itself. An alternative understanding of equipoise as an ethical requirement of clinical trials is proposed, and its implications are explored.

Many of the problems raised by the requirement for equipoise are familiar. Shaw and Chalmers have written that a clinician who "knows, or has good reason to believe," that one arm of the trial is superior may not ethically participate.[6] But the reasoning or preliminary results that prompt the trial (and that may themselves be ethically mandatory)[7] may jolt the investigator (if not his or her colleagues) out of equipoise before the trial begins. Even if the investigator is undecided between A and B in terms of gross measures such as mortality and morbidity, equipoise may be disturbed because evident differences in the quality of life (as in the case of two surgical approaches) tip the balance.[3-5,8] In either case in saying "we do not know" whether A or B is better, the investigator may create a false impression in prospective subjects, who hear him or her as saying "no evidence leans either way," when the investigator means "no controlled study has yet had results that reach statistical significance."

Late in the study—when P values are between 0.05 and 0.06—the moral issue of equipoise is most readily apparent,[9,10] but the same problem arises when the earliest comparative results are analyzed.[11] Within the closed statistical universe of the clinical trial, each result that demonstrates a difference between the arms of the trial contributes exactly as much to the statistical conclusion that a difference exists as does any other. The contribution of the last pair of cases in the trial is no greater than that of the first. If, therefore, equipoise is a condition that reflects equivalent evidence for alternative hypotheses, it is jeopardized by the first pair of cases as much as by the last. The investigator who is concerned about the ethics of recruitment after the penultimate pair must logically be concerned after the first pair as well.

Finally, these issues are more than a philosopher's nightmare. Considerable interest has been generated by a paper in which Taylor et al.[12] describe the termination of a trial of alternative treatments for breast cancer. The trial foundered on the problem of patient recruitment, and the investigators trace much of the difficulty in enrolling patients to the fact that the investigators were not in a state of equipoise regarding the arms of the trial. With the increase in concern about the ethics of research and with the increasing presence of this topic in the curricula of medical and graduate schools, instances of the type that Taylor and her colleagues describe are likely to become more common. The requirement for equipoise thus poses a practical threat to clinical research.

RESPONSES TO THE PROBLEMS OF EQUIPOISE

The problems described above apply to a broad class of clinical trials, at all stages of their development. Their resolution will need to be similarly comprehensive. However, the solutions that have so far been proposed address a portion of the difficulties, at best, and cannot be considered fully satisfactory.

Chalmers' approach to problems at the onset of a trial is to recommend that randomization begin with the very first subiect.[11] If there are no preliminary, uncontrolled data in support of the experimental treatment B, equipoise regarding treatments A and B for the patient population P is not disturbed. There are several difficulties with this approach. Practically speaking, it is often necessary to establish details of administration, dosage, and so on, before a controlled trial begins, by means of uncontrolled trials in human subjects. In addition, as I have argued above, equipoise from the investigator's point of view is likely to be disturbed when the hypothesis is being formulated and a protocol is being prepared. It is then, before any subjects have been enrolled, that the information that the investigator has assembled makes the experimental treatment appear to be a reasonable gamble. Apart from these problems, initial randomization will not, as Chalmers recognizes, address disturbances of equipoise that occur in the course of a trial.

Data-monitoring committees have been proposed as a solution to problems arising in the course of the trial.[13] Such committees, operating independently of the investigators, are the only bodies with information concerning the trial's ongoing results. Since this knowledge is not available to the investigators, their equipoise is not disturbed. Although committees are useful in keeping the conduct of a trial free of bias, they cannot resolve the investigators' ethical difficulties. A clinician is not merely obliged to treat a patient on the basis of the information that he or she currently has, but is also required to discover information that would be relevant to treatment decisions. If interim results would disturb equipoise, the investigators are obliged to gather and use that information. Their agreement to remain in ignorance of preliminary results would, by definition, be an unethical agreement, just as a failure to call up the laboratory to find out a patient's test results is unethical. Moreover, the use of a monitoring committee does not solve problems of equipoise that arise before and at the beginning of a trial.

Recognizing the broad problems with equipoise, three authors have proposed radical solutions. All three think that there is an irresolvable conflict between the requirement that a patient be offered the best treatment known (the principle underlying the requirement for equipoise) and the conduct of clinical trials; they therefore suggest that the "best treatment" requirement be weakened.

Schafer has argued that the concept of equipoise, and the associated notion of the best medical treatment, depends on the judgment of patients rather than of clinical investigators.[14] Although the equipoise of an investigator may be disturbed if he or she favors B over A, the ultimate choice of treatment is the patient's. Because the patient's values may restore equipoise, Schafer argues, it is ethical for the investigator to proceed with a trial when the patient consents. Schafer's strategy is directed toward trials that test treatments with known and divergent side effects and will probably not be useful in trials conducted to test efficacy or unknown side effects. This approach, moreover, confuses the ethics of competent medical practice with those of consent. If we assume that the investigator is a competent clinician, by saying that the investigator is out of equipoise, we have by Schafer's account said that in the investigator's professional judgment one treatment is therapeutically inferior—for that patient in that condition, given the quality of life that can be achieved. Even if a patient would consent to an inferior treatment, it seems to me a violation of competent medical practice, and hence of ethics, to make the offer. Of course, complex issues may arise when a patient refuses what the physician considers the best treatment and demands instead an inferior treatment. Without settling that problem, however, we can reject Schafer's position. For Schafer claims that in order to continue to conduct clinical trials it is ethical for the physician to offer (not merely accede to) inferior treatment.

Meier suggests that "most of us would be quite willing to forgo a modest expected gain in the general interest of learning something of value."[15] He argues that we accept risks in everyday life to achieve a variety of benefits, including convenience and economy. In the same way, Meier states, it is acceptable to enroll subjects in clinical trials even though they may not receive the best treatment throughout the course of the trial. Schafer suggests an essentially similar approach.[5, 14] According to this view, continued progress in medical knowledge through clinical trials requires an explicit abandonment of the doctor's fully patient-centered ethic.

These proposals seem to be frank counsels of desperation. They resolve the ethical problems of equipoise by abandoning the need for equipoise. In any event, would their approach allow clinical trials to be conducted? I think this may fairly be doubted. Although many people are presumably altruistic enough to forgo the best medical treatment in the interest of the progress of science, many are not. The numbers and proportions required to sustain the statistical validity of trial results suggest that in the absence of overwhelming altruism, the enrollment of satisfactory numbers of patients will not be possible. In particular, very ill patients, toward whom many of the most important clinical trials are directed, may be disinclined to be altruistic. Finally, as the study by Taylor et al.[12] reminds us, the problems of equipoise trouble investigators as well as patients. Even if patients are prepared to dispense with the best treatment, their physicians, for reasons of ethics and professionalism, may well not be willing to do so.

Marquis has suggested a third approach. "Perhaps what is needed is an ethics that will justify the conscription of subjects for medical research," he has written. "Nothing less seems to justify present practice."[4] Yet, although conscription might enable us to continue present practice, it would scarcely justify it. Moreover, the conscription of physician investigators, as well as subjects, would be necessary, because, as has been repeatedly argued, the problems of equipoise are as disturbing to clinicians as they are to subjects. Is any less radical and more plausible approach possible?

THEORETICAL EQUIPOISE VERSUS CLINICAL EQUIPOISE

The problems of equipoise examined above arise from a particular understanding of that concept, which I will term "theoretical equipoise." It is an understanding that is both conceptually odd and ethically irrelevant. Theoretical equipoise exists when, overall, the evidence on behalf of two alternative treatment regimens is exactly balanced. This evidence may be derived from a variety of sources, including data from the literature, uncontrolled experience, considerations of basic science and fundamental physiologic processes, and perhaps a "gut feeling" or "instinct" resulting from (or superimposed on) other considerations. The problems examined above arise from the principle that if theoretical equipoise is disturbed, the physician has, in Schafer's words, a "treatment preference"—let us say, favoring experimental treatment B. A trial testing A against B requires that some patients be enrolled in violation of this treatment preference.

Theoretical equipoise is overwhelmingly fragile; that is, it is disturbed by a slight accretion of evidence favoring one arm of the trial. In Chalmers' view, equipoise is disturbed when the odds that A will be more successful than B are anything other than 50 percent. It is therefore necessary to randomize treatment assignments beginning with the very first patient, lest equipoise be disturbed. We may say that theoretical equipoise is balanced on a knife's edge.

Theoretical equipoise is most appropriate to one-dimensional hypotheses and causes us to think in those terms. The null hypothesis must be sufficiently simple and "clean" to be finely balanced: Will A or B be superior in reducing mortality or shrinking tumors or lowering fevers in population P? Clinical choice is commonly more complex. The choice of A or B depends on some combination of effectiveness, consistency, minimal or relievable side effects, and other factors. On close examination, for example, it sometimes appears that even trials that purport to test a single hypothesis in fact involve a more complicated, portmanteau measure—e.g., the "therapeutic index" of A versus B. The formulation of the conditions of theoretical equipoise for such complex, multidimensional clinical hypotheses is tantamount to the formulation of a rigorous calculus of apples and oranges.

Theoretical equipoise is also highly sensitive to the vagaries of the investigator's attention and perception. Because of its fragility, theoretical equipoise is disturbed as soon as the investigator perceives a difference between the alternatives—whether or not any genuine difference exists. Prescott writes, for example, "It will be common at some stage in most trials for the survival curves to show visually different survivals," short of significance but "sufficient to raise ethical difficulties for the participants."[16] A visual difference, however, is purely an artifact of the research methods employed: when and by what means data are assembled and analyzed and what scale is adopted for the graphic presentation of data. Similarly, it is common for researchers to employ interval scales for phenomena that are recognized to be continuous by nature—e.g., five-point scales of pain or stages of tumor progression. These interval scales which represent an arbitrary distortion of the available evidence to simplify research, may magnify the differences actually found, with a resulting disturbance of theoretical equipoise.

Finally, as described by several authors, theoretical equipoise is personal and idiosyncratic. It is disturbed when the clinician has, in Schafer's words, what "might even be labeled a bias or a hunch," a preference of a "merely intuitive nature."[14] The investigator who ignores such a hunch, by failing to advise the patient that because of it the investigator prefers B to A or by recommending A (or a chance of random assignment to A) to the patient, has violated the requirement for equipoise and its companion requirement to recommend the best medical treatment.

The problems with this concept of equipoise should be evident. To understand the alternative, preferable interpretation of equipoise, we need to recall the basic reason for conducting clinical trials: there is a current or imminent conflict in the clinical community over what treatment is preferred for patients in a defined population P. The standard treatment is A, but some evidence suggests that B will be superior (because of its effectiveness or its reduction of undesirable side effects, or for some other reason). (In the rare case when the first evidence of a novel therapy's superiority would be entirely convincing to the clinical community, equipoise is already disturbed.) Or there is a split in the clinical community, with some clinicians favoring A and others favoring B. Each side recognizes that the opposing side has evidence to support its position, yet each still thinks that overall its own view is correct. There exists (or, in the case of a novel therapy, there may soon exist) an honest, professional disagreement among expert clinicians about the preferred treatment. A clinical trial is instituted with the aim of resolving this dispute.

At this point, a state of "clinical equipoise" exists. There is no consensus within the expert clinical community about the comparative merits of the alternatives to be tested. We may state the formal conditions under which such a trial would be ethical as follows: at the start of the trial, there must be a state of clinical equipoise regarding the merits of the regimens to be tested and the trial must be designed in such a way as to make it reasonable to expect that, if it is successfully concluded, clinical equipoise will be disturbed: In other words, the results of a successful clinical trial should be convincing enough to resolve the dispute among clinicians.

A state of clinical equipoise is consistent with a decided treatment preference on the part of the investigators. They must simply recognize that their less favored treatment is preferred by colleagues whom they consider to be responsible and competent. Even if the interim results favor the preference of the investigators, treatment B, clinical equipoise persists as long as those results are too weak to influence the judgment of the community of clinicians, because of limited sample size, unresolved possibilities of side effects, or other factors. (This judgment can necessarily be made only by those who know the interim results—whether a data-monitoring committee or the investigators.)

At the point when the accumulated evidence in favor of B is so strong that the committee or investigators believe no open-minded clinician informed of the results would still favor A, clinical equipoise has been disturbed. This may occur well short of the original schedule for the termination of the trial, for unexpected reasons. (Therapeutic effects or side effects may be much stronger than anticipated, for example, or a definable subgroup within population P may be recognized for which the results demonstrably disturb clinical equipoise.) Because of the arbitrary character of human judgment and persuasion, some ethical problems regarding the termination of a trial will remain. Clinical equipoise will confine these problems to unusual or extreme cases, however, and will allow us to cast persistent problems in the proper terms. For example, in the face of a strong established trend, must we continue the trial because of others' blind fealty to an arbitrary statistical bench mark?

Clearly, clinical equipoise is a far weaker—and more common—condition than theoretical equipoise. Is it ethical to conduct a trial on the basis of clinical equipoise, when theoretical equipoise is disturbed? Or, as Schafer and others have argued, is doing so a violation of the physician's obligation to provide patients with the best medical treatment?[4, 5, 14] Let us assume that the investigators have a decided preference for B but wish to conduct a trial on the grounds that clinical (not theoretical) equipoise exists. The ethics committee asks the investigators whether, if they or members of their families were within population P, they would not want to be treated with their preference, B? An affirmative answer is often thought to be fatal to the prospects for such a trial, yet the investigators answer in the affirmative. Would a trial satisfying this weaker form of equipoise be ethical?

I believe that it clearly is ethical. As Fried has emphasized,[3] competent (hence, ethical) medicine is social rather than individual in nature. Progress in medicine relies on progressive consensus within the medical and research communities. The ethics of medical practice grants no ethical or normative meaning to a treatment preference, however powerful, that is based on a hunch or on anything less than evidence publicly presented and convincing to the clinical community. Persons are licensed as physicians after they demonstrate the acquisition of this professionally validated knowledge, not after they reveal a superior capacity for guessing. Normative judgments of their havior—e.g., malpractice actions—rely on a comparison with what is done by the community of medical practitioners. Failure to follow a "treatment preference" not shared by this community and not based on information that would convince it could not be the basis for an allegation of legal or ethical malpractice. As Fried states: "[T]he conception of what is good medicine is the product of a professional consensus." By definition, in a state of clinical equipoise, "good medicine" finds the choice between A and B indifferent.

In contrast to theoretical equipoise, clinical equipoise is robust. The ethical difficulties at the beginning and end of a trial are therefore largely alleviated. There remain difficulties about consent, but these too may be diminished. Instead of emphasizing the lack of evidence favoring one arm over another that is required by theoretical equipoise, clinical equipoise places the emphasis in informing the patient on the honest disagreement among expert clinicians. The fact that the investigator has a "treatment preference," if he or she does, could be disclosed; indeed, if the preference is a decided one, and based on something more than a hunch, it could be ethically mandatory to disclose it. At the same time, it would be emphasized that this preference is not shared by others. It is likely to be a matter of chance that the patient is being seen by a clinician with a preference for B over A, rather than by an equally competent clinician with the opposite preference.

Clinical equipoise does not depend on concealing relevant information from researchers and subjects, as does the use of independent data-monitoring committees. Rather, it allows investigators, in informing subjects, to distinguish appropriately among validated knowledge accepted by the clinical community, data on treatments that are promising but are not (or, for novel therapies, would not be) generally convincing, and mere hunches. Should informed patients decline to participate because they have chosen a specific clinician and trust his or her judgment—over and above the consensus in the professional community—that is no more than the patients' right. We do not conscript patients to serve as subjects in clinical trials.

THE IMPLICATIONS OF CLINICAL EQUIPOISE

The theory of clinical equipoise has been formulated as an alternative to some current views on the ethics of human research. At the same time, it corresponds closely to a preanalytic concept held by many in the research and regulatory communities. Clinical equipoise serves, then, as a rational formulation of the approach of many toward research ethics; it does not so much change things as explain why they are the way they are.

Nevertheless, the precision afforded by the theory of clinical equipoise does help to clarify or reformulate some aspects of research ethics; I will mention only two.

First, there is a recurrent debate about the ethical propriety of conducting clinical trials of discredited treatments, such as Laetrile.[17] Often, substantial political pressure to conduct such tests is brought to bear by adherents of quack therapies. The theory of clinical equipoise suggests that when there is no support for a treatment regimen within the expert clinical community, the first ethical requirement of a trial—clinical equipoise—is lacking; it would therefore be unethical to conduct such a trial.

Second, Feinstein has criticized the tendency of clinical investigators to narrow excessively the conditions and hypotheses of a trial in order to ensure the validity of its results.[18] This "fastidious" approach purchases scientific manageability at the expense of an inability to apply the results to the "messy" conditions of clinical practice. The theory of clinical equipoise adds some strength to this criticism. Overly "fastidious" trials, designed to resolve some theoretical question, fail to satisfy the second ethical requirement of clinical research, since the special conditions of the trial will render it useless for influencing clinical decisions, even if it is successfully completed.

The most important result of the concept of clinical equipoise, however, might be to relieve the current crisis of confidence in the ethics of clinical trials. Equipoise, properly understood, remains an ethical condition for clinical trials. It is consistent with much current practice. Clinicians and philosophers alike have been premature in calling for desperate measures to resolve problems of equipoise.

Notes

1. Levine, R.J. *Ethics and Regulation of Clinical Research.* 2nd ed. Baltimore: Urban & Schwarzenberg, 1986.
2. *Idem.* "The use of placebos in randomized clinical trials. *IRB: Rev Hum Subj Res* 1985; 7(2):1–4.
3. Fried, C. *Medical Experimentation: Personal Integrity and Social Policy.* Amsterdam: North-Holland Publishing, 1974.
4. Marquis, D. "Leaving therapy to chance." *Hastings Cent Rep* 1983; 13(4):40–7.
5. Schafer, A., "The ethics of the randomized clinical trial." *N Engl J Med* 1982 307:719–24.
6. Shaw, L.W., Chalmers, T.C. "Ethics in cooperative clinical trials." *Ann NY Acad Sci* 1970; 169; 487–95.
7. Hollenberg, N.K., Dzau, V.J., Williams, G.H. "Are uncontrolled clinical studies ever justified?" *N Engl J Med* 1980; 303:1067.
8. Levine, R.J., Lebacqz, K. "Some ethical consideration in clinical trials." *Clin Pharmacol Ther* 1979; 25:728–41.
9. Klimt, C.R., Canner, P.L. "Terminating a long-term clinical trial." *Clin Pharmacol Ther* 1979; 25:641–6.
10. Veatch, R.M. "Longitudinal studies, sequential designs and grant renewals: what to do with preliminary data." *IRB: Rev Hum Subj Res* 1979; 1(4): 1–3.
11. Chalmers, T. "The ethics of randomization as a decision-making technique and the problem of informed consent." In: Beauchamp, T.L., Walters, L, eds. *Contemporary Issues in Bioethics.* Encino, CA: Dickenson, 1978:426–9.
12. Taylor, K.M, Margolese, R.G., Soskolne, C.L., "Physicians' reasons for not entering eligible patients in a randomized clinical trial of surgery for breast cancer." *N Engl J Med* 1984; 310:1363–7.
13. Chalmers, T.C. "Invited remarks." *Clin Pharmacol Ther* 1979; 25:649–50.
14. Schafer, A. "The randomized clinical trial: for whose benefit?" *IRB: Rev Hum Subj Res* 1985; 7(2): 4–6.
15. Meier, P. "Terminating a trial—the ethical problem." *Clin Pharmacol Ther* 1979; 25:633–40.
16. Prescot, R.J. "Feedback of data to participants during clinical trials." In: Tagnon, H.J., Staquet, M.J., eds. *Controversies in cancer design of trials and treatment.* New York: Masson Publishing, 1979:55–61.
17. Cowan, D.H. "The ethics of clinical trials of ineffective therapy." *IRB: Rev Hum Subj Res* 1981; 3(5):10–1.
18. Feinstein, A.R. "An additional basic science for clinical medicine. II. The limitations of randomized trials." *Ann Intern Med* 1983; 99:544–50.

I am indebted to Robert J. Levine, M.D., and to Harold Merskey, D.M., for their valuable suggestions.

THE ETHICS OF CLINICAL RESEARCH IN THE THIRD WORLD

Marcia Angell

An essential ethical condition for a randomized clinical trial comparing two treatments for a disease is that there be no good reason for thinking one is better than the other.[1,2] Usually, investigators hope and even expect that the new treatment will be better, but there should not be solid evidence one way or the other. If there is, not only would the trial be scientifically redundant, but the investigators would be guilty of knowingly giving inferior treatment to some participants in the trial. The necessity for investigators to be in this state of equipoise,[2] applies to placebo-controlled trials, as well. Only when there is no known effective treatment is it ethical to compare a potential new treatment with a placebo. When effective treatment exists, a placebo may not be used. Instead, subjects in the control group of the study must receive the best known treatment. Investigators are responsible for all subjects enrolled in a trial, not just some of them, and the goals of the research are always secondary to the well-being of the participants. Those requirements are made clear in the Declaration of Helsinki of the World Health Organization (WHO), which is widely regarded as providing the fundamental guiding principles of research involving human subjects.[3] It states, "In research on man [*sic*], the interest of science and society should never take precedence over considerations related to the well-being of the subject," and "In any medical study, every patient—including those of a control group, if any—should be assured of the best proven diagnostic and therapeutic method."

Angell, M. "The Ethics of Clinical Research in the Third World." From the *New England Journal of Medicine* 337: 847–849.

One reason ethical codes are unequivocal about investigators' primary obligation to care for the human subjects of their research is the strong temptation to subordinate the subjects' welfare to the objectives of the study. That is particularly likely when the research question is extremely important and the answer would probably improve the care of future patients substantially. In those circumstances, it is sometimes argued explicitly that obtaining a rapid, unambiguous answer to the research question is the primary ethical obligation. With the most altruistic of motives, then, researchers may find themselves slipping across a line that prohibits treating human subjects as means to an end. When that line is crossed, there is very little left to protect patients from a callous disregard of their welfare for the sake of research goals. Even informed consent, important though it is, is not protection enough, because of the asymmetry in knowledge and authority between researchers and their subjects. And approval by an institutional review board, though also important, is highly variable in its responsiveness to patients' interests when they conflict with the interests of researchers.

A textbook example of unethical research is the Tuskegee Study of Untreated Syphilis.[4] In that study, which was sponsored by the U.S. Public Health Service and lasted from 1932 to 1972, 412 poor African-American men with untreated syphilis were followed and compared with 204 men free of the disease to determine the natural history of syphilis. Although there was no very good treatment available at the time the study began (heavy metals were the standard treatment), the research continued even after penicillin became widely available and was known to be highly effective against syphilis. The study was not terminated until it came to the attention of a reporter and the outrage provoked by front-page stories in the *Washington Star* and *New York Times* embarrassed the Nixon administration into calling a halt to it.[5] The ethical violations were multiple: Subjects did not provide informed consent (indeed, they were deliberately deceived); they were denied the best known treatment; and the study was continued even after highly effective treatment became available. And what were the arguments in favor of the Tuskegee study? That these poor African-American men probably would not have been treated anyway, so the investigators were merely observing what would have happened if there were no study; and that the study was important (a "never-to-be-repeated opportunity," said one physician after penicillin became available).[6] Ethical concern was even stood on its head when it was suggested that not only was the information valuable, but it was especially so for people like the subjects—an impoverished rural population with a very high rate of untreated syphilis. The only lament seemed to be that many of the subjects inadvertently received treatment by other doctors.

Some of these issues are raised by Lurie and Wolfe elsewhere. They discuss the ethics of ongoing trials in the Third World of regimens to prevent the vertical transmission of human immunodeficiency virus (HIV) infection.[7] All except one of the trials employ placebo-treated control groups, despite the fact that zidovudine has already been clearly shown to cut the rate of vertical transmission greatly and is now recommended in the United States for all HIV-infected pregnant women. The justifications are reminiscent of those for the Tuskegee study: Women in the Third World would not receive antiretroviral treatment anyway, so the investigators are simply observing what would happen to the subjects' infants if there were no study. And a placebo-controlled study is the fastest, most efficient way to obtain unambiguous information that will be of greatest value in the Third World. Thus, in response to protests from Wolfe and others to the secretary of Health and Human Services, the directors of the National Institutes of Health (NIH) and the Centers for Disease Control and Prevention (CDC)—the organizations sponsoring the studies—argued, "It is an unfortunate fact that the current standard of perinatal care for the HIV-infected pregnant women in the sites of the studies does not include any HIV prophylactic intervention at all," and the inclusion of placebo controls "will result in the most rapid, accurate, and reliable answer to the question of the value of the intervention being studied compared to the local standard of care."[8]

Whalen et al. report the results of a clinical trial in Uganda of various regimens of prophylaxis against tuberculosis in HIV-infected adults, most of whom had positive tuberculin skin tests.[9] This study, too, employed a placebo-treated control group, and in some ways it is analogous to the studies criticized by Lurie and Wolfe. In the United States it would probably be impossible to carry out such a study, because of long-standing official recommendations that HIV-infected persons with positive tuberculin skin tests receive prophylaxis against tuberculosis. The first was issued in 1990 by the CDC's Advisory Committee for Elimination of Tuberculosis.[10] It stated that tuberculin-test-positive persons with HIV infection "should be considered candidates for preventive therapy." Three years later, the recommendation was reiterated more strongly in a joint statement by the American Thoracic Society and the CDC, in collaboration with the Infectious Diseases Society of America and the American Academy of Pediatrics.[11] According to this statement, "... the identification of persons with dual infection and the administration of preventive therapy to these persons is of great importance." However, some believe that these recommendations were premature, since they were based largely on the success of prophylaxis in HIV-negative persons.[12]

Whether the study by Whalen et al. was ethical depends, in my view, entirely on the strength of the preexisting evidence. Only if there was genuine doubt about the benefits of prophylaxis would a placebo group be ethically justified. This is not the place to review the scientific evidence, some of which is discussed in the editorial of Msamanga and Fawzi.[13] Suffice it to say that the case is debatable. Msamanga and Fawzi conclude that "future studies should not include a placebo group, since preventive therapy should be considered the standard of care." I agree. The difficult question is whether there should have been a placebo group in the first place.

Although I believe an argument can be made that a placebo-controlled trial was ethically justifiable because it was still uncertain whether prophylaxis would work, it should not be argued that it was ethical because no prophylaxis is the "local standard of care" in sub-Saharan Africa. For reasons discussed by Lurie and Wolfe, that reasoning is badly flawed.[7] As mentioned earlier, the Declaration of Helsinki requires control groups to receive the "best" current treatment, not the local one. The shift in wording between "best" and "local" may be slight, but the implications are profound. Acceptance of this ethical relativism could result in widespread exploitation of vulnerable Third World populations for research programs that could not be carried out in the sponsoring country.[14] Furthermore, it directly contradicts the Department of Health and Human Services' own regulations governing U.S.-sponsored research in foreign countries,[15] as well as joint guidelines for research in the Third World issued by WHO and the Council for International Organizations of Medical Sciences,[16] which require that human subjects receive protection at least equivalent to that in the sponsoring country. The fact that Whalen et al. offered isoniazid to the placebo group when it was found superior to placebo indicates that they were aware of their responsibility to all the subjects in the trial.

The *Journal* has taken the position that it will not publish reports of unethical research, regardless of their scientific merit.[14, 17] After deliberating at length about the study by Whalen at al., the editors concluded that publication was ethically justified, although there remain differences among us. The fact that the subjects gave informed consent and the study was approved by the institutional review board at the University Hospitals of Cleveland and Case Western Reserve University and by the Ugandan National AIDS Research Subcommittee certainly supported our decision but did not allay all our misgivings. It is still important to determine whether clinical studies are consistent with preexisting, widely accepted ethical guidelines, such as the Declaration of Helsinki, and with federal regulations, since they cannot be influenced by pressures specific to a particular study.

Quite apart from the merits of the study by Whalen et al., there is a larger issue. There appears to be a general retreat from the clear principles enunciated in the Nuremberg Code and the Declaration of Helsinki as applied to research in the Third World. Why is that? Is it because the "local standard of care" is different? I don't think so. In my view, that is merely a self-serving justification after the fact. Is it because diseases and their treatments are very different in the Third World, so that information gained in the industrialized world has no relevance and we have to start from scratch? That, too, seems an unlikely explanation, although here again it is often offered as a justification. Sometimes there may be relevant differences between populations, but that cannot be assumed. Unless there are specific indications to the contrary, the safest and most reasonable position is that people everywhere are likely to respond similarly to the same treatment.

I think we have to look elsewhere for the real reasons. One of them may be a slavish adherence to the tenets of clinical trials. According to these, all trials should be randomized, double-blind, and placebo-controlled, if at all possible. That rigidity may explain the NIH's pressure on Marc Lallemant to include a placebo group in his study, as described by Lurie and Wolfe.[7] Sometimes journals are blamed for the problem, because they are thought to demand strict conformity to the standard methods. That is not true, at least not at this journal. We do not want a scientifically neat study if it is ethically flawed, but like Lurie and Wolfe we believe that in many cases it is possible, with a little ingenuity, to have both scientific and ethical rigor.

The retreat from ethical principles may also be explained by some of the exigencies of doing clinical research in an increasingly regulated and competitive environment. Research in the Third World looks relatively attractive as it becomes better funded and regulations at home become more restrictive. Despite the existence of codes requiring that human subjects receive at least the same protection abroad as at home, they are still honored partly in the breach. The fact remains that many studies are done in the Third World that simply could not be done in the countries sponsoring the work. Clinical trials have become a big business, with many of the same imperatives. To survive, it is necessary to get the work done as quickly as possible, with a minimum of obstacles. When these considerations prevail, it seems as if we have not come very far from Tuskegee after all. Those of us in the research community need to redouble our commitment to the highest ethical standards, no matter where the research is conducted, and sponsoring agencies need to enforce those standards, not undercut them.

Notes

1. Angell, M. "Patients' preferences in randomized clinical trials." *N Engl J* Med 1984; 310:1385–7.
2. Freedman, B. "Equipoise and the ethics of clinical research." *N Engl J Med* 1987;317:141–5.
3. Declaration of Helsinki IV, 41st World Medical Assembly, Hong Kong, September 1989. In: Annas GJ, Grodin MA, eds. The Nazi doctors and the Nuremberg Code: human rights in human experimentation. New York: Oxford University Press, 1992:339–42.
4. "Twenty years after: the legacy of the Tuskegee syphilis study." *Hastings Cent Rep* 1992;22(6): 29–40.
5. Caplan, A.L. "When evil intrudes." *Hastings Cent Rep* 1992; 22(6): 29–32.
6. "The development of consent requirements in research ethics." In: Faden, R.R., Beauchamp, T.L. *A History and Theory of Informed Consent*. New York: Oxford University Press, 1986: 151–99.
7. Lurie, P., Wolfe, S.M. "Unethical trials of interventions to reduce perinatal transmission of the human immunodeficiency virus in developing countries." *N Engl J Med* 1997; 337:853–6.
8. The conduct of clinical trials of maternal-infant transmission of HIV supported by the United States Department of Health and Human Scrvices in developing countries. Washington, D.C.: Department of Health and Human Services, July 1997.
9. Whalen, C.C., Johnson, J.L., Okwera, A., et al. "A trial of three regimens to prevent tuberculosis in Ugandan adults infected with the human immunodeficiency virus." *N Engl J Med* 1997; 337:801–8.
10. "The use of preventive therapy for tuberculosis infection in the United States: recommendations of the Advisory Committee for Elimination of Tuberculosis." *MMWR Morb Mortal Wkly Rep* 1990; 39(RR-8): 9–12.
11. Bass, J.B. Jr, Farer, L.S., Hopewell, P.C., et al. "Treatment of tuberculosis and tuberculosis infection in adults and children." *Am J Respir Crit Care Med* 1994; 149:1359–74.
12. De Cock, K.M., Grant, A., Porter, J.D. "Preventive therapy for tuberculosis in HIV-infected persons: international recommendations, research, and practice." *Lancet* 1995; 345:833–6.
13. Msamanga, G.I., Fawzi, W.W., "The double burden of HIV infection and tuberculosis in sub-Saharan Africa." *N Engl J Med* 1997;337: 849–51.
14. Angell, M. "Ethical imperialism? Ethics in international collaborative clinical research." *N Engl J Med* 1988; 319:1081–3.
15. "Protection of human subjects," 45 CFR 46 (1996).
16. International ethical guidelines for biomedical research involving human subjects. Geneva: Council for International Organizations of Medical Sciences, 1993.
17. Angell, M. "The Nazi hypothermia experiments and unethical research today." *N Engl J Med* 1990; 322:1462–4.

CHAPTER 10

ALLOCATION OF MEDICAL RESOURCES AND JUSTICE ISSUES IN HEALTH CARE SYSTEMS

THE PROSTITUTE, THE PLAYBOY, AND THE POET: RATIONING SCHEMES FOR ORGAN TRANSPLANTATION

George J. Annas

In the public debate about the availability of heart and liver transplants, the issue of rationing on a massive scale has been credibly raised for the first time in United States medical care. In an era of scarce resources, the eventual arrival of such a discussion was, of course, inevitable. Unless we decide to ban heart and liver transplantation, or make them available to everyone, some rationing scheme must be used to choose among potential transplant candidates. The debate has existed throughout the history of medical ethics. Traditionally it has been stated as a choice between saving one of two patients, both of whom require the immediate assistance of the only available physician to survive.

National attention was focused on decisions regarding the rationing of kidney dialysis machines when they were first used on a limited basis in the late 1960s. As one commentator described the debate within the medical profession:

> "Shall machines or organs go to the sickest, or to the ones with most promise of recovery; on a first-come, first-served basis; to the most 'valuable' patient (based on wealth education, position, what?); to the one with the most dependents; to women and children first; to those who can pay; to whom? Or should lots be cast, impersonally and uncritically?"

In Seattle, Washington, an anonymous screening committee was set up to pick who among competing candidates would receive the life-saving technology. One lay member of the screening committee is quoted as saying:

Reprinted from *The American Journal of Public Health*, Vol. 75, No. 2 (1985), pp. 187–89.

> "The choices were hard … I remember voting against a young woman who was a known prostitute. I found I couldn't vote for her, rather than another candidate, a young wife and mother. I also voted against a young man who, until he learned he had renal failure, had been a ne'er- do-well, a real playboy. He promised he would reform his character, go back to school, and so on, if only he were selected for treatment. But I felt I'd lived long enough to know that a person like that won't really do what he was promising at the time."

When the biases and selection criteria of the committee were made public, there was a general negative reaction against this type of arbitrary device. Two experts reacted to the "numbing accounts of how close to the surface lie the prejudices and mindless cliches that pollute the committee's deliberations," by concluding that the committee was "measuring persons in accordance with its own middle-class values." The committee process, they noted, ruled out "creative nonconformists" and made the Pacific Northwest "no place for a Henry David Thoreau with bad kidneys."

To avoid having to make such explicit, arbitrary, "social worth" determinations, the Congress, in 1972, enacted legislation that provided federal funds for virtually all kidney dialysis and kidney transplantation procedures in the United States. This decision, however, simply served to postpone the time when identical decisions will have to be made about candidates for heart and liver transplantation in a society that does not provide sufficient financial and medical resources to provide all "suitable" candidates with the operation.

There are four major approaches to rationing scarce medical resources: the market approach; the selection committee approach; the lottery approach; and the "customary" approach.

THE MARKET APPROACH

The market approach would provide an organ to everyone who could pay for it with their own funds or private insurance. It puts a very high value on individual rights, and a very low value on equality and fairness. It has properly been criticized on a number of bases, including that the transplant technologies have been developed and are supported with public funds, that medical resources used for transplantation will not be available for higher priority care, and that financial success alone is an insufficient justification for demanding a medical procedure. Most telling is its complete lack of concern for fairness and equity.

A "bake sale" or charity approach that requires the less financially fortunate to make public appeals for funding is demeaning to the individuals involved, and to society as a whole. Rationing by financial ability says we do not believe in equality, but believe that a price can and should be placed on human life and that it should be paid by the individual whose life is at stake. Neither belief is tolerable in a society in which income is inequitably distributed.

THE COMMITTEE SELECTION PROCESS

The Seattle Selection Committee is a model of the committee process. Ethics Committees set up in some hospitals to decide whether or not certain handicapped newborn infants should be given medical care may represent another. These committees have developed because it was seen as unworkable or unwise to explicitly set forth the criteria on which selection decisions would be made. But only two results are possible, as Professor Guido Calabrezi has pointed out: either a pattern of decision-making will develop or it will not. If a pattern does develop (e.g., in Seattle, the imposition of middle-class values), then it can be articulated and those decision "rules" codified and used directly, without resort to the committee. If a pattern does not develop, the committee is vulnerable to the charge that it is acting arbitrarily, or dishonestly, and therefore cannot be permitted to continue to make such important decisions.

In the end, public designation of a committee to make selection decisions on vague criteria will fail because it too closely involves the state and all members of society in explicitly preferring specific individuals over others, and in devaluing the interests those others have in living. It thus directly undermines, as surely as the market system does, society's view of equality and the value of human life.

THE LOTTERY APPROACH

The lottery approach is the ultimate equalizer which puts equality ahead of every other value. This makes it extremely attractive, since all comers have an equal chance at selection regardless of race, color, creed, or financial status. On the other hand, it offends our notions of efficiency and fairness since it makes *no* distinctions among such things as the strength of the desires of the candidates, their potential survival, and their quality of life. In this sense it is a mindless method of trying to solve society's dilemma which is caused by its unwillingness or inability to spend enough resources to make a lottery unnecessary. By making this macro spending decision evident to all, it also undermines society's view of the pricelessness of human life. Afirst-come, first-served system is a type of natural lottery since referral to a transplant program is generally random in time. Nonetheless, higher income groups have quicker access to referral networks and thus have an inherent advantage over the poor in a strict first-come, first-served system.

THE CUSTOMARY APPROACH

Society has traditionally attempted to avoid explicitly recognizing that we are making a choice not to save individual lives because it is too expensive to do so. As long as such decisions are not explicitly acknowledged, they can be tolerated by society. For example, until recently there was said to be a general understanding among general practitioners in Britain that individuals over age 55 suffering from end-stage kidney disease not be referred for dialysis or transplant. In 1984, however, this unwritten practice became highly publicized, with figures that showed a rate of new cases of end-stage kidney disease treated in Britain at 40 per million (versus the US figure of 80 per million) resulting in 1500–3000 "unnecessary deaths" annually. This has, predictably, led to movements to enlarge the National Health Service budget to expand dialysis services to meet this need, a more socially acceptable solution than permitting the now publicly recognized situation to continue.

In the US, the customary approach permits individual physicians to select their patients on the basis of medical criteria or clinical suitability. This, however, contains much hidden social worth criteria. For example, one criterion, common in the transplant literature, requires an individual to have sufficient family support for successful aftercare. This discriminates against individuals without families and those who have become alienated from their families. The criterion may be relevant, but it is hardly medical.

Similar observations can be made about medical criteria that include IQ, mental illness, criminal records, employment, indigency, alcoholism, drug addiction, or geographical location. Age is perhaps more difficult, since it may be impressionistically related to outcome. But it is not medically logical to assume that an individual who is 49 years old is necessarily a better medical candidate for a transplant than one who is 50 years old. Unless specific examination of the characteristics of older persons that make them less desirable candidates is undertaken, such a cut off is arbitrary, and thus devalues the lives of older citizens. The same can be said of blanket exclusions of alcoholics and drug addicts.

In short, the customary approach has one great advantage for society and one great disadvantage: it gives us the illusion that we do not have to make choices; but the cost is mass deception, and when this deception is uncovered, we must deal with it either by universal entitlement or by choosing another method of patient selection.

A COMBINATION OF APPROACHES

A socially acceptable approach must be fair, efficient, and reflective of important social values. The most important values at stake in organ transplantation are fairness itself, equity in the sense of equality, and the value of life. To promote efficiency, it is important that no one receive a transplant unless they want one and are likely to obtain significant benefit from it in the sense of years of life at a reasonable level of functioning.

Accordingly, it is appropriate for there to be an initial screening process that is based *exclusively* on medical criteria designed to measure the probability of a successful transplant, i.e., one in which the patient survives for at least a number of years and is rehabilitated. There is room in medical criteria for social worth judgments, but there is probably no way to avoid this completely. For example, it has been noted that "in many respects social and medical criteria are inextricably intertwined" and that therefore medical criteria might "exclude the poor and disadvantaged because health and socioeconomic status are highly interderpendent." Roger Evans gives an example. In the End Stage Renal Disease Program, "those of lower socioeconomic status are likely to have multiple comorbid health conditions such as diabetes, hepatitis, and hypertension" making them both less desirable candidates and more expensive to treat.

To prevent the gulf between the haves and have nots from widening, we must make every reasonable attempt to develop medical criteria that are objective and independent of social worth categories. One minimal way to approach this is to require that medical screening be reviewed and approved by an ethics committee with significant public representation, filed with a public agency, and made readily available to the public for comment. In the event that more than one hospital in a state or region is offering a particular transplant service, it would be most fair and efficient for the individual hospitals to perform the initial medical screening themselves (based on the uniform, objective criteria), but to have all subsequent non-medical selection done by a method approved by a single selection committee composed of representatives of all hospitals engaged in the particular transplant procedure, as well as significant representation of the public at large.

As this implies, after the medical screening is performed, there may be more acceptable candidates in the "pool" than there are organs or surgical teams to go around. Selection among waiting candidates will then be necessary. This situation occurs now in kidney transplantation, but since the organ matching is much more sophisticated than in hearts and livers (permitting much more precise matching of organ and recipient), and since dialysis permits individuals to wait almost indefinitely for an organ without risking death, the situations are not close enough to permit use of the same matching criteria. On the other hand, to the extent that organs are specifically tissue- and size-matched and fairly distributed to the best matched candidate, the organ distribution system itself will resemble a natural lottery.

When a pool of acceptable candidates is developed, a decision about who gets the next available, suitable organ must be made. We must choose between using a conscious, value-laden, social worth selection criterion (including a committee to make the actual choice), or some type of random device. In view of the unacceptability and arbitrariness of social worth criteria being applied, implicitly or explicitly, by committee, this method is neither viable nor proper. On the other hand, strict adherence to a lottery might create a situation where an individual who has only a one-in-four chance of living five years with a transplant (but who

4) customary approach

could survive another six months without one) would get an organ before an individual who could survive as long or longer, but who will die within days or hours if he or she is not immediately transplanted. Accordingly, the most reasonable approach seems to be to allocate organs on a first-come, first-served basis to members of the pool but permit individuals to "jump" the queue if the second level selection committee believes they are in immediate danger of death (but still have a reasonable prospect for long-term survival with a transplant) and the person who would otherwise get the organ can survive long enough to be reasonably assured that he or she will be able to get another organ.

The first-come, first-served method of basic selection (after a medical screen) seems the preferred method because it most closely approximates the randomness of a straight lottery without the obviousness of making equity the only promoted value. Some unfairness is introduced by the fact that the more wealthy and medically astute will likely get into the pool first, and thus be ahead in line, but this advantage should decrease sharply as public awareness of the system grows. The possibility of unfairness is also inherent in permitting individuals to jump the queue, but some flexibility needs to be retained in the system to permit it to respond to reasonable contingencies.

We will have to face the fact that should the resources devoted to organ transplantation be limited (as they are now and are likely to be in the future), at some point it is likely that significant numbers of individuals will die in the pool waiting for a transplant. Three things can be done to avoid this: 1) medical criteria can be made stricter, perhaps by adding a more rigorous notion of "quality" of life to longevity and prospects for rehabilitation; 2) resources devoted to transplantation and organ procurement can be increased; or 3) individuals can be persuaded not to attempt to join the pool.

Of these three options, only the third has the promise of both conserving resources and promoting autonomy. While most persons medically eligible for a transplant would probably want one, some would not—at least if they understood all that was involved, including the need for a lifetime commitment to daily immunosuppression medications, and periodic medical monitoring for rejection symptoms. Accordingly, it makes public policy sense to publicize the risks and side effects of transplantation, and to require careful explanations of the procedure be given to prospective patients *before* they undergo medical screening. It is likely that by the time patients come to the transplant center they have made up their minds and would do almost anything to get the transplant. Nonetheless, if there are patients who, when confronted with all the facts, would voluntarily elect not to proceed, we enhance both their own freedom and the efficiency and cost-effectiveness of the transplantation system by screening them out as early as possible.

CONCLUSION

Choices among patients that seem to condemn some to death and give others an opportunity to survive will always be tragic. Society has developed a number of mechanisms to make such decisions more acceptable by camouflaging them. In an era of scarce resources and conscious cost containment, such mechanisms will become public, and they will be usable only if they are fair and efficient. If they are not so perceived, we will shift from one mechanism to another in an effort to continue the illusion that tragic choices really don't have to be made, and that we can simultaneously move toward equity of access, quality of services, and cost containment without any challenges to our values. Along with the prostitute, the playboy, and the poet, we all need to be involved in the development of an access model to extreme and expensive medical technologies with which we can live.

ALCOHOLICS AND LIVER TRANSPLANTATION

Carl Cohen, Martin Benjamin, et al.

Alcoholic cirrhosis of the liver—severe scarring due to the heavy use of alcohol—is by far the major cause of end-stage liver disease. For persons so afflicted, life may depend on receiving a new, transplanted liver. The number of alcoholics in the United States needing new livers is great, but the supply of available livers for transplantation is small. *Should those whose end-stage liver disease was caused by alcohol abuse be categorically excluded from candidacy for liver transplantation?* This question, partly medical and partly moral, must now be confronted forthrightly. Many lives are at stake.

Reasons of two kinds underlie a widespread unwillingness to transplant livers into alcoholics: First, there is a common conviction—explicit or tacit—that alcoholics are morally blameworthy, their condition the result of their own misconduct, and that such blameworthiness disqualifies alcoholics in unavoidable competition for organs with others equally sick but blameless. Second, there is a common belief that because of their habits, alcoholics will not exhibit satisfactory survival rates after transplantation, and that, therefore, good stewardship of a scarce lifesaving resource requires that alcoholics not be considered for liver transplantation. We examine both of these arguments.

THE MORAL ARGUMENT

A widespread condemnation of drunkenness and a revulsion for drunks lie at the heart of this public policy issue. Alcoholic cirrhosis—unlike other causes of end-stage liver disease—is brought on by a person's conduct, by heavy drinking. Yet if the dispute here were only about whether to treat someone who is seriously ill because of personal conduct, we would not say—as we do not in cases of other serious diseases resulting from personal conduct—that such conduct disqualifies a person from receiving desperately needed medical attention. Accident victims injured because they were not wearing seat belts are treated without hesitation; reformed smokers who become coronary bypass candidates partly because they disregarded their physicians' advice about tobacco, diet, and exercise are not turned away because of their bad habits. But new livers are a scarce resource, and transplanting a liver into an alcoholic may, therefore, result in death for a competing candidate whose liver disease was wholly beyond his or her control. Thus we seem driven, in this case unlike in others, to reflect on the weight given to the patient's personal conduct. And heavy drinking—unlike smoking, or overeating, or failing to wear a seat belt—is widely regarded as morally wrong.

Many contend that alcoholism is not a moral failing but a disease. Some authorities have recently reaffirmed this position, asserting that alcoholism is "best regarded as a chronic disease." But this claim cannot be firmly established and is far from universally believed. Whether alcoholism is indeed a disease, or a moral failing, or both, remains a disputed matter surrounded by intense controversy.

Even if it is true that alcoholics suffer from a somatic disorder, many people will argue that this disorder results in deadly liver disease only when coupled with a weakness of will—a weakness for which part of the blame must fall on the alcoholic. This consideration underlies the conviction that the alcoholic needing a transplanted liver, unlike a nonalcoholic competing for

Reprinted from *JAMA,* vol. 265, No. 10 (March 13, 1991), pp. 1299–1301.

the same liver, is at least partly responsible for his or her need. Therefore, some conclude, the alcoholic's personal failing is rightly considered in deciding upon his or her entitlement to this very scarce resource.

Is this argument sound? We think it is not. Whether alcoholism is a moral failing, in whole or in part, remains uncertain. But even if we suppose that it is, it does not follow that we are justified in categorically denying liver transplants to those alcoholics suffering from end-stage cirrhosis. We could rightly preclude alcoholics from transplantation only if we assume that qualification for a new organ requires some level of moral virtue or is canceled by some level of moral vice. But there is absolutely no agreement—and there is likely to be none—about what constitutes moral virtue and vice and what rewards and penalties they deserve. The assumption that undergirds the moral argument for precluding alcoholics is thus unacceptable. Moreover, even if we could agree (which, in fact, we cannot) upon the kind of misconduct we would be looking for, the fair weighting of such a consideration would entail highly intrusive investigations into patients' moral habits—investigations universally thought repugnant. Moral evaluation is wisely and rightly excluded from all deliberations of who should be treated and how.

Indeed, we do exclude it. We do not seek to determine whether a particular transplant candidate is an abusive parent or a dutiful daughter, whether candidates cheat on their income taxes or their spouses, or whether potential recipients pay their parking tickets or routinely lie when they think it is in their best interests. We refrain from considering such judgments for several good reasons: (1) We have genuine and well-grounded doubts about comparative degrees of voluntariness and, therefore, *cannot pass judgment fairly*. (2) Even if we could assess degrees of voluntariness reliably, we *cannot know what penalties different degrees of misconduct deserve. (3) Judgments of this kind could not be made consistently in our medical system*—and a fundamental requirement of a fair system in allocating scarce resources is that it treat all in need of certain goods on the same standard, without unfair discrimination by group.

If alcoholics should be penalized because of their moral fault, then all others who are equally at fault in causing their own medical needs should be similarly penalized. To accomplish this, we would have to make vigorous and sustained efforts to find out whose conduct has been morally weak or sinful and to what degree. That inquiry, as a condition for medical care or for the receipt of goods in short supply, we certainly will not and should not undertake.

The unfairness of such moral judgments is compounded by other accidental factors that render moral assessment especially difficult in connection with alcoholism and liver disease. Some drinkers have a greater predisposition for alcohol abuse than others. And for some who drink to excess, the predisposition to cirrhosis is also greater; many grossly intemperate drinkers do not suffer grievously from liver disease. On the other hand, alcohol consumption that might be considered moderate for some may cause serious liver disease in others. It turns out, in fact, that the disastrous consequences of even low levels of alcohol consumption may be much more common in women than in men. Therefore, penalizing cirrhotics by denying them transplant candidacy would have the effect of holding some groups arbitrarily to a higher standard than others and would probably hold women to a higher standard of conduct than men.

Moral judgments that eliminate alcoholics from candidacy thus prove unfair and unacceptable. The alleged (but disputed) moral misconduct of alcoholics with end-stage liver disease does not justify categorically excluding them as candidates for liver transplantation.

MEDICAL ARGUMENT

Reluctance to use available livers in treating alcoholics is due in some part to the conviction that, because alcoholics would do poorly after transplant as a result of their bad habits, good stewardship of organs in short supply requires that alcoholics be excluded from consideration.

This argument also fails, for two reasons: First, it fails because the premise—that the outcome for alcoholics will invariably be poor relative to other groups—is at least doubtful and probably false. Second, it fails because even if the premise were true, it could serve as a good reason to exclude alcoholics only if it were an equally good reason to exclude other groups having a prognosis equally bad or worse. But equally low survival rates have not excluded other groups; fairness therefore requires that this group not be categorically excluded either.

In fact, the data regarding the post-transplant histories of alcoholics are not yet reliable. Evidence gathered in 1984 indicated that the 1-year survival rate for patients with alcoholic cirrhosis was well below the survival rate for other recipients of liver transplants, excluding those with cancer. But a 1988 report, with a larger (but still small) sample number, shows remarkably good results in alcoholics receiving transplants: 1-year survival is 73.2%—and of 35 carefully selected (and possibly nonrepresentative) alcoholics who received transplants and lived 6 months or longer, only two relapsed into alcohol abuse. Liver transplantation, it would appear, can be a very sobering experience. Whether this group continues to do as well as a comparable group of nonalcoholic liver recipients remains uncertain. But the data, although not supporting the broad inclusion of alcoholics, do suggest that medical considerations do not now justify categorically excluding alcoholics from liver transplantation.

A history of alcoholism is of great concern when considering liver transplantation, not only because of the impact of alcohol abuse upon the entire system of the recipient, but also because the life of an alcoholic tends to be beset by general disorder. Returning to heavy drinking could ruin a new liver, although probably not for years. But relapse into heavy drinking would quite likely entail the inability to maintain the routine of multiple medication, daily or twice-daily, essential for immunosuppression and survival. As a class, alcoholic cirrhotics may therefore prove to have substantially lower survival rates after receiving transplants. All such matters should be weighed, of course. But none of them gives any solid reason to exclude alcoholics from consideration categorically.

Moreover, even if survival rates for alcoholics selected were much lower than normal—a supposition now in substantial doubt—what could fairly be concluded from such data? Do we exclude from transplant candidacy members of other groups known to have low survival rates? In fact we do not. Other things being equal, we may prefer not to transplant organs in short supply into patients afflicted, say, with liver cell cancer, knowing that such cancer recurs not long after a new liver is implanted. Yet in some individual cases we do it. Similarly, some transplant recipients have other malignant neoplasms or other conditions that suggest low survival probability. Such matters are weighed in selecting recipients, but they are insufficient grounds to categorically exclude an entire group. This shows that the argument for excluding alcoholics based on survival probability rates alone is simply not just.

THE ARGUMENTS DISTINGUISHED

In fact, the exclusion of alcoholics from transplant candidacy probably results from an intermingling, perhaps at times a confusion, of the moral and medical arguments. But if the moral argument indeed does not apply, no combination of it with probable survival rates can make it applicable. Survival data, carefully collected and analyzed, deserve to be weighed in selecting candidates. These data do not come close to precluding alcoholics from consideration. Judgments of blameworthiness, which ought to be excluded generally, certainly should be excluded when weighing the impact of those survival rates. Some people with a strong antipathy to alcohol abuse and abusers may, without realizing it, be relying on assumed unfavorable data to support a fixed moral judgment. The arguments must be untangled. Actual results with transplanted alcoholics must be considered without regard to moral antipathies.

The upshot is inescapable: there are no good grounds at present—moral or medical—to disqualify a patient with end-stage liver disease from consideration for liver transplantation simply because of a history of heavy drinking.

SCREENING AND SELECTION OF LIVER TRANSPLANT CANDIDATES

In the initial evaluation of candidates for any form of transplantation, the central questions are whether patients (1) are sick enough to need a new organ and (2) enjoy a high enough probability of benefiting from this limited resource. At this stage the criteria should be noncomparative. Even the initial screening of patients must, however, be done individually and with great care.

The screening process for those suffering from alcoholic cirrhosis must be especially rigorous—not for moral reasons, but because of factors affecting survival, which are themselves influenced by a history of heavy drinking—and even more by its resumption. Responsible stewardship of scarce organs requires that the screening for candidacy take into consideration the manifold impact of heavy drinking on long-term transplant success. Cardiovascular problems brought on by alcoholism and other systematic contraindications must be looked for. Psychiatric and social evaluation is also in order, to determine whether patients understand and have come to terms with their condition and whether they have the social support essential for continuing immunosuppression and follow-up care.

Precisely which factors should be weighed in this screening process have not been firmly established. Some physicians have proposed a specified period of alcohol abstinence as an "objective" criterion for selection—but the data supporting such a criterion are far from conclusive, and the use of this criterion to exclude a prospective recipient is at present medically and morally arbitrary.

Indeed, one important consequence of overcoming the strong presumption against considering alcoholics for liver transplantation is the research opportunity it presents and the encouragement it gives to the quest for more reliable predictors of medical success. As that search continues, some defensible guidelines for case-by-case determination have been devised, based on factors associated with sustained recovery from alcoholism and other considerations related to liver transplantation success in general. Such guidelines appropriately include (1) refined diagnosis by those trained in the treatment of alcoholism, (2) acknowledgment by the patient of a serious drinking problem, (3) social and familial stability, and (4) other factors experimentally associated with long-term sobriety.

The experimental use of guidelines like these, and their gradual refinement over time, may lead to more reliable and more generally applicable predictors. But those more refined predictors will never be developed until prejudices against considering alcoholics for liver transplantation are overcome.

Patients who are sick because of alleged self-abuse ought not be grouped for discriminatory treatment—unless we are prepared to develop a detailed calculus of just deserts for health care based on good conduct. Lack of sympathy for those who bring serious disease upon themselves is understandable, but the temptation to institutionalize that emotional response must be tempered by our inability to apply such considerations justly and by our duty *not* to apply them unjustly. In the end, some patients with alcoholic cirrhosis may be judged, after careful evaluation, as good risks for a liver transplant.

OBJECTION AND REPLY

Providing alcoholics with transplants may present a special "political" problem for transplant centers. The public perception of alcoholics is generally negative. The already low rate of organ donation, it may be argued, will fall even lower when it becomes known that donated organs are going to alcoholics. Financial support from legislatures may also suffer. One can imagine the effect on transplantation if the public were to learn that the liver of a teenager killed by a drunken driver had been transplanted into an alcoholic patient. If selecting even a few alcoholics as transplant candidates reduces the number of lives saved overall, might that not be good reason to preclude alcoholics categorically?

No. The fear is understandable, but excluding alcoholics cannot be rationally defended on that basis. Irresponsible conduct attributable to alcohol abuse should not be defended. No excuses should be made for the deplorable consequences of drunken behavior, from highway slaughter to familial neglect and abuse. But alcoholism must be distinguished from those consequences; not all alcoholics are morally irresponsible, vicious, or neglectful drunks. If there is a general failure to make this distinction, we must strive to overcome that failure, not pander to it.

Public confidence in medical practice in general, and in organ transplantation in particular, depends on the scientific validity and moral integrity of the policies adopted. Sound policies will prove publicly defensible. Shaping present health care policy on the basis of distorted public perceptions or prejudices will, in the long run, do more harm than good to the process and to the reputation of all concerned.

Approximately one in every 10 Americans is a heavy drinker, and approximately one family in every three has at least one member at risk for alcoholic cirrhosis. The care of alcoholics and the just treatment of them when their lives are at stake are matters a democratic polity may therefore be expected to act on with concern and reasonable judgment over the long run. The allocation of organs in short supply does present vexing moral problems; if thoughtless or shallow moralizing would cause some to respond very negatively to transplanting livers into alcoholic cirrhotics, that cannot serve as good reason to make such moralizing the measure of public policy.

We have argued that there is now no good reason, either moral or medical, to preclude alcoholics categorically from consideration for liver transplantation. We further conclude that it would therefore be unjust to implement that categorical preclusion simply because others might respond negatively if we do not.

AGING AND THE ENDS OF MEDICINE

Daniel Callahan

In October of 1986, Dr. Thomas Starzl of the Presbyterian-University Hospital in Pittsburgh successfully transplanted a liver into a 76-year-old woman. The typical cost of such an operation is over $200,000. He thereby accelerated the extension to the elderly of the most expensive and most demanding form of high-technology medicine. Not long after that, Congress brought organ transplantation under Medicare coverage, thus guaranteeing an even greater extension of this form of life-saving care to older age groups.

This is, on the face of it, the kind of medical progress we have long grown to hail, a triumph of medical technology and a new-found benefit to be provided by an established entitlement program. But now an oddity. At the same time those events were taking place, a parallel government campaign for cost containment was under way, with a special targeting of health care to the aged under the Medicare program.

It was not hard to understand why. In 1980, the 11% of the population over age 65 consumed some 29% of the total American health care expenditures of $219.4 billion. By 1986, the percentage of consumption by the elderly had increased to 31% and total expenditures to $450 billion. Medicare costs are projected to rise from $75 billion in 1986 to $114 billion in the year 2000, and in real not inflated dollars.

There is every incentive for politicians, for those who care for the aged, and for those of us on the way to becoming old to avert our eyes from figures of that kind. We have tried as a society to see if we can simply muddle our way through. That, however, is no longer sufficient. The time has come, I am convinced, for a full and open reconsideration of our future direction. We can not for much longer continue on our present course. Even if we could find a way to radically increase the proportion of our health care dollar going to the elderly, it is not clear that that would be a good social investment.

Is it sensible, in the face of a rapidly increasing burden of health care costs for the elderly, to press forward with new and expensive ways of extending their lives? Is it possible to even hope to control costs while, simultaneously, supporting the innovative research that generates ever-new ways to spend money? These are now unavoidable questions. Medicare costs rise at an extraordinary pace, fueled by an ever-increasing number and proportion of the elderly. The fastest-growing age group in the United States are those over the age of 85, increasing at a rate of about 10% every two years. By the year 2040, it has been projected that the elderly will represent 21% of the population and consume 45% of all health care expenditures. Could costs of that magnitude be borne?

Yet even as this intimidating trend reveals itself, anyone who works closely with the elderly recognizes that the present Medicare and Medicaid programs are grossly inadequate in meeting the real and full needs of the elderly. They fail, most notably, in providing decent long-term care and medical care that does not constitute a heavy out-of-pocket drain. Members of minority groups, and single or widowed women, are particularly disadvantaged. How will it be possible, then, to keep pace with the growing number of elderly in even providing present levels of care, much less in ridding the system of its present inadequacies and inequities—and, at the same time, furiously adding expensive new technologies?

The straight answer is that it will not be possible to do all of those things and that, worse still, it may be harmful to even try. It may be harmful because of the economic burdens it will impose on younger age groups, and because of the skewing of national social priorities too heavily toward health care that it is coming to require. But it may also be harmful because it suggests to both the young and the old that the key to a happy old age is good health care. That may not be true.

It is not pleasant to raise possibilities of that kind. The struggle against what Dr. Robert Butler aptly and brilliantly called "ageism" in 1968 has been a difficult one. It has meant trying to persuade the public that not all the elderly are sick and senile. It has meant trying to convince Congress and state legislatures to provide more help for the old. It has meant trying to educate the elderly themselves to look upon their old age as a time of new, open possibilities. That campaign has met with only partial success. Despite great progress, the elderly are still subject to discrimination and stereotyping. The struggle against ageism is hardly over.

Three major concerns have, nonetheless, surfaced over the past few years. They are symptoms that a new era has arrived. The first is that an increasingly large share of health care is going to the elderly in comparison with benefits

for children. The federal government, for instance, spends six times as much on health care for those over 65 as for those under 18. As the demographer Samuel Preston observed in a provocative 1984 presidential address to the Population Association of America:

> There is surely something to be said for a system in which things get better as we pass through life rather than worse. The great leveling off of age curves of psychological distress, suicide and income in the past two decades might simply reflect the fact that we have decided in some fundamental sense that we don't want to face futures that become continually bleaker. But let's be clear that the transfers from the working-age population to the elderly are also transfers away from children, since the working ages bear far more responsibility for childrearing than do the elderly.[1]

Preston's address had an immediate impact. The mainline aging advocacy groups responded with pained indignation, accusing Preston of fomenting a war between the generations. But led by Dave Durenberger, Republican Senator from Minnesota, it also stimulated the formation of Americans for Generational Equity (AGE), an organization created to promote debate on the burden to future generations, but particularly the Baby Boom generation, of "our major social insurance programs."[2] These two developments signalled the outburst of a struggle over what has come to be called "Intergenerational equity" that is only now gaining momentum.

The second concern is that the elderly dying consume a disproportionate share of health care costs. Stanford economist Victor Fuchs has noted:

> At present, the United States spends about 1 percent of the gross national product on health care for elderly persons who are in their last year of life. ... One of the biggest challanges facing policy makers for the rest of this century will be how to strike an appropriate balance between care of the [elderly] dying and health services for the rest of the population.

The third concern is summed up in an observation by Jerome L. Avorn, M.D., of the Harvard Medical School:

> With the exception of the birth-control pill, each of the medical-technology interventions developed since the 1950s has its most widespread impact on people who are past their fifties—the further past their fifties, the greater the impact.[4]

Many of these interventions were not intended for the elderly. Kidney dialysis, for example, was originally developed for those between the age of 15 and 45. Now some 30% of its recipients are over 65.

These three concerns have not gone unchallenged. They have, on the contrary, been strongly resisted, as has the more general assertion that some form of rationing of health care for the elderly might become necessary. To the charge that the elderly receive a disproportionate share of resources, the response has been that what helps the elderly helps every other age group. It both relieves the young of the burden of care for elderly parents they would otherwise have to bear and, since they too will eventually become old, promises them similar care when they come to need it. There is no guarantee, moreover, that any cutback in health care for the elderly would result in a transfer of the savings directly to the young. Our system is not that rational or that organized. And why, others ask, should we contemplate restricting care for the elderly when we wastefully spend hundreds of millions of dollars on an inflated defense budget?

The charge that the elderly dying receive a large share of funds hardly proves that it is an unjust or unreasonable amount. They are, after all, the most in need. As some important studies have shown, moreover, it is exceedingly difficult to know that someone is dying; the most expensive patients, it turns out, are those who are expected to live but who actually die. That most new technologies benefit the old more than the young is perfectly sensible: most of the killer diseases of the young have now been conquered.

These are reasonable responses. It would no doubt be possible to ignore the symptoms that the raising of such concerns represents, and to put off for at least a few more years any full confrontation with the overpowering tide of elderly now on the way. There is little incentive for politicians to think about, much less talk about, limits of any kind on health care for the aged; it is a politically hazardous topic. Perhaps also, as Dean Guido Calabresi of the Yale Law School and his colleague Philip Bobbitt observed in their thoughtful 1978 book *Tragic Choices*, when we are forced to make painful allocation choices, "Evasion, disguise, temporizing … [and] averting our eyes enables us to save some lives even when we will not save all."[5]

Yet however slight the incentives to take on this highly troubling issue, I believe it is inevitable that we must. Already rationing of health care under Medicare is a fact of life, though rarely labeled as such. The requirement that Medicare recipients pay the first $500 of the costs of hospital care, that there is a cutoff of reimbursement of care beyond 60 days, and a failure to cover long-term care, are nothing other than allocation and cost-saving devices. As sensitive as it is to the votes of the elderly, the Reagan administration only grudgingly agreed to support catastrophic health care costs of the elderly (a benefit that will not, in any event, help many of the aged). It is bound to be far more resistant to long-term care coverage, as will any administration.

But there are other reasons than economics to think about health care for the elderly. The coming economic crisis provides a much-needed opportunity to ask some deeper questions. Just what is it that we want medicine to do for us as we age? Earlier cultures believed that aging should be accepted, and that it should be in part a time of preparation for death. Our culture seems increasingly to reject that view, preferring instead, it often seems, to think of aging as hardly more than another disease, to be fought and rejected. Which view is correct? To ask that question is only to note that disturbing puzzles about the ends of medicine and the ends of aging lie behind the more immediate financing worries. Without some kind of answer to them, there is no hope of finding a reasonable, and possibly even a humane, solution to the growing problem of health care for the elderly.

Let me put my own view directly. The future goal of medicine in the care of the aged should be that of improving the quality of their life, not in seeking ways to extend that life. In its longstanding ambition to forestall death, medicine has in the care of the aged reached its last frontier. That is hardly because death is absent elsewhere—children and young adults obviously still die of maladies that are open to potential cure—but because the largest number of deaths (some 70%) now occur among those over the age of 65, with the highest proportion in those over 85. If death is ever to be humbled, that is where the essentially endless work remains to be done. But however tempting that challenge, medicine should now restrain its ambition at that frontier. To do otherwise will, I believe, be to court harm to the needs of other age groups and to the old themselves.

Yet to ask medicine to restrain itself in the face of aging and death is to ask more than it, or the public that sustains it, is likely to find agreeable. Only a fresh understanding of the ends and meaning of aging, encompassing two conditions, are likely to make that a plausible stance. The first is that we—both young and old—need to understand that it is possible to live out a meaningful old age that is limited in time, one that does not require a compulsive effort to turn to medicine for more life to make it bearable. The second condition is that, as a culture, we need a more supportive context for aging and death, one that cherishes and respects the elderly while at the same time recognizing that their primary orientation should be to the young and the generations to come, not to their own age group. It will be no less necessary to recognize that in the passing of the generations lies the constant reinvigoration of biological life.

Neither of these conditions will be easy to realize. Our culture has, for one thing, worked hard to redefine old age as a time of liberation, not decline. The terms "modern maturity" or "prime time" have, after all, come to connote a time of travel, new ventures in education and self-discovery, the ever-accessible tennis court or golf course, and delightfully periodic but gratefully brief visits from well-behaved grandchildren.

This is, to be sure, an idealized picture. Its attraction lies not in its literal truth but as a widely accepted utopian reference point. It projects the vision of an old age to which more and more believe they can aspire and which its proponents think an affluent country can afford if it so chooses. That it requires a medicine that is singleminded in its aggressiveness against the infirmities of old age is of a piece with its hopes. But as we have come to discover, the costs of that kind of war are prohibitive. No matter how much is spent the ultimate problem will still remain: people age and die. Worse still, by pretending that old age can be turned into a kind of endless middleage, we rob it of meaning and significance for the elderly themselves. It is a way of saying that old age can be acceptable only to the extent that it can mimic the vitality of the younger years.

There is a plausible alternative: that of a fresh vision of what it means to live a decently long and adequate life, what might be called a natural life span. Earlier generations accepted the idea that there was a natural life span—the biblical norm of three score years and ten captures that notion (even though, in fact, that was a much longer life span than was then typically the case). It is an idea well worth reconsidering, and would provide us with a meaningful and realizable goal. Modern medicine and biology have done much, however to wean us away from that kind of thinking. They have insinuated the belief that the average life span is not a natural fact at all, but instead one that is strictly dependent upon the state of medical knowledge and skill. And there is much to that belief as a statistical fact: the average life expectancy continues to increase, with no end in sight.

But that is not what I think we ought to mean by a natural life span. We need a notion of a full life that is based on some deeper understanding of human need and sensible possibility, not the latest state of medical technology or medical possibility. We should instead think of a natural life span as the achievement of a life long enough to accomplish for the most part those opportunities that life typically affords people and which we ordinarily take to be the prime benefits of enjoying a life at all—that of loving and living, of raising a family, of finding and carrying out work that is satisfying, of reading and thinking, and of cherishing our friends and families.

If we envisioned a natural life span that way, then we could begin to intensify the devising of ways to get people to that stage of life, and to work to make certain they do so in good health and social dignity. People will differ on what they might count as a natural life span; determining its appropriate range for social policy purposes would need extended thought and debate. My own view is that it can now be achieved by the late 70s or early 80s.

That many of the elderly discover new interests and new facets of themselves late in life—my mother took up painting in her seventies and was selling her paintings up until her death at 86—does not mean that we should necessarily encourage a kind of medicine that would make that the norm. Nor does it mean that we should base social and welfare policy on possibilities of that kind. A more reasonable approach is to ask how medicine can help most people live out a decently long life, and how that life can be enhanced along the way.

A longer life does not guarantee a better life—there is no inherent connection between the two. No matter how long medicine enabled people to live, death at any time—at age 90, or 100, or 110—would frustrate some possibility, some as-yet-unrealized goal. There is sadness in that realization, but not tragedy. An easily preventable death of a young child is an outrage. The death from an incurable disease of someone in the prime of young adulthood is a tragedy. But death at an old age, after a long and full life, is simply sad, a part of life itself.

As it confronts aging, medicine should have as its specific goal that of averting premature death, understood as death prior to a natural life span, and the relief of suffering thereafter. It should pursue those goals in order that the elderly can finish out their years with as little needless pain as possible, and with as much vigor as can be generated in contributing to the welfare of younger age groups and to the community of which they are a part. Above all, the elderly need to have a sense of the meaning and significance of their stage in life, one that is not dependent for its human value on economic productivity or physical vigor.

What would a medicine oriented toward the relief of suffering rather than the deliberate extension of life be like? We do not yet have a clear and ready answer to that question, so long-standing, central, and persistent has been the struggle against death as part of the self-conception of medicine. But the Hospice movement is providing us with much helpful evidence. It knows how to distinguish between the relief of suffering and the extension of life. A greater control by the elderly over their dying—and particularly a more readily respected and enforceable right to deny aggressive life-extending treatment—is a long-sought, minimally necessary goal.

What does this have to do with the rising cost of health care for the elderly? Everything. The indefinite extension of life combined with a never-satisfied improvement in the health of the elderly is a recipe for monomania and limitless spending. It fails to put health in its proper place as only one among many human goods. It fails to accept aging and death as part of the human condition. It fails to present to younger generations a model of wise stewardship.

How might we devise a plan to limit health care for the aged under public entitlement programs that is fair, humane, and sensitive to their special requirements and dignity? Let me suggest three principles to undergird a quest for limits. First, government has a duty, based on our collective social obligations to each other, to help people live out a natural life span, but not actively to help medically extend life beyond that point. Second, government is obliged to develop under its research subsidies, and pay for, under its entitlement programs, only that kind and degree of lif-extending technology necessary for medicine to achieve and serve the end of a natural life span. The question is not whether a technology is available that can save the life of someone who has lived out a natural life span, but whether there is an obligation for society to provide them with that technology. I think not. Third, beyond the point of natural life span, government should provide only the means necessary for the relief of suffering, not life-extending technology. By proposing that we use age as a specific criterion for the limitation of life-extending health care, I am challenging one of the most revered norms of contemporary geriatrics: that medical need and not age should be the standard of care. Yet the use of age as a principle for the allocation of resources can be perfectly valid, both a necessary and legitimate basis for providing health care to the elderly. There is not likely to be any better or less arbitrary criterion for the limiting of resources in the face of the open-ended possibilities of medical advancement in therapy for the aged.

Medical "need," in particular, can no longer work as an allocation principle. It is too elastic a concept, too much a function of the state of medical art. A person of 100 dying from congestive heart failure "needs" a heart transplant no less than someone who is 30. Are we to treat both needs as equal? That is not economically feasible or, I would argue, a sensible way to allocate scarce resources. But it would be required by a strict need-based standard.

Age is also a legitimate basis for allocation because it is a meaningful and universal category. It can be understood at the level of common sense. It is concrete enough to be employed for policy purposes. It can also, most importantly, be of value to the aged themselves if combined with an ideal of old age that focuses on its quality rather than its indefinite extension.

I have become impressed with the philosophy underlying the British health care system and the way it meets the needs of the old and the chronically ill. It has, to begin with, a tacit allocation policy. It emphasizes improving the quality of life through primary care medicine and well-subsidized home care and institutional programs for the elderly rather than through life-extending acute care medicine. The well-known difficulty in getting dialysis after 55 is matched by like restrictions on access to open heart surgery, intensive care units, and other forms of expensive technology. An undergirding skepticism toward technology makes that a viable option. That attitude, together with a powerful drive for equity, "explains," as two commentators have noted, "why most British put a higher value on primary care for the population as a whole than on an abundance of sophisticated technology for the few who may benefit from it."[6]

That the British spend a significantly smaller proportion of their GNP (6.2%) on health care than Americans (10.8%) for an almost identical outcome in health status is itself a good advertisement for its priorities. Life expectancies are, for men, 70.0 years in the U.S. and 70.4 years in Great Britain; and, for women, 77.8 in the U.S. and 76.7 in Great Britain. There is, of course, a great difference in the ethos of the U.S. and Britain, and our individualism and love of technology stand in the way of a quick shift of priorities.

Yet our present American expectations about aging and death, it turns outs, may not be all that reassuring. How many of us are really so certain that high-technology American medicine promises us all that much better an aging and death, even if some features appear improved and the process begins later than in earlier times? Between the widespread fear of death in an impersonal ICU, cozened about machines and invaded by tubes, on the one hand, or wasting away in the back ward of a nursing home, on the other, not many of us seem comforted.

Once we have reflected on those fears, it is not impossible that most people could be persuaded that a different, more limited set of expectations for health care could be made tolerable. That would be all the more possible if there was a greater assurance than at present that one could live out a full life span, that one's chronic illnesses would be better supported, and that long-term care and home care would be given a more powerful societal backing than is now the case. Though they would face a denial of life-extending medical care beyond a certain age, the old would not necessarily fear their aging any more than they now do. They would, on the contrary, know that a better balance had been struck between making our later years as good as possible rather than simply trying to add more years.

This direction would not immediately bring down the costs of care of the elderly; it would add new costs. But it would set in place the beginning of a new understanding of old age, one that would admit of eventual stabilization and limits. The time has come to admit we can not go on much longer on the present course of open-ended health care for the elderly. Neither confident assertions about American affluence, nor tinkering with entitlement provisions and cost-containment strategies will work for more than a few more years. It is time for the dream that old age can be an infinite and open frontier to end, and for the unflagging, but self-deceptive, optimism that we can do anything we want with our economic system be put aside.

The elderly will not be served by a belief that only a lack of resources, or better financing mechanisms, or political power, stand between them and the limitations of their bodies. The good of younger age groups will not be served by inspiring in them a desire to live to an old age that will simply extend the vitality of youth indefinitely, as if old age is nothing but a sign that medicine has failed in its mission. The future of our society will not be served by allowing expenditures on health care for the elderly endlessly and uncontrollably to escalate, fueled by a false altruism that thinks anything less is to deny the elderly their dignity. Nor will it be served by that pervasive kind of self-serving that urges the young to support such a crusade because they will eventually benefit from it also.

We require instead an understanding of the process of aging and death that looks to our obligation to the young and to the future, that recognizes the necessity of limits and the acceptance of decline and death, and that values the old for their age and not for their continuing youthful vitality. In the name of accepting the elderly and repudiating discrimination against them, we have mainly succeeded in pretending that, with enough will and money, the unpleasant part of old age can be abolished. In the name of medical progress we have carried out a relentless war against death and decline, failing to ask in any probing way if that will give us a better society for all age groups.

The proper question is not whether we are succeeding in giving a longer life to the aged. It is whether we are making of old age a decent and honorable time of life. Neither a longer lifetime nor more life-extending technology are the way to that goal. The elderly themselves ask for greater financial security, for as much self-determination and independence as possible, for a decent quality of life and not just more life, and for a respected place in society.

The best way to achieve those goals is not simply to say more money and better programs are needed, however much they have their important place. We would do better to begin with a sense of limits, of the meaning of the human life cycle, and of the necessary coming and going of the generations. From that kind of a starting point, we could devise a new understanding of old age.

References

1. Preston, S.H. 1984. "Children and the elderly: divergent paths for America's dependents." *Demography* 21:491–495.
2. "Americans for Generational Equity." *Case Statement*. May 1986.
3. Fuchs, V.R. 1984. "Though much is taken: reflections on aging, health, and medical care." *Milbank Mem. Fund Q.* 62:464–465.
4. Avorn, J.L. 1986. "Medicine, health and the geriatric transformation." *Daedalus* 115:211–225.
5. Calabresi, G., and Bobbit, P. 1978. *Tragic Choices*. W. W. Norton, New York, NY.
6. Miller, F.H., and Miller, A.H., 1986. "The painful prescription: a procrustean perspective." *N. Engl. J. Med.* 314:1385.

WHY SAYING NO TO PATIENTS IN THE UNITED STATES IS SO HARD

COST CONTAINMENT, JUSTICE, AND PROVIDER AUTONOMY

Norman Daniels

If cost-containment measures, such as the use of Medicare's diagnosis-related groups (DRGs), involved trimming only unnecessary health care services from public budgets, they would pose no moral problems. Instead, such measures lead physicians and hospitals to deny some possibly beneficial care, such as longer hospitalization or more diagnostic tests, to their own patients—that is, at the "micro" level.[1] Similarly, if the "macro" decision not to disseminate a new medical procedure, such as liver transplantation,

Daniels, N. "Why Saying No to Patients in the United States Is So Hard: Cost Containment, Justice, and Provider Autonomy." From *The New England Journal of Medicine*, 314: 1380–1383 (May 22, 1986).

resulted only in the avoidance of waste, then it would pose no moral problem. When is it morally justifiable to say no to beneficial care or useful procedures? And why is it especially difficult to justify saying no in the United States?

JUSTICE AND RATIONING

Because of scarcity and the inevitable limitation of resources even in a wealthy society, justice—however we elucidate it—will require some no-saying at both the macro and micro levels of allocation. No plausible principles of justice will entitle an individual patient to every potentially beneficial treatment. Providing such treatment might consume resources to which another patient has a greater claim. Similarly, no class of patients is entitled to whatever new procedure offers them some benefit. New procedures have opportunity costs, consuming resources that could be used to produce other benefits, and other classes of patients may have a superior claim that would require resources to be invested in alternative ways.

How rationing works depends on which principles of justice apply to health care. For example, some people believe that health care is a commodity or service no more important than any other and that it should be distributed according to the ability to pay for it. For them, saying no to patients who cannot afford certain services (quite apart from whether income distribution is itself just or fair) is morally permissible. Indeed, providing such services to all might seem unfair to the patients who are required to pay.

In contrast, other theories of justice view health care as a social good of special moral importance. In one recent discussion,[2] health care was seen to derive its moral importance from its effect on the normal range of opportunities available in society. This range is reduced when disease or disability impairs normal functioning. Since we have social obligations to protect equal opportunity, we also have obligations to provide access, without financial or discriminatory barriers, to services that adequately protect and restore normal functioning. We must also weigh new technological advances against alternatives, to judge the overall effect of their introduction on equal opportunity. This gives a slightly new sense to the term "opportunity cost." As a result, people are entitled only to services that are part of a system that on the whole protects equal opportunity. Thus, even an egalitarian theory that holds health care as of special moral importance justifies sometimes saying no at both the macro and micro levels.

SAYING NO IN THE BRITISH NATIONAL HEALTH SERVICE

Aaron and Schwartz have documented how beneficial services and procedures have had to be rationed within the British National Health Service, since its austerity budget allows only half the level of expenditures of the United States.[3] The British, for example, use less x-ray film, provide little treatment for metastatic solid tumors, and generally do not offer renal dialysis to the elderly. Saying no takes place at both macro and micro levels.

Rationing in Great Britain takes place under two constraints that do not operate at all in the United States. First, although the British say no to some beneficial care, they nevertheless provide universal access to high-quality health care. In contrast, over 10 percent of the population in the United States lacks insurance, and racial differences in access and health status persist.[4,5] Second, saying no takes place within a regionally centralized budget. Decisions about introducing new procedures involve weighing the net benefits of alternatives within a closed system. When a procedure is rationed, it is clear which resources are available for alternative uses. When a procedure is widely used, it is clear which resources are unavailable for other uses. No such closed system constrains American decisions about the dissemination of technological advances except, on a small scale and in a derivative way, within some health maintenance organizations (HMOs).

These two constraints are crucial to justifying British rationing. The British practitioner who follows standard practice within the system does not order the more elaborate x-ray diagnosis that might be typical in the United States, possibly even despite the knowledge that additional information would be useful. Denying care can be justified as follows: Though the patient might benefit from the extra service, ordering it would be unfair to other patients in the system. The system provides equitable access to a full array of services that are fairly allocated according to professional judgments about which needs are most important. The salve of this rationale may not be what the practitioner uses to ease his or her qualms about denying beneficial treatment, but it is available.

A similar rationale is available at the macro level. If British planners believe alternative uses of resources will produce a better set of health outcomes than introducing coronary bypass surgery on a large scale, they will say no to a beneficial procedure. But they have available the following rationale: Though they would help one group of patients by introducing this procedure, its opportunity cost would be too high. They would have to deny other patients services that are more necessary. Saying yes instead of no would be unjust.

These justifications for saying no at both levels have a bearing on physician autonomy and on moral obligations to patients. Within the standards of practice determined by budget ceilings in the system, British practitioners remain autonomous in their clinical decision making. They are obliged to provide the best possible care for their patients within those limits. Their clinical judgments are not made "impure" by institutional profit incentives to deny care.

The claim made here is not that the British National Health Service is just, but that considerations of justice are explicit in its design and in decisions about the allocation of resources. Because justice has this role, British rationing can be defended on grounds of fairness. Of course, some no-saying, such as the denial of renal dialysis to elderly patients, may raise difficult questions of justice.[2] The issue here, however, is not the merits of each British decision, but the framework within which they are made.

SAYING NO IN THE UNITED STATES

Cost-containment measures in the United States reward institutions, and in some cases practitioners, for delivering treatment at a lower cost. Hospitals that deliver treatment for less than the DRG rate pocket the difference. Hospital administrators therefore scrutinize the decisions of physicians to use resources, pressuring some to deny beneficial care. Many cannot always act in their patients' best interests, and they fear worse effects if DRGs are extended to physicians' charges.[6] In some HMOs and preferred-provider organizations, there are financial incentives for the group to shave the costs of treatment—if necessary, by denying some beneficial care. In large HMOs, in which risks are widely shared, there may be no more denial of beneficial care than under fee-for-service reimbursement.[7] But in some capitation schemes, individual practitioners are financially penalized for ordering "extra" diagnostic tests, even if they think their patient needs them. More ominously, some hospital chains are offering physicians a share of the profits made in their hospitals from the early discharge of Medicare patients.

When economic incentives to physicians lead them to deny beneficial care, there is a direct threat to what may be called the ethic of agency. In general, granting physicians considerable autonomy in clinical decision making is necessary if they are to be effective as agents pursuing their patients' interests. The ethic of agency constrains this autonomy in ways that protect the patient, requiring that clinical decisions be competent, respectful of the patient's autonomy, respectful of the other rights of the patient (e.g., confidentiality), free from consideration of the physician's interests, and uninfluenced by judgments about the patient's worth. Incentives that reward physicians for denying beneficial care clearly risk violating the fourth-mentioned constraint, which, like the fifth, is intended to keep clinical decisions pure—that is, aimed at the patient's best interest.

Rationing need not violate the constraint that decisions must be free from consideration of the physician's interest. British practitioners are not rewarded financially for saying no to their patients. Because our cost-containment schemes give incentives to violate this constraint, however, they threaten the ethic of agency. Patients would be foolish to think the physician who benefits from saying no is any longer their agent. (Of course, patients in the United States traditionally have had to guard against unnecessary treatments, since reimbursement schemes provided incentives to overtreat.)

American physicians face a problem even when the only incentive for denying beneficial care is the hospital's, not theirs personally. For example, how can they justify sending a Medicare patient home earlier than advisable? Can they, like their British peers, claim that justice requires them to say no and that therefore they do no wrong to their patients?

American physicians cannot make this appeal to the justice of saying no. They have no assurance that the resources they save will be put to better use elsewhere in the health care system. Reducing a Medicare expenditure may mean only that there is less pressure on public budgets in general, and thus more opportunity to invest the savings in weapons. Even if the savings will be freed for use by other Medicare patients, American physicians have no assurance that the resources will be used to meet the greater needs of other patients. The American health care system, unlike the British one, establishes no explicit priorities for the use of resources. In fact, the savings from saying no may be used to invest in a procedure that may never provide care of comparable importance to that the physician is denying the patient. In a for-profit hospital, the profit made by denying beneficial treatment may be returned to investors. In many cases, the physician can be quite sure that saying no to beneficial care will lead to greater harm than providing the care.

Saying no at the macro level in the United States involves similar difficulties. A hospital deciding whether or not to introduce a transplantation program competes with other medical centers. To remain competitive, its directors will want to introduce the new service. Moreover, they can point to the dramatic benefit the service offers. How can opponents of transplantation respond? They may (correctly) argue that it will divert resources from other projects—projects that are perhaps less glamorous, visible, and profitable but that nevertheless offer comparable medical benefits to an even larger class of patients. They insist that the opportunity costs of the new procedure are too great.

This argument about opportunity costs, so powerful in the British National Health Service, loses its force in the United States. The alternatives to the transplantation program may not constitute real options, at least in the climate of incentives that exists in America. Imagine someone advising the Humana Hospital Corporation, "Do not invest in artificial hearts, because you could do far more good if you established a prenatal maternal care program in the catchment area of your chain." Even if correct, this appeal to opportunity costs is unlikely to be persuasive, because Humana responds to the incentives society offers. Artificial hearts, not prenatal maternal-care programs, will keep its hospitals on the leading technological edge, and if they become popular, will bring far more lucrative reimbursements than the prevention of low-birth-weight morbidity and mortality. The for-profit Humana, like many nonprofit organizations, merely responded to existing incentives when it introduced a transplantation program during the early 1980s, at the same time prenatal care programs lost their federal funding. Similarly, cost-containment measures in some states led to the cutting of social and psychological services but left high-technology services untouched.[8] Unlike their British colleagues, American planners cannot say, "Justice requires that we forgo this procedure because the resources it requires will be better spent elsewhere in the system. It is fair to say no to this procedure because we can thereby provide more important treatments to other patients."

The failure of this justification at both the micro and macro levels in the United States has the same root cause. In our system, saying no to beneficial treatments or procedures carries no assurance that we are saying yes to even more beneficial ones. Our system is not closed; the opportunity costs of a treatment or procedure are not kept internal to it. Just as important, the system as a whole is not governed by a principle of distributive justice, appeal to which is made in decisions about disseminating technological advances. It is not closed under constraints of justice.

SOME CONSEQUENCES

Saying no to beneficial treatments or procedures in the United States is morally hard, because providers cannot appeal to the justice of their denial. In ideally just arrangements and even in the British system, rationing beneficial care is nevertheless fair to all patients in general. Cost-containment measures in our system carry with them no such justification.

The absence of this rationale has important effects. It supports the feeling of many physicians that current measures interfere with their duty to act in their patients' best interests. Of course, physicians should not think that duty requires them to reject any resource limitations on patient care. But it is legitimate for physicians to hope they may act as their patients' advocate within the limits allowed by the just distribution of resources. Our cost-containment measures thus frustrate a legitimate expectation about what duty requires. Eroding this sense of duty will have a long-term destabilizing effect.

The absence of a rationale based on justice also affects patients. Resource constraints mean that each patient can legitimately expect only the treatments due him or her under a just or fair distribution of health care services. But if beneficial treatment is denied even when justice does not require or condone it, then the patient has reason to feel aggrieved. Patients will not trust providers who put their own economic gain above patient needs. They will be especially distrustful of schemes that allow doctors to profit by denying care. Conflicts between the interests of patients and those of physicians or hospitals are not a necessary feature of a just system of rationing care. The fact that such conflicts are central in our system will make patients suspect that there is no one to be trusted as their agent. In the absence of a concern for just distribution, our cost-containment measures may make patients seek the quite different justice afforded by tort litigation, further destabilizing the system.

Finally, these effects point to a deeper issue. Economic incentives such as those embedded in current cost-containment measures are not a substitute for social decisions about health care priorities and the just design of health care institutions. These incentives to providers, even if they do eliminate some unnecessary medical services, will not ensure that we will meet the needs of our aging population over the next several decades in a morally acceptable fashion or that we will make effective—and just—use of new procedures. These hard choices must be faced publicly and explicitly.

References

1. Diagnosis-related groups (DRGs) and the Medicare program: implications for medical technology. Washington D.C.: U.S. Congress, 1983. (Office of Technology Assessment OTA-TM-H-17.)

2. Daniels, N. *Just Health Care.* New York: Cambridge University Press, 1985.
3. Aaron, H.J., and Schwartz, W. B. "The painful prescription: rationing hospital care." Washington D.C.: The Brookings Institution, 1984.
4. President's Commission for the Study of Ethical Problems in Medicine and Biomedical and Behavioral Research. Securing access to health care: ethical implications of differences in the accessibility of health services. Vol. 1. Washington D.C.: Government Printing Office. 1983.
5. Iglehart, J.K. "Medical care of the poor—a growing problem." *N Engl J Med* 1985; 313:59–63.
6. Jencks, S.F., and Dobson, A. "Strategies for reforming Medicare's physician payments: physician diagnosis-related groups and other approaches." *N Engl J Med* 1985; 312:1492–9.
7. Yelin, E.H., Hencke, C.J., Kramer, J.S., Nevitt, M.C., Shearn, M., and Epstein, W.V. "A comparison of the treatment of rheumatoid arthritis in health maintenance organizations and fee-for-service practices." *N Engl J Med* 1985; 312:962–7.
8. Cromwell, J., and Kanak, J. "The effects of prospective reimbursement on hospital adoption and service sharing." *Health Care Financ Rev* 1982; 4:67.

THE DOCTOR AS DOUBLE AGENT

Marcia Angell

In earlier times—that is, before 1980—it was generally agreed that the doctor's sole obligation was to take care of each patient. The doctor was the patient's fiduciary or agent, and the doctor was to act only in the patient's interest. Now all that has changed. Many of us—economists, governmental officials, corporate executives, even ethicists, and yes, even many doctors themselves—now believe that doctors have other obligations that compete with their obligation to the patient. In particular, they believe that doctors have acquired an obligation to save resources for society. Doing so requires doctors to practice with one eye on costs, which may mean sometimes denying beneficial care that they would surely have provided in earlier times.

According to the new view, doctors are no longer simply agents for their patients. They are now agents for society's needs as well. They are, in short, *double agents*, expected to decide whether the benefits of treatment to their patients are worth the costs to society. Many distinguished ethicists have enthusiastically embraced this new ethic (Callahan 1990; Morreim 1991). To them, keeping an eye on the price tag means saving scarce resources for other, more important uses.

How did this extraordinary shift in our view of doctors' obligations come about? Is it just coincidence that it began with our first realization—roughly in the mid-1970s—that our seemingly endless resources were in fact finite? And is it just coincidence that it accorded with the wishes of the third-party payers—who discovered during the 1980s that they had severe and growing budgetary problems? In short, can it be that the ethical underpinnings of the practice of medicine have been scrapped in a single decade for financial reasons? Is economics driving ethics?

I'll begin with my conclusions. I believe that doctors *are* now asked to be double agents and that their dual obligation is a recent construct, which arose out of the economic difficulties of the large third-party payers. I will argue that we embrace this new ethic at our peril. Even if

---

Angell, M., "The Doctor as Double Agent." *Kennedy Institute of Ethics Journal* 3(1993), 279–286.

we as a society decide that health care should take a smaller piece of the national economic pie, there are ways to do this that do not entail rebuilding—and perhaps destroying—almost overnight, the ethical underpinnings of the profession.

HISTORICAL REVIEW

First, a quick review of how we got here. This requires an economic analysis, since my thesis is that economics is now driving ethics. The economic history of health care in the United States can be divided into three phases. First, there was the phase of the true market, lasting until roughly World War II. Patients paid doctors out-of-pocket for their medical care. If the price was too high, the doctor was confronted with an unhappy patient. Even after private insurance companies began to flourish in the 1930s, the premiums were still paid out-of-pocket and so patients continued to feel the costs, although the pain was blunted. Fortunately, medical care was fairly inexpensive. Unfortunately, it was also relatively ineffective, compared with the power of modern medicine.

The second phase was marked by the entry of big business into the health care picture. Big business began to offer health insurance as a fringe benefit in order to evade the wage and price controls in effect during World War II. Offering health insurance was tantamount to increasing wages, and furthermore, it was not taxed. The connection between employment and health insurance was thus an historical accident that haunts us still. But the important effect of this connection for the discussion here is that it insulates patients from the costs of medical care. Neither doctors nor patients had to worry any longer about the costs of medical care. With the enactment of Medicare and Medicaid in 1966, this insulation from costs spread to the poor and, most importantly, to the elderly—a politically powerful group. By the end of the 1960s, anything resembling a true market in health care had vanished. Nearly everyone was covered by third-party payers—government, business, and private insurance companies. And medical care was becoming both more expensive and more effective. Despite the increasing costs, the third parries happily paid the charges, with few questions asked.

The third phase began with the realization that health care costs were consistently rising far more rapidly than the GNP. Now that patients and doctors and hospitals were insulated from accountability, there were no limits on the expansion of the health care industry in this country. It was open-ended and nearly risk-free, absorbing an ever greater share of our domestic spending. While national expenditures for other social goods, such as education, stagnated or declined, expenditures for health care rose rapidly—from roughly 6 percent of the GNP in 1965 to nearly 10 percent in 1980 to 13 percent in 1991 (Stoline and Weiner 1993).

Not only was there nothing to stop the inflation, but there were features that virtually guaranteed it. These included the piecework, fee-for-service reimbursement system that is greatly skewed toward high-technology procedures and specialists. Doctors, of course, act as both providers and purchasing agents, so these highly paid specialists could easily generate their own business. For example, the cardiologist who recommends coronary angiography to a patient also bills for it.

COST CONTAINMENT

In the 1970s, the Arab oil embargo made Americans realize that our resources were finite. Health care costs began to occupy the attention of some experts and policymakers. By the 1980s, it became clear to nearly everyone that we could not indefinitely sustain rising health care costs, and for the first time, efforts were made to control them. "Cost containment" crept into the lexicon, and by the end of the 1980s the *New England Journal of Medicine* probably received more manuscripts about cost containment than about cancer. The efforts to control costs were spearheaded by the major third parties—government and big business. They were responding essentially to budgetary problems, not to moral problems. They went about cost containment in a number of ad hoc, uncoordinated ways, as briefly mentioned below. None of them was notably successful. In fact health care costs rose even faster—I believe, *because* of cost containment efforts, not despite them.

Regulation by third parties, including managed care, simply led to the growth of an expensive and intrusive new bureaucracy. Efforts to foster competition led to increased marketing, not to lower prices. And attempts to limit demand through higher deductibles and copayments simply shifted costs and limited care, primarily to the most vulnerable. Efforts by insurers to avoid risks also shifted costs. In general, savings to one part of the system were costs to another. In fact, the dominant characteristic of the American health care system is that there is no system. There is just a hodgepodge of arrangements, existing independently, often working at cross purposes, and generating enormous administrative costs. Indeed, administrative costs—billing, marketing, underwriting, claims processing, utilization review—now consume more than 20 cents of the health care dollar (Woolhandler and Himmelstein 1991).

Why do I recapitulate this sorry history of the economics of the American health care system? I do so because it is important to understand the context in which doctors are being invited to act as double agents. They are invited to do so in an open-ended, inherently inflationary system (or, rather, nonsystem) that spends roughly 40 percent more per citizen on health care than the next most expensive health care system in the world and at least twice as much on administrative costs. Further, this system is embedded in a society that routinely spends billions and billions on such goods as tobacco, television ads, and cosmetics. Clearly, we as a society are not facing scarcity; instead we are facing the inefficient and frivolous use of vast resources.

SAVING FOR THIRD PARTIES

What precisely is the doctor supposed to do as double agent? In a nutshell, doctors are supposed to tailor their care of patients to save money for third parties. For example, under the DRG system of hospital reimbursement for Medicare patients, doctors are supposed to be agents for the hospital, discharging patients as rapidly as possible and keeping services to a minimum so that the hospital can game the system. In many HMOs doctors are expected to keep costs as low as possible, and some HMOs even directly reward doctors with bonuses when the HMO comes out ahead. They may also withhold a portion of doctors' salaries if they refer patients to specialists too often or use too many tests and procedures. Thus, doctors are agents for the HMO and have a direct incentive to undertreat their patients, just as in the fee-for-service system they have an incentive to overtreat them. Other forms of managed care also deter doctors from delivering care. Those that require utilization review often make it so complicated and difficult to get approval for hospitalization or procedures that the doctor is reluctant even to try. And it should be noted that nearly all medical care these days is managed in one way or another, by which I mean it is subject to efforts of insurers to limit care.

In essence, then, doctors are increasingly being asked, in one way or another, to save money for a third party—and sometimes for themselves—by scrimping on the medical care they deliver. But the pressure is seldom described in these terms. Instead, it is described as practicing "cost-effective" medicine. "Cost-effective" is the new watchword. It used to be a technical term that referred to the least expensive of two equally effective alternatives, or to the most effective of two equally costly ones. Now it is simply a shorthand for any attempt to save money. The word sounds fine, and who can object to it?

JUSTIFICATION FOR DOUBLE AGENTS

But how can we justify asking doctors to deprive their patients of care, including clearly beneficial care that in other circumstances they would not hesitate to provide? Just as the problem is new, so are the ethical justifications.

First, it is claimed that limiting care is what society wishes, and that the medical profession has an obligation not only to accept the will of society but to further it. Doctors are simply anticipating and delivering what is expected of them by the body politic, despite the fact that individual patients may want something else when they are sick.

Second, it is argued that because third parties now pay for nearly all medical care, they have gained a legitimate voice—indeed, the overriding voice—in how much medical care patients should receive. I find this a peculiarly American argument. Essentially the message is that whoever pays the piper calls the tune. The purest example of this view is the Oregon plan for rationing the care received by Medicaid patients. This is often described as a decision to allocate scarce resources rationally and justly, but it is, of course, nothing of the sort. It is instead a matter of taxpayers deciding to limit the care received by the poor, on the grounds that the taxpayers are funding it. Those who drew up the priority list of medical services are not those to whom it would apply. Even if we were to accept the idea that paying for medical care confers the right to limit it, we should remember that most patients do in fact still pay for their medical care, just as they always did. They simply pay in advance and indirectly, through their work or their taxes. The third parties are not using their own money.

The third justification for doctors to be double agents is the most compelling. It appeals to the doctor as good citizen or, more dramatically, to the doctor as occupant of a metaphorical lifeboat with limited supplies. According to this view, resources saved in denying patients expensive medical care could be used to provide less expensive care to a larger number of patients. Or it could be used for even more important public purposes, such as education. This line of argument has been put forward most persuasively by Dan Callahan (1990) who contends that Americans have overvalued individual health care compared with other social goods.

ARGUMENTS AGAINST DOUBLE AGENTS

Despite these justifications, I see five serious problems with the view that doctors should act to contain costs, patient by patient. First and most simply, this view of the role of doctors is based on the premise that resources in our health care system are in fact scarce. But, of course, they aren't. The mere fact that we spend so much more on health care than all other advanced nations is proof that our health care resources are plentiful. Given that in 1990 we spent about $2,566 on every man, woman, and child in the United States, and Canada spent only $1,770, we can hardly claim inadequate resources (Schieber, Poullier, and Greenwald 1992). And since Americans and Canadians are subject to the same ailments and have roughly the same outcomes, we must assume that our system is grossly inefficient. Clearly, the answer to an inefficient system is not to stint on care, but rather to restructure the system to make it more efficient.

Second, enlisting doctors as ad hoc rationers presumes that resources saved by denying health care would be put to better use. But in our system there is absolutely no reason to think that it would. As Norman Daniels (1986) has pointed out, in the United Kingdom or Canada, resources saved by denying care would be used for presumably more valuable health care, but that is not the case here. In the U.S., we do not have a closed system in which funds taken from one form of health care are diverted to another that is deemed to be more important. Instead, funds not used for health care may find their way into any sector of the larger economy, to be used for anything—e.g., defense, education, farm subsidies, or personal savings. Furthermore, even funds that remain within the health care system might not be used for more effective care; instead, money saved on, say, heart transplantation may very well find its way to a hospital's public relations office or to higher salaries for administrators. Under these circumstances, it is very difficult to sustain an ethical argument for doctors acting as double agents. The only principled way to ration health care is to close the system and establish limits that apply to everyone—not just to the poor.

Third, asking doctors to be double agents overlooks an important symbolic function of health care. Our society was founded on the principle that individuals enjoy a set of basic rights that cannot be denied them. As medicine has become increasingly effective in preserving life, medical care has come to be counted among these rights. Thus, doctors are seen to preserve a basic human right, namely life, just as criminal lawyers are seen to preserve liberty by defending their clients. Lawyers do not decide part way through a trial to call it quits because it's just too expensive to go on with it. In both situations, there has been a consensus that the single-minded focus on the patient or the client serves the broader interests of society. This argument is particularly compelling in a society as unequal as ours. People will tolerate the vast inequities in income and privilege in this country only if they feel assured that their irreducible set of rights is truly protected. It has been suggested that high technology medicine may serve precisely such a reassuring function in our society. And public opinion polls tend to support this view (Blendon 1991). The public, in contrast to the third-party payers, does not feel that we are spending too much on health care, only that we are not getting our money's worth.

Fourth, when doctors act as double agents, they are merely acting on their own particular prejudices. They are deciding that this or that medical service costs too much. This is not a medical judgment, but a political or philosophical one. Another doctor (or a plumber or electrician) might make quite a different judgment. This is no way to allocate health care.

And fifth and perhaps most important, the doctor as double agent is not honest. Sick people need and expect their doctors' single purpose to be to heal them. The doctor-patient relationship would not survive a candid statement by the doctor that only care that seems to the doctor to be worth the money will be provided. Anything short of full efforts to heal the individual patient, then, must involve a hidden agenda—an ethically indefensible position.

CONCLUSION

In sum, we should be loath to abandon or modify the patient-centered ethic, and we should be wary of ethical justifications for doing so. Unfortunately, history shows us that ethics in practice are often highly malleable, *justifying* political decisions rather than *informing* them. Necessity is the mother of invention, in ethics as well as in other aspects of life. For example, in 1912, when the AMA thought salaried practice was a threat to the autonomy of the profession, its Code of Ethics pronounced it unethical for physicians to join group practices. Now, some 80 years later, we are again hearing that it is a matter of ethics for the medical profession to carry out what is essentially a political agenda. But ethics should be a little more stable than that. Ethics should be based on fundamental moral principles governing our behavior and obligations toward one another. If a doctor is ethically committed to care for the individual patient, that commitment should not be abridged lightly. And it should not be nullified by a budgetary crunch. Doctors should continue to care for each patient unstintingly, even while they join with other citizens to devise a more efficient and just health care system. To control costs effectively will in my view require a coherent national health care system, with a global cap and a single payer (Angell 1993). Only in this way can we have an affordable health care system that does not require doctors to be double agents.

References

Angell, Marcia. 1993. How Much Will Health Care Reform Cost? *New England Journal of Medicine* 328: 1778–79.

Blendon, Robert J. 1991. The Public View of Medicine. *Clinical Neurosurgery* 37: 2563–65.

Callahan, Daniel. 1990. *What Kind of Life? The Limits of Medical Progress*. New York: Simon & Schuster.

Daniels, Norman. 1986. Why Saying No to Patients in the United States Is So Hard: Cost Containment, Justice, and Provider Autonomy. *New England Journal of Medicine* 314: 1380–83.

Morreim, E. Haavi. 1991. *Balancing Act: The New Medical Ethics of Medicine's Economics*. Boston: Kluwer Academic Publishers.

Schieber, George J.; Poullier, Jean-Pierre; and Greenwald, Leslie M. 1992. U.S. Health Expenditure Performance: An International Comparison and Data Update. *Health Care Financing Review* 13 (4): 1–15.

Stoline, Anne M., and Weiner, Jonathan P. 1993. *The New Medical Marketplace: A Physician's Guide to the Health Care System in the 1990s*. Baltimore: Johns Hopkins University Press.

Woolhandler, Steffie, and Himmelstein, David. 1991. The Deteriorating Administrative Efficiency of the U.S. Health Care System. *New England Journal of Medicine* 324: 1253–58.

INSTITUTIONAL RESPONSES TO MEDICAL MISTAKES: ETHICAL AND LEGAL PERSPECTIVES

Andrew E. Thurman

I have been a health care lawyer for more than 20 years. During that time, I have been faced repeatedly with the issue of how much disclosure my client, a health care institution, should make to a patient (or a patient's surrogate when the patient lacks capacity) regarding a clinically significant medical error. In my experience, it is best for the patients, the institution, and the practitioners within it to adopt and implement a policy of disclosure in such situations.

We intuitively understand that honest admission of medical mistakes, when such mistakes are of clinical significance, is the "right" thing to do. However, in practice, health care providers do not always make such admissions (Kohn, Corrigan, and Donaldson 1999). Practitioners who choose to remain silent present various rationales for their decision. The most common reasons are that such admissions are particularly difficult for health care providers such as physicians, that such admissions may implicate other clinicians, and that such admissions may increase liability exposure (Bogner 1994, pp. 373, 379).

This article first explores the ethical and legal foundations for the premise that the admission of clinically significant medical mistakes is the right thing to do. I then analyze the rationales for failures to make such admissions. This analysis leads to the conclusion that the premises that admission of errors by practitioners is particularly difficult or that it leads to increased liability are without objective foundation. Additionally, admission of errors rarely need implicate other practitioners if such admissions are limited to only those errors that are the responsibility of the practitioner or institution directly involved. In short, admission of clinically significant medical mistakes by practitioners and institutions is not only sound ethics, but probably also good risk management.

Thurman, A. Institutional Responses to Medical Mistakes: Ethical and Legal Perspectives. *Kennedy Institute of Ethics Journal* 11: 2 (2001), pp. 147–156.

THE ETHICAL BASIS FOR ADMITTING MISTAKES

Although one aim of a for-profit health care institution may be to make money for its shareholders, that goal is achieved by providing health care services to those willing to entrust themselves to the care of the institution. A for-profit institution can also have an educational mission, including both the education of those in its service area on health issues and the education of erstwhile providers. The missions of non-profit health care institutions typically include providing for the health care needs of the community and providing health care education to the community and providers.

In either case, the missions of health care institutions are incompatible with "covering up" clinically significant medical errors. As Kapp (1997, pp. 758–59) said:

> Hiding or rationalizing, rather than acknowledging, medical errors is ethically harmful for at least three reasons. First, it interferes with the desirable process of turning errors into educational "treasures" from which both erring physicians and their colleagues might learn and grow professionally. Second, it hurts patients by depriving them and their physicians of information that could potentially be valuable in correcting errors and otherwise improving treatment of present and future patients. ... Patients' families may also be cheated. For instance, fear of uncovering errors that might lead to litigation probably assists in accounting for a decrease in the number of autopsies performed today, thereby diminishing many opportunities for physicians to learn, to comfort families with explanations of the patient's death, and to alert families of discovered genetic risks. Finally, purposeful deception undercuts and attacks the essential fabric of the fiduciary or trust nature of the physician/patient relationship by directly violating the ethical principle of fidelity or truthfulness.

While the "healing" mission directed toward individual patients may not be impacted adversely by failing to admit errors, particularly if the clinical consequences of the errors are insignificant or remediable, other aspects of institutions' missions are negatively implicated. An institution cannot effectively carry out its educational mission or its fiduciary responsibilities if it "covers up" errors. In order to understand clinical health care, as well as health care delivery and other policy issues, lay community members, providers-in-training, and providers all must be familiar with the occurrence and consequences of medical errors.

If the covering up of medical errors is discovered, then the institution's mission is compromised in perhaps an even more fundamental way. The mission of health care institutions, particularly charitable institutions, is grounded in trust. Patients entrust themselves to health care institutions willingly because they perceive, correctly, that the institution has a fiduciary obligation to take care of them. Honesty is at the heart of that obligation: the institution will either take good care of the patient, or explain why they failed to do so and fix it. If potential patients and the community do not trust the institution, then the relationship becomes, at best, one of suspicion, and, at worst, adversarial. In either event, the institution is unable to achieve its mission.

The institution has a specific patient-based ethical obligation to admit clinically significant mistakes. A health care institution has an obligation to inform individual patients or their surrogates of issues that have implications for the patients' health status or course of treatment. If an error has a clinical consequence, the patient needs to know it in order to participate meaningfully in continuing treatment decisions. The lawsuit of a professional football player against his team and team doctors is a high-profile example (*Krueger v. San Francisco Forty-Niners*, 189 Cal. App. 3d 823, 234 Cal. Rptr. 579 (Cal. Ct. App. 1987)). The player asserted that had he been accurately told the extent of his knee injury he would not have continued playing as the team and the team doctors encouraged. He played on and was permanently crippled. The court ruled that he had a cause of action against both the team and the team doctors, though neither had caused the original injury. It can hardly be gainsaid that a hospital has more of a fiduciary obligation to its patients than does a professional football team to its salaried employees.

THE LEGAL BASIS FOR ADMITTING MISTAKES

The legal obligation for certain direct clinical providers, such as physicians, to admit mistakes with clinical consequences is clear. The doctrine of informed consent is imbedded in the health care law of the United States. This doctrine places an obligation squarely upon the physician to inform the patient of their condition and the risks, benefits, and alternatives to the treatment being recommended. This obligation includes within it the obligation to inform the patient of current medical mistakes with clinical consequences, whether committed by the physician or not, since the patient needs the information in order to give adequate informed consent, particularly in the area of continued reliance on certain providers (see, e.g., LeBlang and King 1984; Vogel and Delgado 1980; Kapp 1997).

Although the institution may not have a direct legal duty to disclose clinically significant medical errors under the doctrine of informed consent, in most states the institution has a legal obligation to ensure that adequate processes are in place for legitimate informed consent to occur. This duty certainly encompasses a legal obligation to guarantee that there is an adequate process in place for patients to receive the necessary information concerning clinically significant medical errors to give adequate informed consent to their continuing, post-error treatment (see, e.g., *Thompson v. Nason Hospital* 527 Pa. 330, 591 A.2d 703 (1991)). Moreover, the institution often does have a direct legal obligation to report significant medical errors to third parties, such as the joint Commission on Accreditation of Health Care Organizations (JCAHO), if the error is a "sentinel event," which JCAHO (2000) defines as "an unexpected occurrence involving death or serious physical or psychological injury," or to a state agency if state statutes so require (for a representative example, see 28 Pa. Code Section 51 et. seq.). Although it has not been directly tested in court, it appears likely that a court would hold that an institution has a legal obligation to ensure that patients are appropriately informed of clinically significant medical errors.

As a practical matter, institutions are better served to assume the obligation to disclose errors to patients as a result of remedial processes such as that of the JCAHO or state reporting requirements, rather than have that obligation placed upon them by the courts in a punitive fashion, as has happened to physicians. In a landmark case, the failure to disclose a clinically significant error was held to create a cause of action distinct from the underlying malpractice claim resulting from the error itself (*Simcuski v. Saeli*, 44 N.Y.2d 442, 377 N.E.2d 713 (NY 1978)). According to the lawsuit allegations, a surgeon inadvertently severed a shoulder nerve during a procedure. Instead of admitting the error and providing available treatments, the surgeon told the patient that the loss of sensation and motility was a common surgical aftereffect that would wane with physical therapy. The patient did not discover this was misinformation until the damage was permanent and the period in which a malpractice case could be brought against the surgeon had passed. The patient sued the surgeon for both malpractice and fraud after the three-year malpractice statute of limitations had run, but within the six-year statute of limitations for fraud. The court held that the suit was timely and also held that if the patient could prove that the surgeon had been intentionally deceitful and thereby had deprived the patient of potential relief of the condition, the patient could recover damages for fraud, including potentially punitive damages, in addition to or *without having to prove* malpractice.

BARRIERS TO ADMITTING MISTAKES

Three frequently cited barriers to informing patients of medical errors are: (1) the provider's difficulty in confessing mistakes; (2) the fear of implicating other providers; and (3) the possibility of liability exposure.

At the risk of sounding unsympathetic, the thesis that it is particularly difficult for providers, especially physicians, to admit to errors has nothing more than subjective support from some providers themselves. Many of us, regardless of profession, dislike having to confess error. Although the experience may be educational for others, or ourselves, it is often accompanied by shame, a fear of potential punishment, or a feeling that power or stature has been lost. Using this aversion as a rationale for not following through on an ethical and legal obligation to patients in our charge is not acceptable to society and certainly has never been advanced successfully as a legal defense in a malpractice or deceit claim.

The desire to avoid implication of other practitioners is a more concrete barrier. Although there may be times when a qualified practitioner can assess the appropriateness of prior care with a high degree of accuracy, particularly when an obvious error is involved, complete certainty about whether and by whom a mistake was made is rare. A study has shown that practitioners who engage in retrospective reviews of care differ widely in their assessments (Localio et al. 1996). Rather than offering speculation in the guise of information or assessment, the better course is to confine observations about prior care to an assessment of the patient's current condition. However, such practice should not be used as an excuse for not informing the patient of errors that are the responsibility of the present practitioner or institution. An excellent and frequent example is that of a foreign body left in a surgical patient. Once discovered, usually the best course of action (unless the patient is exceptionally frail) is to remove it, which obviously requires another surgery. The risks, benefits, and alternatives (essentially, leave it in or take it out) should be explained to the patient, and, if consented to, the procedure should be performed expeditiously. It is neither required nor clinically useful to engage in a discussion of whose fault it is, particularly since blame often can be allocated fairly to more than one member of the surgical team. In my experience as a hospital lawyer, if the patient tolerates the second procedure well and is not charged for the second procedure, then little or no liability attaches. (As an aside, the patient sometimes wants the charges for the original procedure written off. If the second procedure goes well, I do not usually do so; in more than 20 years that decision has yet to cost the institutions in question.)

There is a very specific dilemma with this situation: Does an institution have an obligation to inform the patient of a clinically significant error by a member of its staff, including medical staff, even if the staff member objects to the provision of the information? Clearly, in light of the physician's obligations regarding informed consent, the best alternative is to convince the physician to inform the patient directly if it is physician error that is involved. Often the involvement of a medical staff officer or committee can be useful in encouraging the physician to meet this obligation. However, if the staff member persists in refusal, then as the legal officer of an institution, I assert that the institution's ethical and legal obligations require disclosure over the objections. Using the specific example of the New York case mentioned above, I think it likely that if the institution knows of an error and its potential consequences and fails to inform the patient, then the institution has the same legal exposure for fraud as the erring physician.

The final barrier is the perception that disclosure increases liability exposure. There has been some study of this contention. The weight of the available analysis by lawyers, risk managers, and practitioners is that a policy of dealing honestly and forthrightly with the patient reduces liability exposure. Kapp (1997) provides an excellent survey of the available literature and studies, including the opposing arguments.

Although actual liability exposure will be unique to each incident and each decision to reveal or conceal, experience has taught me that over time an honesty policy is less costly. A simple decision tree illustrates this point. The choices are to tell the patient or not tell the patient. If the patient is told, a claim may result, but the claim cannot include sustainable allegations of lack of informed consent or dishonesty by the providers. Moreover, if the patient is told and the error is corrected, the patient may be less inclined to sue, and if there was no damage as a result of the error, probably does not have a sustainable cause of action.

On the other hand, if the patient is not told, there are two possibilities. First, the error may never be discovered, in which case liability is entirely avoided. However, in light of the increasing third-party reporting requirements, the increasing sophistication of patients, and the apparently increasing proliferation of plaintiff's malpractice lawyers, non-discovery is not a good bet, and becomes increasingly risky as the level of clinical consequence of the error increases. The second possibility, that the patient is not told and does discover the error, has considerable negative consequences. The patient is likely to be more hostile and suit-prone because of the legitimate feeling that the physician's and institution's fiduciary obligation to him or her has been violated. As illustrated by the New York case cited above, there are additional potential causes of action, such as fraud for the failure to be forthright. These additional counts potentially increase the cost of settling or trying the case. The erring providers are, in the hands of a skilled plaintiff's attorney, made to look extremely unsympathetic at trial. Juries are notoriously punitive to providers perceived to be dishonest. Furthermore, in many states, such as New York and Pennsylvania, "mere" medical malpractice does not expose the practitioner to punitive damages; fraud does (*Simcuski v. Saeli*, 44 N.Y.2d 442, 377 N.E.2d 713 (N.Y. 1978)). Finally, publicity about the event, and the potential loss of public trust in the institution, can be disastrous.

Because each situation is extremely fact-based, there is unlikely to be conclusive agreement on the effect of disclosure on liability. But it has never been demonstrated effectively that a policy on non-disclosure reduces liability; the weight of opinion is that the opposite is true. Therefore, the liability issue cannot be used as an effective counterweight to the legal and ethical obligation to disclose.

INSTITUTIONAL PROCESS FOR HANDLING ERRORS

Institutions should adopt written policies providing appropriate mechanisms for disclosing medical mistakes that have clinical consequences for patients. The benefit of a written policy is twofold: first, it makes the institution's stance a matter of public record; second, it reduces the possibility of individualized responses to situations that might arise.

Let us examine again the case of the foreign body—e.g. a clamp—left in a patient following surgery, assuming in this case the existence and implementation of an institutional policy on disclosure. The policy should provide that once a mistake has been identified, the attending physician should be immediately notified by administration, risk management, or nursing, unless he/she is already aware. An initial immediate discussion with the attending by a member of one of the aforementioned groups should focus on at least two points: the clinical course to address the mistake and the timing and content of the disclosure to the patient/surrogate. Then there should be disclosure to the patient pursuant to the policy.

The attending should be the discloser, and the disclosure should take place as soon as the patient's clinical condition permits. Ergo, the patient is informed by the surgeon that a clamp was left behind, and that infection can develop around it, or it can move, or cause other problems. The risks and benefits of leaving it or removing it, in light of the patient's clinical condition, are discussed between patient and doctor. The surgeon recommends a course of action, and the patient consents or refuses. Assuming the agreed action is removal, the surgery takes place. The patient may, under the circumstances, prefer that another surgeon perform the procedure, and, assuming another physician with the necessary expertise is available, the patient's desire should prevail. Conceivably, the patient may want the procedure to be performed at another facility, either by the same or a different surgeon. In this case, the clinical implications of moving the patient should be discussed thoroughly with him or her. If the desire remains, it should be honored, and the institution should be prepared to bear any costs involved.

Discussion of fault adds nothing to this process and should be explicitly avoided. For the purpose of determining the clinical course, there is no need to even identify the original surgical team, although a request by the patient that others be used should be honored, and the patient easily can find out later whether it was through review of the medical records.

The attending surgeon should be strongly encouraged to be the discloser, as the attending knows the clinical course best and presumably has the strongest relationship with the patient. If the attending is unwilling to inform the patient and is unwilling to designate another willing physician to do so, then disclosure should be made by an appropriate institution-employed physician or medical staff officer, and the same process should be followed. It is important that the discloser be a physician so that the best possible discussion of the clinical issues can be achieved. Furthermore, in most states, true informed consent can only be as a result of discussion between a patient and physician (see *Valles v. Albert Einstein Medical Center* 758 A.2d 1238 (2000)). Physician disclosure also has the added benefit of focusing the discussion on clinical issues as opposed to management or liability issues.

Generally speaking, the attending should not have the authority to "veto" disclosure. The only exception would be an assertion that the patient is so frail that disclosure will cause clinical harm. Such an assertion should be carefully reviewed by a physician not involved in the patient's care, and should be upheld only in a genuinely apparent case.

In order for the institution to be able to disclose clinical information to a patient over the attending's objection, it is important that the policy be in writing and that all medical staff members be aware of the institution's policy. The policy should also provide that as disclosure is institution policy, those who promote or participate in such disclosure are immune from institutional retaliation and will be protected by the institution.

CONCLUSION

Providers and institutions have a legal and ethical duty to disclose their own medical errors when there are clinical consequences. Although such a policy may cause discomfort, perhaps conflicts between institutions and their staff, and in rare circumstances increased liability, there are no countervailing factors of sufficient weight to mitigate the appropriate execution of that duty.

References

Bogner, Marilyn Sue. 1994. Human Error in Medicine: A Frontier for Change. In *Human Error in Medicine*, ed. Marilyn Sue Bogner, pp. 373–79. New York: Lawrence Erlbaum Associates.

JCAHO. 2000. *Joint Commission on Accreditation of Healthcare Organizations Sentinel Event Policy*. JCAHO: Chicago.

Kapp, Marshall B. 1997. Medical Error vs. Malpractice. *De Paul Journal of Health Care Law* 1:751–72.

Kohn, Linda T.; Corrigan, Janet M.; and Donaldson, Molla S., eds. Committee on Quality of Health Care in America (Institute of Medicine). 1999. *To Err is Human: Building a Safer Health System*. Washington, DC: National Academy Press.

LeBlang, Theodore, and King, Jane L. 1984. Tort Liability for Nondisclosure: The Physician's Legal Obligations to Disclose Patient Illness and Injury. *Dickinson Law Review* 89:1–18.

Localio, A. R.; Weaver, S. L.; Brennan, T A.; et al. 1996. Identifying Adverse Events Caused by Medical Care: Degree of Physician Agreement in a Retrospective Chart Review. *Annals of Internal Medicine* 125:457–64.

Vogel, Joan, and Delgado, Richard. 1980. To Tell the Truth: Physician's Duty to Disclose Medical Mistakes. *UCLA Law Review* 28:52–68.

GUIDELINES FOR DISCLOSURE AND DISCUSSION OF CONDITIONS AND EVENTS WITH PATIENTS, FAMILIES AND GUARDIANS

UPMC Presbyterian Policy and Procedure Manual

I. INTRODUCTION AND BACKGROUND

In the course of hospital care, an extensive amount of clinical information is generated. It includes diagnostic findings, treatment options, responses to interventions, and professional opinions. The information can be positive or negative. Clinical events may or may not be caused by clinicians and consequently may be iatrogenic (caused by medical treatment), nosocomial (occurring in the hospital) or natural events.

In accordance with the informed consent policy (# 4011), Patients' Bill of Rights (# 0154, section II H), and the Guidelines on Forgoing Life Sustaining Treatment (# 4007), patients have the right to information regarding their condition and care. Physicians and other caregivers are obligated to provide accurate information as expeditiously as possible. While it is usually easy to provide positive information, negative information is more difficult to disclose, especially when the cause is iatrogenic.

"Therapeutic privilege" has been invoked to explain why certain negative information might be withheld. By invoking therapeutic privilege, the physician refrains from full disclosure to protect the patient from the effects of receiving the information itself. The use of therapeutic privilege is increasingly being called into question because it decreases patient autonomy and reduces trust.

The following recommendations are provided to clinicians to help guide delivery of sensitive information, positive and negative. Specific recommendations are provided for situations where the information is about an unfavorable or adverse event, or where the information might best be characterized as "bad news."

II. DEFINITIONS

Unfavorable Event or Unfavorable Condition

For the purposes of these guidelines, an unfavorable condition is an occurrence or diagnosis that results in or is likely to result in a significant negative outcome, and/or a significant alteration in the care plan.

Reprinted with permission from the Ethics Committee, University of Pittsburgh Medical Center-Presbyterian Hospital.

An unfavorable event in this context is *not* the same as a sentinel event, which in policy #4025 is defined as, "a serious, unexpected, adverse patient event which has resulted in, or if repeated would have a significant probability of resulting in, loss of life or serious physical or psychological injury, that is judged to be a warning of an underlying problem involving hospital facilities, policies, procedures, systems or personnel."

Adverse Event

An unfavorable event for the purposes of these guidelines is also distinguished from the FDA definition of the term "adverse event," which is a reportable negative effect of a drug or device potentially resulting in death, hospitalization, or medical or surgical intervention. (See policy #4022 Safe Medical Device Act.)

Examples of unfavorable events or conditions for the purpose of these guidelines include a new diagnosis of cancer, a perioperative myocardial infarction, or unintended delivery of an incorrect medication that results in clinical change.

Examples of events not covered by these guidelines are intravenous saline infiltration and medication dosing errors that have no clinical impact on care.

Latrogenic

Event caused by the treatment of a healthcare provider.

III. GUIDELINES AND PRINCIPLES

It is appropriate that UPMC Presbyterian support basic principles for patient and family notification regarding all clinical events and conditions, including unfavorable ones. Physicians must be honest because that is a cornerstone of the patient-physician relationship, and because it fosters patient autonomy.

UPMC Presbyterian supports the following AMA position regarding patient information:

> It is a fundamental ethical requirement that a physician should at all times deal honestly and openly with patients. Patients have a right to know their past and present medical status and to be free of any mistaken beliefs concerning their conditions. Situations occasionally occur in which a patient suffers significant medical complications that may have resulted from the physician's mistake or judgement. In these situations, the physician is ethically required to inform the patient of all the facts necessary to ensure understanding of what has occurred. Only through full disclosure is a patient able to make informed decisions regarding future medical care.
>
> Ethical responsibility includes informing patients of changes in their diagnoses resulting from retrospective review of test results or other information. This obligation holds even though the patient's medical treatment or therapeutic options may not be altered by the new information.
>
> Concern regarding legal liability which might result following truthful disclosure should not affect the physician's honesty with a patient. (Council on Ethical and Judicial Affairs. Patient Information. In *AMA Code of Medical Ethics*, pp. 141–42. American Medical Association: Chicago, IL, 1998.)

IV. GENERAL RECOMMENDATIONS

1. UPMC Presbyterian and its physicians have a duty to tell the truth and should inform the patient of all pertinent clinical information including significant unfavorable events or conditions, regardless of causation or etiology. This duty also extends to the patient's family and/or guardian as appropriate depending upon normal standards of confidentiality and surrogacy.
2. The responsible attending physician should notify the patient, family and/or guardian of the condition or event within a short time frame (usually within hours). Although the

physician may delegate this task to an appropriately qualified member of the Care Team, the responsibility for appropriate notification remains with the attending physician.

3. A single person (usually the attending physician) should be selected to speak with the patient, family and/or guardian to ensure a consistent message. Other staff should be called in for corroboration, reinforcement, clarification, and support. Social Work is especially experienced in this role.
4. Legal Services and the Ethics Consult Service are available to assist with patient/family communication issues and determining who should be present for such discussions, as well as assisting with any other legal or ethical concerns or problems related to the case. Their involvement is strongly recommended, and required if information is to be withheld. (See policy 4007 "Guidelines on Forgoing Life Sustaining Treatment," and policy 5128 "Placebos.")
5. The Family Crisis Support/Palliative Care Service staff is particularly well qualified to assist in the delivery of "bad news" to patients and families regardless of the cause.

V. RECOMMENDATIONS FOR IATROGENIC AND NOSOCOMIAL ADVERSE EVENTS AND UNFAVORABLE CONDITIONS

1. It is expected that immediately after an event, all the circumstances and consequences of the event may not be known. Therefore, the physician should both notify the patient, family and/or guardian of the event and advise that as additional pertinent information is ascertained, they will be updated. The information should include only facts related to the patient's condition, or which are required for informed decision making. It should not include confidential peer-review information or ascribe fault or blame, either to the physician or others.
2. The physician notifying the patient, family and/or guardian should refrain from hypothesizing or speculating about the event or its causes until they are clearly known.
3. It is appropriate to tell the patient, family and/or guardian that any iatrogenic reportable event will be investigated. (See policy #4023, Initial Investigation Report Procedure.)
4. If the event is perceived to be iatrogenic, then immediately after discovering the adverse event or condition, Risk Management should be notified.
5. The timing, content and persons present at any discussion of an adverse event or condition should be clearly and carefully documented. For example, specific diagnoses and treatment recommendations should be included.
6. Speculation about how an iatrogenic unfavorable event or condition might have occurred should not be included in any patient record. Factual information regarding the event should be recorded on an IIR (Form #1480-0000-0792, Item 05110) (also see Policy #4023, Initial Investigation Report).

RISK MANAGEMENT: EXTREME HONESTY MAY BE THE BEST POLICY

Steve S. Kraman and Ginny Hamm

In the context of hospital operations, the term *risk management* usually refers to self-protective activities meant to prevent real or potential threats of financial loss due to accident, injury, or medical malpractice. When a malpractice claim is made against an institution in the private sector, risk managers coordinate the defense against patients, their dependents, and their attorneys. The medical institution and the patient often become adversaries, and patients and attorneys frequently seek punitive as well as loss-based damages.

One can assume that, as in divorce proceedings, anger at a perceived betrayal of trust is part of patients' motivation. Hickson and colleagues (1) found that of 127 families who sued their health care providers after perinatal injuries, 43% were motivated by the suspicion of a cover-up or by the desire for revenge. In a survey of 149 randomly selected patients in an academic internal medicine practice, Witman and coworkers (2) found that almost all of the respondents wanted their physicians to acknowledge even minor errors; many stated that they would respond to an unacknowledged moderate or severe mistake by filing a lawsuit. Other authors have cited breakdowns in physician–patient (3) and hospital–patient (4) relationships as motivation for litigation.

Medical lawsuits are expensive. Press and DeFrances (5) studied all of the federal tort trials and verdicts (including those involving the Veterans Affairs system) that occurred during 1994 and 1995 (5). They found that 90 of the 283 federal medical malpractice cases that reached verdicts (32%) resulted in awards to the plaintiff. Of the 90 awards made, the median amount was $463, 000, 26 exceeded $1 million, and 12 exceeded $10 million.

Under the Federal Tort Claims Act (6), the United States is not liable for punitive damages. However, federal judges have wide discretion in determining awards. The upper limit on the size of an award is determined by the plaintiff's claim and by the applicable state law of damages. In cases that involved egregious negligence and resulted in awards of millions of dollars, we inferred that the high assessments were substitutes for punitive awards. Press and DeFrances (5) found that a mean of more than 2 years was spent in litigation in each of the 283 cases studied; this length of time represents additional expense and effort for all participants. For the entire Veterans Affairs medical system, the average cost of liabilities between 1990 and 1997 was $720, 000 for court judgments, approximately $205, 000 for cases settled at suit or by general counsel, and $35, 000 for local settlements. Lower payments are associated with locally negotiated settlements; therefore, it makes financial sense to avoid litigation.

A special report from the Bureau of Justice Statistics (7) studied the 75 largest counties in the United States. In these counties, 403 medical malpractice cases were won by plaintiffs; the mean award was $1,484, 000, and 24.8% of the awards exceeding $1 million. Although much of this award money was meant to compensate plaintiffs for economic losses, a substantial proportion was undoubtedly intended to punish defendants for perceived gross negligence or outrageous behavior.

The self-protective model of risk management is not universal. In 1989, the Board of Directors of the Royal Victoria Hospital in Montreal, Quebec, Canada, approved guidelines for disclosing medical errors to patients

Reprinted with permission of the American College of Physicians–American Society of Internal Medicine from *Annals of Internal Medicine*, Vol. 131, No. 12, 21 December 1999, pp. 963–67.

and their families (8). The guidelines, which proposed honesty about errors, were produced by the hospital's clinical ethics committee to provide a framework that would enable staff to disclose incidents to patients in a helpful manner. Currently, significant incidents continue to be disclosed to patients or families in accordance with the guidelines. However, no system has been used to track practitioners' adherence to the guidelines or to examine the guidelines' financial consequences (O'Rourke P. Personal communication).

Wu and colleagues (9) comprehensively reviewed the benefits of telling patients the truth and reviewed the possible consequences to the physician and the patient under various circumstances. They did not specifically address the responsibility of the medical institution; however, because health care institutions, like physicians, serve the patient, the ethics of their activities should be similar.

In 1995, the Department of Veterans Affairs rewrote the section of its policy manual that dealt with risk management policies; this material is now incorporated into a section called Patient Safety (10). Referring to patient injury caused by accidents or negligence, the new wording stated that "the medical center will inform the patient and/or the family, as appropriate, of the event, assure them that medical measures have been implemented, and that additional steps are being taken to minimize disability, death, inconvenience, or financial loss to the patient or family." The manual also stated that "District Counsel will advise the medical center Director about informing the patient and/or family of their right to file ... Application for Compensation and Pension ... or to file an administrative tort claim. ..." In circumstances involving malpractice or accidental injury, the Department of Veterans Affairs requires its facilities to continue their safeguarding relationships with patients and to provide advice about the available remedies, which may include claims against the government. Although this policy is ethically laudable, its financial effects could be counterproductive. However, one Veterans Affairs facility, the Veterans Affairs Medical Center at Lexington, Kentucky, has operated under such a policy since 1987. We examined the use of this policy at the Lexington facility from 1990 through 1996 and found that on the basis of this center's experiences, the economic outcome could be positive.

EXPERIENCES OF ONE VETERANS AFFAIRS MEDICAL CENTER

The Veterans Affairs Medical Center in Lexington is affiliated with the University of Kentucky College of Medicine and provides primary, tertiary, and long-term care to approximately 18,000 veterans. During the study period, services performed included invasive cardiologic procedures, orthopedic procedures, cardiac surgery, and neurosurgery. Ninety residents support the activities of the clinical services, and approximately 400 physicians have staff privileges. The Lexington facility is one of two Veterans Affairs medical centers in Kentucky and is a tertiary care referral center for patients from smaller nearby Veterans Affairs facilities. Available beds (excluding nursing home beds) have decreased from 924 to 407 over the past 10 years.

In 1987, after losing two malpractice judgments totaling more than $1.5 million (partly because of inadequately prepared defenses), the management of the Lexington center decided to use a more proactive policy in cases that could result in litigation. This new policy was intended to better prepare the risk management committee to defend malpractice claims by identifying and investigating apparent accidents and incidents of medical negligence. However, when investigation identified an incident of negligence of which the patient or next of kin was apparently unaware, ethical issues arose. The committee members decided that in such cases, the facility had a duty to remain in the role of caregiver and notify the patient of the committee's findings (Appendix). This practice continues to be followed because administration and staff believe that it is the right thing to do and because it has resulted in unanticipated financial benefits to the medical center.

Since this policy has been in place, many settlements have been made. Five settlements involved incidents that caused permanent injury or death but would probably never have resulted in a claim without voluntary disclosure to patients or families. Many other settlements involved patients who had expressed dissatisfaction with an outcome; after investigation, the committee agreed with the patient and initiated a settlement. All cases were negotiated on the basis of reasonable calculations of actual loss. Thorough, timely case reviews allowed the committee to defend against nuisance claims—claims without merit that institutions sometimes settle without contest only to avoid the cost and work of a lawsuit.

During the 7-year period that we examined in detail (1990 through 1996), the Lexington facility had 88 malpractice claims and paid out an average of $190,113 per year (a total of $1,330, 790 for 7 years). The average payment per claim was $15, 622. Seven claims proceeded to federal court and were dismissed before trial. One claim proceeded to trial and was won by the government.

The financial consequences of this somewhat radical policy of full disclosure seem moderate. Although satisfied with this outcome, we attempted to determine the facility's position on the liability scale as a result of this risk management policy. It is difficult to compare the risk liability of different health care facilities without comparing workload, inpatient days, size and complexity of the facility, numbers and types of surgical procedures, and regional differences in propensity to sue. Because much of this information was unavailable, robust comparisons were not possible. Instead, we compared the tort claim experience of the Lexington facility with that of all similar Veterans Affairs medical centers located east of the Mississippi River ($n = 38$) during the same 7-year period. Complete information on tort claims was unavailable from 1 of these hospitals, and 1 hospital had opened only recently; therefore, we based our comparison on the remaining 35 facilities. All of these facilities, including the Lexington facility, primarily perform tertiary care and are closely affiliated with medical schools.

We obtained tort claim data from the Department of Veterans Affairs Tort Claim Information System (Office of General Counsel, Department of Veterans Affairs) and reviewed the data from 1990 through 1996. We estimated exposure to risk by examining the 1996 complexity-adjusted facility workload for each of these medical centers. This is at best a rough measure, but more accurate indicators, such as inpatient days and number and kinds of surgical procedures, were not available for the period in question. Results of our assessment are shown in the Figure.

We also contacted the risk managers or regional counsels of the other 35 facilities to ask about their risk management processes. Two of the facilities currently manage accident and negligence cases in a manner similar to that used at the Lexington facility; however, from 1990 through 1996, no centers used a similar method. Risk managers stated that they encouraged physicians to be honest and forthcoming with patients, but it seemed that no organized effort was made to standardize or track the notification of affected patients.

DISCUSSION

Despite following a policy that seems to be designed to maximize malpractice claims, the Lexington facility's liability payments have been moderate and are comparable to those of similar facilities. We believe this is due in part to the fact that the facility honestly notifies patients of substandard care and offers timely, comprehensive help in filing claims; this diminishes the

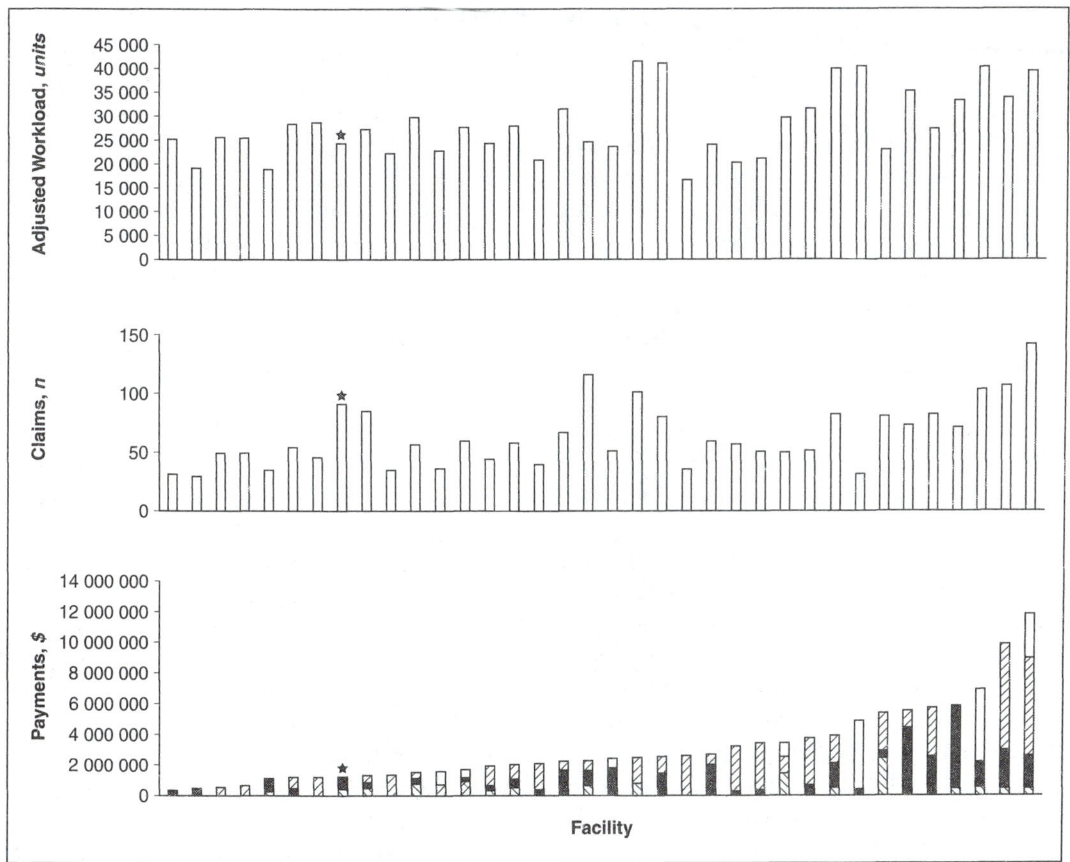

Total malpractice claims and liability payments made from 1990 through 1996 by 36 Veterans Affairs medical centers located east of the Mississippi River. Workload was calculated by the Allocation Resource Center (Budget Office, Department of Veterans Affairs) and is adjusted for sharing, referrals, and patient complexity. In bottom panel, white filler represents payments that resulted from court judgments; left-slanting diagonal lines represent claims settled during litigation before a judgment was made, black filler represents claims settled at the national level by Veterans Affairs general counsel; right-slanting diagonal lines represent claims settled locally by Veterans Affairs district or regional counsel. * Veterans Affairs Medical Center, Lexington, Kentucky.

anger and desire for revenge that often motivate patients' litigation (3). In our experience, plaintiffs' attorneys, after fast confirming the accuracy of the clinical information volunteered by the facility, are willing to negotiate a settlement on the basis of calculable monetary losses rather than on the potential for large judgments that contain a punitive element. This can benefit a facility by limiting settlement costs to reasonable amounts. It also fairly compensates patients who have been injured because of accident or error. This is important because such compensation is deserved but is infrequently offered (11).

The hidden expenses of litigation are also substantial. We estimate that it costs the government $250,000 for a single malpractice case (from initiation through an appeal, including costs of medical experts, travel, and other incidental expenses). A local settlement, however, involves only an attorney, a paralegal specialist, and a few other hospital employees.

We realize that many factors affect the number of negligence claims, settlements, and litigation judgments involving medical facilities. Although none of the other Veterans Affairs facilities used the same risk management process as the Lexington facility during the period in question, some facilities may have used one or more similar components. We also acknowledge the limitations of an analysis of only one facility. For obvious reasons, health care facilities are reluctant to publish their experience in this area, and we are aware of no previous report that describes the details of a consistent risk management philosophy and its results.

Malpractice payments are determined by many factors that are unrelated to medical care, such as the patient's willingness to sue, the expertise of the attorneys representing the medical facilities, the attorneys' willingness to negotiate settlements, and the presence or absence of publicity that could stimulate patients' interest in litigation. It is difficult to accurately compare the Veterans Affairs experience with that of the private sector, but the special report from the Bureau of Justice Statistics (7) indicates that the average medical malpractice judgment in the private sector ($1,484,000) is considerably greater than that in the Veterans Affairs system ($720,000).

Would a policy of full disclosure be acceptable in the private sector? Federal and private employment in the health care industry differ in several important ways. The Veterans Affairs medical system provides comprehensive, virtually free universal coverage. The system can also offer such benefits as remedial treatment and even monthly disability payments by designating that the patient is "service connected" because of injuries caused by Veterans Affairs–administered treatment. Such remedies are not dependent on a lawsuit and are unavailable in the private sector. Government health care practitioners are protected from personal liability by the Federal Tort Claims Act and are not personally named in cases of negligence that occur during the ordinary course of their activities. In addition, they pay no malpractice premiums. However, when they are involved in a payment resulting from negligence or malpractice, government physicians are reported to the National Practitioner Data Bank and state licensure boards and must acknowledge their involvement with malpractice cases on all future employment applications. Repeated or egregious incidents of negligence can, as in nongovernmental facilities, result in limitation, suspension, or revocation of clinical privileges, which can also be reported to the National Practitioner Data Bank and to state licensure boards.

If there is a barrier to the adoption of a humanistic risk management policy by nongovernmental hospitals, it may be the involvement of many private malpractice insurers, each of which is interested in paying as little money in settlements as possible. We believe that these insurers would have to be convinced of the economical benefits of such a policy before they would consider adopting it.

The experience of the Lexington facility suggests but does not prove the financial superiority of a full disclosure policy, and we hope that this report will spur a more detailed examination of the issue. The Veterans Affairs medical system is the largest integrated health care system in the country, and current policy mandates a risk management process similar to that used in the Lexington facility. If this type of process is implemented and followed, more convincing data on this question may become available within the next few years.

We conclude that an honest and forthright risk management policy that puts the patient's interests first may be relatively inexpensive because it allows avoidance of lawsuit preparation, litigation, court judgments, and settlements at trial. Although goodwill and the maintenance of the caregiver role are less tangible benefits, they are also important advantages of such a policy.

APPENDIX

Notifying a Patient of Negligence

When the risk management committee identifies an instance of accident, possible negligence, or malpractice, it investigates the facts. This investigation includes an interview with the involved physicians, the chief of the relevant clinical service, and other personnel, as appropriate. If the committee finds that malpractice or substantial error resulted in loss of a patient's function, earning capacity, or life, plans are made to notify the patient or next of kin. The patient, surrogate, or next of kin is called (usually by the chief of staff), is told that there was a problem with the care in question, and is asked to come to the medical center at his or her convenience for an explanation. The telephone conversation provides only enough details to indicate the seriousness of the matter (including, if necessary, a statement that a medical mistake was made and that an attorney may accompany the patient or family if desired).

Face-to-Face Meeting

The subsequent meeting is with the chief of staff, the facility attorney, the quality manager, the quality management nurse, and sometimes the facility director. At the meeting, all of the details are provided as sensitively as possible, including the identities of persons involved in the incident (who are notified before the meeting). Emphasis is placed on the regret of the institution and the personnel involved and on any corrective action that was taken to prevent similar events. The committee offers to answer questions and may make an offer of restitution, which can involve subsequent corrective medical or surgical treatment, assistance with filing for service connection under 38 United States Code, section 1151 (a law that confers service connection on the basis of disability resulting from medical care), or monetary compensation.

Claims Assistance

After the meeting, the patient, surrogate, or next of kin is assisted in filing any necessary forms and is given the names and numbers of contact persons who can answer any additional questions. If the patient or next of kin has not already retained counsel, they are advised to do so. The committee is then equally forthcoming with the plaintiff's attorney so that the attorney's review of the medical record will confirm the information that was volunteered. The facility's attorney and the patient's attorney work to reach an equitable settlement on the basis of reasonable calculation of loss.

References

1. Hickson, G.B., Clayton, E.W., Githens, P.B. and Sloan, F.A. "Factors that prompted families to file medical malpractice claims following perinatal injuries." *JAMA*. 1992; 267:1359–63.
2. Witman, A.B., Park, D.M. and Hardin, S.B. "How do patients want physicians to handle mistakes? A survey of internal medicine patients in an academic setting." *Arch Intern Med*. 1996; 156:2565–9.
3. Penchansky, R.V. and Macnee, C. "Initiation of medical malpractice suits: a conceptualization and test." *Med Care*. 1994; 32:813–31.
4. Rubin, B. "Medical malpractice suits can be avoided." *Hospitals*. 1978; 52:86–8.
5. Press, A.H., and DeFrances, C.J. Federal Tort Trials and Verdicts, 1994–1995. Bureau of Justice Statistic's Special Report. Washington, DC: U.S. Department of Justice, Office of Justice Programs; December 1997. NCJ-165830.
6. United States Code Annotated. Vol. 28. St. Paul, MN: West; 1988.
7. DeFrances, C.J., Smith, S.K., Langan, P.A., Ostrum, B.J., Rottman, D.B., and Goerdt, J.A. Civil Jury Cases and Verdicts in Large Counties. Bureau of Justice Statistics Special Report. Washington, DC: U.S. Department of Justice. Office of Justice Programs; 1995. NCJ-154346: 1–14.
8. Peterkin, A. "Guidelines covering disclosure of errors now in place at Montreal hospital." *CMAJ*. 1990; 142:984–5.

9. Wu, A.W., Cavanaugh, T.A., McPhee, S.J., Lo, B, and Micco, G.P. "To tell the truth: ethical and practical issues and disclosing medical mistakes to patients." *J Gen Intern Med*. 1997; 12:770–5.
10. Patient safety improvement. Department of Veterans Affairs VHA Manual. 1051/1; 1998.
11. Localio, A.R., Lawthers, A.G., Brennan, T.A., Laird, N.M., Hebert, L.E., Peterson, L.M., et al. "Relation between malpractice claims and adverse events due to negligence. Results of the Harvard Medical Practice Study III." *N Engl J Med*. 1991; 325:245–51.